Aspects of Human Settlement Planning

Aspects of Human Settlement Planning

Edited by
Habitat Conference Secretariat

PERGAMON PRESS
NEW YORK / TORONTO / OXFORD / SYDNEY / FRANKFURT / PARIS

Pergamon Press Offices:

U.S.A.	Pergamon Press Inc., Maxwell House, Fairview Park, Elmsford, New York 10523, U.S.A.
U.K.	Pergamon Press Ltd., Headington Hill Hall, Oxford OX3, OBW, England
CANADA	Pergamon of Canada, Ltd., 75 The East Mall, Toronto, Ontario M8Z SW3, Canada
AUSTRALIA	Pergamon Press (Aust) Pty. Ltd., 19a Boundary Street, Rushcutters Bay, N.S.W. 2011, Australia
FRANCE	Pergamon Press SARL, 24 rue des Ecoles, 75240 Paris, Cedex 05, France
FEDERAL REPUBLIC OF GERMANY	Pergamon Press GmbH, 6242 Kronberg/Taunus, Pferdstrasse 1, West Germany

Library of Congress Cataloging in Publication Data

Main entry under title:

Aspects of human settlement planning.

    1. City planning--Addresses, essays, lectures.
2. Land use--Planning--Addresses, essays,
lectures. I. United Nations Conference on Human
Settlements, Vancouver, B.C., 1976.
HT166.A84   1977   309.2'62   77-9877
ISBN 0-08-022011-8

Printed in the United States of America

Contents

Foreword

The organization of Habitat: United Nations Conference on Human Settlements involved the amassing of huge amounts of documentation: from governments, the many branches of the UN system, non-governmental organizations, and scores of private experts in all fields related to the conference issues. This paper mountain of data, analysis, theory and opinion was distilled into the few hundred pages presented at the conference as policy and background papers which the delegates used in their deliberations. But the process of distillation, while inevitable, entails enormous loss of material which is of great value in its own right. It is for this reason I applaud the decision of Pergamon Press to publish the two works on *Aspects of Human Settlement Planning*, which are drawn from these background studies.

Largely as a result of Habitat, I believe that human settlements will be more widely recognized as an important branch of social science. This is an interdisciplinary science, involving planning, social and political theory, government management, architecture, engineering and many other special fields. It will also be a science in which academic and social research in the years to come will be eagerly studied by governments at all levels. The two most important characteristics of the 20th century have been population growth and the phenomenal pace of urbanization. When world population reaches 8,000 million early in the next century, as it almost certainly will, it is probable that 70 percent or more of that number – or nearly 6,000 million people – will live in urban areas. How these urban areas are organized, and whether or not they will offer a satisfactory quality of life, are among the most important issues facing the human species. And let us also realize that the answers to these questions are not foreordained. The human habitat of the future will be the result of decisions either taken or avoided.

These two works, plus the *Global Review of Human Settlements* already published by Pergamon Press, and the key documents of the conference itself, are all indispensable to any study and understanding of human settlements, both as to conditions existing today and trends leading into the future. As Secretary-General of the Habitat conference, I would like to express my gratitude to all who have contributed to these works: those whose papers appear under their own names and those in the UN system whose efforts are anonymous. These documents also are a further testimonial to the tremendous contribution of the late Professor Duccio A. Turin of Italy, who as Deputy Secretary-General of the conference was most responsible for organizing the support of all whose views are presented here.

Enrique Peñalosa

Part I
A Collection of UN Studies

1

Popular Participation for the Improvement of the Human Environment in Marginal Settlements*

The growth of marginal settlements is closely linked to the rapid urbanization that has taken place in most developing countries over the past three decades. Urban population growth in these countries is in part due to natural population increase within urban settlements and in part to rural migration to urban centers, particularly the largest cities. The confluence of these two trends has resulted in an annual population growth in many cities of six percent — two to three times the national rate. The rate of population increase in marginal settlements is, commonly, twice or three times the rate of urban demographic growth.

The steep decline in infant and other mortality rates in urban areas and continued high birth rates have maintained the high rate of natural population growth. That death rates have fallen despite overcrowding, unsanitary conditions and inadequate health services is largely a consequence of the control of infectious diseases. Cityward migration is a result of "push" factors in the rural areas that have forced people to give up agricultural-rural pursuits and "pull" factors associated with city life. In Mexico, for example, the attraction of higher wages in the city combined with a deterioration of employment conditions in the rural areas have led to an unabated heavy influx of people into Mexico City whose annual growth rate over the past twenty-five years has been about 5.5 percent. Similarly, industrial development in Turkey's cities has spurred rural-urban migration which accelerated markedly between 1951 and 1954. In many countries, political developments have also encouraged cityward migration. The ouster of the dictatorial regime in Venezuela in 1958 was immediately followed by a resurgence of migration to Caracas. Facilitating this influx of migrants are the kinship networks in urban areas which often provide material assistance and information to the migrants which help them to adapt to their new urban environment. According to projections of the United Nations Population Division, urban population growth is expected to continue unabated in developing countries. The present pattern, particularly in developing countries, is that the bigger the unit of settlement, the faster it grows. Towns grow more rapidly than villages, cities faster than towns, cities of more than a million faster than cities with less than a million; and multi-million cities, with more than 2.5 million people, fastest of all. The result is that by the year 2000, twenty-five other metropolitan areas will join New York and Tokyo in the super-city class, i.e., a "super-conurbation" or a connected metropolitan area with more than 12.5 million inhabitants. Of these, no fewer than 18 will be in developing countries. Mexico City, Sao Paulo and Shanghai appear to be the first to achieve this category, followed by Peking, Bombay, Calcutta, Seoul, Buenos Aires, Rio de Janeiro and the spreading complex of Cairo-Giza, with Karachi-Teheran, New Delhi, Bangkok, Manila, Lima, Bogota and Djakarta not far behind. With the exception of Teheran, where government policy is to prevent the creation of marginal settlements, all these metropolitan areas have substantial and growing squatter populations.

Urbanization is a necessary but not sufficient cause for the growth of marginal settlements. The latter were not spawned during the urbanization process in what are now the developed societies. There are several reasons for this: the particular status of property in these societies precluded the illegal seizure of land for the

---

*Abridged verson of a background paper for Habitat contributed by the Social Development Division of the Department of Economic and Social Affairs (Symbol A/Conf. 70/B/3; 15 March 1976).

construction of privately-owned shelter; demographic growth kept pace with economic development and the expansion of employment opportunities in urban areas; and expanding industrialization centred in these areas and generated sufficient capital to finance the construction of low-cost housing which provided a tolerable level of existence for workers and their families who crowded into the slums of these fast-growing cities. In constrast, the rate of urban population growth in developing countries is appreciably greater than the rate of expansion of urban employment opportunities.[1] Much new industrialization is capital-intensive requiring a minimum amount of labour of a skilled nature. Concomitant with this has been the growth of urban poverty resulting from the high incidence of unemployment and underemployment. Given these circumstances of inadequate economic development, it is not possible to finance the construction of much needed low-cost housing for the urban poor. The inaccessibility of conventional low-cost housing to the poor has created the necessary condition for the growth of marginal settlements in most cities in developing countries.

It is generally recognized that unrestricted operation of market forces in most developing countries has had a deleterious effect on urban growth. One aspect of this is the frenzied speculation in urban real estate which has been brought on by spiraling inflation, undiminished demand for housing and the absence of alternative channels for investment. As a result, the price of urban land in developing countries is prohibitively high and bears no relation to the income of the vast majority of the people. Housing to serve the needs of the poor cannot be built on such land which is either held for speculative purposes or becomes the site for luxury housing or commercial buildings. Complicating the problem of providing services to the urban poor are the low population densities that are found in these cities; particularly in Latin America. In large measure, this is due to the movement of the more affluent people away from the central city to the peripheral areas of the city for reasons of convenience, privacy and agreeable environment. Because of their close ties with political groups and government agencies, the middle class and rich are usually successful in securing services. The cost of providing such services to the sparsely populated peripheral areas poses a severe strain on the limited resources of government. The latter, as a result, is pressed to provide the barest of services to the densely populated central areas of the city wherein are located the slums which house the poor. Under these circumstances, squatters have at best only a marginal claim against the already strained supply of social, educational and environmental services.

The Growth of Marginal Settlements

Today, marginal or squatter settlements are probably the fastest growing types of human settlements in developing nations with their overall rate of growth being approximately 12 percent. Much of the growth of squatter settlements tends to take place in and around medium to large cities. In Turkey, for example, there were about 240,000 *gecekondu* (squatter houses) in 1960 which housed 13.5 percent of the total urban population. Five years later the figure rose to 430,000 *gecekondu* and their 2,365,000 inhabitants accounted for 21.8 percent of the urban population. It is estimated that in metropolitan Manila, about a third of 4.8 million people live in slums and squatter settlements. According to a 1968 survey, more than one-third of the population of Dar es Salaam's 273,000 population live in slums and squatter areas. Almost half of Guayaquil's population or 360,000 were living in squatter settlements in 1968. Out of a population of 2.8 million, approximately one-quarter of Lima's population were barrio residents. It is projected that while Brazilian cities with 100,000 population and over are expected to double in twelve years, *favelas* are expected to increase six times. To judge from the evidence at hand, squatter settlement growth is not a passing phenomenon but a widespread and significant form of human settlement.

Official policies and middle class public opinion in most developing countries tend to view marginal settlements as anomalous or pathological phenomena which should be curbed or suppressed. Although these views still have wide currency, they are not pursued with the same vigour as they had once been. Nonetheless, the negative outlook about marginal settlements persists often making it difficult to develop a coherent policy relating to this form of human settlement. The reasons for this are not hard to come by. Unsightly and unsanitary conditions in many of the settlements offend the aesthetic values of the middle class political elites. Their unplanned growth is viewed as detrimental to the orderly growth of the city. There is a widely held view that marginal settlements are breeding grounds for crime and vice which could spill over the city.

[1] Urbanization in the Second United Nations Development Decade, United Nations, New York, 1970 (UN Sales publication E.70.IV.15), Chapter 1; Press, 1962.

Many middle class people who inhabit the "modern" parts of the city and are generally unaware of conditions inside marginal settlements harbor the belief that as social tensions in the settlements increase, so does the incubus of revolution. Underlying these views are certain assumptions about the inhabitants of marginal settlements. The rural peasant, wrenched from a tightly structured rural society, is unable to adapt to the shock of urban life for want of resources and assistance from friends and relatives. The shock and isolation of urban life, so it is believed, cause personal disorientation and political anomie. Given the glaring disparity between the expectations of the peasant and the abysmal conditions of urban living in marginal settlements, he is prone to political radicalism and revolutionary activities.

There is considerable evidence that these views do not accurately reflect conditions prevailing in most squatter settlements. Several comprehensive studies reveal that a substantial degree of social cohesion exists in squatter settlements and that their residents behave in socially responsible and politically rational ways. According to Mangin's study of barriadas in Lima, the educational level of their inhabitants is higher than that of the general population of Peru and great stock is placed in securing a better education for their children. There is considerable family stability and the incidence of delinquency and vice is low. People are generally poor but incomes tend to improve over time, aided in part by an entrepreneurial spirit shown by not a few of the residents for establishing small businesses. People are not, as a rule, fatalistic about the future and believe they are not without some influence in shaping the direction of life in their community. This future-oriented outlook is underscored by the widespread tendency among the residents to save money where possible, secure better educational opportunities for their children, and improve their homes. People living in marginal settlements tend to act collectively or establish organizations to protect their interests; traditional forms of mutual aid common to rural communities often are practiced in squatter settlements. There are few signs, moreover, that squatters as a group are given to radicalism or revolution. On the contrary, squatters tend to view their community as a base for improving their lives through organized self-help and mutual aid activity with the assistance of government, and not as a springboard for revolutionary activity.

Official attitudes towards squatters are often rooted in mistaken beliefs about their lifestyles and an inability to view the squatter settler phenomenon as a response to the problems of urbanization. In regard to the latter, there is considerable evidence that the establishment of squatter settlements by the urban poor is a rational response which corresponds to their needs for shelter, economic security and social status. A better understanding of who squatters are and of their priorities in adjusting to life in an urban setting can place this view in a clearer perspective. Contrary to popular belief, the people who organize and live in marginal settlements are not recent arrivals from rural areas. Many of them had lived for varying periods in smaller towns and cities reflecting the well-documented pattern of step-wide migration. In many cities, moreover, a substantial majority of the marginal settlements' population had first lived in the centre city slums for a number of years prior to moving to the periphery of the city as shantytown dwellers. During this period as a slum-dweller, the urban migrant learns about the ways of city life and in the process begins to define his own goals about the kind of shelter and community he wants to live in. Intra-city migrants, as a result, are better skilled and educated than most rural migrants, and have a greater capacity to adapt to conditions of urban life. These personal assets tend to serve the urban migrant in good stead when he proceeds to make his life in a marginal settlement where the improvement of the community is often contingent upon a resourceful and adaptive citizenry.

These intra-city settlement patterns were first described by Turner who postulated that they are based on "a functional relationship between social needs and environmental forms" characteristic of the migrant population at various stages of urban integration. Urban migrants, according to the Turner study which is based on Peruvian case studies and data from other developing countries, have three functional priorities by which they evaluate their need for shelter and community. These are (1) location; (2) security of tenure; and (3) amenity. The relative importance of these priorities changes over time as the migrants become integrated into the urban environment.

Location has the highest priority to the newcomer who is anxious to gain a bridgehead in the unfamiliar urban environment. Having few resources or skills, the "bridgeheader" moves to the slum areas of the central city which are within walking distance to what he has greatest need for: employment opportunities and food markets. A job and steady income are his chief concerns at this stage of settlement. The reception areas for recent migrants, which Turner refers to as "provisional settlements," are the primary setting for their acculturation to urban life. For the security of employment and reasonably steady income, the migrant is prepared to pay a high rent for crowded and unsanitary shelter which probably differs little from what he is accustomed to. The bridgeheader attaches little importance to housing "amenities" during this period and his shelter takes care of his minimal needs for sleeping, eating and storing his few possessions. He has no interest in improving his shelter and shows little concern for the broader community in which he lives. After a period of anywhere from five to ten years of living in provisional settlements, the urban settler is anxious to consolidate his gains. His priorities are changing and the trade-off between ready access to employment and markets for life in a slum area become less attractive. By this time, moreover, the migrant often is paying a substantially higher percentage of his income in rent and is often subject to pressure from the landlord who is anxious to rebuild and use the property for commercial purposes. The migrant is acutely aware that loss of his job for reasons beyond his control would place him and his family in a precarious position. It is at this stage that the migrant is seeking security of residential stability. The conventional housing market, as was previously noted, is largely foreclosed to him. To gain this security, he is prepared to squat and live on a piece of land on the periphery of the city. It is at this stage that the slum dweller is prepared to exchange the convenience of central location for the security of tenure by joining with others, at no small risk, to become a squatter and fight for title to a piece of land.

After achieving, and not without struggle, a reasonable degree of security of tenure, the urban migrant can begin to invest in the construction of a home. Spared the need to make monthly rent payments, he can invest this money in building and improving his home. He builds his home progressively, according to his own values of space and amenity, and can regulate these expenditures with his income. With more space and sunshine than he had before, there is a net improvement in the migrant's immediate physical environment. Home possession, moreover, serves to increase his stake in the community, providing a strong incentive to become involved in its development. Once settlers secure a reasonable assurance of tenure, they view their community as being their *permanent* home, and not, as was the case of the slum, a *temporary shelter*. Permanent settlements are future-oriented; they are perceived by their inhabitants as offering sufficient opportunities for expansion and improvement. The marginal settlement, for all its shortcomings, is a self-improving community. The addition of a new house, the paving of a road or the construction of a school generally provides a new facility or service where none had existed before. This stands in sharp contrast to the centre city slums which are physically deteriorating, and despite high rents, offer few amenities or space. Air and water pollution pose serious environmental and health risks. In these precincts, it is not uncommon to find sewage seeping through crumbling water mains and sanitation removal and disposal severely neglected. Because of the bureaucratic constraints of the urban environment and the lack of citizen interest in improving it, strategies of popular participation for community improvement generally are met with indifference.

National Policy and Marginal Settlements

Public policy towards the formation of squatter settlements ranges from the eviction of squatters and destruction of their homes to acceptance of these settlements along with programmes to provide them with social services. A restrictive policy is in force in many countries though there is growing tendency to adopt a more tolerant attitude. In Hong Kong, authorities are committed to a policy of clearance and resettlement of squatters. Selective enforcement of anti-squatting legislation is in evidence in some countries. In Nairobi, the government has taken a stand against squatter settlements located near the centre of the city by burning them down, while permitting squatters to settle in Mathare Valley which is on the outskirts of the city. Squatters often are aware of the government's differential response and their choice of a site will be dictated by this consideration. Peru adopted a law in 1961 declaring that any barriada formed by invasion after September 1960 would not be eligible for government assistance or recognition. The Peruvian law appears to have as its main purpose stabilizing barriada growth and controlling their location. In Mexico during most of the period since the early 1950s when *paracaidismo* (squatting, but translated literally, "parachuting," as onto a plot of land) became frequent within the Federal District, most land invasions have been resisted by government authorities, sometimes using riot police and even bulldozers. The resistance encountered by squatters has usually been proportional to the number of squatters involved in an invasion and/or the political influence of the owner of the invaded land. Invasions of land in the public domain — riverbeds, railroad right-of-ways, etc. — have generally met with less resistance from the authorities. Government policy toward squatting in the Mexico City urban area has shifted since 1966 from unmitigated hostility and confrontation to acquiescence and even active assistance in the improvement of illegally formed settlements. The current government approach to established squatter settlements involves expropriating the invaded land, if it is privately owned, and selling it to the invaders at below-market prices. The Department of the Federal District claims to have expropriated and released to squatters some 23.9 million square meters of land between 1966 and 1970 alone. Public policy in Turkey has evolved to a point where the government now recognizes the importance of *gecekondus* to the urbanization process, although a substantial element of public opinion and the press view them as a disfigurement of the city and detrimental to established values.

There appears to be taking place a change in attitudes, if not policies, toward squatter settlements. In part, this change reflects a growing awareness by government that in the absence of alternative forms of low-cost dwellings, a policy of repression is both futile and self-defeating. Government eviction attempts are often ineffective in the long run since the invaded land is often reoccupied by those who participated in the initial invasion or by another group. The lesson is becoming clearer that a social structure cannot be replaced or destroyed unless the functions of that structure either lose relevance or are replaced. Given the enormity of the demand for low-cost housing and the gross inadequacy of resources to provide such shelter, there can be little hope that the conventional approach of building standard housing will solve the problem. What is needed is a participatory approach to urban settlement and housing systems. This is already partly acknowledged in a growing number of countries which have promoted such an approach toward housing. During the 1950s, governments increasingly encouraged aided self-help housing programmes, and, more recently, have been attracted to the sites and services approach. The latter takes into account the all to obvious but often ignored fact that the urban poor "can and do house themselves without direct control or direct housing assistance by government." The marginal settlement, in all its ramifications of providing housing, services and community to poor urban settlers, is the broadest possible application of the participatory approach albeit in an unplanned way. It is increasingly being viewed as an adaptive approach to the needs of the urban poor to build their own housing and create their own community. The marginal settlement, as Mangin noted, has to be seen not as a problem arising from rapid urbanization but as a solution to certain of the problems associated with it.

Using techniques of popular participation, the urban poor, in an effort to solve their individual housing problems, are in effect contributing to solving the problems of urbanization in developing countries. This form of self-help housing in marginal settlement is an important source of capital formation in these countries. Despite this, powerful opposition still holds sway against marginal settlements. In many developing countries, the political and administrative elites in the housing "establishment" view them as antithetical to their middle class values and detrimental to their professional interests. This establishment generally remains committed to minimum modern standard structures and installations. This "nice community" approach is based on three assumptions: "that high structural and equipment standards take precedence over high space standards; that households can and should move when their socio-economic status has changed so that they can afford to have a larger (above minimum) standard dwelling; and that the function of a house is, above all, to provide a hygienic and comfortable shelter." While these assumptions are valid for the developed countries, Turner observes, they do not hold true for countries in the developing world. Despite this, housing administrators and architects, many of whom have studied in developed countries and seek to emulate their standards, indiscriminately impose the "minimum modern standard" form of housing as the model for the people in their own society notwithstanding its inappositeness for the great majority of people. That they persist in this approach is not surprising, considering that they generally do not view popular participation or improved citizen access to decision-making processes as important or urgent issues.

Popular Participation in Marginal Settlements

Marginal settlements are often characterized by a high degree of formal and informal organizational activities. Numerous studies have pointed out the high propensity of people in these communities to band together to deal with collective and individual problems. The level and intensity of such activity varies over time. In new settlements, for example, such activity is generally pitched at a high level as people join together to ward off possible efforts by the authorities to oust them; voluntary concerted action is also in evidence in the construction of necessary community facilities and services. As a settlement becomes more developed and its inhabitants better established, the level of popular participation slackens. Nonetheless, the level of citizen involvement remains greater than that in established urban settings. In the latter, organizational activities — particularly along ethnic, religious and place of origin — remain strong but they tend to have as their primary purpose promoting personal contacts and leisure activities. Participation to promote development is severely circumscribed because work activities are organized more often through the division of labour or through contracts. Developmental activities are highly bureaucratized and this severely limits the scope of citizen initiative; the impersonalization and atomization of life that result from urbanization discourage collective forms of voluntarism that characterize life in rural areas and which are often rooted in marginal settlements. What accounts for the propensity toward popular participation and the particular forms it takes will now be examined.

Citizen participation in environmental improvement in marginal settlements may take a variety of forms. These include individual self-help activity (e.g., building one's own dwelling or improving it), participation in informal mutual assistance networks (based on kinship and proximity relationships) within the community, collective community level self-help efforts (e.g., grading a road or installing a provisional water supply system), and individual or collective activity to secure assistance from the government or other external organizations. Particular attention will be paid in Part II to resident involvement in mutual assistance networks and organizations and externally-oriented efforts to secure assistance, a process which shall be referred to as "demand-making."

Despite government pronouncements attributing great importance to popular participation in promoting development, its realization is no simple matter.[2] It assumes the existence of societal values that encourage voluntary co-operative behaviour. The *cayapa* in Venezuela, the *imece* in Turkey and *bayanihan* in the Philippines, are examples of such voluntarism which are embedded in the societal values and promote participant behaviour. Popular participation, moreover, cannot take place in the absence of approbative policies of government which give it legitimacy. Unless such support is forthcoming at the political and bureaucratic levels, popular participation will have but limited application. The people themselves have to have an interest and capacity for participation and that their efforts periodically secure results by an understanding and responsive government. Where their demands elicit no results, they are likely to resort to violence or, alternatively, sink into apathy. These are essential but often insufficient factors for promoting popular participation in urban areas. As has already been noted, the propensity for citizen involvement in development in cities is held in check because bureaucratic controls and the impersonality of life styles are far advanced and co-operation is generally achieved through division of labour and contract.

Significantly, some of these inhibiting factors are absent or exist in modest degree in marginal settlements. There are, in addition, certain other factors that further strengthen the participatory mode in these settlements. First among these is the very act by urban migrants of banding together to seize the land on which they proceed to build their homes and create a community. At times this is done when one or more families simply squat on land they claim as their own, or acquire a right to the land by purchasing title which may or may not be valid. In the Philippines, until 1971, squatting had been carried on in a covert manner, unlike the more familiar land "invasions" that are fairly common in Latin America and parts of Africa and Asia. Establishing a settlement is, under these circumstances, the result of a collective decision involving voluntary participation and group solidarity which are vital to the enterprise's success. As a rule, the site to be selected, the timing of the invasion and preparations for settling and forestalling possible eviction are well planned. Whether public or privately-owned land is seized will in part depend on the attitude of the government. In many countries, vacant public lands are favoured over privately-owned property because of the more tolerant attitude of the government. Where resistance may occur, the leaders of the invasion will seek the support of prominent political groups or appeal to the media to dramatize the plight of the settlers. Holidays are preferred because politicians are often reluctant to confront squatters when the mood of the day is for national solidarity or for celebrating. Prior to the invasion, it is not uncommon for the organizers to engage law school students and young engineers to carry out land title searches and conduct tests of subsoil conditions; as the invasion is in progress, these leaders decide which land is to be assigned to individual members of the group for dwellings, and for the location of streets, schools, dispensaries and churches.

Squatter settlements, for all their differences in size, population, income levels and mode of formation, have one attribute that is common to most of them: their illegal origins and juridically ambiguous status. Although government in an increasing number of developing countries is revealing a more tolerant attitude toward such settlements, their establishment is still not generally openly sanctioned. Even where squatter settlements are permitted under the law as in Peru or Turkey, it is still common for settlers to run the risk or threat of violent confrontation with the police or army; title to the land is often shrouded in legal uncertainty

---

[2] *Popular Participation in Decision Making for Development*, United Nations publication, Sales No.E.75.IV.10.

and the task of securing formal tenure to the land is formidable. Being outside the pale of the law often exposes the settlers to harassment by the police. This external threat has the effect of causing people to organize in order to resist efforts to oust them. Where tenure to the land is uncertain, this perceived external threat serves as the single most important unifying force in the community. It is also the major preoccupation of local organizations. Success in establishing a community is the most tangible sign of the benefits that can accrue to the people as a result of their collective efforts. It gives them a sense of being able to control their fate. This act makes them feel a member of the community with a stake in its development.

The initial act of organizing the settlement is generally significant in terms of its future development. It is during this formative phase that leadership comes to the fore and begins to assert itself. By allocating in an authoritative manner land to the settlers and negotiating with official agencies, the leaders act in a virtually official capacity. Their formal mandate to do this is often obscure though they appear to have the backing of the residents. As formal institutions evolve, there is often some provision for the selection of local leaders as is the case of the *muhtar* in Turkey. Both formal and effective power may be centered in one individual or group, or, as is often the case, a strong leader emerges such as the *cacique* in Mexico and in other Latin American countries who, by dint of close ties with the established political groups, is acknowledged as the *de facto* settlement leader. Leadership, as shall be discussed below, is a key factor in promoting popular participation in the settlements. The ability of local leaders to articulate and aggregate community demands will, in large measure, influence how government responds to these demands.

There is a strong propensity among people in squatter settlements to form associations, which, because of a tendency to factionalism, tend to proliferate. These groups often take the form of multipurpose mutual-aid societies, one of whose main functions is to bring pressure to bear on the government to grant squatters legal title to the land they live on. As the community becomes older, organizational activities become more differentiated and complex, reflecting the changing lifestyles and demands of its inhabitants. Women's and youth's associations spring up as well as business, religious, ethnic and political organizations. In Bombay and in other Indian cities where strategic resources are largely secured through political channels, it is not surprising that political parties are among the foremost institutions in the shantytown. Formal representative institutions are also provided for in marginal settlements in certain countries, a recognition of the special role accorded to them by the government. Upon declaration of martial law in the Philippines, Presidential Decree 86 was issued amending the Barrio Charter by providing for the establishment in the shantytowns of *barangays* or community assemblies. These are grassroot assemblies composed of leaders elected directly by the people. The Association for Improving the Gecekondu (Gecekonduyu Güzellestirme Dernegi) in Turkey has similar functions representing the interests of the settlement, and like the *barangays*, its board members are formally elected by gecekondu members in conformity with the national law governing the establishment and functioning of associations. The success of institution-building in these and other settlements can be measured by the ability of the settlements to survive the initial pangs of birth; to gain access to higher decision-making authorities for resources and, ultimately, legitimacy and to promote citizen participation in community affairs.

Participatory Development: Model for Development in Squatter Settlements

Participation revolving around the range of economic, social and environmental needs of the people affords a considerable potential for sustaining citizen involvement in community affairs. Creating a participant community around these needs of the people is in substantial measure what marginal settlements are about. Residents of these communities quickly discover that they have no other alternative but to participate in local activities. Participant norms, as has been observed, begin to take root in the very formation of the settlement. They often develop apace with the growth of the community, although there are periods when they falter or are discredited for want of results, or because of a paternalistic attitude by government. Participatory behaviour extends to a wide range of functional activities that are vital to the collective and individual needs of the individual. The lack, or in many cases, the absence of government-supplied social and public safety services associated with urban life oblige citizens in marginal settlements to adopt two courses of action in order to provide for the collective needs of the community. The first is to organize themselves and provide, where possible, minimal community services. In the shantytowns of Manila during the 1950s, for example, the people organized police patrols to protect the residents against crime. Under a traditional system of community protection called the *ronda*, it was expected that every able-bodied man in a family volunteer several nights a month to serve in a group which would protect the community. In the absence of judicial services in a squatter settlement in Nairobi, the squatters adapted a traditional method for conflict resolution in certain types of cases mainly involving debt collection, civil disputes and theft of property. The ability of the residents to perform such services in these and other functional areas is often due to the rural origins of many of the settlers who are accustomed to volunteering for community-related activities. The *gecekondu* in Turkey, for example, possesses within its structure, powerful elements borrowed from traditional village culture which help maintain communal solidarity and mobilize popular participation. The second course of action to secure community services is to engage in demand-making activities, i.e., join with other settlement residents in petitioning the government through established political or administrative channels to allocate more resources for improvement purposes and/or to grant the settlers formal title to their land.

It is clear from the foregoing analysis that a marginal settlement is fertile ground for promoting a development-oriented self-image on the part of the inhabitants. Participation in establishing the settlement gives its founders a sense of being able to shape their own physical and social environment. This image is further reenforced by building and improving their own shelter. This sense of independence contrasts sharply with the dependent position of those who move into government-provided high-rise dwellings and have to look to the official authorities for improvements in their dwellings and, not infrequently, compassion for tardy rent payments which often exceed their ability to meet. With a stake in the community, the settler is often motivated to co-operate with others for improvements in the community. This provides opportunities to the settlers, many of whom have considerable experience as urban dwellers, to put this experience to good use by joining with others in the process of seeking resources from government for community improvements. The marginal settlement, many of whose residents are also of recent rural origins, provides scope for traditional mutual-aid activities associated with rural life, which could not be undertaken within the conventional urban setting. These activities strengthen development-oriented characteristics of the residents. By moving into a settlement and building a house, the settler demonstrates a rational-instrumental view of the world rather than a fatalistic one. This is reflected in his disposition to defer immediate gratification, organize local institutions, trust others and assume moderate risks. These attributes correlate positively with a strong development outlook. By working co-operatively with others to improve their own lot and that of the community through the political process, the residents improve their political competence in dealing with political and administrative authorities. This can also have a spill-over effect by making administrative authorities more responsive to community demand-making. Where this occurs, it will increase citizen confidence in government and strengthen existing inclinations to work through established political and administrative channels. Where the political system is unresponsive, it will undermine confidence in the system and generate cynical attitudes toward government.

How Marginal Settlement Dwellers Define Their Needs:
The Agenda for Citizen and Governmental Action

What kinds of problems or needs relating to human environment are felt to be most important by residents of marginal settlements? By what methods do they go about resolving these problems? These are among the major issues that were raised in the first part of the study. Practical answers were sought by conducting case studies of popular participation in marginal settlements in Mexico City, Manila and in Turkey. The first case study is based on observations in six low-income settlements or *colonias proletarias* and a *ciudad perdida* — a shantytown in which most residents rent their plots of land from legal owners. The second focuses on five urban barrios (communities) in Tondo, Manila. These barrios are located in the Tondo foreshore land area, reclaimed by the Philippine government since 1940 and inhabited by low-income squatters following World War II. The study of *gecekondus* in Turkey is broader in character and analyzes the issues of citizen participation within a national context.

The survey reported in Table 1, drawn from the study of six *colonias proletarias* in Mexico City, reveal that security of land tenure was the salient need in the two squatter settlements (Colonia Nueva and Colonia Periferico) where official recognition of individual occupancy rights had not yet been secured. In the four officially recognized communities (Colonia Texcoco, a low-income *fraccionamiento*; Colonia Esfuerzo Propio, a government site-and-services project; Unidad Popular, a conventional public housing project; Colonia Miiitar, a legalized squatter settlement), virtually no one perceived security of tenure as a key need. In these communities, the provision or improvement of basic urban services — particularly piped water, sewerage systems and paved streets — were regarded as the most important needs, followed by community facilities such as schools, public markets and health care centres. Such problems as environmental pollution, lack of parks and other recreational facilities, and inadequate public transportation were salient only in the two most highly developed communities (Unidad Popular and Colonia Militar); and even in these settlements, deficiencies in water supply and in community facilities such as schools and public markets were viewed as more serious. The overall frequency with which needs for water and sewerage systems, paved streets and security of tenure were mentioned as the most important community-related deficiencies by residents of these *colonias* corresponds closely with the findings of other studies of perceived needs among residents of low-income settlements in Latin American cities. The overriding importance attached by residents of officially unrecognized squatter settlements to the problem of insecure land tenure is not surprising in view of the fact that the opportunity afforded by such settlements to become owner of a homesite constitutes one of the primary motivations of the squatters for moving there in the first place.

One of the most striking findings in the Mexico City settlements study, as well as other studies of "spontaneous" settlements in Latin American cities, concerns the relatively low priority attached by settlement residents to securing better (i.e., larger, more permanent) housing. It is clear that they regard security of land tenure, basic services such as piped water, and infrastructure improvements such as paved streets as more urgently needed than a spacious house built of permanent materials. Only 3 out of 678 migrants interviewed in the Mexico City research communities (excluding the *cuidad perdída*) mentioned "poor housing" as the most important problem confronting people in their settlement. Among residents of squatter settlements and low-income subdivisions, construction of permanent houses proceeds, but only at a pace commensurate with a family's financial resources. Most families would be extremely reluctant to assume the long-term financial burden that payments on a government or commercially built house would impose on them, even if they were able to acquire such housing. Instead, they prefer to build and improve their own houses as time and money become available, even though the basic construction period may last for ten to fifteen years.

Several other needs rank considerably lower in the low-income settler's order of priorities than one might expect. For example, electricity is rarely cited as a key community need, even by residents of squatter settlements and subdivisions lacking regular electrical service, because of the ease with which the settlers can "hook up" to power poles and transformers in nearby residential or commercial-industrial zones. Nearly half of the migrants interviewed in Mexico City and virtually all of those residing in the youngest squatter settlement and the low-income subdivision obtained their electricity in this "unauthorized" fashion; only 4 percent lacked electricity in their houses.

With regard to the need for more or better public schools, it may seem surprising that low-income settlers who value education highly for their children, if not for themselves, do not place schools at the top of the agenda for their community. In all of the communities included in the studies, children had access to one or more public schools in an adjacent *colonia* if not within their own. Even in the most recently established squatter settlements which were studied, residents had constructed their own make-shift school and obtained a teacher whose salary was paid by the official political party (PRI). In general, despite extreme overcrowding in many primary and secondary schools, the performance of the Mexican government in building public schools and providing teachers for community-built schools has been more impressive than in any other problem area affecting Mexico City's low-income neighbourhoods.

In the barrios in the Tondo foreshore, land tenure occupies the most salient position in the priorities of the settlers. This is followed by demands for improved roads, drainage, water, electricity, garbage collection and health services. The importance of these demands is underscored by the area's vulnerability to typhoons and the high incidence of fires.

In Turkey, the law governing *gecekondus* directly affects the nature of citizen demand-making. Thus, the first practical step after the *gecekondu* dwelling has been established is to prevent its destruction by city authorities because of what is commonly called "ruhsatsiz insaat" or building without a permit. Once the physical survival of the *gecekondu* is assured through a variety of orthodox and unorthodox means, the squatters' next concern is to qualify the *gecekondu* as a rehabilitation or "islah" settlement. This is a basic decision on the part of the city authorities because it assures not only the survival of the *gecekondu* but also qualifies it to receive technical aid from the city and national government. The rehabilitation decision is often

Table 1. Most Important Community Problem Perceived by Migrants in Mexico City, by Community[a]

Problem	Colonia Neuva	Colonia Periférico	Colonia Texcoco	Colonia E. Propio	Unidad Popular	Colonia Militar	All
Water supply	23.4%	12.6%	32.5%	12.0%	35.6%	7.9%	20.1%
Sewerage	11.0	28.7	41.7	14.5	0.0	0.9	16.9
Security of tenure	46.7	45.8	0.8	0.0	0.0	2.6	16.5
Medical care facilities	2.0	0.0	10.4	20.5	13.6	13.2	10.0
Street pavement	2.3	8.9	7.5	19.6	3.4	2.6	7.7
Public markets	0.0	0.0	0.0	12.9	0.0	28.1	7.2
Schools	9.1	1.1	0.0	0.0	1.7	25.3	6.4
Environmental problems[b]	0.0	0.0	0.0	4.3	23.7	0.0	3.6
Electricity	1.0	0.0	5.0	3.4	0.0	0.0	1.8
Police protection	0.0	1.1	2.1	0.8	3.4	0.9	1.2
Garbage collection	0.0	1.9	0.0	0.0	0.0	3.5	0.9
Other	4.4	0.0	0.0	11.9	13.6	7.2	6.8
None	0.0	0.0	0.0	0.0	5.1	7.9	1.9

[a]The number of respondents (N) represented in the table is 663. Inter-community differences are statistically significant, by Chi-square test, at the .001 level. Column percentages may not total 100.0 because of rounding. "Don't know" and unascertained responses are excluded. The question was as follows: "Think now about the most important needs and problems of (this community). In your opinion, what are the most urgent or serious problems and needs of this community? (Probe:) Of these problems or needs which you have mentioned, which do you think is the most important?"

[b]Includes air pollution, insects, unstable subsoil conditions, and overcrowding.

the prelude to the formal granting of the "tapu" (land title) although in some cases, the title may be issued before issuance of the "islah." *Gecekondus*, which do not qualify as rehabilitable due to the terrain, the low quality of the buildings or the cost of bringing utilities there, are subject to "tasfiye" or liquidation, although even in these cases the decision may be altered. The rehabilitation decision forces the *gecekondu* settlement to conform to the master plan drawn by the city planners. The cost of rehabilitation which entails an investment in equipment and manpower is high, especially for the government. During rehabilitation a number of dwellings are usually torn down to make room for streets and other physical amenities necessitating the relocation of some inhabitants to new housing sites. As a rule, *gecekondu* residents do not object to this operation because it brings them *de jure* recognition, integrates the settlement into the city and makes them beneficiaries of city amenities, such as water, electricity and the sewage system, although some of these may be provided even before the settlement's full rehabilitation gets underway.

The second category of demands of *gecekondu* residents concerns the physical improvement for the entire community. Among these demands, building and paving roads, providing public transportation (bus service), establishing sewage systems, bringing water and electricity to the settlement take the first priority. The building of schools, mosques, dispensaries and other facilities for social and health services tends to have a second order of importance to the *gecekondu* dwellers who can use the facilities available in the adjacent old city district. The same holds true for health services. Regardless of the *gecekondus'* legal status, sanitation officials of the municipal and central government provide the dwellers with efficient sanitary services such as vaccine and periodic checks of the water for the control of smallpox, malaria, cholera, water pollution, etc. In a number of *gecekondus*, there are health clinics built by the dwellers themselves although the personnel is provided by the government at its own expense. As a result of these measures, Turkey has experienced few cases of epidemics in the *gecekondus* despite overcrowding in these settlements. Matters of household and individual hygiene are regarded as the *gecekondu* dweller's personal responsibility. However, community leaders often play supervisory roles in reminding the dwellers to whitewash the houses, disinfect the outhouses, clean the street, etc. In a number of cases, cleaning the *gecekondu* settlement as a whole may be undertaken as a community project.

THE CONVERSION OF FELT NEEDS INTO CITIZEN PARTICIPATION

Whether a given problem or need relating to the quality of the human environment becomes the object of citizen participation to secure assistance from the government or some other institution external to the community depends on a variety of factors, including (a) the nature of the problem, (b) the availability of resources internal to the community for dealing with it, and (c) resident perceptions of the scope of governmental responsibility in that problem area.

In Mexico City and other major Latin American cities, there is strong evidence that residents of low-income settlements regard housing *per se* as an *individual* (or, at most, family or extended family) responsibility. This observation also holds for Manila, the *gecekondus* in Turkey, as well as marginal settlements throughout the developing world. Housing in these settlements is a private and not a public responsibility. Thus, housing deficiencies rarely become the object of community-wide organizational activity, whether such activity is internally oriented (self-help projects) or aimed at securing external assistance from the government or some other source. It has been found that even in government site-and-service projects, technical assistance in housing construction by government-employed architects or skilled workers is not welcomed by project dwellers and may even be regarded as interference to be resisted. This resistance may derive partly from a lack of flexibility and insufficient respect for the preferences and specific housing requirements of low-income families on the part of the government advisers and technicians, but basically it appears to stem from the settler's conviction that housing problems are his own business.

Community-level self-help approaches are sometimes regarded by the settlers as most appropriate in dealing with such problems as public safety and street layouts. Public safety in the barrios in Manila is often viewed as a responsibility of the settlers. In two of the squatter settlements covered by the Mexican case study, residents had organized regular night-time security patrols to protect themselves against intruders, including would-be squatters who laid claim to their land. In all of the three squatter settlements, residents had also collaborated to lay out and grade streets, either with picks and shovels or with rented earth-moving machinery. In the low-income subdivision, residents provided both labour and most of the materials for installing a provisional water distribution system (public hydrants at intervals of two blocks). In all three of the squatter settlements, residents were responsible for building the first schools and community meeting halls, and in one of them a sizable permanent church and small plaza were built with labour and materials provided by the settlers. In the *cuidad perdida,* the settlers had succeeded after several years of ups and downs in maintaining a community health centre staffed by volunteer nurses and medical students from the National University, but the initiative for construction of the centre was supplied by a group of non-resident, middle-class women who began it as a charity project.

Before residents of low-income urban settlements decide to seek developmental assistance from the government or some other non-local agency, several conditions must generally obtain. First, the settlers must view individual or community-level self-help efforts as inappropriate or inadequate to the solution of the problem at hand. Second, they must view the problem as one particularly susceptible to solution through action by external agencies. Finally, the settlers must perceive a strategy or channel through which to articulate their needs and influence the behaviour of external officials controlling the resources they require.

In the case of Mexico City, Manila and the *gecekondus* in Turkey, it is clear that many kinds of felt needs among residents of low-income settlements are not viewed by them as needs to be satisfied through governmental action; such needs rarely become the object of what has been termed "demand-making" attempts. Their satisfaction is viewed by the settlers as the responsibility of the individual, the community, or perhaps some informal group internal to the community (e.g., the kin-based mutual assistance network). Alternatively, despite the urgency of such problems as unemployment, seeking government assistance may not be viewed as an effective way of dealing with the problem, either because of the complexities and delays involved in obtaining government help or perhaps because of low governmental responsiveness to requests for that kind of assistance. By contrast, securing land tenure rights and obtaining access to basic urban services are problems not viewed as being susceptible to solution through individual, network or community-based self-help efforts.

When residents of low-income settlements in Mexico City contact government officials in search of assistance, they are most likely to be concerned with legalizing the settlement and obtaining individual land titles. Nearly two-thirds of the contacts with officials reported by migrants residing in the six *colonias proletarias* were concerned with the need for security of land tenure. Second in frequency were petitions for potable water. A number of contacts with officials were initiated to request postal service, paved streets, electricity, schools, public transportation, sewerage disposal systems, improved garbage collection, and other community-related services or improvements. Mexican government officials report that in the more remote low-income settlements, there is stronger demand for schools, since children in these settlements have no access to school facilities available in nearly developed communities. Community clinics and other health care facilities are in little demand, apparently because the settlers prefer to utilize the better-equipped government hospitals and health centres closer to the central city. Demands for electrification remain infrequent, largely because, as noted above, the Federal Power Commission is tolerant of illegal hookups into the regular power lines.

Thus, the vast majority of the demands upon government emanating from these settlements are demands articulated in the name of an entire community, for non-divisible, "public goods" benefitting all residents of the community. Highly particularistic requests for jobs and other special dispensations benefitting only the individual petitioner or his relatives constitute an insignificant proportion of the settlers' demands. Again, it must be emphasized that the low frequency of particularistic demand-making reflects not only the urgency with which the low-income settler views such community-related problems as insecurity of land tenure and an inadequate water supply, but also his perceptions of what kinds of needs are *most amenable* to satisfaction through governmental action.

Although low-income settlement dwellers may take it upon themselves individually to contact government officials to present request for aid, most evidence from Latin American cities, including Mexico City, indicates that such individual demand-making is quite infrequent. Instead, the overwhelming majority of contacts with officials are made by the settler as a member of a delegation of residents from his community. These delegations are typically recruited from among the members of the community's improvement association, and are led by the officers of this association. If no such leadership and organizational resources are available to the settler, he is much less likely to engage in demand-making activity. Among the migrants interviewed in the six Mexico City *colonias*, those who had participated in community improvement organizations were *five times* more likely to have engaged in demand-making than the non-participants in such organizations.

Community improvement organizations and their leaders provide important psychological support for the low-income settler seeking to make demands on government. Participation in collective demand-making efforts greatly reduces the amount of individual initiative required, and provides the settler with a clear strategy for articulating his needs and influencing the behaviour of government decision-makers. Moreover, to the extent that community-based organizations are successful in securing benefits through collective demand-making attempts, they strengthen the settler's perceptions of the political system as being subject to manipulation and increase his sense of political efficacy. Such attitudes and perceptions increase his propensity to engage in future demand-making attempts.

Apart from formal voluntary associations dedicated to seeking community improvements, it is evident that strong local leaders can significantly increase the capacity of the low-income settlement to manipulate its social, economic and political environment. Leadership performance can greatly affect the outcomes of demand-making attempts, the length of time needed to accomplish certain developmental objects, the quality of relationships maintained between a settlement and governmental agencies, and the level of citizen participation within the settlement over time.

The impact of local leadership is most pronounced in those settlements ruled by *caciques*, strong and autocratic leaders who are recognized by both the residents of the communities in which they operate and government authorities as being the most powerful person in the community. Public officials usually deal with the *cacique* to the exclusion of other potential leaders in all matters affecting the community. The *cacique* also possesses *de facto* authority to make decisions binding upon the community he controls, as well as informal police powers and powers of taxation (usually described as "taking up a collection" to finance a given project, service or activity). Thus in some respects, *caciquismo* represents a sort of informal government-within-a-government, controlled by a single dominant individual who is not formally accountable either to those residing in the settlement under his control or to external political and governmental authorities.

In Mexico City and in other cities in Latin America where *caciquismo* holds sway, the *cacique* usually gains power through self-imposition, with the acquiescence — and occasionally the active support — of a majority of community residents. Since he (or she) holds no elective post and is not dependent on supra-local officials for appointment, he may remain in power until he voluntarily renounces his leadership role or is removed by force. The *cacique's* principal aim is to increase his personal wealth and that of his closest aides; and despite the poverty of most of its inhabitants, the settlement which he controls usually offers a rich harvest of opportunities for financial gain. In three of the squatter settlements studied in Mexico City, local *caciques* had been deeply involved in a variety of illicit money-making activities, including trafficking in lots or permits to occupy land within the settlement, fraudulent collection of money for personal use, commercial exploitation of local mineral resources, and the charging of special fees for access to basic urban services such as electricity (once "regular" electrical service had been installed). While illicit land deals are by far the most important source of income for *caciques* in many settlements, the frequent collection of donations ("cuotas" or "cooperaciones") from the residents may be equally lucrative. *Cuotas* collected by *caciques* in other surveyed settlements were usually tied to specific community projects or needs such as installing a provisional water supply system, repairing the community meeting hall or grading the main street; but it was evident that the sums collected were far in excess of the amounts actually expended by the *caciques* for these purposes.

The *cacique* in a low-income settlement is usually regarded by his followers with a mixture of respect, cynicism and fear. He is expected to use his power to line his own pockets whenever possible, but self-enrichment is overlooked as long as certain standards of performance are met. Demonstrated performance in securing concrete material benefits for the community is particularly important in this respect. In dealing with certain problems such as the legalization of land tenure within the settlement, the *cacique* may be confronted with a painful dilemma: the residents expect him to make a certain amount of progress toward resolving such a problem over a given period of time; yet the fixation of land tenure arrangements by governmental action may sharply diminish the *cacique's* own opportunities for extracting personal economic rewards through control of land use within the settlement. So he may engage in considerable footdragging in his efforts to secure official action to deal with the tenure problem. In the long run, however, the *cacique* must clearly "produce" on such salient concerns as reducing insecurity of land tenure within the settlement. If he fails to do so, he will find it increasingly difficult to maintain the allegiance of his followers and to forestall potential challenges to his leadership.

The *cacique* usually heads his community's improvement association and customarily identifies himself to outsiders as president of this body. Depending on how seriously he regards the association as a community institution and not just as an instrument of personal rule, the *cacique* may have an important and positive impact on the vitality of such an organization over time. As head of the improvement association, the *cacique* has wide authority to establish priorities for community development. In a very real sense, he is responsible for defining the community's objectives and organizing them into an agenda for negotiation with external authorities. The *cacique's* performance of his role as improvement organization leader also helps to legitimize his control over the allocation of many of the benefits secured from external political and governmental sources among community residents.

Caciques may also contribute importantly to the development of community norms regarding participation in self-help projects and political demand-making activity. Especially if participation in activities organized by the *cacique* is viewed by residents as being necessary to prevent the imposition of negative sanctions by him, extraordinarily high levels of resident participation may be achieved. Thus, the success of some *caciques* in mobilizing citizen participation can be explained largely by their success in solving what has been termed the "public goods dilemma" of community organizers. "The benefits of collective neighbourhood organization efforts are non-divisible public goods, and if there is no way to coerce all the members of the aggregate into paying their share of the costs of these goods — that is, in organizational participation — or unless there is some way to *exclude the non-contributor from the benefits of the collective goods*, there is very little incentive for the rational self-interested person to make a purely voluntary contribution to such efforts."

It is important to note that the *cacique* of a low-income settlement is usually linked as a client to one or more patrons in the government-official party apparatus, usually upper-echelon functionaries in the various offices of the city government or official party having responsibility for dealing with the problems of low-income neighbourhoods. The friendship and goodwill of these persons are cultivated assiduously by the *cacique* through a variety of means. Like all such clientage arrangements, the relationships between the *cacique* and his external patrons are based on reciprocal exchange of mutually valued goods and services. As well as granting him a large measure of autonomy in the running of local affairs and the allocation of government benefits within his community, the *cacique's* patrons represent a source of power and resources which may have an extremely important bearing upon his overall influence within the community. The *cacique* also relies on his patrons to expedite administrative actions favourable to the community and maintain an acceptable flow of material benefits to the area. In return, the *cacique* can be counted upon by his patrons to mobilize large numbers of people within the area under his control to attend official party meetings and rallies, public appearances of the President and other high-ranking officials, inaugurations of public works, and other civic events. Since the patron is usually in competition with other ambitious *politicos* to demonstrate to higher authorities a capacity to "move people" and otherwise turn out grassroot support for the regime, the *cacique's* "available masses" take on special importance. The *cacique* is also expected to maintain control of his settlement — to keep order, avoid scandals and public demonstrations embarrassing to the government, and head off any other types of occurrences which might disrupt social tranquility or undermine confidence in the regime. He also has obligations to "orient" his followers politically (i.e., propagandize on behalf of the regime and strengthen local identification with it) and to organize the participation of his followers in elections, voter registration campaigns, and other forms of officially prescribed political activity. Finally, the *cacique* is expected to assist the regime in minimizing demands for expensive, broadscope benefits which might "load" the political system beyond its responsive capacities. He does this by encouraging his followers to view the community as an entity isolated from other *colonias proletarias* in the city, with problems and solutions particular to that community. By defining the problems confronting the community in such parochial terms, the *cacique* helps to ensure that demand-making by community residents will remain focused upon short-term, community-specific needs. Flagrant violation of any of these basic terms of the informal contract between the *cacique* and his official patron may be punished by a withdrawal of the patron's support and recognition, which may undermine the *cacique's* influence within his community.

The existence of widespread *caciquismo* in both urban and rural communities in Mexico and other Latin American countries has become an increasingly controversial issue among public officials in recent years, some of whom worry that continued reliance on *caciques* for control and electoral mobilization of the poor fosters political alienation and identification of the regime with the exploitative behaviour of *caciques* among the masses. From the standpoint of the poor, too, the costs and benefits of *caciquismo* as a form of local leadership are quite mixed. The economic costs of this form of leadership to individual residents of a low-income settlement can be quite high. Yet the residents of such communities especially the more recently formed squatter settlements, know that they confront a number of urgent developmental problems which must be resolved if their community is to survive and mature into an environment that satisfies their needs for security of land tenure, basic urban services and improvements. The evidence from *colonias proletarias* in Mexico City which were studied suggests that strong leadership — whether of the *cacical* form or some other type — can significantly increase the capacity of the low-income community to manipulate the political system in order to secure assistance in community development.

In Turkey, leadership and institutions in the *gecekondu* have formal as well as an informal cast. The *gecekondu* possesses formally established associations and elected leaders. The latter represent the community as a whole and speak on its behalf. These leaders may belong to a regional, kinship or religious group but are elected by the entire *gecekondu* on the basis of their achievement and capabilities regardless of their former family status in the village, town or country of origin. In the case of *gecekondus* with a large population, leaders may represent a specific *mahalle* or district. All elected leaders become part of the governing board of the *Gecekonduyu Güzellestirme Dernegi* (Association for Improving the Gecekondu — AIG). In some cases, this association may take the name of *Gecekondu Yardimlasma Dernegi* (Association for Mutual Assistance — AMA). The head of AIG or AMA is considered the head of the *gecekondu* and is its most important leader. In a number of isolated cases outsiders may also be elected to head AIG largely because of their professional abilities and connexions in the municipal and national government. The head of AIG may not be personally known to the *gecekondu* residents, and he may not muster the direct personal influence of the traditional communal leader or of the *muhtar*. He is brought to the chairmanship of the AIG largely because of his contacts in the government and his ability to get things done. In contrast to communal leaders who emerge naturally through day to day contact with *gecekondu* inhabitants, the head and board members of AIG are elected in conformity with the national law governing the establishment and functioning of associations.

The AIG chairman and board members appear to be elected by all members of the association (all *gecekondu* residents of a certain age are eligible to become members) while in reality their election is decided by a handful of traditional leaders and other interested parties concerned with the survival of the community. The election takes place in the headquarters of AIG. This establishment is built in common by all *gecekondu* dwellers and serves as a hall for wedding ceremonies, festivals, lectures, meetings of the AIG board, and even study. The chief purposes of AIG are to formulate demands on behalf of the entire *gecekondu* community, to establish communication with municipal and government officials. AIG also has the responsibility of mobilizing the population and of assuring its participation in a variety of self-help projects designed to develop and improve the quality of life in the *gecekondu* through such projects as paving roads, digging trenches for water pipes and building schools. However, as shall be discussed later, AIG directs more of its efforts toward securing support for a common line of action and pressuring authorities rather than toward achieving popular participation in specific self-help projects. The emphasis placed on government assistance rather than reliance on the human resources of the *gecekondu* itself is the consequence of the traditional concept of "father-state" whereby the state (*devlet*) is acknowledged to have a preeminent role in the affairs of its citizens, as well as the bargaining for votes between AIG leaders and political parties. Often AIG leaders feel that they can gain far more by striking a bargain with a winning candidate or with a political party than by relying on the goodwill of the community. A successful deal with outside authorities brings more prestige to the leaders than the tedious and frustrating job of mobilizing the community for some self-improvement projects. A leader's position in the community is assured if he can obtain the *tapu*, that is, the title to the land. This he may achieve by maneuvering and bargaining with outside agencies, such as the officials of the municipal and national government and political parties. Consequently, the elected leaders are often technically unprepared or do not care to mobilize the community for other than political action. In cases in which the AIG chairmen are well prepared and sufficiently motivated, they can go a long way in securing popular participation for self-improvement. For instance, the chairman of the AIG in the Gülveren *gecekondu* in Ankara, a man with mid-level education (the overwhelming majority of AIG leaders seem to have only elementary school education, often incomplete) was instrumental in securing community participation in building roads and bringing water to the settlement. He also established a co-operative within the *gecekondu* to purchase the land from private owners and instituted a typing course for girls in the community to prepare them for secretarial jobs.

Another institution of fundamental importance in the political, social and economic life of the *gecekondu* is the *muhtarlik* headed by the *muhtar* or the headman of the city precinct in which the settlement is established. The *gecekondus* are built usually in the vicinity of an old city district and administratively become part of its *muhtarlik*, that is, the precinct or city ward. A city is divided into *kaza* (districts) *nahiye* or *bucaks* and *muhtarlike*. The *muhtarlik* is also the basic administrative unit of the central government as well as of the municipality. The city also has a municipal administration (*belediye*) headed by an elected mayor (*belediye reisi or baskan*). The *muhtar* of a city ward (the village is administered also by a *muhtar*) is instrumental in formulating the demands of his precinct including those of the *gecekondu* and transmitting them to the municipal or national government through a rather involved hierarchical channel. The officials' point of contact in the ward is also the *muhtar*. In addition to these functions, the *muhtar* performs a series of other official duties; issuance of certificates of domicile, verification of certain occurrences, etc. Thus, a *muhtar* sympathetic to the *gecekondu* may greatly facilitate its communication with official agencies and help to influence the decisions of the government and municipal authorities capable of satisfying the *gecekondu* demands.

The *muhtar* is elected every four years by all the eligible voters in his precinct, including the *gecekondu* dwellers. Consequently, in a number of cases, the *muhtar* may belong to an established city group and yet may be elected through *gecekondu* support, while in other cases, especially when the population of the *gecekondu* exceeds that of the old district, he may be a *gecekondu* resident. In a number of cases the *gecekondus* have formed their own *muhtarliks* but the government has discouraged this practice since the main purpose in establishing this office was to gain additional political leverage for pressure to satisfy demands.

Formal affiliation of the *gecekondu* dwellers with political parties is extremely rare. Probably about 1-5 percent of the population of voting age is formally registered with a political party. Yet their participation in politics is very high. Participation by *gecekondu* residents in elections is about 10-15 percent above the national average, and in view of their large numbers they can provide some 40-60 percent of the votes cast in the large cities of Turkey. It is, therefore, quite understandable that all political parties and individual politicians in the city spare no effort trying to secure their support. Significantly, a special twist of the election system gives the *gecekondu* leaders unusually strong political leverage. Political parties do not have offices in the *gecekondus* since the opening of party branches in city wards and *bucaks* was prohibited after the military takeover in 1960. Parties have branch offices only in *kaza* and *vilayet* (province) seats. Consequently, these leaders, especially the AIG officers, are well situated to provide grassroot contact and support to the political parties and the politicians of their choice, despite the fact that AIG is forbidden by law to engage in politics. The leaders' main problems are to achieve and maintain a united political front and deliver the *gecekondu* vote as a bloc to a chosen party or candidate. During election periods *gecekondu* leaders are actively involved, on the one hand, in assessing community opinion, formulating demands for services and deciding which candidates to support while on the other, attempting to maintain political unity in the community.

A number of *geckondu* dwellers are members of occupational organizations, sports associations or other groups established for a specific purpose, such as building mosques or schools. Yet, the number of people joining such formal organizations is very low. The total number of *gecekondu* residents who are members of some formal organization seldom exceeds 10-15 percent of the entire settlement population. The percentage of younger people of 20-30 years of age who join formally established culture, even political associations, is twice that of the next older age group.

The settlers' choice of demand-making targets exhibits an accurate understanding of the nature of government decision-making processes in Mexico City, Manila and Turkey as well as in other countries where the situation of marginal settlements was reviewed, despite the fact that a multiplicity of agencies from the national and local levels usually have some jurisdictional responsibility in settlement affairs. In the Philippines, community development workers from national and city government agencies have been actively involved in Tondo in the past 15 years. In Mexico City, demand-making by settlers reveal a clear understanding of the highly centralized nature of official decision-making processes. In attempting to influence the outcomes of this process, "both efficiency and security argue that it is wise to seek support and decisions as close to the centre as possible, lest time be wasted with those who don't count and whose decisions may subsequently be overturned." Thus, residents of a community seeking a water supply system may send copies of their petition to a *delegado*, to the head of the city's water department, and to other middle-echelon officials, but will seek to negotiate directly with the mayor (Regente) of Mexico City or one of his closest deputies. Direct approaches are also made occasionally to the President during his inspection tours in various parts of the city, as well as to the First Lady and top-level assistants to the President, and copies of all major community petitions are routinely sent to the office of the President. Of course, access to officials with personal political power and decisional autonomy is more difficult to obtain; yet the potential rewards flowing from contacts with such officials are likely to be far more substantial and immediate than any benefits provided by their subordinates.

If these and other inducements fail to produce the desired results, the petitioners may attempt to exert indirect pressure on the government by publicizing their needs through the mass media. One major newspaper in Mexico City, for example, maintains a section for "complaints and petitions" directed at public officials by residents of predominantly low-income neighbourhoods, and delegations of residents from such communities often visit the newspaper's offices to present copies of their petitions to the government or to request news coverage of the situation in their community. The resulting stories may be highly embarrassing to unresponsive bureaucrats. Another indirect tactic, less frequently used, involved asking official party functionaries to intercede with government officials responsible for acting on their petitions. Negotiations with the government for recognition of land tenure rights and installation of basic urban services are usually quite complex and require frequent attention by the petitioners over a long period of time. A government decision to "regularize" an illegally formed community must be followed by a number of additional administrative acts before individual tenure rights can be considered secure. These actions include expropriation of the land (if privately owned before it was invaded or illegally subdivided); completion of technical studies to determine the feasibility of installing certain types of services and improvements; completion of a census of current occupants of land within the settlement; surveying and subdivision of the land into parcels assigned to individual residents; and determination of land prices, service assessments, and terms of payment. At any of these stages in the regularization of the settlement, serious difficulties and delays may develop; hence, the necessity for numerous follow-up visits to check on the processing of the community's petitions and to cultivate personal relationships with the officials in charge.

The competition for government attention from many other communities whose needs are equally acute is often fierce, but persistence and skill in negotiating with officials can often make a great difference, particularly in a city where the allocation of government benefits to low-income areas is not covered by routinized developmental or planning criteria. In the case of Mexico City, there have been no clear administrative guidelines for determining which low-income neighbourhoods will receive which services and improvements, and when. Neither has there been any single government office in the capital having overall responsibility for planning and resource allocation for low-income areas of the city. Many government agencies and individual politicians and bureaucrats act, or claim to act, in behalf of the *colonias proletarias*. These conditions are clearly reflected in the highly idiosyncratic responses made by officials to petitions from low-income neighbourhoods within the city. Official behaviour toward such communities has fluctuated sharply from overt hostility to benevolent permissiveness with top-level changes in city (and State of Mexico) government personnel. Stubborn refusals to urbanize a squatter settlement on technical grounds that topography or subsoil conditions would make the introduction of basic services prohibitively expensive have given way virtually overnight to a decision to provide all necessary services. While affording certain opportunities to lower-class petitioners, the absence of formally established guidelines by which needs are evaluated and the availability of multiple access points within the government bureaucracy may create other kinds of obstacles, especially for low-income communities whose leaders have failed to develop connexions with high-ranking officials. The particularism of bureaucratic behaviour, which is a widespread phenomenon in developing countries, makes it difficult for settlers in these communities to get a firm commitment for improvement programmes.

Data available from the six settlements that were studied in Mexico City reveal the rewards of citizen participation. Following this analysis, an assessment will be made of government effort to upgrade marginal settlements by focussing on its efforts to grant tenure and encourage self-help housing and the construction of physical overhead.

During the past decade, and especially since the Luis Echeverria administration took office in December 1970, officials have worked diligently to cultivate an image of accessibility and responsiveness to the needs of the poor in Mexico City, even though their responses to petitions from low-income neighbourhoods may often take the form of symbolic reassurances (e.g., making inspection tours, committing the problem at hand to technical study) rather than allocations of material benefits. Petitioners from low-income settlements are seldom refused access to lower- or middle-echelon officials; and those interviewed who had visited a government or PRI office overwhelmingly reported that they were treated courteously and fairly by the officials they contacted. Furthermore, over two-thirds of the migrants interviewed in six *colonias proletarias* who had participated in demand-making attempts believed that such attempts had been successful, in the sense of having contributed to the solution of some community problem. Table 2 summarizes the outcomes of demand-making attempts by residents of the communities that were surveyed over the period since settlement of each community began, as reported in interviews with community leaders. Colonias Nueva, Periferico and Militar are squatter settlements; Colonia Texcoco is a low-income subdivision; Colonia Esfuerzo Propio, a government site-and-services project; and Unidad Popular, a conventional public housing project. While the leaders of these communities tend to depict any benefit received by their community as the outcome of demand-making attempts rather than governmental initiative, detailed investigation — including interviews with the relevant government decision-makers — confirms that most of the benefits cited by community leaders would not have been provided in the absence of persistent petitioning. Records still in the possession of community leaders are too incomplete to permit a rigorous cost (in time, money, etc.) benefit analysis of demand-making efforts by these communities. But lest it be assumed that these communities have benefitted from a typically high level of governmental responsiveness, it should be noted that most of the benefits which they have received are the result of dozens of written petitions and personal visits to a variety of government offices, often extending over a period of five to ten years. Moreover, many serious needs of the communities surveyed have gone unmet. Even today, functioning sewerage systems, schools, public markets and health care facilities are inadequate or nonexistent in three of the six communities. In some cases, these unmet needs reflect an absence or suspension of demand-making efforts by community residents; in others, a lack of skill or commitment among community leaders has led to unproductive negotiations with the authorities. Still other unmet needs reflect a sheer lack of responsiveness by government officials to persistent petitioning.

As noted above, the Mexican government since 1970 has adopted a policy of actively assisting established squatter settlements and clandestine subdivisions to legalize their tenure situation and acquire basic urban services. Nevertheless, the actual commitments of government resources for implementation of this up-grading policy have fallen far short of the needs. Even though more than 157 *ciudades perdidas* and other types of spontaneous settlements have been eradicated by the government since 1970, at least 500 to 600 such settlements remain within the metropolitan area, and probably no more than a quarter of these have benefitted substantially from government regularization and urbanization efforts.

No fewer than three separate government agencies and commissions have been created since 1970 for the purpose of regularizing established spontaneous settlements: CORETT (Comision Regularizadora de la Tenencia de la Tierra), FIDEURBE, and the Fideicomiso Nezahualcóyotl (set up especially to deal with land tenure disputes in the numerous *fraccionamientos* which comprises the *municipio* of Ciudad Netzahualcóyotl). The performance of these organs has been widely criticized by organizations of squatters, subdivisions' residents, and "urban" ejidatarios, who accuse the officials employed in the regularization agencies of taking bribes from landowners and subdividers whose interests are affected by their work and even from individuals seeking to promote new squatter invasions. Considerable resentment has also been generated by the new payments which the regularizing agencies require of individual settlers for providing land titles and urban services. In most cases, the legal mechanism employed by the agencies has been to expropriate the land occupied by a spontaneous settlement and resell it to the settlers. Many settlers view these assessments as unjust over-payments since they have already paid someone else (subdividers, invasion organizers, *ejido* owners) for the land. They argue that the government should attempt to extract payment from these individuals rather than penalize those now occupying the land, many of whom were unaware of the irregularities in tenure rights when they purchased their lot. On the other hand, there has been little or no opposition to the regularization assessments among squatter settlement residents who have not previously paid anyone for the land they occupy.

The urban planning and development agency of the State of Mexico, AURIS, has also attempted since 1970 to stimulate permanent housing construction and other types of self-help activities in spontaneous settlements within its jurisdiction. Following a policy advocated by John F.C. Turner the agency has sought to maximize individual incentives for self-construction of houses, with the owner-builder proceeding according to his own design and at his own pace. AURIS provided technical assistance to the settlers, as well as specialized or skilled labour for some aspects of the construction (e.g., plumbing) and low-cost building materials (offered at wholesale prices). Credit for housing construction was also included in the agency's original plan, but thus far it has lacked the resources to provide such credit. Apparently, the only aspect of the programme which has succeeded in gaining widespread acceptance among the settlers is the sale of low-cost building materials.

Table 2. Outcomes of Settlers' Demand-Making Attempts by Community

Colonia Nueva	Colonia Periférico	Colonia Texcoco	Colonia E. Propio	Unidad Popular	Colonia Militar
Destruction of stone wall erected by former landowner to restrict access to community	Introduction of regular bus service	Installation of provisional electricity supply system	(None — water and sewerage systems, electricity, and other services and improvements installed at government initiative)	Installation of water purification plant	Government recognition of land tenure rights
Reconstruction of houses destroyed by fire	Installation of provisional water system	Construction of secondary school		Postponement of property tax payments	Installation of electricity for individual dwellings and street lighting
Expropriation of land occupied by community (first step toward legalization of community)	Construction of primary school	Installation of provisional water supply system		Construction of two primary schools, one secondary school	Installation of sewerage system
Construction of primary school	Installation of regular electricity supply system and street lighting	Construction of child-care centre		Installation of several public telephones	Construction of primary school
Installation of regular electricity supply system	Pavement of main street			Paving of some streets	Paving of streets
	Installation of one public telephone				Installation of public and private telephones
	Expropriation of land occupied by community				

Technical assistance by agency architects and specialized labour by agency-employed artisans have not been welcome. As noted above, low-income settlers are likely to resist any such interference in construction and design of their dwelling.

The results of other AURIS programmes aimed at encouraging self-help efforts in spontaneous settlements (street building, installation of water pipes, etc.) have also been mixed. Agency officials have encountered a wide range of responses, from enthusiasm through apathy to resistance. In some cases, the agency's promotional efforts have elicited what its officials term an "unrealistic community response" — i.e., demands for expensive or inappropriate improvements. In other cases, a positive initial response by communtiy residents has been followed by paralysis due to internal conflicts. Like other government agencies, AURIS has been hesitant to stimulate the development of community action groups which become true "advocacy" groups for spontaneous settlements, going beyond small-scale self-help projects to demand large-scale infrastructure investments by the government. But the agency's efforts in self-help promotion are too experimental and too recently initiated to permit any definitive evaluations or predictions about their eventual success.

FACTORS AFFECTING THE LEVELS AND DURATION OF CITIZEN PARTICIPATION IN COLLECTIVE SELF-HELP AND DEMAND-MAKING ACTIVITIES

Data gathered from the study of six *colonias proletarias* in Mexico City show that about 26 percent of the total sample of migrants interviewed in these communities had participated in some form of community self-help activity in the *colonia* where they were interviewed. The migrants did not differ markedly from their Mexico City-born neighbours in frequency of participation in community self-help and demand-making activity. Participation by residents of these *colonias* was somewhat lower than in similar lower-class settlements which have been studied in Lima, Peru and Rio de Janeiro, Brazil, but higher than in low-income settlements studied in Santiago, Chile, during the 1960s. The Mexico City settlers' participation rate also exceeded that of a citywide sample of lower-class adults residing in the provincial city of Jalapa, Mexico, and — by more than a 3-to-1 margin — that of a national sample of urban-dwelling Mexicans interviewed in 1959.

Among the settlers interviewed in Mexico City, the incidence of participation in community self-help and demand-making activity varied considerably from one settlement to another. For example, the proportion of migrants who had engaged in demand-making ranged from 45 percent in the youngest squatter settlement to 10 percent in the low-income subdivision. These inter-community differences can be attributed partly to the nature of the developmental problems which each community has confronted (e.g., demand-making has been more frequent among migrants living in squatter settlements because of the extended negotiations required for government recognition of land tenure rights in such communities); but, as shall be argued below, differences in a variety of other community characteristics appear to be equally important in determining the individual resident's propensity to participate.

Data from the communities surveyed in Mexico City showed that migrants who participated frequently in community self-help and demand-making activities did not differ significantly from their less participant or nonparticipant neighbours in terms of such standard socio-economic characteristics as educational level attained, income level, occupational status and length of residence in Mexico City. (This section is based entirely on data gathered through personal interviews with a random sample of 747 residents of the six *colonias proletarias* in Mexico City. The findings are reported *in extenso* because of their wide applicability to participants in community improvement reported by other investigators of marginal settlements in other cities in a wide range of countries.) The recognized leaders in these communities are, however, more likely than their most participant followers to be self-employed (small retail merchants, professionals, technicians, artisans), and to have relatively high and stable incomes. These individuals are, of course, better equipped than the average resident in terms of time and resources to play a leadership role in community affairs. Retail merchants, most of whom own and operate stores in the communities where they live, have the added advantage of an occupation which bring them into frequent personal contact with large numbers of community residents. The distance of the settlers' workplace from their place of residence had little relationship to their frequency of participation in community affairs; in fact, those who participated most frequently in demand-making activities were somewhat more likely than their neighbours to live long distances (ten kilometers or more) from their work place.

Some interesting differences emerge between the more highly participant settlers and their less participant neighbours in terms of several general attitudinal characteristics. The participants are considerably more likely than non-participants to exhibit such traits as a propensity to plan for the future, a capacity to project one's self into the social or political roles of other people (empathy), a felt need for achievement, a sense of control over one's environment (the opposite of fatalism), and a propensity to take risks in order to achieve desired goals. All these traits are generally regarded as indicators of attitudinal modernity. The participants are also more likely to possess a higher level of generalized trust in people and a stronger preference for working collectively rather than individually to satisfy important needs than the non-participants.

A willingness to take sides in conflict situations has been identified as an important characteristic of certain types of political activists in the United States. The data gathered among low-income settlers in Mexico City also showed that those who engage frequently in demand-making and community self-help activities are considerably more likely than their less participant neighbours to take sides on controversial issues and to be willing to place themselves in situations of inter-group or inter-personal conflict. Since both demand-making and community self-help activities sometimes result in conflicts of opinion or of personalities, the participants' tolerance for conflict equips them well for their role.

The way in which the settler relates himself to his community is one of the most important factors influencing his propensity to participate in demand-making and community self-help activities. The participants are more strongly integrated into their community, both socially and psychologically, than non-participants. Participants tend to view themselves as permanent residents of the community in which they currently live, have a personal sense of "belonging" to the social system of the community, take a personal interest in community problems, and interact frequently with neighbours and relatives living in the community. The active participants in demand-making and community self-help projects have also made a greater personal investment — both material and psychological — in their community. They are much more likely than non-activists to own their own homes rather than rent them, to have built their houses with their own labour, to have used permanent building materials in the construction of their houses, and to have obtained the land which they occupy through participation in a land invasion. They have, in short, a larger personal stake in activities aimed at defending or improving the community as a whole.

Activists also differ markedly from non-activists in terms of their perceptions and evaluations of their community. They are more likely to perceive a high level of solidarity among residents of the community and are more sensitive to community norms of behaviour. They express a higher level of personal satisfaction with their community as a residential environment, and they are also more likely than non-participants to view their community as being upwardly mobile in a developmental sense. This finding is consistent with those of several other studies of low-income urban settlements in Latin America, which also discovered a significant relationship between settlers' perceptions of rates of community development and the incidence of community-related political activity. If after a number of years the settler feels that his community has failed to develop and that its long-term prospects for government assistance and security of land tenure are unfavourable, he has little incentive to become involved in activities aimed at securing community improvements.

The data from Mexico City also show that participant settlers are much more conscious of the identities and activities of local leaders and tend to evaluate the performance of these leaders in a positive way. Participants appear to be more responsive than the average resident to the mobilizing and organizing activities of community leaders. In several of the settlements in Mexico City, it was evident that confidence in the ability of local leaders to bargain effectively with public officials was an extremely important factor in persuading residents to "stick their necks out" by engaging in petitioning for government aid in community development. But even those settlers who were less charitable in their evaluations of the performance of local leaders were usually aware of the sanctions which these leaders were often capable of imposing (e.g., loss of one's plot of land in a squatter settlement). The costs of participating in community affairs, measured in time, money or discomfort at being exposed to conflictual situations, may reduce the individual settler's responsiveness to the leader's appeals for participation; but in communities where leaders are in a position to reward those who participate and penalize those who fail to do so, any cost/benefit calculation regarding such participation must include the costs of non-participation as well.

A certain level of awareness of how the political system operates and how its outputs affect one's personal life is generally assumed to be a necessary precondition for most kinds of civic participation. In the settlements studied in Mexico City, those who had participated most frequently in demand-making efforts had far greater knowledge about politics and government institutions than non-participants, and were also more likely to perceive the relevance of government and politics to the satisfaction of personal and community needs. However, settlers who had engaged more frequently in community self-help activities than in demand-making exhibited low levels of political consciousness; their orientation toward the political system was considerably more parochial than that of the frequent demand-makers.

Numerous studies have shown that persons whose attitudes toward the political system are strongly positive or supportive of the system are much more likely to engage in political activity than those whose political attitudes are less system-supportive. The data for low-income settlers in Mexico City also reveal a strong relationship between civic participation and positive orientations toward the political system. Activist settlers surpass the non-activists by considerable margins in their esteem for national political and governmental institutions, their tendency to support the official party (PRI) in elections, and their willingness to trust the government "to do what is best." The activists exhibit less cynicism about the behaviour and motives of politicians and government officials and are more likely to believe that public officials are concerned about the welfare of the poor. They tend to view officials as being responsive to requests for assistance from the average citizen, and exhibit a greater sense of political efficacy or confidence in their own ability to influence the actions of public officials.

Settlers who have engaged most frequently in demand-making are generally more supportive in their attitudes toward the political system than those who have participated only in community self-help activity. The demand-makers, of course, have had the experience of personal contact with public officials, and their strongly positive orientations toward the political system may represent outcomes of this personal contact with government decision-makers. However, one might also argue, reversing the order of causation, that contacting of officials, perhaps more than any other mode of civic participation, seems to *require* a strongly positive set of orientations toward the political system. Those who would engage in demand-making activity must believe that public officials want to know the needs and grievances of the average citizen and will respond in a nonpunitive fashion to citizen influence attempts. They must have confidence in both the willingness and capacity of the government to provide whatever assistance is being sought. In short, they must take an optimistic view of the opportunities afforded by the political system to satisfy some of their needs through petitioning.

As noted above, most of the civic participation engaged in by residents of low-income settlements in Mexico City is of a collective nature. Those who are concerned with demand-making and community self-help efforts usually participate as members of task-oriented groups. Thus, it could be expected that exposure to certain kinds of collective learning experiences and affiliation with voluntary organizations would increase the likelihood that an individual will become involved in collective action. The data gathered in six *colonias proletarias* and elsewhere confirm this expectation: demand-makers and frequent participants in community self-help activities are drawn disportionately from that portion of the sample which had participated in a land invasion. They are also more likely than nonparticipants to have witnessed at least one attempt by the government or a private landowner to evict the occupants of illegally occupied land, whether in their current community of residence or elsewhere in Mexico City. Thus, the invasion experience appears to be a more important factor predisposing the settler toward civic participation if it has met with strong resistance. This finding contradicts the argument that negative sanctions accompanying a land invasion have a depressant effect upon political involvement among the invaders. A more comprehensive measure of exposure to collective stress situations — land invasions, eviction attempts by the government or landowners, widespread flooding, major fires and other disasters affecting large numbers of community residents — reveals even more clearly the politicizing effects of such experiences. Stressful situations affecting the residents of a settlement increase their psychic investment in the community — an investment which they may seek to protect through civic participation.

As was noted above, settlers who are members of voluntary organizations tend to participate more than those who are not, irrespective of their socio-economic characteristics or attitudes toward the political system. This is especially true of settlers who belong to organizations whose concerns are in some way related to political activity, such as political parties, labour unions, and community improvement organizations. But even involvement in *non*-politically relevant organizations such as church groups, parent-teachers associations and other types of social service organizations appears to stimulate participation in community problem-solving. This probably occurs because organizational affiliation in general serves to locate the individual settler in networks of social communication and interaction which are important in sensitizing him to community norms regarding participation. For those who belong to community improvement organizations, these organizations facilitate participation in activities such as demand-making by reducing the amount of individual initiative and other kinds of "costs" entailed in petitioning.

2
Health and Environment in Human Settlements*

By Dr. A.E. Martin
In collaboration with staff members of the World Health Organization

FOURTEEN VITAL QUESTIONS

Ideally, a report on the state of health in human settlements should discuss and compare in terms of positive health, as defined in the Constitution of the World Heatlh Organization, the state of health in the different types of human settlement throughout the world. Health, however, has so far defied all attempts to quantify it for statistical purposes. It is necessary therefore to approach the subject from a negative angle and analyse the hazards and influences which affect health. To a degree this has already been done in detail in "Health Hazards of the Human Environment" published by WHO in 1972. In the following pages the subject is carried a stage further and an attempt is made to determine how far these influences and hazards are affecting human health in the various types of settlements, and to assess their relative importance.

The health services in many parts of the world are still in the early stages of development, with the result that there is frequently a dearth of reliable statistics suitable for international comparison. Reliance has therefore to be placed on the results of special surveys and studies extrapolating them when necessary from one country to another.

For the convenience of the reader the principal findings are summarized in the answers to the following fouteen vital questions.

1. **Which types of settlement would offer the healthiest conditions in which a parent would wish to bring up a family and, conversely, which would be the most detrimental to health?**

Ideally, a person would wish to bring up a family in a settlement (1) where the environmental and epidemiological conditions were such that the individuals were not submitted to any local health hazard e.g., communicable diseases, including waterborne and foodborne infections and diseases spread by poor sanitary and environmental conditions, chemical hazards, e.g., air pollution, adulterated or contaminated foods, or physical hazards, e.g., earthquakes or hurricanes; (2) with efficient preventive health services to safeguard against health hazards that may still arise, e.g., vaccination and immunization facilities, maternity and child welfare services, health education facilities, occupational health services; (3) with good medical care services, general family doctor, hospital and consultant facilities with appropriate supporting services; (4) with good social welfare services ensuring adequate financial provision for sickness, for unemployment, for old age, and in the event of premature death of the wage earner; (5) with good social services, including care for the physically or mentally handicapped, home help services (to provide domestic help where needed by reason of sickness or old age), and geriatric services; (6) with a satisfactory standard of living and quality of life. This should be such as to ensure sufficient quantity and variety of food, satisfactory housing and satisfying employment together with pleasant surroundings, facilities for recreation and social intercourse, and also a stable administration and government, all providing for the full enjoyment of life, development of personality

*Abridged version of a background paper for Habitat contributed by the World Health Organization. (Symbol A/Conf. 70/B/2; 21 October 1975.)

and freedom from undue stress and anxiety. Such an "ideal" environment, however, could result in the individual members of the family not having a sufficient stimulus and challenge to develop adequate character and personality.

An environment which is the most detrimental to health would be to a great extent the converse of the above. The actual poorness of the quality of any given combination of harmful factors becomes a matter of a value judgement in which individuals would differ markedly in what they wanted to avoid for themselves and their families.

2. What sort of health differences are to be expected between human settlements in different parts of the world?

The differences are very great. On the basis of a study of mortality in children under five, carried out between 1968 and 1971 in 10 American countries by PAHO, great differences are found between developing areas and the more developed areas which had good health and social services and good standards of living. In this study children were chosen, as they are the most susceptible to deleterious health conditions. The findings would be applicable to many other parts of the world.

It was shown that there were very large differences in child mortality particularly in the post-neonatal period (i.e., between the ages of one month and one year). The greatest differences were in deaths from communicable diseases and more particularly from diarrhoea. Thus, in one area investigated in a Latin American country, deaths from diarrhoea in children under 5 were approximately 1000 times as great as in a healthy suburban area in North America. Measles was also a very important cause of death in the Latin American countries.

Nutritional deficiency was found to be the predominant underlying or associated cause of death, making children more susceptible to the effects of the various diseases. In some areas two-thirds of the deceased children had shown evidence of malnutrition. Nutrition of the mother was also an important factor, since it led to infants of low birth weight, among whom it was shown that there was an excessive mortality during the first month of life. Such conditions of malnutrition are to be found in many developing countries.

The provision of piped water and adequate sanitation was shown to be an important factor. There is a greater likelihood of children dying in houses without these facilities.

An inverse relationship existed between the deaths and the educational status of the mother, the latter probably being a reflection of the effects of socioeconomic status.

More children died in crowded houses, although socioeconomic and cultural factors may have been largely responsible for this.

Mortality was greater in the rural areas studied in Latin America than in the associated urban areas and it was thought that even greater differences would have been found if more isolated rural areas had been investigated.

3. Do similar differences operate in adult life?

National statistics indicate that many developing countries have higher proportions of adults who die during early and middle adult life. A comparative study was made between 1962 and 1964 of mortality at ages 15-74 in 10 Latin American cities, and in San Francisco, USA and Bristol, England. This demonstrated that there were generally higher death rates in the Latin American towns, particularly in the age range 15-45. Analysis of deaths by cause showed an excess of deaths from infections and parasitic diseases, including tuberculosis, in the Latin American towns and one of them had a high death rate from Chagas' disease (American trypanosomiasis).

4. Are health conditions worse in rural than urban areas?

In most parts of the world, yes. The American study of deaths in childhood showed higher mortality rates in the rural areas. It is likely that this pattern would be found in most developing countries with poor and inadequate water supplies, inadequate sanitary facilities and poor health care services and frequently higher communicable disease rates in the rural areas.

In developed countries cities have often higher mortality rates than rural areas. In these countries good health care services, good water supplies, sanitation and housing are to be found in the rural areas. Frequently there are important differences in socioeconomic class distribution, with a larger proportion of persons of low socioeconomic class (who have higher mortality rates) located in the towns, particularly the slum areas of towns. A proportion of people in the higher socioeconomic class may migrate into suburban areas and rural areas near to the towns, which have good health services; these areas may have particularly good health records.

5. Deficient water supplies and poor sanitation have been mentioned as important causes of ill health and excess mortality. How important are they?

A WHO survey has shown that a high proportion of the population in developing countries, particularly in rural areas, are without a piped water supply or reasonable accesss to an adequate water supply and have inadequate sanitary facilities. It has frequently been shown that lack of safe water and sanitation is associated with an increased incidence of and mortality from communicable disease, in particular diarrhoeal disease. Diarrhoea is the most prominent cause of infant mortality, being responsible for a high mortality in many developing countries, while in contrast many developed countries with good environmental conditions have very low rates. As a group the gastrointestinal infections, cholera, enteric diseases, salmonellosis, dysentery and parasitic intestinal infections resulting from poor sanitary conditions are responsible for a large proportion of the world's communicable diseases. In addition to the more direct routes of infection, lack of water for washing and fly infestation associated with bad sanitation result in contamination of foods and, in consequence, food borne infections.

6. What other aspects of housing may affect health?

In certain areas housing may provide facilities for the breeding of specific vectors of disease, e.g., the triatomid bug responsible for the spread of Chagas' disease in Central and South America, mosquitoes capable of carrying malaria, or rats capable of carrying plague, typhus, jaundice and other diseases. Houses should protect from excessive heat or cold, which may be harmful to health, and new housing may not always pay adequate attention to this. Overcrowding can contribute to the spread of airborne infections. Old and dilapidated property may be associated with higher accident rates.

7. How may human settlements affect mental health and wellbeing?

The amount of mental ill health in a community is difficult to quantify. Conditions which cause stress are known to affect mental (as well as physical) health. Thus, excessive noise, crowded housing — particularly where members of different families share accommodation — and oppressive landlords may increase stress. Overcrowded slum areas are frequently associated with serious behavioural difficulties in some members of the community. Life at the top of high-rise tenement buildings may cause stress on the mother since she has difficulty in supervising the children, and may also be associated with a feeling of loneliness. Badly planned new housing schemes, by giving inadequate opportunities for social intercourse, may deleteriously affect the psychological and social development of the family, more particularly of the young members of the family. New housing schemes, particularly if associated with compulsory removal of population groups, may cause increased loneliness, especially in old people.

8. Have any harmful effects of new settlements been found?

New settlements established without adequate consideration of possible health hazards may cause troubles. Thus, the creation of artificial lakes or reservoirs may result in serious troubles from schistosomiasis, a parasitic disease that is spread in damp conditions by freshwater snails and that causes a serious chronic debilitating ailment which may affect 50 percent or more of the population resident in the area. In such situations onchocerciasis, another parasitic disease, may also cause a high prevalence of blindness. The unregulated and unplanned growth of new settlements (e.g., squatter settlements near to towns) may be associated with communicable disease hazards caused by lack of pure water, poor sanitation and the breeding of disease vectors. Malnutrition due to poverty, which is so common in such settlements in developing countries, increases susceptibility to such diseases. Settlements of this kind also produce serious social and mental health problems.

9. What methods are, or will be, most likely to provide adequate health services in human settlements?

No single approach can be successful. To ensure that a population is adequately covered, there must be a threefold attack: (1) to ensure that adequate health care facilities are available and that the population is well informed about them and uses them; (2) similarly, to ensure that adequate preventive health services exist; this will include the provision of adequate environmental health services, including good housing, water and food hygiene and protection from hazards; (3) the proper integration of the health services with other government and administrative services to ensure that health problems are taken into consideration and given due weight when decisions on economic, occupational, and social policies are being made. Community participation is often the only means by which improvements on the scale needed may be achieved. The need for a comprehensive approach is shown by the importance which must be attached to adequate nutrition, requiring integrated planning by economic, agricultural and health interests. In particular, a concerted attack must be made on malnutrition.

10. How may health care facilities be improved in developing countries?

There is a great shortage of all types of health service personnel and of adequate clinic and hospital facilities, particularly in the more remote areas of developing countries. It is now realized that these services cannot for some time be provided on the scale or pattern of those of the more developed nations. In the meantime urgent measures are needed in these areas and these must take the form of providing and training various categories of medical auxiliaries and aides, including village health auxiliaries or "primary health workers" who would be locally based and locally trained. They would probably work under the supervision of higher level auxiliaries who would form part of the health team under professional control. Appropriate simple equipment and drugs would be provided. Such a system of providing primary medical care will require considerable reorientation and expansion of training facilities. Once established, standards can be raised by training "on the job" and by periodic training and refresher courses.

11. Are there any hazards associated more specifically with life in the more developed types of human settlement?

The greater life expectancy in such settlements and the lower death rates from communicable diseases result in a different age structure of the population with a higher proportion of the middle-aged and elderly. Consequently there is a higher prevalence rate of and mortality from the degenerative diseases: the degenerative cardiovascular diseases, malignant neoplasms, diabetes, and mental disease. There is also evidence that increased mental stresses, and differing social customs and eating habits have produced a disproportionate increase in certain diseases; lung cancer has increased and hypertensive heart disease is tending to occur at an earlier age. The increase in the numbers of motor vehicles has resulted in a marked increase in accident rates.

12. Are some occupations hazardous?

Certain forms of work carry important health risks such as lead poisoning, silicosis and asbestosis, and stringent precautions have to be taken to protect the worker, his family, and sometimes people resident near the works. In some countries the precautions may not be adequately enforced. Small businesses in particular are difficult to control and small workshops may be found with just one or two workers who are using a hazardous substance and who may live and work in the same building. A careful watch always has to be maintained for new chemical hazards in industry. In rural areas, activities such as agriculture and forestry can involve quite serious occupational hazards (e.g., sylvatic yellow fever, malaria, schistosomiasis, and onchocerciasis).

13. How important are chemical hazards?

These can be very important. Thus, inadequately controlled air pollution from domestic coal burning resulted in a heavy mortality in the London smog of 1952; the Los Angeles type of photochemical smog associated with motor vehicle fumes causes serious nuisance on account of its irritating effects, coupled with damage to vegetation; chemical contamination of water or food by, for instance, organomercury, can cause serious health effects.

14. Is it not possible to produce more accurate statistical information on many of these problems?

Accurate figures susceptible of international comparison are difficult to collect, particularly from developing countries where birth and death registrations cannot yet be properly developed, and causes of death cannot be recorded properly when medical care does not extend to the entire population. The value of the two American studies mentioned above lies in the fact that special checks were made of the accuracy of the figures – a procedure which can only be followed for research purposes.

Very little information concerning sickness incidence is available in most countries and information on, for instance, hospital admissions, is of little value for comparative purposes. For international control purposes information on cases of serious communicable disease such as cholera, smallpox, plague and yellow fever is collected. For the most part information on disease prevalence can only be obtained by special local surveys, e.g., of schistosomiasis. Such surveys are an expensive but valuable method of collecting information.

Information is available on numbers of doctors, nurses, clinics and hospital beds in different areas but where these are so deficient that health care cannot reach all members of the community information on sickness and mortality can only be based on estimates.

In developed countries a great deal of effort is put into collecting accurate information on causes of death and care is taken to assess reliability. More advanced epidemiological investigations are then possible. Such investigations of environmental problems have yielded a great deal of valuable information; nevertheless many environmental problems still remain unsolved because the complexity of the data is such that statistical techniques capable of dealing with the problems have not yet been developed.

THE EFFECTS OF URBANIZATION: ECOLOGICAL ASPECTS

In a recent inter-American investigation of mortality in childhood, the existence of higher death rates in rural as opposed to urban areas was mentioned, and it seemed likely that, had more isolated rural areas been chosen, even greater differences would have been found. Indications of similar differences exist in many parts of the world, particularly in the developing and the less urbanized developed countries. The evidence indicates that the principal factors responsible for the differences are the less satisfactory, and sometimes absent, preventive medical and health care facilities in some of the rural areas, the frequent absence of adequate and safe water supplies, poor sanitation and, associated with this and other factors, the higher rates of communicable disease. The standard of education, including health education, is lower, primitive customs often result in higher health risks and the general standard of living and of nutrition in the rural areas may be lower.

In contrast to this an opposite gradient is sometimes found, and though there are exceptions, this may be more typical of many of the developed countries, particularly those with urban problems. Some 300 years ago it was noted that London had higher mortality rates than rural England. Although the London death rates have now fallen to a low figure, the urban-rural difference has persisted in other parts of the United Kingdom.

The gradient is particularly prominent with certain diseases. The explanation here — and this is likely to apply to other countries that have this mortality pattern — is probably that rural and suburban areas have a good standard of living and good water supplies and sanitation. Public health, health care and educational services are good and there is a low incidence of and mortality from infectious disease. The higher urban mortality is related particularly to the slums and decaying areas of the older towns and cities, whereas the health indices of the the more spacious and wealthy areas are often better than those of the rural areas as well as of the more crowded working-class and slum areas. An important factor influencing these area differences is the social class variation in mortality, linked primarily to socioeconomic factors. Thus, the professional and managerial class at one end of the scale will in general have better indices than the unskilled working class at the other. Allied to this are distinct occupational class differences in mortality (England and Wales, Registrar General, 1971b).

A feature of the incomplete planning of the industrialization of a country is that many people will be attracted by the higher rates of pay and the social amenities of the cities, so that there is a marked rural-urban migration; the cities, unable to cope with this influx, become grossly overcrowded, and on the outskirts large unplanned settlements without water, sewers, roads and other amenities, and with the very minimum of shelter constructed of the cheapest available materials, often spring into existence. These "shanty" or in more affluent areas "caravan" towns present their own problems over and above those of the old, established urban areas and require separate consideration.

Allied to the problems of the shanty towns are those of new or "transitional" settlements often associated with natural or man-made disasters such as earthquakes, fire, war, or enforced migration of populations due to revolution or politically imposed circumstances. Such temporary settlements may spring up overnight, sometimes on most unsuitable sites. They are frequently in isolated positions where the occupants cannot rely on services from a nearby town, and the situation will call for speedy government or even international understanding and help. Another type of new settlement is associated with agricultural development and this often follows the construction of man-made lakes. New settlements on the shores of these lakes have been seriously affected by diseases such as malaria, schistosomiasis and onchocerciasis.

Some of the environmental causes of ill health may be easy to define on a simple cause-and-effect basis. Thus, a polluted water supply or deficient sanitation is often the direct cause of an outbreak of waterborne or foodborne communicable disease. Often, however, it is not possible to ascribe a single cause to the unhealthiness of a district and the effects may be related to a complex interaction between numerous factors (WHO, 1974b). The problem of determining the relative importance of the factors is so difficult and involved that statistical methods that can provide a complete answer are not yet available. Most of the work on the subject comes from studies in developed countries and has consisted of either straightforward comparisons between two or more areas of different type or studies of a population group which has been transferred from a slum area to one of new housing, a comparison being made of health indices before and after the move, using a second population group which has remained behind in the slum area as a control. The results of such surveys have frequently shown some improvement in health after resettlement; but in other surveys the results have been indeterminate, particularly when a search has been made for possible effects of the move on mental health (Martin et al., 1957; Martin, 1967; Taylor & Chave, 1964; Wilner et al., 1962; WHO, 1974b; Worth, 1963).

These surveys have usually been carried out in developed countries; when both areas concerned have had adequate and safe drinking water and waterborne sanitation the incidence of communicable disease has been low and limited mainly to the common childhood infections; there have been reasonable health care services, and the state of nutrition has been reasonable. Under such conditions the main benefit of resettlement in improved housing has been the removal from an area of deteriorating and dilapidated property and characterized by gloomy and depressing surroundings, overcrowding, noise, high delinquency rates, and the difficulties many parents have in bringing up a family in these surroundings. The move, however, tends to disrupt family relationships and friendships with neighbours and the new area is often felt to be a social desert in which it is hard to establish new social relationships. Such resettlement schemes may carry important socioeconomic implications. Thus, in one of the earlier surveys undertaken in England at a time of unemployment and considerable undernutrition, the health of the population was found to have deteriorated after the move, and this was attributed to the additional financial strain imposed on the families in the new environment (M'Gonigle, 1933). From the evidence it is apparent that when resettlement schemes are under consideration it is necessary to take a comprehensive view of the situation and plan the move so that possible

Table 1. Mortality by Social Class, England and Wales 1959-1963

Class	Standardized mortality ratio* (males)
I. Professional etc. occupations	76
II. Intermediate occupations (between I and III)	81
III. Skilled occupations	100
IV. Partly skilled occupations	103
V. Unskilled occupations	143

*Death rate adjusted to make age structure of England and Wales and expressed as a ratio to the corresponding death rate for England and Wales (E & W 100).

Source: England and Wales, Registrar General, 1971b.

harmful social and socioeconomic effects are prevented.

In countries with higher rates of communicable and particularly enteric disease, and where gross overcrowding is more common, the beneficial effects of rehousing are likely to be associated with more dramatic and easily demonstrable improvement in health. Thus Worth (1963) showed how in Hong Kong a move from villages to squatter settlements was accompanied by a reduction in gastrointestinal infections but an increase in respiratory disease, while a subsequent move into new housing produced an improvement in health. Also in Hong Kong, Mitchell (1971) showed how overcrowding was associated with an increased prevalence of symptoms of mental disorder.

Another type of epidemiological study of the multifactoral nature of environmental problems is more sophisticated. Suitable environmental, climatic, socioeconomic, education, and other indices are obtained for a number of areas and mathematical associations and correlations are worked out between these and various indices of health. Such studies may give some indication of the relative importance of various environmental and socioeconomic influences but the large numbers of factors concerned make this type of approach difficult. Recent thought has been directed towards the systems analysis approach, but the absence of suitable methods of measuring some of the parameters, coupled with the complexity of the problem, have not yet made it possible to produce a solution. Nevertheless, it has been possible to delineate the relations between some of the factors influencing health, both directly, and indirectly through their action on other factors. Thus, to take a single example, the mental ability of a family may have a direct effect on the state of nutrition of its members, on hygienic practices in the family, and on the household health care of the members, all of which will affect health directly. A low level of mental ability may also affect the standard of education in the family, and both may affect occupational status, leading in turn to poverty. Poverty also may affect health through poor nutrition, or through inability to pay for medical care. Poverty may also result in a family gravitating to poor quality, insanitary housing, again having a direct influence on health. Thus a complicated "web of causation" is seen to exist.

Although these epidemiological investigations present some of the most complex problems in preventive medicine, it is possible to draw some broad conclusions, some on a firm factual basis, others of a more tentative nature, which nevertheless enable priorities to be established and practical programmes designed.

The Effects of Climate

On a global basis it is apparent that climate has a major effect in determining the healthiness of some parts of the world. As a result of its direct effect on flora and fauna it affects food production, and hence has an effect on nutrition.

Protection against the extremes of weather is one of the important functions of housing. Air conditioning is becoming increasingly common in many developed countries, but as a global solution to the vagaries of climate is obviously impractical and uneconomic. Much therefore has to depend on the suitability of the house, its materials, design and structure, to provide its occupants with adequate protection. Mass production, often prefabrication, of houses is a cheap and economic way of dealing with the needs of a community but care is obviously needed to ensure that such housing is suitable for the climate in which it is to be erected.

There is a close association between climate and communicable diseases and the distribution of many of the major diseases — cerebrospinal meningitis, malaria, yellow fever, schistosomiasis and others — is influenced by a climate providing conditions favourable to the vectors. Other less obvious relationships are also well known. Thus, even in temperate climates gastrointestinal infections such as typhoid or paratyphoid fevers, Salmonella food poisoning, dysentery and infantile diarrhoea are more common in the summer, as also are poliomyelitis and certain enterovirus infections. Respiratory infections such as the common cold, influenza and pneumonia are more common during the winter, possibly owing to the greater chances of the spread of airborne infection in closed rooms. In extreme northern areas the long Arctic nights force the population to spend lengthy periods in their living accommodations and high rates of respiratory disease have been reported by a number of authors (WHO, 1974b).

Climate has also an important association with air pollution. Temperature inversions prevent the dispersion of pollutants, a factor associated with the health effects of both the London and Los Angeles type of pollution. Bright sunshine also has an important bearing on air pollution as it promotes photochemical reactions in the atmosphere which are an important factor in the Los Angeles type of smog and in the production of certain types of persistent haze.

Obvious direct effects of extremes of climate on mortality are relatively rare as the body has considerable powers of adaptation. However, the sudden onset of extreme heat or cold will not infrequently be associated with a number of deaths, particularly in persons not accustomed to these types of extreme, and recent work in California has indicated that the effects of extremely hot weather may be greater than had been thought. Thus, in three very hot periods in Los Angeles it was calculated that there were 546, 946 and 580 more deaths than would otherwise have been expected (Oechsli and Buechsley, 1970).

The amenity aspects of warm, sunny, temperate climates must not be overlooked. Such areas are increasingly popular for residence and with improved travel facilities more and more people are choosing such locations for holidays.

The Physical Structure of Houses, the Housing Environment, Crowding

The outstanding features of slum property, shanty towns and similar areas are general dilapidation, lack of repair, poor workmanship and materials, and the failure of occupants to cooperate in upkeep. Few attempts are made to remedy the effects of willful destruction or vandalism. It is easy to condemn such properties as "unhealthy" but it is more difficult to analyse the reasons in depth. The buildings are obviously more likely to give rise to accidents as a result, for instance, of defective flooring or stairs, falling roof tiles, unsafe walls, or may even collapse, and children and old people are particularly liable to have accidents. There may be a high prevalence of gastrointestinal infections due to leaking or absent sanitation, or accumulations of filth and refuse that encourage vermin such as rats, or insect infestations. Dampness may result in moulds giving rise to allergies; and in temperate climates a damp house will be cold and clammy, and this may be a contributory factor increasing the illness prevalence rates.

The use of lead paint in a house may result in a hazard of lead poisoning in children and although this is greatest in dilapidated property, cases may sometimes occur in well-maintained houses. A considerable amount of research is at present taking place in the USSR, Czechoslovakia and Poland on the safety of new organic materials used in housing and household effects. Other hazards may arise in any house as a result of defective heating, lighting or cooking equipment, giving rise to dangerous carbon monoxide fumes or danger of electric shock. Fire hazards may be associated with particular materials, with poor design of houses or equipment, or with the storage of fuel in dangerous places.

In human settlements the general housing environment is important. Good planning will result in an appreciable reduction in road accidents and excessive motor traffic or the burning of fossil fuels for heating and cooking in residential areas will give rise to serious air pollution. Housing should not be too close to industrial areas where noise, odours, or air pollution will give rise to hazards or loss of amenity.

In certain parts of the world the house and its immediate environment provide facilities for the breeding of vectors of disease. Thus, in Central and South America Chagas' disease is spread by triatomid bugs living in cracks in the structure of the house; similarly, in various parts of the world leishmaniasis is spread by the sandfly, (*Phlebotomus papatusii*) which also lives in cracks and crevices. In malarious areas, water storage tanks, often on the roof, pools of water, or water in discarded cans and utensils, may provide breeding places for mosquitoes. More generally, warm climates will encourage the breeding of houseflies and similar insects and these can contribute much to the spread of gastrointestinal infections.

Man has brought rodents with him into practically every human settlement from the smallest villages to the largest cities. Rodent populations have both an economic and public health importance; they are reservoirs of plague, murine typhus, leptospirosis and rat bite fever among other diseases and, in addition, their depredations in homes and food stores cause severe economic losses to the community, quite apart from those caused by field rodents to growing crops. While control of rodent populations can be achieved by rodenticides, the best method of control is to deny them food and harbourage by improving community sanitation.

Many investigations have shown a relationship between health and overcrowding and it is plain that in an overcrowded room or house more people will be exposed to any infection that may be introduced. Some investigations, however, have not shown a clear-cut increase in risk. The relationship is obviously complex and other factors, such as the state of health and nutrition of the occupants and their degree of immunity to certain diseases, must play a part. In some diseases such as influenza or the common cold all members of the household will, regardless of overcrowding, encounter a dose sufficient to convey the infection to a susceptible person. The same is true for childhood infections such as chickenpox or measles, where the organism has a very high degree of infectivity. Quite apart from communicable diseases, overcrowding is liable to add appreciably to mental stresses, particularly when rooms are shared by several families.

Water Supplies

Although water covers the greater part of the earth's surface, shortages of usable water for domestic, industrial and agricultural purposes are becoming more frequent in most parts of the world. Even in many of the developed countries in temperate regions having an apparently adequate rainfall the demand for water is constantly mounting and producing shortages. The introduction of piped water and adequate wastewater disposal systems immediately increases the average domestic consumption of an area. Industries usually demand an even greater share and even in countries with a satisfactory total annual rainfall the judicious use of irrigation will increase food production by prolonging the growing season into the drier months of the year. Sources of pure water in such countries are often limited and rivers are becoming progressively more polluted, requiring more sophisticated and expensive techniques to produce usable water.

In developing countries the position is acute. The size and rapidly growing nature of the problem led the World Health Assembly in 1959 to launch a "spearhead programme" to promote the provision of safe water in adequate quantities to communities lacking it. A survey of urban water supplies in 75 developing countries, undertaken by WHO in 1962, showed that of an urban population of some 10 million in these countries, about 41 percent had no access to piped water within a reasonable distance of their homes (Dieterich & Henderson, 1963).

A further survey undertaken in 1970 covered both urban and rural water supplies in most of the developing countries, and showed the extent to which the provision of rural water supplies was lagging behind that in urban areas. Nearly two-thirds of the rural population had neither access to safe water nor adequate excreta disposal facilities (Fig. 1). The health problems associated with these shortcomings are particularly important. Targets for future development have been set for the Second United Nations Development Decade, and the report showed that if progress in establishing new water supplies continued to accelerate at the 1962-1970 rate it would fall short of the United Nations target, although in most regions of the world it would be sufficient to compensate for the expected increase in population. Considerable regional differences existed and there was a very uneven distribution in the availability of external finance. Thus, during the 5 years 1966-1970, nearly half of the total external assistance was received by the Latin American countries, and at the other extreme South-East Asia received only 2 percent of the total assistance needed (Pineo & Subrahmanyam, 1975). This situation is now changing.

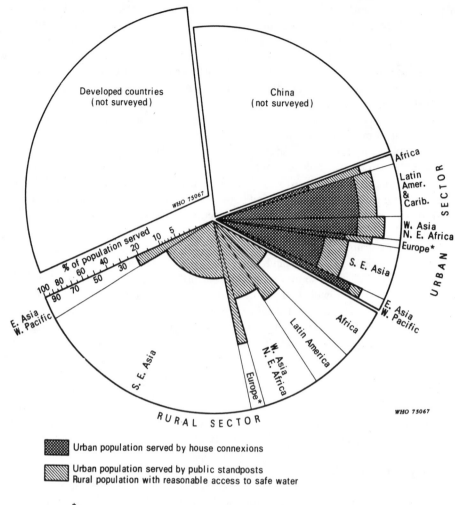

**Fig. 1. Community Water Supply Situation in Developing Countries, 1970
(extrapolated from survey of 91 countries)**

Source: Pineo & Subrahmanyam, 1975.

Water Pollution

Microbiological pollution of drinking water provides one of the easiest ways by which pathogenic organisms may be transferred to man. The readiness with which organisms excreted by a patient or carrier of enteric diseases can, under conditions of poor sanitation, contaminate rivers, springs, wells and other sources of drinking water accounts for a considerable amount of communicable disease throughout the world. Surface water is often used for nearly all purposes in many developing countries, where it is frequently a source of drinking-water and simultaneously a medium for the disposal of various kinds of wastes. Since entire communities will often rely on a single water source, the contamination of a supply, perhaps by a single person, can result in the dissemination of the disease to many hundreds of people, thus accounting for the explosive type of outbreak so typical of waterborne epidemics.

Modern techniques of water treatment and monitoring make it possible, given adequate raw water, finance, technical manpower and equipment, to provide safe supplies. Unfortunately, as shown in the preceding paragraphs, in many parts of the world even untreated piped supplies are not available.

Risks are always present and even in countries with comprehensive networks of piped supplies and experienced qualified staff, breakdowns may occur; and not all water treatment plants are as yet so fully automated that the supply is automatically cut off in the event of a breakdown in treatment. Modern knowledge of virus diseases suggests that the dosage of disinfectant (e.g., chlorine or ozone) may sometimes be insufficient to kill pathogenic viruses. After it leaves the treatment plant, water may sometimes be contaminated, as for instance by repair work on water mains, or by accidental cross-connections with pipes containing untreated water. A common cause of trouble is due to periods of negative pressure in the mains, when contamination may be sucked in from sewage polluted soil, or for instance through hosepipes intended for filling water tanks or ponds. Such hazards are particularly liable to occur when, because of water shortage, supplies are being distributed intermittently.

Chemical pollution is now attracting much attention. Because of expense many authorities undertake relatively few water analyses, and more attention obviously needs to be devoted to the subject. Threshold limits have been drawn up by international, national, and other authoritative bodies, and research is currently being undertaken on many of the lesser known trace substances that may occur in water supplies. Among the common pollutants lead is important. In some countries many of the older properties have lead water piping and water cisterns and soft water may dissolve sufficient lead to cause subclinical and occasionally even overt cases of lead poisoning. Other toxic metals include cadmium and mercury, which may be derived from industrial contamination. Traces of arsenic or radon may be derived from mineral strata.

Considerable attention is now being paid to nitrates, which are present in water as a result of the oxidation of nitrogenous matter in sewage, the use of nitrogenous agricultural fertilizers, the precipitation of air pollutants, or occasionally the solution of mineral deposits. Amounts above 50 ppm of nitrate may give rise to methaemoglobinaemia in infants during the early months of life. Traces of other substances which will occur in drinking waters include pesticides and detergents.

Wholesome water from different areas will contain a wide range of trace substances which in some circumstances may have a beneficial effect on the body and in higher concentrations may be harmful. Thus, fluorides in concentrations of about 1 ppm have a valuable anticaries effect on teeth; in gross excess, however, they will produce symptoms of fluoride toxicity and in some parts of the world excessively high levels are found. Another example of the apparent beneficial effect of trace substances is the negative correlation which has been found in some countries between the hardness of water supplies and the amount of cardiovascular disease in a community.

An important cause of worry to many water engineers is accidental pollution as, for instance, when a factory accidentally discharges some toxic substance into a river, or a lorry containing chemicals overturns. Increasing attention is also being paid to the medical implications of the recycling of water, for with growing populations using purified river-derived water, water may be extracted from, and sewage effluents discharged into, a river at many points and precautions have to be taken against a possible harmful build-up of substances in the water.

Marine pollution, particularly of coastal waters, is now causing much anxiety; in addition to the effects which it may have on marine ecology, it may lead to undesirably high levels of heavy metals (lead, cadmium, mercury) and organic substances in fish and shellfish consumed by man. Similarly, sewage contamination may lead to the contamination of shellfish with pathogenic organisms including, in particular, the salmonella-typhoid group.

Sanitation

The group of communicable diseases spread as the result of the excretion of pathogenic organisms in either human faeces or urine includes many of the world's most serious epidemic and endemic diseases: cholera, typhoid fever, other salmonellosis and the dysenteries, and many of the parasitic protozoal and helminth infections. Their contribution to the sum of human sickness is considerable, yet the nature of the route of transmission offers points at which control, in theory at least, can easily be exercised.

The primary point is at the place and time of defaecation. Almost invariably the person contaminates his fingers whilst cleansing himself, and unless therefore he washes, there is a direct route of infection to further victims, either by the contamination of food or via household utensils and furniture. Unfortunately, the habit of washing is difficult to promote, particularly where there are no piped water supplies or where supplies are limited or intermittent, or where water has to be purchased by volume.

A common method of sanitary disposal in many developing countries is by the bored hole latrine, where a simple structure is placed over a specially dug hole in the ground. Much then depends on the nature of the subsoil and the amount of use. Ideally the faecal matter decomposes and soaks harmlessly into the soil. In some cases, however, with an unsuitable soil, the hole rapidly fills and pollution of the surface around the latrine may result. In other cases, with a badly sited latrine, seepage may result in the contamination of a spring or watercourse which may be used as a source of drinking water.

In some primitive communities without sanitation, defaecation may take place in fields and areas not far from the home, or the latrine may be unsatisfactory and flyborne infestation may lead directly back to the home or to food shops. The exposure of the faeces on the ground gives the opportunity for many of the intestinal parasites to continue their life cycle. Finally, the faeces, or organisms from the faeces, may be washed into wells and streams, and thus contaminate drinking water.

In other circumstances faecal matter may be removed from the household environment by discharge directly into a watercourse, or, if a sewage system has been provided, the effluent, still containing pathogenic organisms, may discharge into watercourses ultimately used as drinking water sources.

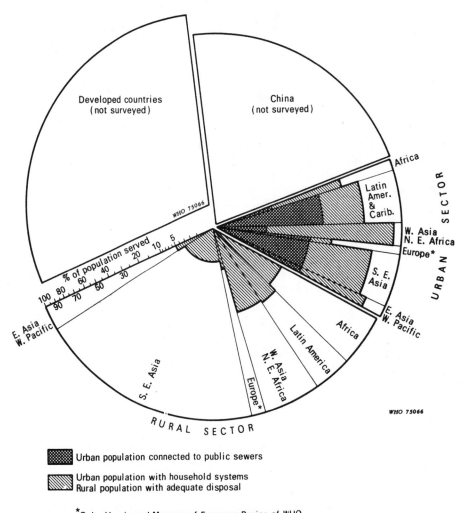

Fig. 2. Excreta Disposal Situation in Developing Countries, 1970 (extrapolated from survey of 61 countries)

Source: Pineo & Subrahmanyam, 1975.

A demand for an adequate sanitary disposal system usually follows shortly after the provision of piped water. In developing countries, the WHO survey of conditions in 1970 showed how far the provision of adequate sanitary disposal services lagged behind (Fig. 2). The survey also showed that the provision of adequate finance was not the only obstacle to be overcome. If a scheme is to be a success, the community itself must feel that it wants the facilities and that they offer something better than the previous mode of life. There must be community participation and this frequently involves health education and obtaining the cooperation of the leaders of the community.

Communicable Diseases Associated With Contaminated Water or Food or With Insanitary Conditions

The inter-American survey of mortality in childhood demonstrated the importance of communicable diseases of gastrointestinal origin and evidence from countries throughout the world indicates that they are a major, probably *the* major, cause of preventable mortality and ill health and that they affect mainly the tropical, subtropical and developing countries. The financial and technical problems of prevention on the vast scale required are enormous. Some of the principal diseases and the problems associated with their control are outlined below.

Cholera is the classical example of a waterborne disease. It is a condition characterized by extreme diarrhoea in which the body rapidly becomes dehydrated. Untreated cases may have a 50 percent fatality rate. The principal endemic area of infection has been the Ganges-Brahmaputra delta of India and during the period 1817-1923 six major pandemics originated from this area, spreading along the trade routes of Asia, Africa and Europe. The mortality associated with these pandemics rivaled that of all other infectious diseases with the single exception of the influenza pandemic of 1918-1919. A seventh pandemic started from an endemic focus in Indonesia in 1961 and was associated with a different biotype of vibrio — the El Tor. Infection spread north as far as Korea and the Philippines, and westwards through India, Afghanistan, Iran, southern USSR and Iraq. Though introduced into a number of Western European countries, Japan and Australia, it did not gain a foothold, owing to good sanitation. The El Tor biotype has now largely replaced the classical *Vibrio Cholerae*.

Cholera is primarily a foodborne and waterborne disease and introduced suddenly into a new community will often show the characteristic explosive onset of a massive waterborne outbreak. The subsequent pattern of the outbreak will be determined by often inadequate water supplies and poor sanitation, the outbreak may follow a more protracted course and cholera may become endemic in the area. Under such conditions the attack rate becomes distinctly higher for children, owing to the immunity developed by adults.

Cholera affects primarily individuals of the lower socioeconomic class and the proportion of cases showing symptoms is low compared with the total number infected. The El Tor biotype is more resistant than the classical vibrio; it remains viable in water for a longer period and infected persons tend to excrete it for a longer time. In many outbreaks of cholera the provision of copious supplies of uncontaminated water has been sufficient to terminate the outbreak but the characteristics of the El Tor biotype may account for the experience in several outbreaks recently, where poor sanitation and bad personal habits have played a major role. Thus, in a rural area of East Bengal, in an outbreak of classical cholera in 1968 and 1969, persons living nearby a safe water supply were shown to have had a pronounced degree of protection, whereas in an El Tor outbreak the following year the availability of pure drinking water did not appear to affect the prevalence of the disease (Sommer & Woodward, 1972). In the 1972 Singapore outbreak 94 percent of the patients were living in modern sanitary, highrise apartment flats and had a safe water supply (Velimirovic et al., 1975). In an outbreak in Manila, 93 percent of some 700 patients investigated had a safe municipal water supply available, though only 36 percent had a direct house connexion. A large proportion of the patients were in crowded unsatisfactory housing and 39 percent were in squatter dwellings with very poor or absent hygienic facilities (Velimirovic et al., 1975).

In a study by Azurin & Alvero (1974) it was shown that over a period of 5 years the provision of sanitary facilities for human waste disposal can reduce the incidence of cholera by as much as 76 percent.

Compared to the high case fatality rate in untreated patients, modern treatment of the disease, based primarily on adequate fluid replacement and effective antibiotics, is extremely effective. Unfortunately, medical treatment is often not available.

As experience with the El Tor biotype has already shown, there is a real danger of further spread of this condition to new areas, where it may become endemic. Preventive measures — a safe and adequate water supply, good sanitation, fly control and good hygienic habits — are the obvious and effective measures in controlling the disease.

Acute Diarrhoeal Disease of Childhood

The importance of acute diarrhoea in young infants and its association with malnutrition was clearly demonstrated in the inter-American investigation referred to above, where it was shown to be the major cause of mortality in early life. The same problem appears throughout the developing world and to a smaller degree in some of the less advanced developed countries. In contrast, the prevalence of serious cases of infant diarrhoea in the more developed countries is low and the mortality even less. The subject was dealt with in the WHO monograph "Interactions of Nutrition and Infection," Chapter 6 (Scrimshaw et al., 1968) and in the report of the WHO diarrhoeal diseases advisory team (van Zijl, 1966). The WHO team carried out investigations in 7 developing countries and their work demonstrated the great importance of pure water supplies and sanitation in controlling diarrhoea. They showed that it was the very young children who were particularly at risk and laboratory investigations in each country demonstrated the proportions of infections due to the various pathogens.

Because of the difficulties in collecting reliable statistics there is little accurate evidence of the prevalence and fatality rates of acute diarrhoeal diseases in many developing countries. In northern Punjab, Gordon and his colleagues (1961) investigated the problem in 11 villages over the period 1956-1960. Because of the unreliability of the local statistics they made their own investigations into causes of death and found that acute diarrhoea was the commonest cause of death (all ages), with a death rate of 187 per 100,000. The villages had a mean infant mortality of 162 per 1000 live births, diarrhoea being the commonest cause of infant death. Most fatalities occurred during the second six months of life, the high mortality rate continuing until the age of 18 months, and case studies demonstrated the association with weaning. Out of a group of 20 children who for various reasons were artifically fed from birth, only one survived and she suffered from no less than 5 attacks of diarrhoea.

In a follow-up of this work, a survey has been carried out to demonstrate the effects of providing the underfed infants with nutritionally adequate weaning food and of improved control over infectious diseases. The infants showed a marked increase in anthropometric measurements as compared with a control group, but it has not yet been possible to assess the effect of the measures against infectious diseases, owing to fluctuations in the prevalence in the control group (de Sweemer, 1975).

The problem was also investigated during the period 1958-1964 among the rural Mayan populations of the Guatemala highlands. Again, excess mortality during the second 6 months of life was apparent and, although the mortality rate fell, the attack rate continued high until the age at which the children entered school (Mata et al., 1967). This investigation has since been continued to demonstrate the relationships between nutrition and infectious diseases.

Work on the causes of the diarrhoea has been done in many parts of the world and indicates a variety of agents: shigelloses, salmonelloses, enteropathogenic *Escherichia coli*, probably some enterovirus infections, and helminthic and protozoal infections. In many cases no causal agent was found, and even when a pathogenic agent was isolated there was often doubt about its role, since the same agent was found in healthy infants.

Preventive measures again are the obvious ones — a copious safe water supply, proper and effective sanitation, control of flies, health education in child care and hygiene, and prevention of malnutrition. Sanitary measures must be thorough: thus it has been shown that dangers exist from the use of porous earthenware storage jars for cooling the drinking water and that pure tap water drawn into them frequently becomes contaminated with faecal organisms (van Zijl, 1966).

Typhoid and Paratyphoid Fevers, Shigelloses and Salmonelloses

Water authorities live with the constant threat that, despite the most painstaking precautions, there may at some time be a human or technical failure which will result in contamination of the public water supply by some pathogenic agent. Typhoid fever is the most serious disease likely to be conveyed in this way, but outbreaks of partyphoid and Shigella infections and of infectious hepatitis may also occur. Cholera has already been discussed. The outbreak may be the result of a breakdown in the treatment plant permitting pathogenic organisms in the raw water to pass into the distribution system, or of contamination of the water after treatment. Many outbreaks are due to an apparently pure water being put into supply either with no treatment or with inadequate treatment.

The Zermatt typhoid outbreak of 1963 provides a good example of the explosive nature of a waterborne outbreak, of the way in which it can affect large numbers of people, and of the deficiencies which can arise in the treatment of the water.

In the Zermatt outbreak described by Bernard (1965) there were 437 identified cases (260 tourists — the majority from abroad — and 177 local residents) and 3 deaths. The village has some 2200 inhabitants with an additional tourist population that fluctuated between 3000 and 5000 at the time of the outbreak. The water was treated by filtration and chlorination but subsequent investigations showed that the latter had been faulty and the water under-chlorinated. It was not possible to determine the cause of the outbreak conclusively as there were two possibilities, neither of which could be excluded. Water entering the treatment plant was found to be subject to sewage pollution from a workers' hostel at which one of the workers had suffered from an illness which could have been typhoid. The second possibility lay in the existence of a fractured sewer from which it was subsequently shown that sewage was percolating into the holding tank at the treatment station.

Earlier in this study, the various ways in which poor sanitation might result in increased rates of gastrointestinal infections were discussed. The extent to which this can, in fact, happen was demonstrated in a survey of Kentucky mining villages undertaken by the United States Public Health Service (Schliessman et al., 1958). The villages were classified into 3 groups, A, B and C, according to the quality of the housing, sanitary disposal facilities and water supply; the socioeconomic circumstances of the householders were also taken into account. The groups of pathogens studied included sigelloses, salmonelloses, enteropathogenic *E. coli* and various intestinal parasites. The shigelloses and, among the parasites, the tape worm (*Ascaris lumbricoides*) and the whipworm (*Trichuris*), were the commonest pathogens found. Diarrhoea was found to be considerably more prevalent in families living in group C accommodation, the percentage found with shigella infection was higher, and infection occurred most frequently in the 0-4 age group, particularly among those 2 years of age. Moreover, in group C, infections were found to occur earlier and later in the season than in groups A and B. *Ascaris* and *Trichuris* infections were also commonest in group C and in the 5-9 year age group 60 percent of faeces examined were positive for *Ascaris* and 57.3 percent for *Trichuris*. More detailed analysis of the data showed a progressive gradient both as regards *Ascaris* and Shigella infections and the acute diarrhoea mortality rate, houses with indoor water and flush toilets having a low prevalence, those with indoor water and privies having a higher. The highest prevalence was in households where water had to be obtained from a distant source.

The importance of housefly infestation was not clearly demonstrated in this study, although earlier studies quoted by the authors had shown that control of houseflies was associated with a reduction in diarrhoeal disease. Among the socioeconomic factors, crowding, family size, and education of the housewife were found to have an influence on the disease prevalence.

Schliessmann (1959) showed similar relationships between the prevalence of Shigella infections and the location of household water supplies and the type of sanitation in surveys in Guatemala, and in California and Georgia (USA). Similar relationships have also been found in the various countries investigated by the WHO diarrhoeal diseases team (van Zijl, 1966).

Typhoid, paratyphoid, Salmonella and Shigella infections are principally transmitted by food. All are characterized by the excretion of the organism during and for some time after the attack and in the case of the first two conditions the person may become a chronic carrier excreting the organism possibly for life. Salmonella and Shigella infections are widespread, often accepted by a patient as a temporary indisposition, and in consequence the size of the problem and even the existence of large outbreaks can pass unnoticed. Bad hygienic habits frequently result in further cases in the household, and food sold in shops, markets and restaurants is easily contaminated by carriers. Flies also may convey the organism direct from faeces to food, or the organism may be conveyed by contaminated water or utensils. When once an item of food becomes contaminated, the organism under the right conditions will multiply. Thus, for instance, food such as cooked meats exposed for sale in a market or shop in a hot climate may become heavily contaminated and the organism can then be conveyed on the hands, knives and working surfaces to other foods.

Salmonellae occupy a somewhat special position, for some 1200 separate serological biotypes have been identified, usually host-adapted to one or more species in the animal world and many of them nonpathogenic for man. Some, however, may cause large scale outbreaks of gastroenteritis in man. Thus *Salmonella typhimurium* may affect every bird on a large chicken farm and, since the organisms in the interior of the carcass can survive light cooking, quite large outbreaks can occur. The same organism is frequently present in duck eggs. In Sweden in 1953 an outbreak spread by the contamination of meat carcasses from a single slaughterhouse caused 8845 identified cases with 90 deaths.

Clostridial and Staphylococcal Food Poisoning and Brucellosis

These infections must also be mentioned as important causes of foodborne illness. The organism *Clostridium welchii* is commonly present on carcasses of meat, the spores are relatively resistant to cooking and the organism will proliferate when the meat is left in warm conditions or cooled slowly. Staphylococci are the common organisms found in septic wounds or sores and can therefore easily be conveyed to food and result in food poisoning. The various strains of brucellae affect cattle, sheep, goats, and swine; they are the cause of disease in farm workers, and infection may frequently be conveyed via milk to large numbers of the population, causing the disease.

Infectious Hepatitis

It is believed that this disease — caused by a virus — is usually transmitted by airborne infection. It can, however, be spread by the contamination of milk or water. Since viruses are generally more resistant to chlorination than bacteria the disease may more easily be spread by a faecally contaminated water supply which is under-chlorinated. One such outbreak, when there was massive sewage pollution of a river from which the drinking-water was derived, occurred in Delhi in 1955. Over 7000 cases of manifest jaundice were reported to the health authorities but it is believed that the total number of cases must have been some 29,000; 65 deaths occurred in hospital and the total deaths in the outbreak were estimated at about 90 (Viswanathan, 1957).

Intestinal Parasites

Intestinal parasites are of great importance, particularly in tropical and subtropical countries. In some areas a particular parasite may infect more than 50 percent of the population and although most are not important causes of death they may have a profound debilitating effect, producing a marked reduction in the work capacity of the community. They cause much pain, inconvenience and sickness and some may cause damage to organs such as the liver, kidneys, brain and eyes. In some countries the effects are so serious that entire areas are rendered uninhabitable.

The following are the more important intestinal parasites whose ova are excreted in the faeces or urine.

Schistosomiasis (Bilharziasis)

The trematode worm *Schistosoma* occurs in most African countries, in some of which it has a profound influence on the health of affected populations, and some species are prevalent in parts of Asia, Africa and South America. Globally it is estimated that some 200 million people may be affected and current evidence shows that in some areas the prevalence of schistosomiasis is increasing as a result of the creation of artificial lakes and irrigation schemes. The adult worm lives in the portal and pelvic veins, and ova are discharged in either the urine or faeces. Should these reach fresh water the life cycle can continue by infection of the intermediate host, a freshwater snail which discharges free-swimming cercariae capable of penetrating the human skin and reaching the blood circulatory system. In addition to general systemic weakness, malaise, loss of weight, abdominal pain and distension, and enlargement of the spleen and liver, the condition frequently results in complications due to the presence of ova in various organs and subsequent scarring. The disease may carry an appreciable mortality, particularly in children and adolescents, and in later life it may be a cause of cancer of the bladder. Infection is mainly through the skin as a result of working, bathing or playing in contaminated water. Control of the spread of the disease is difficult; it consists of, *inter alia*, care in the disposal of faeces and urine so that the ova do not enter fresh water likely to contain the intermediate host; the provision of fresh water for drinking, bathing and the washing of clothes; the treatment of snail breeding places with molluscicides; the drainage of marshes and pools, etc.; the provision of protective clothing for persons having to enter contaminated water; and education of the population on the nature of the infection and methods of protection.

Amoebiasis (Amoebic Dysentery)

This disease is caused by an organism, *Entamoeba histolytica*, and has a world-wide distribution, the endemic areas being mainly in the tropical and subtropical areas of Africa, Asia, and Central and South America. It is particularly likely to occur in areas with contaminated drinking water and poor sanitary facilities, especially in areas where the standards of living and of general hygiene are low and malnutrition common. It is thus likely to be found in many squatter settlements. Under suitable conditions it may infect 50 percent or more of the population. It may also be found in many temperate areas where the infection usually runs a milder course and the proportion of asymptomatic cases is higher. Cysts passed in the faeces of infected persons may survive for considerable periods and cause the spread of infection by the contamination of food and drinking-water. Symptoms of acute infections are those of typical dysentery, with diarrhoea and the passage of blood and mucus, and in most circumstances the mortality associated with the disease is low. The organism may enter the wall of the large intestine, causing ulceration and local inflammatory lesions, and may produce abscess of the liver, lung or brain. Untreated, the chronic infection may persist, with continued excretion of the organism, for years.

Ancylostomiasis (Hookworm Infection) and Other Helminthic Infections

Hookworm is a further common parasite of tropical climates throughout the world, which may also affect workers in temperate climates engaged in warm, moist tunnels and mines when insanitary habits result in faecal contamination. The worm inhabits the small intestine, ova being excreted in the faeces. Contaminated soil around or near the houses is the most important source of infection, further infections being caused by the larvae penetrating the unbroken skin. Symptoms may be caused during the complicated migration of the larvae via the blood stream, lungs and air passages to the gastrointestinal tract, but the most typical symptom is the severe anaemia which may result from massive infections. In 1947, it was estimated that the global incidence of infection was 450 million people (Stoll, quoted by Woodruff, 1974).

Faecal pollution of the soil caused by children and adults in human settlements with poor or no sanitary facilities are also responsible for ascariasis and trichuriasis. These infestations are worldwide, although more likely to occur in hot climates. Taeniasis is spread by bad food habits, i.e., the undercooking of meat. In the context of human settlements parasitic infestations are of interest, since in undernourished families the degree of undernourishment may be increased and this may result in a greater susceptibility to other diseases.

Air Pollution

The classical example of the effects of urban air pollution on man is the London fog of December 1952, which was estimated to have resulted in nearly 4000 deaths in persons already suffering from serious respiratory and cardiac diseases in the Greater London area. A persistent temperature inversion had resulted in a rapid build-up of pollutants, particularly black carbonaceous matter (soot) and the oxides of sulfur and nitrogen, derived partly from industrial sources but mostly from domestic heating discharging smoke at a relatively low height. Investigations during the ensuing decade showed that even moderate increases of smoke and fumes were accompanied by detectable increases in mortality and morbidity. Similar, though smaller, episodes have been identified in New York and other large cities. In the United Kingdom, legislation designed to promote the burning of smokeless fuels in domestic premises and to improve control over the heights and emissions from industrial chimneys has led to a great improvement in the situation and the acute health effects noted in London during the period 1952-1962 are now no longer found.

The problem is not only one of the acute effects of pollution, since investigations have shown that continued residence in heavily polluted towns is associated with raised levels of chronic respiratory disease, bronchitis in particular. Infants and children are especially susceptible and lung damage in early childhood is likely to show up again in late middle age, particularly if the person is a heavy smoker. Any association between lung cancer and urban air pollution, however, is difficult to demonstrate epidemiologically, although urban lung cancer rates are usually higher than rural, and air pollutants are known to contain traces of carcinogens. Any effects, if present, tend to be overshadowed by the pronounced association between lung cancer and tobacco smoking.

Air pollution is not only a hazard of developed countries and both industrial and domestic emissions may create trouble even in remote areas. Thus, when a high prevalence of nontuberculous lung disease was investigated in villages in the New Guinea highlands, high levels of smoke, aldehydes and carbon monoxide were found in the native huts (Cleary & Blackburn, 1968).

In many cities motor vehicles are now the major polluters of the atmosphere. The Los Angeles type of smog has become particularly notorious in many areas where atmospheres, heavily polluted by vehicle fumes, are exposed to intense sunlight. This effect is accentuated by particular geographical and climatological conditions which increase the process of smog formation. In Los Angeles, for example the frequent occurrence of temperature inversions promotes the building-up of pollutants. The result is a complex photochemical reaction producing an atmosphere with an intensely irritating effect on the eyes and nasal mucosa. Not only is the smog a serious nuisance to the populations of the affected towns but it has also an important effect on vegetation and subsequently may result in reduced food production.

Motor vehicle emissions contain a number of substances which in sufficient quantity are harmful to man. Carbon monoxide is well known as the cause of accidental or sometimes suicidal fatalities when car engines are left running in closed garages. It is not infrequently present in concentrations of 100 ppm or more in busy city streets, and may also be present in houses from defective cooking or heating equipment. Its principal source in man's personal environment, however, is cigarette smoke. It is not now considered that in the concentrations normally found in man (as the compound carboxyhaemoglobin in the blood) it has any effect on mental alertness or activity, but there is evidence that continued exposure, as in heavy smokers over a period of many years, may have an effect on the cardiovascular system.

Nitrogen oxides are similarly emitted as a result of fuel combustion. They are present in motor exhaust fumes, they may occur in the domestic environment from cooking and heating apparatus, and they are also present in industrial emissions. The amounts in the urban environment are usually well below those regarded as hazardous in factory atmospheres, but countries which suffer particularly from the Los Angeles type of photochemical smog are keen to reduce the amounts of nitrogen oxides from motor vehicle fumes and from other sources, since they, in association with hydrocarbons, are essential precursors of the photochemical oxidants.

Lead and other toxic elements are now engaging increasing attention as are pollutants. Lead is added to gasoline in many countries, and there has been much scientific argument on how far the resulting lead pollution of the environment may produce an undesirable increase in the lead content of the body. Its use brings about some reduction in the amount of gasoline consumed and to this extent it is an aid in dealing with the energy crisis, but many countries consider that a reduction or even the total elimination of lead in gasoline is necessary. A more important source of lead in the human environment is pollution from lead refineries and smelting works. Where these have been sited near to human habitations, raised blood lead levels in children have not infrequently been found.

Airborne cadmium and arsenic and other toxic elements may also pollute the atmosphere and be deposited in the neighbourhood of some metal smelting and refining works and cause problems. In the past, asbestos has escaped into the environment in the neighbourhood of asbestos mines and works, and has been responsible for cases of mesothelioma, a rare form of cancer, in people living in the vicinity. A somewhat similar cancer hazard has now been shown to exist in the vicinity of factories dealing with vinyl chloride. Fluorides are a common source of trouble from industrial emissions and fluorosis in farm animals in not infrequently found in the vicinity of aluminium smelting plants, fertilizer works and some ceramic factories. Cases of human fluorosis have also been identified, which again emphasizes the need for careful control over industrial emissions.

The list of chemical substances producing potential air pollution hazards could be extended. Some pollutants, such as dust from cement or lime works, are usually more a nuisance than an actual health hazard. Similarly, industrial noise or odours are a nuisance and should be limited as far as practicable on amenity grounds. Moreover, it must be borne in mind that nuisances produce mental stress.

Pollution of the Soil and Solid Waste Disposal

Man-made contamination of the earth's surface by quarrying, mining and smelting activities is particularly important in some areas. Thus lead, copper, zinc, cadmium, and nickel may interfere with the growth of vegetation and crops, and sometimes, as in the case of lead or asbestos, produce a direct hazard to man.

Industrial pollution of soil is of increasing concern. Acute problems can arise from accidental breakdown of plant, as for instance a breakdown in the filtration plant at a weed-killer factory, resulting in airborne emissions of the weed-killer with profound effects on neighbouring crops. Accidents in transport not infrequently happen, and a serious situation can arise when a tanker containing some noxious chemical overturns, contaminating the soil and watercourses or underground water-bearing strata.

Disposal of solid industrial wastes is most frequently by dumping, and industrial tips have to be adequately protected from access by children, farm animals and wild life. The site for an industrial dump should be carefully selected, and seepage into underlying strata and run-off of contaminated rainwater into local watercourses must be prevented. Some chemicals may have to be specially treated and inactivated before disposal.

Old mineshafts are sometimes used for the disposal of liquid or semi-liquid wastes and slurries, but consideration must be given to the possibility of contaminating underground water supplies or of the toxic material emerging in a watercourse some distance away or gaining access to other underground workings.

Disposal at sea has been extensively used in the past, but the importance of protecting the marine environment is being increasingly realized. The poisoning of Japanese fishermen and their families (Minamata disease) by organomercury in fish as a result of the disposal of industrial waste is a dramatic illustration of the dangers.

It is now appreciated that the disposal of industrial wastes cannot be left to industry alone. Careful thought must be given to the best method of disposal and if necessary a suitable site made available. Adequate supervision must be exercised and records maintained so that in future years the existence of a hazard at a particular site may be known and unsuitable uses of the land prevented.

Sewage sludges and sewage effluents present some problems. Under suitable conditions they provide valuable agricultural fertilizers, but injudiciously spread in a fresh state they may constitute a hazard to farm animals (e.g., cysticercosis), or to man by the contamination of growing crops (e.g., by salmonellae). Heavy metals, (lead, cadmium, mercury) are known to be concentrated in sewage sludges, and in industrial areas the agricultural use of unsuitable sludges may result in reduced yields and a slow build-up of undesirable heavy metals in the ground.

Noise

In occupational medicine the effect of loud noise, particularly pure tone noise over a limited range of frequency, has been recognized for many years. Yet until comparatively recently little attention has been paid to the problems of noise in the general community. The intensity of sound in a discotheque is often such that it can induce a temporary deterioration in the threshold of hearing which may persist for some hours.

In the community generally it is the psychophysiological and psychosocial effects that are important. Noise frequently leads to disturbance of sleep but, depending on a person's psychological approach or state, considerable adaptation can take place. A person exposed to continuous traffic noise outside his/her bedroom window will probably adapt more easily than a person who is similarly exposed to the noise of intermittent low-flying aircraft. The important aspect is the extent to which irritation and annoyance are caused and the extent to which these can result in increased stress. In some people the stress may be produced as a subconscious effect without the person himself being aware of either annoyance or irritation. Thus, a person whose work involves concentrated thought may suffer from a feeling of harassment and stress as a result of working in a noisy atmosphere. Stress is a recognized factor influencing mental health, but unfortunately these aspects are difficult to quantify and measure. Although a number of epidemiological investigations have been undertaken, it has not yet been possible to assess how far adaptation can take place in different types of personality or how far noise may act as either an underlying cause or a precipitating factor in mental stress.

HUMAN SETTLEMENTS: MORTALITY, DISEASE AND ILL HEALTH

Communicable Diseases

The importance of communicable disease as the major cause of excess mortality and of high morbidity rates is apparent throughout the developing world. The resulting loss of human productivity has important effects on the countries concerned. In many cases, by restricting the output of food, and sometimes by preventing the development of whole areas of a country, it may create a vicious circle, since the loss of productivity may contribute to malnutrition, thus making the population weaker and more susceptible to the diseases. To a very large extent the communicable diseases are, or should be, preventable, though the economic, manpower (professional and otherwise) and technical problems involved are enormous.

One group of diseases, the zoonoses, is apt to cause serious difficulties in control. These are the infections transmissible under normal conditions between vertebrate animals and man. Some, such as the dog tapeworm (*Dipylidium caninum*) or *Toxocara* (an occasional cause of blindness in man) are normally infections of domestic animals; others such as brucellosis and hydatidosis are normally diseases of agricultural animals and their control requires the cooperation of veterinary officers. The difficulties, however, arise where the reservoir of infection is in wild animals. Thus, the virus of yellow fever is enzootic in forest monkeys of tropical Africa and America and the virus of rabies may be found in wolves, jackals, and foxes, as well as in the domestic dog. Chagas' disease presents a cycle of transmission in wild animals (opossums, armadillos, etc.) as well as in domestic animals (dogs and cats). Such infections are then difficult to eradicate and create a hazard to the population of human settlements in infected rural areas.

The gastrointestinal diseases whose control is so obviously dependent on good water, sanitation and good hygiene have already been discussed above. It remains now to consider the more important examples of other infectious conditions whose distribution throughout the world is markedly affected by environmental conditions, and which are therefore an important factor influencing the development of human settlements.

Malaria

Malaria was long recognized as the chief health problem of most tropical and subtropical countries. Shortly after the establishment of WHO it appeared that new methods of control over the mosquito vector, coupled with the availability of more effective antimalarial drugs, would make eradication of the disease possible. This was clearly demonstrated in some countries and the concept of eradication was adopted and approved by the World Health Assembly in 1955. At that time malaria prevalence and mortality from the disease were estimated to be about half what they had been 12 years earlier (WHO, 1959). By the end of September 1974 the disease had been eradicated from 36 entire countries or territories containing some 41 percent of the population of the original malarious areas of the world. Progress in Central and South America has been good but in some parts of the world, hampered by lack of finance and by technical difficulties, it has been very slow and uneven. In the WHO African Region, 232 million people live in originally malarious areas and of these only 5 million live in areas for which eradication is claimed, while an additional 20 million are protected by some measure of control, but 207 million people live in areas without any specific antimalaria measures. In Africa, malaria is still responsible for about a million child deaths per year (WHO, 1975).

Tuberculosis, measles, influenza, pneumonia, infectious hepatitis, meningococcal meningitis

In contrast to malaria, these are examples of diseases whose distribution is worldwide, but their effects on the populations of developing countries are particularly severe. Malnutrition, overcrowding, debility arising from the coexistence of other diseases, and unfavourable climatic conditions all play a part in producing high prevalence and mortality. Moreover, financial stringency and deficiencies in health care frequently prevent the adoption of vaccination schemes against tuberculosis and measles, the drug treatment of cases of tuberculosis or of pneumonia, or the proper home or hospital nursing care of all these conditions. While many of the developed countries are experiencing a marked fall in notifications of new cases of tuberculosis, in some areas in Africa, Asia and Oceania the annual incidence of new cases is as high as 250-300 per 100,000 inhabitants.

Onchocerciasis

This non-fatal disease is due to a small filarial worm which is prevalent over a belt stretching across Central Africa, south of the Sahara from Sierra Leone to Ethiopia and as far south as Angola and Zambia. In the Americas it affects localized areas of Central and the northern part of South America. The adult worm lives in the subcutaneous tissues, where it forms a nodule characteristic of the condition. An adult worm will liberate some million microfilariae each year and these migrate through the skin, not infrequently reaching the eye and causing occular disturbance and blindness. The parasite is spread by an intermediate host, the *Simulium* fly. In the Volta River basin of West Africa, an area of 700,000 km^2 covering parts of 7 countries, it is estimated that among the 10 million inhabitants of the area more than one million are affected: at least 70,000 of them are incapacitated for work by blindness and many more suffer serious visual impairment. As a result large areas of this fertile basin are unproductive and uninhabited. (WHO, 1974a). Control of the disease is difficult, since up to the present no chemotherapeutic agent has been found that is suitable for mass therapy and, since the worm may continue to discharge microfilariae for as long as 15 years, vector control will have to continue for many years.

Other filarial infections

Other filariae are widespread through tropical and subtropical countries, the worms having a life history somewhat similar to that in onchocerciasis. *Wuchereria bancrofti*, the most widely distributed of the human filarial parasites, occurs in many parts of India and the Far East, in tropical Africa, in the tropical Americas and in many of the Pacific islands. The condition is apt to result in disturbances of the lymphatic system which may progress to elephantiasis, a condition where one or more limbs, the scrotum, breasts or vulva may become grotesquely enlarged. The fear of such development in a person suffering from this form of filariasis is very liable to produce anxiety and other psychological symptoms.

In some areas of Africa up to 60 percent of the population has been found to be infected with microfilariae and since the condition is transmitted by common mosquitoes, in particular *Culex fatigans*, it is very likely to occur in human settlements in damp areas. Squatter settlements and shanty towns are particularly liable to become new foci of infection.

Leprosy

Historically leprosy was a disease so dreaded that the patient was excluded from the community and placed in a leper hospital or colony. Today the disease is endemic mostly in tropical and subtropical areas, China and Korea, with a few endemic foci in other temperate regions. The highest prevalence is in the Far East, with India and China contributing about half the world total of between 12 and 20 million cases. It is a disease characterized by a long incubation period, usually 3 to 5 years, with lengthy periods often elapsing before recognition. It is associated with poor socioeconomic conditions and in most cases is transmitted by family contact. Effective modern treatment has altered the outlook and it is now practicable to render patients noninfective at an early stage so that they may return to their homes. Nevertheless, an increased prevalence has recently been reported, associated with crowded human settlements in tribal, rural, slum and urban areas of Burma, India and Sri Lanka and other South-East Asian countries, and, according to recent information from the WHO Regional Office for South-East Asia, surveys among schoolchildren have revealed incidence rates as high as 3 percent.

Smallpox

After 8 years of work, the smallpox eradication campaign has achieved remarkable success. In 1970 there were 15 endemic areas; the following year the last case on the American continent was notified, and by 1974 the number of endemic areas had been reduced to 4, with 75 percent of the cases occurring in one country (WHO, 1974a). The success of this scheme gives hope that other eradication or control schemes, some perhaps on a local basis, may in turn be attended with similar success.

Noncommunicable Diseases

With many noncommunicable diseases considerable geographical, urban-rural and social class differences are apparent in both prevalence and mortality rates. Sometimes this may be due to a localized natural occurrence of some toxicant. Thus arsenic, radon, excess fluoride or excess nitrate may occur in a local drinking water supply; alternatively there may be a local deficiency, as in the case of a lack of iodine which occurs in some goitrous areas. Food habits may also affect the prevalence of noncommunicable diseases. Thus in Iceland the consumption of highly smoked fish was associated with an increased prevalence of cancer of the stomach and in some areas of Africa cancer of the liver is associated with aflatoxin, a carcinogen produced by moulds on certain foods. The increase in dental caries in many countries is associated with excessive consumption of highly refined carbohydrate foods. In many cases diabetes appears to have an association with excessive food consumption. The effects of man-made pollutants has already been discussed. The association of air pollution and in particular the personal localized pollution produced by tobacco smoking is associated with bronchitis, cancer of the lung, and heart disease.

Usually however the environmental factors in the etiology of noncommunicable diseases are complex. In many cases apparent area or regional differences are due in part to differences in the age and sex constitution of the population; associated with this, the diminished rate of communicable disease in the more developed countries results in the population having a higher proportion of the late middle-aged and elderly, who are more likely to be affected by the degenerative diseases. Geographical differences may sometimes be attributed, in part at least, to differences in the quality of medical care or differences in disease nomenclature. Racial and geneological differences may also be important in some diseases.

With coronary, arteriosclerotic and other degenerative cardiovascular diseases many etiological factors are involved and much still remains to be learned. Stress undoubtedly plays an important part, both as a factor precipitating acute episodes and as a factor contributing to the increased prevalence of these diseases in some countries during recent years. The diseases are in general more common among the affluent, i.e., the upper socioeconomic groups, and this in turn will contribute to many of the area differences in mortality which have been noted. These diseases have also important relationships with obesity, tobacco smoking, and excess alcohol consumption. In tobacco smoking carbon monoxide probably plays an important part. There are also more fundamental factors probably associated with disturbances in biochemical metabolism at the cellular and molecular levels, manifested *inter alia* by the excess production of cholesterol indicating a disorder of the lipid metabolism. A recent international survey promoted by WHO demonstrated that atherosclerotic lesions of the blood vessels were frequently present in quite young people, the development of the condition in women usually being 20-30 years behind that in men. The concept that atherosclerosis of the adult originates in early childhood is being increasingly widely accepted (WHO, 1974a).

The apparent association of cardiovascular mortality with the consumption of soft water has already been noted. It has been found in a number of countries, though these are exceptions, and differences in cardiovascular pathology have been identified in a comparative study of a hard and a soft water city. No clues have yet been found to indicate the mechanisms which might create these differences.

From the point of view of human settlements, there is no evidence that, apart from the environmental factors mentioned above, the physical environment itself has any specific relationship with degenerative heart disease.

Rheumatic heart disease is a separate problem. Its prevalence in developed countries has diminished greatly, but it is still an important problem in many tropical and subtropical countries. It is a condition which is frequently the aftermath of streptococcal infection and its prevalence is therefore likely to be associated with differences in health care and in particular with delay or failure in giving effective antibiotic treatment.

Another infectious disease associated with serious effects on the heart is American trypanosomiasis (Chagas' disease). In Brazil it has been estimated that up to 80 percent of the chronic cases of this disease may have cardiac sequelae.

There are considerable regional and area differences in cancer prevalence. In the Americas neoplasms of the uterine cervix are responsible for the largest number of cancer deaths in women, and there are great differences in the mortality rates for cancer in the various New World countries. Cancer of the colon and rectum occurs more frequently in industrialized countries. In Africa, where at one time it was considered that cancer prevalence was relatively low, it now appears to be as great a problem as in many other parts of the world and in some areas as many as 40 percent of the surgical beds for adults are occupied by cancer patients.

Accurate reporting of cancer is an important factor in understanding the environmental aspects of the condition and surveys sponsored by or with WHO assistance are now taking place in many parts of the world (WHO, 1974a).

Nutrition

The important influence of nutrition on health in human settlements has been repeatedly mentioned. It is now necessary to examine the subject in greater detail. The dietary deficiencies most concerned are those due to the lack of protein which contributes to the growth of the body, and carbohydrate and fat which provide energy. The deficiencies are manifest in two varieties of protein-calorie malnutrition.

Kwashiorkor

This is a condition which is primarily due to nutritional imbalance in early childhood, the diet, though yielding carbohydrate calories, being low in protein material. The time of greatest danger is the weaning period, when the child is growing rapidly in relation to its size and is not yet adapted to its new diet, which is all too often deficient in nutrients. The expense of protein foods, the dietary customs in many countries, which fail to provide adequate protein for young infants, and the occurrence of concurrent infections, especially diarrhoeal diseases, all contribute to the high prevalence and seriousness of the condition. The infant tends to be oedematous with generalized subcutaneous fat giving a chubby "moon-face" appearance; growth is retarded and there is wasting of the muscles. The child is miserable, suffering from loss of appetite and vomiting and passing loose bulky stools. The hair and skin often assume a lighter colour and there may be a "flaky paint" rash.

Nutritional marasmus

This condition occurs when the diet is low in both protein and energy (calories). The child suffers from severe retardation of growth and wasting of both muscles and subcutaneous fat. The typical appearance is that of "skin and bones." Often in severe cases the child is little more than half the normal weight for its age.

The retardation of growth is characteristic of these forms of malnutrition. Jelliffe (1968) in reviewing the literature shows the extent to which newborn African infants have low average birth weights, due largely to malnutrition of the mother, although other factors such as symptomless malaria in the mother may influence an infant's birth weight.

During the first six months after birth the infants often thrive, but this is followed by a marked deterioration in the second semester of life. The relationship of maternal malnutrition to low birth weight was shown in the Netherlands shortly after the liberation, in Leningrad during the siege, and, more recently, in the Guatemala survey (Mata et al., 1975). The beneficial effects of giving nutritionally adequate weaning foods has been discussed above.

Scrimshaw and his colleagues (1968) have reviewed evidence of the relationship between nutrition and infectious diseases and concluded that infections are more likely to have serious consequences among persons with clinical or subclinical malnutrition, and infectious diseases have the capacity to turn borderline nutritional disease into severe malnutrition. In this way malnutrition and infections can be mutually aggravating and produce more serious consequences for the patient than would be expected from a summation of the independent effects of the two. More definitive evidence is now emerging from the Guatemala survey, where it has been shown that neither the provision of an adequate diet nor the prevention and control of infection will yield the expected results independently. Moreover, both the nutritional measures and those for the prevention and control of disease should be directed to the pregnant mother as well as to the infant after birth. It is pointed out also that the assessment of the effects of these factors on mental development still awaits investigation (Mata et al., 1975). Evidence in favour of such an association was discussed at a symposium of the Swedish Nutrition Foundation held in 1973.

Human Settlements and Mental Ill-Health

As with physical illness, the effects of housing, the environment, crowding, and socioeconomic and other conditions in producing or exacerbating mental ill-health are complex and difficult to identify. There are similar multifactoral influences and these are themselves closely interlinked. Moreover, psychiatric symptoms are of a subjective nature and difficult to quantify for the purposes of epidemiological study.

Again, as with studies of physical ill-health, surveys have mainly taken the form of observations on communities living in poor environmental circumstances, often compared with communities living in better environmental conditions, and observations on the effects of moving populations from poor to improved environmental conditions, a further group being left in the poorer environment to act as a control population. Results from such studies have been somewhat varied, so that it is not easy to detect consistent trends.

A number of studies have indicated that in overcrowded city areas of low quality housing there are higher rates of admissions to mental hospitals. Evidence also suggests that overcrowding, particularly the sharing of accommodation by members of two or more families, may give rise to an increase in superficial symptoms of stress, while not affecting the prevalence of the more serious symptoms of mental disorder. The moving of population groups into new and improved housing has, in most of the studies, had comparatively little effect on the prevalence of symptoms of mental ill-health.

In the poorer areas of cities there is not only the bad physical environment, the dilapidated structures, the depressing visual outlook, the noise from traffic, industry and fellow mankind, and the overcrowding, but there is also the associated poverty that has led a family to take up residence in such an area. There are often accompanying feelings of friendlessness, alienation and frustration. Some members of the community, however, retain the enterprise and ambition to continue the struggle to move up in the social scale. The community is composed of many types of mankind and crime rates and alcohol and drug abuse are more in evidence. The population is unstable and badly integrated as compared with rural areas and better quality urban districts. In some slum areas, however, particularly in older cities, there is a surprising element of stability, families having remained in close, friendly proximity to each other for many years, and the forced relocation of such families is likely to result in considerable stress and loneliness as a consequence of the disruption of the community.

There is evidence suggesting that in any population group there is a more or less consistent proportion of individuals predisposed to psychiatric breakdown. In stable, well-integrated communities, many such people do not progress to the stage of overt mental disorder, and minor degrees of mental illness are more likely to receive supportive care from the family or other members of the community. In the disintegrated hetero-geneous populations of city slums and shanty towns, such people will receive less care and understanding and be subjected to greater stress from both the physical and socioeconomic conditions prevailing there. In city populations many people with behavioural difficulties or psychotic tendencies will be forced down the scale to end up in the worst areas. The prevalence of excessive mental ill-health in such areas is not therefore solely the effect of the conditions prevailing there.

Many studies indicate the importance of stress, and this can often explain the apparent contradictions in some of the findings. Even in stable, well-integrated communities, some members will find themselves unable to live up to the demands which they feel are being placed upon them by the community, and such communities may at times place great strains on their nonconforming members.

The relative effects and interrelationship of physical environment, crowding and emotional stress are important. London experienced a considerable influx of immigrants from the Caribbean in the 1960s and later of Indians and Pakistanis from Uganda. The housing shortage forced many of them into dilapidated furnished accommodation, often sub-let by unscrupulous primary tenants. Considerable overcrowding occurred according to the standards laid down by the London boroughs. The paramount troubles, however, arose not from the physical environment or from the overcrowding as such, but from the difficult personal relationships which developed between the occupants themselves and between the occupants and their landlords. A number of studies have also been undertaken in Hong Kong. Here, in contrast to London, the overcrowding is far greater, individual rooms being shared by several families and beds often being shared with non-kinsmen. Again the findings showed that it was not the physical conditions and overcrowding which *per se* created emotional strain and unhappiness, but that these conditions did have an effect when operating alongside other factors such as poverty. Similarly, correlations have been reported between the floor level on which the dwelling was situated and emotional strain – an association which has been noted in studies of highrise flats. These findings therefore may be summarized as indicating that housing has an effect on patterns of social relationships, and that individuals respond to the strained social relationships, anxieties, stresses and strains which the housing conditions have helped to create.

Occupation and Ill Health

Man's occupations have a profound influence on his health and longevity. It has been known for many decades that certain occupations carry serious health risks, and in the course of the years continued improvements have been effected. The more obvious ill-effects led to the earliest action: the high prevalence of tuberculosis in the cutlery and pottery industries, phosphorus poisoning in the manufacture of matches, arsenic poisoning in the paper industry, and lead poisoning in the manufacture of paints. As time has progressed, the list of hazardous occupations has lengthened and methods of control have become more effective. Parallel with action against specific hazards has been action to control hours of work, particularly of women and children, and action to reduce the risk of accidents. Legislation governing workmen's compensation has encouraged employers to see that workpeople conform to the safety requirements laid down, but nevertheless it has often been found difficult to get both employer and employee to conform to the requirements conscientiously in order to obtain the maximum protection.

The employer is concerned primarily with the economics of his business, and employees, despite careful health education and continued exhortation, are often unable to take a long-term view and to appreciate that precautions taken now will avoid ill health in perhaps 10 or 20 years. International medical meetings and occupational health conferences, and, in recent years, the coordination of international activities by ILO, WHO and other bodies, have encouraged countries to adopt more adequate precautions.

It is unfortunate that most of the hazards have been identified only as a result of the occurrence of a sufficient number of cases to indicate the existence of the danger. With improved epidemiological methods, and statistics of the health of both active and retired workmen, more accurate data may be obtained so that new or unidentified hazards can be found at an early date, sometimes when only a very few cases have occurred. Thus, within recent years, it has been possible to identify new occupational conditions such as mesotheliomata, a rare form of cancer due to the inhalation of asbestos fibres, haemangiosarcomata, due to exposure to vinyl chloride in the plastics industry, and bladder cancer in the rubber and chemical industries. Unfortunately, it is rarely possible to identify an industrial hazard before a new chemical is introduced into industry, though, with modern methods of testing for carcinogens, mutagens and teratogens, there are hopes that this may sometimes be possible.

The diseases affecting workers in most industries do not necessarily originate from specific occupational factors, although the workers may contract the infection in the working environment or it may be aggravated by working conditions. In developing countries the prevalence of certain communicable diseases is sometimes higher than in the general population. This is not infrequently the case with tuberculosis. A rate of between 5 percent and 7 percent has been reported, for example, in some Asian countries, and is probably the result of various nutritional, economic and environmental factors associated with lack of proper health care.

In developed countries effective systems have usually been introduced to control the well-known occupational hazards and either eliminate or reduce them to a minimum, although negligence and lack of discipline are still liable to cause occupational accidents and disease, and efforts are continually being made to find new methods to reduce these as far as possible. With modern advances in technology fresh problems continually arise.

In many developing countries conditions are often far from satisfactory and even the most elementary precautions are frequently found to be neglected. Thus, the control of dusts is often inadequate. Recent reports from one South American country showed that, of 48,000 workers exposed to dusts in the manufacturing industries, 5.6 percent required compensation in 1972. In the mining industry very considerable numbers were found to be suffering from pneumoconiosis and silicosis, and in asbestos works no less than 23 percent were found to have radiographic signs of asbestosis. These are all diseases leading to chronic ill health as a result of fibrosis of the lungs. Tuberculosis is a frequent complication, and asbestosis has an added risk of the development of cancer. In the same country 4.3 percent of a sample of workers from the lead industry were considered to be suffering from lead poisoning.

In another South American country, 21.9 percent of lead workers examined were found to have signs of excessive lead absorption and, in yet another country, in 3 lead works from 22 percent to 100 percent of the workers were similarly affected. Reports of poisoning by mercury, arsenic, carbon tetrachloride and benzene — all highly toxic substances — are not infrequent. In another country it was found that of some 10,000 patients admitted to hospital in 1967, 56 percent were diagnosed as suffering from occupational disease. The same sort of story may be found in many countries throughout the developing world.

Accidents are among the most common causes of occupational disability. Frequently employers and employees alike tend to accept the risk as inevitable, and unless it is someone's duty to be constantly on the alert for hazards and studying methods of preventing them, accident rates continue to be high.

Risks are not confined solely to factories. Of recent years there has been a growing realization of the hazards from vegetable and other organic dusts in both agriculture and its associated processing industries. Large numbers of people are exposed to dusts from cotton, flax, hemp, jute, coconut fibres, rice germs, bagasse, tea, cocoa, paprika and wood and the list of resulting hazards includes respiratory allergies, asthma, bronchitis, and pulmonary irritation. Many infectious and parasitic diseases are also prevalent. Thus anthrax is commonly reported from the handling of infected animals, wool and hides. Pesticides are also a frequent cause of poisoning. These risks are not confined to the worker, for his family and particularly his children are often involved. Dusts may be taken home on his clothing, or the family may work with him for long hours in the fields.

It is particularly difficult for occupational health services to reach the smaller industries, such as the workshop employing just two or three men. These are often conducted on a family basis; long hours are worked, and the families, often living on the same premises, are thus exposed to the same hazards as the workers themselves.

Risks are not always confined to the workpeople and their families. Traces of toxic substances may escape into the factory environment and cause cases in local residents. This has happened in the case of asbestos, beryllium and vinyl chloride, and raised blood lead levels have been found in mothers and children living close to lead refineries. Minamata disease, due to industrial wastes in Japan, has already been mentioned. It is apparent that there is a clear case for close cooperation between environmental and occupational health services. Epidemiological methods evolved in one may be useful in the other, and knowledge of hazards in one should encourage a search for similar hazards in the other.

In most countries it is difficult to assess the size of the problem. Some have introduced schemes for the notification of specified industrial diseases, but usually the only information available comes from applications or awards for compensation, and such figures as exist invariably understate the position, for the worker himself is anxious to continue to earn the maximum wages and defers reporting his condition for fear of being suspended or discharged.

Countries with good systems of recording vital statistics sometimes classify deaths according to occupation. Social class differences have already been discussed. When deaths are classified according to individual occupations, some surprising differences are found. In addition to the occupational factors themselves, allied socioeconomic and other influences are likely to have played a part, and this possibility is further borne out by the fact that similar mortality trends are often found in the workers' wives.

Economic losses from occupational diseases and injuries are substantial. For example, in the USA they cost nearly $9000 million in 1969 and in the United Kingdom in 1967 there were 900,000 compensated cases of occupational disease and injuries, resulting in a loss of 23 million work days, compared to 3 million lost through strikes. In 1968 in the Republic of Korea compensation was awarded in respect of 21 percent of mineworkers, and in Chile some 18 percent of insured workers had occupational disabilities treated by the health service, with an estimated loss of 6.8 million workdays and a cost of $73 million.

Accidents

In many countries accidents have now become one of the most important causes of death and incapacity and since they frequently occur in early and middle adult life the economic loss to a community is often very considerable.

Road traffic accidents are among the principal causes of the increase in accident rates, and their importance in one of the most highly developed countries is shown by figures from the USA for the year 1968. Of a total of 1,930,082 deaths, 114,864 were due to accidents, and of these 54,864 were due to motor vehicles. At the ages of 5-34 accidents were the largest single cause of death and, of these, from a half to two thirds were associated with motor vehicles.

More detailed information of the pattern of motor vehicle accidents comes from England and Wales. Mortality among males is higher than females and, while the peak in deaths between the ages of 10 and 34 is very obvious in the former, it is barely detectable in the latter. This is probably due to the larger numbers of males who drive motor vehicles, particularly in connexion with their work, and possibly to the greater tendency of young males to take risks. With both males and females there is a pronounced rise in old age, when the elderly find themselves less able to appreciate approaching hazards. Similar patterns are detectable in other countries, and the numbers of persons injured also presents a similar picture.

Although a considerable amount of information has been assembled in many developed countries, particularly in Europe (United Nations, Economic Commission for Europe, 1972), international comparisons on a global basis are difficult since, in many countries, a considerable proportion of the population may be located in rural areas with comparatively few traffic problems. Figures of persons killed, expressed as a rate per million population, and per million cars registered, are available from some countries. Considerable differences are apparent between countries and, as shown by the WHO survey of 1962 (Norman, 1962) and various national surveys, these are not only related to the numbers of cars but also to the state of the roads, the condition of the motor vehicles, and the personal characteristics and training of the drivers. Countries which have spent money on road safety, on the testing and approval of cars, and on testing drivers are at an obvious advantage, as also are those which have taken action to deal with alcoholic drivers.

Although at present road traffic accidents are primarily a problem of developed countries, it is apparent that they present a problem which is affecting to a greater or lesser degree almost every country of the world, and will become progressively even more serious in developing countries as the numbers of cars in these countries increase.

The pattern of domestic accident statistics for the USA and for England and Wales show the importance of domestic accidents as a cause of injury and death compared with other accidents and demonstrate the predominance in children under 10 years of age and in the very old. Females, particularly elderly females, are more affected than males. The British survey showed them to be a more important cause of death at the extremes of life than road accidents in England and Wales, and similarly in the USA they were shown to be a more important cause of injury than road accidents. More recent information, and figures for international comparison, are scanty since few countries classify their statistics for domestic accidents separately. A survey undertaken by WHO in 1963 shows the preponderance of accidents due to falls, to fire and to poisoning in most of the countries investigated (Backett, 1965). In this survey the general problem was reviewed and recommendations for reducing the numbers of domestic accidents were made. Similar surveys have been made by a number of national authorities.

Although the pattern will vary from country to country, the same situations and principles will apply in each. Houses, furniture, and domestic equipment are often faulty in design. Large old-fashioned multistorey houses present problems, particularly if the houses are in bad repair, and when crowded together in cities present a serious fire hazard and consequent danger to the occupants. The flammability of housing materials is a problem of particular concern in the rural areas of many developing countries. Although not strictly a cause of "domestic" accidents, the proximity of water presents a hazard to children from drowning. In rural areas children are very prone to accidents caused by agricultural machinery.

The Delivery of Health Care

The great differences in the delivery of health care in developed and developing countries and in urban and rural areas of many of the developing countries have been known for many years. Recently attention has been focused on the planning, organization, and administration of health care services in individual countries, an aspect which has been considered in the successive WHO Reports on the World Health Situation, and it is hoped that this will enable countries to provide a more effective administrative structure for the more rapid and effective development of health care services. At present the situation in many countries is desperate and considerable areas of the world still have only the most primitive medical services.

The world situation can be reviewed most effectively by examining the numbers of physicians in relation to the population. While there has been a marked improvement over the period 1950-1970 in the total number of countries with more than one physician per 1000 inhabitants, there are many countries with less than one per 10,000 and indeed, with the growing population in many of the latter countries, the position appears to be deteriorating.

A consideration of the numbers of hospital beds per capita is a less satisfactory way of demonstrating the situation, since there are difficulties in defining a "hospital bed" and much will also depend on the extent to which beds in a hospital are used and the average length of stay in hospital. Nevertheless, the figures show that vast differences exist. Many of the developed countries have more than one hospital bed per 100 population, whereas 14 countries have less than one bed per 1000 population. Bangladesh in 1968 had only one per 8120 population and Afghanistan in 1970 one per 6890. It is apparent that in a number of countries distance and shortage of beds will make it impossible for many of those in need to receive hospital treatment.

Severe deficiencies in health care facilities are apparent in the isolated rural areas of many countries; yet valid comparisons between urban and rural areas are difficult. A chart comparing the numbers of health personnel and of hospital beds in selected urban areas of some countries, comparing them with the remainder of the country, was published in the World Health Statistics Annual for 1964 and more recent information on the proportions of beds in general hospitals and in rural hospitals and medical centres was given in the Fifth Report on the World Health Situation. This information, however, is hard to interpret and requires a knowledge of the individual countries. In most countries there is an important trend towards concentrating hospital beds and consultant services in the larger provincial hospitals to facilitate the more effective use of medical time and specialized equipment. With improved transport facilities these hospitals are able to cater for the population of considerable areas and small district hospitals are either being closed down or are dealing only with cases requiring less specialized care.

Outside the catchment areas of the larger hospitals it is more difficult to organize efficient hospital services. In some cases it may be possible to employ visiting specialists and in others the care must be largely provided by medical auxiliaries. Occasionally, particularly in developed countries, serious cases may be flown to hospital from the more isolated areas by helicopter.

ECONOMIC AND FINANCIAL ASPECTS

The information in this document shows the enormous problem of providing the various types of human settlements with efficient and effective health services. A correlation exists between the gross national product and life expectancy in a country. This of course is the obvious corollary to the fact that health services are expensive, and also that the developing world which, by and large, has the lowest range of gross national products is situated in the tropical and subtropical zones where medical services are faced with the most acute and pressing technical problems. The complicated relationship between economic development of a country and the organization of its health services was analysed in the recently published Fifth Report on the World Situation (WHO, 1975).

A danger exists that the market economy countries — those countries whose outlook is devoted towards increasing their foreign trade — will give priority to their economic development at the expense of their health and social services. Nevertheless, pressures for better services build up within a country, and the increase in wage earnings tends to make more money available for these services, particularly if the expenditure is increasing more rapidly than the gross national product of many countries. Between 1950 and 1963 health expenditure represented on an average about 4 percent of a country's gross national product. It is now between 6 percent and 8 percent in most of the developed countries. Developing countries vary considerably and the figure is not infrequently between only 1 percent and 2 percent.

Comparatively little is known of the circumstances and pressures which determine the method of evolution of a developing country's health care service. The developed countries have each pursued their individual line of development, with the result that there is great variation in the administrative and economic structure of their services. The developing countries tend to follow a more uniform pattern, which is not simply a response to a demand determined logically on priorities. In the initial phase the service has usually been based on the conception of free provision of both health care and preventive health services. As the country develops this encounters increasing demands from the population. A middle class, employed by commerce, the banks, insurance companies, hotels, and government agencies, grows up consisting of many of the better educated and more intellectual members of the community. To satisfy their needs private practice develops which may be entirely separate, or alternatively, it may be permitted as a branch of the health service; the latter is likely to be encouraged by the government as a means of providing more money for the development of its service. At this stage there is a danger that the private sector may develop with its own finances, to the economic and probably the functional detriment of the public service. Most countries, however, find some means of syphoning off at least some of this money to the public service, usually by the creation of some form of social insurance scheme. Difficulties are experienced in bringing in the independent workers, the families without means, and frequently much of the rural population. These at present often remain a government responsibility in so far as they are unable to provide for themselves.

The problem of how to guide the development of these services is engaging the attention of many governments at the present time and there is an obvious need for comparative studies and research.

The development of the environmental services also has its own economic and financial problems. The sections of this document on water supply and sanitation indicate the size of the task and, although much help has been given by the international agencies and international cooperation, there is still an enormous field to be covered. Many of the environmental services are primarily the responsibility of the local authorities.

Communities most in need are often those with the least financial resources. The provision of services in a slum or shanty town will be expensive on account of the number of people and the size of the installations required. At the other extreme, rural installations and services may be expensive in relation to the small numbers of people requiring the service. In developing countries the costs will be particularly heavy in relation to the gross national product.

In such circumstances it is important that available money should be well spent. Good administration is therefore needed, together with an accurate assessment of priorities. The provision of expensive equipment, though impressive and suggestive of progress, may not always be the best solution. Simpler equipment, easier to operate by untrained or semi-trained staffs, will often provide an acceptable service without making an undue drain on available resources. The value of community participation, already emphasized in preceding paragraphs, and the utilization where possible of local materials may make many otherwise over-expensive schemes practicable.

PRIORITIES

From the information given in this document it is apparent that there are 4 major factors influencing the health of human settlements:

(1) the inadequacy of the health care services in many parts of the world;
(2) the effect of malnutrition in affecting health and, more particularly, in rendering people more susceptible to the effects of other medical conditions;
(3) the ravages of communicable disease, still the major cause of illness and premature death in the developing world, especially in young children;
(4) the existence of environmental hazards which have a profound effect on health and mortality, particularly in the contribution they make in the spread of communicable disease.

These factors are all so closely interrelated that it is not possible to judge between them. There are, in addition, a number of basic factors which have an important bearing on each of the above. These are:

(1) the shortage of food in the developing world;
(2) the inadequacy of the financial provision for health services;
(3) the need for expansion and reorientation of the services for training health personnel;
(4) the need for research into improved ways of controlling, diagnosing and treating disease and into the understanding of, and improved methods of, administration, organization and development planning of the health service.

Health care services: The inadequacies are apparent from the data on the shortage and sometimes complete absence of doctors, nurses, health auxiliaries, clinics and hospital beds serving many parts of the world. The shortage can only be met by reorientating much of the training in developing countries to increase the numbers of medical auxiliaries and health aides in order to provide a basic or primary health care service.

Malnutrition: It is beyond the scope of this document to examine the shortage and maldistribution of food. The evidence overwhelmingly indicates that malnutrition plays a predominant role in influencing both disease prevalence and mortality. A vicious circle is created in that the diarrhoeal diseases in particular exacerbate the state of malnutrition.

Communicable disease: Although there have been great advances in communicable disease control, these diseases still have a profound negative influence not only on health, but also on the working capacity of a population, and in some areas development is held up until more effective control can be established.

Environmental health: Undoubtedly the major environmental influence is the lack of adequate pure water supplies and satisfactory sanitation. Without these a large number of communicable diseases cannot be adequately controlled.

The interrelationship of other environmental factors is complicated, but the importance of two is outstanding:

(i) Crowding has an important effect on the prevalence of communicable disease and has an influence on mental health, mainly as a result of the creation of stress.

(ii) Air pollution has been shown to have important health influences, particularly in the urban areas of developed countries and in the vicinity of industry. The control of air pollution must include attention to planning. By this means it is possible to obviate the effects of many of the problems some of which are already beginning to have important influences in the developing world.

To assess the effect of the physical structure of human habitations it is necessary to subdivide the subject into a number of separate influences. These include:

(i) the capacity of the house and its environment to harbour and encourage vectors of disease;

(ii) the likelihood of an unsatisfactory or dilapidated structure causing accidents;

(iii) the adequacy of the protection from excessive heat, cold or damp;

(iv) the possibility of the structure giving rise to allergic manifestations (e.g., from moulds) or toxic effects from materials used in the structure of the building;

(v) the effects of the agglomeration of houses, e.g., in slums and squatter settlements;

(vi) the influence of the housing environment, e.g., the existence of traffic, hazards to children from water, and natural physical hazards such as landslides or earthquakes.

These and other influences combine to create the state of healthiness or unhealthiness of the housing environment. The weight to be attached to each factor will vary with the local conditions. It is important not to overlook the effects of the environment on mental health and wellbeing, the importance of the amenities and the effect of the physical environment on influencing the social relationships of an individual or a family with the community.

Three other subjects are of importance:

(1) *Accidents and accident prevention:* The numbers of persons killed or disabled by road or occupational accidents or accidents in the home is growing, and their control and prevention must be considered a major health requirement.

(2) *Occupational health*: The totality of ill health and premature mortality caused by man's occupations is considerable and precautions are often either lacking or neglected. The evidence indicates that conditions are particularly bad in many developing countries. This is tragic because great improvements could often be achieved with relatively little expenditure by adequate legislation and efficient administrative and managerial control. In many situations there would be an economic advantage by the resulting fall in sickness rates and industrial compensation.

(3) *Chemical hazards and hazards from consumer goods*: Constant watch must be maintained for new chemical and other hazards from the expansion in technology. Without adequate investigation and control new methods of producing consumer goods and the introduction of new substances will inevitably produce new hazards.

Information: Throughout this document shortages of adequate statistical information to assess the importance of hazards has been apparent. Accurate information is essential if hazards are to be identified and priorities assessed in order to assist planners and decision makers. Studies are needed to show the best methods of collecting information and conducting surveys.

3
Planning and Improvement of Rural Settlements in Developing Countries*

This chapter reviews major issues in the area of settlement planning and improvement. It discusses alternative approaches which have been suggested and examines different types of settlement projects, particularly those in which FAO has been involved. In most cases, only partial data were found to be readily available: the housing component of some projects, for example, is recorded in considerable detail, while the economic base component is neglected. More frequently, in the case of the FAO materials, the reverse was true: the agricultural or farm land tenure issues are documented in some detail, but the housing and its layout, tenure of homestead plots, etc., are neglected. The major criterion used in analyzing issue areas and in identifying important alternative approaches was that they should be "habitat-related."

The major areas of issues are considered hereafter as Economic, Social, Physical Planning and Implementation factors.

ECONOMIC FACTORS

Economic considerations in settlement planning relate to the habitat component in two major ways. They determine the resources available for housing the population, and hence the level of housing and services which can be provided.

A. Economic Base

The production activities of rural settlement are primarily agricultural, and the major concern of much of the work of the FAO. This paper deals primarily with economic activities in rural settlements as they determine or influence the habitat component of the rural settlement, and not in detail with other aspects of rural economic planning.

In projects for the settlement or development of newly cultivated, irrigated or redistributed land, in most countries, especially without marketable resource wealth, planning and management of production system is crucial [1]. Although the analysis in this paper focuses on planning and improving the habitat component of rural settlements, it is necessary to keep in mind, that, as Sabry insists, in a national settlement programme planning for agricultural production should receive priority because a proper agricultural programme can, in many instances, buy good social services [2].

The practices necessary to maintain productivity with traditional technology, provide low yields and produce little beyond the subsistence of the cultivators. Extension of such systems over new areas produce

---

*Taken from a background paper for Habitat contributed by the Food and Agriculture Organization (Symbol A/Conf. 70/B/10; 4 May 1976).

only meager surpluses. Clearly development requires that traditional systems be drastically revised or replaced. New systems of water and land utilization and associated human settlements have drastically different requirements for their viability than either the traditional peasant systems or the simplified models of Western capitalist agriculture. Thus, in Iran, land reforms made life better for many, but reduced the remaining landless to a precarious condition that forced them to migrate in increasing numbers. To stem this tide, the government, with wealth from its petroleum resources, is emphasizing agro-industries and decentralized growth poles and to increase productivity it is promoting new corporate production structures. In Ethiopia's Awash Valley development scheme, large-scale land development by concessionaires made no provision for the infrastructure, housing, and services required by the inevitable squatter settlements which sprang up and only slightly more for the nomad settlement scheme. Only recently have the human settlements implications been fully realized by government and project authorities [3].

Few, if any, developing countries are able to support schemes of resource development or rural development indefinitely unless they are quickly made economically viable. Therefore, land and water development policies must also take into account the desired social, physical and economic requirements for the associated settlement system (the Nickere District Rice Scheme in Surinam is an example) [4]. Many large dam construction projects for the purposes of power generation, urban water supplies, and even for crop production have failed to meet production expectations because they had stopped at the end of the major canal systems, leaving the farmer to cope with secondary distribution, field layouts and levelling, draining, and a wide range of other unfamiliar farm practices. On the Chambal Irrigation Scheme in India, proper water management and land development were not introduced for more than a decade after construction was completed. Major land and water development investments, at a minimum require for their productive use, such measures as survey, development and consolidation of land holdings, water management and creation of new or reorganized settlements. An area authority is required for farm and rural development coordination, including improvements in human habitat, and to assure the adequate resource organization, infrastructures, and availability of input services, marketing and processing services, social infrastructure and phased town and village planning which meets current and foreseeable probable future needs of the population. Land use planning with various community needs in view is an important element. Effective provisions for the continued management, maintenance and coordination of use of the structures and infrastructures related to economic and other activities of the population are essential.

The expected productivity of a development programme should determine the planned levels of facilities, social services and housing which can be provided in the settlement. Even if improvements and services are subsidized initially, the planning should seek to ensure that adequate additional income will soon exist to support the new facilities.

Target income (as a measure of agricultural productivity) is closely linked under given conditions with the size of holding in the settlement. The main determinants of size of holding to be provided as identified in the Near East Region include:

"Size of family, quality and production potential of land, availability of land and size of population, type of farms and farming enterprise, managerial skill and financial capacity, existing man-land ratio in the region, standard of living in the country ... and quantity of water (irrigation and drinking) and rainfall [5]."

However, such factors do not adequately explain the range of holding sizes in land settlement programmes in the region in 1965 which ranged from two to 16 hectares for irrigated land; and up to 50 hectares per family for unirrigated lands. In the Sudan, the variation ranges from 15 to 40 acres for irrigated lands and to over 1,000 acres for rainlands.

Other factors related to size of holding which must be taken into account in new settlement layouts include the system of farming adopted (intensive or extensive) and the number of families which must be accommodated in the settlement project.

The viability of some rural settlements depends on fishing and on forestry rather than farming. In many developing countries, small scale fishing operations are a principal source of employment in rural coastal areas and make a vital contribution to national diet. In fact, 25 percent of the world's fish catches and 40 percent of the catch used for food is provided by small craft.

The improvement of incomes from fisheries for coastal rural settlements usually requires the creation or improvement of an infrastructure of roads and/or harbours to facilitate access to markets (fresh fish are highly perishable) or of plants to process the catch (e.g., canning or drying) for later sale. Recognizing this, the FAO has proposed a programme of technical improvement, including development of institutional infrastructure (cooperatives for marketing, credit schemes), technical assistance, and provision of roads, water supply and housing to fishing settlements [6].

Income from fisheries can provide the economic base for housing and settlement development. At Kariba Lake, for example, in the period after the dam was completed, the high productivity of the fisheries on the lake enabled considerable capital accumulation as represented by village stores [7]. However, factors determining capital accumulation for other facilities and home improvement have not been studied in this or similar situations. For both landlocked and coastal nations income development and income diversification for fishing villages requires integration into regional plans and provision of infrastructure to allow for marketing the catch [8].

As already noted, FAO has information for several countries and/or has directly assisted projects designed to settle forest populations, provide alternative sources of income and improved social services as part of a package approach to afforestation, forest management, and better resource utilization. In Tunisia, people living in forest areas are gathered around a focal point (e.g., school or first-aid station) for an area of about 300 hectares in order to improve the forest resources and increase the productivity of agriculture. Each forest worker is to have an area for a vegetable garden and to build his house [9]. However, reports do not indicate any policies by the government to assist home building and planning. Futhermore, such regional projects require integration into regional development programmes.

In Turkey, as part of a Rural Development programme, about 3200 forest villages comprising about two million people come under a Directorate General of Forest Villages with the objectives: to develop agriculture where soils are suitable; promote animal husbandry; provide additional employment opportunities in forest operations; and protect and develop the forests. In Thailand, a Forest Industry Organization has set up forest villages to: prevent further land clearing, organize labor for afforestation, provide social services, encourage settled agriculture; protect the environment, and slow down rural-urban migration.

In Nigeria, the development of agrisilviculture based on forest villages in forest areas has provided more work at convenient distances between forests and village services. In Nepal and India, hill tribes have been relocated in consultation with the settlers on lands suited for agriculture. In India, housing, bullooks, implements and sanitary and educational facilities plus training in cottage industries are provided. In Latin America, colonization in forest areas is to be found, especially in Peru, Venezuela and Mexico. Inadequate information is available to assess the adequacy of village and homestead layout and design and the devices of assistance on this aspect.

There are also examples of more comprehensive diversification of the rural economy from countries with a communal base for the rural economy. Diversification of the rural economy, including the location of industries in the rural areas and other measures to provide a diversified economic base for rural settlements improvements within the framework of regional planning [10] have been fundamental principles of planning in Israel. In China, different types of enterprises and industrial sidelines are commonly found in the rural communes, including tool making, carpentry, handicrafts, electric bulbs and lubricants [11]. Rural industries also provide opportunities for workers to learn skills which they may later employ when needed in larger urban centres. There, and in other socialist countries, increasing encouragement is being given to rural cooperatives and communes to save and reinvest agricultural profits in local industries.

This form of diversification of the economic base in rural areas has not so far been adopted on a large scale in other developing countries. However, it is one approach to rationalization of labor and resource utilization and to increasing income levels in rural areas where the potential for agricultural productivity is limited. Elsewhere some work has been done on development of local crafts (tie dying, fabric design, printing) and skills. The economic potential of such activities has usually been considered primarily as a source of cash income for women in rural areas [13].

At any point in time, some choice, is required between saving and investment in basic production capacity and provision of consumer goods and services for producers and their families.

B. Agricultural Policy and Programmes

The type of farming planned for rural communities based on agriculture depends on the target income. Voelkner has proposed a range of types of settlement schemes grouped by approximate levels of target incomes for irrigated agricultural settlements in Ethiopia's Awash Valley:

Self-help subsistence settlements, in which settlers are to provide their own minimum food subsistence.

Planned small-holder subsistence settlements in which settlers are to develop suitable land resources traditionally and prepare them for modernization. (The objective is to achieve maximal subsistence and some surplus.)

Planned small-holder, modern simple irrigation, individual or cooperative settlements, in which the objective is to achieve the highest productivity possible from the land and for the settlers to attain modern levels of living and productivity. Subsistence agriculture is replaced by modern agriculture with either diversified or specialized products. The agricultural output is to include "surplus for national consumption and some export."

Planned large scale capital intensive cooperative or corporation schemes based on modern mechanization and often complex irrigation. The objective is to develop high productivity potential of land and water resources and products for import substitution and/or exports [14].

The farmer's (settlers) concern for ensuring adequate subsistence food supplies, especially in new settlements, may initially limit the scope for self-help construction of housing and infrastructure — hence the value of food aid in self-help projects. But, as Voelkner points outs, settlements can be upgraded (to higher income levels) in stages. Similarly Sabry suggests the need to provide sufficient land for the production of subsistence crops even when cash crops are to be grown; especially during the initial stages of a project [15].

In subsistence level agricultural settlements, only very limited local resources are available for infrastructure, social services, and housing construction and improvement. Self-help and local materials are the main inputs and any additional resources needed should probably be in the form of grants rather than loans, since the settlers cannot be sure of having cash to repay loans for improved living conditions. As a base for refugee settlements, minimal subsistence farming may be a necessity. The World Food Programme (WFP) provides food aid to refugees until land has been cleared and self-sufficiency in subsistence foods is attained [16]. Furthermore, in refugee settlements, agricultural and settlement policies need to take account of the refugees concepts of the permanence of his status and his hopes of returning home, as well as the perspective of the planners [17]. A number of WFP projects studied (Zambia, for example) also include plans for more permanent settlement and subsequent upgrading to "maximal subsistence farming" with the introduction of some cash crops [18].

In Kenya, in irrigated settlements for growing cash crops with improved technology, the needs of the extension services influenced the housing pattern planned for the farmers. Thus it was decided that:

"The best results have been obtained by settlement in small villages closely tied to a topographical unit. Individual housing on each working makes it difficult to get people together and villages accommodating between 75 and 100 families provide the optimum situation [19]."

Agricultural projects with target incomes for settlers present special opportunities for testing techniques and general feasibility of higher standards of housing, supporting facilities and other settlement improvement [20]. However, their value for such purposes is dependent upon adequate feed back and evaluation, especially with regard to their habitat aspects. Furthermore, the necessary national administrative coordination between different ministries concerned may be only possible by means of a special authority (e.g., a river valley authority or a commune system) or by means of strong central and local administrative coordinating bodies.

In the settlement of nomadic populations, the importance of at least a partial continuation of a nomadic way of life is frequently emphasized [21]. The agricultural system for pastoral peoples is frequently designed to permit continuation of their livestock-rearing activities. Where the agricultural system adopted involves continued, even though possibly reduced, migration movements of the livestock, accompanied by part of the family or tribe, the settlement plan must take this into account. Traditional forms of housing may continue to be used by the mobile population, but improved habitat and access to social services and infrastructure are a major attraction for substituting a settled for a mobile way of life. Christodoulou has discussed criteria and alternative agricultural systems for nomadic settlers [22]. However, little is known about the trade-offs between settlement and income earning possibilities as perceived by nomads themselves, except that, livestock represents important elements of social and economic systems which they are most reluctant to give up. Even when eager to settle and to own an agricultural and housing unit, nomads may also prefer to use part of their land for livestock [23]. Furthermore,

"Pastoralists utilize effectively 714 million hectares of pastureland in the arid and semi-arid regions of the Near and Middle East and Sahel and Sudan zones of Africa and produce nearly 90 percent of the meat for a population of 350 million people ... If these people are settled and made farmers it will not be possible to use this pastureland and produce meat for this human population. However, through partial settlement of nomads and pastoralists these huge grazing areas can be utilized through development of new systems of nomadic and transhumant animal production which can be managed by part of the tribes ... Other members of which can stay in settled areas [24]."

Pursuit of such a policy may require development of services to the mobile habitat of the nomadic groups to which, so far, inadequate consideration has been given although examples are known in Syria, Sudan and other Near Eastern countries. But in the projects reviewed, improvements in nomads' living conditions were only undertaken after their settlement.

Adequate space and facilities plans for the marketing of farm products are essential in all but subsistence level schemes. Effective arrangements usually include construction of physical structures and transportation improvements. Facilities and organizations for their management must be provided to assemble, process and prepare for shipment. Access to markets will be required. Inadequate marketing arrangements are often a factor limiting offtake, and hence productivity, from rangeland livestock herds. The more perishable the product, the more important all these become, especially to reach distant markets – e.g., for fish some fresh fruits and vegetables and milk products. The provision of an adequate transportation network of all-weather roads (or in some cases airstrips, railroads, and harbors) is often a limiting market factor. Lack of any of these "market" facilities may be a restraint to production, increasing incomes and hence longer-term availability of resources for financing and maintaining other infrastructure and social services. For this reason, they frequently receive priority in infrastructural improvements for rural settlements.

The planning of agricultural programmes, with an emphasis on food production, is the focus of most of FAO's activity relating to rural settlements. The implications of the economic base for habitat improvement and maintenance (and *vice versa*), though recognized, have often not been adequately considered in projects for which FAO assistance is provided. Nor, indeed are these factors generally considered together by national or other international agencies charged with the improvement of rural settlements. Rather, i.e., the tendency is to treat production and habitat aspects independently.

C. Land Tenure

The conditions by which land is owned and used are basic to the economic structure of both planned and existing rural settlements and may strongly influence attitudes and behavior toward habitat improvement. As determinants of security for investment in improvements, the income which can be generated by the land and of the distribution of that income, the land tenure pattern in a settlement strongly influences the amount of local resources which will be available for habitat improvement and who will receive it [25]. In the projects examined, considerable attention was given to land tenure and use conditions of the farmlands. Their importance as issues in land reform and settlement has recently been verified in FAO case studies [26].

However, the implications of alternative forms of homestead plot tenure and conditions of use usually have been neglected. Many parallels and contrasts with farmland tenure are of great importance in programmes involving housing improvement. Land tenure conditions in rural settlements do not always correspond to housing tenure conditions, especially for landless labourers and nomads. In nomadic and transhuman societies, the "habitat" is often "owned" by the family or sub-tribe, while grazing land may be collectively owned and used. Cultivated land, especially land with tree crops, has additional aspects of "ownership." Moreover, in various other settlement types such as socialist communes, the homestead plot frequently provides land for subsistence crops, small animal production, cottage industries and other income supplementing activities.

In settlement planning and improvement projects, the tenure and use systems adopted for the habitat need not be the same as that adopted for farmland. However, the rural family does need a feeling of security of tenure with regard to its home and associated plot. Under a dispersed farm residence pattern, farmland and house are usually treated as a unit. For example, in Libya, FAO advisors proposed that the ex-Ente farms be allocated as a "farm unit and its premises — land, house, stable, wells, cistern ... etc.[27]." On the other hand, in both the Israel "Moshav Shitufi" (collective work settlement) and in the rural communes in China, collective farming is usually combined with individual housing arrangements, combined, in the latter case, with private gardening plots for production of vegetables, cash crops and small animals [28]. In the early Tanzanian Pilot Settlement Schemes, individual farmers were given rights over homestead and production plots, while the village cooperative society retained all rights over land on which public and farm buildings were built [29].

In settlement projects where housing (of various standards) is provided, various forms of tenure have been granted including freehold (often in conjunction with freehold individual family farm cultivation patterns) and leasehold. In leasehold, the development authority retains ownership of the plot and housing unit and usually sets conditions as to the standards of construction and additions to the house. Restrictions are also sometimes placed on ownership and use of the homestead plot. For example, in the Volta Project, it was the intention to eventually issue title of ownership. In the meantime, settlers had been forbidden to rent out or sell the houses as they are not yet legally their property [30].

Tenure insecurity has been a problem in schemes where homestead plots are separate from the owned farm holding. Only when this security exists can the settler be expected to invest substantially his time, effort, materials and money to improve or construct his house or improve other aspects of his environment (surely one factor in the problem of improving squatter settlements) [31]. In the Volta River Project, for example, the inhibiting and unsettling effects of a lack of "ownership" have been noted and a freehold title to the settlers or their heirs recommended [30].

An unsatisfactory legal solution may force the settlers to search for unauthorized means to circumvent orders imposed by a settlement authority. Clearly the implications of existing alternative forms of tenure for homestead plots, their relationship to farmland tenure, and their problems and possibilities ought to be examined for settlement (layout) plans and house improvement programmes.

SOCIAL FACTORS

This section reviews the major planning issues related to the social organization of settlements (planned or improved) as part of a rural development policy. Some of these, e.g., the selection of settlers, apply primarily or exclusively to new, planned settlements. Others, such as the choice of supporting services to be provided for the welfare of families in the community, and the role of settlers in participating in management, apply to both new settlements and improvements on existing ones.

A. Social Structure of Groups in Settlement

Detailed studies of the social structure of settler groups or host populations in areas affected by settlement schemes, have been carried out in a number of countries (in some cases by FAO Technical Assistance experts). The main groups studied have been nomadic or seminomadic groups in Africa and the Near East (for example, Voelkner's study of the Afar, in Ethiopia and Abdallah's study in the Baggara area of the Sudan), and the populations of areas flooded by major dam schemes or in settlements affected by irrigation projects [32]. Such studies were sometimes designed to determine tribal structure, as in Cyrenaica, Libya, preparatory to resettlement or reform of land tenure since tribal claims over their lands are recognized by the Libyan government and compensation payment required an understanding of local tribal structures [33]. In other instances cursory attention has been given to habitat patterns and housing preferences (e.g., Abdallah, op. cit.). In some cases Voelkner (1974), Castelli-Gattinara (1973), and Van Heck (1973) present housing patterns, preferences and requirements detailed enough to be of some help to housing planners [34]. Also Brausch, Crook and Shaw (1964) provided adequate details to develop proposals for improvement of settlements in the Gezira scheme, but their recommendations were not implemented [35]. Studies of social structure before resettlement can be utilized to minimize disruption to existing social structures, a condition some authorities consider will facilitate further development [36]. In the Volta Lake Resettlement Project, data was collected to determine as far as possible preferred relocation sites and tribal neighbours. This information was considered to have minimized subsequent development inhibiting disunity [37]. For the Tabqa Reservoir one proposed alternative was to compensate the evacuees and allow them to arrange their own relocation.

Social surveys may also identify structures or institutions which can be advantageously changed, e.g., adaptation of attitudes of old slaveowners and feudal masters and the substitution of more democratic social structures [38].

Settlement (e.g., of nomads) and involuntary resettlement (e.g., of populations of areas inundated by dams) has both intended and unintended effects on both individuals and social structures. Yacoub observes in relation to Bedouin settlement:

> "Once the habits of mind and the symbolic relationships which are inherent in nomadism and sustain it are described (sic) by sedentarization, the individuals themselves become more receptive to migration to the big cities in search of fancied advantages" [39].

In the Volta Project, Afriye and Butcher consider inadequate housing contributed to an increased incidence of divorce and of separated households and Scudder has noted other reactions to the stress of relocation [40].

The type and process of settler selection may be critical for the success or failure of the project as Meliczek suggests [41], and helps determine the housing and social services requirements of the settlement. The housing needs of projects for settling teenage youths are not the same in the short term as for settling whole families. In cases of forced relocation, such as dam resettlement projects, there is little scope for choice except by offering cash or resettlement (as at Volta Lake and Tabqa Reservoir) thus allowing some degree of self-selection [42]. In some cases, the selection of settlers may be dictated by longterm policy: in China several hundred thousands (at least) educated youths have been settled in the countryside in a reverse migration process for merging intellectuals with peasants as "the only way of fostering successors to the cause of the proletariat", ensuring the future of the Chinese revolution and utilizing intellectuals in the modernization of the peasants [43].

The criteria most frequently utilized in settler selection include: education, skills, health, character, age and family status with consequent bearing on the type of accommodation required and on the social structure of the settlement. The age and sex structure may approximate or be very different from that in traditional settlements. Occupational skills other than agricultural may be sought or kept out. If housing and other structures are to be built by self-help methods, then it is advantageous if settlers with appropriate skills can be attracted. If a cooperative shop is to be provided, then competing shopkeepers may be discouraged. Financial status is sometimes important, either to select needy beneficiaries and to correct social and economic injustice; or, on the contrary, because (as in some settlements in Kenya and the Sudan) settlers are expected to provide their own working capital [44].

Another selective factor has been the desire to settle under the conditions provided. Where settlers are to be provided with food or capital in the initial stages, before any crops can be grown, persons interested in the immediate gratuities or services may be attracted, but leave as soon as the flow of food aid is ended. One way to tackle this problem (as on some World Food Programme supported projects) is by giving food aid as a return for work on land development, housing and other settlement improvements, rather than as a gratuity.

Where selected settlers are not heads of households but individuals, such as unemployed youths, they may be accommodated initially in camps rather than individual houses. Such camps can be designed for subsequent use as housing. On the Land Reclamation Project related to the Aswan Dam, the WFP evaluation report recommended that "the principle should generally be followed of constructing all new migrant labour camps (for reclamation labour) in the form of villages." The migrant labourers can subsequently be given priority as settlers [45].

An alternative selection scheme to minimize the trauma of constructing a complete new social system with strangers, is the selection of settlers from the same social groups, tribes or villages. This could be particularly critical to reduce returnees and "deserters" under transmigration and nomadic settlement schemes.

B. Relationship with Host Community

The problems of relationships between settlers and the existing population or other claimants for use of the land requires careful planning in new settlement. This principle diminishes in countries with very large areas available for settlements, and over which there are few or limited claimants to right of ownership or use (e.g., in some parts of Latin America, Malaysia, and Indonesia) and where local identities and cultural differences are small. In Africa, there is no "unowned" land, and therefore, unoccupied areas always belong to someone. In order to minimize the potential conflicts, the initial living conditions in the new settlement should not be much higher than those of the surrounding community, but good enough to compete with alternatives perceived by those to be settled. Otherwise there is a danger of making the "host community" (people living close to the sites of new settlements or resettlement villages) jealous and antagonistic [46]. A study of the Vahpo area (a village constructed for the settlement of farmers displaced by the Volta Reservoir) revealed serious conflict between "host" and "settler" communities that careful planning might avoid. It was also found that conflict was greatly influenced by the degree of social and cultural integration between settler and host communities. The FAO expert consultation on agrarian structures in Africa considered that inter-communal conflict is influenced by:

> "(a) the ethnic links which existed between settler and host communities (b) the degree of landlessness or land 'hunger' of the settler community and the extent of land abundance of the host community at present and in the future (c) the willingness of the host community to accept the settler community and to give it part of their land and (d) the degree of homogeneity of the settler community [47]."

In other projects studied, attempts were made to minimize potential conflicts by giving the "host" population access to the supporting services, and institutions were being built in the new settlements (schools, clinics, extension workers' etc.) [48].

C. Supporting Services

This section deals with what are often called "supporting services," leaving the related facilities provisions to be dealt with later. The most commonly provided service in rural settlements is agricultural extension (briefly discussed above under economic issues). However, other important forms of support for the family and for the community (especially in new settlements) are not directly related to the productive activities of the village or settlement but are important components of integrated improvement programmes. The UNDP/ FAO Technical Report on the Ghab Region of Syria recognized that "All the planning and expenditure that have gone into the project will have little impact on the social life of the settlers unless their living conditions are improved" by the provision of essential services in the principle villages, albeit in gradual stages [49].

In Tanzania, integrated village plans through the government's Ujamaa and Cooperative Division include "women trained in home economics at all levels engaged as trainees in the Ujamaa villages." They are concerned with nutrition, child care, budgeting, and reduction of women's work load in the home [50]. Such services often include various forms of both formal and informal education including schools for children, functional literacy for adults, and training of women in home improvement, management and family life education. Programmes for women usually need to cover other aspects of women's activities such as agricultural production (food crops, animal husbandry, poultry raising, bee keeping) marketing, health care and first aid, and leadership in community and cooperative organizations. One recent evaluation of rural development programmes concludes that:

> "Women's training programmes frequently miss the important point that the traditional role of an African woman has often been quite different than in the West. Women have constituted an important portion of the productive rural labour force" [51].

The range of supporting and social services provided in a given settlement project will depend, in part, on the resources available, in part, on peoples expectations and needs, and on their impact on accomplishment of other projects and community goals. As noted above, FAO recommended for the Ghab Valley region a phased development of social services from a minimum base acceptable to the settlers.

Where construction techniques involving self-help are incorporated into village planning, for housing units and/or communal facilities, an important function of supporting services, including home economists, extension workers and other adult educators, is the teaching of new or improved construction techniques. In more capital-intensive planning and improvement projects, where finished or semi-finished housing units are provided

— information on techniques which can be used to maintain, furnish and improve the housing units will be needed [52]. Many examples exist of settlement projects where this factor was neglected and as a result buildings deteriorated rapidly. Lack of maintenance can also be due to inadequate incomes and designs otherwise inappropriate to the needs of the occupants.

Encouraging the development of vegetable garden plots (in communities where these are not customary) has been recommended as one way in which extension workers can help improve nutritional standards and increase the efficiency of use of the homestead plot [53]. However, more follow-up studies are needed to determine the effort, length of time, and other conditions for success of such introductions. Furthermore, and as already suggested above, extension services must avoid traditional (especially imported) sex role, stereotypes and reach both men and women.

In the Paraguay Programme of land settlement, the wide range of supporting services included credit, marketing and storage facilities, and training in agriculture and home economics to the settlers [54], and plans to assist new settlers in house construction. In other projects this latter aspect is largely neglected. Home economists were not, for example, much used in the Volta River Resettlement Project, and an array of services recommended for Syria's Ghab Valley Project did not include home management and other services for families, related to habitat maintenance and improvement.

D. Participation and Management Roles [55]

In many of the early settlement programmes examined (the Gezira Scheme, and the early programmes in Kenya, for example) the settlers had little if any say in project planning or operations, neither its agricultural/ economic aspects nor in the habitat component. Techniques for farming were chosen by the project planners and housing provided for the settlers in patterns laid out beforehand. In the Ghab Valley settlement plans, central house construction contracts were recommended to realize economies of scale [56]. In some schemes, however, as in Tanzania's Ujamaa villages, an emphasis is seen on the role of the settlers in planning and operating their own villages, in collaboration with cadres or community organizers. Here, the settlement community is, in principle at least, given considerable access to decision making and to the productive resources available. However, administrative and political targets sometimes override a commitment to voluntarism [57]. When projects do not involve a large component of outside investment, as in spontaneous settlement processes, the settlers make decisions about what to produce, where to settle, where to set their houses. But this evidence indicates that in many traditional African communities, this planning was done by the community through the medium of the chief [58]. Investigation of it could reveal insights about the ability of settlers to plan spontaneously and the role for technical assistance to improve the effectiveness of the planning process.

With increasing frequency, some parts of decision-making and management are decentralized and the settlers are allowed a limited say in planning and management processes. In this study, and where noted, it was usually reported to be valuable in improving the quality of decision making, even though time consuming [59]. For instance, the group itself may be best qualified to weed out "undesirables" in the final selection of settlers [60], and individuals may choose with what groups they wish to live in proximity [61].

In some cases, the community has participated in developing housing and settlement plans suited to their needs: in the Tema Manhean resettlement of a complete fishing village in Ghana, the architects were "subjected to a good deal of intelligent criticism" by local authorities and village representatives. As a result of criticism and suggestions, new plans were prepared which came closer to meeting the needs of the villagers to be resettled [62].

Both Butcher and Castelli-Gattinara recommend consultation with the relocatees (a) to inform them ahead of time of the relocation situation and procedures, (b) to allow them choices of compatible groups of fellow settlers or hosts, choices of plots, and where possible (c) the choice of government relocation or self-relocation with compensation [63].

The social survey provides an indirect and sometimes the only initial kind of participation insofar as it informs decisionmakers accurately of the distribution of needs and desires of the population. For example, in the Volta and Tabqa Dam and Lake Nasser Fisheries Development Centre projects such surveys provided valuable guidance for settlement and the introduction of technical fisheries and agricultural practices.

Self-management was an objective of many planned settlement projects, after a transition period which ranged up to as much as 20 years (in the highly mechanized irrigated settlement in the Awash Valley). However, in projects where the government undertakes most or all the organizational responsibility in the early stages, transfer of decision making and responsibility can be difficult: e.g., in the Jafr Pilot Project for Bedouin settlement in Jordan [64]. This difficulty arises because of the establishment of a conflicting set of expectations, and may be exaggerated by the unwillingness of the project management to give up complete control and to risk strong opposition to their policies [65].

The distinction between management, technical staff, and other residents of the settlement, can be exaggerated or minimized by the housing assigned to them. In Indonesia, the plans for the Penatang Panggang Transmigration Project proposed locating staff housing in the village centre and relatively isolated from the settlers. Such staff housing in a tight enclave is not uncommon, and is likely to exaggerate staff feelings of superiority over the settlers and the social distance between them [66]. At times, however, staff housing has been used as a positive factor. In Malaysia, the Federal Land Development Agency (FELDA) Handbook states that FELDA Staff are to receive extra allowances if they are required to use normal settlers' houses as accommodation [67]. In a range management scheme in Nigeria, services were provided to the nomadic Fulanis, a base camp was erected to house veterinary staff and a store established where the Fulani could sell milk, buy essential foodstuffs, collect supplementary feed for livestock and obtain routine treatment. This may provide a first step in reducing the movements of nomadic groups, and on which other social and extension services can be built, including the use of mobile units to reach them in their temporary camps.

E. Participation and Communications

Participation of the population concerned and clear and continuous communication between them and the "experts" and officials is often not recognized as important or is treated as a residual category. Frequently, participation and communication are considered as separate issues with the extreme position being that "communication" is a problem of mass media, or getting across the details of plans and policies already made and "participation" is the actions of the people in carrying them out. In fact, true communication between the populations concerned and officials, planners and leaders can really occur only during their joint participation. A wide range of techniques to assure appropriate participation are available. However, without organization of activities in a way that encourages rather than penalizes criticism, participation may be sullenly withheld, or simulated to please administrators and real communication is blocked. Social scientists are trained to detect the differences and have assisted in numerous ways (a) by surveys and other studies that summarize and differentiate opinions and perceptions of official policies and plans (sometimes erroneous ones that need correcting), and define resources availabilities (b) by helping to set up the appropriate climate and situations in which two-way communication can take place, and by (c) determining the accuracy of the officials understandings of the position and attitudes of the people affected, (d) providing guidelines for selection of settlers in ways to assure success of new projects, and (e) by suggesting appropriate adjustments in policies to make them compatible with local needs and perceptions.

PHYSICAL PLANNING FACTORS

The design and layout of the habitat component of existing (traditional) rural settlements are frequently the work of local leaders and officials with no or little formal training in planning or experience in the improvement of settlement conditions. This kind of activity is not usually documented, particularly in FAO reports oriented primarily to production goals. As a result, this section of the paper (based on research on documented cases), necessarily examines planning of the physical component as undertaken by professional planners who have been involved in the settlement projects. For a more complete picture this information should be supplemented with information on the approaches and methods adopted in projects planned by non-professionals.

A. Regional Context

In almost all of the settlement (and resettlement) programmes that were reviewed, regional planning aspects were, in varying degrees, taken into consideration. This was mostly expressed by the location, pattern and size of the new settlements within their area of immediate influence and, to a lesser extent, with their relationship in the wider region. The plans for the Ghab Region in Syria are a good example. Reconciliation of national vs. farm economic goals of planners are also covered, but possible impact on surrounding areas was not mentioned.

The existing distribution pattern and size of rural settlements in most developing countries can hinder social and economic development. The population of "villages" can be as small as 20 inhabitants (e.g., Tanzania or Ghana) and distances between them more than 5 or 10 km. Moreover, in many cases where settlements are located along roads linking well-developed agricultural areas with ports, large areas are left outside the sphere of influence of both the settlements and the link roads as in Ethiopia [68]. Because of this, *inter alia*, attempts have sometimes been made to restructure the settlement pattern. In many of the settlement projects examined, for example, village population sizes were enlarged by regrouping existing settlements and a hierarchical pattern of settlement networks was introduced in areas where the existing pattern was haphazard [69]. The general concept of central villages and hierarchical growth poles used in more developed and more densely populated countries, was adapted to local conditions although in many cases the unit population sizes were necessarily smaller. The basic concept of distributing services according to a "rational" settlement pattern, however, was essentially the same. In Sudan, for example, where central villages and their immediate agricultural surroundings have been proposed as the basic planning units for rural development, the average size of the unit is 5,000 people and that of its village component, 200 per village [70]. For the Ghab in Syria, an eventual population of 1,500 families was proposed, but incorporating into the plan already established villages and dispersed farm homes. New villages would be sited on non-irrigable land, and accessible to drinking water and farmlands with no one further than 5 km from his land. Such villages are considered large enough to form local governments and provide basic services (water, sewage, electricity, streets, etc.). A central township was proposed as an administrative headquarters. Possible future growth was considered, as well as housing for persons in private and public services, small industries, etc., but concepts of growth poles and major market towns were not utilized.

In the resettlement project of Densu River Dam at Weija, Ghana, the concept of regrouping smaller villages into large units capable of economically supporting social services and utilities, was utilized to determine physical (spatial) settlement criteria [71]. A survey of physical and socio-economic conditions was made of an area considerably larger than the zone of inundation in order to determine the capacity and potential of surrounding towns and villages for assimilating some of the smaller ones to be flooded. A structure of settlement hierarchies was thus established. The population formerly living in villages of 36 to 700 inhabitants was regrouped in a two-tier settlement structure with a population of 1,500-2,000 people in the higher tier and up to 500 people in the lower [72].

The same approach was used in the Volta River Dam Project. Here 740 settlements with an average population of a 100 people, were regrouped in 52 settlements with an average population of 1,320 people, ranging from 14 to 826 houses in each village. The regional framework originally proposed and indicating the location size and role of each settlement in the Volta basin as a whole, was not strictly followed in implementation, but provided a theoretical framework for the final area development plan [73].

In Israel, specific population sizes of settlements are an important criterion for regional integration. In new settlement areas major rural centers serve a population of 6,000-9,000 at a radius of 1-15 km. At a lower scale, centers of 1,300-1,500 inhabitants provide only daily services, while even smaller settlements of 70-80 families are sited close to one another in order to support a service center for 250-300 families (i.e., 1,300 to 1,500 inhabitants) at a distance not more than 1.5 to 2 km [74]. Such criteria have formed the basis of establishing the regional development policy of the country. However, as noted elsewhere in this paper, integration of settlement projects with national and regional plans (wherever these exist) has generally occurred only in the case of larger (area-wise) settlement projects.

B. Siting and Location

Criteria for the location of new settlements or of existing settlements to be improved and expanded were more or less similar in all the projects examined. Health conditions, quality of the agricultural resource base and soil, climate, water supply accessibility to farmlands or other employment sources and to services, preservation of social and cultural ties, preference of settlers, etc., are among the most common. However, the weight given to each criterion was found to vary with each case and occasionally such factors were, as in the case of political refugee settlements, located away from frontiers.

Limited resources for capital investment and level of technology on the one hand, and on the other the importance of water both for agricultural and domestic use, and proximity to water supply is usually given high priority in rural settlements in the developing countries. Health conditions and micro-climate are also basic factors for the siting of any human settlement, but are of paramount importance in tropic and sub-tropic areas, many of which are infested by tse-tse fly, and other indigenous health hazards. (For instance, Ghana, Sudan, Tanzania and Indonesia experience some of these difficulties.)

Countries which have abundant unexploited land, e.g., Tanzania, Malaysia and Indonesia, and especially some Latin American countries, have a greater flexibility in establishing new settlements. In contrast, in agricultural land-hungry countries, like Greece, Israel, Korea, India and Bangladesh, the number of potential sites for new settlements is restricted because of the need to be near agricultural land, but at the same time, avoid occupying fertile soil [75]. Also, areas liable to natural disasters such as flooding (e.g., Penatang Panggang in Indonesia) and earthquakes (i.e., parts of Greece) must be avoided when locating new settlements, or the much higher security measures required taken into account.

Preservation of cultural, ethnic and even community and family ties has been strongly emphasized in most settlement projects examined, since most of the developing countries include different tribal or ethnic groups which have still kept their identity. Such aspects have even been seriously considered in ethnically homogeneous countries. In Greece, for example, the relocation of villages subject to earthquakes or land sliding has tended to be on sites close to communications lines but near the endangered villages and as close as possible to their agricultural lands. Only where the villages were isolated, almost inaccessible and the land too poor were people moved to another region [76].

Where prospective settlers participate actively in site selection, preferences are influenced by ethnic and cultural ties and the experience from the Volta Project indicates that "as far as possible (settlements should) be sited within the geographic area from which the villages derive their livelihood," and within the same cultural (tribal) area [77].

Accessibility to larger towns and services is also indispensable for any form of development, even in subsistence farming areas. L. Huszar [78] considers that, even if a settlement is designed to cater for local needs only, its services and especially markets will be used by throughtraffic thus providing additional income. For this reason new settlements may be advantageously located on throughroads, or throughroads provided as access to new areas where practical. It would seem that this was considered in the Syrian Ghab Region.

C. Size of Settlements and Services Provided

The services provided are influenced by, and may in turn influence the accessibility and size of a settlement, as in the Kenya and Syrian cases already cited [79]. But it should be borne in mind that existing conditions impose restrictions on the implementation of a policy of grouping or regrouping with efficiency of services in mind. Even in the Volta Project where 80,000 people were to be settled and where considerable financial and organizational help was provided, sizes of villages had to reflect other limiting factors, such as an acceptable walking time to farmlands and the settlers' willingness to join with others to form larger communities [80]. This, however, does not negate the principle of locating services by considering the most advantageous location vis-a-vis the intended clientele. It has also been suggested that in improving existing settlements, existing service and market centers should be identified and reinforced where necessary by providing additional services [81].

Criteria for deciding on settlement size has been discussed by Yalan, Geogulas, Huszar and others [82]. Proposed settlement sizes differ in the various projects examined according to prevailing physical and socio-economic conditions, but it is not entirely clear how these conditions are determined. The planners for the Ghab region recommended a change from an existing settlement size of "a few dozen to over 1,000 houses to large compact villages of 1,500 houses." In general, it seems that a population of 1,000-1,500 inhabitants is considered necessary for a settlement that can provide basic services, such as a primary school, or a health center. A settlement of this size can also provide some beginning differentiation in employment, i.e., a certain proportion of the population is not exclusively and directly employed in agriculture and/or, in some cases, forestry or fisheries, but in supporting services (e.g., government extension services, education, commerce, etc.). Examples of this size of population include Israeli settlements — both Moshav and Kibbutz, some of the earlier "pilot" settlements of Tanzania, dam settlement projects in Ghana and others. However, the services which can be supported depend on transportation means, proximity of larger centers or smaller satellite villages, and level of the economy.

If circumstances do not permit such concentrations of population, smaller units are sometimes situated close enough to one another to share a common service center. In the Tanzania Pilot Settlement Programme where three or four sub-villages of 65-80 families are served by a rural center in their midst providing services for all farmers and houses for non-agricultural families [83]. In both cases distance between houses and community services in the center is planned not to exceed 900 meters. In Israel the multi-unit Moshav usually comprises three moshavim around a commercial service centre. Each unit has 60 farmer families and some families employed in services, so that the total population of the settlement unit consists of about 180 families employed in agriculture and 60 employed in services [84].

Services provided at this type of center usually include (sites for) a primary school for 100-150 children, government services such as a post office, police station, health center and community hall, church or mosque, market, recreation, agricultural machinery repair shop and storage, as well as technical infrastructure such as roads, communal water supply and communal septic tanks. In some of the cases examined, apart from the size of the population, existing levels of services and their locations were used as guides for standards for the provision of services in the new or improved settlements [85].

The problem of balancing these theoretical planning concepts against the cultural and family ties, especially if settlers are drawn from nearby communities, is illustrated by Italian experience in the Metaponto. There, the settlers preferred to remain in surrounding traditional villages for services and social life rather than utilize the newly provided service centre, and preferred to utilize isolated farmsteads as seasonal dwellings and on-farm storage.

Larger villages serving as sub-regional centres, are sometimes planned to provide higher level services such as middle or high schools, demonstration farms and agricultural training centers, clinics, banks and offices [86]. Services of higher order can also be maintained through the operation of joint regional services and enterprises by cooperation between smaller units. Various patterns of rural regional cooperation have been developed in different places throughout the world. For instance:

"a special form of inter-regional cooperation has emerged which consists or organizational frameworks incorporating 50 to 200 villages around interregional physical centers, planned for storage, marketing and processing of agricultural produce and raw materials on a larger scale for a wider rural area. These Rural Regional Councils are the municipal bodies of the agricultural regions, generally comprising between 1 to 15 agricultural villages. The fact that qualified and skilled personnel live in many of these centers, located in the rural areas, creates mutual bonds between the farmers and technicans thus attracted from the city [87]."

However, despite the assumed economic and social advantages of concentration, there are instances where a prevailing dispersed settlement pattern should be retained. In some cases, where people prefer to live in isolated homestead clusters, or in small villages, provisions of social and economic services can be less costly than measures to change drastically an already existing settlement pattern [88]. In small villages, with a population of up to 500 people, one multi-purpose community building with 10-14 rooms can accommodate meeting hall, mass-education office, health office, adult literacy class, day nursery, post office, shops, etc. The school, also catering for children living outside the village, can be located in a different building and provide a minimum total of 100-150 places [89]. These buildings can be used temporarily by the settlers for accommodation during the self-help construction of housing.

Similarly, in small villages of 80 families in Israel, despite the better communication network, certain basic services, such as community hall, dispensary, kindergarten, playground, stores, workshops and stations for farm produce, are provided in the village centre. Usually schools are established at bigger centres with 300-600 pupils brought by special transport from surrounding villages [90]. Such dispersion of services to smaller centres must eventually consider economies of scale and public cost vs. economy of client travel, local control and convenience, with some trade-offs in quality and quantity of services to small villages vs. more central places.

In other areas, with semi-nomadic population and where settlers prefer to live on their own rural property in scattered settlements with more limited social contacts, certain facilities could be mobile, such as selected medical services and educational assistance [91]. Although the dispersed farmstead settlement seems to represent an increasingly more expensive system to service as development proceeds, the best solution to be applied must be determined bearing in mind the social values and consequences involved, rather than economic cost alone.

D. Pattern and Layout of Settlement

As already noted, land tenure influences land use and patterns of agricultural activity, which, in turn, influence the settlement pattern. Dispersed larger size individual farms encourage scattered settlement farms, while groups of adjoining family farms or communally owned or cooperatively cultivated land, more readily form gathered settlements. The basic advantages and disadvantages for the two patterns are well stated by Yalan:

> "In the scattered settlements the homestead is situated in the center of the farmer's lands, providing most convenient conditions from the point of view of 'agro-distances', but creating unfavourable conditions from the point of view of social, organization and security distances.

> The gathered settlement on the other hand, is more favourable to the social organizational and security aspects, but requires longer 'agro-distances' [92]."

Both are considered in the multi-unit moshavim layout in Israel where distances to farm land range from 600 mts. to 2,200 mts.

Considering the Near East, in 1965, one group of experts concluded that for farm holdings of less than five hectares and distances of not more than 2-3 kms between the center village and the farmlands, a gathered system is preferable and much less costly. For holdings of between 5 and 20 or 30 hectares. the distance from the centre village to the farm will necessitate a considerable amount of time and energy unproductively wasted and the presence of the farmer on the farm represents a more economic alternative [93]. In general, holdings of more than 30 hectares can only support an extensive system of farming and constant presence of the farmer may not be required [94].

The social aspects loom larger for planned rural settlement projects, especially those considering the habitat component. In the Penatang Panggang Study [95] in Indonesia for example, village layout plans followed a strictly linear form with the farmlands extending at the back of the houses, and allowing for a maximum distance of 1.5 km. between house and farm, but maximum distance between houses and services was 3.5 km. Obviously, however, there are differences in agro-distances depending on the type of farming (intensive, extensive, irrigated, etc.) and on the size of the individual holding, level of economic development, and the mode of transportation. The need to reduce walking distance can become less crucial as incomes rise and bicycles and other transportation (such as power boats and ferries on rivers and lakes) become available. In the Indonesia study, walking was the assumed mode. Bicycles would increase the distance possibilities and the efficiency of the centers. Studies of pattern changes over time and with development of infra-structure on the Canadian Prairies, have been well reported [96]. The advantages in efficiency of agricultural operations, enjoyed from living on farm holdings, must be balanced in settlement planning against the social considerations and the lower cost of providing infra-structure in concentrated settlements.

Immediately related to distance between homesteads and farm holdings and services are village density and size of house plot. In Penatang Panggang, Indonesia, in addition to a 4 hectare farm holding, each farmer is allocated a one hectare homestead plot consisting of a house and garden area of 2,500 square meters and arable land for cultivation. Of the 2,500 sq. mts., 500 are for the house and domestic activities. Yalan describes a similar situation in a more developed country where 1.5-2 acres of agricultural land are included in the farmstead plot while additional farmland belonging to each farmer is divided into several plots situated in big blocks for "homogeneous cultivation [97]."

It is not surprising that in most of the settlement projects examined house plots are smaller. In Greek settlement projects, for instance, rural house plots range from 400 sq. mts. in flat areas to 200 sq. mts. in land with slopes. Vassilikiotis observes that this is an intentional policy to discourage the keeping of livestock close to the living quarters. In societies where livestock is an important part of the household economy, this arrangement may present serious difficulties unless satisfactory alternatives are made available. For instance, a large part of China's food protein from animal sources is produced on home plots.

In the Volta Project initially, house plots were originally 60' or 70' by 100' (i.e., about 650 sq. mts.), which resulted in a density ranging from 9 to 30 persons per acre. At a later stage, smaller plots were used, i.e., 50' by 75' or 350 sq. mts. in area, resulting in higher densities and a lowering of costs for construction and maintenance of roads and services [98].

Planned size of plot and density should also be influenced by the tradition and life style of the settlers. In some Ujamaa villages in Tanzania where one acre homestead plots were assigned to the settlers, following traditional practice, they expressed a preference for smaller (1/4 acre) plots because it made possible greater community interaction and socialization [99]. Likewise tribal and social structure of the settlers requires consideration. In all of the four Ghanian projects examined, the layouts provided distinct neighbourhoods for each tribe or ethnic group. The Volta Project studies utilized sociograms to distribute settler groups on new sites according to their desired proximity to other groups [100]. In some cases, however, not enough "buffer" area was provided between the different tribal wards, making village expansion difficult and creating conflict [101].

For functional as well as social reasons, facilities for supporting services are normally situated near the village center. The area required may vary with population numbers and the kind and number of services provided. For example, a small Israeli village of about 80 families has a center of 40,000 sq. mts. (10 acres), whereas the area proposed at Penatang Panggang for 500 families is about 20 acres. It would seem that the initial functioning of a centre may be inhibited by too wide spacing, but may allow more possibilities for future growth and expansion of services.

Finally, recreational open space is sometimes provided in the village layout. However, adverse climatic conditions and the presence of animals in the village, may make maintenance of plants and green acres a problem [102]. Therefore, with the exception of playing fields, other open space (e.g., parkland) is not usually provided.

E. Housing Design and Standards

Traditional patterns in family life play an important role in the design as well as the size of the house. Thus extended or polygamous households demand more rooms, since each couple or each wife usually needs a separate space. In some cases, wives prefer to live in a separate hut or building on the same plot, or even in a different house, and the arrangement of buildings, walls and fences both within and between house plots may have important social meanings. In many instances, the verandah or porch provide covered access between rooms, additional living space and is used for preparing and cooking food. In general, among many rural communities, any room providing a reasonable standard of privacy and shelter is regarded as living space and used as a sleeping room, not necessarily because of overcrowding [103]. Surveys are needed to identify these traditional arrangements.

Capital investment in housing seldom has a high priority in developing countries, except for some capital intensive, externally financed projects. Therefore, many settlement project communities are expected to house themselves but usually with some assistance in material aid or technical advice. This type of policy, does not guarantee the completion of some form of shelter within a given time. Therefore, in some emergency cases as well as some capital intensive schemes, housing is provided entirely by the sponsoring agency (government). In some cases, a "core" house of one completed room together with a roofed area for a second room, a cooking area and a porch is provided by the responsible authority. The settler is then expected to complete the house by himself with or without some assistance in the form of building materials and technical advice [104].

Frequently new houses and settlements under government assistance have to comply to set standards. As in Ghana's Tema Manhean resettlement villages [105] and in Greece where minimum standards (e.g., size, form, materials) have been set, they have often taken inadequate account of prevailing circumstances. As a result, settlers make the best housing they can, given available resources and social needs. However, better incomes in the future, exposure to new values and standards, and education create demands for better living conditions. For this reason, house designs as well as the house plots in planned settlements must permit gradual improvement and expansion [106]. As Butcher argues, in many regions, the traditional rural house is an organism which must be capable of growth as the space needs of the household increase. Possibilities for expansion are particularly important in households with extended families, which are initially given a smaller or a "core" house. Comparison of "before and after" completion occupancy rates in the Volta Project found to be 1.44 and 2.35 persons per room respectively, proves this point [107].

Size and shape of plots (as well as house designs) are frequently not planned to provide flexibility for expansion while considering social requirements. Thus, Castelli-Gattinara found initial project houses unsuitable on social grounds. Sometimes, rooms are situated along one or two of the sides of a rectangular plot leaving the third for later expansion. This design reduces the area for the yard and the possibilities of using it. In most cases, however, plots are rectangular and space for expansion is left at the back or inside the rectangle. This shape provides greater flexibility. Moreover, careful selection of the ratio of the two sides can reduce cost in the future provision of utilities (water lines) and road construction. Standard-unit room, window and door sizes are sometimes recommended to simplify construction and encourage a local building materials industry [108].

Choice of materials for construction depends mainly on cost and availability. For walls, "sandcrete or landcrete" blocks have often been used in African projects. Asbestos cement or corrugated tin is often used for roofing. Somewhat sturdier and more expensive cement blocks and reinforced concrete roofs were recommended for the Ghab. In many countries in Africa, wood is avoided because of termites [109]. However, adequate control methods against insects are now available.

In Indonesian projects, as in much of Asia, wood is suggested for the main house frame, as well as the wall partitions. In addition to the desirability of creating familiar forms and reducing overall costs, the use of local materials has been encouraged, because it offers more opportunities for employing local skills and building methods and the creation of local industries and enterprises for diversification of employment [110]. Furthermore, a better utilization of forests for building materials is possible in many developing countries by utilizing lesser known species after proper preservative treatment. Finally, regarding methods of construction, prefabrication of standard components seems to be considered the best solution both from the speed and economic points of view [111].

F. Productive Waste Management

With some notable exceptions of small-scale re-cycling systems (e.g., the Chinese use of pig manure in aquaculture), waste disposal through the public sector has been traditionally approached from a defensive standpoint, particularly from a disease prevention orientation. Seldom are waste materials seen as a source of useful products. Furthermore, economies of scale discourage efforts to devise systems justifying necessary investments for organic wastes utilization in rural villages and rural towns. Domestic and industrial wastes in communities of 2000-3000 people can, however, be substantial and could be processed for fertilizer, energy (bio-gas, electricity), animal feeds, building materials and organic compounds. Such exploitation should be approached on a community or total industry basis, rather than an individual household or private enterprise basis. Frequently, legal sanctions are required and even public assistance for designing technical solutions.

IMPLEMENTATION FACTORS

Aspects of implementation analyzed in this section cover: management of the planning and execution as well as the on-going stages after completion, cost and financing, and phasing and timing of work (primarily as they relate to the development and running of the community rather than its farmlands, fisheries or other economic occupations).

A. Management

Management systems are to a large extent dependent on prevailing governmental and institutional frameworks which in turn depend on the political systems concerned. The generalizations discussed hereunder are drawn from the experience of the studies examined and, thus, did not include studies in *all* political systems.

Management of planning and execution of rural settlement projects is usually undertaken by a specially formed governmental "authority" or "committee" sometimes supplemented by a committee of the people to be settled. Power and participation of each of these two groups differ from country to country, but, generally, participation of the settlers, and self-help which used to be less important in earlier projects, has increased quantitatively as well as qualitively (see Social Factors, d) "Participation and Management Roles").

The role of international organizations — such as the FAO — in management is usually the provision of expert advice to supporting governmental and non-governmental institutions, in such matters as agriculture, fisheries, forests, etc., but increasingly with a multi-purpose or integrated project framework.

Participation by government in management is always present. Even where a more or less autonomous planning and implementation authority has been created, responsibility for settlement decisions with political implications can be shared but not given up. Moreover, some (and usually considerable) financial support and technical support is derived from the government. Finally, central government agencies are often essential to provide skilled manpower needed in establishing and managing settlement projects. Central government involvement is more significant during the planning stage than local representation, although, in most cases examined, local people were consulted about the location of the settlement concerned, and sometimes about the design of housing and other facilities.

Often in the execution stage the central government (and/or authority) is either responsible for all necessary activities, or provides assistance for distribution of plots, developing the farmlands, utilities and social facilities, leaving housing construction to the settlers. Several analyses of alternative forms of government assistance for housing were found [112]. Even when self-help is used, the level of management and assistance for housing provided by the government or subsidized through local entrepreneurs — to government-paid and supervised construction of a complete unit or a house core. However, in some cases, durable materials, such as bricks or reinforced concrete are considered socially necessary (seemingly the case in the Ghab project) and should be used provided they can be produced locally and cheaply in small production centers, preferably as a joint enterprise by a group of the settlers. Such an arrangement can improve housing conditions, and provide training in new building techniques, as well as extra employment and income.

Instead of cash loans, provision of prefabricated materials can help to ensure utilization of housing funds for intended purposes. Such materials have included concrete hollow blocks for walls, reinforced concrete beams for roofs, door and window frames, sanitary latrine parts, etc. New ideas in construction techniques can be best achieved through local artisans. This can be done by training courses combined with the construction of demonstration houses, organized by the government, in local production-cum-training centers, or by extension workers in the village [113].

Assuring an adequate and continuing supply of necessary building materials may well be an essential government function, the potential of well-managed natural forests or farm forestry as a source of building materials is particularly important for developing countries which have to rely on imports for other materials such as steel and cement. Wooden building materials are being successfully used for permanent rural settlements. The easy workability and handling of wood and diversity of its application make it a particularly desirable raw material for building components in those rural areas where high concentration of technology and mechanization is economically not justified. This applies particularly to rural areas where "self-help" schemes based on simple equipment and wood supply from nearby forests can be used for rural housing and other constructions. Where wood is scarce and more expensive, other materials such as bricks, stone, bamboo matting, etc., may substitute but wood is still appropriate in locally constructed farm and village homes for framing, roof beams and even partitions and insulating wall panels. For locally made home furnishings there are few substitutes.

Another important government management function is the initial "re-establishment" of settlers. Education and familiarization moves have to start long before it occurs, if possible, and trained personnel have to help during the evaluation process, the transportation to the new site and the "settling-in" process [114].

After the completion of works and the establishment of farmers on their land so that they are able to grow their first crops, management functions are gradually transferred to local authorities, e.g., decentralized agencies of central government and the organizational system of the settlers (i.e., cooperatives, village committee, etc.).

In some countries local cooperatives play very important functions in organizing the life of the settlement. In China, for example, local communes prepare and finance local development and welfare plans [115] and commune work brigades may prepare building materials and even help with construction [116]. Ujamaa villages in Tanzania rely on their cooperatives to undertake all activities for running and organizing agricultural production and marketing [117].

Special single purpose development corporations or multi-purpose area authorities may be created. District governments or authorities sometimes undertake responsibility for development control. However, as will be discussed in the next part of this paper, this seems to entail serious difficulties. Finally, another important function usually undertaken by central or district government is the provision of supporting services. These include training and education of settlers to help them to adjust to the new living conditions of the settlements and to increase the productivity of both men and women and to strengthen family structures. In some countries, such as China, such matters are handled through locally designated representatives (perhaps designated by the local cooperative, work group, or labour brigade) to take special courses or go on observation tours to learn new techniques [118]. As a rule, management of the agricultural production component of rural settlements seems to receive greater attention than the management of other affairs [119].

Unfortunately, the documents examined gave relatively little information on the continuing management of the habitat component. The many habitat factors in the Ghab Planning Project in Syria, notwithstanding farm management, received much better treatment. For example, it appears that the organization and distribution of labour and activities concerned with improving living conditions generally have not been an issue of central concern, even though this can have implications for agricultural productivity. For example, the management of time devoted by women to various activities is especially important if they are expected to contribute to farming as well as the well-being of the home. Also, on projects in house construction, road building, and the provision of utilities — labour requested of the community is not always carefully managed to avoid conflicts with agricultural production activities. Finally, little information was found on the management of maintenance functions to ensure continuation of tolerable standards (see below, "Maintenance Factors".)

B. Phasing

Phasing of activities is often crucial to the success of settlement projects. However, both the number of different agencies and groups and the multiplicity of tasks involved make phased coordination difficult.

Just as eventual economic viability of the agricultural component is to a large extent dependent on a series of carefully interrelated and phased actions, so social viability of a new or a resettled community depends on, at least, an equally complex set of activities with often crucial scheduling sequences. Furthermore, the identification and elimination of conflicts arising in joint phasing of production (economic) and social-related functions are required at an early stage in the management of the settlement project. Frequently, conflicts have arisen: (a) over temporary accommodation for settlers while they build their own houses, and (b) between labour demands on the one hand for land clearing and cultivation of the first food crops and for house construction on the other.

Based on the Volta Dam Resettlement experience, FAO has published a manual describing step by step the activities involved in resettlement and their phasing for use by officials and planners responsible for resettlement. (This manual might well be a model for a further series, describing "how to" carry out other settlement planning and management functions.) It utilizes network analysis to describe phasing and logical sequence of activities. As an indication of the complexity of the task, 40 major steps are specified which the resettlement officer and his staff must execute in a dam resettlement project before evacuation can take place. Each of these steps includes many activities [120].

C. Costs and Financing

The costs of habitat improvement projects were not covered in enough detail in the materials reviewed to provide the basis for systematic analysis or reliable conclusions. However, some examples can be instructive.

Indisputably, costs in planned settlement projects have frequently been high, and understandable, in emergency situations where swift action rather than low cost is paramount. Moreover, in the large dams of Africa, a type of project on which cost data are available, gross initial under-estimation of settlement costs has been characteristic with final costs ranging from $160 per settler in the Kariba Dam project to as much as $2,000 per settler in Egypt [121]. In land settlement projects financed by the World Bank, costs per family reportedly range from $1,327 (in Kenya) to $13,667 in one Malaysian project [122].

These wide differences in costs reflect different approaches, differing degrees of administrative efficiency and even different methods of accounting, e.g., the inclusion or exclusion of particular factors from the estimates. Settlement-related projects are often financed by a number of sources (national and international) and the tasks involved are carried out by many different agencies, making difficult any comparisons of documentary evidence. Meaningful comparisons, for instance — depend on whether school construction was included in the costs, or borne by the Ministry of Education as part of its normal budget. The same is true of other social and supporting services. Therefore, only very wide differences in costs (on the basis of currently available information) can shed light on relative factor costs. In addition, inflation and fluctuating exchange rates make comparisons over time difficult. Nonetheless, some of the reasons for the high cost of settlement projects may be found by comparison with traditional settlement processes.

Spontaneous settlement has always been a feature of life in much of Africa. When land is exhausted from intensive cultivation and invaded by weeds, the village or group relocated (settled) elsewhere, utilizing their labour, a few simple tools and usually leaving the fallow to regenerate itself.

The high costs of planned settlements obviously reflect policies very different from those influencing spontaneous settlements. The Kariba Dam project is exceptional with the final cost of resettlement estimated at $160 per caput in Southern Rhodesia and $220 in Northern Rhodesia [123] (now Zambia). In this case the resettlement population was regarded as "an expensive nuisance" which had to be moved in order to flood the valley and provide hydroelectric power. Resettlement was necessary for the population in the area to be covered by the reservoir but

"the basic strategy was to resettle the population under conditions more or less equal to their previous state. The people and their goods were physically moved to resettlement sites where they were expected to build new farms and houses by themselves [124]."

Differences in policies between the two countries included compensation paid to settlers in Zambia only and provision by the government of thatch and poles in Southern Rhodesia. But in both cases the costs were low as compared with later projects in the region. In contrast, in other African countries, dam resettlement was often approached as an opportunity for development with a simultaneous increase in productivity and levels of social services. The earliest project examined where this approach was fully adopted was Aswan [125]. Here the planners made provision for modern housing, infrastructure and social services, modern irrigation works and mechanized agriculture at levels much higher than other rural areas. The result was much higher per capita costs. The costs of constructing housing and public building was 38.6 percent, 44.5 percent and 40.5 percent of total settlement costs in projects in Ghana, Sudan and Egypt respectively.

These high costs included a substantial compensation component for inundated land and houses. In the Volta Project, for example, settlers were compensated (though sometimes after long delays) for the loss of their houses by either cash or a replacement house in the new settlements. The costs of the new housing were much greater than the value of the abandoned traditional houses (which had no market value in that culture).

Costs of facilities of the habitat component in other settlement projects have not been as high as the Volta and the Aswan cases. In refugee settlements aided by the World Food Programme, for example, costs are mainly those required to support the refugees at subsistence level until the first crops are ready, plus the costs of minimal social services and utilities. The level of housing provided is not, as in the dam projects, outstandingly "better" than or at least more expensive than what they had in their places of origin. Initial cost estimates for substantially better housing in the Ghab region ranged from $225 - $335 per family for public buildings and services and $1,100 to over $3,300 for housing. The lower cost was based on an initial core house of concrete blocks and reinforced concrete roof and it was assumed the cost for building by government and by individual settlers would be the same [126].

Unfortunately, no cost data were available on the habitat component of settlements in China or of Ujamaa villages in Tanzania. In both these countries, relatively large scale village building projects have been undertaken, and there is expressed political commitment underlying policy to spread resources widely, rather than investing concentrated amounts in small areas. This suggests that per capita investment other than labour on the habitat component is relatively low. Certainly, in the case of Tanzania's Ujamaa villages investment in housing is of the same order as in traditional settlements.

Though the costs of new settlements are generally high it is argued that they may still compare favourably with costs of job creation in other sectors. El Ghonemy has estimated that in some Middle Eastern countries, the cost of $960 per acre for land settlement compares favourably with $5,940 to employ an extra person in industry and $5,214 in other sections [127]. However, later remedial action to rectify water-logging salinity and improper soil and water management may considerably augment initial cost figures. For the Ghab project in Syria, costs were estimated at over $4,800 per acre, not including any land acquisition costs. In some countries food production and employment requirements may outweigh basic investment calculations in any case.

It would seem that the high-cost (capital-intensive) settlement projects have not made a significant contribution to alleviating depressed rural conditions or problems of landlessness, even in countries where land is abundant. In fact, high costs conflict with policies to alleviate the problems of large numbers of the rural poor. In particular, high costs accompany attempts to transform the level of housing by a significant order of magnitude. The costs of less dramatic improvements are very much less, have a greater chance of success and can play a roll in providing benefits of development to more people. The implications of the above discussion may be even more true for established rather than for new settlements.

Budgeting the costs of settlement planning and improvement projects is important. Major mis-estimates are not uncommon, sometimes because attempts are made to continue a failing project. In Madagascar (Malagassy Republic), e.g., over $20 million in foreign aid (mainly from private French sources and from the Fonds Europeén de Dévelopment) were given to a land settlement project in which after over eight years about 2,500 "settlers" and 550 "labourers" were living. Some settlers, however, had only 0.2 hectare per family and the average was only 0.61 hectare per family [128]. According to Butcher, the mis-estimation of resettlement costs for the big Africa dam projects were great. In the Volta Dam Project in Ghana actual costs were 2.3 times estimated costs, in the Kainji Dam in Nigeria, three times and for Kariba Dam six times [129]. The reasons for these miscalculations include the lack of adequate feasibility surveys and social surveys in the planning of projects [130], and probably the initial lack of any calculations for many human needs and the initial capital costs of establishing social services [131]. The cost of recurrent as well as capital components in settlement planning and improvement projects is frequently neglected in budget preparation. This factor is even more important in improvement projects (where capital costs are less) than in planned settlement projects. People may be able and willing to construct a clinic or school building by self-help means, but not able to pay for the staff and materials needed to keep these institutions running, especially where developed country standards rather than improved local ones are used.

The sources of financing for settlement programmes and other habitat improvement projects are on the whole similar to those for other large-scale development projects. They include international sources (bilateral aid and multilateral funding from the IBRD and the UNDP, for example, and food aid from the World Food Programme); national sources (usually government funding); and the resources of the settlers themselves, both in money (though this is a limited source, especially where programmes are designed to aid the rural poor) and in kind, through investment of their labour in construction of housing, public buildings and infrastructure. Recommendations for financing the Ghab Project show clearly where the major costs lie for settlement improvement in an irrigated area. Land and water development is the major component. Facilities for services ($300/family) is estimated as under 1/3 of minimum housing provisions ($1,100/family). However, a wide range of economy measures are proposed including temporary and simpler permanent structures, multi-service buildings, effective full or partial recovery of development costs from recipients, long-term phasing of essential services, and food aid for building and construction work [132]. World Food Programme food aid often plays an important role in providing for the nutritional needs of settlers and their families until the first crops can be cultivated [133], and in mobilizing labour for capital construction work.

D. Maintenance Factors

No specific attention to maintenance was noted in this study during the planning and implementation of settlements. However, housing and related facilities may well deteriorate simply from lack of organization and management of the maintenance work involved and/or an unrealistic assessment of the possibilities of the inhabitants. For instance, the women in Africa frequently have this responsibility in addition to a great deal of the farm work and childcare. When economically active males migrate for employment, the women may have little time left from cooking, childcare and farm work for such maintenance activities.

Therefore, the ability of settlers to maintain and improve the standards of their habitats is dependent not only on income and other economic factors but also on the organizational abilities of the rural communities for undertaking the work required and providing for supplies of non-local materials; on available advice and assistance; on the availability of skills required for maintenance; and on the appropriateness of the facilities provided.

While cooperatives can be adapted for the building, storage and maintenance and improvement of private dwellings and cooperatively owned processing facilities for at least part of the population, the maintenance of most local families is not likely to be provided for on a consistent basis without effective local government with access to adequate sources of revenue.

In the planning and implementation of new settlements, maintenance should be considered to assure against overplanning, particularly in terms of the abilities of the residents. Such considerations could influence both design and materials with important considerations for overall costs.

THE EXPERIENCE IN PERSPECTIVE

This section notes the role of evaluation in the planning and improvement of rural settlements and identifies crucial elements which need to be taken into account in assessing the habitat component. Finally it summarizes the extent of the FAO's involvement with this component of rural settlements.

An Overview

In reviewing available materials on the improvement of the "habitat component" of settlements, relatively few cases of careful, long-term evaluation and assessment of project performance were found. The instances in which there had been an evaluation (e.g., Syracuse University, Tanzania Project 1965-1968) and Afriye and Butcher (1971) on the Volta Resettlement) concerned newly planned settlements and not the improvement of existing ones.

Evaluation should include both on-going monitoring to provide feedback into project work and so improve performance, and *post facto* detailed assessment of project achievements — their strengths and weaknesses. It can thus provide valuable inputs to subsequent work on rural habitat improvement.

The reasons for the comparative rarity of detailed evaluation include national or local political sensitivities, e.g., fears that assessment will reveal embarrassing problems of failures. In settlement schemes this would potentially preclude assessment of projects. In any case, internal evaluations, guided by external consultants are more conducive to corrective measures in on-going programmes. Large projects are almost bound to have weaknesses as well as strengths, even when their overall performance is relatively successful.

Another reason for resistance to "outside" evaluation is fear by "internal" authorities that inappropriate or inadequate criteria will be adopted. As Moris points out, economics criteria alone, for example, are not sufficient. Moreover, where resources are scarce, there may be reluctance to allocate them for "internal" evaluations. Some projects were not assessed because they were not yet complete, or on-going assessments were discontinued. Other projects were planned but never implemented.

The present analysis has identified major elements of the habitat component which need to be taken into account in any evaluation. They include:
— Careful planning at each stage of such aspects as —

    i.   Site layout and the choice of elements to be included in the settlement (social and supporting services, infra-structure).

    ii. Housing design and the choice of housing types to be introduced. This should be done on the basis of careful survey of the population needs and preferences, local conditions, probable speed and direction of development, social and population trends, etc.

— Plan preparation has been found to be crucial, both to the success of projects and to their development costs. Relatively small expenditures on careful and detailed plan preparation can lead to major subsequent savings, and/or avoid major lapses and waste in effort.

— Implementation and management of projects needs careful consideration. The numbers of identifiable groups as well as individuals involved, and the complexity of the tasks and decisions in a large scale settlement project, can put excessive demands on the management capacity of the organizations responsible for their establishment, improvement, etc. The type of scheme involved, the "nature" of the group settled, and the levels and phasing of facilities completion, all contribute to demands on the management of the project.

— The role of community participation requires consideration in each stage of the project. The community can play a valuable part in providing inputs at the planning stage and in evaluating the process and its outcome. Georgulas, among others, has suggested some possible forms of such participation. The process can be facilitated by experienced social scientists. Above all, the community itself should take over responsibility for the management of the settlement and its habitat component, as soon as possible.

— Evaluation should include assessment of the impact of the project on households or families, as well as on individuals and on the community as a whole. The move to a new settlement, and major changes in a familiar living environment, are both stressful situations, in which community organizers, extension workers, home economists, or other individuals with comparable training, have an important role to play in helping households to adjust, especially if important social or economic systems changes are required.

— On-going evaluation — ideally based on initial benchmark studies, surveys and other activities intended as inputs to the planning and implementation process — can contribute to improving performance, especially during any period of intensive investment. Scudder, for instance underlines the importance of prefeasability social and demographic surveys to provide the baselines for future evaluation. At the end of project works, and (if possible) again several years later, assessments are needed to establish effectiveness of the project relative to its objectives.

— Evaluations should be "locality-specific," i.e., relating to each of the villages in the settlement project. (Within the same project or programme, there are frequently some "successful" and some "unsuccessful" habitats.) In assessing them and depending on the heterogeniety of the settlements each component and each village may require separate consideration, whereas agricultural productivity may, perhaps, be assessed for the project as a whole.

From the foregoing it is then clear that evaluation requires on-going (or periodic) field work over relatively long periods of time, since project maturity develops only slowly. It is important, also to adopt realistic evaluation criteria, using as points of reference conditions in the existing rural settlements, and development experience under similar conditions.

NOTES

1. For example, in Saudi Arabia, the Harad settlement cost $25 million for the first phase alone, i.e., for housing 1,000 Bedouin families. See Yacoub, S.M., (1971) "Sedentarization and settlement of the Nomadic Populations in Selected Arab Countries: A preliminary survey," (mimeo), Faculty of Agricultural Science, American University, Beirut.

2. Sabry, O.A. (1970) "Starting Settlements in Africa" in *Land Reform 1970*, No. 1. pp. 52-81, FAO, Rome.

3. See van Lier (1968) *op. cit.* (especially pp. 68, 70-71 and 99ff).

4. See van Dusseldorp, D.B.W.M. (1971), *Planning of Service Centres in Rural Areas of Developing Countries*, Publication 15, International Institute for Land Reclamation and Improvement, Wageningen (The Netherlands).

5. El Chonemy, M. Riad (ed.) (1966), *Report on the Development Centre on Land Policy and Settlement for the Near East*, p. 23, UNDP/FAO Report No. TA 2160, FAO, Rome.

6. FAO (1974), "Small Scale Fisheries," Paper prepared for Item 5 of the provisional agenda, Committee on Fisheries (COFI/74/9), FAO, Rome, 10/74.

7. See Scudder, Thayer (1974), "The Development of the Kariba Lake Fisheries: The Government Role," (mimeo) California Institute of Technology (Research partly supported by FAO).

8. See also Fisheries Department, FAO (1974), "Perspective Study of Agricultural Development for Nepal: Working Paper on the Fisheries Sector," Rome.

9. See FAO/SIDA, "Villages Forestiers . . .," Footnote No. 34, Chapter I, above.

10. See especially Weitz, R. (1963) "Agriculture and the Rural Development in Israel," Israel, P. 113, *et. seq.* and Pohoryles, Samuel (1973), "The Changing Model of Rural Development and Planning of Rural Areas," paper for the FAO Conference on Planning of Rural Areas, held at Leon, Spain, May-June 1973, Ministry of Agriculture, Jerusalem, 5/73.

11. Tschudi, A.B. (1971), "Peoples Communes in China" in *Norsk Geogr.*, Tidsskrift (27) pp. 5-37.

13. See ECA/FAO/Netherlands Government (1973) *Report on Five Workshops for Trainers in Home Economics and other Family Oriented Fields — Eastern and Southern Africa*, Rome, particularly Chapter IX.

14. Voelkner, H.E. (1974) "The Social Feasibility of Settling Semi-Nomadic Afar on Irrigated Agriculture in

the Awash Valley, Ethiopia," Informal Technical Report 23, Development of the Awash Valley Phase III, UNDP/FAO/ETH 72/006, FAO, Rome.

15. Sabry, O.A. (1970).

16. For example, see, WFP Refugee Settlements – *Burundi 249* (establishment of a viable agricultural area to support the refugees, population of 25,000 persons) WFP/IGC: 12/6/73, 20 March 1972: *Tanzania 256* (Settlement of 17,600 refugees, enabling them to attain self-sufficiency in food production), WFP/IGC:18:10:33, 15 October 1970; *Tanzania 441* (Settlement of 10,000 refugees on their own farms of 5 acres each, to produce basic subsistence food as soon as possible and later cash crops) WFP/IGC: 17/10/19, 4 March 1970; and Zaire 712/Q (Resettlement of Sudanese refugees), WFP/IGC:26/11 Add C2, August 1974.

17. See, e.g., WFP: *Zaire 712/Q, op. cit.*

18. FAO (1969) "Note on Installation of Refugees in Zambia," in Land Reform 1969, No. 2, Rome.

19. Giglioli, E.G. (1967), "Planning of Settlements in Irrigated Areas – Aspects of Planning Irrigated Settlement in Kenya," paper for Seminar on Problems and Approaches in Planning Agricultural Development, Addis Ababa, 10-11/67, (Seminar sponsored by UN Economic Commissions for Africa and the German Foundation for Developing Countries).

20. See Yacoub (undated), *op. cit.*, and FAO/UNDP, "Plan of Operations": Syria-Euphrates Pilot Irrigation Project.

21. See, for example, Ministère de l'Agriculture et de la Reforme Agraire (1971),"Republique Algerienne: Enquête sur le Nomadism, 1968, Resultats principaux Séminaire de Saida, 4-6 May 1971.

22. See Christoudoulou, D. (1970), "Settlement in Agriculture of Nomadic, Semi-Nomadic, and Other Pastoral People: Basic Considerations from a World View" in *Land Reform 1970*, No. 1, FAO, Rome.

23. Yacoub, Salah M. (1971), "An Evaluation of the Jafr Pilot Project for Bedouin Settlement," Paper for the FAO expert consultation on the settlement of Nomads in Africa and the Near East, Cairo 17/71.

24. Demirüren, A.S., Interview, FAO, Rome, April 1975, See also Demirüren, A.S. (1974), "The Improvement of Nomadic and Transhumant Animal Production Systems." (AGA/MISC/74/3) FAO, Rome.

25. For a description of the different impacts of an agricultural programme under different tenure systems, see Wetterhall, Hans (1974).

26. See also Sabry (1970), p. 55; FAO (1976) *Draft Sixth Report to ECOSOC on Progress in Land Reform* – Summary p. 13, and *Report on the FAO Expert Consultation on Emerging Agrarian Structures in Africa, op. cit.*

27. See Radna, A.N.K. (1969) "Land Tenure System in the Northern Part of Eastern Region," in Report to the Government of Libya, Development of Tribal land and Settlements projects, Vol. IV *Final Report of Experts, Institutional Aspects of Land Settlement*, FAO Rome.

28. Yalan, E., et. al. (1963), *Land Planning of the Agricultural Cooperative Village*, Rural Building Research Centre, Haifa; Crook, Frederick W. (1975), "The Commune System in the People's Republic of China, 1963-74," in *China: A Reassessment of the Economy* – A compendium of Papers Submitted to the Joint Economic Committee, Congress of the United States. Washington, D.C., 10/7/75; and Joan Robinson (1975), *Economic Management in China*, Anglo-Chinese Educational Institute, Modern China Series No. 4.

29. FAO/(1969), *Land Settlement: Report to the Government of Tanzania*, No. TA 2706, FAO Rome.

30. Afriya, E.K., and Butcher, D.A.P. (1971), *Socio-Economic Survey of the Volta Resettlement, Four Years After the Evacuation*. Report for the Government of Ghana.

31. See Afriye, and Butcher, *op. cit.*, p. 38, and FAO (1969), UNDP/FAO Technical Report on *Planning of the Integrated Development of the Ghab Region – Phase 1*, Syrian Arab Republic. Rome.

32. See Volkner (1974); Abdallah, M.I.A. (1972),"Final Report on Tribalism and Nomadism Within the Baggara Country in the Sudan," (mimeo) FAO, Rome; Butcher D.A.P. (1970), "The Social Survey," in Chambers (ed.), "The Volta Resettlement Experience," Pall Mall, London; and Castelli Gattinara, G.C. (1973), "Studies on Socio-Cultural Cum Institutional Factors Affecting Settlement of the Population from the Tabqa Reservoir and Adjacent Areas of the Euphrates River," Final Report of the Sociologist, The Euphrates Pilot Irrigation Project, AGS/SF/SYR. 67/522, Raqqa (Rome).

33. FAO (1969), Report to the Government of Libya, Development of Tribal Lands and Settlements Project, Vol. IV: *Final Report of Experts on Institutional Aspects of Land Settlement*. Rome; See esp. section I: "The Development of Government Farms in the Eastern Region of Libya."

34. Voelkner (1974), Castelli Gattinara, G.C. (1973) and van Heck C. (1973), *Settlement of the Lake Nasser Fishermen* (FI: DP/EGY/66/558 Technical Report 3). Lake Nasser Development Center, Aswan/FAO, Rome.

35. Brausch, G., Crooke, P. and Shaw, J. (1964), Bashaqra Area Settlements 1963 — University of Khartoum.

36. See Scudder, Thayer (1973), "Summary Resettlement" in Ackermann, White and Worthington (eds.) MAN-MADE LAKES: THEIR PROBLEMS AND ENVIRONMENTAL EFFECTS, Geophysical Monograph 17, American Geophysical Union, Washington, D.C.

37. Butcher (1970), Afriye, E.K., and Butcher, D.A.P. (1971).

38. Christodoulou, D. (1963), "Problèmes posés par les Regimes et la Sedentarisation des Populations Nomades," paper presented to the Réunion Technique d'Etude sur le Nomadisme et la Sedentarisation, Geneva, April 1964, FAO, Rome.

39. Yacoub, Salah M. (1970), "Nomadic Populations in Selected Countries in the Middle East and Related Issues of Sedentarization and Settlement," (mimeo) UN Economic and Social Office in Beirut.

40. See Afriye, E.K., and Butcher (1971). Also see Scudder (1973) on other symptoms of "stress."

41. Meliczek, Hans (1969) "Selection of Settlers for Land Settlement Schemes" in *Land Reform 1969*, No. 2, FAO, Rome.

42. See Afriye, E.K. (1969) "Report on the preliminary social survey of four Krachi Areas G.E. (Gone Elsewhere) Villages," Volta Lake Research Project, (202/368) Ghana, and Castelli-Gattinara (1973).

43. "Educated Youths in the Countryside." Hong Kong Union Research Service (1972) 69 (3) 29-43.

44. See Meliczek (1969), *op. cit.*, pp. 42-49.

45. World Food Programme (1972), Egypt 535. *Land Reclamation Development and Settlement*, Interim Evaluation. 7/72.

46. See Butcher, D.A.P. (1971), *An Operational Manual for Resettlement*. FAO, Rome, p. 28.

47. FAO (1973), *Report of the FAO Expert Consultation on Emerging Agrarian Structures in Africa*. Dakar, Senegal, November-December, and FAO (1970) *Etudes en vue du developpement agricole de la Region du Kara, Togo* (ESR:SF/TOG8 Rapport Technique 5) Rome.

48. World Food Programme (1969) Turkey 084: *Establishment of 2 new villages and improvement of 16 existing villages* (WFP/IGC/16/8/19), (Rome, 10/69).

49. UNDP/FAO Technical Report (1969), S.A.R., p. 175.

50. See FAO (1974), Report on the FAO/SIDA Workshop for Intermediate Level Instruction in Home Economics, FAO/SWE/TF/136 Kenya, May 1974, Rome; and Musoma, B. (1971), "Report on a study of Child Health and Nutrition in Butiama Ujamaa Village" Buhara Home Economics Training Center (mimeo).

51. Lele, Una (1974), *The Design of Rural Development: Analysis of Projects and Programmes in Africa*, IBRD Africa Rural Development Study — Studies in Employment and Rural Development No. 1. Washington, D.C.

52. See Nelson, L. (1971), "Home Economics in Agrarian Reform" (mimeo), paper prepared for the Latin American Seminar on Land Reform and Colonization" (FAO/UNDP), Nov.-Dec. 1971; and Haglund, E. (1965), *Housing and Home Improvement in the Caribbean*, FAO and the Caribbean Commission, Rome.

53. See, Guurts, Ema (1973), "Rapport en Gouvernement du Dahomey, L'Amélioration de la Nutrition par la création des Jardins Familiaux." FFHC/FAO88/AFP:FFHC. FAO, Rome.

54. World Food Programme (1973), "Paraguay — Land Settlement in Seven Areas Progress Report," Rome.

55. Participation as a mode of implementation is discussed under a subsequent section: "Implementation Factors."

56. UNDP/FAO Technical Report (1969), S.A.R., p. 175.

57. See, Awiti, Adnu (1974) "Some Notes on Tanzania Rural Development Strategy: A case of Ujamaa Villages of Iringa Region," paper for Expert Consultation on New Forms of Organization and Structure of Agricultural Production. German Foundation for International Development, West Berlin; UNDP/FAO Technical Report (1969), S.A.R., p. 18; and Reggam, Z. (1967), "Agrarian Reform in Algeria" in *Land Policy in the Near East*. FAO, Rome.

58. Based on observations by H.A. Fosbrooke, FAO Sociologist in "The Role of Tradition in Rural Development," *Botswana Notes and Records*, No. 3. p. 188-191, and on the not-so-happy results of spontaneous settlement observed in the Ghab Region of Syria. See UNDP/FAO Technical Report, Syrian Arab Republic, (1969).

59. See, Voelkner (1974), on consultation with the Afars on the house designs prepared for the Awash Valley, and FAO (1969), Report to the Government of Tanzania: *Land Settlement*, UNDP/FAO No. TAZ 700, Rome.

60. Sabry, O.A. (1970).

61. See Butcher (1971), p. 46 and Van Heck (1973), p. 43.

62. Amerteifio, G.W., Butcher, D.A.P., and Whitham, D. (1967), *Tema Manhean, A Study of Resettlement*, Accra, Ghana.

63. Butcher (1971) and Castelli-Gattinara (1973).

64. Yacoub, S.M. (1971), p. 3.

65. See FAO (1969), Report to the Government of Tanzania, p. 7.

66. See Huszar, Brammah and Ass. (1974), "Penatang Panggang Transmigration Study." FAO/UNDP Project INS/72/005 — Planning and Development of Transmigration Schemes, p. 60.

67. Government of Malaysia (1974), FELDA Manual on Scheme Administration, Malaysia, Jan. 1974.

68. For a discussion of this aspect see, Pioro (?), "Growth Poles and Growth Theory as Applied to Settlement Development in Tanzania" in Kuklinski, A., (ed.) (1972) *Growth Poles and Growth Centres in Regional Planning*, U.N. Research Institute for Social Development (UNRISD) Geneva.

69. See UNDP/FAO, Technical Report (1969), S.A.R., especially pp. 172-181.

70. Al-Sammani, M., *et. al.* 1971, "A Study of Central Villages and their Served Envelope as Planning Units for Rural Development in Sudan," *Ekistics*, Vol. 32, Athens.

71. See Amissah, S.B. (1973), "Community Involvement in Resettlement Projects in Ghana," in *Town and Country Planning Summer School Report of Proceedings*, R.T.P.I., London.

72. *Ibid.*

73. See Kalitsi, E.A. (1971), "Regional Planning in the Volta River Basin," in *Town and Country Planning Summer School Report of Proceedings*, R.T.P.I., London; and Kalitsi, E.A. (1970), Organization of Resettlement in Chambers, R. (ed.), *The Volta Resettlement Experience*, Pall Mall, *London 1970*.

74. Yalan, E., (ed.) (1961), *Private and Cooperative Agricultural Settlement Physical Planning*, International Seminar on Rural Planning, Haifa.

75. See FAO/UNDP Technical Report (1969), S.A.R., page 129.

76. Interview and unpublished material of E. Vassilikioti, Ministry of Public Works, Dept. of Housing, Greece, 1975.

77. Kalitsi (1970).

78. Huszar, L. (1970) in R. Chambers (ed.), (1970).

79. See Giglioli, E.G. (1964) and FAO/UNDP Technical Report (1967), S.A.R., page 129.

80. Huszar, L. (1970).

81. Amissah, S.B. (1973).

82. See Yalan, F. (1963), *Land Planning of the Agricultural Cooperative Village*, Rural Building Research Center, Haifa; Georgulas, N., "Settlement Pattern and Rural Development in Tanganyika," *Ekistics* Athens, August 1967, and Huszar, L. *op. cit.*

83. Georgulas, N. (1967), *The Tanganyika Settlement Agency* (unpublished dissertation), Syracuse University, pp. 61-99.

84. Yalan, E., (ed) (1961).

85. See Butcher, D., Huszar, L., Ingersool, T.G. (1968), "Bui Resettlement Study: Ghana," in *Ekistics*, Vol. 25, No. 3, Athens (1968).

86. Huszar, Brammah and Ass. (1974).

87. Hilburg, Maos and Prion (1967), "Physical Planning and Sanitation for Rural Villages and Communities," United Nations Paper for the Rural Housing Seminar held at Venezuela, April 1967.

88. Georgulas, N. (1967), "Settlement Pattern and Rural Development in Tanganyika" in *Ekistics*, Vol. 25, No. 141.

89. Butcher, D., Huszar, L., Ingersool, T.G. (1968).

90. Yalan (1963).

91. El Ghomey (1966).

92. Yalan (1961).

93. El Ghonemy (1963). However, this also depends on the levels of social and commercial services assumed.

94. See El Ghonemy (1963), pp. 348-9.

95. Huszar, Brammah and Ass. (1974).

96. See Government of Saskatchewan (1955), *Report of the Royal Commission on Agriculture and Rural Life*, Vol. 4, "Rural Roads and Local Government," Fig. 25; and Vol. 12, "Service Centers," pp. 23-27.

97. Yalan (1961).

98. Huszar, L. (1970).

99. Proctor, J. (ed.) (1974), *Building Ujamaa Villages in Tanzania*, University of Dar-es-Salaam, Tanzania Publ. House.

100. Butcher, D.A.P. (1970).

101. Amarteifio, *et. al.* (1966).

102. Huszar, L. (1970), also Amarteifio, G.W. *et. al.* (1966).

103. Voelkner (1974), Castelli-Gattinara (1973) and UNDP/FAO Technical Report (1969), S.A.R. and Amarteifio, G.W. *et. al.* (1966) and particularly Butcher (1970).

104. Danby, M. (1970) "House Design" in Chambers (1970). See also UNDP/FAO Technical Report (1969) S.A.R.

105. Amarteifio, G.W. *et. al.*, (1966)

106. See Butcher (1970), Castelli-Gattinara (1973) and UNDP/FAO: SAR (1969).

107. Butcher (1970).

108. Amarteifio, G.W., *et. al.* (1966), and Huszar (1970).

109. *Ibid.*

110. Huszar, Brammah and Ass. (1974).

111. *Ibid.* and Danby (1970).

112. See Huszar, Brammah and Ass. (1974); Castelli-Gattinara, (1973); and UNDP/FAO SAR Technical Report (1969).

113. Chandrasekhar, B., *et. al.* (1967) "Towards Re-thinking Rural Housing" in *Ekistics*, No. 141, Athens, 8:67 (1967).

114. Kalitsi (1970).

115. Aziz, S., *et. al.* (1973) "The Chinese Approach to Rural Development" in *International Development Review*, Vol. XV, No. 4.

116. Myrdahl, Jan. (1965), *Report on a Chinese Village*, Wm. Heineman Ltd.

117. Temu, P. (1973) "The Ujamaa Experiment," in *Ceres* Vol. 6, No. 4, FAO, Rome.

118. Myrdahl (1965).

119. For example, see Yeager (1965), "The Settlement Manager and Citizens' Participation," in Proceeding of the Syracuse University Village Settlement Conference, University College, Dar-es-Salaam.

120. Butcher (1971).

121. Butcher (1971).

122. IBRD (1974), "IBRD Bank Policy on Land Reform," Report No. 440, IBRD, Washington, D.C., May 1969 (Table 3.1).

123. Jenness, J. (1969), "Reservoir Resettlement in Africa," (mimeo), p. 5, FAO, Rome, September.

124. Scudder, Thayer (1965), "The Kariba Case: Man-Made Lakes and Resources, Development in Africa," in Bulleting of Atomic Scientists, pp. 6-11, December.

125. Jenness (1969).

126. UNDP/FAO SAR Technical Report (1969), p. 183. (exchange rate used: L.S. 4.5 = US$ 1.00).

127. El Ghonemy, M. Riad, (1971) "Land Settlement as a Developmental Instrument Towards Attacking Poverty in the Middle East," (mimeo), FAO Regional Office for the Near East, Cairo.

128. World Food Programme, (1971) *Madagascar, 087*, "Pilot Land Settlement Scheme on the Lower Mangohy River," WFP/IGC 19/9 Add. 24, FAO, Rome, February.

129. Butcher (1971).

130. Scudder (1965).

131. Lele (1974).

132. UNDP/FAO S.A.R. (1969) p. 187.

133. UN/FAO World Food Programme (1972), "Ten Years of World Food Programme Development Aid: Rome, 1963-72. p. 7. Land Settlement schemes represent 9 percent of WFP's commitments and land development a further 16 percent.

4
Employment and Human Settlements*

The major trends in the location and development of human settlements are determined by contemporary patterns of work, fundamentally by man's need to work. It is the concern of the ILO with the world of work that defines the organisation's interest in the field of human settlements. In a sense, the essential role of the ILO is that of helping people cope with the relatively new industrial environment of the expanding cities and with the changing work patterns and social relationships in rural areas brought about by technical changes in agriculture.

Where people live depends on where gainful work opportunities are available. Geographical shifts in population are due mostly to the search of millions of individuals to improve their access to more gainful work opportunities, either within their own countries by moving from poorer areas to richer areas and from the countryside to the towns, or internationally by moving from poorer to richer (or at least better organised) countries. This poses some basic questions which are among the major concerns of the ILO: how best to utilise the manpower potential represented by the massive geographical transfers of migrants to increase production, incomes and well-being; how to train people for productive activity in the human settlement and work contexts where they will find themselves; how to cope with technological change so that it can be combined with the work potential of existing human resources instead of displacing them; how to improve the conditions of work created by the new modes of living, new methods of production and new geographical localisations of work and habitat.

This paper is not intended as a description of all the ILO's activities related to human settlements. It presents our views on three sets of problems on which the ILO has been doing significant work and which we consider central to the discussion on human settlements: migration and employment, technology and employment, and interactions between working conditions and environment.

Migration and Employment in the Developing World

Two kinds of migration patterns are relevant to the present state of human settlements: spatial patterns and time patterns. The spatial pattern of migration which has received the most attention in recent years is the massive flow of populations from rural areas to the major cities which has resulted in the phenomenal growth of the larger cities in most of the developing countries. It is this massive inflow of populations from the rural areas that impinges most clearly on the life styles of the urban elites and on the responsibilities of government agencies. The time dimension of migration varies over a wide continuum of "temporary" settlement from commuter status at one end to permanent residence at the other. At any point in time, a migrant is anyone who is not in his place of origin. But the nature of being an "immigrant" changes significantly with length of residence. It is, consequently, often convenient to distinguish "recent" migrants with up to perhaps five years of residence from "settled" migrants of longer residence.

*Abridged version of a background paper for Habitat contributed by the International Labour Office in Geneva. (Symbol A/Conf. 70/B/8; 26 February 1976.)

Analysts have distinguished a number of explanations for the massive flow of rural-to-urban migration — all of which boil down to the search for a better life." One fundamental cause is the pressure of increasing population on rural resources, which has led in some instances to increasing rural poverty even in absolute terms. But the trigger for movement is the expectation — usually justified — that poverty is both less intense in the cities and that the chances are greater in the cities than in the countryside of escaping from poverty. The key factor is the perception of differences between urban and rural living which are favourable to the former — differences in income, differences in opportunity, differences in the degree of individual freedom from social pressure of family, village and tribe (which has as its reverse side loss of social support), differences in possibilities for entertainment in the broad sense. It is in the cities where new things happen in the modernising world, where power is centred, where investments are made, where rapid changes occur. It is possible to offset some of the advantages of the cities by a massive diversion of resources from city-centred to rural-based activities. But the dynamic of most major contemporary societies is essentially an urban one and the attraction of the cities will continue to be a powerful one for a long time to come.

Man is a working animal and the differences cited above — in income, in opportunity, in range of activity — are reflections of differences in the range of urban employment opportunities as compared to rural. The bulk of non-agricultural activity is urban-centred, particularly the modern, formally organised branches of manufacturing, construction, trade, finance and government services. It is these formal sector activities which represent the glamour and the promise of the big city to members of the labour force of both urban and rural areas. In fact, in most of the developing world, the number of urban formal sector jobs increases less rapidly than the urban labour force and the great majority of the latter works in informal sector activities. These activities — small-scale commodity production, petty trade, services — generate lower incomes than the formal sector but permit a large segment of the labour force to stay on in the cities where their own chances — or those of their children — appear to them to be much better than in the countryside or in the villages. Levels of open unemployment are high in urban centres in many of the developing countries, but employment (or underemployment) in the informal sector provides an alternative which the out-migrants from rural areas evidently prefer to staying at or returning home.

Rural-to-urban migration has had a number of significant impacts on the localities of out-migration as well as on those of in-migration. One well-known aspect of the migration phenomenon is that the bulk of those who migrate are young adults. In some cultures these young adults are predominantly male, in some they are more in balance between the sexes, and in some females predominate. In situations where the young females move as well as the males, the natural increase of the urban population is reinforced and the urban problems of education, housing, health and other social services are intensified. Where the young females tend to stay at home in the village, the children of the rural migrants in the urban labour force remain rural.

Another aspect of rural-to-urban migration is that it generates income transfers between the migrant and his family in the village. These transfers are two-directional, although usually the net movement is strongly from the city to the rural areas of origin of the migrants. The income transfers take many forms, the most obvious being cash remittances from the migrant to his family. There is also a form of urban-to-rural transfer in kind: the hospitality offered to visitors from the rural place of origin, visitors who often intend to become longer-term migrants themselves. In the other direction, there are often rural-to-urban income transfers, often in kind, to help support the new migrant while he is studying or looking for employment. The transfer is thus often an inter-generational one: the elders of the family make an initial investment in the migrant; the return on this investment takes the form of the cash remittances he sends home later on. There is indeed some question in the case of single migrants in the city as to what is the locus of expenditure decision making: is a single individual living in the city an independent urban consumer or is he an urban part of a rural household?

The rapid growth of the urban populations of the developing world, particularly in the larger cities, has created great discrepancies between obvious needs and limited availabilities, discrepancies which are all the more visible because of the demographic concentration in the larger cities. Shortages of decent housing and or urban infrastructure facilities are endemic in the larger cities of the Third World, which also suffer high levels of unemployment and underemployment, reflecting the fact that the manpower requirements of modern manufacturing and other formal sectors of the urban economy fall far behind the demand for jobs.

The most visible indicator of the Third World's shortage of urban housing and urban infrastructure is the enormous rash of slums and shantytowns that have grown up within and on the outskirts of the major cities of Asia, Africa and Latin America to accommodate the new in-migrants. The concentration of shantytown populations in and around the larger cities has created health hazards for the more prosperous city dwellers as well as for themselves, hazards whose resolution requires extensive installation of costly water supply, sewerage and drainage systems which are not necessary when populations are scattered in a rural setting. The peri-urban shantytowns have in many cities also created physical barriers to orderly expansion of the urban centres, a development that has led to the realisation of the need to plan and provide infrastructure for slums as well as monumental avenues in the physical expansion of the large cities of today.

There are several dimensions to the imbalance between the size of the population in the working ages and the demand for manpower in the formal sector. One is relatively high rates of urban open unemployment in most of the developing countries. Another is relatively low rates of labour force participation, particularly among women, which reflect the "discouraged worker" syndrome that accompanies unemployment. A third is underemployment which may take several forms, among them time worked, inadequate income earned, and low requirements for the work performed compared with the abilities and training of the worker. Of these, the most prevalent is probably the inadequate incomes earned by many of those who put in long hours of work in informal sector activities.

There is an obvious potential link between the need to satisfy the infrastructure needs of the expanding cities, particularly of their mushrooming slums and shantytowns, and the need to create larger volumes of productive employment in the cities. Urban physical development will necessarily play an increasing role in urban employment generation in the developing countries.

Some Policy Issues

Those concerned with urban policy must live with the paradox that in the short- and medium-term, success in improving conditions in the cities will attract even greater number rural-to-urban migrants and increase the scope of the urban problem. There is no escape, in an urban-centred civilisation from the necessity to keep the cities habitable and functioning. A fundamental issue is how to allocate limited resources so as to achieve something approaching balanced urban and rural development. Urban development is needed to meet the physical and social needs of the inevitably growing urban populations. Rural development is needed both for the benefit of the existing rural populations and for the support that the countryside gives to the urban centres. Improvement in conditions in rural areas is not only important in itself for improving living standards of the rural populations, it is an essential element in slowing down rural-to-urban migration if conditions in urban areas do continue to improve. Increased agricultural production, which by its nature is primarily a rural activity, is essential for sustaining the urban economy. In effect, what is needed is integrated urban and rural development.

Public policy choices for reducing the flow of migrants to the cities boil down either to improving rural conditions relative to urban conditions, or to taking police measures to keep unwanted rural migrants out of the cities. Rural development based on a technological and social transformation of agriculture is a necessary condition for raising rural incomes and improving physical conditions in rural areas, thereby effecting an improvement in the absolute level of rural living even if not necessarily a reduction in the relative gap between rural and urban living standards. If rural levels rise and urban levels stay the same, the relative gap will of course diminish; but it is unlikely that urban levels can be held down if the general economy progresses. An actual worsening of urban conditions is not an aim that most governments will consciously pursue. The other extreme is merely to keep migrants out of certain big cities by administrative measures. Most of the developing countries have neither the political will nor an administrative structure capable of carrying out such an action. The upshot is that it is almost certain that migration will continue.

Public policy must therefore consciously focus on absorbing the new additions to the urban labour force at tolerable productivity and income levels. Among the possible approaches, at least three are worth serious consideration: encouragement of informal sector producers; the use of urban construction as an instrument for economic development and employment promotion; and dispersion of urban growth to smaller cities and towns.

One way to achieve these aims is to encourage the output of marketable goods and services by small-scale informal sector producers — who usually use more labour-intensive techniques than formal sector enterprises. Such encouragement involves a range of possible measures.

Among these measures is the reversal of existing negative policies which now discriminate against informal sector economic activity: banning of certain activities on aesthetic ground (e.g., prohibition of hawking in downtown areas) or for the convenience of the more prosperous members of urban society (e.g. banning of bicycle rickshaws from main streets of the city in order to relieve automobile traffic congestion); premature efforts to impose regulatory norms and standards (e.g. apprenticeship regulations, health and sanitation codes, restrictive licensing) on informal sector activities which would be stifled by their application; government subsidy and special treatment of large-scale units operating in competition with informal sector producers and traders (e.g., the limited amounts of official credit at low interest rates available to large firms while the small-scale producers and traders can obtain credit only from the local moneylender at high interest rates; direct access to import licences and raw material allocations for large enterprises while the small enterprises must obtain their inputs at retail prices in the local market; tax concessions for large investments which only larger firms are in a position to make).

Another negative policy worth reversing is slum clearance (as opposed to slum improvement) whether its ultimate purpose is beautifying the city, creating a traffic artery, establishing a port or industrial site, or building a middle- or upper-income housing project. Elimination of the slum destroys, at least temporarily, the informal sector economic activities that take place in it and the investments made there by the slum dwellers.

Possible positive measures to support informal sector activity include encouragement of small enterprises through provision of vocational and management training, organisation of credit facilities and co-operatives, preferential and "reserved" government procurement from small-scale producers, encouragement of sub-contracting by formal sector units, and city planning that includes sites and services facilities.

The training aspects are of special interest to the ILO which at present is reorienting its technical assistance activities in the fields of vocational training and management training to focus directly on the special problems of the very small-scale establishments in the informal sector. At the same time, the ILO is actively engaged in a series of field studies of the informal sector in a number of urban centres in Asia, Africa and Latin America. These studies are aimed at gaining a better understanding of the problems of the informal sector producers for the formulation of effective policies to assist them.

The provision of "sites and services" areas in the physical planning of Third World cities could be a significant element in programmes to develop the production and income capacity of the urban informal sector. Such an approach includes the laying out of sites for industrial parks for which basic infrastructure — water supply and drainage, road access and electricity — is provided, as well as of larger sites for self-built housing and the spontaneous economic activities that spring up in a poor urban community. Informal sector producers of goods and repair services can be accommodated in industrial parks by the advance construction of small workshops for rent, as is done in some towns in Turkey, or simply by provision of empty lots with access to the basic infrastructure, leaving to the individual entrepreneur the task of creating his work facility. On the other hand, a good deal of the informal sector's economic activities are attached to the dwelling. The provision of sites and services facilities for settlement, as an alternative to the spontaneous creation of slums subject to arbitrary destruction in the case of a later slum clearance project, will encourage self-financed investment in both housing and informal sector workplaces in new communities.

The need to provide the flood of new urban residents with infrastructure facilities and housing can be considered both as a burden and as an opportunity. It is a burden in the sense that the creation of urban infrastructure requires resources and effort. It is an opportunity in the sense that clearly defined and realisable needs can be transformed into effective demand for additional output of goods and services and for additional employment within manageable resources constraints. With the possible exceptions of structural steel shapes for major pieces of construction (e.g., bridges), steel rods for reinforced concrete, and cement, the raw materials used in construction are in most countries primarily locally produced. The creation of urban infrastructure will therefore create employment for local labour and generate domestic incomes with a minimum of first-round spill-over of demand into imports. The incomes generated will create secondary demands for other goods and services most of which are or can be locally produced as well. The real question with regard to resources is whether the other parts of the economy, particularly agriculture, will be able to respond to increases in demand by increasing the supply of goods and services they produce.

The rural exodus is a phenomenon that can at best only be slowed down, but it should be possible to influence the direction taken by the rural migrants. If employment possibilities and urban amenities can be made available in smaller towns as alternatives to the big cities, the most important factors motivating migrants in choosing their destinations can be changed. The big cities attract additional manpower because of the variety of job possibilities inherent in the size of the labour market; capital is attracted by the size of the market and the availability of manpower. What are needed are ways to offset the economic attraction of size of place itself.

To some extent the growth of specific localities is "natural" or fortuitous. It occurs because of pre-existing factors: proximity to natural resources (including prosperous agriculture), favourable location as a transport centre, the accident of dynastic foundation of a political capital. It occurs because of a spill-over of activity from overcrowded large urban centres which become unmanageable. It occurs because of the presence of a particularly dynamic group of entrepreneurs. But a certain amount of decentralisation of economic activity can be encouraged through planning and the provision of proper incentives.

Among the elements that can enter into effective spatial planning for employment creation is the fact that governments have a choice as to where they can direct public resources devoted to the creation of urban infrastructure; and there may be long-run advantages in going against the economic dynamic of centralisation. Another is that effective rural development itself requires the development of viable smaller towns to provide urban types of service facilities to the surrounding rural areas. Success in fixing local manpower in smaller urban centres will have cumulative local effects through further income generation and the creation of new employment opportunities.

One of the present areas of research of the WEP urbanisation and employment programme is infrastructure requirements for small urban centres of less than 20,000 population in an essentially rural setting. The needs of these smaller settlements have been neglected up to now, as have their role and potential contribution to over-all development goals. If rural development is to be integrated into regional and national development, it will be necessary to bridge the economic and political gaps which disadvantage the rural population and contribute to migration to the primate cities and their growing dominance over the rural hinterland. Specifically, what is needed is an effective, functional hierarchy of viable market centres and smaller towns oriented towards agriculture and rural industry and capable of absorbing the surplus rural population in productive, and as much as possible, labour-intensive employment. Seen in terms of welfare and equity considerations, the patent deficiency in social and economic infrastructure in the rural areas suggests a great potential for employing local labour and resources to support the growth of smaller urban centres. Furthermore, decentralised urbanisation suggests a logical alternative to migration to the already overburdened large cities, since it may be considerably cheaper to provide adequately for a given population when it is distributed among smaller towns. However, not only is there very little useful information available about actual or comparative costs of providing and maintaining infrastructure facilities in urban centres of different sizes, the entire question of the adequacy of facilities has begun to be reexamined to determine what levels of service the government can afford and the population reasonably support. Devising coherent strategies for comprehensive development on a national scale will thus require adequate knowledge of the endowments and functional requirements of the smaller towns at the lower end of the urban hierarchy. Through this project we hope not only to start generating reliable knowledge about smaller urban centres, but to devise workable methods which will enable government planners to undertake similar studies essential in formulating programmes of decentralised urbanisation.

TECHNOLOGY AND EMPLOYMENT

"Another development requires another approach to technology. This is true in Third World and industrial countries alike. However, just as another development does not imply jettisoning all that has been achieved to date, so too another approach to technology would not only be innovative but also use, adapt and build on substantial elements of existing technologies. However, it would also diverge from them in several basic orientations: it should aim at: meeting needs; providing meaningful employment; sustaining ecological viability; and making the best possible use of the specific resources of local eco-systems. It should be diversified so as to relate to the needs, resources and capacities of different societies and communities; be more closely linked to science; be broadly participatory and draw on the contributions of workers and peasants as well as specialised professionals.

Thus, science and technology would contribute to identify socially and environmentally sound alternatives for the production and use of resources, goods and services."

(Source: *What now: Another development*, the 1975 Dag Hammarskjold Report, prepared on the occasion of the Seventh Special Session of the UN General Assembly, p. 17.)

"Another development" implies embracing improvements in living standards and the quality of human life in human settlements; the removal of poverty in general, and the preservation of non-renewable and renewable resources. Since in the Third World today the quality of life at present is particularly low in the rural areas where most of the population lives, the pertinent question to ask is: do any policy instruments, referring to technology or urbanisation, result in improving the lot of the target groups — the rural poor? The quality of life in the rural areas is poor in the first place beacuse of the lack of satisfaction of basic needs, e.g., drinking water, sanitation, education and building materials, etc. The satisfaction of these needs is limited partly because of the extreme poverty and low incomes of the rural poor; and partly also because most public expenditure is allocated to the improvement of the cities. This urban bias in planning is now well recognised. But what can be done to reduce this bias directly, and indirectly? The shift of more public resources to rural instead or urban areas may partly redress this imbalance and improve the average quality of human life directly. There are also indirect ways, however. One way is to promote and encourage the utilisation of technologies appropriate to the socio-economic conditions of each country in that they properly mobilise existing resources and/or generate new ones — e.g., creation of energy through water, sun and tides.

The use of these technologies in the poverty-stricken rural areas can create higher incomes and employment. One of the reasons for very low current incomes is the very low productivity of the activities in which the inhabitants of rural settlements are engaged. If the technological levels of these activities are upgraded through appropriate innovations, which are within the cash resources of the subsistence economy, the quality of life through higher incomes and better access to social services would improve. This may in turn have an indirectly favourable effect by reducing migration to the cities. Lower pressures on the already overcrowded cities would also raise the quality of urban life.

One can further argue that employment by itself is also a component of the quality of life since it gives the employed a sense of purpose in life (what has been called "the recognition aspect" of employment) and sense of security. Thus, to the extent that appropriate technologies are employment-generating, they should contribute also to raising the quality of life in this second sense.

In the light of the above relationships between alternative technological choices, quality of human settlements, rural-urban migration and employment, we now consider the following main aspects of a technology policy: utilisation of local materials and other resources; stimulating the manufacture of more appropriate products, be they final consumer goods or intermediate products; and preserving the environment through adoption of pollution-free technologies and products.

Utilisation of Local Resources

One of the main characteristics of appropriate technologies is the use of local inputs that are often abundant and/or can be used more efficiently through local skills, and an economical use of scarce and imported resources. To meet these criteria may often call for technological self-reliance and self-help activities. One of the means by which quality of life in human settlements can be improved is through the provision of adequate housing and social infrastructure, e.g. transportation and road network. These are precisely the activities in which the development and use of indigenous materials through appropriate technologies is by now well established. For example, ILO studies on road construction within the framework of its World Employment Programme have clearly demonstrated the feasibility of improving traditional techniques through local initiative and skilled manpower. The traditional bullock cart was modified to enable it to transport and unload soil more easily. Similarly, manually operated scrapers in the Philippines were made of indigenous bamboo material which is available in abundance in the country. In the case of the building of houses, there may indeed be even a greater scope for substituting local for imported material, and for using domestic raw materials such as the pressing of building blocks from groundnut shells. For example, in the case of the foundations of houses, an ILO study[1] reports on an innovation, namely, *hyperbolic parabaloid shell foundation* which is not only labour-absorbing but also economises on concrete. From Mexico, where the innovation was developed, it has spread to Kenya, India and other countries. Similar other examples of innovations which utilise local domestically produced material components exist for other components of building.

Public policies and plans therefore need to be so tailored that they encourage the most economic use and development of indigenous building materials. The use of such materials will of course depend on the distribution of these resources regionally and/or globally. It is in the public interest therefore to develop both

[1]W. Paul Strassman: *Building technology and employment in the housing sector of developing countries* (Geneva, ILO, June 1975), mimeo.

regional and national plans for the exploitation of domestic building and other material resources. This public effort would not duplicate or supplant local initiative in using domestic materials; but only supplement it to make sure that local initiative is fully mobilised and supported through any research that may be needed or through regular supplies of materials in areas where they may not be immediately available.

Public intervention thus may be necessary only to make sure that resources that are locally available — both material and human — are utilised optimally. These would otherwise remain unexploited or unemployed, if imported instead of local materials were used.

Appropriate technology in construction, which among other objectives is meant to utilise domestic resources optimally, is also closely related to environmental considerations. In the first place, lowering the cost of housing through technological innovations will tend to increase the housing stock from a given amount of resources. This will improve the quality of life in so far as it is low because of the lack of shelter or because of very poor shelter. Secondly, density of settlement varies among alternative building technologies or systems. The quality of life in settlements may be improved by lowering density. Most modern building technologies, e.g. industrialised systems building, are economical only at very high levels of density. Therefore they may be less appropriate in developing countries than the low-rise housing which requires less advanced building technologies appropriate to the available local materials and skills. Such local materials would include bamboo, various types of clay, mud and stone and so on. But the first task must be the clear rejection of an unnatural subjective valuation of desirable modernity being represented by aluminium roofs over steel or cement housing. Too inflexible a respect for tradition may of course be inefficient. But even more so, reverence for the architectural profession, already tainted by a false sense of universalisation fuelled by cupidity, is an expensive excess in the rural areas of the developing world.

Stimulating Energy-Saving Technologies/Products

Taking the avoidance of environmental pollution into account in the selection and adaptation of technologies in developing countries further complicates the technological choice problem in industry, agriculture and construction. This complication has been aggravated by the new price of energy in world and domestic markets. Many developing countries have been compelled to reduce both oil imports and imports of other producer and capital goods. Usually the domestic demand for energy has been reduced by higher prices to consumers, leading to domestic inflation and diminished levels of investment and output. There is therefore likely to be a relative deceleration in economic growth rates among the many developing countries which are not exporters of oil. Despite the seriousness of the situation it is possible, however, to argue that the term "energy crisis" is to some extent an overly negative misnomer. The argument runs as follows. Like the industrialised countries, many developing countries have in the past become dependent on cheap energy supplies; but unlike the developed country experience, in any case dominated by labour shortages in recent years, the existence of cheap supplies of energy has reinforced the other distortions typically found in developing economies. Cheap energy has tended to further encourage capital-intensity to a degree not compatible with full employment. The pressure on policies for economic development brought about by higher petroleum prices may therefore be regarded as constructive in the sense that a built-in distortion is corrected. To take an example from the agricultural sector, tractorisation has been brought to a halt in some developing countries: and this is not necessarily regrettable if the tractors are not economically feasible anyway, given the manpower available, as has sometimes been found to be the case after careful examination.

The higher price of crude oil, and of fuel and electricity derived from it, will render more feasible than before technological alternatives in which more labour is employed. In some manufacturing plants in developing countries it may now be more clearly desirable to use labour for in-plant materials handling and other auxiliary activities outside the main core process. On the other hand, in a few industries the most capital-intensive technology costs will be reduced relative to other technologies because the economies of scale with respect to the energy input are the most significant. Such an industry is fertilizer production.

There is therefore a need in most developing countries to re-evaluate technological choices in industry and adapt the more modern technologies to economise on energy, substituting labour in its place. The ILO technology programme will be paying further attention to this problem in the biennium 1976-77. Indeed, in this particular field a key research project has recently been launched on "Technology, employment and higher oil prices in Sri Lanka." This project examines the employment and output implications of higher petroleum prices within, firstly, the macro-economic framework and, secondly, certain industrial sectors by case studies. The project is intended to draw conclusions about the policies which might turn the higher oil prices to good effect, in bringing about employment generation by more labour-intensive technological choice. Among such policies may be included the pricing of petrol, diesel fuel and electricity, and research and development policy in certain sectors where there is a good prospect of energy saving per unit of output; but these are just two of the possibilities in the policy direction. Another project envisaged in the future will concern alternative technologies in urban transportation.

Again, this project is designed to evaluate the real social cost of different forms of transport (e.g., bicycle versus car or public buses) in urban centres, and the comparative benefits in terms of the satisfaction of basic needs. The resource, employment and income distribution implications of various strategies of urban transport planning will be examined, probably by case studies of one or two specific urban areas. Traffic pollution, including gaseous by-products, noise, and other effects of congestion, will be costed as far as it is possible to do so. (Although the imputed cost of such pollution is not yet ranked high in developing countries, it will in the future be increasingly taken into account as urbanisation proceeds.)

The corresponding need in the rural sector is for measures to establish small-scale energy sources to satisfy basic needs. Examples of such sources include methane gas generators with cow dung as the raw material, simple windmills for rural irrigation and small-scale electricity generation and efficient small-scale solar capture devices which can power pumps, kitchen stoves and water heaters. There is considerable scope for energy generation along these lines if suitable locations are chosen so that the techniques and equipment are both useful and feasible from the social and cultural point of view. Such small energy sources, with low capital costs, may stimulate and strengthen self-reliance in rural areas. Once established in a village, that village is no longer dependent on public supplies, an advance which may enable the central government to divert public investment towards the satisfaction of other basic needs, such as education and health.

Preservation of the Environment

The transfer, without adaptation or some degree of selectivity, of the modern technology of developed countries to developing countries will inevitably bring in its train the same environmental disruption as has been revealed already in the industrialised world. It is possible, and the opportunity should be taken, to avoid the technological cycle of research and development leading to production, then pollution, then more research and development and, finally, anti-pollution measures. Developing countries are better placed to embark upon socially responsible policies of industrialisation which attach due weight, in the assessment and selection of technologies, to the preservation of the environment and the full use of industrial waste materials which would otherwise be harmful. Positive managerial decision making to ensure the use of industrial by-products is to be encouraged; and the experience of China in this respect may be well worth examining more closely.

Technological choice and environmental considerations are even more inextricably linked when we consider the international dimension. For example, the processing of natural fibres by relatively labour-intensive industries in developing countries is to be preferred to the capital-intensive production of synthetic fibres in the already industrialised world. And pollution of the oceans of the world may be reduced below the level which it would otherwise attain by processing more raw materials in the producing countries than is presently the case. As in other examples, this one carries significant employment benefits for the peoples of developing countries, as well as the obvious environmental benefit, a global one. The implications of concern for the environment for the international division of labour will no doubt be taken into account in the deliberations of the Tripartite World Conference on Employment, Income Distribution and Social Progress and the International Division of Labour to be organised by the ILO in June 1976.

The Case of Employment and Technology in Building

The case of building technology raises a number of interesting questions related to employment: Do owners, architects, builders and artisans in developing countries choose techniques that take full advantage of the available labour force? What employment options are given by the conventional technology? How much of a price or wage change is needed before one switches from one method to another? Will rapid wage increases, on balance, help or harm the labour force?

A close look at housing costs shows that more developed countries choose less labour-intensive housing. Higher quality housing incorporates more expensive materials and equipment, which automatically lowers the share of on-site labour even if employment and wages remain unchanged. Moreover, development means urbanisation and multi-storey apartments in larger cities, and as one goes from one storey to four to eight, the share of on-site wages in structural cost falls from 29 to 26 to 24 percent (in conventional Colombian and Mexican building). Superficial statistical analysis would attribute the fall exclusively to rising wages and an elasticity of demand for labour far above unity, when, in fact, both changes are partly the result of development as a whole.

The goal of an employment-promoting policy is not just to raise on-site construction work, but *any* kind of remunerative employment. Hence, the indirect labour content of materials and equipment has to be seen as offsetting lower on-site employment. Estimating the labour in the materials, and the materials that go into the materials *ad infinitum*, is an elaborate statistical procedure; and so far, studies exist only for Brazil, Mexico and the United States, although others are under way elsewhere. In Mexico around 1970, the indirect labour content was about 35 percent of all man-years in a single-family house (without off-site construction work, urbanisation and sales) and in the United States it was 55 percent. In Mexican low-cost housing, the indirect labout share was only around 30 percent, but for luxury housing it rose to 40 percent. For apartments, the percentage was a few points higher, especially for high-rises.

But the rise in indirect employment does not offset the fall in on-site employment. In Mexico, indirect labour costs rose only from 13 to 16 percent of structural cost as quality changed from low cost to luxury, while direct labour costs fell from 32 to 20 percent: a net loss of 9 percent (from 45 to 36 percent).

A decline in the wages share of building and a fall in the growth rate of construction employment should not immediately provoke a policy of lowering real construction wages, perhaps by letting them lag behind inflation. The falling wages share may be due to a shift in the composition of output — higher quality and higher rise dwellings that may be desired or inevitable. This may reflect urbanisation and a rising middle class. If the shift in composition is undesired, a change in mortgage credit policy might reverse it and restore the labour intensity of building as well. Whether or not employment is thereby restored depends on whether or not the volume of building falls by a critical amount with the shift to labour-intensive dwellings.

If there is no shift in composition, there is still no case for a restrictive wage policy just because substitution is under way. Labour costs may be high because of inefficiency as much as high wages. Training of workers and managers must therefore keep up with, and even anticipate, rises in construction demand. Such demand is likely to accelerate at the middle income level of economic development, together with urbanisation and the need for infrastructure. The sensible vogue for seeing construction as a leading sector — given disappointment with agriculture and manufacturing — will contribute to this pressure. Mechanisation, because of failure to expand training programmes, should not negate the very employment-generating characteristics that originally helped make construction an appealing sector. Conventional technology, with its vast variety of substitution possibilities, harbours threats to employment and the welfare of workers if training programmes are inadequate and if there is undue interference with labour markets raising wages prematurely. But that is not the only kind of intervention, nor the only kind of technology, hence not the only theme of this study. In addition to conventional technology, novelties can be promoted or retarded.

Examination of a large sample of innovations of the past two decades shows that private firms are fully capable of importing the rather humdrum off-shelf innovations that do not take further local adaptation or research. The more creative changes that improve organisation, or perfect traditional methods, and that might depend on substantial scientific research, are strongly associated with public agencies, such as building research stations and productivity centres. These innovations were not remarkably more complex: nor, since complexity was associated with risk, were they riskier, although they may have appeared risky to the less well-informed in the private sector.

One benefit of the more public, science-based research was its tendency to lower material costs, while all other innovation types mainly reduced labour costs. Science-dependent innovations were good at developing new uses for indigenous materials or adaptations to fit local peculiarities, such as foundation types. By definition, off-shelf innovations could not achieve anything like that. Since off-shelf innovating is cheap and involves little risk in the narrow sense, it would, nevertheless, be foolish to discourage this way of bringing in useful advances that might have been heavily science-dependent abroad.

On the other hand, off-shelf and innovations that adapt advanced methods from abroad with little reference to local materials should not be encouraged with special licences and subsidies. These innovation types, unlike all others, are likely to increase equipment cost and be capital-intensive. Unfortunately, public support, including research and special subsidies, has often vainly tried to adapt unsuitable advanced methods. The most flagrant case is that of prefabricated Industrialised System Building (ISB).

To oppose advanced systems of prefabrication for walls and floors under all circumstances would be wrong. For schools, hospitals, office buildings and apartments in advanced countries, ISB has been logical and successful. Modular co-ordination and prefabrication of many components will always be desirable. But ISB is not optimal for all circumstances, specifically those of developing countries.

With a 5-year volume of 1,500 to 2,000 dwelling units in 4-5 storey apartments at one site, the best ISB could theoretically reach the cost range of conventional "low-cost" housing of $35-45 in 1970 dollars per square metre. No more than 3 percent of the on-site jobs would be lost, or 100 man-years.

That is the most that can be hoped for in developing countries. The vast majority of systems need a much larger volume, far exceed conventional costs, and displace hundreds of additional workers. Two decades of failures with such systems in developing countries have passed; and yet, as governments come and go, and as memory fades while salesmanship persists, ISB again and again comes in for another try. Only recently did an African president announce a bold new programme of prefabricated housing.

The misleading appeal of ISB has many facets. One is human fascination with anything neat and systematic that seems to replace chaos. Another appeal is that speed per dwelling unit is easily confused with cost or with the annual rate of building that a country can afford. A saving of six months of construction time should be rated as worth no more than about 6 percent of the price of a dwelling. Nothing in an abstract formulation of a building system gives a clue to inexperienced policymakers about start-up delays, on-site interruptions, breakage rates and other problems that arise in practice.

Innovation that takes the form of organisational changes paradoxically reduces and therefore preserves the labour-intensity of efficient building methods. Normally, it appears that half of labour time is spent on activities that do not make the building grow. A capital-intensive method that cuts the labour force by half, eliminates half of both productive and paid-for but wasted time. *Organisational* innovations are supposed to eliminate the wasted time without the capital expenditure. Some organisational changes nevertheless go with simple adapted tools such as the trowels developed in India. Others go with a change in design like the cavity wall with vertically set bricks, tested in Madras. Organisational changes range from such job studies to altering the sequence of operations, rationalisation, modular co-ordination, quality control, proper testing of materials, and building code reform. Some of these save materials cost as well as labour. Most organisational improvements seem neglected in developing countries. It seems easier to adopt something tangible that does not call for subtle changes in behaviour. Yet the intangible changes are less risky since attempts to improve organisation seldom cost much and rarely fail.

To sum up, conventional building technology allows labour to be replaced in a wide variety of ways. The elasticity of substitution is probably not far from unity.

Cost-reducing innovations may also lower man-hours per unit. Since competition is typical in construction, prices should fall with cost, and given elastic demand, a rise in employment should follow.

Whether they are copies, improvements, adaptations or drastic reorganisations, the best cost-reducing, quality-raising innovations should be welcome. If they produce cheaper, safer, more convenient and more attractive dwellings, they are appropriate technology. But even ultra-appropriate innovations will be more effective if they are part of an appropriate housing sector strategy. The greatest barrier to improving the housing stock is not inability to design better dwellings and construction methods, but clumsy housing sector institutions.

WORKING CONDITIONS AND ENVIRONMENT

Work and human settlements are closely linked. Survival is the first necessity and man seeks above all the means to preserve it — food — and to protect it — human settlements. Food and human settlements require that man works; he works to establish himself; he acts on the environment and uses it to protect himself; he also establishes himself to live and to work, in order to carry out, under the best possible circumstances, the activity which will ensure him sustenance, safety and, if possible, well-being.

The multiplicity of interrelationships is complex and unsettled. Only a few among them may be touched upon here.

Worker's housing will first of all be examined quickly.

The following will then be studied in succession: instances where work and residence are apart from each other and the resulting consequences; instances where work and residence are close to each other, with particular reference to the environment shared by work and human settlements.

Workers' Housing

The problem of workers' housing, which has both social and economic dimensions, is most often expressed in quantitative terms since it is recognised that a housing policy affects to a great degree the success of employment and economic development policies. But the qualitative aspect also assumes great importance. The supervision of healthful housing conditions is critical since human settlements not only depend on the number or technical characteristics of accomodation, but also on the conditions in which they are used: overcrowding can render unhealthy an otherwise suitable flat.

The safety and health standards which dwellings should put into effect concern the working man in particular for two reasons: first, housing conditions are closely related to working conditions, and, second, it is the category of workers of modest income whose work is often unpleasant which endures the least favourable housing conditions.

It will be enough to recall that housing should satisfy conditions of safety and hygiene and, if possible, of comfort, with differing degrees existing between these various imperatives since the first condition to be fulfilled is that housing does not collapse or is not blown up by explosion or fire, and that following this it allows its occupants a sufficient volume of air.[2]

It is not rare that fires or explosions due to defective electrical wiring or makeshift heating methods, or accidents caused by lifts in poor condition, persons asphyxiated, etc., are brought to light in poor quality housing and particularly in shanty-towns. The overcrowding and poor health conditions of the "working class neighbourhoods" of cities has long since been made known.

The shortage of housing — or its deterioration — are not the only dangers. For several years, the employment in the construction industry — housing as in other types of building — of new products whose reaction to fire is very poorly known (degree of inflammability and fire resistance, heat released combustion-produced substances, etc.) present severe risks for inhabitants, workers, the public, neighbouring areas and fire-fighting personnel alike. These risks are all the more serious given that the size of buildings and the number of persons they house are constantly increasing.

Housing, Sleep and Conditions of Work

Of the various facets of this question, particular emphasis should be placed on that which is no doubt best known and which, furthermore, is linked in a special way to conditions of work: sleep. It is this problem which maintains a current events flavour. On the one hand, general health conditions are making progress even if they are far from satisfactory in every case; on the other, there are more and more jobs, in industry or the service sector, which cause nervous tension; this fact makes the kind of rest which brings sleep more necessary and at the same time more difficult.

If the first physiological studies concerning fatigue and rest date only from the end of the last century, the need for rest to compensate for work-caused fatigue has always been recognised, and it is at the very foundation, in all countries, of that important part of social legislation which are the laws concerning rest.

In order to fully recover from nervous fatigue, and without after effects — fatigue as a result of either the kind of work or the physical or psychological conditions in which it is performed — sleep must occur under conditions which permit it to be normal, that is, full and of sufficient length; these conditions refer in particular to noise level and hours of sleep. An important factor of working and living conditions about which it will prove more and more indispensable to be aware concerns the progressive replacement of muscular fatigue by mental fatigue in a number of industries as a result of increasing mechanisation and more and more sophisticated organisation.

[2] The International Labour Organisation adopted in 1961 Recommendation No. 115 concerning Workers' Housing. This Recommendation examines inter alia: the objectives of a national housing policy, the responsibility of public authorities and employers, financing, housing standards, and town, country and regional planning.

Sleeping hours, on the other hand, exercise a profound influence on the nature of sleep itself. This is demonstrated both by various basic studies concerning sleep and the work of physiologists who take an interest in the case of workers who are subject to irregular working hours or rotating or night shift work. It is known that man, as with the majority of living beings, has his biological activity regulated according to a 24-hour rhythm ("biological rhythm"); the link, in man between the external rhythm and the different physical and mental functions is very complex.

A number of complaints from workers who are subject to irregular working hours as with a number of various findings — absenteeism, in particular, cited by management or industrial physicians — have led to scientific research. Studies have thus been carried out on the irregular working hours of major line railwaymen.

But the majority of these studies concern workers who are tied to night work or rotating shift work. Its incidence is spreading and affecting a large number of industrial workers — not only labourers but also clerks and managerial staff — in industrialised countries; it is also spreading to some services. It is estimated that in France, for example, 20 to 30 percent of all wage earners work in shifts. Rotating shift work was previously justified for obvious emergency reasons (in the case of hospitals, fire protection, safety and police); for reasons of public service (transport, postal service); by the nature of the article produced or the service provided (bakeries, newspaper printing, nightwatchmen); or because of technical constraints which require a continuous running of industrial machinery to avoid damage to equipment (so-called "non-stop" factories such as steel, chemical, petrochemical, plastics and synthetic textile industries). Today, however, it is used more and more as a justification for economic and financial reasons (quick amortisation of equipment which is increasingly more sophisticated, onerous and short lived). In addition, there is the essential research in developing countries for the creation by this means of a greater number of jobs with the same level of investment.

All of the studies made show a number of effects which are linked directly to this working hours format. There is first of all an over-all sleep deficit among shift workers; thus, for example, the later one goes to bed the shorter the sleep (an individual awakens at approximately the same hour regardless of the time he has gone to bed); meanwhile, for the worker who must begin work during the night, bedtime is hardly advanced. Secondly, it has been determined that the sleep of shift workers was less good and that the number of REM sleep periods (delta waves brain activity) was less than normal. Further, it is shown that the result of the observations of several researchers agree in establishing that the various "indexes" (heart beat rate, blood pressure, etc.) maintain, in instances of night work, their nightly low points and "that there is never a genuine inversion of rhythms; thus night work cannot benefit from the psychosomatic activation which facilitates day work; given equal work, one should therefore anticipate that the former will be more tiring than the latter." Sleep during the day, being shorter, is also often broken sleep; for night workers, the rhythm of hunger interferes with that of sleep.

The repercussions for each night or shift worker will vary, of course, in relation to other elements, often outside the work environment, such as the quality and location of housing, duration and mode of transport, type of food, non-work activities, state of psychological balance, etc. The nature of human settlements is at the top of the list of these elements.

Human Settlements, Working Life and Private Life

A worker's residence is not merely the place where he sleeps or regains strength which he will spend anew at his trade the following working day or night. It is above all the place where he lives and conducts for the most part his social relationships. He brings there the cares and pleasures which his work brings to him. Beyond this, and in a more profound way, work can be the source of fulfilment or, on the contrary, of frustration whose consequences inevitably affect the personal, familial and social life of the individual worker.

The feelings of inadequacy or maladjustment of man and of the professional, familial and social life he leads can make itself felt at home or in his relationships with his friends or neighbours. They can also be felt in the undertaking where he works: absenteeism is the most frequent example: turnover, conflicts with colleagues or superiors may also be symptoms whose real basis cannot at all, or may only in part, be attributed to professional reasons; numerous studies dealing with a clinical examination of occupational accidents have demonstrated the role of the background of individuals as a promoting factor.

It is not possible to separate the surroundings which make up the human establishment and the life which goes on there. The more the human community increases — villages, cities, magapoles — the greater the specialisation of the duties of each inhabitant and the quantity of services which its existence implies in this aggregation calls for infrastructure which becomes the indispensable complement to housing, the means of adjustment between the working and private life. The means of collective transport are, to a great extent, made necessary by the daily travel between residence and workplace; day nurseries and crèches become increasingly necessary, their absence or their remoteness able to pose such problems for mothers of families that they prefer not to work or, as in certain Asian countries, they take with them their young children who spend their day in a corner of the workshop.

The result is therefore that as urbanisation progresses, the level of individual and collective needs rises on the one hand while awareness of them and their fulfillment grow more complex on the other. Legislative and statutory provisions in the social field cannot provide solutions in this respect entirely on their own. Human establishments should include suitable infrastructure and establish the administrative and managerial capabilities which permit a fulfillment of these needs. But the very idea of "suitable" and desirable raises very complex questions. The localisation of human settlements is one of these. The worker of limited financial means generally has no possibility of breaking out of small accommodations: he must find a flat on the outskirts of the city as the only thing which corresponds to his financial status; this involves lengthy travel with all of the corresponding consequences (to be developed further below) for himself, his health, his family; consequences likewise for the presence and cost of the means of transport, the availability and cost of social infrastructure of social life, the establishment of "bedroom communities" and the segregation of population according to income, to mention only the main points.

The authorities are thus faced with two types of problems. The first concerns an awareness of the needs and aspirations of people and the necessary liberty they must be given to exercise their individual options: this person cannot put up with the distance between home and work while another, in exactly the same position, appreciates either the quiet of a residence outside the city or even the simple matter of being separated from his place of work which gives him the feeling of escape from its problems and constraints. But this kind of possibility of choice exists only for the most favoured workers, those who live in small cities and those whose income allows them to pay higher rents or to save in order to secure their own housing. The situation of the low-income majority requires that public authorities intervene, and this is the second type of problem: Which housing policy to adopt? Where to build? What type of urban-planning to adopt? How to act on the price of land? The sizeable effort carried out in different countries to face up to the growth of population in cities, which is a product of both demographic factors and the movement of rural populations towards the large centres, demonstrates that a housing-creation policy is not confined to an already difficult quantitative problem consisting of providing a roof and decent surroundings to all new arrivals in the city. Nor can such a policy limit itself to the application of several major, straightforward though theoretical principles such as that which consists in grouping together a population in the greater urban centres as was provided for in the "Charter of Athens," established by the assembly of the International Congress of Modern Architecture in 1933. It was this assembly which defined the necessary separation of four functions: living, working, recreating and moving about. It has been shown that the inhabitants of the "great urban centres," built up in these areas, do not necessarily find in these places the necessary jobs. This in itself maintains the daily, sometimes numerous and lengthy, to-and-fro movements with the former workplace in these industrial areas. Furthermore, the well-to-do populations in Europe continue to prefer the city centre with the ensuing very pronounced social segregation. The "separation of duties" leads to these buildings, often constructed in a stereotypical fashion, becoming "bedroom communities" where the "liveliness" sought by the designers remains artificial. Social infrastructure above all is often insufficient and poorly suited to the needs of the wage-earning populations in such centres.

A large movement seeks to question this concept and to replace it with the will to create true urban centres which are not "an analytical projection, that is, a situation where all of the elements are isolated from each other," but a synthesis, where human settlement, employment and leisure are better integrated. Furthermore, the establishment of social infrastructure adapted to the needs of workers is both a social and an economic necessity.

Human Settlements and Work Where the Two are Separate from Each Other

Every human settlement is the scene of movement, a large part of which is made up of journeys between home and work. These journeys whose length, complexity and the time devoted to them increases progressively as the urban fabric grows more crowded and spreads out, is a phenomenon to which greater attention should be paid. Commuting between home and work raises two types of problems: commuting accidents and the health and family problems posed by movement between home and work.

It has been determined in numerous countries, according to the ILO Encyclopaedia of Occupational Health and Safety, that if the frequency of accidents occurring between home and place of employment (number of accidents occurring divided by the number of hours of risk exposure) is sometimes less than that of occupational accidents in a strict sense, the first group is on the contrary more serious than the second.[3]

It is necessary to distinguish in the social cost of commuting accidents, the economic loss in the number of work days lost, disabilities and death, etc., and not merely the cost of accident compensation. In fact, commuting accidents are not always compensated for as such. If the tendency is increasingly in favour of including commuting accidents in the special system of compensation for occupational accidents in a strict sense, such has not always been nor is it still the case. According to available information, at present in 69 of the 128 member states of the ILO, commuting accidents are compensated for as occupational accidents.

In a few states, commuting accidents are taken into consideration under exceptional circumstances, chiefly if the journey takes place in a vehicle supplied to workers by the employer. Such a definition of commuting accident is very restrictive. The fact should not be ignored nevertheless that in the majority of countries where commuting accidents are not yet in the same category as occupational accidents properly so called, the other branches of social security are still quite undeveloped or even, at times, non-existent.

The difficulty in combating commuting accidents stems from innumerable variables which are taken into consideration and the difficulty in interpreting available statistics and of carrying out detailed studies on public highways in order to establish the circumstances. Furthermore, unlike occupational accidents where the role of the heads of undertakings is essential, responsibilities are more diffuse in the case of commuting accidents. Lastly, in each country there are characteristic climatic conditions, road systems and means of transport whose respective occurrence is quite varied. In certain regions, human settlements are so close to the place of employment that the risk of commuting accidents is notably reduced. The standard of living influences the means of transport and, as a consequence, the number of accidents.

The time spent travelling regularly increases for a growing number of workers: this is a natural and universal observation as there is a constant growth of towns. Millions of workers spend several hours each day on public transport, queueing or travelling by their own means; a growing number must rely on several methods of transport for a single journey which demands a succession of periods of wait and hurry. In the big towns of African countries, workers travel on foot for what are often very long distances. The Director-General of the ILO expressed himself in thie way in the Report which he presented to the 60th Session (June 1975) of the International Labour Conference:

> Everything that is done to reduce hours of work, both by the ILO and all those persons concerned, is aimed at ensuring that people have sufficient time for rest and relaxation. However, the ratio between work and rest presents problems in big towns ... At the beginning of the century the claim for the reduction of hours of work was reflected in the slogan '8 hours' work, 8 hours' leisure, 8 hours' rest.' It could not be foreseen at the time that many workers were going to spend two, three or four hours per day on travel that would be as long and tiring for them as it would be costly for the community. This is a new problem to be borne in mind, for one cannot turn a deaf ear to the claims of those who think that such a large proportion of time devoted to travel should be taken into consideration when hours of work are being determined. Moreover, the inhabitants of these suburbs of major cities often form less of a community than a large collection of individuals whose way of living and actual lives are excessively moulded by the conditions in which they work. There is evidence of a disturbing number of nervous breakdowns and various disorders, unacceptable living conditions and, in particular, inadequate social services. Although

---

[3] L. Cloquet, "Commuting Accidents" in *Encyclopaedia of Occupational Health and Safety* (Geneva, ILO, 1971), p. 11.

this situation as yet affects only a minority of workers, it is worsening and neither national authorities nor the ILO can ignore it.[4]

The circumstances in which this travel takes place are not without their repercussions on workers' living conditions. For a certain privileged few, travel to and from work may be considered a period of relaxation (short distances on foot or by car on lightly travelled roads). For the majority and, in particular, for workers of modest means in large towns, these journeys are a source of physical or nervous fatigue or both at once. This problem is as yet poorly understood and its importance is probably not appreciated as it should be; it is different for each individual; there exists no trade union or pressure group to latch on to it; finally, for many, it is considered part of the natural order of things to which one is obliged to submit. However, awareness begins to the extent that this problem is growing worse everywhere in the world.

The interferences between working life, hours of work and place of employment, and the personal, family and social life are thus numerous, closely related and emanating from both directions. Many are the observers and scientists who have stressed these relationships. P. Cazamian writes:

> The more difficult it is for a worker to reconcile his working life with the role he must play in private life, the more his physical state feels the effects; he grows more anxious, more in conflict with himself, thinks less of himself. There is thus a relationship between the degree of difficulty perceived by the worker and his psychic balance ... If one considers more precisely the intrusions of the working life with certain specific roles maintained in private life, one notes that the more the roles of husband-wife, father and citizen are disturbed, the more this affects significantly the worker's psychic balance.

Is it possible to complete this evaluation of the increase in travel time, until now understood in purely economic terms (increased costs for petrol, transportation, amortisation) by an appreciation of workers' dissatisfaction or of the various difficulties which can result for him and his family? This latter approach raises difficult and unresolved problems; it is good, however, that they have not been resolved hastily as the danger is great, in wishing to quantify everything, to put aside more systematically than before phenomena which are exactly those which it is suggested be known better.

Human Settlements and Work Where the Division Between the Two Is Indistinct

Life in rural areas is characterised by the close proximity of human settlements and the place of employment. There is a certain romanticism in industrialised countries towards work on the land — the idea of a healthy environment, flexible time schedule, the existence of communities where one lives and works — which at times tends to forget the hazards and difficulties which agricultural workers face.

Furthermore, in developing regions, the quick tempo or urban population increase and the resulting problems often hide the fact that the majority of inhabitants still live in rural areas.

It does not appear that the economic and social development plans in use in developing countries have understood the results of such a geographic and occupational distribution of the population. Indeed, physical pressures (for example, safety), social ones (the social evils of urbanisation are more visible than rural poverty) and political pressures (favoured and politically influential people are concentrated in large towns) have seen to it that priority, as regards economic and social investment, has been too often given to the urban sector. This tendency has contributed to a deterioration in the standard of living of the rural population.

Leading a marginal existence in rural areas, while clearly less visible, affects many more people than the same existence does in urban areas. This marginality shows up in each of the essential elements of the standard of living of rural populations: food, housing, health and education. It harms the normal development of the individual and his productive capacities. In this sort of human settlement, at once vast and dissimilar,

---

[4]Making Work More Human, Working Conditions and Environment. Report of the Director-General to the International Labour Conference (Geneva, International Labour Office, 1975), pp. 33-34.

that is the rural sector of developing countries, it is impossible to separate living conditions, working conditions, income and means of maintenance.

In industrialised as in developing countries, agriculture is characterised by the seasonal nature of the work to be performed during certain and, most often, very limited periods. Such a volume of work at times requires very considerable effort; and the fact of being governed by weather conditions and the consequences of weather for farming which restrict or entirely do away with rest periods, while the need to be nearly always present on the land being worked acts as a constraint for the farmer and a source of nervous tension.

Moreover, everywhere where modernisation has taken place in agriculture, there has also been a sharp increase in occupational accidents and disease, either through an increase of traditional risks or through the appearance of new risks. It has been observed in several industrialised countries that the occupational accident rate in modern agriculture is now just below that for mining and construction. The rapid expansion of mechanisation in agriculture in industrialised countries and in several developing countries, while it has fortunately reduced the cost of energy and improved yields, has given rise to hazards which seemed until now to be restricted to industry. The most spectacular accidents are those involving wounds, falls, crushing and the overturning of tractors.

In addition, there are the effects of noise, vibration and prolonged nervous tension to which tractor drivers and their assistants are subjected. The other dominant feature of present-day agriculture is the increasingly frequent and world-wide use of chemical products such as fertilizer, weed killer and pesticides. The use of pesticides in particular poses serious problems insofar as there is currently a real escalation in their use: spraying occurs more frequently, products have a higher toxicity and the amounts used are larger and larger. This is a disturbing phenomenon and not merely because of the immediate effects but likewise due to the less well-known, long-term consequences on the environment and the human organism.

A large number of workers other than farmers live and ply their trades in the same location. Human settlements thus often include a work function which was even greater in the past since this phenomenon is in decline. Often using vegetable or animal materials to make ornaments, clothing or other products (carpets, tables, etc.) which required the use of simple tools, cottage industry at times takes on more elaborate forms: this is the case where the manufacture of a product is distributed according to an exact organisation among several craftsmen and the item produced moves from house to house. Cottage trades, suffering from the competition of mass production, are tending to decline. Those which do not disappear survive with difficulty and questions of health, safety and the upkeep of the premises are far from being of primary importance.

Small-scale industry groups a large number of people in the world. The independent worker both lives and works under the same roof, in adjoining premises; he employs the members of his family and possibly takes on a few workers.

Many of these small industries use old methods, have hardly any access to occupational medicine or to any sort of medical or nursing services; social infrastructure is practically non-existant. The working environment is generally poor and often presents dangers. In many cases work is performed in poor environmental conditions which are harmful to both production and health.

Every type of occupational accident or disease caused by work is found, according to the activity performed, in the small family establishments and cottage industries. These risks are increased, on the one hand, due to the absence of measures for detection and prevention which goes hand-in-hand with ignorance and neglect of danger, and on the other by long exposure to dangerous substances for workers and their families. This quasipermanent exposure is all the more serious since it concerns children who, it is recognised, are much more vulnerable than adults and whose development can be seriously affected by certain situations. Furthermore, diseases resulting from poor quality housing and sanitation are often encountered in such establishments; these conditions are transferred to and worsened within the atmosphere of the workshop where particularly vulnerable individuals such as old people, young persons and the handicapped are exposed.

The workers in these small undertakings have very limited means, or none at all, to defend their rights to better living conditions; trade unions, particularly those in developing countries, take their power from the support of large concentrations of workers more so than from that of employees of small factories. Nor do the serious employment problems which run endemically rampant in many of these countries prompt those concerned to be the least bit demanding whether concerning the nature of the work or the risks attached which are often simply considered inherent to the work itself. Family ties and the protective feeling applied to any job which guarantees a living and permits the individual to escape from misery accentuates further the dependence of these workers.

This aspect is still further pronounced in the particularly distressing case of the employment of children, still very widespread in spite of legislative measures taken by States.[5]

Broadening the Notion of Environment

Many are the outlying districts of large towns which bear the mark of an era of disorderly growth. There one finds, side by side, often closely intermingled, workshops, warehousing districts and living quarters, everything in dilapidated and filthy condition: all the disadvantages for inhabitants found in one spot. Another sort of housing is conceived and built by the large undertaking for its personnel: in this case there is the advantage of proximity to the place of employment, favourable conditions for renting or purchasing property; but there may also be the feeling of an omnipresent undertaking which in its extreme can be quite distressing from a psychological standpoint.

Even in instances where place of employment and residence are separate, there is less and less of a sharp division between the working and living environment.

At the outset of the Industrial Age, the limited size of production units, the nature of the products dealt with and the simple techniques used limited the negative effects on the worker. It is true that in the old industrial regions (northwestern Europe, northeastern United States) urban complexes closely joined industry and human settlements; the environment, for the most part steelworks, mines and cokeworks, was particularly frightening, and it remains the same in every case where workers live in close proximity to these factories — the holdover from an era when employers sought to stabilise the workforce they required. This situation changed but slowly; today the attempt is made everywhere, even when the grouping of large numbers is required not far from a large industrial centre, to provide intervening space to screen out noise, smoke and other forms of pollution.

Nevertheless, to an increasing degree, the interpenetration of the previously separate living and working environments is being emphasised. This phenomenon, which appears indisputable but whose consequences are not entirely known, manifests itself in several ways.

First, the amounts of toxic products used are in themselves a factor in generalising hazards; the ever-increasing release of industrial wastes, either in the air or water, widen the area of possible contamination; previously limited to workers or near neighbours, this area can readily reach populations quite unaware of the existence of the polluting source.

Second, the two environments have both become increasingly complex due, in particular, to the proliferation of new products, and have had as yet poorly understood effects on man. The enormous problem posed by the extraordinarily rapid and general development of the chemistry of organic and organo-metallic compounds, the chemistry of metals and the petrochemical industry, and the hundreds of new products which every year find applications in industry and agriculture are used, in the great majority of cases, before their toxicity and their danger are known. The hazards are so great that it appears that for certain products, and by no means the least dangerous ones, their effects on health do not show up until after long periods of exposure — as with vinyl-chloride-caused cancers (approximately 20 years) or blue asbestos (15-20 years) — which make protective measures or product replacement all the more difficult.

A third observation, stemming from the first two, concerns the interpenetration of the working and living environments. On the one hand, the living environment of some represents the working environment of others in urban centres where the smallest action relies on the proper functioning of a number of activities or services performed by others: the traffic policeman in Tokyo, for example, is obliged to wear a respiratory mask because of the city's air pollution; the refuse collection employee or telephone repair serviceman working on lines in underground conduits are exposed to germ-caused injuries and infections. Thus the

---

[5] The International Labour Organisation adopted in 1973 a Convention (No. 138) and a Recommendation (No. 146) concerning Minimum Age. The Convention provides inter alia (Article 1) that each Member shall specify a minimum age for admission to employment which shall not be less than the age of completion of compulsory schooling and, in any case, shall not be less than 15 years. As an exception this age may be specified to be 14 years under certain conditions and as a first step, and (Article 7) national laws or regulations may also permit the employment or work of persons 13 to 15 years of age on light work, under the condition that this work is not likely to be harmful to their health or development and not such as to prejudice their attendance at school nor their participation in vocational orientation or training programmes.

products or the types of dangers can be the same at work and in the city both for the worker and the members of his family. The worker can bring home with him in his clothing, hair, etc., pathological agents to which he has been exposed at his place of employment (lead, silica, acids, various chemical products) or the bacteria of sickness contracted at work (tuberculosis). Certain products may be found simultaneously in the working and living environments: such is the case with lead, the amount of which in the atmosphere continues to increase and which presents particular dangers for children. Furthermore, each environment is said to be made up of various substances which join together; the results of this union themselves combine forces without it being known, in fact, just what these groupings are.

CONCLUSION

The working and living environments do not interact only momentarily. Work and human settlements are both marked by man's struggle against uncertainty, a struggle which, doubtless, from the moment when immediate needs such as hunger have been satisfied, explain the variety of conscious and unconscious behaviour of the private and working life. It has been observed that the possibility for acquiring a certain technical expertise, the characteristics of numerous repetitive tasks and the uselessness of the experience therein acquired to fill other similar jobs clearly are important factors in the disturbance of the worker. The need for security and progress are beyond a doubt deeply ingrained in the nature of man.

5
Education and Human Settlements*

This section which seeks to base itself equally on qualitative as much as on quantitative data reveals manifold contradictions in the field of habitat and education, the main ones being the disparity between MDR and LDR and the town-country gap and the man-woman gap. But the hoped for emergence of a twenty-first century global and universal civilization makes it indispensable that each country and its culture make a substantial and specific contribution to both architecture and urbanism and to the methods and objectives of education.

The causes of these deprivations in the sphere of human settlements and education lie in the international division of labour, the discrepancy between town and country and in the exploitation of the working classes. Specific educational practices can succeed only if these are first integrated in a more substantive sharing and dissemination, which also aspire to a new cultural, social and educational balance.

If one stops short with stereotyped thinking in regard to the cost of education or the arrangements for the urban and rural areas, then we will never find a solution to the MDR and the LDR gap. But if one has confidence in working populations, inasmuch as they are the bearers of cultural values, the innovators for a community and also responsible for their own educational experience, then the benefits and worth of educational systems will quite surpass the simple expectations of commonplace financial investments.

There exist several possibilities and options which, in the long run, will allow us to minimize the startling inequalities in the domain of housing and education. Among these are the acquisition of cultural autonomy, freedom from imitations of foreign models of consumption, the founding of a new global economic order, a new equilibrium between urban and rural and the upgrading of inherent endowments and cultural values.

In the MDR, the shortfalls of conception of pure economic growth and its re-assessment furnish us with a historic occasion to re-equilibrate the social system through the development of democratic life and the vigour of cultural forces. Thus, in their turn, the school and town variables dependent on production will accordingly be able to orient industrial society.

THE ASSESSMENT

A. World-Wide Trends in Housing and Education: Qualitative and Quantitative Aspects.

Contrary to the methodologies frequently used in reports of an international range, the study that follows is not circumscribed by quantitative comparisons and parallels.

Under the guise of highly scientific forms, estimates and decisions of significance are propagated through statistical usage, as a consequence of which the most advanced countries appear to be universal models. In the

*Abridged version of a background paper for Habitat contributed by the International Labour Office in Geneva. (Symbol A/Conf. 70/B/8; 26 February 1976.)

elucidation of world-level relationships between human settlements and education, qualitative criteria become as important as quantitative criteria.

Each of these separate cultures are creators of architectural forms and moulders of spatial solutions genuinely adapted to local environments. Besides this, the traditional elements of housing also include the active contribution of various populations as well as the framework of their lives (material location, artisanship, self-constructed buildings). Modern techniques and their fruition, which take into account the above functional elements, satisfy requirements and reduce costs. This has already been realized in Egypt under the direction of Hassan Fathy. Many similar projects are extant in other countries of the Third World. For example, there are the regional centres for research, for the improvement of techniques vis-à-vis materials at Baghdad, Kumasi, Teheran, Lomé and Roorkee.

In education as a whole, certain modes of knowledge and instruction, not as specialized or as standardized as in Western civilizations, also have a viability and congruence at certain local levels. An example of this is expertise in the field of agriculture. To deny such cultural resources because of a circumscribing matrix of superstition or to refuse to re-utilize supplementary modes of imparting knowledge only because they differ from the accepted methods entails a considerable wastage. Moreover, this wastage cannot be assessed or discerned through the mode of criteria which is based on the cultural system of more advanced countries. But this immediately becomes evident in the course of an investigation, both qualitative and quantitative, of the social subjects assessed.

Quantitative comparisons are essential to ascertain the phases and to hasten the awareness of the immense effort required to enable less-developed countries to achieve victory over misery and poverty.

Qualitative considerations upgrade spiritual richness, the ecological balance of man and his environment and the equilibrium of pre-industrial social relations, which contain such valuable educational contents that it is not merely a question of preserving these behind tourist show-windows or in ossified reactionary regimes.

Regarding this entity of human values, the interdependence of human commonalty and the flow of everyday life which contains the art of living, the advanced countries can profit from backward countries to solve their own post-industrial problems, such as those of self-alienation which stem from urban life and industrial nuisance.

In this manner, the search for a new equilibrium in the developed regions can nourish and maintain itself on cultures from all over the world. Similarly, the "take-off" of the less developed countries can draw sustenance from the experience of more advanced countries. These two complementary tasks could lead to much desired repercussions in the policies of housing and education.

The world-wide urbanization of whole populations, linked to industrialization, can currently proceed at a quick pace — that is, at a growth of 40 percent over a 10-year period, appertaining to towns with populations of over 20,000 inhabitants.

Singularly, in highly developed regions, it is possible to foresee the trend towards a complete urbanization by the end of this century.

The massive growth in school enrolment is also evident on the world level. The total of educational institutions, in 1970, received over 500 million enrolments (against 320 million in 1960), which consumed 16 percent of the global budgetary resources.[1]

At the primary level, the world's student population surpassed 254 million in 1960, and exceeded 351 million in 1970.

The goal of primary education for everyone in the LDR is a possible objective for 1985.

For secondary education the global figures for school enrolments grew from 66 million in 1960 to 130 million in 1970 and the rate of annual growth for enrolments is anticipated at approximately 3.2 percent until 1985.

Table 1 below gives the information classified, by continents, for the general evolution of secondary education.

For higher education there has been a considerable increase in the enrolment of students. It topped 11,600,000 in 1960 and 26,850,000 in 1970, which is an average annual world increase of 8.8 percent. Table 2 below gives the total figures and the rate of growth by continent.

Education is, in effect, one of the main indicators of the development of urbanization. A comparative

---

[1] Report for the UNESCO Commission on Education: "Three Billion Students." R. Faure. Editions UNESCO Fayard.

Table 1   Enrolment and Average Rate of Annual Growth of Primary and Secondary Education.

REGIONS	Year	Primary education		Secondary education	
		Enrol-ments	Average annual growth rates*	Enrol-ments	Average annual growth rates*
			%		%
WORLDWIDE	1960	254,649	–	66,111	–
	1965	310,266	4.0	101,323	8.9
	1970	351,425	2.5	130,011	5.1
	1985	468,902	1.9	209,330	3.2
MDR	1960	134,763	–	45,218	–
	1965	145,864	1.6	64,794	7.5
	1970	150,451	0.6	72,498	2.3
	1985	162,388	0.5	93,196	1.7
LDR	1960	119,886	–	20,893	–
	1965	164,402	6.5	36,529	11.9
	1970	200,974	4.1	57,513	9.5
	1985	306,514	2.9	116,134	4.8
AFRICA	1960	18,543	–	1,767	–
	1965	25,814	6.8	3,139	12.2
	1970	33,094	5.1	5,098	10.2
	1985	50,991	2.9	12,797	6.3
ASIA	1960	91,984	–	25,157	–
	1965	119,291	5.3	38,929	8.0
	1970	137,625	2.9	47,886	4.2
	1985	215,975	2.9	86,536	4.0
LATIN AMERICA	1960	26,517	–	4,038	–
	1965	34,403	5.3	6,725	10.7
	1970	43,546	4.8	10,709	9.8
	1985	64,435	2.6	24,919	5.8

*These percentages are for the average annual rates of growth for the three periods 1960-1965, 1965-1967 and 1970-1985.

study covering 36 countries, made in the 1960s by the United Nations, discloses a coefficient of correlation of $R = 0.70$ between the percentage of the urban population and the indices for schooling.[2]

Quantitative forecasts in education and in the field or urbanization are conditioned by the cultural contexts of different peoples and ethnic groups. These forecasts are further modified by every single change in the international economic and political *status quo*.

The statistical notion of disparity in the field of education between developed countries and the third world are, in this context, made doubly relative:

(a) Because advanced countries are not models meant for servile imitation: the determinative cultural contribution of illiterate countries intervenes and their spiritual quality can enrich humanity by its vocal and tangible skills, by its art and cosmogony, in the same measure as the intellectual prowess of a more literate civilization which has achieved modern technology; and

[2] Urbanization and Economic and Social Change in International Social Development, Review No. 1. United Nations, 1968, p. 27.

Table 2   Number of Students in Higher Education and the Rate of Growth.

REGIONS	NUMBER OF STUDENTS			MEDIUM RATE OF ANNUAL GROWTH		
	1960	1965	1970	1960-1970 %	1960-1965 %	1965-1970 %
WORLD-WIDE TOTAL	11,594,714	18,353,726	26,843,947	8.8	9.6	7.9
Africa	135,055	247,098	373,884	10.7	12.9	8.6
Latin America	569,151	914,078	1,614,790	11.0	9.9	12.1
North America	3,778,908	5,890,425	9,140,130	9.2	9.3	9.2
Asia	2,295,797	3,731,289	5,943,943	10.0	10.2	9.8
Europe	4,690,874	7,380,138	9,502,270	7.3	9.5	7.1
Oceania	124,929	190,698	268,930	8.0	8.8	7.1
MDR	9,399,190	14,677,813	20,778,381	8.3	9.3	7.2
LDR	2,195,524	3,675,913	6,065,566	10.7	10.9	10.6

Note: These figures do not take into account the following countries:

AFRICA: South Africa and Southern Rhodesia

ASIA: The People's Republic of China; The Democratic People's Republic of Korea; The Democratic Republic of Viet-Nam.

(b) Because the possibilities and options of development expand along with new vigorous relationships of economic and political power. The actions of countries who are exporters of basic raw materials fortell a redistribution of planetary resources such as will increase the capacity of third world countries to finance the endeavour required in the field of education.

B. Disparities in the Field of Education and Human Settlements

Official statistics with reference to the models of education in developed countries reveal that the qualitative and quantitative gap between the MDR and the LDR is in the process of widening. Official norms disclose that this gap is also evident in environment, sanitation and in over-population.

Lack or weakness of policies in the field of health, sanitation and housing have unfortunate consequences on the viability of economic investments in education. The percentage of children between the age of 5 and 14 (school-attendance age) is very high in the countries of the Third World. Similar percentages for the age group 25 to 45 years (individuals most valuable from the economic point of view) is, on the contrary, weaker than in MDR. That is to say the educational systems of the Third World prepare a certain percentage of children who do not participate, or else remain for a restricted period in the labour market. For example, in Japan in 1970, 16 percent of the population fell into the age group 5 to 14 years, while in Central America the percentage was 28 percent. In Japan, for the same year, 32 percent of the population was of the age group 25 to 45 years; in Latin America, for the same age group the proportion was only 21 percent.

It was foreseen, between 1970 and 1985, that the total number of children under 15 years of age would increase fo 450 million throughout the world and of these, 400 million would be in the LDR. The rate of population growth for the age group 5 to 24 years is 30 percent for a 10-year period for the LDR, in contrast to 10 percent in the MDR.

At the same time, between 1970 and 1985, it was foreseen that the increase in the active population would be 42 percent in Africa, 48 percent in Latin America, 34 percent in Asia and 16 percent in the rest of the world.

This means that Africa, Latin America and Asia are likely to be faced with a rapid increase in expenses for education, followed by the increased need for capital required to create new posts, together with other specific investments in the field of professional training.

Another relevant factor is the rate of school attendance after six years of schooling. In 1960, in the MDR, 93 percent of boys between 6 and 11 years continued with their schooling, and so the forecast is — 99 percent for 1980. For girls, the figures were 91 percent in 1960 and will be 99 percent in 1980. In the LDR, these figures attain only 62 percent for boys in 1960, with a decrease forecast for 1980. For girls, the figures were 52 percent in 1960, with a slight increase forecast for 1980.

The situation is even more unequal in the MDR in regard to the ratio of students who enter school and of those who remain until the end of the 12-year period, 1975-1987: 49 percent for boys and 39 percent for girls in the MDR. During the same period, the comparative figure is 11 percent for boys and 7 percent for girls in the LDR.

Moreover, one must not forget that there is already a most perceptible disparity in the field of education. In 1968, $132 billion ($380 per inhabitant) was invested in the MDR and $12 billion ($11 per inhabitant in the LDR. The widening of this disparity leads the education systems to increasingly more uneven levels.

One must not, however, assume that these disparities are confined to school systems. The educational structure outside the school system creates inequalities even more striking, simply because the principal investments of the LDR have been in the schools and in universities. As an example, let us take two countries, in 1971, which fall into the first and second categories. As regards libraries, a country in the first category with a population of approximately 10 million inhabitants had a network of around 9,000 which loaned 50 million documents. The second country, with a population of approximately 16 million inhabitants, had two with an annual loan of 9,400 documents.

In the field of education, there also exist striking disparities between town and country and between urban centres and the peripheries. The ratio of schooling to the retention of students in schools is higher in the towns than in the country and the exodus of youth and adults also indicates that the initial educational investments in the rural sphere finally end up for the profit of the urban centres. For the year 2000, one can forecast urban populations of 81 percent for the MDR and 43 percent for the LDR. As far as it appertains to the MDR, the construction of schools shows an increase in urban and semi-urban zones, even in rural zones where school enrolment for the 1960s has been extremely poor. Let us remember, on this point, that even if the reduction of rural population maintains a 5 to 10 percent rate between 1965 and 1985, it will not show any decrease in real terms.

The demographic analysis of populations shows that the town-country gap further increases between MDR and LDR and that rural populations will continue to be more significant in LDR.

With regard to this disparity between town and country in the field of education, particularly significant is the ratio that exists between those who enter primary school and those who complete a comprehensive course, in both town and country. For example, in Colombia, with an index at the national level of 17.3 percent, the figure for town is 27.3 percent and for country 3.7 percent. In Guatemala, with a national index of 25.4 percent, the figure for town is 49.6 percent and for country 3.5 percent.[3]

In relation to the educational establishments, children from an urban environment in Latin and Central America are able to complete the whole course at the primary level at the same school, at a proportion of 88 percent against 34 percent for the rural area because of inadequate scholastic facilities.

The marriage age, comparatively higher in towns, is also a factor that has to be taken into account because it bears a positive relation to the level of schooling.

The variable social class, in all socieites, plays a role in whatever concerns school establishments and the quality of housing. In the LDR semi-urban zones, social classes will show a narrowing because educational services are apt to develop in a more selective manner in centres than in the rural areas. Social demands are sharpened without the reciprocal development in the educational infrastructure. In the LDR, urbanization, particularly in the towns, is not accompanied by any increase in revenues such as would permit a significant investment in education. The percentage of children without schools (58 percent in 1965 and 30 percent in

[3] See *Statistical Measurement of Educational Wastage*, UNESCO.

1985, and which, in absolute numbers, will increase from 164 million in 1965 to 405 million in 1985) will be composed of peasant children, untrained labour and urban unemployed, in environments devoid of social, cultural and educational institutions.

Sex variables also play a role in schooling. If, in the MDR, this variant is not sufficiently important at the level of higher education, in the LDR, however, this factor unquestionably discriminates against women at every level.

C. Achieving Autonomy of Education and Culture and Consequences for Human Settlements

The tendency towards an independence of education and culture from its economic logic and bureaucratic pressures is, on the whole, strengthened in both rich and poor countries. During the 1960s the social agitations and contestations of university students and later those of secondary school students impinged upon a great number of developed societies: Japan, North America, Western and Eastern Europe. These aims and the distinctive national disputations of a new type of social struggle are less important than the deep-hidden currents which become evident from them. The mass of students and their percentage in the most developed countries became a new factor in the chronicles of humanity. Thus, in North America, since 1970, there are more than 400 students for every 10,000 inhabitants. (See table 3 below.)

Even more important is the enrolment of a significant portion of youth in higher educational institutions. For the class age-group 20-24 years, table 4 below shows that almost 20 percent of young Europeans and approximately 50 percent of young North Americans take up higher education.

To this quantitative phenomenon is added a qualitative realization which one also discerns in science and research of developed countries. Physicians, biologists and experts in social sciences are increasingly stepping in, in order to control the use which is made of their scientific research. Institutions in the education and science sector seek to affirm their own independent influence, because of their strength and struggle to emancipate themselves from both techno-structure and military complex.

Autonomy of education and culture has already had repercussions upon settlements. School and educational settlements are conceived in closer relation with the other human settlements. The campus, isolated and peripheral, no longer has its significance at a time when the educators and educated strive to play an appropriate role in political, social and economic life.

In the long run, educational institutions in the MDR are called upon to have a radical transmission, such as will justify an influence even upon the modalities or urbanization.

In the less developed regions, the aims of education are no longer the training of productive elements

Table 3   Number of Students Per 10,000 Inhabitants

REGIONS	1960	1965	1970
WORLD-WIDE TOTAL	55	73	97
Africa	7	9	12
Latin America	27	37	57
North America	190	275	402
Asia	27	34	48
Europe	73	109	135
Oceania	98	134	159
MDR	99	146	197
LDR	19	25	35

Table 4 · Student Enrolment in Relation to the Population: Age-Group 20-24 Years.

	1960			1965			1970		
	MF	M	F	MF	M	F	MF	M	F
WORLD-WIDE TOTAL	6.3	8.3	4.2	9.5	12.0	6.9	11.7	14.1	9.1
Africa	0.8	1.3	0.2	1.0	1.7	0.4	1.4	2.2	0.6
Latin America	3.2	4.5	1.9	4.5	6.0	2.9	6.7	8.6	4.8
North America	30.6	38.5	22.7	39.1	47.6	30.6	48.0	56.0	40.0
Asia	2.8	4.2	1.3	4.2	6.0	2.3	5.7	7.9	3.3
Europe	8.8	11.1	6.5	16.8	20.1	13.4	17.8	20.0	15.5
Oceania	15.1	21.5	8.2	18.6	26.1	10.8	18.6	25.1	11.8
MDR	12.5	16.1	8.9	21.2	26.1	16.2	24.5	28.6	20.2
LDR	2.0	3.0	1.0	3.0	4.2	1.7	4.2	5.7	2.5

M: Male enrolments in relation to the population of the same sex-age — 20-24 years.

F: Female enrolments in relation to the population of the same sex-age — 20-24 years.

ruled only by the criteria of short term productivity of initial investment. Other variables come into consideration, particularly the involvement in political, social and cultural life. The original experience of the Chinese Cultural Revolution should be regarded in this perspective.

Because of the increase in the absolute figures for rural populations in the statistical expectations for the year 2000, the reshaping of educational models of certain countries of the third world implies an upgrading of the intrinsic value of the rural areas, within the framework of a policy designed for a balanced management of land use. If the right to education for all humanity becomes the aim of educational systems, the rural areas will take first priority in educational assessments; one will have to ask peasants and labour to participate vigorously in the formation of educational systems, the objective of which is the strengthening of the participation of the masses, from a social, cultural and political viewpoint, in the making of society. The schools of rural China are seeking to identify themselves with local conditions and specific needs of the population with mobile schools erected on boats, travelling schools under tents and in the mountain regions, that are but a few examples of original approaches to achieve education of scattered populations far from urban centres.

Some important experiences of decentralized educational activities in the rural areas took place through voluntary activities in literacy in the interior of different countries: Cuba, Tanzania, Ethiopia, Senegal and others. The aim was and is to allow the participation of the whole population in the building of their society and the rupture of the differences in educational systems between town and country. The voluntary participation of school and university students working as educators surpassed the normal scope of expansion of the educational system linked to the increase in the GNP.

The enhancement of the educational role of workers with their technical skill and social and political awareness is also another approach which permits the establishment of new relations between town and country and among the social classes. The peasants and workers accordingly have the means to shape the educational, cultural and political life of their country. In this case, it is no longer the metropolis or the civil servants of a centralized bureaucracy that dominates and advocates the policies and function of education. The method of Freire and the educational "nuclearization" of Peru, the "Ujamaa" villages of Tanzania and those of the liberation movement in the ex-colonies of Portugal (Angola and Mozambique) are, from the cultural and educational standpoint, but examples of educational work based on an active participation of the peasants of these countries.

Under these conditions, the peasant population is concerned with the educational activities and inclined to participate in a direct and free manner to create the schools and to transform them into active centres of production and vice versa (educational evaluation of centres).

If one is struck with the stereotyped thinking about the cost of education, there will never be a solution regarding the disparity between the MDR and the LDR; but if one places confidence in populations inasmuch as they are bearers of culture and active members of a community accountable for their own educational experience, then the value and worth of educational systems will surpass the simple logic of financial investments.

CONDITIONS FOR ALTERNATIVES

A. The Necessity for Alternatives in the Global Reallocation of Resources to Achieve Reductions in Disparities in Housing and Education

These preliminary remarks permit us to observe that, at a global level there is an increasing disparity within the domain of education itself. The alternatives in the one pedagogical sphere do not appear to be a remedy to reduce this gap. The preliminary needs, in the first place, must forestall or permit the reinforcement of the economic, social and educational policies. Beginning with this reconstruction, one is able to foresee functional educational systems helping the development of these societies.

The dependence, to a large degree, of the economies of several countries and the social and international division of labour are the chief factors causing malfunctioning of these educational systems. That is, the rapid growth of services, the stagnation of a deformed industrialization and the lack of investments in agriculture merely help to strengthen such educational systems whose objectives are the duplication and the prolongation of a parasitic tertiary class.

If one compares the situation in 1975 with that existing at the beginning of the century, one is aware that the disparity between *per capita* incomes is still growing. This means that the international exchange has worked out to the profit of the MDR. The international division of labour accentuates and provokes inequalities in education. A striking thesis has been set out[4] which foresees the world divided into three kinds of countries: firstly, the countries with primary education, producing basic raw materials; secondly, countries which have attained a level of secondary education and can carry out production and processing of basic materials; lastly, at the highest level where everyone has both university degrees and work in industries constituted to undertake intensive research. The requirement in the quality of a labour force has turned into an element which strengthens division of labour.

In taking up and re-examining this international division of labour, the first aim is to reduce the town-country gap in those developing countries.

A more equitable income policy at this level is an indispensable condition to reduce disparities between the educational choice offered in towns and rural areas.

An integrated economic policy, centred upon the development of non-sectoral rural areas linked to the development of crafts and industry with strong emphasis on manpower, will become a necessary requisite for an independent start and for the autonomous growth of many societies. These economic claims and priorities allow a deeper integration and equality between the urban and rural populations and, moreover, give them means to escape from their precarious state of penury.

It is fitting to remember that the rural population, though diminishing in percentage (5 percent to 10 percent between 1965 and 1985), will still increase in total numbers. If one accepts the above integrated economic policy, then the peasants will be able to organize their own educational centres according to their practical needs, make room for a folk and rural culture and, in the educational programmes, upgrade the oral tradition so as to introduce into their systems of education such educators who will affirm this culture and whose competence is linked to the actual and living needs of the development of rural communities. Some African countries are already committed to this course of procedure.

Due to lack of finances within these communities and the need to invest capital in agriculture and basic industrialization, the demand is for less costly educational structure, so that the effects of production complement the meagre budgets: all this without, in any way, working at cross-purposes with these educational centres, which will remain at the disposal and service of the community for all possible requisite training.

[4]J. Galtune, C. Beck and J. Jaastad "*Educational Growth and Educational Disparity*," UNESCO, 1974.

A policy of transportation will allow the integration of the urban and the rural communities, so as to lead them out of their educational and cultural isolation.

In order to achieve a new global sharing and allocation of resources, the objective must not only be quantitative and the methods not just aimed at getting things to work and limited to the struggle against the economic preponderance, but it should equally be an educational and cultural affirmation in each country of the LDR, and this latter remains the basic requirement for the destruction of existent machinery of exploitation.

The causes responsible for the human settlement and education gap lie in the international division of labour, the friction between town and country and the exploitation of the working class. Any exacting measures undertaken in the domain of education will succeed only if these are assimilated into more comprehensive actions which also aim at new cultural, social and economic equilibrium.

Cultural dependence often indicates the acceptance of foreign models of development foisted on the dependent country. These models, over the decades, have appeared as the only practical ones but, in truth, they have yielded meagre results and, in the main, have served to worsen the dependence of the host country.

It is clear that the basic and preliminary condition for a new sharing of the world's resources lies in the capacity of each country to rediscover its very own model of development. This reappropriation makes it possible to surmount the problem of policy of aid, and also aims at preserving a policy of national and regional independence. That is, the enlargement, at the regional level, of the work for economic and political independence will also be an opportunity for a new sharing out of resources in most of the LDR.

The acquisition of cultural independence by the LDR can also create most important economic results: independence from foreign models of consumption, new equilibrium between town and country, development and autonomy of national leaders and opinion makers and the upgrading of natural and cultural work.

The denial of cultural freedom results in ill effects not only in the cultural domain. For example, take the consumption in the domain of human settlement and of education. This is a consumption which is in the process of increasing quantitatively in most countries of the world, but this increase often occurs in a restricted manner and consequently impairs the development of these societies. These imported and costly educational models are imposed upon many countries, and causes minority groups to consume an inadmissible portion of the GNP and national budget to satisfy their educational needs. This occurs sometimes in the management of the areas used for construction and sometimes for luxury school edifices propped up by policies of real estate speculation. It also weighs heavily upon the economy of several countries, diverting critically needed wealth for the use of urban minorities.

B. The Alternatives in the More Developed Regions (MDR)

Since the end of World War II, economic growth in the MDR has had a priority to which the school and town have had to adapt themselves. The policy of full employment of State assisted industrial investment and economic growth for the sake of growth, have been the unwritten rules of governments inspired by Keynesian thinking.

In the 1970s, the prospect of a prolonged economic crisis came as a challenge to the established model, coupled with the threat of inflation and unemployment. The concept of an important social and cultural qualitative development, in this instance, has appeared as an alternative to the quantitative growth of supplies and public services. The qualitative adaptation of the need for manpower alone allows readjustments by sectors and avoidance of stasis in opportunities for employment. That is, if the State succeeds in guaranteeing employment for all in the coming years, then the only function proper to towns and management of human settlements will be that of education and development.

Material and human resources exist in developed countries. A forceful effort can lead to a reorientation as States take cognizance of the urgent need to have another kind of civilization. At that time, democratization of the socio-political life and the opening up of educational and cultural opportunities will correct the obsessions of production-consumption and also the hypertrophy of economic life at the very heart of the MDR.

From the outset, the reversals of prospects show, for example, that Tokyo, with a prodigious economic rise in the 1950s and the 1960s was also confronted by a brutalizing urbanization of the habitat with a population of 14.9 million inhabitants for greater Tokyo. This has resulted in a total disequilibrium of industrial investment and its dependent sectors and of what the Japanese have named "social investment." Today, resources are channelled into housing, education and public services. This social investment corresponds to the qualitative alternatives demanded by the citizens of post-industrial societies.

On the other hand, the outlook of a total urbanization in the most developed regions is being increasingly admitted as a testimony to the description of the Oecumenopolis — the universal city — heralded by Doxiadis. This modern megalopolic complexity of overcrowding and congestion, of the multiplication of social problems and incidence of crime, is epitomized by New York.

What, in this over-all picture, is the alternative to the inordinate agglomeration of 20 million inhabitants for whom all the facilities available do not succeed in giving them even essential services, except at the cost of an enormous wastage?

In the field of education alone, restricted to the town not including its suburbs, official statistics indicate that 1,122,000 children and 70,000 teachers daily crowd into 900 schools that are run with the assistance of 43,000 municipal employees; 440,000 children go to private schools while 147,000 students and 9,000 professors/staff attend the 23 universities attached to the town. The blockage of an ungovernable school system has forced towns strongly to decentralize the administration and to depend, instead, upon local associations which possess both educational and administrative independence. There exist two ways in which this gigantism, the blockage as well as the slow-grinding wheels of bureaucracy, can be mastered: by means of reducing the density of the urban network and by democratizing social life up to the level of districts and municipal sections. The responsibility of the burden of education, and also of transportation and re-housing leads to radical restructuring of the towns by its inhabitants. Herein resides the chance to control unmanageable metropolitan cities. However, this way of participating and of decentralizating the hardcore of decision-making conjures up a financial obstacle: the indebtedness of towns. The following regional capitals of Western Europe in 1974 clearly illustrate this position:

Municipal indebtedness

Frankfurt . . . . 1,500 million DM
Genoa . . . . 50 billion lires
Grenoble . . . . 357 million francs
Manchester . . . . .420 million pounds/sterling

The debts and liabilities contracted end up by tying the hands of the organizers of these towns, vis-à-vis the State or private capital. The social tensions and the complexities which surround cultural and ethnic minorities are inherent problems of large towns. Often the decay of old and ancient localities works towards a concentration of the subproletariat or "lumpen" confined to ghettos, which worsens social segregation. The willingness — notably by busing — to reintroduce a mixture of national groups into the schools does not suffice, for it is necessary to work out a policy formulated for the rehousing of immigrants or of racial minorities, and devise a type of schooling for these children which hinges on dual cultural models.

In the fight against traditional or hereditary culture, these complexities partake of a broader cognitive awareness. For, even if the gross number of graduates from the working class increases steadily, there will still remain a considerable inequality facing schools. The developed socialist countries have managed to rectify this inequality, but even the example of the recent Polish reform of such systems demonstrates that this task requires a substantive and sustained effort. The aim and object of this equality of opportunities is not so much cultural as economic and social structural reform.

In order that this economic growth may proceed swiftly on to social and cultural development, it has become imperative to attain a profound change of relations between different groups and classes. But urban populations need to master the distinctive architectural outlook of the new human settlements.

The problem posed by the speeding-up of history and today's amazing techniques deployed for urban and rural development, can be mastered by education and by self-management, which should become the objective of all the inhabitants faced with a collective apprenticeship for the management of their new environments.

C. Alternatives in the Less Developed Regions (LDR)

The new international economic order is preliminary to alternatives in the LDR. But, it is also necessary to consider the nature of the cultural, technical and educational conditions. That is, the possibilities of the latter should also become a decisive element in the dynamism of the new international economic order.

The wealth and the cultural and educational potential of the LDR do not display quite the same features as are seen in the MDR. The opportunity for participation and the obstacles to this participation have conflicting characteristics, which are necessary to set out and specify.

The utilization of potential resources of the traditional environment in the LDR operates on two complementary levels:

(a) The traditional social structures can be re-employed as a means to popular participation;

(b) The architecture and the technology of traditional environments can also lend themselves to re-utilization in rural and semi-rural areas, i.e. as materials, local workmanship and suitably adapted forms.

In the suburbs of Dakar, five urban zones make up the quarter known as "Pikine." This includes the "Pikine ancien," the "extension," the "loti récent," the "cités" and "irrégulier" with a population of 200,000 inhabitants of whom many live in slums and insalubrious shanties. So it is clear that any influx of rural people to the suburbs of Dakar merely swells the percentage of idle labour. School equipment and facilities are almost non-existent. Some schools are scattered about the semi-urban complexes; there are from two to three Koranic schools in each quarter. The schemes for the renovation of the slums, particularly of Pikine "irrégulier," utilize the artisans and local talent for constructions by concentrating on the amelioration of health and sanitation and of collective facilities.

With regard to the European-type school, architects and urban experts involved admit that these schools merely turn out unemployed and migrants. So, without neglecting indispensable literacy, it demands that one accept the help of existent organizations and functional groups: on the one hand, of political organizations like the Union Progressiste Sénégalèse, on the other, of traditional organizations. Thus, local leaders, chosen by the people, the council of leading figures, the organizations for mutual help, the ethnic organizations (notably the Toucouleurs) or women's committees are capable of introducing a new dynamism into the projects of renovation, as well as the religious organizations, the Dahiras, the traditional meeting places (the "tours de thé") and the theatrical and recreational associations which participate in the transmission of education and in undertaking complete charge of the project for renovating Pikine.

Similar experiments can be observed in many countries of the Third World.

The alternative is actually to profit from the revolutionary and the creative potential of the people whose endowments and talents exceed the monetary and economic worth. There exists a cultural, social and technological skill which needs to be effectively exploited. In these communities, there often exist several levels of solidarity conducive to a collective and mutual apprenticeship.

The above alternative demands bringing education even closer to the needs of the communities and of their development. Buildings, public works, agriculture, health, are the pressing requirements of these family units and of their communities. Education should be capable of responding to these needs by transforming and adapting its contents, its structure and its methods.

The alternative proceeds by a strengthening of the systems of information and transmission. The upgrading of local languages plays a central role because an introduction of these into the educational experience makes it possible, from that moment, to avoid discrimination, the division and segregation of those social groups who have not mastered foreign languages.

A policy on the means of traditional and modern communications, congruent with the aims and scope of development, is also a solution to problems of social and geographic segregation; cultural dependence or independence is closely bound to the quantitative and qualitative choice of information and communication policies.

The project of the policy of "life-long education" becomes the melting pot for educational policies. The crisis of teaching in schools has its origin not only in its present inefficiency or in the rising cost of education, but equally in the shallow and restricted systems of education.

Thus, societies in a state of crisis or in the process of change and transformation, the people who are fighting for their independence, do not neglect their learning or their education, and the acquisition of knowledge is not circumscribed by time or circumstances.

An innovative role for leaders is a necessary condition for alternatives in the domain of education. These will need to draw their justification from the working class, they will have to be integrated into the masses and, furthermore, free themselves from the domination of foreign models.

One must also consider new relations between education and production. In traditional peasant life, these relations are always constricted because education is never conceived as something isolated; modern schooling advocates a clear, incisive break between work and education; in contrast to this, modern industry and the tertiary group have tried to re-introduce the harmony and balance between education and production, but through a narrow professional training which, in the LDR, promotes interest in only a segment of the population.

The solution is not to be found in this way, but in the creation of new and functional relations between production and training, above all in agriculture and also in the traditional sectors of the economy of these countries.

In Indonesia, an effort has been made to promote cottage and handicraft industry, in order to ameliorate the conditions of village life. Similar pilot experiments have been carried out in India, within the framework of the Bhoodan movement, where the aim is not to gain diplomas or even to acquire expertise parallel to Western techniques, but rather the knowledge and skill which are of practical use. In certain African countries, the co-operatives for both production and integrated vocational training lead pupils firstly to cultivate and commercialize their products and secondly to use their resources effectively to produce sports and cultural facilities.

ENLARGING THE CONCEPT OF EDUCATION

A. Human Settlements and Education Confronted with Changes in Ways of Living.

The policies for human settlements and for education, influenced by the changes in the ways of living, in their own turn reactivate the daily lives of the users. But this logic is dependent upon its specific position within the developed regions and the less developed regions. In the MDR, this means financing technology and administration for the housing of existing populations. But the inhabitants of large cities today seek collective facilities and the possibility of varied assurances for achieving numerous kinds of fulfilments within an aesthetic framework of life. The free movement to urban living with its rapid rate of increase has essentially become a problem of the quality of life in the human settlements. This concept covers a broad span of leisure, of interesting work as well as economic growth and technical change better mastered, therefore less brutalizing. The substantive development of education is considered to be attained in the MDR, and this, in the collective awareness of the advanced countries, represents one of the pillars of "gross national happiness," as evoked by Sicco Mansholt, to which urbanism and a distinctive architectural outlook should equally contribute.

In the LDR, the substandard facilities in housing and schools remain the fundamental issue. The change in the way of life takes place at the crucial junction of a traditionally well-balanced but conservative society and a new-born industrialization too often over-dependent upon foreign sources. The exigencies of a sustained rise in the standard of living in the less developed countries replace the aspiration of the MDR for a better quality of life. To maintain this *status quo*, the LDR require sizeable capital and investments in the LDR which, with rare examples (for example in Africa) have to face a demographic increase of 2.5 to 3 percent.

Part of the task of educating classes of huge numbers of young students is to anticipate both urban and rural employment and to solve the problems of slum towns and insalubrious settlements, if one wants to move out of the confines of a pre-industrial society which can stand to benefit from modern technology.

To circumscribe and seize these problems more fully, it is necessary to make certain definitions more precise: the concept of education and the concept of people held accountable for education.

Education, for a long time associated with the development of mental faculties, today takes on an enlarged meaning for the individual and the group. From a socio-psychological approach, education includes all activities which promote the fulfilment of individual and collective opportunities, as well as physical and manual skills along with sensitive, artistic and intellectual ability.

How should one class those responsible for education? The essential criterion is that of the chief function of these educators:

(a) Whether the educational function is the chief one: for example the school.

(b) Whether the educational function is a secondary one: in the factory, the phases of vocational training are secondary in respect to the needs of production.

Another important criterion in the study of the relationship of educational and human settlements is that of the local placement of educators:

(a) Whether the work of these educators is localized: one speaks of an establishment with an educational function (this is the case of the schools or of the factories mentioned above).

(b) Whether the work of these educators is diffused and their spatial placement is not a determining factor. One speaks of an institution with an educational function: this is the case of the family or various and different social movements.

By combining the two criteria, functional and spatial, this study employs a fourfold classification of educational structures:

Local placement	Educative function	
	Primary	Secondary
Determinant	Type 1	Type 2
Non-determinant	Type 3	Type 4

Classification of Educational Structures

Type 1: Institutions exclusively educational

Usually, these institutions are schools (primary and secondary schools and university) or out-of-school education (for example: family planning centres). These are usually public institutions. The choice of their setting is thus manageable and, to this extent, it can influence the pace and operating conditions of urbanization, especially on the measures that make operative that paradigm centralization-decentralization.

Type 2: Institutions designed for secondary education

The work of these institutions has an impact on every sector of social life: economic, political and even health. But what is important is that they can offer a portion of their material and human resources according to the circumstances, to the process of being educated. Thus, a hospital annexed to a faculty of medicine will create a new university-hospital which will work to diversify its functions so as to assure the training of future physicians.

Types 3 and 4: Social structures and movements

In order to present these hypotheses, types 3 and 4 are herewith regrouped in social structures and movements with an educational function. That is, whether the educational impact is, or is not, their chief purpose, the family, associations, unions or, even more, mass communications, all institutions of this kind have common ground: their localization in human settlements is not a determining factor in their activity; however, they are able considerably to influence changes in ways of living. Because they can transmit and modify ideals and values, these structures and social movements modify the socialization of the individuals according to the distinctive conditions of the MDR and LDR.

An analysis of the propensity of these educational systems permits us to note the contradictions, on the one hand, between the change in the ways of life and the new prospects of education (learning), and on the other, the rigidity of educational systems. In particular, the analysis of the tendency in the nursery and the primary level makes evident the amplification of the concept of education a necessary alternative.

The extension of nursery education and a new role in this field for the departments of national education show, in several countries, the transformation of the family system and the role of women who refuse to play only a family role and who participate more in community life. Urbanization and industrialization are the other factors in the promotion of a generalized nursery educational system whose development encounters resistance among those who want to preserve the traditional role of the family and the financial constraints in the poorest communities. But the tendency towards the extension and the integration of the nursery sector into the education system is common to many countries, and statistics attest to a definite progress in the pre-primary domain.

At the same time, traditional primary schools, especially in low-income countries, have become a source of unemployment which hits increasingly harder those who have finished the primary phase than illiterates or those who have not finished their primary education. Consequently, the need to re-examine the contents and the working methods of primary schools, whose purely preparatory nature for studies of secondary teaching does not correspond to the needs of the development of several societies. This development has its initial stages in the transformation of a primary school into an educational centre whereby the whole population can share educational activities and where the educators respond to the needs of training, as expressed by the communities, on work, housing, health, transport, leisure and artistic life.

The aim of many educational systems is to reformulate their concepts on basic education. This has already been the object of experiments in several countries. The overcoming of the contradictions between town and country, between intellectual and manual work, between peasants, labourers (factory workers) and civil servants is facilitated by a different concept of initial education.

Regarding the introduction of the peasant/worker culture into educational activities, it is essential to integrate learning carried out in educational institutions into the understanding of everyday life (for example: practical education in Gabon). But these educational institutions do not seem equipped to keep alive the oral tradition of these cultures, their scientific acquirements nor the wealth of their profound experience of life.

Basic education must extend beyond the limits of primary schools in order to become an education to which everybody has access: infants, youth and adults. Futhermore this basic education cannot be considered as anything but the first stage of a global project for lifelong education. Communities, parents, workers and migrant workers all need educational programmes which go further than mere basic initial training.

The international social division of labour is deepened by a basic education which is not designed to give an equitable response to the needs of all those which could profit from it: from the outset, among the educational systems, there are privileged students who have the opportunity to continue an uninterrupted schooling within the educational system.

The educational policy in the LDR was aligned towards universal education at the primary level and, generally, one can state that both school and university systems have been privileged. Minimal investments have been reserved for non-formal education which is better placed to respond to the specific developmental needs of every country. Moreover, investments in secondary and university education have been confined to towns causing an exodus to the towns by people who would not, otherwise, have left the rural areas in such massive numbers; this could have been avoided if adequate social and educational facilities had been foreseen for the rural areas.

The orientation towards universal schooling has not yielded the results anticipated. Several countries have invested 4 percent of the GNP and 18 to 20 percent of national budgets in education (see Table V). In the LDR, on an average, not more than half the adult and infant population profits from education.

In the LDR, the forecasts of the 1960s for the rates of schooling to be achieved in 1970 have not been realized. Take, for example, the case of Africa: the Addis Ababa plan anticipated a growth rate of 15 percent for the secondary level, and 71 percent for the primary level, but the rate achieved was in fact 6.34 percent and 46.16 percent, respectively.

In the case of the Addis Ababa plan for Africa and the Karachi plan for Asia, the demographic underestimate has been a decisive factor, but it is necessary to take into account the poor performance of the educational systems and the increase in the disparities within the same regions; that is, the decentralization of the educational systems has not taken place in Africa, Latin America, not even in Asia, and the internal disparities of these regions have increased.

B. Educational Institutions and Human Settlements (MDR)

In post-industrial countries, the growing needs for more comprehensive economic aspirations have been the target of many tentative approaches; 24 social and basic necessities assuring the well-being of the populations have been regrouped by OECD under eight headings: health; development of personality by acquisition of knowledge; quality of everyday life; leisure; welfare and available services; ecological environ-

Table 5   Investment and Recurrent Cost of Education

	Total expenditure in percentage of the G.N.P.		Percentage of the total government expenditure		Recurrent costs in percentage of total recurring costs		Investment in percentage of the total investments incurred	
	1966	1971	1966	1971	1966	1971	1966	1971
Afghanistan	–	–	–	12.3	–	15.6	–	–
Burma	–	3.2	–	18.5	–	18.8	–	7.5
Costa Rica	–	5.2	–	28.8	–	–	–	–
Dominican Republic	2.7	2.7	14.5	14.4	18.1	20.0	1.8	6.1
El Salvador	–	3.6	–	25.5	–	28.5	–	23.8
Greece	–	2.6	–	9.8	–	–	–	–
Guatemala	–	1.8	–	14.5	–	18.0	–	5.1
Indonesia	–	2.1	–	18.8	–	18.8	–	5.1
Korea	4.2	5.4	17.9	18.2	–	–	–	–
Mali	–	3.7	–	25.7	–	25.6	–	5.8
Nicaragua	–	2.2	–	20.0	–	–	–	–
Pakistan	–	1.8	–	7.1	–	–	–	5.9
Phillippines	3.0	2.1	28.3	17.7	–	–	–	4.6

ment; security; and participation in cultural life. The social indicators of quality of life, in the first place, concern architecture and urbanism responsible for housing and those cultural, educational structures responsible for education.

There is a fundamental need for innovation. It is remarkable to verify that creativity manifests itself first in institutions of types 3 and 4.

The phases of diffusion of the innovations produce a delay in the time required for transmission and, in principle, it works according to the following pattern:

$$\text{Types 3 and 4} \longrightarrow \text{Type 2} \longrightarrow \text{Type 1}$$

Innovation in the Educational and Cultural Sectors

It is clear that the educational innovations and initiatives take place first in institutions responsible for the socialization of all age groups, and that this encourages the traditional schools to reform pedagogy, or simply school architecture; here we have a phenomenon which proves that, in the urban and educational society, the transmission of knowledge affects all aspects of urban life and that its boundaries coincide with the main social practices. The important concept in the actual structural plans of polyvalent areas is useful for describing the multiple ways of using the urban centre. Educational facilities are integrated into the main local and regional facilities.

The concept of polyvalent space is exemplified in the house of glass in Dronten, Holland. The architecture possessing such transparency in this vast central space is also the hub of local activity. Every day, this area is the setting for the people's market, a sports-ground for children, a theatre and a conference hall for adults. This innovative use of space, now such a rarity, in response to need, also contributes to saving funds. During the two-and-a-half days when the school is empty, the premises can be put at the disposal of the community, provided that an effective control over the facilities can be exercised.

Apart from this, the hierarchy of urban centres, according to the scope of their influence, enables one to establish the requisite criteria valuable to the hierarchy concerned with educational facilities. The primary centre is for university and research use (between 200,000 and one million inhabitants).

In the secondary centre, there are secondary (high) schools and colleges for vocational education (between 20,000 and 100,000 inhabitants). At the level of the tertiary central ring, families avail themselves of the primary and pre-primary facilities. The boundaries which define these levels of "centrality" vary from one country to the other, but it is important to note, at the same time, that the idea of the "Russian dolls" by interlocking and dovetailing, also applies to the urban and educational plan. This same observation, applied to developed regions, reveals that, in the field or urbanism, the structure and the elements of urban centres again reflect the new impact of education. Education and culture work by a fusion of contemporary urban forms while they diffuse only the information in industrial towns. In this manner, one of the main new French towns, Lille-Est, conditioned to absorb 10 percent of the demographic growth of the regions in the North, i.e. a target of 100,000 inhabitants in 1985, is, today, already polarized by the university and the higher tertiary class. Here, the educational facilities have been envisaged in order to create the structure of the urban centres and human populations.

The growth of personality and leisure and the increase in opportunities for education require innovative concepts in the framework of the post-industrial megapolis. The dissemination of education establishments throughout the urban complex is only one aspect of the problem. It is imperative to reduce the density of populations, for example, by integrating them into the green belts. It was quite fitting that the Green Belt Act was initiated in London, capital of the country which started industrialization, and this collective willingness to solve the contradiction of town-country also made London the first great city to preserve rural zones in the perimeters of the great urbanization. This concept of the green belt is also to be found in Moscow, in Ottawa (the Greber Plan in 1950 with 50,000 acres of territory in the south of the city) in the Polish towns and in Western Europe. The green belts penetrating right into the heart of the towns are natural zones of equilibrium functioning as "lungs" of the great metropolis. This applies on every occasion to areas almost wholly managed by agriculturists but on which the managers impose facilities for rest and recreation. The example furnished by Ranstadt is interesting, because Holland has the world's highest population density. This ring of urbanization functions as an inter-meshing of 70 towns (like Amsterdam, Rotterdam and The Hague) with a green centre at Ranstadt. The large areas of forests and parks, natural and protected, make possible a visual assuagement and psychological solace for the residents of high-density metropolitan zones.

In England and Wales, 17 percent of the territory has been made into parks or zones of exceptional natural beauty. The policy of national parks in all heavily industrialized towns irrevocably includes the conservation of land. Faced with the challenge of excessive concentration of populations, scarcity of space and hyper-organization, it is necessary for the inhabitants of the more developed regions to think up a new way of life and somehow learn a creative adaptation to their new environment.

C. Educational Institutions and Human Settlements (LDR)

Substandard educational facilities and scarcity of housing are one of the aspects of poverty in the countries of the third world faced with pressing and even hopeless deadlines, if there is delay in the establishment of a new world economic order.

Growth and rise in living standards are basic priorities. But the road to development has not been defined by all industrial countries of the western hemisphere. There does not exist any immutable way or fixed scale which can lead an agrarian society to a post-industrial level. Many diversified experiences have been established and from this it is necessary to learn specific ways and means for every individual nation.

The countries of the Third World have inherited, from the colonial period, an education system based upon Western models leading to wastage of resources. In the same way, the dependent urbanization in Africa, Latin America and South East Asia favours large towns and ports linked to world-wide trade.

The influx of uprooted rural populations to the slum towns, which encircle the metropolis, further worsens social disparities. In theory, the regulation of the movement of migrant workers pre-supposes a decentralization of activities, where the rural management and village schools play a decisive role.

The developed countries have experienced two contradictory phases: an excessive urbanization followed by reduction of population density in towns so that the citizens could better be situated in the complexes of human settlements. These two phases have exacted a heavy price regarding damage to ecological environment and in the aggravation of social frictions. The question arises whether or not it is possible for some of the Third World countries to industrialize and, at the same time, achieve a town-country equilibrium.

Since the beginning of their socio-economic take-off, the Chinese model of de-urbanization advocates the industrialization of the countryside by means of small scale units of production.

Some precise experiences have been undertaken throughout the Third World, but without the planned and systematic character of the "great leap forward" of 1958. In China, industrialization was first carried out in coastal urban centres, thereby reinforcing inequalities between the littoral regions and the interior of the country. The total number of towns with populations of over a million inhabitants grew from 9 to 17 during this period, showing a rapid growth of urban population which is demographically estimated at the minimum rate of 7.6 percent/year for the period 1949 to 1960.

The reversal of tendencies of the 1960s was not merely a quantitative de-urbanization. The creation of popular communes and the diversification of rural areas, especially for education, has for the last 15 years induced a massive return of populations to the country. However, the total figures of density of towns remains considerable. The lesson we can extract is that the creation of an original model has allowed fundamental transformations in the reorientation of management and activities: those of the economic sector, of political mobilization and also education — beginning with country and rural populations.

The Chinese de-urbanization does not possess a more universal applicability than the western models: however, it does illustrate the scope of using specific national ways and means.

The enrolment of children in primary schools, without taking into account their separation from the family environment, introduces both wastage and excessive prolongation of the school attendance (repetition of grades). The first consequence of this is that these schools turn out students who are socially maladjusted, uprooted from their own environment and faced with the impossibility of finding employment in the urban sector. In some cases, as in Morocco, families have been spontaneously active in controlling this form of wastage: the family will not invest in education for more than one child per family.

Another problem particular to the LDR is that of remanagement of the suburbs and urban and semi-urban slums. This is the case in Caracas (3 million inhabitants of which over one third live in "ranchos" or shanty towns). The Government is disposed to limit these by its policy of buffer zones of self-made facilities and by transit camps. But one can nevertheless see that the number of these "ranchos" will have doubled between 1961 to 1990, the date by which they will occupy approximately 15,000 acres in the metropolis of Caracas.

The basic problem is to re-think and reformulate educational systems and their contents, in terms of autonomous development, free from the traditional models of the highest developed countries. The overcoming of the town-country contradictions implies a popular experience, decentralized, unique and, thus, differentiated from the parallel experiences of advanced countries. The progressive upgrading and enhancement of informal education, which is the new element in several countries, requires land use and education policies which also allow the upgrading of the structures of Types 2, 3 and 4 and the development of fresh relations between the above and Type 1. With such a prospective outlook human settlements and the attendant problems can develop into a major theme of research and social and educational action.

6
Weather, Climate and Human Settlements*

H.E. Landsberg

Shelter against atmospheric vagaries, next to clothing, is one of the oldest technological inventions of mankind. No part of the world is safe from adverse or even dangerous weather events. The list is long and the threats to millions of people and their dwellings compelling. In modern times floods, hurricanes (typhoons, cyclones), tornadoes, severe thunderstorms and lightning, and blizzards are no longer considered inevitable acts of an angry deity but calculable and predictable risks that can and must be incorporated into planning for housing and settlements. One of the functions of the world's weather services is the issuance of timely warnings against the weather hazards and to advise on safety measures to be taken for appropriate building and housing construction.

But the protection of life and limb, while foremost in the tasks of meterological services, is not the only way in which they can help in the planning of settlements. Weather and climate are all-pervasive. They control comfort of people as well as efficiency of workers. Housing needs to be designed to optimize health and comfort conditions indoors. Urban areas exercise their own effects on the atmosphere, some of them quite undesirable. These have to be taken into account in planning new towns and in revamping old cities. Energy needs for heating and cooling are directly governed by the atmospheric environment which, in turn, may eventually furnish a substantial proportion of the energy needed through use of solar radiation and wind power.

WEATHER DISASTERS

Hurricanes, Typhoons, Cyclones

Of all weather hazards tropical storms, which bear the different names indicated in the heading in various parts of the world, are the most destructive. They principally affect the coast lines of East Asia, Australia, Central and Eastern North America and many islands in tropical and subtropical waters. The toll of deaths, unfortunately, is still high and averages annually in the thousands. In recent memory four examples stand out.

In November 1970 a Bay of Bengal cyclone struck the coastal area of Bangladesh (then East Pakistan) and swept an estimated quarter million people to their death. In June 1972 hurricane "Agnes" moved from Yucatan to the heart of Pennsylvania, accompanied by torrential rains. The death toll was 129 and 120,000 had to flee their homes. Damages were about 3 1/2 billion dollars. In September 1974 hurricane "Fifi" struck at Honduras with a 50 cm rainfall causing floods that killed about 5,000 persons. At the end of 1974 a devastating tropical cyclone drove nearly half of the population of Darwin, Australia, from the town.

*Abridged version of a background paper for Habitat by the World Meterological Organization. (Symbol A/Conf. 70/B/1; 23 September 1975.)

116

Over historical times the list of such disasters is long; in earlier decades they were aggravated by inadequate, or complete lack of, warning.

The portions of the world that are particularly threatened, with the probability of tropical storms striking near land areas, include some of the most densely populated shore lines on earth. The annual occurrences are extremely variable — for example, in the last 45 years in the North Atlantic tropical storm frequency has varied between 3 and 21 per year. Equally variable are the tracks followed by the storms. For planning, it is exceedingly essential to note that some coastal areas within the reach of tropical storms are not visited by even one of these unwelcome visitors in years or even decades. This often leads to complacency about the danger, and land is developed with inadequate safeguards. An historical example is the settlement of shore areas in New England. A devastating hurricane of 1815 was just a dim memory when the area was disastrously struck in 1938. Some lessons were learned but inadequately, because in 1954 again much damage was inflicted in the same region by another furious attack, even though loss of life was less because of better warnings.

Primary and secondary effects of tropical storms vie with each other in causing damages. The primary onslaught is by the high winds near the center of the tropical storm. In a full-fledged hurricane these exceed, by definition, 34 meters per second (120 km per hour). Peak gusts often exceed 67 meters second (240 km per hour). Roofs and windows cannot withstand these wind pressures, unless protected and anchored. Insufficiently stressed structures, such as broadcast towers, frequently collapse in such wild gales. The other primary effect of tropical storms are torrential rains. Storm totals of 5 to 20 cm of rain in one to three days are not uncommon and the almost unimaginable extremes were shown.

The rains have several consequences. They lead to landslides, with often disastrous results. They also cause flash floods that inundate farm land, wash away houses and bridges, and disrupt communications and traffic. Further, the rains percolating into the soil weaken the rooting systems of trees, so that the high winds can easily topple them. Shallow-rooted trees are usually the first victims of tropical storms. The clouds that accompany the fringes of severe tropical storms not infrequently spawn tornadoes that cause havoc in their own way.

However, the most menacing hurricane-created side effects are the storm surges, often erroneously called storm "tides." These are created by the waves driven up the beaches from deep to shallow water along the shore. The high winds cause swells and waves in the deeper water. As these run up the shores they become formidable walls of water. They can breach dikes and chains of dunes. They smash most human structures in their path, beach even large vessels, and inundate the low-lying lands near the shore, often for several kilometers inland. Unless people are evacuated from the endangered spots, mass drowning are the outcome. For planning purposes, estimates where such storm surges may strike can guide land use and minimize later damages. At least 500 million people are presently exposed to occasional strikes by damaging tropical storms.

Severe Local Storms

While tropical storms ordinarily have damaging diameters of 50 to 200 kilometers, severe local storms rarely exceed 5 kilometers and usually are only 1 kilometer or less in their effective diameter. Most of the local storms originate from convective activity which causes tall clouds which can grow to heights of 20 kilometers. These tall clouds are the sources of thunderstorms and tornadoes. Not all parts of the world are equally afflicted by thunderstorms. Some areas, e.g., the west coast of South America, are completely free from this weather phenomenon, while in some parts of Indonesia they are a nearly daily occurrence. All thunderstorms have electrical manifestations. Cloud-to-ground lightning is the principal effect. It is in itself a minor killer (for example, in the United States of America 200 persons lose their lives annually by lightning). Lightning is a major cause of forest fires and occasional house fires, which need not occur because adequate protective devices exist. Damage to electric transmission lines is probably the most notable effect of lightning. Many modern communities place their electric distribution system underground but lines from power plants overland are still generally carried overhead. Estimates of lightning frequency observed nocturnally from satellites showed over land about 7,000 strokes per night. Daytime lightning is likely to be several times this number.

Many of the tall, thunderstorm-spawning clouds are also the seat of hail formation. In areas where thunderstorms are infrequent hail, if it accompanies a thunderstorm, is usually small in size and, although it may be damaging to crops rarely affects structures. But there are a number of areas which are severely affected by hail (certain parts of W. Africa, India, Central U.S., Southern Soviet Union) where hailstones maximally reach 2.5 to 5 cm diameter once a year, and once per decade grow into projectiles of 7.5 cm diameter that pelt down. Obviously such large stones will ruin glass structures, such as green houses, damage roofs and vehicles, and severely affect livestock.

But the most devastating of all storms, the tornadoes, are also given birth by the mammoth thunderclouds. It has been estimated that for the whole earth they reach about a 1,000 in number during the year. Most of them pack winds in excess of 50 meters per second (180 km per hour). In the most destructive it has been estimated, though never measured, that winds of 150 m/sec (540 km/hr) caused the devastation. By and large, tornadoes have short tracks, commonly not exceeding 16 to 50 km in length; but a few have travelled as much as 500 km. Such long distances are more apt to be covered by families of tornadoes, associated with the same storm system.

A collection of tornado reports is not entirely adequate but a chart covering four years of observations shows location of tornadoes in the 1963-1966 period, after Fujita. From this distribution and the damages caused one can estimate an expected maximal wind speed from these storms in various parts of the world. Again, the information is likely to be inadequate in some regions. Yet it shows two features: certain coastal areas in East Asia and Eastern North America show effects of tornadoes associated with tropical storms; these have already been alluded to. However, the interior areas of North America, Western and Central Europe, Southern and East Central Australia, and other smaller sectors have notable tornadoes. Some densely populated areas are again affected. Hundreds of lives are lost per year, thousands are injured, and property losses run into hundreds of millions of dollars annually.

Much is known about structural damages caused by tornadoes. In structures built from reinforced concrete even tornadic winds cause only minor damage, mostly broken windows. Steel frame buildings suffer damage to windows, roofs, and siding but do not collapse. Masonry building usually suffer major damage. Their bricks or blocks are loosened and transformed into formidable missiles. Wood frame buildings often collapse, lose their roofs and are lifted off their foundations.

Major Floods

Floods are rather ubiquitous. They affect all stream and river courses. In spite of attempts at regulation through reservoirs, dams, and flood walls exceptionally large amounts of runoff cannot be completely contained and still cause floods. In such exceptional events coincident dam breaks can occasionally vitiate all efforts of man to protect his life and works.

In the areas afflicted by tropical storms, floods usually occur as a consequence of the torrential rains accompanying these storms. Not infrequently two or even three of these storms follow a similar track in short succession and unload terrific amounts of rain on the same area. There are records of such events in the Philippines, Japan, China, Bangladesh, the Eastern United States.

Similarly, repetitive heavy rains, sometimes for days and even weeks on end, are noted in some years in regions affected by summer monsoons. The classical area for such conditions are in Southeast Asia and India. In the latter country these conditions start far upstream where the high mountain chains force the monsoonal air currents to ascend and dump their water contents.

Floods prevalent in temperate and high latitudes are also seasonal. These occur mostly in spring at the time of snow melt. They can generally be anticipated and estimated in magnitude from the accumulated snow cover. However, in some years heavy falls of warm rains, with a deep melting snow cover on frozen ground, can lead to such intense and rapid surface runoff that extraordinary flood crests develop in the river systems. These may overwhelm protective works and often lead to severe flooding and major damages. Historically river basins have been the site of agricultural development, because of fertile soils, and of major settlements, because of the ease of transportation and communication. Many of the largest cities in the world are riparian. In these settlements river flood plains have been more and more used for domiciles and industrial development. This may go along for decades without serious problems but then some evil week nature's vengeance may wipe out much of such development. Settlement of flood plains on streams and rivers can, for new developments, only be strongly discouraged. The existence of flood plains is the best evidence, even in the absence of long meteorological records, of possible major flood events.

In mountainous areas flash floods on smaller streams are a common occurrence. They develop not only response to snow melt but as a consequence of almost any intense rainfall, such as experienced from a deteriorating tropical storm, a stalled frontal system or occlusion, or a thunderstorm-induced cloudburst. In contrast to the usually timely and accurate flood predictions by hydrometeorological services for major river valleys, flash flood forecasts for such isolated mountain streams are often not available. Small settlements may thus become cut-off and inundated without warning. Recreational summer camps have suffered severe consequences. An aggravating condition in some areas is denudation of slopes by indiscriminate lumbering or by forest fires. Increased rapid runoff is usually one of the first consequences of such events.

Effects of Urbanization on Flash Floods

Urbanized areas are a special case of altering the flood-protective devices provided by nature. Soil and vegetation are natural sponges for intercepting precipitation. Actively growing vegetation will, in fact, reevaporate a major portion of the fallen water back into the atmosphere. The remainder seeps slowly through litter and humus into the deeper soil layers. Some of it is incorporated into the ground water and only a relatively small fraction runs into the river. The lag built into this system, except for the case of frozen soil, is considerable. It retards the surface and underground runoff by days or even weeks.

In urbanized areas the situation is radically changed. Vegetation is stripped off and soils are compacted. Most of the natural surface is replaced by a new surface of roofs, asphalt, stone, and concrete. These materials are deliberately non-absorptive and impermeable. They are designed to drain rain off as promptly as possible. Storm drains and drainage ditches direct the water from major rainstorms on the shortest route to the nearest river. In many urban areas more than 50 percent of the surface is impermeable and often storm drain systems are inadequate to hold the runoff from cloudbursts. This makes streets, drainage ditches and tributary stream channels carry churning freshets that inundate low-lying areas and flood basements.

Improved planning of urban areas can greatly reduce such incidents. Vegetated areas, such as parks, trees, flowerbeds, judiciously spread through a town and more adequate design of storm drainage systems should be planned for.

Weather Warnings

Loss of life and injuries from weather hazards have been greatly reduced in recent years by timely warnings. These warnings have become possible by a common, international system, the World Weather Watch. Over a century of cooperation between the National Weather Services has led to this admirable development. First through the International Meteorological Organization and now through the World Meteorological Organization systems of weather observations and weather communications have been planned and implemented under a unified scheme.

Data collected on land and sea and from the upper air are communicated through a single world code into world weather centrals which are interconnected and, in turn, disseminate worldwide information to regional and national centers for preparation of forecasts and dissemination of warnings. To these centers flow weather messages from thousands of observing stations. The World Weather Centrals: Melbourne, Moscow, and Washington, not only collect and disseminate basic data but also produce generalized numerical projects of atmospheric flow patterns, produced by high-speed digital computers. These projections give guidance to the local forecasters for the preparation of their local predictions, which can pinpoint any dangerous developments more precisely in time and space.

Weather forecasters everywhere have been immensely strengthened by powerful observational tools that permit recognition of severe storms and storm systems. Among these devices are weather satellites and weather radar. The weather satellites are now so perfected that after only a few years of experience (since 1960) no major storm, even if spawned in the vast empty areas of the oceans can escape attention. They permit continuous tracking and issuance of early advisories when these storms seem to be headed for coast lines. These weather satellites, whether geostationary or orbiting, can yield what their scanning cameras see to surface receivers in any place on earth. The wide-spread distribution of such receivers over the globe indicates not only the perceived need for this information but the far-flung potential for protection of life from this network.

For detailed local warnings against hurricanes, tornadoes and other severe storms serve pickets of weather radar installations. These can begin to track the adverse atmospheric manifestations within a radius of about 300 km and plot their course. Usually eyes of hurricanes and spiral rain bands are clearly marked so that there is no doubt of position and course. Severe thunderstorms and squall lines can be readily traced and tornado formation is often indicated by a characteristic hook echo on the radar scopes. Although the short range of radar does not permit projections and forecasts for more than a few hours it can help in issuing warnings of immediately imminent dangers.

The foregoing clearly indicates that the weather services are capable of coping with the problems of forecasting damaging storms and are potentially able to protect new and old settlements from weather surprises. Yet in many areas of the world, especially the developing regions, means for timely and quick dissemination of the warnings are inadequate, protective shelters are lacking, and procedures for evacuation of people insufficient. There is much yet to be implemented in this connection.

CLIMATE AND ENERGY USE

Heating Needs

Although mankind originated in the tropics, the invention of clothing, fire, and shelter enabled gradual poleward expansion of settlement. Discovery of the change of energy of coal, natural gas, and petroleum to heat, either directly or via conversion to electricity, has made the heating of homes and buildings a reliable technology. It has essentially permitted the settlement of the whole globe. Only the availability of energy derived from fossil fuels at reasonable prices has made this possible. Settlements in cold regions can only be maintained where such fuels are available for heating. As they become exhausted or too expensive, substitute sources of heat have to be found. In some areas geothermal heat can be exploited. Atomic energy — with some as yet not fully assessed risks — can also serve. But many eyes are now focussed on the inexhaustible and non-polluting atmospheric sources. These will be separately dealt with below.

Space heating is a necessity where average daily temperatures fall for appreciable periods of time below 18°C. The heating, and consequently fuel, requirements are a linear function of accumulated values of mean daily temperatures below 18°C. This gives the heating degree value. Although other weather elements besides temperature also exercise an influence on heating needs, such as solar radiation, cloud cover, and wind they cancel each other over any appreciable interval of time, say, a month.

Although there are considerable swings from year to year, the variability, as indicated by the standard deviation of a series of observed annual values, is least in the coldest areas and greatest in the marginal zones along the regions where heating is needed only for short periods in winter. In a developed industrial nation (U.S.A.) the annual needs for domestic space and water heating are about $2 \cdot 15 \times 10^{16}$ Watt (84×10^{11} BTU) for offices and shops $1 \cdot 23 \times 10^{16}$ Watt (48×10^{11} BTU) and are a bit over one half of the industrial energy consumption of 6.42×10^{16} Watt (250×10^{11} BTU).

Nearly 1 billion people in other countries live under climatic conditions comparable to the moderate and higher latitude locations in the United States of America. As their development and population expansion approaches that of the U.S.A. energy needs for heating of homes and work places will also approach those given above.

Cooling Needs

Even though man, as already stated, is a creature originating in warm climates, there are definite upper temperature limits to survival. High atmospheric moisture content will lower this limit because it prohibits the cooling by the evaporation of perspiration from the skin. Efficiency radically deteriorates in high temperatures and industrial hygiene laws often restrict working hours in hot environments. Climate obviously governs such conditions. This and the general desire for comfort has led in many regions to the installation of cooling devices. These include refrigerators for the preservation of foods. Air conditioning also is gradually spreading, usually starting with hospitals, where such cooling can help greatly in the healing process. In addition it is highly beneficial in schools and buildings of mass assemblies, such as theaters, and finally apartment houses and individual dwellings. Degree days above a given threshold, such as 18°C, are again a good measure of the energy required for cooling. The estimate of annual energy use for cooling purposes of residences, offices and shops in the United States of America is currently about 2.9×10^{16} Watts (11.9×10^{11} BTU) for the former and 4.6×10^{16} Watts (17.83×10^{11} BTU) for the latter. This is roughly 4 percent of the total energy used in the U.S.A. This type of climatization, even though it has been occasionally designated as luxury, is readily compensated by the savings in food spoilage, improved efficiency of workers, and protection of the health of the very young and the very old fraction of the population. These latter two groups have undeveloped or impaired heat regulation mechanisms, respectively. Living and comfort conditions in vast areas of the globe could be vastly improved if the power demands could be met. An assessment of global cooling degree days shows that areally about 1/2 of the land surface of the earth, with 1.5 billion inhabitants requires some cooling in dwellings and work places to afford an optimal environment.

Solar Energy

The needs for space heating and cooling forcibly bring the energy needs to the fore. Fossil fuel resources are limited; their burning inevitably causes air pollution, if only an increase of atmospheric carbon dioxide. Their combustion also leads to heat rejection into the atmosphere-ocean system. Although global effects of such added pollution and heat is likely to be small for a few decades to come, the local and regional effects are not trivial. Hence the search for alternative energy sources is well warranted on meteorological grounds alone.

It is only natural to investigate the feasibility of turning to the inexhaustible, pollution-free natural sources of energy. In forefront of these is the life-sustaining radiation received by the earth from the sun. This energy, as received at the surface of the earth is indeed stupendous. The areas with the highest income of energy from the sun are the deserts of subtropical latitudes. These are notoriously sparsely populated. Elsewhere the solar radiation is intermittent and disrupted by cloudiness. In polar regions we have, in addition, the seasonal and elsewhere the diurnal change between dark and light hours.

The periodic or aperiodic interruption of sunshine makes this source of energy rather difficult to incorporate into power systems. Even though the sun has heated domestic water supplies for years through suitable roof tanks or green houses in sun-rich areas, such direct conversion of the solar radiation is not suitable for large-scale power production. More complex home heating systems, with use of heat storage beds for the sunless periods, are already available. Yet, while the fuel is free, the cost of such installations is high. In the longer run, it seems likely that direct conversion of the incident solar radiation to electricity by photovoltaic cells will become a major contender in the field. Great strides have been made to supply power for space craft and space stations through these devices. Solar electric conversion panels are costly but the current generated can be directly fed into a net or stored in batteries. It can be anticipated that this technology will develop rapidly.

Wind Energy

The other, once popular but now neglected, atmospheric energy resource is the wind. The windmill, that was once a substantial link in the food processing chain, is now mostly a picturesque tourist attraction rather than a power source. The sail ship that for centuries furnished the only ocean transportation has still speedy descendants for a great racing sport.

However, in the past 30 years, experimentation has not ceased to harness wind power, first on the mountains of New England and then in Denmark. In both these areas strong winds of relatively high reliability made them meteorologically attractive. These installations were propeller-driven generators on towers. They again, were too expensive to be competitive in a market where fossil fuels were cheap.

Available meteorological information clearly indicates that close to the surface wind speed is a very fickle element, alternating frequently from near calm to strong, gusty pulses. This is hard to manage in generating systems of electricity. Meteorological observations clearly show that variability of wind speed decreases rapidly with height while average speed increases. This mandates that wind power installations have to be elevated. Even a 100 meter high tower rarely experiences the nocturnal calms that are so common near the ground.

Even then some areas of notoriously low wind speeds are not suitable for wind power installations.

The standard height of measuring winds is 10 meters above the ground. As a crude first approximation one can estimate that the wind energy available at 100 meters is about twice as high as at 10 meters. Obviously there is a very wide range of wind conditions. Generally, coastal areas are favored by the high wind speeds but mountain-protected inland regions score low. Areas where frequent meteorological changes take place or where major planetary winds, such as the trades, prevail are potentially quite favorable for wind power. New propeller designs have improved the power yield and a promising vertical-axis wind turbine has been tested. The latter has the great advantage that it needs not be directed into the wind and that the generator can be at the surface. For small communities and isolated settlements the future potential of wind power installation is considerable.

CLIMATE AND BUILDING CONSTRUCTION

The meteorological environment has to be taken into account to achieve safe and adequate design of dwellings and other buildings. The most important factors are temperature, wind and precipitation conditions.

Walls and Roof

The outer shell of the house has to bear the brunt of the weather. Perhaps its first function is to keep precipitation out but more than that it prevents penetration of moisture to the inside when strong winds drive heavy rains against the walls. This requires suitable combinations of building materials (wood, brick, stone, metal, glass, plastics). In snowy regions roof design is a particular art. The roof should shed as much snow as possible but it still has to have the bearing strength to stand up to the maximal snow load of the region. In this connection, one should be aware that one can not use the maximal snow depth on the ground as a safe upper limit of roof load because a snow layer on a roof can absorb several times its own weight in form of water from late season rain. This can lead to a collapse of inadequately designed roofs.

Wind loads on buildings and structures can be estimated from meteorological records. To give a broad general estimate, one can expect wind speeds of 25 m sec^{-1} about once per year and 50 m sec^{-1} about once in twenty years in coastal zones. Inland the corresponding figures are 20 m sec^{-1} for once a year and 30 m sec^{-1} for once in twenty years. There are some areas in the lee of mountains where aerodynamic forces can bring about damaging down-slope winds of strengths comparable to those experienced near the coasts.

Wind statistics are usually available as wind speeds averaged over a short time interval, say 5 to 10 minutes. From maximal values noted over the years one can estimate the maximum wind gust to be expected in a strong wind. These gusts have to be considered for their impact on structures, especially tall buildings and towers.

In the tornado-prone areas special precautions have to be taken. Roofs have to be properly anchored and so designed that collapse of high structures in the neighborhood, such as chimneys, does not cause penetration. The high wind pressure against walls, windows, and doors usually causes the greatest amount of damage. It has been suggested to reduce the glass surfaces because they are the first to go and are often smashed by the inevitable debris flying around in high winds. Wall construction with better supports and reinforcements may be required. The explosive force of a pressure difference between the inside of the building and the low pressures of the passing tornado can also cause collapse but can be counteracted by venting. It has been suggested that in the endangered areas the venting should be at least 1% of the floor area of the house area, i.e., for a house of 1200 m^2, there should be 12 m^2 venting. Buildings with free-span roofs are particularly endangered because the lift forces of the wind and the interior overpressure may lift the whole roof off. Traditionally, homes in the areas under tornadic threat have had storm cellars as refuges. Public buildings, especially schools usually have tornado shelters in the basement or in the interior under short-spanned roofs, away from all windows and doors.

Roofs and walls are also of great importance with respect to the heat exchange between the house or building or its environment. Some of this will fall under the heading insulation. But here our concern is with the radiation-absorbing qualities of the outer surfaces. If they are dark they will readily absorb solar radiation, warm up, and transmit heat to the inside. If walls and roofs are white on the outside they reflect much of the incoming energy and the building material does not heat up excessively. This immediately suggests that these outer surfaces in sunny, warm climates should be light. In cold climates dark surfaces are advantageous. The problems arise in climates where winters are cold and summers warm but on balance it appears better to plan for summer protection when the sun is high above the horizon and its radiation intense. In winter clouds often prevail and little energy is available from the low-standing sun.

Special problems are offered by the glass surfaces of windows. They reflect little radiation, although specially treated glass is now available that transmits less energy than ordinary glass. All radiation that gets through the glass is trapped as heat inside. The glass is completely opaque to the interior's heat radiation. Thus glass surfaces can, to a limited extent, aid in cold regions in transferring solar energy to the inside. But in warm, sunny seasons and climates glass surfaces add a large cooling burden. Outside reflecting shutters or shading devices have to be provided to avoid excessive heating inside and the overloading of climatization devices.

Insulation

An important function of the outer shell of housing is the damping of outdoor weather fluctuations. In former times this was accomplished by thick walls. Presently the same aim is pursued by insulation and air spaces. Material of high heat capacity and low heat conductivity best fulfills the needs, which are imposed in many climates by variations in radiation and air temperature outdoors that necessitate alternating heating and cooling indoors. Many materials used in structures, such as stone, concrete, and ordinary bricks have relatively high heat conductivity and low bulk heat capacity. Metal, often used for roof construction is particularly poor in this respect. It will, for example, heat up to an extraordinary degree under the influence of direct insolation. All these materials require inside covering with materials imparting thermal inertia. Among these are wood, mineral fibres (rock wool) and polystyrene. Air spaces between the outer structural material with the insulation attached and interior plaster board or panelling provides an effective heat transfer barrier. This type of construction provides for conservation of heating fuel and reduction of cooling needs.

The roof construction needs the greatest attention as regards insulation. In sunny climates, and especially those where summers are hot, most roofs are heat collectors and attic spaces, if present, can have temperatures up to 50 or 50°C. Without adequate insulation this unwanted heat diffuses to the living spaces below, causing discomfort and may require artificial cooling. Heavy layers of insulation, preferably with a reflecting aluminum cladding are needed to avoid this extra thermal load.

Windows interrupting the outer wall surfaces offer special independent problems. We have already referred to the need for shading to avoid excessive absorption of radiation. In warm sunny climates excessive outside fenestration and sky lights have to be avoided. Considerable attention has also to be paid to orientation of windows. In many areas windows directed toward a shaded inside court (patio) have a time-tested advantage.

Windows also offer special problems in cold climates. Aside from shuttering used at night, storm windows offer substantial insulating qualities because of the low conductivity of the dead air space between the two glass surfaces. This insulation can be enhanced by double panes with a vacuum between them. Such windows, while effective, unfortunately, are quite expensive. On the inside the use of curtains and drapes also adds to the insulation. Obviously, air leakage, often found around poorly fitted window frames has to be avoided or corrected.

Ventilation

In hot climates ventilation can reduce the heat load on the inhabitants and increase comfort. This can, of course, be provided by fans which bring about air motion artificially. But natural ventilation is often the only available resource for causing some cooling sensation. With efficient ventilation air temperatures of 29 to 32°C are quite comfortable, but above that, especially with high relative humidities some artificial cooling is essential. In desert areas natural ventilation has to be frequently interrupted because of blowing sand and dust. Nocturnally natural ventilation can often cool houses efficiently. A rule of thumb indicates, that if cross ventilation is provided the air flow through the house is about 30 percent of the outside wind speed. Without cross ventilation, that is in rooms with single windows and closed doors, wind flow will be less than 10 percent of the external wind speed. This manifests the importance of cross ventilation. The fact that wind speeds at night are invariably lower than in day time further underlines this postulate. Sometimes more satisfactory results can be achieved by placing apertures at various heights through the walls that, when opened, will enhance circulation.

After cooling at night through ventilation it is often possible in suitably insulated and shuttered houses to preserve for a while the cool night air indoors by closing all openings after sunrise. Comfort for nocturnal rest can, in warm climates, also be provided by sleeping porches. Full advantage should be taken in coastal areas of the day time sea or lake breezes for ventilation and cooling. This requires close attention to orientation of houses and openings, as well as city block arrangements. Mountain breezes that nocturnally flow downhill, bringing cool air, may offer ventilation opportunities in some regions.

AIR POLLUTION

Sources, Transformations, Sinks

Almost all human activities cause some air pollution. Settlements nearly always are prolific sources of air pollution. The origin may be stationary point sources, such as smoke stacks of mills, factories, refineries and power plants, domestic furnaces and incinerators. Mobile sources include primarily motor vehicles, steam trains, aircraft, and ships. They bring a veritable plethora of substances into the air, many of which undergo chemical transformations in their life history in the atmosphere.

It should, however, not be overlooked that perhaps half of all man-caused air pollution is the result of agricultural activities. These result in soil blowing, and contamination from suspended fertilizers and pest control substances. There are also some exhaust products of farm machinery and an enormous amount of suspensions from the slash-and-burn agricultural practices in some regions.

Atmospheric processes alter, disperse, and eliminate these pollutants. Some of them are oxidized, some hydrated, and some undergo photochemical reactions. In the latter process irradiation by certain wave lengths in the sun light acting on exhaust gases, especially oxides of nitrogen and hydrocarbons, can lead to formation of ozone and other irritating compounds. These also promote the formation of "smog", which — although most notorious from the experience of Los Angeles, California — is notable in many other urban areas of the world. Avoidance and remedial action require great attention to the meteorological setting of planned or existing communities.

Horizontal and vertical motions of the air move and dilute the polluted urban and industrial atmospheres. In this transport process many particles fall out or are intercepted by shrubs and trees. This has led to the planting of shelter belts along major traffic arteries to reduce the pollutants from exhausts. Such barriers have also noise-reducing properties but for both tasks they have to be sufficiently high, wide, and dense. Single hedges help little and protective strips of at least 10 meters height and 100 meters width with low permeability should be planned for.

By far the most effective eliminator of air pollutants is precipitation. Aerosols are incorporated into cloud droplets and fall out with them or the raindrops intercept and wash out impurities.

Endangered Areas

The wind disperses and dilutes air pollutants quite effectively but there are many localities where wind is permanently or temporarily weak. Many of these are located in the high pressure belts of the subtropical zones. Others lie in mountain troughs and valleys where air often stagnates. Such stagnation is usually accompanied by low level temperature inversions. In the cold, heavy air hugs the ground, with warmer air aloft. The cold air is not easily lifted off and pollutants accumulate; they cannot move readily through the boundary between the cold and the warmer air, which acts as an effective lid. Such conditions are quite common at night but are usually replaced by warming of the layer of air near the surface by the sun's radiation. But in winter, in mountain valleys high fogs form at the inversion boundary and the stagnant conditions may persist all day. In sub-polar and polar latitudes this can continue for days on end and will be noted even in shallow terrain depressions.

In summer and subtropical latitudes, especially inland, stagnation caused by inversions is common but inversions are usually at higher levels thus permitting mixing of pollutants through a greater depth. But in these regions photochemical action on the pollutants is common. Using weather statistics on wind motions, inversions and sunshine conditions one can estimate the atmospheric air pollution potential. A chart of the climatological air pollution potential over the globe would show many areas that are poorly endowed with dispersal properties of the air for pollutants. Their climate has frequent episodes of limited dispersion, which may last three days or longer. These intervals have low-level inversions and wind speeds of generally less than 4 m/sec. In many areas terrain plays a major role. Considering air as an essential natural resource there are already now communities that have stressed their air resources to the limit. Further expansion of these metropolitan areas could lead to further serious deterioration of air quality, unless the most stringent controls on emissions are instituted. New settlements, both as regards location and size, must be planned with the full incorporation of meteorological information on limitations to local dispersal of air pollutants.

Rainwater Contamination

Air motions distribute pollutants far and wide through the atmosphere. Although they dilute the pollutants rapidly with distance from the point of origin and render them relatively harmless from a hygienic point of view, they may nonetheless affect areas and settlements far downwind. This influence is exercised through the washout by rain that may take place hundreds of kilometers away from the sources of the pollutants.

Among man-made substances that have been identified as potentially damaging are sulfur dioxide and oxides of nitrogen. Some of these will become incorporated into cloud and rain drops as sulfuric and nitric acids. Acidic rain, if continued over an appreciable period of time will acidify the soil and affect the plant or crop association that will grow. It can also through run-off affect aquatic life in inland water bodies.

Washed out, too, are many trace substances, especially metals. Some of these, such as lead, have been identified in increasing quantity in recent years in the precipitation forming arctic ice. Elsewhere they can enter the water supplies and food chain. Thus settlements downwind and their inhabitants can be affected by air pollutants from far-away industries and cities. International boundaries are nonexistent for the drifting contaminants.

CLIMATE AND LAND USE

Farm or Town?

There are only limited land resources available on earth. Much land is essentially unsuitable for human habitation and use. Vast areas are desert; nearly nothing will grow there and the absence of reliable water sources make them uninhabitable. Rugged mountain terrain has other limitations and while inhabited by small groups of people, there is generally no arable land.

Most of the important food crops on earth have closely circumscribed climatic limits in which they can be optimally grown. They have specific requirements for water and a minimum period in which they can ripen. That period between the last freeze in spring and the first in autumn, the so-called growing season, sets the poleward limit of agriculture. There is only a limited amount of land suitable for crop production and grazing on the continents. Only relatively small additional acreage can be brought into production without inviting ecological disasters. The logical consequence is that with increasing needs for food in the world, planners will have to protect the available arable land against conflicting use claims.

Already some excellent farm land has succumbed to the encroachment of urbanization. Soil paved over with concrete and asphalt does not yield wheat, corn, rice or vegetables. In areas where severe flooding is relatively rare, low river land that should not be used for construction can well be assigned for farm lands. It seems inevitable that much future urbanization will necessitate tall construction that will house a maximum of persons and their activities on a minimum amount of land, unless land unsuitable for farming is available.

Water Supplies

Water use by humans, their agriculture and their industries is on the rise. In developed countries it has been estimated that the per capita use of water for all purposes is 750 liters per year. The greatest consumption of water is for agricultural irrigation. It is an essential technology for optimal crop production. Personal hygiene, sanitation, and food preparation require substantial, reliable water supplies for urban areas. Similarly, to keep power and industrial production going prodigious amounts of water are needed.

All this water must be supplied from the sky. Only the continuous replenishment of the water reservoirs, artificial or natural, can keep the essential supplies for survival. In some areas there is active mining of water, by use of groundwater. Some of these areas are located in climates where this consumption is not balanced by an equal amount of precipitation, a practice that will eventually lead to the exhaustion of the supply. There are enormous amounts of water locked in the ice masses. Most of these are in the polar regions and no practical means are as yet in sight to use these natural reservoirs. Runoff from glaciers in the mountains of moderate latitude is, of course, essential to the water budgets of many communities.

The income of water from precipitation depends on the weather conditions of a given year or season. We are dealing here with probably the most fickle of all weather elements. It varies from cloudburst to drought. The reliability of rain and snowfall depends greatly on the climate. In some regions with moderate marine climates year to year variations in amounts are fairly small. However, in semiarid and monsoonal areas the swings from one year to the next can be extraordinarily wide. In most regions it is axiomatic that the sections getting the least average rainfall have the highest variability. They have the highest risk to their water supplies. But it is equally important to remember that there is no region which does not occasionally have a drought or periods of excessive rain.

The logical, and extremely important consequence for the planner is that he will have to prepare for adequate water storage in reservoirs. In areas with high evaporation these have to be underground to avoid excessive losses. In communities near the ocean, where cheap power is available, distillation of sea water can tide over a temporary water shortage, but requires a cheap energy source.

Urban areas will more and more compete for water supplies with agricultural irrigation. In the early 1970's about 1.5×10^9 hectares were irrigated. This is about 15 percent of the agricultural land. The major areas are in the U.S.S.R. (233×10^6 hectares), U.S.A. (193×10^6 hectares), India (165×10^6 hectares), and P.R. of China (111×10^6 hectares). In terms of percent of the farm land irrigated they range in major producing countries from 100% in Egypt to 3% in Australia. The needed expansion of crop yields, and requirements of new varieties, call for more and more irrigation.

Urban Planning

Meteorological conditions should be incorporated into urban planning. This applies both to the new development and redevelopment. The problem of building on flood plains has already been alluded to. Presently expensive flood protection works are often resorted to but it may be more economical gradually to withdraw such land from urban development and devote it to other uses, such as agriculture and recreation.

Drainage systems in urban areas have to be designed to permit excessive rainfall to run off without causing damage. Good engineering practice now suggests that these systems have to be designed for the once-in-one-hundred-year storm. Statistical analyses, combined with synoptic considerations, permit to obtain an expected maximum rainfall for such an interval. In order to regulate the run off to avoid sudden rises in river flow, holding reservoirs may be needed and should be planned for. This impounded water can be aerated to supply oxygen demand of aquatic life and used for increasing of river flow during dry periods.

Water supply problems have to be anticipated and in certain areas purification and recirculation, especially of water not destined for human consumption, is mandated.

Air pollution is more difficult to deal with than water problems. But even here proper planning can reduce potential damages from the emissions of major stationary sources. These are apt to be factories, refineries, and power stations. Present zoning systems often confine them in massed form in separate sectors of the urban area, generally downwind using the so-called prevailing wind direction. This last concept is a poor use of meteorological information indeed. The planning should proceed with the wind directions that are associated with meteorological stagnation conditions. The light winds that permit accumulation of pollutants rarely coincide with the "prevailing" wind directions. Further, in many instances, agglomerations of polluting sources in a small area may not only aggravate undesirably high concentrations of toxic substances in the air of some nearby urban sections but also inadvertently modify local precipitation patterns. Trash disposal by incineration should particularly be avoided to keep air pollution within bounds.

Planning of urban transport systems can also have a profound influence on air pollution levels. Wherever large numbers of people have to be moved periodically into congested areas non-polluting electric transportation should be provided. The uncontrollable emissions and movements of individual automobiles with internal combustion engines has to be avoided. Through-traffic arteries have to be planned so that vehicles can move rapidly and smoothly, a mode that will minimize undesirable effluents.

In areas where snow is a common weather element provisions for rapid removal have to be made. Among these is the use of waste heat to melt snow from sidewalks and road beds. Provisions for heating are particularly important at dangerous intersections and on bridges and overpasses. Sidewalks can also be protected by colonnades.

Finally, building codes in cities have to be formulated in the light of the meteorological needs to promote comfort and safety of the inhabitants.

Urban Microclimates

Into the broader scale meso-climate of an urban area are tucked a large number of microclimates. In fact, man's works destroy many natural microclimates and create in their stead new ones. Topography, vegetation, structures and exposure all play a role in determining the microclimate.

In rolling or mountainous terrain topography is the governing factor. It may well decide the allocation of land to various uses. Among the facts to be considered are the temperature inversions that form in lowest terrain features. They cause "frost holes" that affect agriculture but they also are the traps for pollution and the poorest localities for pollutant sources. The ridges have the highest wind velocities, a desirable feature for smoke stacks but less pleasant for dwellings. The equator-facing slopes have maximal exposure to sun, good for reducing heat needs in cold regions but in hot extratropical areas the pole facing slopes may have an advantage. Actually, midslope locations often referred to as the "thermal belt" have usually warmer temperatures, especially at night, because they lie above the valley inversions. They have long been the favorite exposures for orchards and vineyards.

Man's removal of vegetation destroys many desirable microclimates. This process promotes extremes in daily maximum and minimum temperatures. The process is reversible in urban areas to a limited degree by planting again shade trees, which are from a climatic point of view a great asset.

Other acts that affect microclimates are building of dam structures, such as often used for railroad embankments. These impede air flow and often create cold air "lakes." Solid fronts of building can have the same effects. They and dams also inhibit free air circulation.

Depending on street width and building heights, incidence of solar radiation is regulated. In cold climates lower floors in narrow streets may never get a ray of sunshine. Similarly, courts in tall apartment developments are often devoid of sun, a sad situation, if they are to serve as play areas. On the other hand, in areas with abundant sunshine, such as deserts, the mutual shading of houses is a time-honored practice to create a more tolerable microclimate in the streets and indoors.

A fair amount of microclimatic manipulation can be practiced with plantings around houses. Deciduous vines can protect walls from excessive radiation. Shrubbery can act as a snow fence and pollutant screen.

EFFECTS OF URBANIZATION ON CLIMATE

To this point we have considered mainly the influences of weather and climate on dwellings and settlements but it is essential to be aware that human settlements have a "feedback" into their atmospheric environment. In the case of large urban areas this is by no means trivial and for the projected megalopolitan areas can cause regional effects that go beyond the confines of the urbanized area. This is usually the case for the air pollutants produced in a megalopolis. The city produces a gigantic plume, gradually dispersed downwind. At times, such a plume can be traced several hundred kilometers downwind. It is so dilute that it is not likely to cause health effects in humans but that is not certain with regard to other parts of the biosphere. The possible global consequences are being monitored under the auspices of the World Meterological Organizations. Although it is presently not predictable if human atmospheric contamination will lead to global climatic alterations, much as this has been speculated about in recent years, one can hope that this surveillance will give an early warning of untoward happenings.

Heat Island

On the local scale, the formation of an area of higher temperatures compared with rural environs is generally the first obvious manifestation of settlements. This so-called heat island is primarily the result of the alteration of the surface which affects the heat balance of the urbanized space. Less solar radiation is reflected and, since water is drained off and less vegetation exists, there is less evaporation. Urban heat generation, even in high, but subpolar, latitudes, contributes generally less than one third of the energy causing the heat island. The effect is particularly notable in the temperatures of the surface (not identical with air temperature) and can be directly related to the building density. In air temperatures the differences between urban and rural areas reach their highest values in the early night hours after sunset. The values that can be reached occasionally are above 10°C difference between the center of town and rural areas, at the same time. These maximal differences can be directly related to population figures. They occur on clear, calm nights. But even, in the annual averages, large cities have 1 to 2°C higher temperatures than their rural environments.

The heat island has a number of consequences. In cold regions it reduces the number of heating degree days. It may melt falling snow and thus reduce clearing costs. It causes convection that has effects on wind, cloudiness, and rain.

In warm regions or seasons the heat island contributes to discomfort and increases the cooling requirements. In cases of heat waves it adds to higher death rates, especially among infants and the elderly.

Effects of Settlements and Building on the Windfield

The heat island causes a rise of the warm air in the center of the city. This air is replaced by air from the outskirts converging into the city. In some cases it may bring in cleaner air, but in others, it may advect contaminated air from factory districts at the urban periphery.

The major effect of urban areas on the wind circulation is a result of the increased roughness introduced by the building complexes. These induce many smaller and larger eddies which swirl around in the city. The arrangement of streets and avenues will cause channeling of the wind. The result may then be that strong currents flow through one set of streets, while relative calm prevails in the streets at right angles.

The eddy currents that are caused by the buildings, especially the tall ones, can lead to very high wind gusts at street level. They can become so strong that it becomes difficult to walk on sidewalks and to open doors unless special protective overhangs are included in the design.

But the most notable overall influence on air flow by settlements is the general reduction of wind speed. This amounts, on an average, to 10 percent at the surface but the effect is by far more pronounced on the weak winds of 3 m sec^{-1} or less. These may be slowed down by 30 to 40 percent. This means that, when the atmospheric circulation is sluggish, urban air flow essentially stagnates. This, in turn, causes accumulation of air pollutants.

Air Pollution

The urbanized and industrialized areas of the world are major contributors of air pollution. Although they are not the only anthropogenic source, agriculture being the other, the urban areas produce a bewildering variety of pollutants from combustion processes, traffic, incinerators, and the effluents of utilities and factories. The dust pall over urban areas reduces visibility and contributes to fog formation. Some of the exhaust products of motor vehicles interact with sunlight to cause photochemical smog. Hence, there is generally less beneficial sunshine in cities than their surroundings.

Many of the pollutants present in urban areas have known health effects. Most common among these is carbon monoxide from automobile exhaust. Its presence impairs the oxygen carrying capacity of blood. The oxides of nitrogen, resulting from many combustion processes, but again mainly from automobiles, form irritating compounds that affect eyes and mucous membranes. Other nitrogen compounds originate in industrial processes and can cause a number of aggravations from rhinitis to keratoconjuctivitis.

One of the principal urban air pollutants is sulfur dioxide. It is the main obnoxious effluent from the burning of many fossil fuels. In the course of its chemical history in the atmosphere it often transforms into dilute droplets of sulfuric acid. This compound not only can have an effect on fog and cloud formation but also is a known irritant of the respiratory passages. It is suspected of promoting respiratory diseases and can be a main cause of urban cases of chronic bronchitis. The same sulfur fumes also affect many wild and ornamental plants.

Polycyclic hydrocarbons, which are known cancer-producers have been found in polluted urban atmospheres. The list of trace metals that has been determined in the metropolitan areas is bewilderingly long. They have their origin in gasoline additives, abrasion of tires in traffic, and incineration of refuse. Some of them come from coal and oil used in space heating. Chemical factories, refineries, and other manufacturing processes add their share. Many of these pollutants such as lead, mercury, beryllium, cadmium, create known health hazards.

Many of the urban atmospheric suspensions provoke severe allergic reactions. Allergically stimulated asthma attacks are far more prevalent in urban than rural areas. They, as well as other health effects, increase when stagnation situations prevail over cities. These happen when slow-moving high pressure cells settle for a while over urbanized areas. Under clear skies temperature inversions form near the surface. They place an effective lid on vertical convection which is one of the prime dispersers of pollutants. At the same time the winds, which could advect clean air to the urban area, are weak. Thus the pollutants accumulate and provoke serious health episodes.

The meteorological services have the predictive skills to alert the population to these conditions and enable municipal authorities to order such remedial measures as may be called for by this weather-induced menace. The overall problem can also be readily assessed for any existing urban areas and its growth projection. The concentration of any air pollutant is linearly related to a number of variables that are ascertainable. This relation is as follows:

$$X \propto \frac{N\,q}{d\,u}$$

Pollutant concentration (x) is directly proportional to the population number (N) and the average per capita production of the specific pollutant (q) and inversely proportional to the diameter of the urban area (d) and the wind speed (u). For most localities the frequency of low winds is known so that for any projected population and effluent rate fairly realistic estimates of potential local pollution levels can be made.

Urban Effects on Precipitation

The influences of the heat island and urban air pollution combine to affect the precipitation climate of cities. This effect does not become apparent until cities grow above 100,000 inhabitants and does not become really appreciable until they reach the million size.

The formation of fog in cities has already been alluded to but it is also evident that the convection induced by the heat island, particularly in daytime, leads to the formation of cumulus type clouds earlier in the day than in the nearby rural areas. It is not unlikely that some of the hydroscopic substances present among the pollutants also may lead to droplet formation sooner than would be the case if these substances were absent.

These clouds, continuously fed by the city-warmed ascending air currents, will under suitable weather conditions, grow tall and eventually lead to showers. These clouds may be carried by the upper winds, beyond the confines of the city and discharge their rains in the nearby suburban or rural areas downwind. This type of convective urban-induced shower will mostly occur in the warm season.

Under some other weather conditions rain enhancement over urban areas can also take place. This may occur when a rain-producing frontal system slowly drifts over a city. Such a system may well produce only a few millimeters of rain generally. But when its clouds get the added uplift provided by the rising currents of the heat island heavy showers or even cloud bursts can result. As urban areas expand this presently rare occurence will without doubt also increase in frequency.

There is still another way in which urban areas can contribute to their own precipitation. This comes about through cloud seeding. Such events are most likely to occur in the cold season because it necessitates cloud droplets at temperatures below freezing for seeding to become effective and initiate precipitation. Clouds with suitable droplets are common in cold regions in winter. These clouds are often very stable and suitable natural nuclei that may induce the precipitation process at the prevailing droplet temperature may be scarce. But when such clouds drift over cities they may meet a veritable volcanic outburst of freezing nuclei. These particles are present in profusion apparently from automobile exhaust and from industrial effluents. With the updrafts of the heat island lifting them to cloud level they may well induce added precipitation.

Minimization of Urban Effects on Weather

Even though, aside from high concentration of air pollutants, the effects of urban areas are not a major menace now, one can view the prospect of metropolitan areas of 20 million inhabitants and conurbations of many times that number of people only with great uneasiness. One would not like to see the heat island and its consequences grow to regional size. One would certainly not want to see the air pollutants grow by another order of magnitude. Contemplation of the run-off characteristics of many more square kilometers of paved-over land alarm because of their flood-producing potential. One can speculate only with misgivings about the multiplication of damages and injuries that major natural storms will cause in the communities of the future, stacked high with humans.

From the meteorological point of view what remedies could be recommended? The principal effort should be radical remedies for air pollution. Because it seems to be difficult to control many small sources, one would expect a non-polluting transportation system, probably electric. It is easier to control effluents from a few power stations than those of millions of vehicles. For stationary pollution sources smoke sewers should be constructed. The effluents can collectively be better controlled than individually.

The heat island and runoff problems should be counteracted by reducing the percentage of impermeable surfaces. This can be achieved by better land use, such as providing parking under houses, apartments, and business buildings. Multiple story parking garages will have to take the place of parking lots.

All lateral spread of buildings should be replaced by use of the vertical dimension. In this respect use of subsurface structures will have to see vast expansion. One would particularly hope to see more green surfaces interspaced into the urban scene and must urge a revival of the use of shade trees on streets and avenues. The green surfaces should not be restricted to lawns or playgrounds because, although they are better than paved-over places, trees have a far more profound influence on the heat balance. In hot, dry areas one would like to see the development of novel shading and deflecting devices.

7
The Protection of Human Settlements from Natural Disasters*

A component of the development process which has often been overlooked is the effect of natural phenomena on the development efforts of disaster-prone countries. Modern science and technology are only beginning to make inroads on this problem, both from the point of view of assessing the real costs and over-all impact, and devising and applying preventive measures for the benefit of individual countries and entire regions.

Such measures are designed to benefit primarily regions most affected by natural disasters, particularly developing countries, and contribute, over the longer-term, to the achievement of an important objective: the prevention of the terrible loss of life and the reduction of the enormous physical destruction of human settlements in all countries subject to natural disasters. There are, of course, additional areas where planning and preventive steps could be taken. However, the first and most basic problems in the field of disaster prevention are those related to the planning, building and management of human settlements.[1]

This paper, taking as its premise that natural disasters constitute a development problem, proposes steps which the international community and individual governments can take to help mitigate the effects of destructive natural phenomena on the economic development of disaster-prone developing countries. It refers briefly to the International Strategy for Disaster Prevention proposed by the Office of the United Nations Disaster Relief Co-ordinator, which should be an integral part of national development planning, and recommends measures to improve the protection of human settlements from natural disasters.

This document is designed to pinpoint a major impediment to development which is of grave concern to the community of nations and suggests ways to begin to cope with the problem as it affects human settlements.

NATURAL DISASTERS AS AN ECONOMIC DEVELOPMENT PROBLEM

Throughout history natural disasters and other emergency situations have inflicted heavy loss of life and property, affecting every people and every country. Only in recent years has the international community become aware of the degree to which the losses resulting from natural disasters affect the economic development of disaster-prone developing countries. In a number of cases, in terms of gross national product, the losses caused by disasters have tended to cancel out any economic growth. Moreover, estimates have

*A background paper for Habitat by the Office of the United Nations Disaster Relief Co-ordinator (Symbol A/Conf. 70/B/7; 24 February 1976.

[1]For more information on this subject, the reader may refer to the three volumes entitled *Guidelines for Disaster Prevention*, published in 1976 by the Office of the United Nations Disaster Relief Co-ordinator, United Nations, Geneva, and available at HABITAT: United Nations Conference on Human Settlements.

shown that the direct and indirect damage from the effects of natural phenomena have caused some countries actually to lose ground in relative terms. The accumulating evidence has led to the conclusion that natural disasters should be viewed fundamentally as a problem of economic development.

During the last two decades the world public has become increasingly alarmed by natural disasters, which have tended to be more and more destructive as they affect ever-larger concentrations of population. The dual phenomena of rapid urbanization and high rates of population growth have contributed to increase the physical devastation and loss of life from disasters, particularly in developing countries which experience frequent recurrences of large-scale catastrophes. The sheer magnitude of the human problem in disaster-prone areas, manifested by the continuing expansion and relentless concentration of population in urban slums and squatter settlements, shows unquestionably that preparedness and post-disaster relief measures are by themselves not sufficient. The actual and potential consequences of disasters are now recognized as a formidable obstacle to the economic and social development of the stricken area. Much greater emphasis must henceforth be placed on pre-disaster planning and prevention.

General Assembly resolution 3362 (S-VII) emphasizes the responsibility of the international community towards disaster-stricken countries in these words:

> "Special attention should be given by the international community to the phenomena of natural disasters which frequently afflict many parts of the world, with far-reaching devastating economic, social and structural consequences, particularly in the least-developed countries."

This admonition concerns both donors and stricken countries. Although there is mounting evidence of consequences to economic growth, social and political stability, as well as to the daily lives of the peoples affected, far too little is known about the actual direct and especially the indirect effects of natural disasters — or, more precisely, the over-all effects of natural phenomena, particularly on the economies of poor countries.

These phenomena affect all countries and all peoples, whatever their social and cultural pattern, political orientation or economic system. In one recent year, for example, more than 111,000 people died and 215 million others were affected as a result of natural disasters. Most of this toll occurred in developing countries.

There are 50 to 60 developing countries in all regions of the world which can be characterized as very disaster-prone. In these countries, damage caused by disasters far exceeds in absolute terms the external bilateral and multilateral assistance received. The Office of the United Nations Economic Commission for Latin America (ECLA) in Mexico, for example, has estimated that in the five countries of the Central America Common Market, disaster damage has averaged 2.3 percent of the gross domestic product in the 15-year period 1960-1974. This figure does not take into consideration indirect effects, such as the higher incidence of certain diseases, nor many small events, such as limited floods which, taken on aggregate, reach disastrous proportions. Since the countries concerned also have a population growth rate of about 3 percent a year, to avoid an actual decline in the rate of economic growth and remain at a static level of development, they must achieve an economic growth rate of at least 5.3 percent. Very few of these countries actually achieve this rate; therefore, partly because of disasters, most are actually losing ground in relative terms.

Other data and information available in developed countries are fragmentary at best; in most developing countries reliable data on the frequency, intensity and indirect losses attributable to natural disasters are virtually non-existent at this time.[2] What is known only partly reveals the situation. For example, cyclones occur an average of four times a year in the Bay of Bengal. It is estimated that every year about 100 earthquakes occur which are strong enough to produce substantial destruction if their centres are near areas of concentrated human habitation.

Between 1961 and 1974, the cumulative total damage caused by monsoons, tropical cyclones and floods in the ESCAP region was estimated at $US 29,800 million (1974 price), with an annual average damage of $US 2,190 million. Altogether there were some 280,000 lives lost, 485 million people affected, 139 million

---

[2]The Office of the United Nations Disaster Relief Co-ordinator has undertaken a World Survey of Disaster Damage covering the period 1960-1974. The objectives are to provide accurate and up-to-date data from all countries on the effects of natural disasters, to assess the economic impact of such phenomena and to aid in the formulation of the International Strategy for Disaster Prevention.

hectares inundated and 35 million dwellings and buildings damaged. This staggering estimate does not include the damage in Afghanistan, China, Indonesia, Iran and a number of other countries of the region on which no data have yet been collected in a systematic way.

Even these few statistics make dramatically clear the devastation wrought by the effects of natural phenomena in disaster-prone developing countries. The heaviest impact occurs in human settlements of the least developed countries, where the death toll is perhaps a hundredfold higher than in the industrialized countries, and the damage caused, in terms of percentage of GNP, many times higher. Although two thirds of the world's population live in developing countries, it has been estimated that 95 percent of disaster-related deaths occur in these countries. Furthermore, in contrast to the exceptional regional differences in death rates, losses from natural disasters are closely correlated to world income distribution. While as much as three fourths of the global disaster losses occur in the developed countries, the proportional burden of losses in terms of percentage of GNP is much higher in the developing countries.

The international community needs to know more concretely the direct and, especially, the indirect or hidden effects of natural disasters. Consideration must be given, for example, to forced unemployment, crops destroyed, harvests which spoil because they cannot be delivered to centres of consumption, the added nutritional problems, particularly for children, the higher incidence of certain diseases in the wake of disasters, and the medium and long-term impact on the agricultural production cycle of a stricken country.

The destructive effects of natural phenomena must be viewed by the international community not only in humanitarian and broad social terms, but also in economic terms, in view of the admittedly fragmentary but indisputable evidence demonstrating their extraordinary potential to impede economic and social progress. This provides an entirely new element to add to traditional thinking about the causes of under-development, low productivity, economic stagnation and inadequate social development. While it is obvious that the effects of natural phenomena constitute only one of the factors hindering development, they do play a decidedly significant role in disrupting the economies, the social fabric and the human settlements of disaster-prone developing countries.

These same countries have very limited human and material resources to deal with their disaster problems, which is compounded by their lack of ready access to available low-cost technology. In human terms, the effects are even more pernicious. The public is largely ill-informed of even the basic steps necessary for adequate preparedness, and often has no awareness of the most rudimentary preventive measures. There is all too often a fatalistic view of natural calamities, sometimes acquired from centuries of experiencing such phenomena. There is frequently no national organization or even government department with direct responsibility for initiating, directing and co-ordinating disaster-related activities. Many governments also have not accepted the responsibility for initiating appropriate measures and promoting a national consciousness of and an active interest in disaster prevention.

It is evident that there is a need for an international strategy for disaster prevention to channel the technology and human and material resources of the international community toward the common objective of preventing, or at least mitigating, the scourge which natural disasters represent for so many countries. This strategy, which the Office of the United Nations Disaster Relief Co-ordinator has proposed and is currently formulating, will provide the conceptual framework for all national and international action in the area of prevention and mitigation of natural disasters and should be an integral part of national development planning.[3]

THE PROTECTION OF HUMAN SETTLEMENTS FROM NATURAL DISASTERS

In preparing an international strategy for disaster prevention and recommending measures for the protection of human settlements, certain basic premises need to be understood. Many disasters, considered as distinct from the natural phenomena which cause them, can be avoided. Virtually all phenomena liable to cause disasters share one common feature: although it may not be possible at the present stage of scientific

---

[3] For further information, the reader may refer to the series of publications on *Disaster Prevention and Mitigation*, published in 1976 by the Office of the United Nations Disaster Relief Co-ordinator, United Nations, Geneva.

knowledge to forecast, except a few hours beforehand in some cases, *when* they are going to happen, on the other hand, it can often be predicted with a reasonably high degree of accuracy, *where* they are most likely to occur, for example, in flood plains, fault zones or avalanche corridors. Even in the case of such "erratic" phenomena as tropical storms (hurricanes, cyclones and typhoons), it is known that approximately 90 to 95 percent of the human losses and property damage are attributable to the action of water, and not to the effects of wind. This has obvious implications for the location of human settlements of any kind. More often than not, most disasters can be averted if the first step taken is to locate human settlements in areas having the most favourable conditions, in other words, the sites least exposed to disaster risk.

This self-evident statement often needs to be re-emphasized: there is always a choice between a dangerous site and a *less* dangerous one. The best choice can be encouraged by measures which involve negligible cost, such as the adoption and application of appropriate legislation on land use, such as town and country planning laws and zoning regulations, based on vulnerability analyses. The key factor in ensuring that the best choice is made, is to include in any development project a "vulnerability analysis," i.e., an evaluation of all types of risks for the area concerned.

The expenditure on such a study would be negligible in comparison with the total cost of a project. The "multiplier effect" of this prophylactic measure would be enormous, not only from the point of view of lives saved and damage avoided, but also because relief and reconstruction of human settlements would not be necessary. Two facts highlight still further the role which such a simple measure as a "vulnerability analysis" can play in averting future disasters. First, the majority of the poorest countries most disaster-prone are still at the initial stages of urbanization and industrialization; secondly, it has been estimated that settlements, will have to be made available during the next 25 years as during the whole of man's previous history. Therefore, choosing the safest location possible for all types of construction and human activity should be given high priority in national and regional planning of human settlements.

In terms of a community's vulnerability to catastrophe, the growth of population and the advancement of economic and social welfare produces paradoxical consequences. On the one hand, advances in techniques and technology provide better means to make building construction safer and urban development more secure against disasters. The protection and reinforcement of existing infrastructure and buildings will not only help safeguard the well-being of the occupants, but also increase the life-span of the structure. Safer sites for development are more clearly recognized, and advances in knowledge and communication systems make emergency measures for disaster prevention more efficient.

On the other hand, growth in population involves increased urbanization and agglomeration of buildings and activities. This provides bigger targets for disaster phenomena and an increase in the probability of man-made disasters. The likelihood of property destruction and loss of life is considerably increased.

Although reliable figures are not yet available for comparing all natural phenomena, a major portion of damage and loss of life in cyclones is caused by flood waters. For this reason, coastal and river flood plains are considered regions of most potential danger from the viewpoint of general habitation, especially so when flood events can occur in combination with earthquakes, landslides and other phenomena. Areas within river deltas are also at risk when upstream river flooding combines with unusually high sea levels.

It is unrealistic to suggest that all flood plains and other regions at risk should not be occupied or used for human activity. In many cases, habitation of such regions has become a firmly established social phenomenon and, for the most part, endures in economically and socially stable conditions. Moreover, in some regions, it may be impossible to occupy areas other than those having high risk.

The objectives of physical planning, expressed in general terms, are to co-ordinate different aspects and components of the complex process of development and to orchestrate environment-shaping activities towards an harmonious result. The general task of physical planning and design of a given area (region, urban district, rural district, city, village, etc.) is to translate the social and economic aims of development into physical patterns of land-use, and to achieve an appropriate quality of organized environment necessary for human activities, satisfaction and well-being.

The usefulness of physical planning measures for the protection of human settlements against the results of sudden or violent natural phenomena is readily justifiable. In most developing countries the protection of employment and investment against degradation or sudden destruction through appropriate planning constitutes a significant contribution towards economic stability and growth; factories, stores and other institutions of employment should be safeguarded.

In reviewing the application of physical planning for disaster prevention and mitigation in human settlements, two distinct situations must be considered. The first concerns physical planning in the context of existing settlements, and the second embraces the full spectrum of comprehensive planning measures applicable to new areas of development and new settlement planning. Physical planning measures applicable in the first instance are likely to be corrective rather than preventive in the strict sense. As each existing situation differs in all its specifics from every other, this paper emphasizes primarily planning for new development.

A policy maker and a planner will meet in the process of planning a number of conflicting situations, of conflicting demands and criteria and of conflicts of interests between individual citizens and between various social and interest groups. The task of the planner and policy maker is to find the most appropriate solution; this will often be based on compromise and on some trade-offs.

In disaster-prone areas, a physical planner should introduce into planning schemes for the physical development of a given area measures to make settlements safer and to safeguard human life. These measures, beginning with site selection and land-use patterns, may be in conflict with some other interests or criteria of development. The need for one of the most dramatic trade-offs arises at this moment. Some protective measures in the area of physical development patterns will create additional costs. How far to diminish the potential risk and for what kind of additional cost is one of the fundamental questions asked of political decision-makers. It can be answered by planners on the basis of cost-benefit analyses of risks or alternate locations for human settlements and activities to be situated in vulnerable areas.

The Office of the United Nations Disaster Relief Co-ordinator stresses that vulnerability analyses and cost-benefit analyses for disaster prevention and mitigation should be an integral part of national economic and physical planning. These should be undertaken at the project level for all pre-investment studies for physical development in disaster-prone areas, and the vulnerability concept should be introduced as an additional variable to be taken into consideration at the national planning level.

There are many other measures in urban or physical planning which require little additional costs, or even none at all. Some of them may be very logical and simple, i.e., to act in a planned way as opposed to a haphazard one. The adoption of such measures calls for professional expertise, political consciousness and public commitment.

At the present stage of knowledge and technical achievement, preventing the occurrence of natural phenomena which may cause disasters is rarely feasible although this is rapidly changing. In most cases, preventing disastrous consequences is the most practicable course of action. This is in contrast to disasters resulting from human habitation and activity, in which case both prevention of the event and of its possible disastrous consequences can be exercised.

Pre-disaster physical planning is an essential element for the protection of human settlements. To plan efficiently depends largely upon a thorough understanding of the nature and consequences of possible catastrophic events and, particularly, of their impact on the structure of human settlements and the life of the inhabitants. Good physical planning also takes into account the possibility that the occurrence of one disastrous event might lead to the occurrence of one or more further disastrous events, as in a chain reaction, such as an earthquake resulting in a fire and conflagration in an urban area, or river flooding causing pollution, subsequent disease and loss of fertile agricultural land.

A disaster prevention programme involves a complex and comprehensive set of interdependent measures. These necessitate advance planning of physical development, implementation and execution, technical layouts, and effective administration and management.

Measures for the protection of human settlements are based on an understanding of the problem and experience in both the pre-disaster period and in the aftermath of a disaster. Although the measures include planning, building and management stages, they must not be considered in isolation, but as an integrated whole. In the following pages, some specific steps are set forth, based on available knowledge and technology.

The more closely and specifically the planner investigates the problems of protecting human settlements against the potentially disastrous consequences of natural phenomena, the clearer the technical issues become in terms of necessary and essential measures.

Physical planning for disaster prevention and mitigation may take place at different levels. Countries may co-operate at the international level in solving problems of common concern, such as the regulation of river basins or development zones shared by more than one country. The first steps that may be taken are, of course, of a political and economic character. The role of the planner will depend on high-level political decisions. At the national level, physical planning needs and considerations should shape national development policies and plans. In the field of disaster prevention, vulnerability analyses for the spatial distribution of population, communications and all types of services and infrastructure are of primary importance. Planning at the national level permits the political decision maker, the economist and the physical planner to establish regional and local development planning within an over-all cohesive pattern.

Regional planning differs less from national planning in character than it does in scope and scale. Planning at the "local" level provides the policy-maker and the planner with the means to take concrete and specific measures for disaster prevention, particularly since disaster-prone areas are often well localized and predictable.

The process of physical planning for disaster prevention and mitigation in urban and rural human settlements or agglomerations may be broadly described as follows:

(a) The first step is to define the nature of the danger by examining natural conditions and the likely character of phenomena which may have disastrous consequences;

(b) Secondly, the planner and scientist should define areas of differing degrees of potential risk (vulnerability analysis);

(c) The third step is to define land-use patterns and the location of various types of development, selecting the lowest risk areas available for the most important activities and highest concentrations of population. Vulnerability analysis should occupy the main role in site selection and in formulating land-use and, particularly, zoning policy and regulations.

High-risk areas may encompass local, regional and even national scales of potential destruction. As far as natural phenomena are concerned, the main high-risk areas include seismically active zones or seismic faults, river flood plains, tidal wave (or tsunami) flood plains, zones exposed to tropical cyclones, landslides, avalanches and erosion, and the vicinity of active volcanoes. Within this context, the most vulnerable types of development are high concentrations of populations or high concentration of economic activities (mostly manufacturing), key communications and transport networks, and major defence installations.

Whenever it is not possible to avoid a high-risk area altogether, more expensive measures must sometimes be undertaken, such as those related to the structure and design of building. In all cases, the amount and type of protection to be provided is primarily an economic question. Almost any amount of protection can be provided with today's knowledge and techniques, but the main limitation is one of cost. Expensive technology would not only be a step in the wrong direction, but beyond the resources of developing countries. Consider, for example, the very expensive construction of embankments and flood-walls for the protection of settlements on a coastal area against tsunamis, which can be economically justified only in very special cases. It is therefore necessary for political leaders and decision makers to have access to all information available in order to find the most feasible and effective solution.

Since it is known that flooding causes the greatest loss of life in natural diasters, special attention should be given to the technical protection of inundation areas and the protection of buildings and houses located there. Floodway and flood-defence systems should be well maintained; special measures should be taken, such as designing the levels of roads and tracks as high as economically justifiable to assure uninterrupted access to settlements during flooding where existing defence systems cannot provide total security. For the case of potential dam failure, an effective warning system is of the utmost importance. For most areas, increasing security against inundation is primarily a financial problem and also one of adequate supervision of the safety of the project.

In disaster-prone areas, buildings and other structures may be subjected to abnormally heavy loads as a result of the action of horizontal and up-lifting wind forces (tropical storms and floods), and vibrational forces (earthquakes). In some cases, these loads may be large enough to cause the destruction of the building, with consequent loss of life and material damage to property. For this reason special attention must be paid to the design and construction of buildings and other civil engineering structures. Prevention or at least diminution of the disaster effects can be achieved by building legislation and building supervision.

Building codes and regulations for disaster-prone areas should define the special loads which should be taken into account when designing buildings for these areas, including the effects of soil conditions on seismic loads. Up-to-date methods for structural analysis of buildings and other types of construction should also be provided.

The enforcement of building codes is a complicated and difficult process in many countries. Since enforcement of disaster-prevention legislation is a more serious matter than that of normal building codes, a special national or regional authority may be recommended.

The construction of buildings and other types of structures should be strictly supervised to ensure that they are built in accordance with the approved design, with the use of materials of sufficient quality, appropriate construction techniques and in safe areas. Standardization of building materials is one of the most important measures for disaster prevention.

Too little emphasis is given to the study of soil conditions in earthquake zones; for example, soil conditions around high dams must be investigated. A geological survey of the site could determine whether earthquake resistant foundations are needed. Construction of any kind of building in landslide areas in earthquake regions should be prohibited.

A substantial portion of disaster prevention measures concern the damage resistance of buildings. Under certain conditions, building techniques may be preferred which will react to natural forces only to reduce loss of life, and not emphasize the resistance of the building itself.

Since resistance in buildings is of such great importance, design of buildings becomes a major subject in disaster prevention. It is extremely important that preventive measures should not be concerned with architectural style, but with the resistance of buildings to damage and their ability to protect life. Structures in seismic regions, for example, should be designed to be as light as possible, and should be built with the use of ductile materials as often as possible. The most vulnerable structures in tropical storm areas are normally small buildings. In some areas where low-cost one-floor houses are the major form of accommodation, more than 90 percent of all earthquake victims perish in them. Since building materials and construction techniques which are likely to augment damage should be avoided, a problem confronts developing countries which, often for reasons of practicality or economy, use technically unsatisfactory materials available locally.

Building designs adopted in one country as a result of their advantages in resistance to damage may well be incorrect or inadequate in another country, not only with respect to local building traditions and climate, but also technically. In evaluating the desirability of particular designs for buildings, consideration should be given to their resistance, cultural traditions, sources and amount of income and the climate. It will not generally be necessary to adopt the building practice of industrialized countries.

Many techniques of disaster prevention at present have been studied for industrial countries, in particular, but their applicability in all countries has not yet been ascertained. In many cases, there is reluctance to undertake certain measures because of the cost. A complete change of construction practice for low-cost housing is a very difficult economic problem for developing countries, where millions of people are living and will still live in houses very vulnerable to disasters. It is essential that local research into prevention techniques be given due consideration.

The protection of human settlements against the potentially disastrous consequences of natural phenomena comprises measures in addition to those in building and physical planning. These measures concern national community preparedness, forecasting and warning. Relocation, public land acquisition, and administration are functions which have a wider framework than disaster prevention and are mentioned here only as they relate to disaster prevention.

A clear distinction must be made between preparedness and prevention. *Prevention* comprises long-range planning aimed at avoiding the disastrous effects of natural phenomena, whereas *preparedness* is a state of readiness to cope with disasters which cannot be avoided and to minimize their impacts, particularly in terms of casualties. The crucial point in distinguishing prevention from preparedness is the desire to forestall all catastrophes to the extent possible. Preventive measures should be concentrated in areas where the risk is greatest. Costlier preventive measures should be distributed within disaster-prone regions according to the degree of risk, density of population and the amount and concentration of investment.

Pre-disaster contingency planning and preparedness include the establishment of national, regional and local administrative mechanisms, the formulation of rescue and relief plans and the implementation of such plans in times of emergency or catastrophe. Whereas disaster prevention measures are essentially comprehensive and intersectorial in nature, disaster preparedness is specifically organizational in character and should be clearly situated in the governmental structure, preferably close to the source of power, such as the prime minister's office or the office of the president (depending on the socio-political system in question). Phases and measures connected with disaster preparedness, emergency operations, rehabilitation and reconstruction as well as warning, rescue and relief will often be affected by prevention measures or, conversely, will have effects on prevention programmes.

The national authority for disaster preparedness should control and co-ordinate the actions not only of all government agencies involved, but also of all voluntary relief and rescue organizations, including the local Red Cross societies and donor organizations (bilateral and multilateral). Preparedness plans should also include the adoption of emergency measures to keep communication and transport channels open, the stockpiling of relief supplies and emergency shelters, and the earmarking of funds for relief and rehabilitation purposes in advance of any disaster.

In the vertical division of management, it is preferable to give a single national or regional authority jurisdiction over all preventive measures. Experience suggests that only comprehensive measures will be effective, but this should never be an obstacle to action. In many cases, a correct diagnosis of the main needs or difficulties in a region, or with respect to one type of disaster even when the analysis is only partial, will be more fruitful in disaster prevention than a formal administrative attempt at comprehensive measures, which will often require more time and extensive experience.

It may be said that in disaster prevention the importance of regional administration and its relationship to the national level are dictated by the fact that most disasters are regional. Regional management will have concentrated on particular aspects of the region, whereas the national government would have centralized most of the expertise, communications, administration of funds, establishment of comparative standards and the programme of research. At the international level more experience is available on the variations which manifest themselves in each type of disaster. Research on prevention and the exchange of information at the international level is also likely to bring results which cannot be obtained on a national or regional basis.

Forecasting and warning make considerable and unavoidable demands on international co-operation for disaster prevention. However, the fields of preparedness, forecasting and warning are geared to national and regional protection to the extent that they relate to the prevention of disasters in specific human settlements. Tracking and warning systems require close co-operation among meteorological agencies, public authorities, telecommunications and the disaster prevention administration which is concerned with the continuous education of the public. Warnings are effective in saving lives and equipment if the warning arrives in time and if the population is actively convinced of the danger and clearly understands the warning. In many countries, however, fewer people heed the warnings than would be expected, and frequently an inspection system should complement the warning.

Preventive measures vary for specific phenomena causing disasters. Flood damage may be prevented or reduced in a number of ways, including river basin management, afforestation and the introduction of other plant cover. As previously noted, the two most important methods of prevention are land use regulation measures and engineering measures. As a general rule, in places where density is high, engineering works may be more justifiable in economic terms, and control of land use may be more difficult.

International agreements exist in the use and management of international river basins, and disaster prevention adds another dimension to them. Where basin management agreements do not include disasters, the governments involved must reach agreements concerning flood disaster prevention.

It may not be advisable or possible to change the location of economic activities in a disaster-prone area. Relocation becomes a special issue in the case of earthquakes; it may be considered before or after the disaster and may be partial or total. Relocation may become a more serious alternative where an earthquake hazard is combined with risks of landslides and other disasters. Relocation is a drastic and costly undertaking and should be considered when it contributes to resource development within a region. On an urban scale, a decision may be made for partial, rather than total, relocation. On the other hand, whole villages may be relocated as a preventive measure against some types of disasters.

CONCLUSIONS

What conclusions may be drawn from an investigation of the potential impact of disasters upon human settlements? The two principal conclusions are that disasters constitute in many cases an acute economic development problem and that disasters, as distinct from the natural phenomena which cause them (and even that is changing), can frequently be prevented or at the very least mitigated. A third conclusion from the discussion in this paper is that the costs of prevention, especially such a simple step as a vulnerability analysis, are a fractional part of development costs and that, in terms of lives saved and physical damage avoided, the benefits are incalculable. A further conclusion is that insufficient attention has been given to disaster prevention by political decision makers and administrators at every level of consideration, from the international to the local.

Technicians and planners themselves have often looked upon disaster prevention in isolation on a case-by-case basis, and have seldom striven to include prevention in comprehensive planning. Thus, existing human settlements or those in the process of being planned and built, remain excessively vulnerable to disasters in high-risk zones, even to the extent that, following destruction, entire cities have been reconstructed in exactly the same location as before, and with little or no additional precautions for disaster prevention. Land ownership, vested interests and political reasons have all too often forced public authorities to turn a blind eye to disaster prevention. Disaster prevention for human settlements, in addition to being an economic and technical problem, is also a social, human and political one. Without a political will to adopt preventive measures to protect settlements at all levels of national life, little will be achieved in practical or technical terms.

Governments bear the basic responsibility for leadership and decision making for all actions with respect to natural disasters. Governments also carry the responsibility for initiating appropriate measures and promoting a national consciousness of disaster prevention. In many developing countries, in earthquake-prone areas, a long-term programme for the strengthening or reconstruction of houses not resistant to earthquakes should be prepared by the countries involved.

The training and education of the public in disaster preparedness and prevention must be promoted by governments as well as national and international organizations. Education in disaster prevention should begin in primary school by informing pupils about the effects of disasters and methods of protection against them. Every country must incorporate a policy of preparedness and prevention into its national development policy. Both national and regional authorities must be made fully aware of the importance of taking effective steps which will not only save lives and diminish physical damage, but equally important, help safeguard the economic development of the country concerned.

Natural catastrophes are an obstacle to the development of many countries. They affect people; they affect human settlements and the whole human environment. A natural catastrophe can weaken or even destroy the economy of a developing country. Governments must therefore recognize the importance of undertaking a "vulnerability analysis" before executing any new project. This basic step, as well as other preventive measures, is inexpensive and does not require complicated or expensive technology to carry out. Over the long term, measures for prevention and mitigation will benefit the regions most affected and provide an impetus to the attainment of an important over-all objective: the advancement of the economic and social development of peoples throughout the world.

Part II
Expert Reports Prepared for the Habitat Conference

1
Humanizing Human Settlement

Ernest Weissman, Yugoslavia

In both developing and industrial countries, the agglomeration of production and people continues in certain dominant areas at the expense of the rest. The pace of urbanization will of necessity become more rapid as countries adopt industrialization as a national development policy and as advanced technologies improve agriculture. These dynamic processes will continue to widen and deepen the crisis in human settlements, particularly in the developing countries and in the less affluent regions of the industrial world; and the least privileged groups in both will be most affected by it. Yet the crisis is also a manifestation of scientific and technological progress. It represents a promise of abundance as well as a challenge to our ability to accept changes in attitudes and values that would enable the world community to use its immense new productivity for truly bettering the human condition and closing the gap between the affluence of a few countries and the increasing poverty of the rest. The growth potential of world society as a whole multiplies with the advances in science and technology in any country in the world. But the necessary adjustments in the approach to such basic issues as the economy, land and government, for example, are very slow to come. Thus, problems multiply and in spite of ever growing debate, the urgency and hugeness of the issues are yet to be grasped.

Meanwhile, urbanization continues unchecked throughout the world. Developing countries lack the implements: the economic, technical and human resources needed to reduce, through development, the gap between economic and demographic growth; and most industrialized countries appear to be counting on an unlimited elasticity of metropolitan economies and the physical infrastructures, as well as an unlimited capacity of human beings to accept inconvenience and hardship. In the developed market economies, production facilities tend to continue settling near existing consumer markets where sufficient labour and services essential for their success are available. It is true that, in a way, wealth attracts more wealth, but many great cities have already reached the point of economic, social and environmental collapse.

This is the background of the crisis. But, how are we as a world society tackling the complex and admittedly extremely tough problems of human settlements? What role do they play in the context of development and the environment? And what about international co-operation? Some representative approaches are discussed here.

Conceptual Evolution

The commonest approach in settlement planning is still extrapolation from current and past trends. Thus, the megalopolis is being designed and redesigned by architects, planners and futurologists in the spirit of the space age and science fiction. Like their pre-war forerunners, Le Corbusier and Wright, contemporary planners are fascinated by the new forms of settlement made possible by technology. The only point they are able to prove in these exercises is that humans could some day live almost anywhere, in environments of their own making, if they could alter their attitudes, adjust their institutions and learn to apply science and technology for social progress rather than merely tolerate the side effects of their misuse. What these technological designs omit are the social, economic, political and cultural instruments which societies must conceive and mobilize in order to build a better human society and environment. The real challenge is that planning, unlike Utopia, must specify the means for achieving a future state of affairs.

The dichotomy between cultural-based (indigenous) and technology-based (international) models, so general in urban planning, emerges particularly clearly in the new designs for megapolis, whether conceived by Fuller's scientific mind or Tange's creative genius, or by planners and builders who bury their creations underground, miniaturize their cities, suspend them from giant masts, insert them in immense grid-like structures, float them in the seas, or build into the super-highway itself. As long as the dichotomy persists, urban models will exhibit either an economic bias (in terms of cost), or a design bias (in terms of civic monuments). Neither can prevail for too long.

Some urbanists expect world economic integration and the resulting urban concentration to create a super-megalopolitan organism and the emergence of a world city. 'Ekistic Ecumenopolis' would be shaped by the impact of a world population of between 20 and 35 billion, the geography of continents, and the tendency of urban growth to follow linear extensions between "centres of strong ekistic development."[1] The assumption appears to be that technology and incomes will progress spontaneously rather than be guided by human needs, at a time when, it is hoped, world society will have moved from scarcity to relative affluence and adopted the habit of planning economies and technology to ensure a human use of human beings.[2] What is forgotten in this assumption is the fact that, in a sense, the world city already exists, its medium being the transistor operated radio, the communications satellite and other new communication technologies. Information is now, or can be, instant and accessible even to the illiterate.

In their probing into its problems planners recognized early the city's essential role in the industrial society. They also diagnosed the rapidly approaching crisis of cities in transformation. Attracted by the promise of comprehensive regional and urban planning for a rational distribution and redistribution of production and people, they also recognized the opportunity provided by new technologies for the realization of the aspiration of all societies. C.I.A.M.'s charter drafted in August in 1933 puts it thus:

"... Town and country merge into one another and are elements of what may be called a regional unit. Every city forms part of a geographic, economic, social, cultural and political unit (region), upon which its development depends. Towns or cities cannot, in consequence, be studied apart from their regions, which constitute their rational limits and environment. The development of these regional units depends on:

a) *Their geographic characteristics* — climate, land and water, natural communications within the region and with other regions;

b) *Their economic potentialities* — natural resources (soil and subsoil, raw materials, sources of energy, flora and fauna), technical resources (industrial and agricultural production), the economic system and distribution of wealth;

c) *Their political and social situation* — the social structure of the population, the political regime, and the administrative system."

Through history, the character of cities has been determined by special circumstances, such as military defence, scientific discoveries, administrative systems and the progressive development of the means of production and locomotion. The basic factors governing the development of cities are therefore subject to continual changes. All these essential factors taken together constitute the only true basis for the scientific planning of any region. They are:

---

[1] C. Doxiadis; "The City of the Future," *Ekistics*, Vol. 22, No. 128, Athens, July 1966.
[2] N. Weiner; *The Human Use of Human Beings; Cybernectics and Society*, Doubleday, New York, 1954.

a) Interdependent, the one reacting upon the other; and

b) Subject to continuous fluctuations which are due to scientific and technical progress, and to social, political and economic changes.

Whether these fluctuations are forward or backward, from the human viewpoint, depends upon the measure in which man's aspirations toward the improvement of his material and spiritual well-being are able to assert themselves. The persistently neglected potential for a constructive interplay of economics, social and cultural development, new technology, industrialization and agricultural reconstruction is reflected in this statement of the town planning avant-garde of the 1930s.

The many social problems of the growing urban crisis have held the attention of the United Nations from its inception. But the explosive character of the troubled situation in most parts of the world began to be discussed by international bodies only in the 1960s and early 1970s. The United Nations Conference on Human Settlements is the culminating point in this search by the international community for workable arrangements for co-operation. Against this background, the concern of governments and the international community has shifted from isolated aspects of housing, building or town-planning to causes and consequences and the concept of comprehensive environmental development as part of general development.

Preoccupation with these problems has produced a considerable body of doctrine and experience. One could perhaps contend that it was not the lack of ideas, facts or projects that was preventing action commensurate to the world-wide crisis, and that what was missing was mainly the resources needed to demonstrate convincingly the feasibility of action. Nevertheless, United Nations aid which, in 1951, consisted of one rural housing project in a Latin American country, is evident in practically every developing country.

During the last 25 years the trend has moved away from specialized aspects of housing or town planning or building toward comprehensive environmental development. An example of this is the reconstruction in Yugoslavia of Skopje, the capital of Macedonia, a city of 200,000 almost entirely destroyed by an earthquake in 1963. In October 1965, the reconstruction plan was put on exhibition, starting the process of formal adoption by the legislative bodies in November. A variety of new approaches and techniques was applied, ranging, for example, from computer programming for emergency shelter to social surveys, employment and income projections for housing programmes and feasibility studies for transport and urban infrastructure. These techniques were used simultaneously and at a scale sufficient to permit elaboration in a very short time of a comprehensive urban and regional plan.

The reconstruction planning for Skopje is unique in several other aspects: the United Nations Educational Scientific and Cultural Organization provided aid in earth sciences, the International Labour Organisation in the area of environmental health and sanitation, and the United Nations Children's Fund in child and family welfare. The experiences of many lands were applied. United Nations aid made for a more effective use of material, technical and financial aid from national and external sources. The World Food Programme of the United Nations, the Food and Agriculture Organization and the League of Red Cross Societies provided essential extra rations and medical supplies for the rescuers and rescued and for the planners and builders during the emergency. In many ways, this undertaking has become a symbol of international solidarity and may well be a forerunner of practical international co-operation in the field of human settlements at this time of crisis.

Laissez-faire Urbanism

The first three cases discussed below illustrate the phenomenon of the spontaneous agglomeration of activities and people in response primarily to short-term requirements of economic growth and foreign trade. In the affluent countries, in the absence of any specific national policy for human settlements, action to cope with the resulting social and environmental degradation is piecemeal and ineffective, unable to repair the damage or to arrest the trend toward further degradation. In the developing countries, development oriented to external markets tends to increase national economic and political dependency, accelerate rural-urban migration, produce disproportionately large metropolitan concentrations and, in the process, destroy the traditional hierarchy of settlements, their social structure, national institutions and cultural values.

Between 1960 and 1970, the population of the metropolitan areas in the United States of America grew by 20 million, leaving an increase of less than 4 million for the rest of the country. In 1970, metropolitan areas contained over 140 million people, nearly 70 percent of the total population of the country.

The mammoth agglomeration of metropolitan areas on the eastern seaboard of the United States has been the subject of much analysis as have other megalopolitan agglomerations in North America, North Western Europe and Japan. Incipient megalopolitan growth, moreover, is a world-wide phenomenon. As a consequence, the entire hierarchy of cities so elaborately projected by urban theorists and so generally accepted by urban planners is collapsing as the metropolis and its outgrowth, the megalopolis syphon off the economies and people of the small town and rural areas. But the megalopolitan agglomeration seems to be accepted as a new kind of lifestyle, and, to the urban plane, its accidental materialization justifies its continued existence.

Does the concept of megalopolis as the ultimate form of urban settlement tally with the concept of a viable urban environment? Is the megalopolis conducive to social progress and economic growth? Are its alienated lonely people, chronic unemployment, rising crime rates, drug addiction, street violence and racial riots, its seemingly uncontrollable expansion, chaotic physical features and transport desirable models? Here are some life-saving suggestions from a community service to protect citizens against mugging, rape, burglary and murder: "... When walking at night, stay in the centre of the sidewalk or walk in the street. Avoid parked cars and alleys. Listen for footsteps. Glance around often. While travelling on public transportation, sit close to the driver or conductor. Do not have both arms laden with bundles: you have no way to defend yourself. Always lock your car while driving or parked. Never open the door to an unidentified person. Never allow anyone to follow you into the building. Do not get in an elevator which is going down. Wait for it to come back up empty. Muggers and rapists often lurk in basements. Do not ride an elevator with a lone man. If one gets on after you, push the button for the very next floor and get off. . ."[3] And so on.

An assessment of urban problems in the United States a decade ago warned of the hazards of urban neglect. It claimed that nothing short of national concern and deliberate policy would build a better environment. Until that concern and policy emerge, local decisions and individual choices will barely be able to keep abreast of decay. This of course was not an argument for central domination of local affairs, but rather a plea for elevating the cities' problems of employment or national defence, and for giving local authorities the responsibilities and the resources they deserve.

What makes a megalopolis? One United States expert gave the specifications of the New York region as follows: Population density ranges from 77,000 people per square mile in Manhattan, and about 25,000 per square mile in New York City proper, to about 200 per square mile at the edges of the region. Thus, the over-all density of the region is 2,337 people per square mile. Even the part of the region outside New York City has a density of 1,265 per square mile. As defined by the Regional Plan Association, the region covers 6,900 square miles in 22 counties and three states. Its population in 1960 was 16,139,000 persons. With nine percent of the country's population, the region provided 40 percent of all jobs in national wholesaling activities, more than one third of the jobs in finance, one quarter of the business and professional service jobs and one eighth of the jobs in manufacturing. It is highly centre-oriented. Most of the activities in which the region is ultimately dominant — finance, radio and television, advertising, publishing, fashion and corporate headquarters activities — are concentrated in the Manhattan business district to which, every day, more than three million come to work.

Although in some respects New York is unique, it is at the same time a typical megalopolitan agglomeration. The profiles of London, Paris and Tokyo in the market economy or industrialized countries, Moscow, Shanghai, Warsaw, Bucharest, Belgrade and Budapest in the countries with centrally planned economies and of Buenos Aires, Mexico City, Rio de Janeiro, Sao Paulo and Teheran in the developing world, are all similar. All are highly dynamic complexes, controlling their exploding growth with more or less success, and with an ability to create new jobs for their new citizens ranging from the centrally planned and some industrialized countries to the developing countries. But all have a common concern: problems and needs are multiplying at an explosive rate, be they migration, social change, numbers (individuals, families, organizations), movement (of people, goods, ideas), education, health or environmental deterioration. It is not the difference in degree or the variations among them that are important, but the new character of the metropolis and its new role in the maturing industrialized society.

Already in 1966, the Council of Economic Advisers to the President of the United States warned in a

[3] Ann Landers: "Play it safe in every way," *The Boston Globe*, 27 March 1976.

report that the central core of the cities had experienced a gradual process of physical and economic deterioration. As a result of people's desire for more space and home ownership, central cities lost middle and upper income families to the suburbs and became caught in a vicious spiral of spreading slums, rising crime and worsening congestion, creating an almost impossible financial situation for many cities. The report also maintained that, from the point of view of efficiency, investments should have been made in mass transit facilities instead of automobile expressways, which only increase the congestion at the centre.

Those who are seeking to accommodate the forces that, uncontrolled and unchallenged, have created the megalopolis and its accompanying ills, point to the opportunities that it offers for so-called freedom of choice. But they neglect to indicate any viable alternatives for the ordinary citizen, nor do they actually suggest that megapolitan environments, even for affluent societies, are humane in concept and practice, let alone desirable.

Many of the problems of the megalopolis created by economic growth are left unsolved. For example: "Growth *per se* does not provide the public services nor does it help the dependent and disadvantaged who are unable to participate fully in the economy. Far from solving the problems of the urban environment, it makes them infinitely more urgent. Some public services — transportation, manpower training, postal services, research and statistical facilities, for instance — must expand if private growth is to continue. Other services — control of water and air pollution, waste removal and so on — must keep pace if private growth is to be tolerable. Others again — health services, welfare services, help for the dependent — must grow if there is not to be an appalling contrast between private affluence and public squalor."

The situation continues to deteriorate. In the United States, for example, almost every big city is now nearly bankrupt. "The Federal Government, through income and corporation tax, receives the money produced by rising economic activity and incomes and the problems are left to the cities. Various means of correcting this situation have been suggested, most of them calling for the Government to underwrite the cost of providing a minimum income, thus freeing the cities from the present burden of welfare costs."[4]

In the United States the national income has risen from $88 billion in 1929 (or $40.2 billion in 1933) to $510 billion in 1964. Personal income has grown from $228 billion in 1950 to $491 billion in 1964. For 1976 it is estimated at over $1,300 billion. *Per capita* income has grown correspondingly, as has industrial and service investment and the pressure for more goods and services, housing, health and education, as well as for culture, entertainment and recreation. "The city and the fast growing metropolitan belts of America are the locations for these economic and social activities. However, the megalopolis is one of the least planned parts of the American economy. However, private corporations are large enough to embrace the tasks of planning. They assume control of the prices at which they buy and sell and they exercise reasonable influence over suppliers and customers. They do not leave things to the market; they would regard that as leaving it to chance ... when people were insufficiently fed and clothed and sheltered, economics rightly enjoyed a high priority in social calculation. But as we move on to lower orders of need — the wants that can be stimulated only by singing commercials — economics loses any natural claim to priority. Other goals are rightly advanced. And there is no reason to believe that an unplanned metropolis will have any better chance of beauty than an unmade bed ... The problem of the modern city is partly that the age of economics, with its preoccupations with private production, has denied it the public services it needs. It is partly that the same age, with its mistaken assumption of the role of the market, has denied it the planning that is commonplace elsewhere in the economy."[5]

The struggle of New York to survive is a dramatic illustration of the megalopolitan phenomenon. New York's largest deficit is largely due to generous social programmes covering a wide range of services and serving a large part of the megalopolis and the country — from health and education facilities to public housing and care for the old, the poor and the handicapped. The crux of the city's financial crisis is that, although a considerable share of the nation's wealth is created there, it cannot retain enough of the public revenue it generates to solve its problems.

Dispersed Development

In 1960, Japan formulated a long-range development policy against the background of a sustained high rate of economic growth in the post-war period. A doubling of the national income in ten years has been

---

[4] J.K. Galbraith, "The starvation of the city," *The Progressive*, December 1966, New York.
[5] *Ibid.*

projected through intensified industrialization. Subsequently, a regional approach was adopted and nine regions were established, each with its own development target. Twenty-year programmes were then prepared for infrastructural development in each region.

The stated national goals were a continuous and balanced growth of the economy, a rise in the standard of living, and conditions in which all citizens throughout the country could enjoy an affluent life and share equally in the benefits of modern society. In 1960, 1962 and 1964, the United Nations sponsored mutli-disciplinary discussions on urbanization and regional development in which, in co-operation with Japanese practioners, administrators, scholars and representatives of the different interest groups, approaches were formulated and actions recommended with regard to a number of urban, metropolitan and regional issues. Some of these recommendations have already been implemented and others are in the process of implementation.

The intended effort of Japan's ten-year plan and the projected further development was to eliminate economic and social disparities among the regions and between town and country; to close the gap between the incomes of agricultural and industrial producers; to overcome the discrepancies in the economic strength of large and small enterprises; and to create full employment. In the process, the number of full-time and part-time agricultural workers was planned to decline from 40 percent of the country's labour force in 1958 to one-third that number in 1970. Industry, power and transportation were to be expanded and better co-ordinated on a national scale. Japan achieved an amazing post-war recovery, but by the 1960s urban services and utilities in metropolitan areas were at breaking point. The infrastructure and external economies of the cities would have had to be recreated, at high cost, to allow further uninhibited growth. In order to avoid this enormous outlay, a national policy of deliberate dispersion of investment, particularly investment in physical, economic and social infrastructure, was adopted for the different regions.

Central planning, government guidance, orientation towards regional development, and local public and private initiatives for the implementation of national objectives have together evolved somewhat less central-ized patterns of settlement which will, in time, bring to the backward rural areas the benefits of urban life. The basic elements of this policy are:

(a) The establishment, through sufficient infrastructural investment and within the wider regions of the already overcrowded metropolitan areas, of suitably equipped alternative centres for industry, commerce, culture and residence. This would reduce the pressure on central cities now caused by rural migration, physical congestion and other social and environmental problems (examples: Tokyo, the National Capital Region, and Osaka/Kobe, the Kinki Region);

(b) The strengthening of the economies and infrastructure of smaller towns and cities and rural zones, the expansion of their trade and industry, and the improvement of their living conditions through suitable environmental development, improved social, educational and health services and enlarged industrial job opportunities, so as to minimize the need for internal migration thus enhancing the geographical distribution of employment; and

(c) The redevelopment of large metropolitan regions and the reinforcement of their economies by judicious investment in capital-intensive industries and services to raise productivity and the quality of life through better environmental design and better social and cultural facilities, so as to obviate or reduce the need for further physical expansion of central cities.

The Japanese policy of geographical dispersion of the means of production and of people, operating within a free enterprise economic system, has been guided by economic incentives and also necessarily, by economic benefit, often to the detriment of the quality of life and the environment.

Population concentration in urban areas has progressed rapidly in recent years through the transfer to workers from primary to secondary and tertiary industry. As a result, the ratio of the population in urban areas to the nation's total population has climbed rapidly, from 56 percent in 1955 to 72 percent in 1970. There are eight cities with more than one million people, and seven with between 500,000 and 1,000,000. There are 21 cities with from 300,000 to 500,000 inhabitants and 114 with a population from 100,000 to 300,000. The Tokyo metropolitan area (encompassing Tokyo and the three adjacent prefectures) had, in 1970, a population of about 22 million with a radius of approximately 50 kilometres, forming a megalopoli-tan agglomeration of a size and complexity without precedent in the entire history of mankind.

The concentration and expansion of economic activities in the major urban areas has intensified social ills and public hazards. On the other hand, the outflow of population from rural areas has accelerated "depopula-tion" in such areas as education, medical care and disaster prevention. The local communities are less and less able to perform their normal functions.

In the 1960s, economic efficiency and the growth of the national product were the priorities in Japan. At that time, too, 60 percent of the gross national product went into the infrastructural development, a percentage many other countries spend on armaments. This, together with national planning, dynamic regional and local development, and the habit of saving, made the income-doubling miracle come true. With growing affluence, the challenge looms larger. In the 1960s, familiar models tested for economic efficiency created astonishing productivity. Now, new development concepts, a closer partnership of government and citizens and fuller integration of all levels in planning and execution are needed in order to identify opportunities and stimulate and guide further development into socially productive channels.

The nation faces a crucial choice. Development criteria and public investment must now shift from economic to social and environmental needs, from the quantity produced to the human qualities of life desired. The tools are there, and so are the capital, talent and know-how. But social innovation is necessary to prevent growing affluence and the misuse of technology from ushering in a computerized technocracy or an era of conformity because citizens are so programmed, or else environmental decay and degradation may reach a point at which there is no hope of repair.

Incipient Megalopolis

The big cities of developing countries are experiencing similar concentrations of activities and people. The city of Tunis, a metropolitan agglomeration of about one million people, is a good example of economic development and urban growth within the constraints of external economic dependence.

Tunis is the capital city of a lopsided hierarchy of settlements: a network of smaller towns and villages, some linked to one another through intensive interchanges and others isolated in the predominantly agricultural plains of Northern Tunisia. In the nineteenth century, the city's 100,000 inhabitants comprised one-tenth of the country's population. At present, the city holds one-sixth. Tunisia's transition from a pre-industrial economy to a dependent market economy has accelerated rural migration to the capital. As a consequence, the old Arab city, the Medina, with its traditional urban pattern, gradually became enveloped by a new city laid out by the colonial authority in rectangular patterns.

The division of the city of Tunis into Arab and European quarters (physically and socially, we well as in terms of amenities and services) reflected the process of outward oriented development within the limitations imposed by political and economic dependence. In the 1940s, a third element appeared in the form of numerous shanty towns inhabited by landless peasants. This was a direct consequence of a concentration of land ownership and the intensive mechanization of grain production for the world market, both processes characteristic of the consolidation of colonial relationships.

By 1956, Tunis had an urban structure consisting of the Medina, whose traditional functions were vanishing, a colonial city which was the centre of political and economic power, and a series of shanty towns containing the rural people who had fled from rural misery. This urban structure was based on, and an outcome of, social and racial segregation among the French and Italian colonists, the Tunisian landlords, the emerging *bourgeoisie* (active in commerce and the professions), the working class tied to the colonial economy, the unemployable migrants and certain ethnic and religious minorities.

Like other newly independent nations, Tunisia faced the problem of transforming its socio-economic structure from that of a dependent colony into a national economy; turning the capital of a colonial society into an integrated national capital; and transforming the country's settlement network, which had served the interests of a colonial power, into a system designed to promote national development.

At first Tunisia attempted to do this through the planned development of its infrastructural base and through dispersed industrialization. Both elements of this development strategy were intended to reduce and ultimately eliminate regional disparities. A temporary effect of the policy was to ease the pressure of rural migration on the capital city. In the long run, however, they were unable to resolve all the problems created by the collapse of rural communities. Regionalization and co-operatives were added as supplementary development instruments.

These measures redistributed economic activities to a degree and stabilized the flow of migration for a time, but they were unable to eliminate the grave structural imbalances of an outwardly oriented economy built in the colonial era. The division of Tunis continued, the shanty towns continued to grow, new prestigious housing estates sprang up at the expense of shelter for the lowest income groups and the capital acquired some representative structures: an Olympic stadium, a congress hall, many office buildings and so on. However, in spite of these heavy investments, the needed basic restructuring and integration of Tunis as national capital did not materialize.

Since 1970, a new development is being implemented, relying largely on private initiative aided by new legislation and supportive public investment. In the process of reorganizing agricultural co-operatives, a large number of small land-owners have seen their former holdings incorporated in larger units. This, together with additional agricultural mechanization, has resulted in a new wave of migration. The total effect has been a further transfer of rural people from the interior into Tunisia's coastal areas.

A second strategy instrument of the new economic policy was the 1972 investment code enabling foreign based industries to produce, on Tunisian territory, goods destined exclusively for the foreign market. The consequence in terms of human settlements was this: in the absence of alternative incentives, investment tended to locate in the better equipped urban areas, particularly the metropolitan region of Tunis, where there exists an abundant supply of labour, a harbour, an airport, automatic telecommunications, office space, hotel facilities, and some high standard housing. The result: a large part of foreign investment under the new policy is concentrated in the Tunis metropolitan area and the excessive growth of the city and its predominance over the rest of the country continues to increase. Modern structures are multiplying and, at the same time, the shanty towns are extending rapidly. The long term social cost to the nation of this development model may far outweigh the short term economic benefit which is its primary motivation.

The policy of creating favourable conditions for foreign investment has further polarized growth in metropolitan Tunis. The capital city is now becoming more than ever an overgrown center of production and economic power, geared to the requirements of external markets instead of national needs. The former colonial structure has become an "externalized" development based on economic dependence and the resulting urbanization patterns cannot but be a continuation of those of the colonial era.

A combination of *laissez-faire* in economic development and orientation to external requirements and, consequently, economic dependence on external sources, are often determining factors for patterns of settlement in the developing countries. These economic and political factors, together with the consequences of unprecedented population growth and concentration in the metropolitan areas, are giving rise in the developing countries to urban agglomerations which bear all the characteristics of megalopolitan development, minus the resources required to cope with the problems it generates.

Deliberate Settlement

Whether uncontrolled growth occurs in a highly industrialized country or in a developing, pre-industrial country, it leads to social and environmental dislocation and human degradation. Other approaches to development have been conceived and tested in a number of countries over the past few decades. Some of them are discussed below, as illustrations of the crucial issues involved and the instruments that have been applied to implement these approaches in societies with different economic and political systems, operating at different levels of technology and development, and within the different value systems of their respective cultures.

The planning of urban development in the socialist countries of Eastern Europe is usually an integrated part of planned national development. In the redevelopment of existing large metropolitan cities in the Soviet Union, for example, no encouragement is given to new industries, save for communal services and the construction, particularly housebuilding, industry. New industries are preferably located in new or existing medium sized or smaller cities, which are then developed to what is regarded as the optimum size of 200,000 to 250,000 inhabitants. Settlements having enterprises that are interrelated in terms of their use of materials, production processes, products, power transport and utilities, are planned in accordance with regional and sectoral, long range economic development plans. The distribution of the population increment is guided as far as possible into preferred locations through co-ordinated and selective industrial and agricultural development.

In 1970, the national plan anticipated that, over a period of 20 years, industrial production would increase by about 500 percent and agriculture by 250. The plan called for the full electrification, mechanization and automation of industry and agriculture, new production processes, the development of new sources of energy and materials, and a sharp rise in productivity. A balanced pattern of growth, the control of undue concentrations in large cities and an important reduction in urban/rural differences in incomes and amenities was expected to result from this policy. Regional development within the national plan was to be the general frame of reference for all urban development planning.

An indication of the tremendous volume of construction and the amount of resources mobilized for the urban programme in the USSR is the fact that over 800 new towns were built between the early 1920s and the early 1960s, at an annual rate of construction of 3 million dwelling units, or over 14 units per thousand population: the highest rate of housing construction anywhere. Between 1960 and 1980, urban population is expected to rise from 50 to 70 percent of the national total. By 1960 already half the urban dwellers lived in cities of over 500,000. Since very large cities, as well as very small settlements are not easy to equip, and the *per capita* cost for amenities and services being high in relation to the levels of convenience and comfort provided, the distribution of population and the location of industry and agricultural development is being planned in order to obviate overcrowding and congestion. In agricultural areas also, urban type settlements are to be established, equipped with the necessary utilities and services, and with educational, cultural, social and health institutions.

In the USSR, a city of 200,000 to 250,000 people, is expected to offer the following: a convenient and relatively short journey to work, a variety of high standard cultural and social amenities and an economically efficient organization for the building and maintenance of the city. There are, essentially, three types of amenities provided. Those designed for the daily use of the family (for example, kindergarten and junior schools, local shops, repair facilities, markets, sports and playgrounds) are provided in neighbourhoods, within a radius of from 300 to 500 metres; those used periodically (clubs and cinemas, cafés and restaurants, department stores and shopping centres, bank, post and telegraph, pharmacy and clinic, centres for physical recreation and parks) are provided in residential areas or districts of about 900 to 1,000 metres in radius and having a population of 25,000 to 35,000. The third category (which includes theatres, concert and conference halls, specialized shops and large department stores, stadiums and large parks) serves the entire city.

The integration of the different socio-economic functions within the city and the simultaneous development of the required structures, services and systems are basic tenets of settlement planning in the centrally planned economy countries of Eastern Europe. A gradual shift is now under way from the traditional economic cost/benefit approach to a benefit/cost approach. Thus, it is anticipated that the provision of urban services and facilities, including housing, will be less and less guided by strictly economic considerations and may be available ultimately free of charge to the user, although still at a cost to the local economy. Urban and regional development theories, policy and practice are based on the acceptance of a close integration of socio-economic and environmental development, and an understanding of the role of the latter in shaping the physical framework for development generally. Consequently, environmental development in its broadest sense includes housing, communal services and facilities, as well as the necessary infrastructure and environmental protection. The provision of an environment compatible with the resources available and the accepted standards is regarded as a justifiable and indeed productive investment.

Town planning in the centrally planned economy countries of Eastern Europe is carried out in advance of, or at least simultaneously with, new economic development. Every plan, whether national, regional or local, global or sectoral, has its physical and social services counterpart. After nearly six decades of effort, a wealth of practical experience exists and a variety of urban models can be observed at the planning, implementation and real life stages. As a result of this massive experience, as well as growing affluence and rapid scientific and technological progress, the present strong economic and physical bias of settlement planning is likely to be replaced by a more integrated, multidisciplinary approach. The resulting balanced interplay of economic, social, environmental and cultural factors in development planning could then produce viable concepts, theories and models of settlement systems for contemporary industrial society, which would not only be technically efficient but also designed to promote a continuous improvement of the human qualities of life and a considerable reduction in the use of energy and other scarce resources.

Large areas of Poland, the USSR and the other centrally planned economy countries in Eastern Europe were devastated in the Second World War. Post-war efforts to reconstruct the large cities, towns and villages were supported by planned economic growth and by the necessary changes and advances in construction and building material technologies, all of which created conditions conducive to industrialized building. This enabled these countries to replan and rebuild the settlement networks they had inherited, and ultimately to reorganize them in accordance with their new role as agents of further economic growth and as desirable places in which to live.

In framing its Fifth National Development Plan, the Government of Iran adopted a regional approach as a national policy and a supplement to national and sectoral planning. This policy is largely a response to the recognition that, in conditions of rapid economic growth and social change, development planning cannot be effectively implemented unless it includes a geographical dimension.

Eleven regions have been defined and surveyed to identify development trends and determine the broad outlines of further development, consistent with their potential. The analyses include recommendations for regional development policies and for economic and social programmes and projects to be incorporated into the plan. These economic, social, environmental and institutional development strategies for the eleven regions are compatible with and linked to sectoral and national development. A major step in implementing this policy of regionalization is the establishment of regional planning offices. Some 16 to 23 development regions will ultimately be established, possibly one for each province.

The regional offices are responsible for formulating comprehensive plans for their respective territories. This planning, as well as the interregional co-ordination of development within the framework of national sectoral and general objectives, is guided by the national planning agency. Within each region, special areas are being identified, such as agricultural areas and city-centred "micro-regions," where more intensive and detailed planning is required. A research programme has identified 140 city-centered micro-regions with suitable levels of "habitability," where intensive development was already located in the past or could be effectively located now.

One of the purposes of the regional plans is to designate suitable locations for "growth poles," for industry and agriculture, urban centres and services, and facilities for tourism. They also establish criteria for selecting, among potential locations, those which will most rapidly produce the projected socio-economic development in their wider "macro-regions." The plans will also contain detailed development and investment schedules, containing lists of projects and priorities for short-term programmes for each development zone or micro-region, identified on the basis of feasibility studies.

Growth poles, growth centres and zones designated for immediate development are regarded as suitable vehicles for spreading the benefits of economic growth more equally within the regions and throughout the country. The policy is based on the premise that an effective integration of industry, agriculture and social services, as well as the integration of the urban and rural aspects of development, can be conceived in a more concrete way and can be rendered more manageable at the regaional and sub-regional levels than at the national level. The approach is also expected to produce easier ways of implementing plans in the short run, and greater cumulative social and economic effects in the long run.

This regionalization of development is being instituted in Iran against a backdrop of intensified industrialization and rapid urbanization: metropolitanization. The powerful effects of these processes have already created major regional disparities in incomes and living standards. At the same time, large parts of the country are still insufficiently surveyed and their potential in terms of natural resources and human capacities still relatively unknown. To support the regional approach in development planning, the relevant processes and procedures are being restructured in order to facilitate co-ordinated planning and plan implementation, particularly in the regional context; the in-service training of the requisite regional planning teams; and research designed to strengthen the two-way integration of national and regional planning. Regional settlement systems are the instruments through which development, in terms both of economic growth and social change, is expected to be obtained and its benefits distributed more equally throughout the nation.

The current Five-Year Plan of Peru combines a medium term development model, conceived within a longer term projection, with relevant legal, financial and political-administrative action, requisite changes in the environmental structure (the urban/rural settlement system) and the institutional and social reforms needed to alter Peru's society and economy. The latter is to be achieved by directly involving the emerging social groups in the development process, in particular the industrial workers, urban poor and rural people. This effort to encourage public participation is intended to bring about a social transformation whereby these formerly passive, inarticulate and oppressed groups will start to participate through their own autonomous organizations in the control of their country's key resources, the ownership of the means of production and the making of strategic decisions affecting Peruvian society as a whole, as well as in their own fate, and the fate of their families. To achieve this, public authorities are also expected to change from "bureaucrats" to agents of development and change. The Plan's stated purpose is to eliminate existing inequalities and economic and social disparities, rather than to create an industrial society as such.

The Peruvian Plan is firmly based on the concept of specialized development in particular geographical areas which are at the same time closely linked with the rest of the nation and neighbouring countries. Present investment resources are insufficient for the development of all areas of the country. The Plan therefore introduces selective regionalization. Its main objectives are:

(a) To reduce demographic pressure on metropolitan Lima through the selective development of economic, social and physical infrastructures elsewhere in Peru; and

(b) To create alternative growth centres and offer new locations for major projects through the development of additional sites equipped to accommodate them.

The urban and rural underemployed will be able to find jobs in pursuits that are neither typcially urban nor typically rural, but instead intended to develop basic utilities, transport and communicating networks, hydraulic projects and harbours, and similar programmes that can use large inputs of relatively unskilled labour. In order to raise productivity, the Plan envisages supporting these labour-intensive methods by suitably mechanizing the production process at strategic points. These projects and programmes will provide basic training for large numbers of people of rural origin on their way to becoming industrial workers.

The principal features of the Plan are as follows:

(a) Public investment in basic industries and infrastructure will grow over the five-year period to a point at which it can ensure self-sustained economic growth and social development.

(b) Social development is conceived as a process of transformation of a society through institutional reform and through education geared to productivity and the acceptance of change as the vehicle of progress.

(c) Public participation in local and regional development within the larger national Plan will be stimulated and co-ordinated, both territorially and sectorally, in line with vital local needs and available total resources.

(d) Public resources will be reserved for strategically important projects, such as the development of natural resources, infrastructure to support agriculture and industry, and strategically located settlements.

(e) Full employment will be achieved by combining a variety of innovative approaches and technologies (for infrastructural development, environmental improvement, etc.) with labour-intensive techniques.

(f) Imported technology will decline in importance as a result of the intensive development of human capacities, through self-management and participation in urban and rural settlement activities, and the merger and conversion of industrial plants together with the joint provision of essential services and facilities.

These and similar measures will barely begin to cope with the long-standing problems of regional inequality inherent in the existence of an over-extended and overcrowded metropolis in the midst of underdevelopment. The situation is one of environmental decay and social dislocation, growing diseconomies and rapidly increasing economic, social and cultural disparities between the centre and the periphery. The regional development embodied in the Plan seeks to restructure Peru's economy and society by creating political and administrative institutions and a system of settlement designed to reverse the current trends toward centralization, environmental degradation and depressed living conditions in town and country alike. A more equitable distribution of income is expected to result, particularly in areas rich in natural resources and human capacities, where existing urban centres can be strengthened and improved or new ones created.

New Approaches

The gap in incomes and living conditions between the affluent and the developing parts of the world keeps on widening. Currently, seven eighths of the world's wealth is produced, and largely consumed, by one third of its population. By the end of the century, according to United Nations estimates, the other two thirds will have to provide as much urban employment in tolerable environments as the industrialized countries have done in the whole course of their history. And they will have to do this with only one-eighth of the world's gross product. To tackle this task, innovative approaches are needed.

In some countries, for example, squatting is becoming an accepted form of rapid urbanization. The new social organization, which has emerged in some squatter settlements, co-operative in nature, relying strongly on self-help, self-management and direct action, is beginning to be used in a genuine partnership between governments and the people in a number of countries. In other cases, public participation is becoming institutionalized within the general development process, and in connexion with the development and improvement of the quality of life in settlements more particularly. Experience to date shows, however, that such efforts at deliberate urbanization and at mobilizing the people's resources and skills for development purposes require very careful planning. As instruments for implementing national settlement policies, programmes of this kind need to be fully integrated with the other elements of settlement strategies at the local, regional and national level.

Development planning in China is motivated by social criteria and a concern for the human qualities of life. Rural development and a reduction of the differences in living standards between town and country are primary goals. Thus, industries are being dispersed as much as possible throughout the countryside and urban dwellers are encouraged to move with them. In some cases, entire large enterprises with their equipment and staffs have been transferred out of the very big cities, to the benefit both of their overcrowded original community and of their adopted ones. This deliberate strategy of development dispersion, combined with the integration of town and country, industry and agriculture, is consistently pursued. Together with programmes for the social and cultural development of the individual, the family and the community, it has already begun to create highly innovative patterns of settlement and new forms of social relations. These, in conjunction with the new institutional structure resulting from there, are conducive to the attainment of higher levels of living and an improved quality of life.

China's rural development policy is directed to the village as a part of a commune of several villages, the basic unit for the implementation of the national agricultural policy. The land in the commune is owned collectively by its members, but a small amount is privately owned. The annual and long term production goals for the commune are set by the central Government, but day-to-day operations are locally controlled.

Apathy towards increasing production, which was a feature of Chinese village life before the revolution, has largely been overcome. One of the instruments of this change appears to have been the grant of small private plots to each family for raising pigs and cultivating vegetables and bamboo or fruit trees in their spare time. Families may barter or sell this produce at local markets.

The produce of the commune proper is distributed among its members, after determining the share of the members according to their work and productivity (the "work point" system). The rest of the produce is exported to the cities and towns. These exports provide the capital out of which most agricultural development has been financed. This economic self-reliance has been a major feature of Chinese agricultural development policy. Some of the land is irrigated.

Traditionally, animal labour was used to drive irrigation mechanisms and in years of drought, it was common for the cattle population to decline substantially from overwork and undernourishment. Today, most of the irrigation and drainage is mechanized and ponds and tube wells generally provide an ample supply of water. Farm machinery increasingly supplements human and animal labour in the fields.

Most of the nitrogen, phosphorous and potassium fertilizers come from organic sources, principally animal dung and night soil. The total of the nitrogen used is 12 million metric tons per year, which averages about 60 kilogrammes per hectare of cultivated land. Rice, being the favoured crop, gets larger than average applications of manure and fertilizers. This rate of fertilizer use is quite high, comparable to that in many industrialized countries. That most of this fertilizer comes from organic sources reflects the remarkable and careful husbanding of organic manure that has characterized Chinese agriculture for centuries.

Rural development has been pursued in other countries in somewhat different ways. "Arango," a hypothetical village in northern Mexico, may serve as a prototype to illustrate what has been called the "green revolution."[6]

Arango was first established as a collective *ejido* (village), but the land is now held or leased by individual *ejidatarios* (heads of households). The *ejidos* as collectives withered away in the 1940s and 1950s because of government neglect, lack of effective extension services, the desire of the peasants to have their own land, mismanagement and the preferential lending policies of the Ejido Bank to individual *ejidatarios*. The 80 households of Arango (supporting 420 people) have 380 hectares of irrigated land, with an average holding of 4.8 hectares. The smallest farm is four hectares and the largest seven — a remarkably small spread compared with other parts of Latin America and the developing countries in general. There are also 700 hectares of unirrigated land. By the standards of most of the rural populations, Arango is a rich community. It illustrates the dramatic difference that high yielding seeds (particularly wheat), irrigation, fertilizers and fuel have made in agricultural productivity in Mexico and elsewhere.

The Laguna region in which Arango is situated has an arid subtropical climate with hot summers and relatively cool winters. The annual rainfall is only about 30 centimetres. Because of the scanty rainfall, unirrigated land produces a meagre harvest and is therefore not cultivated, particularly as surpluses of wheat are produced by the use of high yielding varieties on the irrigated land. The soil of Arango is shallow and stony, typical of over 50 percent of Mexico. There is sparse shrub and grass cover, some suitable for grazing. The soil is fertile if irrigated, and dry farming is possible in some areas.

---

[6] A. Makhijani, *Energy and Agriculture in the Third World*, Ballinger Publishing Company, Cambridge, Mass., 1975.

Most of Arango's cultivated land is irrigated by an intricate system of canals fed by the Nazas River, which never runs dry; 30 percent is irrigated from the six wells in the *ejido* and the remaining 10 percent from the Aguanaval River which is dry in December and January. Irrigation has freed the *ejidatarios* from the vagaries of the highly variable and scant rainfall of the region and enabled them to use high yielding seed varieties and fertilizers in a farming cycle that is largely under human control. However, the level of the water table in the region is dropping, and there is a danger that the water may cease to be usable in the foreseeable future. Farm machinery is widely employed, as are fertilizers and pesticides. Draft animals mingle with machines in providing labour for farms, but most of the horsepower used for farming comes from machines. In addition, there are mechanical irrigation pumps with a total of about 100 horsepower. Animal dung is not used either for fertilizer or fuel.

The people of Arango use substantially more commercial energy than their counterparts in the villages of most developing countries. Each home has a kerosene lamp, half have potable running water, one fifth have electricity, and one third have gas stoves. Many families spend US $50 or more a year on gas, kerosene and electricity. Two thirds of the people still heat their houses and cook by burning agricultural wastes such as cotton stubble. The largest indirect energy input imported into the *ejido* comes in the form of chemical fertilizer. One hundred and twenty kilogrammes per hectare are commonly used for the high yielding wheat varieties which are in almost universal use in this region.

Most of the agricultural production is exported to the cities either through private traders or through the Ejido Bank. The considerable surplus production is responsible for the relative prosperity of farmers in this region of northern Mexico. In fact, most of the food for Mexican cities and towns is provided by the surpluses of a relatively few farmers who, by and large, live in northern Mexico.

In Karachi, Pakistan's largest city, a comprehensive programme has been developed for creating integrated and self-sustaining urban communities, known as *metrovilles*. The programme is designed to provide housing for low income groups as well as to secure the co-ordination of various other social programmes such as health, education, housing finance, low-cost building techniques, small-scale industries and handicrafts, community development and social welfare.

A *metroville* project which will ultimately house 35,000 people has already been launched on a 200 acre site near an industrial trading estate, and a number of agencies have joined hands in an effort to ensure that all utilities, services and public facilities are available to the *metroville* population. The site is being developed in plots ranging from 80 to 400 square yards, most of which will be supplied with utility walls. The utility wall concept is of particular interest in situations where, owing to lack of funds, the public sector is unable to build complete housing units. These basic walls are later incorporated in the kitchen and bathroom. The idea is that they will at least ensure hygienic living standards, while at the same time giving individuals an opportunity to build their own homes, using materials and techniques they can afford. Further walls can be added in stages and accommodation increased to meet individual requirements.

Rural programmes have a much longer history in Pakistan. Land reform, the "green revolution" and other developments in the agricultural sector were unsuccessful in eliminating underemployment among the landless peasants and small farmers. At the same time, easier access to information — a wide range of educational programmes, including programmes on agriculture, are broadcast in the national and regional languages — made the rural population more conscious of its rights, and more dissatisfied with the lack of amenities in the rural areas. Rural-urban migration increased considerably as a result.

There have been more than two decades of rural programmes in Pakistan which have sought to stem this tide. The Village Aid Programme, started in 1954, was replaced in 1962 by the Rural Works Programme, organized under the provisions of the Basic Democracies Order of 1959. The programme was administered by councils at four levels, the lowest, or union level, consisted of members representing the villages. The three higher levels included members of the bureaucracy and the general public.

In 1972, the Integrated Rural Development Programme was launched. It encompasses practically all aspects of rural life, with the main emphasis on the achievement of self-sufficiency in food production, control of waterlogging and salinity, land reclamation, the procurement of agricultural supplies and credit facilities. The programme operates through centres (each covering an area of 300 to 500 square miles) responsible for transmitting innovations in farming to the 60 to 100 villages under their jurisdiction. This arrangement is expected to aid the small farmer rather than the farmers with larger holdings who benefited most from the previous programmes.

Another programme initiated in 1972 is expected to bring urban facilities to small towns in the rural areas, in order to relieve big cities of the continuing population pressure. These *agrovilles* would offer their inhabitants both urban amenities and opportunities for participation in civic life. In broad outline, the programme envisages the development of existing towns, or the establishment of relatively self-contained new urban settlements, with a balanced range of essential public services and socio-economic and cultural facilities. The *agroville* would function as a market place, offer employment to the inhabitants of the surrounding rural areas, including artisans, and contain establishments for the storage and processing of agricultural produce, small manufacturing industries, repair workshops for agricultural machinery, cotton ginning, rice husking, flour mills and workshops for servicing tractors. If resources permitted, even large industries could be located there. The well planned and systematic development of these centres is expected to remove some of the present inadequacies, end the exploitation of the small farmer and increase the co-ordination and integration of rural and urban activities.

The Government, conscious of the fact that agriculture can never provide full employment for all surplus farm labour, and that the rural areas cannot at present offer an adequate alternative in the way of gainful occupation, is undertaking a programme of rural industrialization to fight against mass poverty and to bring social facilities and amenities to the forgotten rural masses. If rural settlements are linked either to a larger village or to a township supplying some form of social or economic services, the problem of locating these industries can be simplified. One of the objectives of the *agroville* programme is to provide as many of the urban amenities as possible in strategically located rural settlements. Certain locations within the rural agricultural settlements may possess a high degree of social organization, but skilled manpower will still be required to run the industries. In many cases, even the semi-skilled labour required to run small scale or cottage industries is not available in rural areas. Therefore, the plans for these new settlements include basic training institutions such as vocational schools and polytechnics.

Agroville sites are selected by the provinces in consultation with the Federal Government. In selecting sites, due care is taken to ensure that the proposed *agrovilles* are centres or potential growth poles within the regional framework. Once a site is approved, a feasibility study is made, including analyses of present migratory trends, communications, health, education, sewerage and drainage facilities available, water resources, potential for mineral and industrial development and present levels of commercial activity. The study also contains details of the cropping pattern in the surrounding agricultural areas and the possibilities of locating agro-based industries.

In the planning and development of these settlements, the direct focus is on the farmer and the development of agriculture and agro-based industries, as well as increased employment, higher standards of living, better education and other amenities and, of course, increase of productivity in all sectors. These objectives cannot be achieved through random and scattered investments in small towns or villages. Instead, they call for technical judgements of perspective growth points involving geographical, economic, sociological and other aspects. Premature action not based on proper study is likely to lead to excessive costs and waste of scarce capital and energy without achieving the anticipated social returns.

A number of feasibility studies have been completed and plans for some of the *agroville* sites are in preparation. These plans include the basic infrastructure and once this is available, no difficulty is expected in establishing industries along with civic amenities in the area. If the *agroville* development programme is planned and implemented systematically, new jobs are expected to follow for the now underemployed farm labour and the unemployed artisans, semi-skilled and skilled workers in the surrounding rural areas. If this can be achieved, the large influx into heavily industrialized urban areas should be considerably reduced. Rural dwellers undoubtedly prefer to live in their own surroundings provided there are employment opportunities and other amenities.

Tanzania is perhaps the world's best example of the use of a human settlement strategy to accomplish comprehensive developmental objectives. More than 90 percent of Tanzania's population is rural and the *ujamaa*[7] village programme is one of the very few attempts to produce rural based self-reliant development. At the same time, the objective of this strategy is to slow down the growth rate of Dar-es-Salaam and to achieve adequate growth in the regional cenres, balancing the population growth among them by distributing employment opportunities in decentralized patterns. The *ujamaa* concept is Tanzania's answer to the crucially

---

[7]*Ujamaa* is a Swahili word which literally means "familyhood." The term is used to describe Tanzania's form of socialism.

urgent concern of the developing countries in particular to evolve viable alternatives to the conventional development models emphasizing industrialization and foreign trade. The *ujamaa* principle of self-reliance is an innovative approach. It is a rare exception in development planning, where a nation espouses a non-conventional model and commits itself to develop its people's human capacities rather than just industrializing for the sake of the world market demand. China, Cuba, Peru, the USSR and Yugoslavia are some other examples of nations adopting this approach.

The *ujamaa* approach is now being applied in the building of the new capital city, Dodoma, which is replacing the colonial capital, Dar-es-Salaam. Dodoma is planned as the metropolitan centre of a region in which all settlements, rural and urban, including the capital city, are based on the *ujamaa* concept at the neighbourhood and local community level.

Tanzania is committed to the *ujamaa* approach to development and the principle of regionalization. It emphasizes most strongly requisite social changes and political participation of citizens in directing socio-economic and cultural development, as well as in the decision making concerning societal changes, the quality of life and the environment. A structural reorganization of the rural areas of Tanzania into viable socio-economic and political communities was launched in 1967. The *ujamaa* villages are intended to transform now private and scattered production activities into communal planned production.

The *ujamaa* villages are socialist organizations, created by people who decide to live and work together for their common good. They are governed by those who live and work in them. The peasants form these villages either into existing traditional communities or they move on to unused land or regroup their scattered homesteads to establish new villages. Members of *ujamaa* villages own and run their communal farms and other projects such as shops, flour mills, pre-primary and primary schools, dispensaries, and cultural and recreational activities. The size and population of a village depends on the land available. There is no standard pattern of organization for all *ujamaa* villages. Each village is organized in ways compatible with its socio-economic and physical environment. Creative local planning is encouraged.

The main objectives of the *ujamaa* approach are:

(a) To engender awareness among members, organize total opposition to exploitation in any form, and create instead a sense of communal spirit by working together for the benefit of all;

(b) To secure employment and a fair income to every member of the village;

(c) To expand the socialist economic undertakings of the village by establishing communal farms, shops, industries, and commercial and service activities;

(d) To market the products of the village, including those from private plots;

(e) To construct the buildings and offices and buy machines and other equipment needed for the development of the village;

(f) To co-operate with other *ujamaa* villages or para-statal institutions in commercial undertaking in ways compatible with the common good;

(g) To provide to the villagers adult and primary education, medical care, pure water, better housing and other services contributing to an adequate material standard of living and fuller human development; and

(h) To be an example to Tanzanians who are not members, so that they can see the benefit of the *ujamaa* way of living.

A general meeting consisting of all the villagers runs the affairs of the village. The meeting is convened four times a year and the day-to-day management of the village rests with the executive committee elected by the general meeting.

Several short and long term benefits are expected from the *ujamaa* programme. Among these are:

(a) Creation of self-reliant and self-determining communities as a basis for national self-reliance;

(b) Avoidance of exploitation and excessive differentiation in wealth, income and power;

(c) Better utilization of rural labour to realize the potential productivity of peasants working together, specialization of functions, division of labour, work discipline and leadership;

(d) Openness to technical innovation, through increases in scale, and readier access to farmer education;

(e) Facilitating of national planning, both as to the formulation of over-all goals and decentralized implementation;

(f) Creating communities which can relate effectively to government officials and councils following the 1972 decentralization of most governmental functions directly affecting individuals.

Movement to villages is now compulsory, but the transformation of a village into an *ujamaa* village is voluntary.

The results of the *ujamaa* programme to date are many. First, the human settlement pattern has been transformed from one dominated by scattered homesteads and hamlets to one of more compact communities. Access to basic health, adult education, primary education and communication facilities has greatly improved. Access to skills, directly productive knowledge and inputs has increased. Access to food has improved; the change in settlement pattern was useful in identifying and meeting deficits during the 1973-1975 drought.

Mistakes have been made through poor planning and substitution of exhortation and coercion for education and participation. However, these have usually been identified and corrected. Communal action has increased rapidly with regard to infrastructure, new economic activities and new crops. Egalitarianism has also progressed: private plots are unequal in size but not radically so.

Participation within villages has broadened and the degree of rural elite control has declined. The villages have often been able to exert far more influence on the decentralized government structure than on the elite-dominated co-operative unions or the agents of central government bodies before the *ujamaa* period. Village self-reliance has been unequal in terms of goals and achievements. In many cases, it has risen. Ideological development has begun, especially the realization that basic needs can be met. Adult education and improved communication have led to broader and deeper individual and community consciousness.

Tanzanians do not claim to have achieved participatory, self-reliant socialist development but only to have begun the long transition to it. They do not claim that the *ujamaa* core of rural development is complete, but that it has begun to emerge. As regards planning, they believe that the participatory nature of their society demands the evolution of sequences and programmes within the strategic framework rather than the laying down of detailed patterns for the year 2000. The *ujamaa* principle, as applied in development, and the Tanzania National Union network of political action represent important instruments for mobilizing the people's own resources for the development effort and for integrating the socio-economic-environmental stream of technical planning with the societal-cultural (political-financial-legislative) stream of planning within the conceptual framework of self-reliance and human development as fundamental motivations.

Decision making in Yugoslavia is based on self-management and the participation of individual citizens and the collectivities representing the societal interest and territorial entities. Planning on the central (federal) scale is, therefore, only indicative. Long term and medium term plans and objectives are based on and reflect the planning experiences and development trends of the past 25 years. It is firmly based on the development potentials, aspirations and plans of the federated republics and the two autonomous provinces, the country's original planning regions. A further subdivision has been found to be necessary in recent years and is now being realized.

The national plan includes indicative sectoral plans which are more specific as to quantitative and locational objectives, with time sequences for execution, and relative priorities for the allocation of resources. As planning moves from the central scale, via the republic, province and region, to the local scale projects in a given commune, it becomes more detailed, more definitive and more concrete in terms of actual location and product, and more specific in terms of social benefit and economic cost.

Thus, comprehensive development planning in Yugoslavia is a continuum covering all levels and scales. Regional development planning has assumed in this context the dynamic function of identifying, for a given area, development objectives which are consistent with national development goals, policies and strategies and realistic in terms of regional and local potentials and aspirations. In co-ordinating intra-regional and inter-regional development, such planning facilitates the co-ordination of sectoral planning, both regional and national, for a balanced and therefore also a more productive development.

In Yugoslavia, comprehensive regional planning is not, of course, a substitute for all other types of planning. Instead, it aims at integrating the different sectoral plans into a coherent whole; it identifies the critical areas of interaction among related development factors and activities and provides for a more effective and productive interaction through mutually beneficial accommodation and adjustment. A comprehensive approach for coherence, compatibility and internal consistency is a basic prerequisite of all planning, whether territorial (local, or regional and national) or sectoral, or project planning and programming.

The local community is the place in which the citizen participates personally and through the political process in decisions concerning development in his own community. Decisions by other governmental entities can be influenced by the citizen through the political system, through the system of participation in management at the enterprise level, or through other types of producer and service organizations and bodies such as trade unions or professional associations. The incentive for public participation in local or regional development efforts is the availability to the governments of such entities of considerable resources to implement the decisions arrived at through participation.

In Yugoslavia, the region has been established as the intermediate level or scale of planning particularly for settlements in the context of development. This does not imply, however, that the role of local government has diminished. On the contrary, direct contacts between local government and the governments of the republics, the provinces and the federation have been strengthened. Instead of a vertical "line of command" from the central to the regional to the local level of government, and *vice versa*, there is interaction and partnership.

To make this relationship really meaningful, an essential condition must be met. Any decision concerning an area and its people must be subject to approval by the government of the area. Since every investment project ends in a given locality, the community concerned is consulted about it. The local community or commune then approves or rejects the plan, project, or programme after being fully apprised of the economic, social and environmental consequences involved. Thus two sets of checks on federally sponsored projects enter into the process: it is determined first whether the proposed project or programme conforms to the regional plan, and second whether it is acceptable to the local community concerned and conforms to the community's plan. The procedure is, of course, reversed if the initiative is local, and works both ways if it is regional.

This may seem to be an unduly complex process, but experience proves that it can be quite efficient. People learn very quickly to assess whether a suggested development will benefit them and their community, or whether it will affect them adversely. Some of the basic criteria for such an appraisal are: does the proposed intervention improve the living conditions in the community concerned? Does it improve the quality of life for the average citizen? What will the intended economic advantages cost in terms of environmental degradation? What will be the cost in terms of social and human development which must be delayed in order to accomodate the proposed intervention?

Human, social and environmental concerns, coupled with the specifically Yugoslav frame of reference of self-management, lead naturally to a conception of development planning as a continuing process in which the people, government and planners interact productively in reaching requisite decisions. In the recent evolution of a model of this process, in the case of comprehensive development planning for the Belgrade region, these changing and interrelated factors have been accommodated in six phases of a continuing process: formulation of goals and objectives; analysis of relevant information; multi-level and multi-sectoral planning; decentralized plan implementation; suitable monitoring and evaluation; and periodic revisions of all phases in the light of current achievements. This process of continuous development planning, however, operates within another continuum of plan periods, namely: short term, medium term and long term prospective development planning.

The objective is not a single model of a future situation (1985) for the region but rather to develop an appropriate model for the permanent planning of its development. This planning system, which includes sectoral planning in the economic and social fields, relates to yet another continuum, namely, that of territorial entities of different sizes, responsible for complementary overlapping, or parallel functions, to wit the local community, region, republic and nation. The community in the particular context of self-management in Yugoslavia is the actual hub of a system of interrelationships among these four kinds of management authority, rather than at the bottom of four hierarchical levels of government in a vertical line of command. What it amounts to, in terms of methodology, is this:

(a) There is a complete integration of technical (socio-economic, environmental, cultural) development planning with the societal-political action planning for implementation in the short, medium and long term;

(b) A process of decision making involving the people, planners and the societal and governmental entities alike; and

(c) An information and a monitoring system is supporting, on a continuing basis, the processes of projecting the future and planning in response to the immediate needs. In sum, a model of the process of development planning on a continuing basis is being tested, rather than projecting a more or less attainable future situation. The five basic broad contexts in which the analysis of all sectors of development and planning for the region is carried out are: environment, society, economy, linkages (including infrastructure) and the regional settlement network.

Humanizing the Process

The interdependence between settlements and development is well established. However, settlements have usually been residuals, the outcomes of a larger political process of decision making concerning primarily economic growth and sometimes also military strategy. The recognition that settlements are capable of being managed by society through these decision making processes clearly implies that they can be subject to explicit public policy aimed at achieving specific societal goals. Present insight into the role of settlements enables this relationship to influence both the geographical scope and the quality of development as well as the equity of its distribution.

At the present point of societal development, the setting for any further progress has shifted to the great metropolitan concentrations. These exploding urban formations are the places where the essential economic, political and social processes and problems of our societies come together. However, their interaction is becoming increasingly counter-productive. It could be made highly productive through mutual accommodation and adjustment and thus more effective in terms of material wealth, delivery of services, social well-being and the environmental and human qualities of life. The world's great metropolitan regions demonstrate most dramatically the cumulative stresses imposed by man-made development upon nature's ability to recycle the growing concentration of industrial and other man-made wastes. But the interaction of the two environmental systems need not necessarily be destructive of nature and humans. Technologies are known which can stop pollution and other nuisances at their source. The argument that their application is uneconomical cannot stand. How can an economic value be put on human survival and well-being?

Inherent in the present rural-urban environmental crisis are both a challenge to our societies and a promise of abundance through reasoned use of the sciences, technology and economic growth as instruments of human development. The challenge to our world community is this: Will we accept such changes in institutions and values as a condition for development? Are we ready to use our immense new capacities and productivity to improve the human condition everywhere?

Available evidence indicates that the crisis in the world's metropolitan and megalopolitan regions will grow progressively acute; unless, of course, highest priority is given to resolving the crisis by developing new settlement systems or redeveloping existing ones in patterns better suited to the social and human needs of our different societies.

The City-Region Concept

As a result of economic, social and political integration, new rapidly urbanizing entities are being formed in the process of development through industrialization. These territories are urban entities in the socio-economic sense and regions in the geographic and political-administrative sense. A redefinition of the concepts "settlement" and "city" as socio-economic and political entities is now clearly necessary. A broader concept consisting of regional networks of urban agglomerations or settlements systems, suggests itself instead. Carried to a logical conclusion, this approach leads to the concept of the "city-region": an open-ended polycentric regional system of settlements in which separate but interacting residential agglomerations, industrial and agricultural zones, protected landscapes and centres of leisure, learning and culture blend into their wider ecological regions. Society can enrich and develop these regions by mobilizing and developing their resources, and the human capacities of their people, and putting to productive use the social, economic and political potentials of the existing settlements also for regional and national development.

Any development plan or projection of the "mega-system" city-region must encompass at least the following:

(a) A *social system* to further the development of individuals now highly productive, disposing of vastly more time and resources for their own development, more thoroughly informed and therefore better prepared to participate meaningfully in making decisions concerning their own and their community's welfare;

(b) An *economic system* to further the application of science and technology for increasing the productivity of humans and machines and an equitable distribution of material well-being made possible through the creative participation of citizens in the planning and relization of their society's economic growth and their own human and cultural development;

(c) A *political system* to further the identification and formulation of goals and strategies, and to foster the means and methods of development through a continuing dialogue between citizens, planners and the authorities, through due political processes and true participation; and

(d) An *environmental system* to promote the development of human settlements within larger ecological regions (eco-systems), as the physical, socio-economic, political and cultural environment in which new capacities are created and multiplied and the human qualities of life enlarged: an environment in which man intervenes as a creative builder, not a despoiler of nature.

To facilitate meaningful participation in the dialogue and interaction within and among these systems, a highly sensitive and responsible monitoring process is needed. This process should record, assess and integrate into all phases of planned development the potentials and consequences of new technologies, the resulting expansion of industrial and agricultural productivity, the changing values and attitudes and the human need for continued growth and development in dignity and freedom.

Within a city-region any developing centre or area can become the starting point of a planned development of the system. In some cases the aim may be the requisite concentration for economic growth and social welfare. At other times it may be the decongestion of urban agglomerates for higher efficiency, or simply the enlarging of the human quality of life. The city-region can take any shape that regional geography, technology, and human ingenuity can produce. It can adopt any socio-economic structure which the respective political system can create. Its main characteristics, however, must be unqualified flexibility and a capacity to respond readily to continued growth and rapid social change. What is suggested here is not a prescription or image of the future city, but the formulation of ground rules for a continuing dynamic process of unified and coherent socio-economic, environmental and political development of regional systems. Such continuing settlement planning, however, must be an integral part of national and international development and a viable framework for planned local development.

The concept of the city-region ultimately implies comprehensive development of extended rural-urban continua. Such development will require new departures in development planning, professional education and training. Joint research-training projects would tend to bring together the professions concerned through an understanding of their respective roles and contributions to comprehensive development planning. The press and other mass media play a most important role in facilitating citizen participation in the continuing process of city-region development and understanding and acceptance of plans, as well as the understanding and acceptance of the hardships that inevitably accompany development.

The city-region as discussed here establishes ground rules' for a productive interplay of sectoral and territorial interventions within the main stream of development (rather than a "regional" or "community" plan) as a means of producing a human condition which can be progressively improved. The great challenge for the industrial (or "post-industrial") society, then, is the need to mould a socio-economic, physical and political environment that is worthy of human achievements and the potentialities of emerging affluence.

The emerging role of human settlements in the context of development and the environment must be seen both as an inevitable consequence of the interaction of these processes and as a principal means whereby this interaction can be made more productive. If so conceived and practiced, comprehensive planning of city-regions as settlement systems attuned to national development objectives and strategies can become a truly dynamic and highly effective instrument for humanizing the process of development. It would transform the present guessing game of forecasting — often misnamed "the planning process" — into coherent action-oriented planning for human development. Master planning city by city would then be replaced by planned development of city-regions within wider socio-economic and ecological regions. Their urban and rural agglomerations would be linked by means of super-rapid transit networks and "total communication." In fact, if so conceived, planned and developed, city-regions could become highly effective instruments for:

(a) Locating socio-economic and cultural activities where they will be most productive;

(b) Distributing the social and human benefits of development more equitably throughout the region and country;

(c) Maintaining the balance between the adverse effects of development and the capacity of the affected ecological systems to recycle them.

The most often stated objectives of national development are social progress and the improvement of the human qualities of life. The generally accepted instrument for their achievement is economic growth and its prime mover: industrialization. But social progress (the increased ability to satisfy human needs) is not an automatic consequence of economic growth. To obtain it, a society must allocate to social development an appropriate share of the wealth it creates. Dissatisfaction with the blind pursuit of economic growth as the motivation for development has led in recent years to a growing demand for a better balance in national planning between economic growth and social development. Thus, the concept of gross national product (GNP) could now be replaced, or at least supplemented, by a broader concept of national economic welfare (NEW) as the "corrected" version of GNP. Corrected to " . . . subtract from the conventional contributed non-material disamenities that have been accruing as costs to our economy, whether or not they have been charged against the industries and activities that caused them"; and corrected "to add in items irrationally excluded from GNP (such as housewives' services in the house, value of expanded leisure and so forth) . . . It is up to us, the public. If we will it, we can give up half a percent rate of NEW growth. And a good bargain many of us would judge such a trade off." [8]

In recent times our diverse soccieties have produced, in the process of economic development and settlement, a rapid degradation of both the man-made social and the natural physical environment. These adverse experiences have focussed the attention of the international community on the problems of human settlements, economic growth and the environment. It is now more generally accepted that to achieve social progress, our societies must distribute equitably the social benefits they can offer; and to maintain and enlarge the human and environmental qualities of life, the process of settlement must respect the environmental tolerances. These are then the main concerns of development and human settlements. They are nationally important in terms of social and political implications and resources needed. Therefore, national policies and strategies to guide the development of human settlements are also needed.

In the context of development, planning can be defined as follows: a model of an intended situation with respect to socio-economic and cultural activities, their location and linkages and the land structures, landscape and installations which provide the physical environment for them; and a co-ordinated programme of political action with respect to legislative, financial and administrative measures required to negotiate the change from the present situation to that projected by the socio-economic-cultural and environmental model. This implies a commitment to the concept of development through economic growth in the quantitative sense, and social change in the qualitative sense; close integration of the planning for socio-economic and cultural development; and finally, to the concept that the processes of economic, socio-cultural and environmental planning are interdependent and can be made to interact productively with the planning of legal, fiscal and political action for implementation.

Recent experiences in deliberate or planned development have demonstrated the fallacy and gross inadequacy of using the conventional abstractions (like national averages for incomes, production and consumption) as quantitative development indicators. They also demonstrate the outright danger of current attempt to quantify the human and environmental qualities of life in physical terms alone. Different geographical areas within countries vary in their natural environment and man-made endowment; in their physical and economic resources, the technologies they posses, their settlement systems, the rates of productivity and levels of living; in the state of health and education they have achieved, the distribution of power and wealth among societal groups, the social structure and institutions, and in the culture and values that motivate their respective societies and produce particular lifestyles. The totality of these factors (some quantifiable, others not) and the particular constellation within which they interact, account for the apparent uniqueness of regions. It would be futile, therefore, to try to evolve a universal mathematical model for regional development and settlement networks. But it should be recognized that certain key factors are common to all regions and that they interact in a great variety of ways.

Once the existence of regional variations is recognized, national development planning and strategies must try to strike a balance between two extreme positions:

(a) To equalize the human condition in all regions or areas of the country as soon as possible, conceivably at the expense of total economic growth; or

(b) To favour areas most likely to grow fast, maximizing their economic product in the hope of generating, in the long run, the resources needed for progress everywhere.

The decision-making process implied in this dilemma is socio-economic-political. But, there are good

[8] P.A. Samuelson, "From GNP to NEW," *Newsweek*, New York, 9 April 1973.

reasons for regionalizing development also from the viewpoint of the environment. The biosphere is assumed to be a closed ecological system. It has, therefore, by definition, a finite tolerance for man-made development. However, the component parts of the biosphere, i.e. its different ecological communities, operate and interact as open systems. This condition offers a large degree of flexibility for productive interplay between human societies and nature in the continuing process of development. We have seen that human societies can enrich these ecological regions and render them habitable through development. Unfortunately, only rarely have our different societies refrained from overexploiting the resources and overloading environmental capacities in the course of their development. But to achieve a productive interplay of development and the environment has been and is the essence of any regionalization of development.

Many development options are available to societies. The concepts of settlements and habitat here imply regionalization of development, and this implies, in turn, projecting economic, social and physical development in a given area and over a given time for the benefit of the region's people and compatibly with the national benefit to which all regions contribute. In the course of regional development planning viable locations are designated for specific programmes and projects, and requisite linkages among them projected. A suitable framework can thus be established for projects of national significance as well as for those based on local aspirations, initiative and resources. The wide gap between stated national goals and the actual possibilities of realizing them in local situations can perhaps also be bridged in this way. The regional approach may, in addition, help to resolve conflicts among the many sectoral projects and programmes in terms of land requirements and location, or the use of scarce resources; as well as to resolve conflicts arising from the sequence and rate of their implementation, or conflicts opposing man-made development and eco-systems.

The region thus emerges as the physical, economic, socio-political and institutional environment in which local growth potentials can best be mobilized. Whether this process is productive or counter-productive from a nation's viewpoint generally will depend on whether regional growth can be induced where it helps the region and the nation, and stopped where it may harm man or nature. Several propositions can be derived from this recognition:

(a) The process of regional development can be seen as the cumulative effect of a complex system of interacting development activities and factors controlled or influenced by governmental and non-governmental interventions and by collective and individual decisions made at the local, central (national) and intermediate (or regional) levels. Co-ordination and integration could influence especially their interaction thus accelerating (or, if necessary, retarding) the realization of certain development targets.

(b) The regional approach in development planning can facilitate a meaningful disaggregation of a country's plan and its sectoral components, promote the aggregation of local plans and projects within a region, guide action in regions with special problems or potentials, or help to identify existing growth poles and implant new ones in strategic locations. In either case, regional development should promote national development objectives by judiciously combining, for a higher total effect, the inputs from central sources with those of local and regional resources, aspirations and action.

(c) A more comprehensive approach to regional development planning would have to be adopted in these circumstances. Such planning would have to shift from a predominantly sectoral approach (e.g. agricultural, industrial or educational) to integration and adjustment to one another of the different sectoral investments in a region. Thus, the objective of comprehensive regional development planning should be intersectoral integration and mutual accommodation of critical development factors so that their interaction in a given region can be more productive in terms of total development and in the ability to mobilize latent resources, reduce the demand for scarce resources, or to cause less hardship to citizens.

Regional development planning is bound to assume in the future a highly dynamic role of identifying development possibilities and stimulating, guiding and controlling development in harmony with national objectives and strategies and the resources and human skills available, as well as the capacity of eco-systems to absorb the consequences of such development. As a means of co-ordinating regional and interregional development efforts, it adds to sectoral and intersectoral co-ordination of activities the dimension of geographically defined development based on actual resources, people, institutions and infrastructures. In a growing number of countries, regional planning bodies are already beginning to assume greater responsibilities in development planning. But the competence and ability of central bodies must also be increased, particularly in regard to their function of allocating investment resources to the different regions.

Regional development could be used also as an instrument for redistributing the means of production and well-being, thus providing for the requisite social, economic and geographic mobility of the people. A planned redistribution of "external economies" in a region (through suitable adjustments in its settlement system) could then guide human settlements into new environmental and social patterns which would attract not only the rural migrant, but also provide additional employment opportunities. It could draw benefit from size, yet avoid excessive concentration, make urban amenities more accessible to rural people, and bring nature closer to the urban dweller.

The socio-economic development of a region is determined primarily by the distribution pattern of economic and political power within and outside it, and the flow of development benefits within and out of the region depends in turn on this distribution of power. As in the case of both local, sectoral and national development planning, regional development theory and practice often fail to recognize the distribution of economic and political power as the decisive element. As a result, planning methods and techniques grow steadily more complex, often bordering on the esoteric. What is needed instead is to accept the great diversity of factors that influence it. These motivations and factors are present in the different regions in specific constellations. For planning purposes, the boundaries of a region and its "development model" cannot be stereotyped but must be tailored to the development objectives in question: the social and political system, the level of the economy, the technology and the physical and capital resources available.

When implementing a regionalization policy, infrastructural development is crucial. It plays a vital role as it provides the facilities and services judged by a given society to be essential for production and the welfare of the people. The infrastructural system and its individual elements constitute, furthermore, the link between goods and services and the people for whose benefit they are presumed to be produced. Finally, infrastructural development is influenced by existing settlement patterns and, to a very large degree, influences future patterns. There are three types of infrastructural systems: the local (intra-settlement), the regional (inter-settlement) and the national (inter-regional). Access to social and other services transforms shelter into housing. The local physical and social infrastructure in turn links housing with the other functions and services of a society to create a settlement. Inter-settlement networks connect settlements in regional and national settlement systems.

New technologies in infrastructural development provide greater freedom in choosing the locations for various activities and enhancing the quality and accessibility of service. As in other areas of technological advance, freedom of choice, exercised in the interest of individual and corporate gain, has tended to lead to concentration rather than to more equal distribution. The current urban crisis, the depletion of the country-side of the benefit of the metropolis, and the seemingly irreversible degradation of the environment are products of the neglect of the opportunities offered in the past by new infrastructural technologies for choices more desirable in human terms.

An operational integration of infrastructural networks could substantially reduce the financial burden on the community because the more productive components of a regional system would help subsidize the less productive ones, heretofore obliged to operate at a deficit in order to provide service for all. Equal service, equal access, and subsidized service as necessary are concepts rapidly gaining public acceptance. Basic education is already free. In many countries, health services are also free. A growing number of experiments are being made with free public transport to find ways not only of providing equal service but also of reducing or even eliminating the use of private cars in congested urban areas.

The integration of different infrastructural components into unified regional systems necessitates the development of radically new approaches and technologies, particularly in the case of the developing countries, in place of the cost-benefit analyses and other predominantly economic tools now dominating project and programme evaluation. Many of these tools have become inadequate and obsolete in the context of developing countries' problems. Above all, planners must learn how to incorporate human benefit and environmental quality in such analyses as major factors.

Regionalization of the infrastructure and social services is often required for geographical reasons. In addition, it offers economies of scale and technical efficiency. In the case of social services, it also provides possibilities for the very necessary specialization in strategically located regional facilities. To these technical criteria should be added the non-technical ones of quality of service and access for all citizens. These can be expressed in terms of minimum levels of service, available free if necessary to those unable to pay, and charged for at progressive rates for larger users in order to be self-financing. Public subsidies are the inevitable alternative. To ensure equity, quality and accessibility, the users of these services should participate in organizing their distribution and management.

Most economic and social components of infrastructure are growing more dependent on public financing as the original profit margins diminish and turn into deficits. When infrastructural systems operate as private enterprises, they are almost without exception subsidized through public funds, financial incentives or tax relief. This is due to the long time needed for amortization and the relatively low yield. The conflict is yet to be resolved between the principle of providing basic services to the public, either at cost or free, and the unduly high profits that private companies (national and multinational) expect (and indeed, often extract) from infrastructural investments. A similar development is taking place in the environmental field, particularly in the more affluent countries, where, owing to the rapid decline in the human qualities of life in town and country, the initially free "external economies" are tending to become costly "externalities." Here again, the community is expected to pay the cost from its public funds.

The pivotal role played by infrastructure in promoting development and the consequent need for continued comprehensive and flexible planning is obvious. Yet the current explosion of urban problems and the concomitant environmental degradation in so many parts of the world demonstrate vividly the failure of most nations to anticipate or even deal with the great changes in the physical environment inherent in their economic progress. The essential role of infrastructure is that of a dynamic system of linkages designed to facilitate a socially productive integration of the different sectors of the economy of town and country, and region and nation. Regionalization of the city-region concept and integration of the infrastructure and other linkages are the three key instruments for a planned development of human settlements: one which is socially desirable, productive, economical and at peace with the natural environment.

The Rural-Urban System

The classification of settlements as rural or urban implies a false dichotomy. In reality there is a continuum in the scale of settlements, small and large. Similarly, territorial boundaries artifically separate cities and their jurisdictions from the surrounding countryside. These division cannot stem migrations, nor do they divide the environment into separate rural or urban compartments or reduce the interdependence of city and countryside.

Nevertheless, there is a qualitative distinction between urban and rural settlements and their ways of life. Two aspects are particularly important. In the first place, there is abundant historical evidence to the effect that cities generate the creative transformations which make development possible. Secondly, the over-whelming majority of social and economic investment, in both developed and developing countries, is channelled into cities. The preponderance of urban investment, even in countries whose populations may be more than 70 percent rural, is sometimes justified by the theory of the city as a developmental catalyst.

In developing countries in particular, the most articulate political constituency is urban-based. Under-standably, development strategies have gradually assumed an urban bias. For example, the options of most developing countries are: either to concentrate investments in the urban industrial sector in the hope of eventually generating sufficient resources to support a rural development programme; or to adopt an agricultural — and thus primarily rural — development strategy. The former strategy chiefly benefits external economic interests and urban-based "elites." In the main, the associated agricultural modernization resulted in a more or less rapid rural-urban migration. The two options are not mutually exclusive. The issue is rather one of relative priority. It is clear that much greater resources must be allocated to rural development than is now the case. It must also be noted that there is no case on record that any society has been able to turn back the rural exodus permanently.

The majority of people live in rural communities; in many developing countries, between 80 and 95 percent of the population is rural, and each year, the absolute increase in rural population in the developing countries still exceeds the urban increase. These millions will have little choice but to march on the cities if nothing is done. Clearly, no progress can be made in overcoming the human settlement problems if the development of the potential of these millions is not given the highest priority which, with few exceptions, is not yet the case.

At the root of the urban crisis in the developing countries there is a rural crisis and, as is often the case, it is accompanied by an opportunity to change. Through rural development, self-sufficiency in food can be attained and, by deliberately dispersing some non-agricultural activities to villages and small towns, it becomes possible to redistribute sources of income. On this rests the only hope for improving life in the majority of human settlements.

Another key issue, as we have seen, is the distribution of incomes. Population rates are lowest in countries where the economic and social benefits of development are most broadly distributed. In contrast, countries with high population growth rates (even when the average incomes *per capita* are relatively high) have wide income disparities and limited access to social services. The distribution of income, coupled with an intensive effort at education rather than the GNP *per capita*, is the significant determinant of the "demographic transition." It has been argued that, because of their high rates of population growth, many developing countries could never achieve self-sustained development and a level of living sufficient to bring about a spontaneous reduction. The evidence suggests that the most important issue is the political one of equitable distribution of the benefits of development to all segments of the population not yet enjoying them.

The world-wide agricultural revolution, advances in medical technology and modern sanitation are producing increasing numbers of redundant rural people who must find alternative employment. They may do this, first of all, in industries based on agriculture or those supporting agricultural productivity, and later in building, in infrastructural development, and in other industries which could be suitably based in rural areas. This suggests that, in some cases, existing rural settlements could assume the role of growth poles. They could become alternative points of attraction for rural-urban migration, closer to home than the metropolitan cities. In rural-agricultural areas, therefore, settlements should be planned as part of a regional system. As agricultural transformation progresses, the major functions currently performed by the intermediate cities and smaller towns (as service centres and trading places for the farmer's produce, and the goods, implements and services he requires) could be supplemented by these other functions.

Certain settlements located in the agricultural zones far from any larger city meet the requirements for a real test of the concept of the *agroville* as a carrier of agricultural transformation and a link between agricultural and metropolitan regions. Other towns located close to a metropolis, will, of course, have to be planned as component agglomerations of city-regions. The rural zones around such towns will then also undergo a radical transformation. From producing staples, they would move, preferably, to the intensive cultivation of products for metropolitan markets. This may mean more employment, higher productivity and higher levels of incomes and living, and of general well-being than those prevailing in agricultural areas generally. These factors, combined with judicious investment to expand the region's physical, social and economic infrastructure, may deflect at least partially the relentless flow of rural migration, away from the central cities.

The principal issue for the developing countries, then, is to assess how much of their resources they should spend for social and environmental development in connexion with, and as a basis for, industrial and agricultural growth and settlements. A related issue is how to incorporate rural-urban migration and deliberate urbanization into their strategies for the planned development of settlements as essential elements of strategies of national development. The principal issue for the industrialized countries is how to negotiate a real change in the pace of settlement action; how to replace welfare programmes, such as "urban renewal," "slum clearance," or "social housing" with a concerted attack on all aspects of urbanization; and how to do this on a scale sufficiently large to make an impact on their national economies and to give impetus to local and regional growth.

Planning of Human Settlements

Formulating the broad lines of development and a varying degree of economic programming have become accepted functions of government in all countries. This is true whether planning is done by a central agency or by separate public authorities, for example, those which control housing loans or facilitate or restrict the flow of capital into given investment fields. But the current explosion of problems in human settlements in most parts of the world vividly demonstrates the need to anticipate and plan for the necessary changes in the physical environment. This is essential if the full social benefits of economic development are to be obtained. Physical planning — the planning for desirable environmental changes — may in fact help to reconcile the often conflicting requirements between economic growth in the narrow sense and human welfare. But the degradation of the environment by overloading its ecological and social capacities may jeopardize the achievement of the economic goals themselves. Awareness is therefore growing of the close inter-dependence between the two main streams of planned development: the technical and the societal and political.

Urban master planning has been the most common type of settlement planning to date. At first, master plans were designed to co-ordinate various physical development efforts within city limits and gradually economic and then social considerations and developmental assumptions were added. But one major shortcoming of such planning is its strictly sectoral approach to the projection and programming of development. Another is — or was until very recently — the planning of cities in isolation, most of the time disregarding the geographical areas and governmental entities influenced by, and in turn influencing, the city.

Settlements, as we have seen, cannot exist and operate in isolation, without exchanges or contacts with other settlements in a region or nation. The historical process of development has produced a progressive division of labour and specialization of people and settlements, a social stratification of income groups and a functional differentiation and disparity among settlements in terms of evolution of the power to make economic and political decisions. No single set of rules and procedures can be laid down for settlement planning in all socio-economic and political situations. However, experience in the development of settlements as part of regional, local and national planning, provides some insight into the process.

The planned development of settlements usually proceeds in stages. First, a general outline plan may be formulated for a regional network or an individual settlement by establishing basic development directions and targets in harmony with the long term development trends and projections. Such an outline plan should first be built on the most reliable long range economic and demographic projections, covering a period of 15 to 30 or more years, within the framework of planned or anticipated national development. As a land-use plan, it could normally designate general locations and land areas for the different functions and activities in the region, as well as suitable zones for the different forms of cultivation and resource development plans based on capability surveys for agriculture, industry, residence, recreation and transport. Studies should be undertaken of water, soil, and climate, as well as of possibilities for power generation. A power grid and transportation and utility systems should then be laid out, linking these activities and functions (industry, agriculture, residence, culture, etc.) to one another and, as necessary, with the neighbouring regional systems as well as with existing or planned national networks.

A more detailed master plan (medium term development projections) can now be drafted for the regional network of settlements and its component parts, to cover a period of from 5 to 15 years. At this stage, precise locations would be assigned for housing facilities, recreation, education, culture and health as well as for heavy and light industries, agro-industries and service centres. During this phase, feasibility studies help to determine sources of power and alternative solutions for transport and water for the more important economic and social projects on which the viability of all the others depends. These plans for regional networks and individual settlements must also contain specific investment programmes as well as the probable source of investment capital.

In the final stage, detailed action plans (actual investment projects and programmes), tied to given locations, would be prepared for specific areas, projects or programmes. These detailed plans may be designs for residential communities ready for execution; programmes for environmental health; or projects for transport or other services and facilities supporting the different economic, social and cultural functions. They are usually projected in an order of priority depending on resources, and alternatives are based on benefit/cost analyses. They may cover both current short term development programmes and capital investment budgets.

Changing conditions, technological advances and evolution in values make it essential for both the regional master and the general outline plan to be reviewed, evaluated and suitably revised in the light of the concrete achievements of short term investment programmes (covering from one to three years). Where the requisite continued review and evaluation of current achievements is coupled with annual revisions, the existence at any time of valid short and medium term development plans for the regional settlement network, and a long term projection of regional development trends is also ensured.

Most countries lack comprehensive research and training facilities in the technical and managerial disciplines required for regional development and settlement planning. The need for such professional skills at all levels of planning and implementation will become more pressing as development planning gains its rightful place in the governmental hierarchy as an instrument of good government. Post-graduate training, professional education and in-service training are needed in developed and developing countries alike. Research and training centres should be established, to provide the necessary factual and scientific bases for policies and strategies and for the all important effort to ensure civic education and citizen participation in the planning and development processes.

A major problem in this area is the lack of communication among the different disciplines involved. The difficulties are compounded by the lack of communication between those who plan and those who represent the often contradictory objectives of various societal interests and different citizen groups who may support or oppose all or part of the plan. Finally, there is often little contact between the planner and the citizen at large, who will, or should, benefit from the proposed development. A major aim of any comprehensive training and research programme in regional and settlement development, therefore, should be the establishment of communication and "bridge building." A common understanding must be reached by all concerned of the role and purpose of regional development and settlement planning.

Another major function of such programmes would be to train by means of suitable team research enough cadres of technical and administrative personnel. Such research should be geared to advance the understanding of the need for, and methods of, integrating the economic, social and environmental factors that influence the evolution of settlements and their quality and, what is even more important, it should further the comprehension of the political factors conditioning the implementation of plans.

The chief purpose of research and training programmes in the field of human settlements should be to strengthen the technical and other needed capacities of the countries concerned. The principal instrument for attaining this objective is a training programme geared to the different aspects of regional development and settlement planning, and to actual needs at the required staff levels. Such training should be organized in connexion with actual planning and implementation and should be supported by suitable research and information programmes, using the various forms of in-service training as their teaching vehicle. Finally, national centres should be linked to one another within multinational and international research, training and information networks, in order to facilitate the international exchange of experience in the planned development of settlements.

Mobilizing Essential Resources

A review of policies and strategies for urban development around the world reveals that, with only a few exceptions, the various societies are attacking problems of unprecedented complexity and magnitude with tools and resources which proved inadequate even when the pace of change was slower. The exploding urban and environmental crisis cannot be contained by invoking obsolete concepts and constraints which may have been valid in an era of economic scarcity. Restrictive legal practices and the institutional structures of pre-industrial rural societies do not help, nor do the highly centralized intergovernmental relations and administrative procedures of the past. Finally, it is almost useless to rely on a building industry and an underdeveloped urban technology. The most critical of these issues are discussed below.

Land and Water

Industrialization has intensified the problems associated with the use of land and infrastructural development. Land and water are closely related resources and the misuse of one often affects the other. In its need for more land and water, the expanding urban population must reach for ever more distant locations to meet higher requirements. The growing cost of storing and transporting water is multiplied by wasteful uses. Costly methods have had to be applied to purify polluted water or convert sea water, as a result of the misuse of a resource assumed to be inexhaustible. All types of communities need rapidly increasing quantities of water for such legitimate purposes as domestic use, intensive food growing and manufacturing. In urban areas, however, the water from the atmosphere is rushed through storm drains straight into the rivers and seas without even passing through the soil.

A comparative study of land problems and policies in different countries demonstrates the close relationship between urban development and the availability of urban land. It also reveals such manifestations of these problems as the simultaneity of their appearance throughout the world, the many common features of land use and tenure, and striking similarities in the governmental power of eminent domain. Governments possess the necessary powers to deal with the problem of urban land and they are, in general, applying them. The power to acquire land for a public purpose is an inherent sovereign power, power to tax it provides broad possibilities for development control and public revenue, and power to police its use is fundamental to the attainment of general welfare.

Land has traditionally played and still plays a very important role in all pre-industrial societies; but as countries shift from agriculture to industry as their primary economic foundation, it is essential that land-use practices be compatible with the social and economic objectives of long term development. Urban land reform, urgently needed to facilitate national development, is now seriously hampered by outdated traditions and obsolete land policies and laws.

Settlement Technology and Capital Resources

Building accounts for two thirds to three quarters of all investment in fixed capital formation in most countries. Consequently, even a slight reduction in unit costs could release large capital resources for additional productive activities. Human settlements, industrialization and infrastructural development are the largest participants in the often wasteful building process, and the capacity of this group of industries and related technologies therefore influences in large measure the pace and cost of development. The pivotal position of the building industry and related technologies in national development strategy is only rarely recognized. Although no group of industries is more important for national development, the level of building technology is persistently low and methods of production are often primitive in comparison with other industries. In addition, the predominance, particularly in many developing countries, of small enterprises makes it difficult to apply technological improvements more generally. In market economy countries, the savings accruing from advanced technology and economy of scale go to the large producer and are seldom transferred to the user.

For increased efficiency, therefore, important structural changes must be made in this group of industries, hand in hand with research and the judicious transfer of technologies after suitable adaptation from one specific situation to another. The most appropriate means for such adaptation would appear to be pilot projects, in residential construction and urban services and facilities, and in new technological approaches to both, provided they are carried out on a sufficiently large scale and as a continuing operation. The process of modernizing these industries is so complex, and the resources involved so huge, that the required changes can only be achieved through the involvement, and indeed the leadership of national governments. Appropriate technologies combining the input of human labour, machines and power in agriculture and industry could increase employment while at the same time raising productivity. In the all important production of shelter and services, such technologies could be generally applied but to do so, many technical, institutional and bureaucratic obstacles would have to be eliminated.

On grounds of technical efficiency and obsolete economic concepts, all kinds of restrictions on social development are accepted as the price of economic growth. These restrictions might have been justified at a time of scarcity, when social development had to be limited to that which could support a society's economic goals. The task facing the affluent nations today, when they are no longer faced with scarcity, is to define the way and quality of life they desire as societies, and then to decide how much of their lifestyles and resources they are ready to sacrifice (through some form of transfer of capital resources and technology to the developing countries) in order to make the world economy and society more viable. Negotiating the needed shift in attitudes and values in respect of national development and international aid, away from exclusively economic criteria and motives of foreign policy toward social and human development, may well be the international community's greatest challenge during the remaining years of this century.

Institutions and Participation

Much has been said and written in recent years about public participation in settlement affairs and planned development. One of the most vital and potentially highly productive elements of this interaction of citizens and government is, of course, the due political process of decision making, in which the interests and conflicts of individuals, social groups and communities meet, accommodate and adjust to each other, or clash. To be effective as an instrument in this political process, participation needs to be intergovernmental, intersectoral and popular. Since all development factors change continuously, the procedure for intergovernmental co-operation must also remain flexible.

The purpose of government is not only to facilitate but also to promote and plan for change. There are two important ways in which a political and administrative structure can be made sensitive to this need. The first is to invite or, even better, to ensure the participation of the public, the ultimate beneficiaries of any proposed development, and second is to give each entity of government the necessary decision making power and resources required for the initial investment and the effective management and continued development and improvement of the programmes, services and functions for which each is responsible.

The pursuit of short term economic growth and technical and economic efficiency tends to neglect the long term consequences. Changes of the kind described are essential if the threat of "dehumanization" posed by development is ever to be reversed. One of the surest ways to meet this challenge is institutional reform, coupled with increased opportunity for effective participation by all citizens in decisions regarding their own welfare and the development of the settlements in which they live and work, and where they enjoy the fruits of their labour.

2
Expanding the Perception of the Housing Problem in Developing Countries*

S. Angel and S. Benjamin, Thailand

As professionals, we have failed generally to deal effectively with the housing problem in our developing countries; we have been hasty in making recommendations; we have systematically underestimated how much change is required to bring our proposals about; and we have failed to be convincing, even though our ideas may have been logically and technically impeccable. In a sense, by restricting our interests to aspects of housing problems which we were *qualified* to discuss, we have failed to confront it as an ordinary citizen might — by moving to change the political attitudes that stand in the way of effective solutions.

It seems appropriate at this time to stop and make a realistic assessment of the political, social and cultural context in which housing problems need to be solved. Such an assessment must be wider than a strictly professional one, and must provide every citizen with the insights required for political action on housing.

Third World societies are faced with a difficult challenge — *shelter* — the task of assuring that everyone is adequately housed. What we have to examine is whether we are really willing to confront this challenge — to *solve* the housing problem. Many believe that we are solving the problem. We are not. In particular, the low-income housing problem — the task of finding shelter for those of us now living in slums and squatter settlements — is not solved and cannot be solved until attitudes concerning it change in a rather fundamental way.

The core of this paper provides a critical analysis of the prevalent myths surrounding low-income housing, and as such erects a sound basis for an enlightened attitude toward the problem. Seeing through these myths and beliefs is the first step in training a large number of people to deal effectively with the society's housing problem. Given a significant change in attitudes and perceptions, it becomes immediately clear what role each individual can play in solving it, and what specific training, if any, is required. But without such a significant change, training becomes another futile exercise.

We can distinguish two different approaches to the solution of the low-income housing problem — Technological Transfer and Self-Reliance. Technological Transfer is the largely unsuccessful attempt to take housing solutions from developed societies, and modify them for application in the developing world. It has the great advantage of fitting well into elite middle-class aspirations. But it fails on three important counts: Lack of realism as to how adaptive technology is, a complete misunderstanding of people's needs, and a poor use of available resources.

Self-Reliant Technology, the dependence on people's traditional capabilities to build for themselves, is successful in overcoming these three difficulties. It has been widely applied by squatters everywhere, but has failed to win wide acceptance as a solution to housing problems, because it does not conform to elite values.

This presents us with two possibilities. Either we must devise a third, alternative technology which

*This paper is an expanded version of an earlier paper by the same authors entitled "Seventeen Reasons Why the Housing Problem can't be Solved," *Bangkok Post*, June 25, 1974.

answers the economic and social problems as well as being widely acceptable; or we must change our attitudes so that Self Reliant Technology in some form can be widely implemented.

Given the time and resources available, a third technology is probably impossible. So we are left with the prospect of changing our attitudes. But changing attitudes is no mean task. We often hold them close to our hearts, and they are entrenched. We may not want to change them, or we may be afraid to change them.

The set of attitudes to be discussed are connected to each other in a special way (see CHART), because some are more fundamental than others. They fall into three major groups. First we look at professional and technological myths; then at myths related to middle-class and elite values; and finally, we explore myths that have found their way into our institutions.

High Rise

This discussion of low cost housing mythology begins by looking at two myths: the myth of HIGH RISE and the myth of LARGE PROJECTS. The High Rise idea was supposed to offer us two major economies: Savings on land by increasing densities, and savings in construction by using modern methods. Both have proved wrong in most cases. Several recent studies show that building densities are approximately the *same* for multi-storey towers as they are for 3 and 4 storey buildings, given an acceptable level of air, sunshine, open space and services. An American study showed that building costs per sq. ft. *rise* from $20 to $36 as building height increases.[1] A Scottish housing study showed that maintenance costs per dwelling unit in 1970 were £8.39 for low buildings, and £21.35 for towers.[2] This kind of data has been sufficient evidence for the British to substantially stop building high rise public housing.

In cities of the Third World, we expect high rise costs to be even greater, due to the heavy import of

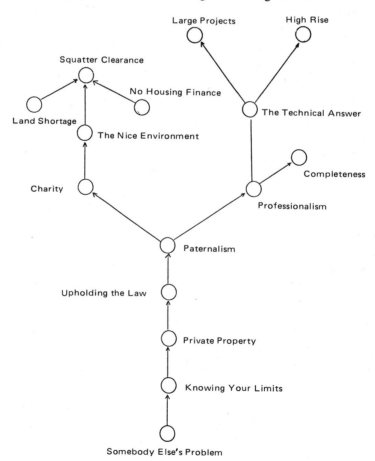

The Structure of Myths Concerning the Housing Problem

[1] Alexander, C., Angel, S., Silverstein, M., Ishikawa, S. and Brams, D., *The Oregon Experiment*, Oxford University Press New York, 1974, Table 3.2: Cost Per Square Foot of Net Usable Space.
[2] Jephcott, Pearl with Robinson, Hilary, *Homes in High Flats: Some of The Human Problems Involved in Multi-Storey Houseing*, University of Glasgow, Edinburgh, 1971, pp. 128.

equipment and materials, the high level of skills and precision required, and the extensive use of capital, often from foreign sources. These high costs usually result in high social costs because they force us to provide less space. And we know, as Patrick Geddes remarked: "the essential need for a house and family is *room* and that the essential improvement of house and family is *more* room."[3] Further social costs are brought about by loss of social contacts, small business opportunities, and the manufacturing work that can take place when families live close to the ground.

Large Projects

Now suppose we can see through the myth of HIGH RISE. We may now be willing to consider low-rise solutions to housing. There still may be an advantage in LARGE PROJECTS, the construction of many similar housing units in one project. Here we expect to find savings because of repetition; by shorter planning and construction time, by buying materials in bulk, and by industrialization.

We may also believe that projects which are physically large and highly visible tend to progress more smoothly than the small physically scattered projects which deal directly with people; that management is a scarce resource in developing countries, scarcer perhaps than capital; and that large construction projects by their monumentality tend to command the attention of ministers and top civil servants when they need urgent decisions.[4]

The result of LARGE PROJECTS should be much cheaper housing but it is not. We have to add to the cost of these projects the high costs of administration and organization. In our developing countries we also have to add the considerable costs of corruption and profiteering. In Venezuela, a cost comparison study found that self-reliant housing cost 4,200 bolivars per unit, 4-storey low quality construction cost 10,200 per unit, and 15-storey low quality cost 16,000 per unit.[5]

LARGE PROJECTS are also expensive in the long run because their management and maintenance costs are high, particularly in the developing countries; they deteriorate rapidly due to much vandalism because their occupants have no stake in them and are often hostile to them; and they are neglected because there is limited public resource and capacity to keep them up.

Belief in LARGE PROJECTS leads to a serious over-simplification of the housing problem, and consequently to the search for *one* answer. Society, however, provides its shelter in a hundred different ways. There are a myriad of individuals, groups, agencies, and institutions that take serious responsibilities for housing people, and that make a significant contribution to the low-income housing stock. These include company houses, dormitories, small plots rented for house construction, orphanages and old-age homes, shophouses, hostels and day hotels, military barracks, quarters for domestics, gardeners and guards, construction site dwellings, and small building additions to name but a few. Most prevalent among those are squatters — people building their own housing communities on unoccupied land.

Highlighting LARGE PROJECTS and taking credit for them inevitably takes credit away from, and weakens, all these activities, instead of strenghtening them. Thus, a government fails to use the natural capabilities of the society to take care of its shelter problems.

The visibility of LARGE PROJECTS is thus a two-edged sword. As social problems and maintenance problems mount, what was once a visible achievement is slowly transformed into an equally visible failure. When individual projects are successful, their visibility spells out concretely a commitment to house everyone in similar projects in the longer run. But, since LARGE PROJECTS invariably commit more resources per family that can realistically be committed, they can only provide for a minority of the low-income population, leaving the rest with rising expectations which are unlikely to materialize.

---

[3] Quoted by Turner, John F.C., "Barriers and Channels for Housing Development in Modernizing Countries," *JAIP*, Volume 33, 1967, p. 167.

[4] This particular formulation of the bias in favour of large project is made by Earl Kulp with regard to agricultural programs in developing countries. See Kulp, Earl, "Essentials of Basic Agricultural Programs," *Ekistics*, Vol. 39, No. 230, January 1975.

[5] Jones, Robert, "Transport, Urban Design and Housing," in Haefele, Edwin T. (ed.), *Transport and National Goals*, The Brookings Institution, Washington, D.C., 1969, Table 2.2., p. 60. Data for the table was obtained from working papers of Corporation Venezelona de Guayana on construction projects in Cuidal Guayana, 1962-64.

Such problems rarely occur with small projects — small groups of houses, each one built and owned by one or several families. These are invariably better kept and improved over time. They are liked and cared for, because they allow people to build for their own special needs — those needs which are systematically averaged out in LARGE PROJECTS. In particular, they allow for traditional family structure to be maintained — a crucial element of social cohesion, and the basis of healthy community life, which cannot be found in large public housing estates.

Taking these considerations into account, we can begin to see through the myth of LARGE PROJECTS. But both this myth and the myth of HIGH RISE are grounded in a more fundamental one — the myth that technology can overcome all these difficulties with new innovations. This is the myth of THE TECHNICAL ANSWER.

The Technical Answer

We are somehow led to believe that given enough trained technicians, time, and money, an ingenious modern solution to low-cost housing can be found. The fact is that we are now producing very low-cost housing, but low-cost housing is not necessarily *low-income* housing. Modern sector construction costs, including overheads, put low cost housing out of range of the poor. In Tanzania, for example, the National Housing Corporation, the country's lowest-cost builder, can build a traditional type house for US$ 2,230. A similar house is being built by squatters for roughly half this figure.[6] In Thailand, the lowest income people, comprising 15 percent of the urban population, earn less than 1,000 Baht (US$ 50) per month.[7] This income group cannot afford to pay more than 120 Baht (US$ 6) for housing each month. No modern construction method can meet their housing needs without heavy subsidies.

Cost reductions through the development of new materials and methods are difficult to come by. And even if we do come up with some invention, there are so many other costs — services, materials, land, energy and skilled labor — that rise fast enough to overshadow these savings. Clearly, modern technology by itself has not yet given us the answer, and very few realists now believe that it will.

The numbers of squatters in our Third World cities are in the millions and estimated to be growing as much as 12 percent annually in some places.[8] Albeit humble, most of these people are building themselves shelter — which we cannot build for them — without the benefit of modern technology. Because this is being done by lay people without professionals, we tend to think that it cannot possibly be a serious answer to this very complex problem. This is the myth of PROFESSIONALISM — our trust in the rational objective expert. We think that economists, sociologists, architects, engineers, and urbanists, all trained to solve special problems are the people most fit to solve housing problems in a comprehensive manner. This is clearly not the case. But before taking a more critical look at this professional attitude, we will first explore a myth generated by this attitude — the myth of COMPLETENESS.

Completeness

The myth of COMPLETENESS, embodies our aesthetic desire to produce finished products — housing units and all their associated facilities, including schools, markets, fire stations, hospitals, recreation centers, public parks, playgrounds, movie theatres, and places of employment. Our attitude is that nothing should be done until everything can be properly planned, financed, and built. Yet we know that the vast majority of Third World housing is built in small increments over long periods of time. Similarly we have observed that communities take shape slowly over time as needs are felt and money becomes available. In Mexico communities have built thousands of schools. In Guyana, they build roads and water supplies. In Peru, squatters plan their own communities and then slowly build them over time, complete with roads, markets,

---

[6]Leaning, John, *Low Cost Housing in Tanzania,* Ministry of Lands, Housing and Urban Development, Government of the United Republic of Tanzania, Dar-es-Salaam, 1971.
[7]"NHA: An Uphill Task to Fulfill Ambitious Plans," *Business in Thailand,* February, 1974, p. 54.
[8]Turner, *op. cit.,* p. 168.

schools, community centers and public open spaces. The people's needs are immediate, they need a roof over their heads and they cannot be expected to wait for months or years while we plan, look for that ever-elusive financing, and build our housing packages.

Professionalism

Now let us complete the discussion of the myth of PROFESSIONALISM by observing two of its major drawbacks. First, it is impossible to train our professionals to solve the housing problems of the poor. And second, even if they were adequately trained, there are simply not enough professionals to fill the demand.

It is impossible because the rich countries systematically decide on the direction of professional training, even within the developing countries themselves. Training is largely at the academic level and is usually restricted to the elite. The elite, in most of our developing societies, has committed itself to modernization and has turned its back on traditional methods and traditional values. Members of this elite insist on "the latest" and "most modern," and refuse to hear about mud huts, wooden houses, or any intermediate technology. These values are not shared by the poor. Hence we can begin to see that our professionals are equipped with the wrong system of values to contribute significantly.

There can never be enough housing professionals because of the magnitude and complexity of the housing problem, and the vast number of details requiring attention.

The housing problem is far too important a problem to be left to our professionals. It is analogous in scope to the daily problem of feeding a city of several million people — transporting adequate food, distributing it, and preparing it, so that each one of us is fed adequately several times a day. Consider the number of people who will go hungry if the task was left to some central planning agency. The professionals burdened with responsibilities for housing were given a problem which they cannot solve, because, as we said before, the solution is not a technical one. They can be, and are, most useful in carrying out special tasks, but their role is limited.

To be realistic about providing housing it seems that we must rely primarily on the energies of our people themselves; for they have the ability and willingness to build their own houses; and there are enough of them to handle the job. But when we begin to talk about relying on the energies of the people, we come up against an even more difficult myth — the myth of PATERNALISM. This myth is a fundamental one. Before we look into it in more detail, we must first examine another chain of principles which are the results of our paternalistic attitudes.

Squatter Clearance

Many of us would like to go on believing that slums and squatters are a social disease infesting our cities. Just like cancer has no place in a healthy body, we are tempted to say that squatters and slums have no place in a healthy city, and that we must uproot and eliminate them.

In reality, when shelter is in critically short supply, squatter clearance to make way for public housing results in a net loss of housing units for a large expenditure of money. A recent investigation in Dar-es-Salaam showed that at a cost of $1.6 million spent over 3-5 years, the number of dwelling units destroyed would exceed by 2,800 the number of units built.[9] In addition, the original squatters did not care or could not afford to move back into the new project. So rather than containing the extent of squatting in the city, the clearance project simply results in the proliferation of new squatter areas. Some squatters in Bangkok claim to have been evicted 5 or 6 times.

When the option of moving to another squatter area no longer exists and squatters are forced to move into housing estates, they are usually made worse off in several important ways. They have to pay a larger share of their money income for housing, they cannot utilize their labor in construction, and they lose the structures and facilities into which they have put a considerable amount of savings. For example, it is

[9]Benjamin S.N., *Squatter Communities in Tanzania*, Ministry of Economic Affairs and Development Planning, Dar-es-Salaam, 1971.

estimated that the present value of structures in squatter areas in Bangkok is of the order of $50-100 million, which amounts to 25-50 percent of the National Housing Authority's total low-income housing budget request up to 1986.[10]

These facts are already well-known. But even if we come to think that SQUATTER CLEARANCE has serious disadvantages, we must still confront three important myths that require it: LAND SHORTAGE, NO HOUSING FINANCE, and THE NICE ENVIRONMENT.

Land Shortage

We have been led to believe that there is a LAND SHORTAGE in cities, and that squatters are aggravating this shortage. First, they pre-empt the use of very valuable land needed for private and public construction projects; second, even assuming low-income housing to be a proper use of land, squatters live at densities that are far too low.

On close examination, we see that there is actually a lot of land in many Third World cities. For instance, a recent World Bank study on urbanization reported that 40 percent of the urban land in Bangkok and Buenos Aires is unoccupied.[11] The problem is one of making this land legally available, at an acceptable price, for those who are forced to squat.

Equally, we find that it is faulty reasoning to blame squatters for pre-empting land needed for essential private development or public works. For *all* land uses, legal or illegal, low, middle or high income housing, businesses, parks and the like, can be equally guilty of pre-empting land and subject to legitimate expropriation for some public good.

Concerning densities, the problem is not that serious in many cities, as studies have shown that squatter settlements develop high densities over time. The implication here is that we have no excuse for not finding land in our cities for squatters, and that we must be willing to allocate space exclusively for this purpose. We shall discuss later why this is not happening.

No Housing Finance

In our conventional banking world, the poor are a bad security risk. They have little material resources for collateral, low savings and frequent debts; their income fluctuates too much, and they are notoriously unreliable in meeting regular payments. For these reasons banks cannot support individual housing loans for low-income people. Instead, they prefer to make large loans for bigger housing projects secured by government guarantees. This is the myth of NO HOUSING FINANCE. The banking interests upholding this myth force us to take a position in favour of LARGE PROJECTS and SQUATTER CLEARANCE.

The poor improve their houses as their families grow, and as they acquire small savings. To take advantage of these energies, and to assist in financing, we need new kinds of loans that can be given in small amounts over long periods of time, and secured by the house itself.

Poor people themselves furnish many good examples of housing finance. One traditional way of financing housing is through a small group of acquaintances who systematically pool their small savings and loan them to one of their members, on a rotating basis. In Thailand, for example, this is called "Len Chaer." It is widespread in low-income communities and has been sophisticated to the point of providing interest to its members. Similar systems are known to exist in Pakistan and several African countries. These collaborative systems have been overlooked, or just neglected, by authorities in search of workable house financing schemes. Yet they are most reliable and virtually without defaults. This traditional system must be reinforced and allowed to proliferate, if it is going to be of value.

On the other hand, efforts at imposing housing cooperatives or credit unions from the outside have not been very effective. Low-income communities view the organizers of such schemes as transient outsiders, and therefore tend to treat them less responsibly.

[10]See Angel, S. and Benjamin, S., "An Alternative Housing Program for Bangkok," Asian Institute of Technology, Bangkok, 1975 (Unpublished).
[11]World Bank *Urbanization: Sector Working Paper*, Washington, D.C., June 1972, p. 38.

This does not mean that the government has no role in housing finance, but rather that it should concentrate its activities in specific areas, such as financing the purchase of land or the installation of public services, which are out of the realm of possibility for small groups. This would serve to reinforce and secure the financing efforts of the people themselves. Furthermore, if we were willing to give loans to numbers of small groups and organizations involved in housing, and to secure bank loans by government guarantees, the potential losses to the government would be far less than the cost of subsidizing constructing public housing.

The Nice Environment

The third myth requiring squatter clearance is that of THE NICE ENVIRONMENT. Many people believe that even if we may find some economic sense in squatter settlements, they are not nice places. They are dirty, disorderly, and rundown. Our image of a nice place is the middleclass area in which we live, where buildings are modern and of high quality, arranged in an orderly pattern with lots of open space and greenery.

It is difficult for us to overcome this bias, because it has to do with our tastes and not with our reasoning. We find it hard to admit that these tastes are middle-class and urban and have little to do with the tastes of lower-income or rural people. In fact, recent surveys find that in many squatter areas the people are quite satisfied with their housing.[12] The reason they look messy is that they are often in a constant process of construction; that they are used as a place of manufacture and work; and that they often use cheap or second-hand building materials. Squatters have lots of problems, but nicer housing and a nicer environment are not very high on their priority list.

Our preoccupation with THE NICE ENVIRONMENT aggravates their housing problem. By insisting on the enforcement of middle-class codes and standards, we make it difficult or impossible for people to build housing which is satisfactory as far as they are concerned. This insistence also results in a refusal to recognize many poor people's housing as part of the country's housing stock, thus artificially exaggerating the need for expensive new construction of public housing.

Charity

Still, even if a NICE ENVIRONMENT is not what is required, many of us feel that something has to be done for the poor. We may feel that it is necessary for those of us who are more fortunate to share our good fortune with them. This sharing should take the form of gifts and contributions, for which the poor should be grateful. In particular, we should help them with a decent house and supplement their income so they can afford to rent it. This is the myth of CHARITY. It is our traditional way of addressing inequality, and maintaining goodwill between rich and poor. Its modern equivalent is welfare — the committment of the government to help the poor on behalf of our more prosperous citizens. Poor people thus become dependent on the government, and lose both self-respect and self-reliance. Many of us feel that it is to our advantage to remain charitable and "do good," rather than be faced with the prospect of satisfying the demands and rights of the poor. Our charitable attitude inevitably discourages the poor from organizing into communities and groups that could take more effective actions to satisfy their housing needs.

Paternalism

So once again we find ourselves talking about relying on the energies of the people themselves to care for their needs, which as we said before is ruled out or discouraged by the principle of PATERNALISM. This myth embodies the idea of the "father-child" relationship. It states that the elite know better and therefore should be allowed to decide and act on behalf of the rest. We persist in believing that the people who have

[12] See for example Morell, Suzan and David, *Six Slums in Bangkok: Problems of Life and Options for Action*, UNICEF, Bangkok, 1972, p. 13; Hongladaromp, Tongchat, *Klong Toey-1973: A House-to-House Survey of the Squatter Slum*, Asian Institute of Technology, Bangkok, 1973, pp. 98-99.

housing problems are less mature, less experienced, and less responsible. They are less organized and less reliable. So we cannot in good conscience leave them to cope by themselves, we must solve their problems for them.

As an example, let us make a rough comparison between the scale of the housing problem in Bangkok, and what the Thai government is planning to do about it. By 1983, the Thai National Housing Authority plans to build 70,000 housing units in Bangkok, for people earning less than 1,500 Baht (US$ 75) a month. It is estimated that the present requirement, just to eliminate the estimated 600,000 squatters who generally fall into this income group, is of the order of 100,000 housing units. Conservatively, by 1983 this figure will have grown by an additional 50-100,000 units.

Even if sufficient capital was available, any responsible government would not expand its public housing activities to totally meet low-income housing needs. Any such expansion will inevitably compromise rural development efforts. It would seriously increase pressures for migration of labour into the cities, instead of providing more and better rural employment opportunities which would keep migration to a minimum. Massive investment in public housing programs has only been possible in the extreme cases of Hong Kong and Singapore, which are both city-states without a hinterland and require large amounts of capital for development.

It is obvious that we cannot meet low-income housing needs by conventional paternalistic means. The low-income people know better what they need, and can better understand the delicate balance between what they need and what they can afford to build at any given point in time. They are quite willing to invest more in their own housing, if we can give them reasonable assurance that their houses will not be destroyed. Instead of attempting to *build* houses for all of the people, we must take *responsibility* for *housing the people*. In other words, we must help the people to help themselves.

But we cannot give squatters any assurances that their houses will not be destroyed because we believe in UPHOLDING THE LAW.

Upholding the Law

Squatters are illegal land occupants. Basically, they have broken the law. So we tend to think that to "recognize" them and to provide them with privileges awarded to law-abiding citizens, such as police protection, education, health, fire protection, water and the like, is an affront to the very principle of law.

This common attitude ignores the nature of law. Laws exist as long as society is willing and able to uphold them. When the majority, or a significant minority in a society, finds certain laws inappropriate they must be changed. Upholding laws after they have been massively broken, and when there is no possibility or need to maintain them, increases the feeling of lawlessness and promotes the breaking of other laws. If those who are forced by circumstances to squat are expected to respect the law, then the law must be changed to respect the circumstances in which these squatters find themselves. This is particularly relevant when we consider laws regarding land ownership.

Private Property

Privately-owned land is private property. It is protected by the law because it symbolizes individual rights: the right to do with our property as we please; the right to benefit from developing it; the right to profit by selling it. However, this attitude cannot be maintained when there is a small minority of land holders and a large majority of landless people. In a situation of land scarcity, those with more land than they need cannot expect the government to fully protect their unused land against trespassers.

Squatters never occupy used productive land, even agricultural land. They occupy unused land held by private speculators or by government agencies. Squatters hold a traditional view of land ownership — the ownership of use; that people have a right only to the land that they can and do use; that one actually establishes ownership through use.

What they lack is the legal tenure that will allow them to build for themselves, to develop their communities, and to obtain the required public services. Thus, some type of urban land reform which will provide the large amounts of land necessary for expanding low-income housing cannot be avoided. This is hardly likely to occur by government purchasing land in the open market. Zoning land for low-income housing, or creating laws for land expropriation are more realistic measures. Limiting the amount of land owned by anyone, or nationalizing land are also important possibilities.

Knowing Your Limits

The trouble is that talking about tenure and land reform is idealistic and unrealistic. Because it does not take into account the real interests of those who hold power, and we believe that their support is essential to any such fundamental reforms. So when experts and professionals are brought in to provide a *scientific* answer to the housing problem they are automatically excluded from dealing with land, as this would mean trodding on the toes of those who hired them.

This, then, is the Principle of KNOWING YOUR LIMITS. Decisions on the proper use of land are largely political, and traditionally favour land-owning interests who predominate in local and national politics. Two typical results: Those in power insure that the most valuable facilities are built on their land; and once their land is developed, they insure that it remains undisturbed by requirements for public improvements. As squatters have neither legitimacy nor power, they are the most politically expedient and economical target for eviction to make way for public improvements. Moreover, as they often occupy lands owned by the powerful people, they fall prey to market and political pressures to build more profitable structures on the land they occupy.

Even if we could somehow overcome the problem of land ownership, there is still one final major obstacle. We find that the bureaucracy, the executive arm of our government, is powerless to act on the housing problem.

Somebody Else's Problem

Ineffective bureaucratic action on housing largely falls under the principle of SOMEBODY ELSE'S PROBLEM. Each division of government has well-defined responsibilities, and cannot overstep its authority. The problem of low-income housing is both a land problem and a housing problem — an economic, legal, and social problem. No one in government can be blamed for not handling it, because it falls outside everybody's jurisdiction. Even those in government who would like to do something about it are powerless, because it falls outside their responsibility. City governments disagree with the national government about responsibilities for squatters; suburban local authorities refuse to share the burden of the central city's housing crisis; government agencies that need land for housing cannot obtain it from other powerful agencies that have large amounts of land. In addition, there is an extreme breakdown of responsibilities, so no one can act with single purpose.

Typically, the answer to this state of confusion is the creation of a national housing corporation with responsibilities for all low-income housing. While such an authority is vitally needed to orchestrate the housing efforts of the nation, it usually militates against them by adopting a strict role of constructing public housing of one type or another. The efforts of all other groups, agencies, and individuals are thus largely frustrated.

Instead of closing off options, the proper role for such a central authority is to open up possibilities for as many groups and agencies as possible, inside and outside government, to take responsibility for the provision of housing. But this is never the case. So while public construction efforts struggle along, low-income people in increasing numbers continue to live without any significant benefit from such efforts. As a result the low-income housing problem remains with us and is unlikely to go away.

CONCLUSION

It is customary to finish a section on housing with a series of recommendations. But we will not. We cannot recommend a new technology because this is not just a question of building more houses, better houses or cheaper houses. We cannot suggest new laws or new policies. We have enough of those. And besides, no matter what policies we are able to articulate and put on the books, they will not be implemented. Or if they are implemented, they will simply be reinterpreted to reinforce entrenched attitudes. Until there is a considerable change in attitudes and perceptions, the housing problem simply cannot be solved. The only serious task, as far as training and education is concerned, is to gradually increase the awareness of as many people as possible regarding the housing problem. Expanding our perceptions is the best form of enlightened education and training.

3
Cities-Within-Cities
A Solution for Metropolitan Areas

Lauchlin Currie, Colombia

"The" urban problem changes both in degree and magnitude as the size of cities grows. The urban problem of a city of 20,000 is obviously quite different from that of a city of 5 million. This paper is concerned particularly with relatively large cities, say of 1 million and up. Such cities are growing very rapidly, and increasingly "the" urban problem will be concerned with the quality of life in large cities. It has been estimated that in 10 years, on the basis of present trends, there will be 12 cities in the world with over 11 million population each. The number with populations over 1 million will be very large.

It is assumed that this growth will occur regardless of whatever efforts may be made to restrain migration or to encourage the growth of smaller cities under 100,000. While there are, it is true, very large cities in developed countries, all of the 12 large cities with the highest growth rates in the world are located in developing countries.

The commonly cited disadvantages and drawbacks of larger cities centre around the urban design created by the threefold forces of the pricing system, inequality of income and personal mobility. These forces have led to sprawling suburbs, highly congested centres,. enormous sums spent (or use of physical resources) on movement, high and rising land values in certain areas and blight in others, segregation, fragmentation of living, and intensification of the sense of deprivation and of the loss of significance of the individual.

There has been a tendency to concentrate attention on one of these elements — congestion — and to identify "the" urban problem with transport and the solution with that of the "traffic" problem. But the relief of congestion in one spot generally only results in more congestion elsewhere, so that solutions of the traffic problem only lead to the need for more costly solutions. Making it possible for more individuals to drive to work in their own cars leads to even greater traffic, greater centralization, more far-flung suburbs, more segregation and more fragmentation and more resources devoted just to movement. The traditional centre loses its efficiency despite higher and higher buildings and higher and higher land values. The growth of lighted areas has matched the movement of fashionable areas.

While the authorities and planners of many cities have come to realize this, they have often drawn the conclusion that the solution is the substitution of mass for individual transport. But it is to be feared that the urban design made possible by the private car is not a design that makes mass transit a viable proposition in most cities. Too many people have adapted their lives to a style that depends on individual transport. If energy is permanently much more costly relative to other things, the present design of cities in developed countries will be a major factor militating against a desirable reorientation of personal and public expenditures. Mass transport may become more viable under the circumstances, but, if combined with single-family homes in distant suburbs, will not obviate the necessity of private cars and their extensive use, and will not resolve other problems of urban life in large cities touched upon here. In fact, as just indicated, successful mass transport, as in London or New York, has exacerbated some of these problems.

The City Cluster Principle of Urban Design

As an alternative to the extension of existing forms, mass transport and more radical national solutions of growth poles or decentralization, it is urged that serious study be given to the urban design variously known as cities-within-cities or a metropolitan area made up of a cluster of compact, walkable, planned communities of sufficient size to be true cities (say 400,000-500,000 in developing countries). In existing large cities, the transition to such a design would admittedly be a difficult and costly undertaking, as all the land within many miles of the centre of a metropolitan area is already urbanized or devoted to high value uses. However, much may be done through remodelling or renovation to regroup activities into what might be called balanced zones. In the case of developing countries, the application of the principle is easier, as the major period of growth is still ahead of the larger cities in such countries, and a city built in what is now a suburb will shortly be incorporated well within the metropolitan area.

The major characteristics of urban cluster design is that each unit in the cluster can be completely planned from the beginning in terms of land use, density, height of buildings, community buildings, open spaces, shopping areas, work places, and internal and external transport systems. It can be made large enough and of sufficient density to provide all the amenities of a fair sized city (say of 400,000) and yet small enough to be compact and walkable. Whatever advantages may be claimed for an intermediate city can in this manner be attained by dwellers in a metropolitan area of 5 or 10 million or more, plus the additional advantages offered for cities of such size. Indeed, many more, as the inequality in living styles, segregation and sprawling character even of intermediate cities can be minimized.

There need be no montonous uniformity, as each city can be fitted into its peculiar physical environment and room left for variation in styles. The objectives are common: preplanning, public ownership, the public capture of the rise in land values created by the new community, walkability and minimizing of movement by mixing living, working quarters, shopping facilities, schools, playgrounds, parks, all within walking distance or very short bus rides. But compromises may be necessary if part of the area is already urbanized, or if it is too difficult to acquire sufficient land for a new planned city within an existing city without demolition and renovation.

One advantage of this design in a rapidly growing city is that it lends itself easily to the accommodation of additional millions to an existing city with a minimum of disturbance, occupation of space or premature obsolescence. While additional millions can be accommodated in a succession of compact cities in a metropolitan area, the traditional centre remains for those activities that require personal contact but, through licensing, can be kept quite compact, and space made for living quarters for office workers. Other activities, not requiring such high value land, may move to the surrounding new cities. Expansion of distant purely residential suburbs may be curbed, but people who prefer that type of life may buy existing homes and continue to commute by car to the traditional centre, as now. Since peak hour movement to the traditional centre can be stabilized, there should be no necessity to build new throughways to that centre, or additional parking areas. Urban commercial traffic will of course expand with the growth of the metropolitan area but this, spread over 12 or 14 hours a day and between a number of centres, requires much less space than does peak hour personal movement.

With the stabilization of the working force of the traditional centre, planners have a firmer basis for drawing up longer term plans for the design of that centre, to be achieved by renovation and the use of the licensing authority, thus, in time, converting it into a type of compact, self-contained (more or less), walkable city, similar to but larger and more specialized than the other cities.

On the matter of size, room must be left for experimentation and variation. It now appears evident that the earlier British New Towns were too small to supply the attributes of a true city, and the trend is toward larger units. The French planning authorities now believe that the new cities should accommodate around 400,000, and this is also the target figure for the new city of Jurong Town in Singapore. A much larger population would necessitate very high densities to keep the city compact and yet provide open spaces and industrial sites. A smaller size would not support a sufficiently diversified and lively commercial centre to compete with the traditional centre. While it is anticipated that the new cities will in turn be composed of neighbourhoods, supplied with shops for staples, and with schools and playgrounds, it would seem important to plan for a large commercial and office centre with sufficient movement to justify a host of specialized shops, professional offices, notaries, government offices and so forth. One lesson that appears to be valid and may be learned from observation of European, Asian and Latin American large cities is that people enjoy, for a change and for a time, the company of a large number of other people who may be complete strangers. It is depressing to be in a stadium watching a match if only a few other people constitute the audience. The same is true of a concert or a play, and is particularly true of a stroll in a crowded thoroughfare with other pedestrians, like parts of the Champs Elysées or Oxford Street or Fifth Avenue. It appears likely that 400,000 people would satisfy this requirement if they were pedestrians and not all sealed in homes, offices or cars as is so often the case in United States cities. The popular housing estates of Singapore, ranging up to 175,000, have wisely provided shopping and outdoor but covered eating areas where residents congregate after work. Naturally the climate also favours this practice, as well as the generally very small apartments.

Cities-within-cities must be distinguished from popular housing. They are designed to be true cities in every sense of the term with industries, offices, shops and a cross-section of the population, and not segregated, dormitory suburbs of popular housing. For those people of low income who work in such cities, rents within their price range can be provided by differential pricing — a hidden subsidy.

The solution is primarily designed to accommodate the growth of cities in a better fashion than now. It is assumed that the existing city will be improved by upgrading, renovation and regrouping of activities, but in any case the new cities will in a few years provide for larger populations than now reside in existing metropolitan areas. The self-help solution, on the other hand, assumes an endless proliferation of poor dormitory suburbs stretching out in all directions, necessitating mass transport and a costly extensive network of public services. By continuing segregation, they make the upgrading of schools and health facilities and diversion more difficult.

Preplanning and Public Ownership

Is this necessary? Cannot the same effect be achieved by zoning requirements and building norms, with private construction and ownership? Experience with private planning guided by zoning and norms in all countries strongly suggests that planning in this way is ineffective, except in the case of some spectacular but relatively small "downtown" areas, as in Park Avenue, New York, or certain areas in Boston, Toronto, Montreal and other cities. The answer seems to lie in the opposition of the profit motive and the public good. The interest of the individual is to use an individual lot in a way that will yield the maximum profit. But this use, if duplicated by other owners, will almost certainly give a result that will yield a lower over-all optimum use of land.

An illustration may make this clear. It is obviously of the highest importance that a main thoroughfare be not permitted to be cluttered by parked cars or with numerous access driveways, that is, that any commercial development or parking should take place some blocks back of the thoroughfare. But it is to the individual interest of the first builders that they locate houses, apartment buildings and shops on the thoroughfare with direct access to it. In a relatively short time traffic becomes so congested that the road ceases, in effect, to be a thoroughfare. This process is widely recognized but it is most difficult for a planning authority to resist "development," and individual developers will be reluctant to turn their backs on the main access routes and start building some blocks away. It is not, after all, certain that this particular area will develop, and nobody will guarantee an individual builder against the consequence of a wrong guess in location or type of building. Builders, therefore, go by present values or values they expect in the immediate future. But the type of building appropriate to these values, say in a new, sparsely built suburb, may be totally inappropriate to the type of building if a city of 400,000 is shortly to occupy the area. If an area develops, pressure is brought on the planning authority to modify the norms to permit greater density and then to modify zoning requirements to permit commercial use. The result is premature obsolescence and demolition of buildings with useful life, and a ragged, unplanned area of higher density that in a relatively short period of time either strangles itself by traffic congestion or must be served by a new system of throughways put in at great expense in an urbanized area.

Public ownership, over-all planning and construction according to plan with the instruments of policy discussed below, permit a city to be planned from the beginning so that the land use pattern can be one to yield the maximum over-all return for the entire site upon completion of the plan. It does not guarantee that mistakes will not be made, but it offers a means of avoiding the costly mistakes of piecemeal development dictated by the existing set of land values.

A second powerful argument for planning and developing a city by a public corporation is that only in this way can there be assurance that the inevitable rise in land values will accrue to the community whose growth gave rise to this scarcity value, and not to individual fortunate or shrewd buyers. If a city has to plan for an increase in population from 3 million to 9 or 10 million (the case of Bogota), the rise in the value of the limited land area resulting both from this growth and a sixfold or more growth in gross income of the area will largely accrue to a relatively few and be a prolific source of large fortunes. If a public corporation retains the ownership of land, it has the opportunity, in an inconspicuous way causing the least social conflict, to bring about a measure of redistribution by providing a hidden subsidy in the rents of the lower income dwellers or by transferring the rise in the social increment to the provision of social amenities, schools, hospitals and so forth.

A third powerful argument for public development is that it provides the most effective way of carrying out two of the major objectives of the design — the reduction of movement and expenditures therefrom, and the lessening of segregation by income groups. For a time, it was thought that all that would be required is that care be taken to ensure not only a matching of jobs with housing and with shops, schools, and recreation facilities, but also matching the type of housing with the anticipated income levels resulting from the job composition. Experience in planned communities in the United States and the United Kingdom, however, clearly indicates that this is not sufficient. Once land and/or apartments are sold, control is lost. Increasingly, if the facilities and amenities are good, people will live in the community and commute considerable distances to work. Others who work in the community will find that it will pay them to sell their apartments and buy in cheaper areas and commute to work. Only by retention of ownership can the corporation managing a community set differential rents to ensure that it pays people who live there to work there, and people who work there to live there. Thus the tendencies toward segregation and peak-hour transport can be countered.

This consideration becomes all the more important if the new cities are only distant by a few miles from the traditional centre and from each other. Without powerful instruments of policy, the pressure to provide easy access to all parts of the metropolis becomes very difficult to resist. The result becomes, as in London, tremendous peak-hour movement and expenditures to provide for this by a network of underground and surface transit going in all directions of the whole metropolitan area. If commuting takes place from suburban satellites 25 miles distant, the pull from the newly planned cities, in many places only 5 to 10 miles or so distant from the traditional centre, will be strong. This suggests that not only should it be possible to vary rents according to income and residence, but that no particular effort should be made to provide excellent and fast means of transport between the centre and the cities. It may be taken as a general rule that the better the peak-hour means of transport, the more the means will be used, that is, the stronger will be the pull of the traditional centre on the one hand and the residential suburbs on the other. The objective should be to make it more difficult and inconvenient, rather than less, for residents of the new cities to commute to work areas outside the cities.

ALLEVIATION OF URBAN ILLS

A. Transport Problems

Let us assume that the design is feasible and that people will both live and work in the same cities, and that in a few years half the population will be located in the new cities and the other half in the existing area. To what extent may this urban design be expected to remove or lessen the objections to metropolises?

Since it is assumed that people will live and work, play, shop and go to schools in the same neighbourhoods and in the new cities, peak-hour commuting, by definition, will be greatly reduced and there will be a great reduction in the urban transport facilities required by a city of, say, five millions with a rising per capita income. It is proposed that the new city internal transport needs be served by a continuous bus service on an exclusive bus way so that all apartments will be within 500 feet of the line; that only narrow access streets be provided, mainly for commercial vehicle use for deliveries; and that few parking areas be provided and those on the fringes. External transport needed to provide access to the traditional centre and other nearby cities will be mainly by bus lines, with the existing or improved arterial network available for commercial traffic and private cars. Since it appears to be a safe assumption that both gasoline for personal car use (or suitable substitutes) will become increasingly expensive, the saving involved in reducing the need for personal car use will become more and more significant as time passes. This continuing and growing saving will be supplemented by the saving in roads and maintenance of roads and parking areas, which have a hidden cost in the competition for scarce space. This combined saving permits an increased allocation of additional resources to education, health and diversions, as well as making a larger portion of personal disposable incomes available for non-transport expenditures. If, in other words, it is feasible to channel future growth of large urban centres into a cluster of compact, walkable cities, the combined future annual savings in transport in comparison with expenditures resulting from expansion of the existing design will be sufficiently large to make possible a significant modification in life styles.

B. Differences in Levels of Living and Social Segregation

Another disadvantage of present urban design, that has been stressed in previous chapters, is the intensification of the deprivation effect that arises from conspicuous differences in styles of living. These differences are particularly marked in the segregation between rich, middle income and poor residential neighbourhoods, and in the manner of transport as between personal automobiles and overcrowded and inadequate bus service. In few sectors is the struggle for status as evident and strong. The gradations in neighbourhoods may be thought to be slight to a casual observer, but are keenly apparent to residents. A personal car no longer gives status in developed countries, but has become a symbol in developing countries of the difference between classes.

The proposed urban design, always assuming that it can be successfully implemented, would contribute to a lessening in conspicuous differences in styles of living. Presumably neither building licences nor mortgage money would be available for high income urbanizations, especially of single-family homes. For people to whom such a status symbol means much, the existing supply of single-family housing would be available for purchase. Others would presumably accept the alternative of renting larger apartments near their work, and walking or using the local bus service operated by the urban corporation.

The urban programme is not primarily designed in itself to do away with differences in income but rather to lessen differences in levels of consumption, which is not the same thing economically but has the same impact in feelings of well-being and in permitting a levelling up in the standards of the lower income groups. To restrict new housing to the low-income groups would, paradoxically, increase segregation and the deprivation effect. What is desired, if possible, is a better social mix, but in a manner in which the differences are not so apparent. This is apparently being successfully done in the new city of Jurong Town in Singapore, where "executive suites" in high-rise buildings are built within a few hundred yards of high-rise popular housing. The main differences are in the size of apartments and interior finish. The mixture of classes is very evident in some of the older European cities (in the West End of London for example and in Edinburgh) though the segregation in London is also severe.

In the planning of new cities-within-cities, provision should be made for apartments for the well-to-do executives and professionals as well as for those occupying the lower paying jobs. This diminishes segregation, lessens commuting by private car, lessens the desire of people rising in the income scale to leave the city, and permits the hidden transfer of excess rents and/or sale values to lower income groups through lower rents. *The development must be viable as an entity but not necessarily in terms of each apartment.* This averaging is one of the features of the Singapore housing estates and will, it is expected, be used even more extensively in the new cities in Singapore and Hong Kong island. For all these reasons, therefore, the new cities should be planned as complete cities and not as popular housing estates, and this implies providing for residence by higher income groups. Indeed, in planning the new cities and ignoring superficial political considerations, the early provision of apartments for higher-income groups and of shops will make it easier to retain ownership while financing the provision of more and more apartments and amenities for lower-income groups. To start with the latter, the natural impulse, would entail difficulties in financing and force the premature sale of land and buildings, thus leading to loss of control of the composition of residents and of the possibility of capturing the social increment in the future.

C. Crime and Social Isolation

Another reason for attempting to secure a better social mix is suggested by the investigation of Oscar Newman into the relation of urban design to crime and vandalism.[1] He found that a heavy concentration of

---

[1] Oscar Newman, *Defensible Space*, (New York, MacMillan, 1972).

low-income families, together with high densities and housing designs (especially the latter) that lead to impersonality and lack of knowledge of neighbours or of people using the same entrance or living on the same floor, appear to encourage crime. Crime rates are generally lower where residents are of different income levels, and the design encourages and permits auto-vigilance. Needless to say, the problem is complex and many factors enter into the growth of urban crime.

Many of the criticisms of large cities are centred on congestion, noise and pollution. The design being discussed here would obviously contribute to a lessening of all these factors. Whether it would contribute to a lessening of the feeling of loneliness and loss of individual significance stressed by many writers is more difficult to demonstrate. It is possible that the sources of feelings of alienation and impotence go much deeper in our society. However, it seems reasonable to suppose that the organization of life in smaller neighbour-hoods in large cities, less changes in residence and less changes in neighbours, members of local clubs and sports groups and so forth will lessen the sense of the lack of significance of the individual to his fellowmen, which many writers identify as the essence of alienation.

The metropolitan area of Vancouver is made up of a number of originally distinct and separate towns that gradually expanded until they formed a single metropolitan area. This origin gave rise to the formation of many aspects of small town life in a large city that still persist. Local bowling alleys are not exclusively masculine affairs but are arranged for the diversion of whole families. Matches between local clubs and firms are frequent and in many respects the establishments, though commercial, are local clubs whose members know each other well. Each of the separate communities have one or more skating rinks, which are a focus of community life in winter, and municipal swimming pools, bowling greens and tennis courts for summer use. It is virtually unheard of to attend school in other municipalities of the area. The author has no basis for asserting that the residents of Vancouver are any happier than those of, say, New York, but certainly the opportunities for knowing one's neighbours and participating in community diversions are much greater. It is significant, however, that a good road network and the universal ownership of private cars are working together to disintegrate the former degree of separateness of muncipalities making up the area.

D. Inequality of Income

Considerable stress was laid on a characteristic of urban growth that is open to serious criticism — the rise in land values accruing to individual owners. This threatens to become a major source of growing inequality, especially in developing countries where the largest growth in numbers and income is still ahead. Something can doubtless be done to capture a portion of this rise, after making allowance for smaller owner occupied properties and for the general rise in prices, although it must be admitted that the experience to date has not been encouraging. The surest way to capture the rise in land values for use by the community whose growth caused it is by public ownership. Stockholm is frequently cited as an example of the possibilities here. However, to assure the capture indefinitely in the future, it is important that the land not be sold but be rented. Since the rent should be susceptible of being raised rapidly to reflect both inflation and the rise in true scarcity value, this means in effect that the buildings, residential, commercial and industrial, should also be rented with full ownership retained by the semi-autonomous public development corporation. In this way, an increasing proportion of the rise in urban land values accrues automatically to the public and not to private owners. This, then, is another means by which differences in styles of living may be lessened and the gains that would otherwise accrue to individuals can be diverted into lower rents for lower-income groups, the provision of schools, hospital facilities and so forth, and investment in other new cities.

E. Misuse of Agricultural and Recreational Land

Emphasis on compactness or high density for living quarters is not only for the purpose of lessening the need for mass and personal transport by car, but also to preserve the lands adjoining metropolitan areas for agricultural and recreational purposes. With the prospective frightening growth in numbers, the space require-ments of the existing pattern of single family suburbs become increasingly large. Hence a valuable feature of the cluster principle of urban design is that it combines compactness and high density with reasonable size, so that each city of say, 500,000, could be contained in some 2,000 hectares or 5,000 acres (the size of the extension will vary with local circumstances). In Colombia, where there is excellent but strictly limited agricultural land near the three largest cities, the prospects are for complete disappearance of this land unless the extension of the cities can be contained and suburban sprawl prevented. While this might not be too serious in economic terms at the moment, it appears that the growth in population will be such that in the future the country will require all the agricultural land it now has at various altitudes. It is only prudent to plan now to preserve these lands before some of the best and most accessible are covered by concrete and asphalt.

F. High Cost of Services

An objection to the present pattern of growth is the costliness of services that a wide extension entails. The cost in terms of transport has already been covered. In perhaps less degree, the water mains, sewage system and power lines are much less costly per person when they serve compact high density areas than when they are spread over a great area. This, then, is another saving of resources that can be devoted to the improvement of health and educational facilities.

G. Architectural Dullness

Since almost all cities of the world of mixed economies now follow the same pattern of growth determined by the pricing system, inequality and the automobile, it is hardly surprising that they tend to lack distinction and to exhibit common and unattractive features. Industry is usually segregated and is expected to be dirty, noisy and extravagant in its use of space. The centre core is generally a cluster of very high rise office buildings. The new suburbs have a ragged character with more vacant lots interspersed by clusters of housing. Other areas often become deteriorated. Roads originally designed to serve residences become lined with shops, advertising and used car lots. Poorer residential areas are too often deadly monotonous. It is a curious fact that the most beautiful or distinguished cities are generally the oldest, a heritage from pre-automobile times.

The proposed design provides opportunity for architects to try out a variety of styles and to plan completely harmonious cities. This opportunity may not be availed of, or it may be foregone in the interests of economy, but at least it is there. The large competition among eight firms for an extension of the planned city of Evry in the Paris metropolitan area indicated the variety of arresting architectural solutions for a common problem, with given parameters of area and density. The basic difference is that there is an opportunity to plan a complete city. Generally, today, architects are limited to the economic use of a single lot, given the land values prevailing at the moment. In many cases, there is no architect. Naturally, architectural design must be conditioned by considerations of cost, but when a whole area is being planned, there is a wide variety in possible designs, groupings, heights and land use.

The ragged appearance, particularly noticeable in rapidly growing cities, arising from changing land use, changing zoning requirements, changing owner expectations, can be avoided by the rapid construction of a new city with inducements that will divert a portion of the rapid growth in population to the occupation of that city. As it approaches completion, other cities can be started. In this way, vacant lots, deteriorated areas, changing use and roads unable to handle future traffic requirements may be avoided.

H. Unequal Facilities for Education and Sports

In some developing countries with mixed economies, education raises delicate social problems. The ideal is, of course, to have all public schools of uniformly high level. But this is an ideal. The fact is that, like most public services, the level of teaching and facilities leaves much to be desired in public schools. Hence all, or as many parents as can afford it, prefer to send their children to private schools, and great differences in the standards of proficiency arise among private schools as well as between public and private. In addition, the system is wasteful as it entails a vast movement of buses every morning and afternoon, passing each other going to and from widely scattered private schools.

Since it is too much to expect that the numbers of public schools and especially the level of teaching can be raised from one day to another, some feasible means of transition would be desirable. The proposed design may facilitate the transition by offering facilities for the residents of a neighbourhood to form co-operative schools or for the urban development corporation to foster primary, secondary and vocational schools, and also universities. This would, in a sense, permit competition in obtaining teachers and in holding students to the neighbourhood, in short, provide facilities for the transition period that may be desirable in some countries.

One particularly objectionable form of inequality that now exists in cities in many countries may be found in the unequal opportunities for sport and diversions. The facilities are generally much more adequate in the wealthy suburbs and very scanty in densely populated inner areas. With increasing numbers and the necessity for compactness and the preservation of agricultural land, facilities for highly space-extravagant sports, such as golf and even football, may be difficult to provide for many in the future. However, in the planning of the new cities, provision could be made for adequate facilities for a wide variety of games that do not require such great extensions of land as golf. Basket-ball, volley-ball, squash, handball, ping-pong, bowling (lawn and alley), swimming pools, roller skating and, in colder climates, ice rinks are some of the possibilities.

A possibility that might be kept in mind is the provision of facilities for amusement areas at some distance from the city in, if possible, a different climate, which each urban development corporation could organize and run for the use of its residents on week-ends and holidays. Such areas might be equipped with sleeping and housekeeping facilities and made available for vacation use to different neighbourhoods at different times, with special bus service arranged by the corporation or neighbourhood associations. Corporation school schedules could even be geared to varying vacation time possibilities.

Integrated planning offers possibilities for different aspects of living that would pose very formidable problems for the administration of a single enormous metropolitan area. Theoretically at least, it is possible to achieve many objectives through planning in mixed economies that are often thought to be possible only in socialist states. In certain respects, the planning is more difficult. In others, however, much could be done to diminish differences in styles of living and raise minimum standards without affecting in any way basic economic motivations or incentives and without sacrificing the true economies of scale and desirable externalities. Planned communities are a logical extension of public housing. The evolution can be clearly seen in Singapore over a relatively short period, from the first small public housing efforts, to the much larger housing estates with shops, schools, restaurants and flatted factories to, finally, fully developed new cities. Other cities need not follow the precise pattern, as it had some undesirable features, but may pass directly to the new city stage.

Finally, the urban design proposed by concentrating building in fully planned communities designed for permanency, provides both the necessity and the opportunity to stimulate and use national savings in a socially and economically desirable manner. A by-product of this use is to assure full urban employment for a long period of years.

IMPLEMENTATION OF THE CITY CLUSTER PRINCIPLE OF URBAN DESIGN

A. Administrative Structure

The integration of national economic and social planning with regional and urban planning requires a governmental and administrative structure that permits and facilitates such integration. In most cases the present structure is inherited from distant and simpler economies when planning on a national scale was unheard of, cities were generally small and compact and the problems of urban growth were those of providing services to people wherever they happened to settle. Newer countries have generally copied the governmental and administrative structure and division of authority and responsibility that were becoming less and less adequate for developed countries. Some changes in this field appear to be indicated in order to further the basic objectives of enhancing the quality of life in cities, of securing a better allocation of financial and physical resources and in lessening differences in the levels of living within and between cities and as between cities and smaller settlements.

The basic assumptions underlying the present distribution of powers appear to be that the main task of a local government is to see that common services of power, water, transport are served, and to share in the tasks of providing a minimum level of education and health and in the preservation of law and order, and, in some cases, in the provision of public housing. Urban planning, or urban design, except for Washington and Paris, is a relatively new concept. The automobile and growth in numbers resulted in a great extension of area which raised new problems not only of allocation of resources but of segregation and differences of levels of living. The response in political terms has been to seek to extend correspondingly the authority of a single local government authority, or to enforce or impose co-operation in some way between and among many separate agencies.

Clearly the division of governmental authority and responsibility appropriate for settlements of the eighteenth century could only, by the most improbable accident, be appropriate for the dispersions, concentrations, numbers and styles of living of the late twentieth century. When it took days and even weeks to pass from one part of a country to another, the role of the national government in "local" affairs was naturally small, and there was more justification for decentralization of authority to local and state governments. Today, even in the largest countries, all places are a few minutes apart by telephone and a few hours by plane. If 95 percent of the people are urban dwellers or attached to urban communities, it would seem evident that the role of the national government, if it is to assume some responsibility for the well-being of the people, must inevitably be broadened, where it has not already been done, to enable it to discharge this responsibility in urban communities. The economic and political justification for intermediate governmental units has consequently shrunk. They remain strong only in special cases and for special historical or ethnic reasons.

Solutions that are still largely influenced by the implicit assumption that any aggregation of people, no matter how great and extensive in area, is simply an extension of a village and its government an enlargement of the early town council and town meeting form of government (or, in Latin countries, of the mayor) result in such political and administrative aggregations as the Greater London Council or the New York City form of government. Efforts are made to treat these areas as a single entity. This is the "natural" response of any city government to the growth of suburbs with different tax rates, different levels of services and yet dependent upon certain common services such as water and transport.

It must be admitted that the problems for which the metropolitan area is proposed as a solution do exist. The headquarters of wealthy corporations can move out of a city and beyond the taxing power of a city. If tax rate differences become significant, the corporation themselves can move, as well as wealthy individuals. Suburbs permit wide differences in services. Hence the common complaint is that the wealthiest suburbs can have the lowest real estate tax rates and supply the best services, while the neighbouring city supplies the residents of these suburbs, who work in the city, with many costly services supported by poorer people.

On the other hand, a single city of 10 million becomes an administrative nightmare, leads to a disproportionate diversion of resources into transport and the diseconomies of size and congestion. Industires move to the suburbs to escape the diseconomies and preserve the economies, and the process is repeated. There are now two and a half million Londoners living beyond the green belt made for the purpose of preventing the extension of the city, and the Greater London Council has followed them and attempts to govern and supply their needs as though they lived in the inner boroughs.

Another serious short-coming of this particular solution is that it is quite compatible with continued differences in styles of living, in levels of services, in segregation and in the vast allocation of resources to transport. In fact, it tends to intensify the undesirable features of cities. In other words, it is not a satisfactory solution for anything other than the imposition of a uniform rate of property tax. Poor metropolitan cities cannot provide a high level of services if the tax base is low. Rich metropolitan areas need not share their good fortune with poorer areas. Even so, the solution might be favoured if the only alternative was endless proliferation of suburbs. This, however, is not the case. There is another alternative.

A national urban policy

The other alternative is based on granting much greater authority to the national government to work out, finance and otherwise implement a desirable national urban policy. An awareness of this need has been growing in recent years in the successive creation of national housing or urban or environmental ministries (variously called ministries of urban affairs, housing and development, environment) and conferring on them increasingly broad powers. The trend has been more difficult where strong state or provincial governmental units are interposed between the national and the local governments, but this difficulty has been in part circumvented by the device of grants-in-aid or conditioned loans.

In any case it is becoming increasingly evident that only the national government and national legislation can bring about more uniform conditions of urban life and provide for a national policy sufficiently strong to counteract the trends stressed in this work. A few rich or powerful governments at a state or provincial level may assist in this process (e.g. New York State or Ontario) but in general there is evident need to establish closer relations between the national government and the local, and to establish regional authorities around metropolitan areas that can be delegated powers for the control of land use.

If the principle is adopted that governmental and administrative organization should be functional and adapted to needs, which seems reasonable, then the forms must be considered in the light of the cluster principle of metropolitan centres and the control of suburban sprawl. To plan, execute and manage a new city requires competence, persistence or continuity in developing a plan, and sufficient independence from local pressure groups to be able to raise and vary rents and public service charges as needed. The sums involved are large and the first requirement is financial soundness to service the large sums that must be borrowed.

A national urban development authority

To meet the various conditions, separate urban corporations for each project are indicated, under the direction of boards whose members will have the competence and can accept responsibility to appoint managers and approve policies, budgets and programmes. However, it is evident that such corporations cannot be completely independent of local municipal authorities. Certain criteria for operation must be laid down and adherence to minimum standards of uniformity must be insisted upon, with power residing in somebody to remove imcompetent or dishonest management. It would seem that such powers of general supervision and responsibility for the planning of new cities, their administrative co-ordination with local municipal and regional authorities and public service companies, and final guarantee of financial capacity can only be vested in a national authority, responsible in turn to the chief executive of the nation — the president or prime minister. This would generally be a ministry or an agency of equivalent rank in the governmental hierarchy.

Such a national agency could have, among its powers, that of elaborating a national urban and housing programme, promoting and channelling savings through to the building of new cities-within-cities, renovating old cities, reducing transport requirements, preventing further urban sprawl, promoting uniform minimum levels of services in cities of all sizes and acting as a mediator in relations between various local authorities and other institutions in matters affecting urban policy. Such an agency could have attached to it a land bank for the acquisition of lands for future new cities or for the renovation of well-located but run-down urban areas. It could advise the president on the nomination of members of the boards of urban corporations, assuring adequate representation of local authorities, the private sector and local residents of new cities. It could have the authority to assess and license land use in areas surrounding metropolitan areas with further power to delegate such licensing authority to specially created regional authorities. The objective here would be to preserve lands adjacent to cities for agricultural and recreational purposes and for future cities.

The national authority could also be the agency for the administration of the recapture of the true rise in urban land values outside the new city zones and for the use of the funds so captured for specified purposes. It could be granted authority to designate areas as sites for possible new cities or smaller improvement projects (such as areas to be renovated) with a certain time, say, five years, during which to conduct studies and decide whether or not to create cities on such sites. During this period it could have the first option to acquire land at the commercial values prevailing immediately prior to the date of designation. The ability to acquire large blocks of land on reasonable terms and conditions and to control its use in other ways is indispensable to the whole concept of urban planning.

Finally, it could be the highest authority in the nation for the preservation of the environmental quality of urban settlements, again with authority to delegate the exercise of such powers as it possesses in the matter of air and water pollution and the prevention of disfigurement of the landscape to properly qualified local authorities.

Short of granting subsidies, it could operate to ensure that intermediate-sized cities are not handicapped in the provision of basic urban services, and have good means of communication with and transport to the rest of the country. Perhaps too great a degree of economic sophistication is required to expect that the governments of developed and developing countries would appreciate that the promotion of mobility of labour from low income to higher income areas may be a much more effective way of raising the average than trying to subsidize industries in handicapped areas. However, subsidies and licences for the location of industries, as in Britain, are of questionable value in developing countries. The political abuse of the powers is too tempting. All areas except the richest will quickly wish to qualify, the cost will mount and national benefits will diminish. In fact, this process has frequently occurred in developed countries with high administrative levels. To leave the location of industries to bureaucrats, or perhaps we should say "government technicians," would almost certainly result in mal-location from an economic point of view. For this reason, these powers are not suggested for inclusion among those given to a ministry of urban affairs.

Urban development corporations

The urban corporations could be formed by the national ministry, which would subscribe the capital necessary to enable them to purchase or acquire land and provide working capital. In countries where the urban growth is very rapid it should be possible to construct and rent residential, industrial and commercial properties rapidly enough to gain revenues to cover the debt service on borrowings necessary for construction of those facilities. The initial over-all plan should not preclude modifications and, with yearly budgets of each corporation, would be submitted for approval to the ministry.

British experience suggests that each project be organized, planned and administered by a separate corporation acting under the general supervision of a ministry of the environment. (We were somewhat critical of some of the basic planning concepts of the New Towns but not of the quality of management.) A city of 400,000 becomes so large and complex as to require a full-time competent staff operating under the watchful eye of a single board of directors. To place several such cities under one management, however, would invite disaster. It is true that in Singapore all the housing estates are planned and administered by one board. However, while this has led to a certain degree of uniformity, it has also led to a lack of diversity and innovation. It is interesting to note that when a new city was planned, this was placed under the Jurong Town Corporation. So even for a single city of two million, it appears desirable to provide for different operating bodies. It may finally be noted that there has been no change in government during the period of intense building activity in Singapore. The New Town of Thamesmead in London has no separate corporation or semi-independent board of directors and the changes in management and policy reflecting changing views of the Greater London Council have generally been thought to have prejudiced the development of this city within a city.

Board of directors

Is is important to note as a prerequisite for cities-within-cities, a management that can combine efficiency with continuity of policy and ability to resist pressure against what may be necessary rises in rents or in other charges. Vast sums must be borrowed and the lenders must have assurance that the project will be financially viable, and that the government will not be called upon to assume heavy subsidies. To pursue the objective of a virtually carless city with a minimum of commuting requires a strong-willed, honest, dedicated and reasonably efficient management, assured of security of tenure as long as it is doing its job efficiently, protected from political pressures, and with a complete understanding of the objectives. These, admittedly, are difficult requisites, especially in a developing country where the administrative levels are not high. It could be that in some countries they are impossible to fulfil. Where, however, there is reasonably efficient private management and a pool of talent on which to draw, the task is simplified. It consists then of providing a board of directors which (a) has a large amount of autonomy, (b) is appointed for longer terms with staggered expiration dates, (c) has power to appoint and remove the manager, and (d) is civic-minded and convinced of the basic soundness of this design for growth.

For the sake of co-ordination it is necessary that representatives of local governments be on the board. However, it is vitally important that policy not be changed with every change in government and especially with every change in mayors or ministers, and that the management be sufficiently insulated to be able to raise and vary rents. So far as possible, it should be able to act as a private body pursuing wider public objectives. The major difficulty, of course, is the selection and nomination of competent but civic-minded private individuals to serve on the board of directors. Obvious conflicts of interest must be avoided (for example, a board members should not be a contractor for any of the construction, or the renter of a commercial or industrial establishment). However, prominent and successful businessmen and professionals, provided they believe in the basic ideas, can generally be relied upon to serve competently and efficiently partly for the sake of their own reputation and partly because many people successful in the private sector are genuinely anxious to contribute something in the public sector if they can do so without becoming salaried employees. The British have recognized this for a long period and have secured a tremendous amount of dedicated work from private individuals serving on Royal Commissions.

It is assumed that the members of the board will be appointed for renewable terms of, say, four years, with some terminating each year. This provision is desirable to give continuity and security of tenure and permit resistance to pressure. The manager will, on the other hand, be appointed or renewed at the pleasure of the board (this is the main effective instrument of control by the management). It would be most desirable to be able to set salaries comparable to those paid in similar positions of responsibility in private industry.

It if is thought desirable that some members of the board be public officials, it is important that some provision be made in advance for the election of the chairman of the board. Otherwise, it will go automatically to the highest-ranking government official on the board and, in his absence, to the next highest-ranking one. It would be far more desirable for provision to be made in legislation that the board should elect its chairman from among the representatives of the nation appointed specifically by the president of the nation. A private member is likely to feel more responsibility, take a longer view, be more in accord with standard procedure, taking votes if and when necessary. The public members can contribute the work and views of their agencies and are probably more sensitive to public opinion, but for this, membership on the board is sufficient.

B. Ownership of Site and Buildings

Another indispensable requisite for cities-within-cities is the ownership of a sufficient area of land to permit of comprehensive and integrated physical planning, construction and management. This may require expropriation powers and, in certain cases, a high degree of ingenuity in adjusting plans to sites that already have some building which, for one reason or another, it would be inadvisable to replace. In Britain legal powers exist whereby the Ministry of the Environment may acquire large blocks of land for New Towns at the values prevailing before the announcement of the development, which is obviously just and equitable. In France, the same result is achieved by the Government being able to place areas for possible new cities in "reserve," which, for a period, gives the Government first option in acquiring the lands at the values prevailing when the lands were placed in reserve.

To have to purchase lots at whatever price "hold-outs" demand would place an intolerable financial burden on the corporation and would defeat some of its social purposes (providing public amenities, lower rents to low income groups, funds for investment in other urban corporations.)

Ownership is not only necessary for comprehensive and co-ordinated planning of a complete community, but is most desirable to capture the raise in the value of land as reflected in higher rents in the future, and also to retain some means of providing incentives and disincentives to influence the composition of the working force and reduce commuting to and from other living and working zones in the metropolitan area. The alternative — licensing, zoning and the use of building norms — forces the planning authority to play a passive role, and invariably results in ragged, piecemeal development and frequent changes in zoning and norms. These traditional instruments can be used as valuable supplements to control the development of areas adjoining a planned community, but in themselves are completely incapable of bringing about the speedy execution of a well planned city.

To plan to retain ownership of buildings and to rent instead of sell requires a drastic change in customary thinking of the role of a developer. Private developers prefer to sell lots and building units as rapidly as possible, as their profit comes from the appreciation of values and not from the difference in rental income and debt service and expenses. Their construction loans are short-dated and are repaid by the rapid sale of property. Their business and concern is developing, not managing, so they are anxious to make their profit and move on to the next development. Our interest, however, is different and lies more in the planning and administration of a community for social purposes. To attain these social purposes, continued ownership appears indispensable.

It will be objected that people prefer to buy rather than rent. This is undoubtedly true in many cases. One generally takes more pride and interest in an owned than in a rented property and it is generally considered to be more profitable to the individual. It is precisely for the second reason, however, that continued ownership by the public corporation is desirable. The combination of fixed debt service payments with rising values due to inflation and growing scarcity of land, has indeed made it more profitable in the past for the individual to buy than to rent. In other words the buyer secured the social increment in addition to making a profit because of the failure of mortages and debt servicing to adjust adequately to inflation. But these benefits are at the expense of other sectors of the economy, savers and insurance policy holders and people without property. It will be suggested later that it would be desirable for the financing to be through savings and borrowings subject to monetary correction for changes in the over-all value of money (indexing). If this is done, one source of profit, that due to the lag in debt service behind the raise in prices, is eliminated. The other source, however, the raise in the social increment, remains and it would seem preferable for many reasons that this should accrue to the community.

Another reason for continued ownership has a politico-psychological aspect. Borrowers may initially be eager to buy via an indexed mortgage. Once having secured their property, however, they are inclined to resent the adjustment to the principal of the mortgage necessary to compensate for inflation and to pay the resulting adjustment to the lenders and the savers. It is a constant danger to the permanence of the adjustment system that a demagogue may seek to make political capital out of organizing resistance among low-income borrowers. This danger is greatly lessened if the borrowers are themselves public corporations, and if the residents are renters rather than owners. People are more or less accustomed to see rents rise with other elements in the cost of living, whereas they are accustomed to have the value of a mortgage remain fixed, declining only as amortization payments are made.

A final objection is that if the public corporation borrows at longer term all that is needed for construction, an excessive proportion of current savings will be tied up. Would it not be better to sell some of the land, and repay construction loans, so that the lending agencies have more to lend to new borrowers, and the urban corporation can more quicly pay off its debt?

This is another case of the fallacy of composition. From the over-all national point of view the cost in terms of absorption of resources is incurred at the time of building. Thereafter the repayment of the loan by sale of assets merely involves transfer payments. The urban corporation is enabled to repay its loan to a lender by the sale to a person who borrows the identical funds from the lender. The over-all debt remains outstanding unless and until it is reduced by current saving out of current income. This may be by an individual making amortization payments on a mortgage or by paying rent to the urban corporation, which in turn makes amortization payments to the lender. From the national economic point of view there is no difference in the two cases. Hence there is no particular advantage in the rapid repayment of its debt, whether construction or mortgage, by the urban corporation. Indeed, there is no particular reason why the financing of the new city should be separated into the two types of loans.

C. Fixing Rents and Other Charges

Since the corporations are non-profit making, other criteria must be provided for the guidance of the board in setting rents and other charges. These criteria could be:

(1) The financial soundness of the corporation and its ability to service all debt and cover operating expenditures;

(2) The ability, over a term of years, to repay the original capital investment;

(3) The ability to rent or sell housing within the economic capacity of the people working in the new city and its area of influence;

(4) The proper maintenance of owned property, and property within its area of influence;

(5) The provision of facilities to enhance the quality of life;

(6) The provision of incentives and disincentives to ensure that people who work in the new city will live there, and will work there;

(7) The ability to avoid segregation of new cities by income groups as far as practicable;

(8) The capacity to assist in providing personal and property security;

(9) The willingness to seek to reduce, so far as possible, daily busing of children to distant schools;

(10) The willingness to seek to encourage the provision of all activities that occasion or necessitate movement of residents outside the city;

(11) The capacity to invest, at the direction or with the concurrence of the minister, in other new cities and improvement projects;

(12) The ability to retain ownership of property to the utmost degree feasible.

Much care must be given to the study of the relations of residents of the new cities to the corporation, especially if residential units, shops and industrial sites are sold to private buyers. The possibility of conflict is perhaps another reason why it would be desirable to retain ownership and rent all properties. It must be expected that elected representatives of residents are more likely to be interested in lower rents and more services, and be opposed to siphoning funds off to aid in the creation of new cities or to aid the existing city to provide services equal to those of the new cities.

D. Controlling Employment and Growth

The rationale of the proposed urban design depends on the existence of sufficient jobs near residences, with the type of residence adapted to the income levels of the job-holders. Hence the feasibility of the whole scheme to reduce movement and create communities depends on the degree of success in attracting and holding the right amount and kind of employment. The employment division must be one of the most efficient of all the divisions of the urban corporations and its studies and activities most soundly based. It must work in close contact with the rental and financial divisions to the end that rents are neither too high nor too low, that industrial properties are adjusted to needs and that every effort is made to secure and maintain activities — commercial, professional and governmental — that are found to result in decreased need for trips outside the city.

It is especially in this activity that close co-ordination is required at national and metropolitan levels. It would be a mistake for one new city to attract only high-paying jobs and avoid low-paying jobs. Every effort should be made to secure and retain a desirable social mix and avoid excessive differentiation of cities by income levels.

It is not only important that sufficient jobs be assured initially to prevent a commuting pattern being formed, but that close study be made of trends of employment in the various activities so that an unbalanced situation of jobs *versus* housing and other facilities does not arise.

All countries with mixed economies have found it difficult and costly to influence the location of employment. But their efforts have almost always been to change the regional location of jobs. To influence the location of plants and activities within a region, or within a metropolitan area, should be much easier since there is no question of foregoing the external economies that mean so much to a firm. The difference, within a metropolitan area, between one city or another or the traditional centre is important for a few activities but a matter of relative indifference for many others. Many activities will depend on the size and activity generated by a new city and no particular efforts need be expended in attracting them. Others are more "seed" industries whose location will generate other jobs in the vicinity, and these are the ones whose location will require the closest study.

A private developer, whether of a satellite planned community or of a residential or office complex, must undergo considerable risk arising from the fact that the facilities he has to offer must be competitive to other locations to the prospective tenants or buyers and he has no control over alternatives. This risk can be considerably reduced if the city cluster principle is adopted as a national or metropolitan plan, since a variety of instruments are then available to guide and influence the direction of growth. Thus, in the exercise of the building-licensing powers, it can be made a policy not to license new suburban urbanizations or the erection of plants unless and until the new urban corporations certify that they are not interested in the location within the new cities or new office buildings in the traditional centre unless or until there is a movement of some employment out of the centre.

This could be a potent weapon. Its exercise has not been very effective to date because of the lack of acceptable alternatives, the lack of control of building permits outside city limits or the dominance of the view that a leading objective of zoning is to protect existing property values and to promote rather than inhibit fragmentation of city life into residential, industrial and commercial zones.

An even more potent weapon whose use might be considered is the direction of flow of mortgage funds within broad limits. Thus it may be a national policy to prohibit or give low priority to mortgage lending by thrift institutions to finance construction in suburban residential areas, and to assign top priority to the financing of construction in new cities.

The higher rate of growth of a city and the more this growth can be guided into one city after another (or even two or three simultaneously), the faster the raise in the social increment and the less risk of financial loss. It is difficult to rent commercial space at high rentals if it is going to take 10 to 20 years for the city to attain its size target. A highly diversified and active shopping area promotes local growth, but it also depends on local growth. The faster and the more this interaction can be stimulated, the more viable the undertaking, and the quicker can new cities within the metropolitan area be undertaken. For this reason the planning of the growth of an intermediate city of, say, 200,000, must be much different than the planning of a city which is already growing at the rate of 200,000 a year.

E. Co-ordination and Flexibility

For a cities-within-cities design of growth, the need for close co-ordination with both the city government of the metropolitan district, the surrounding region and the federal or national government is obvious. Land use adjoining the new city must be harmonized with the land use pattern of that city. Services must be contracted for. Agreement must be reached on the sharing of costs and provision of public facilities. Efforts should be made to promote uniform standards of service for all parts of the area. As for the region, co-operation on the part of the state, provincial, or regional authority is necessary to preserve land for agricultural use and prevent the indefinite spread of residential and unplanned industrial uses of land.

Regional Corporations

The danger of regional corporations is that they may regard themselves as "development" corporations and be anxious to encourage the growth of the region. The objective, however, should be the direct contrary. What is desired is not growth, but rather preservation of the rural, agricultural character of the immediate environs of cities for a radius of some 25 miles or so. Owners anxious for valorization of their properties will undoubtedly bring every pressure on the regional corporation to license land for many uses other than agricultural and recreational. For this reason, any license granted should be subject to approval by the ministry before being granted. In highly suburbanized regions in developed countries, it may be very difficult to prevent further intensive non-agricultural land use. Indeed, some suburbs may be candidates for cities-within-cities. But even in such countries, in view of the increasing cost of energy and the other considerations advanced earlier, it would seem that every effort should be made to confine further growth to compact, walkable cities. Since land values in suburbs are already so high, the regional corporations might be charged with the responsibility of assessing the value of land for agricultural use and this value would be the base for the assessment of the property tax on land so used, rather than its possible urbanization value. If, for any good reason, its use is changed, it could be made subject to the land rise recapture law. Adequate powers should exist to capture the rise in land values of land immediately adjacent to and within the sphere of influence of the new cities.

The reorientation of outlook suggested applies also to the location of plants and places of employment. Instead of their further deployment in areas surrounding cities, much more thought must be given to their location in the new cities and in every way to minimize the use of the personal automobile. The ministry and the regional corporation can play a useful role here. However, the national government must exercise over-all supervision and see that plans and funds are distributed to the different main cities and regions of the country. National leadership must be listed as perhaps the most important requisite for a successful national programme tying together the requirements of a national economic and social programme that affects directly the well-being of the growing proportion of the population that will live in cities.

It would be dangerous to insist on a single set design and density for cities-within-cities. Account must be taken of individual differences in land availability, rapidity of growth, prospects, income levels. For developed countries in particular, the task may appear to be the more difficult one of modifying, renovating, regrouping of activities and the gradual emergence of a series, perhaps not of separate cities properly so called, but at least of better balanced zones that will reduce movement and differences in standards of living. In some cases, the main task may appear to be to attract employment opportunities to working class residential zones; in others, to provide residences, shops, schools and so forth in a predominantly industrial zone, cleaning the industries as this takes place. In some places, an option may be limited by area available and in such cases there may be a good case for providing better balanced zones for only 50,000 to 200,000 people. As long as the objectives are kept clearly in mind, a flexible approach is very much to be desired.

MOBILIZING RESOURCES TO IMPLEMENT THE NEW URBAN DESIGN

When it is said that resources are inadequate to supply popular housing, or that conventional measures do not provide sufficient resources, it is probably that reference is to financial and not physical resources. In developing countries, at least, there is an enormous pool of under-utilized or poorly utilized labour to draw upon, as well as raw materials for building construction, and, less certainly, capacity to make and transport building materials. This is implicitly assumed by the site and services advocates who assume that there are materials and sites available and plenty of under-utilized time of the prospective occupier.

The term may be used in a still different sense, that of inadequacy of funds relative to the effective demand or capacity to pay of the lower income groups. In this sense, the problem merges into that of poverty in general — inadequate housing, public services, health, education, a varied and adequate diet and so forth. The basic solution is a twofold one — adopt policies to increase the incomes and buying capacity of lower income groups and provide incentives to have smaller families and subsidized health and education services. Housing falls in a category between the fully paid-for goods and fully subsidized services, varying according to circumstances and need and the adequacy of other solutions.

The problem, then, is not really one of inadequate physical resources but rather the absence of an institutional framework and public policy that can mobilize such resources in an efficient and modern way and convert building into a large-scale, efficient industry. "Resources" must be understood in a financial rather than physical sense unless and until the volume of building is actually limited by physical shortages.

A. Financing Building

Although a number of planned new cities-within-cities may each appear to be financially viable, together they cannot be undertaken until a large flow of savings is attained and this flow is channelled into building. In most mixed economies in both developed and developing countries, the financial arrangements for channelling resources to the sector appear inadequate. The proportion of the national income available for urban construction is both low and variable. The high percentage necessary to house or rehouse the additional millions of urban dwellers and to provide them with necessary facilities is lacking, as is the steady and high absolute growth that is desirable to provide urban employment and encourage the producers of building material to enlarge capacity in advance of and along with need.

To build a series of permanent cities in rapid succession to handle the tremendous rates of growth facing cities in developing countries requires relatively large sums. In Singapore, for some years, building expenditures were between 10 and 14 percent of a rapidly expanding gross product, so that annual rates of growth of between 20 and 40 percent in building were attained. In the United States, the collapse of the building industry in 1973-1974 and the bankruptcies and the failures of planned satellite communities were traceable to the dearth of mortgage funds arising from the conjunction of inflation and rigid long-term interest rates and rates on savings in thrift institutions. Hence a large and growing source of funds must be listed as a prerequisite.

Probably no single explanation will serve for all countries to account for lack of building. In certain cases, there may be a lack of sufficient effective demand due either to very high costs or very low buying power. In many cases, however, the deficiency appears to be more on the side of supply, not of physical resources, but of financial resources. There are those who place their faith in the forces of the market place and would rely upon those forces for the allocation of resources to various uses, letting the more productive use to incur the highest rates of interest to attract the resources it needs. The difficulty with this theory and policy is that it assumes away a large part of the problem — that mobility is effective. There are a host of institutional and cultural factors that may impede mobility. In labour, for example, workers do not have equal skills or capacities to perform equally any task, nor are they in a position to bid for any job in any part of the country. In developing countries in particular, the mass of completely unskilled rural and urban labour who have little more than their strength to offer has given rise to the phenomenon of dualism, which is only an extreme case of immobility. The greatest single act to raise the standard of living of the totally unskilled in the United States was not a piece of social legislation, but the restriction of immigration. The inflow of unskilled immigrants had exactly the same effect as the large natural addition to the labour force resulting from a very high birth rate in relation to the facilities for education and fixed volume of natural resources.

The mobilization of human resources for building and for the subsidiary and secondarily affected industries is an instrument to promote the greater mobility of labour (moving upward in the income scale) and hence is a "social" measure of prime importance. It is paradoxical and sad to see how frequently people who are most socially motivated advocate policies that defeat their laudable objectives. The rural policy and attitude to migration is one. Another one is the attitude toward building.

The role of savings

Building, necessitating a very large expenditure relative to most people's incomes, requires long-term financing. Neither individual savers nor commercial banks wish to sacrifice liquidity by tying their money up in long-term loans. Hence the need for specialized financial intermediaries who can give liquidity to savers on the one hand and long-term loans to borrowers on the other. How can they afford to do this? Only if savings in the bulk continue to grow steadily so that individual withdrawals of savings are always more than offset by new deposits. The more established the system, the more reliance can be put on monthly repayments of existing loans as a source of funds, but such repayments only maintain the outstanding volume of loans. New savings out of new income are a necessity for continued growth.

The institutional system for financing building evolved out of the early and local small building societies in Britain in which pooled savings supplied member after member with funds to build a house. Then came the mutual savings and loan associations (which long since ceased to be co-operatives in the true sense of the term) and joint stock savings and loan banks, savings banks, trust companies and even in some cases sections in commercial banks.

This institutional development met a real need, and grew in many countries to be a very large system. Yet it was never completely satisfactory. It depended upon the constant growth of deposits to supply the instant liquidity it offered and savers demanded. If, for any reason, this constant growth was interrupted, the system was in trouble and with it, the whole industry. The vulnerability of the system lay in the fact that its assets were invested in long-term obligations at a fixed rate of interest, which could not be readily changed. Hence, implicitly the system relied upon a stable interest rate structure that would permit investment in savings deposits to remain attractive to savers year in and out. But even before chronic inflation became a problem, interest rates would fluctuate somewhat during the business cycle (fluctuations in business activity). It was the savings/mortgage institutions that would first feel the repercussions of rising and falling interest rates, due to the fixity of the interest rates they paid and received. In recent years the institutional framework became particularly inadequate with the growth of inflation, general rise in interest rates as a consequence, and the increasing competition of commercial banks and other borrowers for savings and their consequent diversion from building.

As background, it may be helpful to review in very broad terms the main sources and uses of savings in the United States. The main uses are public "investment," industrial, commercial and agricultural investment in structures and equipment, and residential construction. The sources are taxation, business saving (undistributed profits and depreciation and other reserves) and personal saving (the increase in consumer credit is treated as negative saving). Since the line between government "operating" and "investment" expenditures is so arbitrary or subjective, we will not attempt to separate them here, but merely show that the overwhelming bulk of all public expenditures — transfer, investment and other — is covered by current receipts other than borrowing.

Tables 1, 2 and 3, summarize the trends since 1960 of government (federal and other), business and personal savings. "Forced saving" through taxation was offset by public expenditures, so attention may be devoted to the other two categories. So much discussion has been devoted to the stock and bond markets as sources of corporate financing, that it is startling to observe that generally business saving covers the gross investment in physical assets plus the addition to inventories, and that business gross saving ranges between 10 and 12 percent of the GNP, with some tendency in recent years to remain around 10.5 percent.

The relation between net personal savings and residential construction is more erratic, but again it is

Table 1   Total Receipts and Expenditures, National, State and Local Governments of the United States[a]
(thousand million dollars)

	Receipts	Expenditures	Difference
1960	139.8	136.1	3.7
1961	144.6	149.0	− 4.3
1962	157.0	159.9	− 2.9
1963	168.8	166.9	1.8
1964	174.1	175.4	− 1.4
1965	189.1	186.9	2.2
1966	213.3	212.2	1.1
1967	228.9	242.9	−13.9
1968	263.5	270.3	− 6.8
1969	296.7	287.9	8.8
1970	302.5	312.7	−10.1
1971	322.0	340.2	−18.1
1972	368.2	370.9	− 2.8
1973	419.0	407.4	11.6

[a]Based on the *Economic Report of the President, 1974*, (United States Government Printing Office, Washington, D.C., 1974), p. 328.

Table 2   Business Investment and Savings in the United States[a]   (thousand million dollars)

	Business gross investment in physical assets	Business savings	Difference	Business savings as percentage of GNP
1960	52.0	56.8	4.8	11.3
1961	49.0	58.7	9.7	11.3
1962	57.7	66.3	8.6	11.8
1963	60.2	68.8	8.6	11.6
1964	69.9	76.2	6.3	12.0
1965	80.9	84.7	3.8	12.4
1966	96.2	91.3	−5.9	12.2
1967	91.5	93.0	1.5	11.7
1968	95.9	95.4	− .5	11.0
1969	106.3	97.0	−9.3	10.4
1970	105.1	97.0	−8.1	10.0
1971	110.5	111.8	1.3	10.5
1972	124.2	124.4	.2	10.7
1973	143.4	134.7	−8.8	10.5

[a]Based on the *Economic Report of the President, 1974*, pp. 264 and 272.

Table 3 Personal Savings and Residential Construction in the United States 1960-1972[a]
(thousand million dollars)

	Net personal savings	Residential construction	Difference	Net personal savings as percentage of GNP	As percentage of disposable personal income
1960	17.0	22.8	−5.8	3.4	4.9
1961	21.2	22.6	−1.4	4.1	5.8
1962	21.6	25.3	−3.7	3.8	5.6
1963	19.9	27.0	−7.1	3.4	4.9
1964	26.2	27.1	.9	4.1	6.0
1965	28.4	27.2	+1.2	4.1	6.0
1966	32.5	25.0	+7.5	4.3	6.4
1967	40.4	25.1	+15.3	5.1	7.4
1968	39.8	30.1	+9.7	4.6	6.7
1969	38.2	32.6	+5.6	4.1	6.0
1970	56.2	31.2	+23.7	5.6	8.0
1971	60.2	42.7	+18.3	5.8	8.2
1972	49.7	54.0	+ .9	4.8	6.9
1973	53.8	58.0	−4.8	4.2	6.1

[a]Based on the *Economic Report of the President, 1974*, pp. 264, 268 and 272.

apparent that personal saving is the main source of financing for housing. The rise in personal saving from 6 to 8 percent of disposable income (4.1 to 5.6 percent of the GNP) from 1969 to 1970, and to 8.2 percent in 1971 is reflected in a delayed upsurge in housing expenditures in 1971 and 1972. Calendar year figures conceal highly significant movements in savings, and particularly savings in thrift institutions in 1973 and 1974. The collapse in building in those years was associated not only with a decline in the percentage of income saved but more importantly with a massive diversion of the flow of savings.

The implicit impression which some economists appear to have that the ideal is a large annual flow of savings available to whoever is prepared to bid the highest for them, is a gross simplification. Savings arise from different sources, have different motivations, and meet different requirements. The demand for savings also arises from different borrowers or users to serve different purposes. It is only by accident that the variety of resources and uses happen to coincide, and the interest rate is not a good instrument for assuming that the "right" amount of investment is available in different fields to assure high and steady growth. Much of business investment is motivated by a management's desire to maintain growth and the position or rank of particular companies in particular fields. Sudden rises in profits are rarely disbursed as dividends but are retained, even if only for investment in other companies. The savings of individuals are largely semi-obligatory (premiums on insurance policies, repayments of mortgages and instalment debt). Again, sudden and large gains are generally saved. There is little point in raising one's level of consumption unless one can hope to maintain the new level. The requirements of liquidity by individual savers are far in excess of the funds private savers wish to loan for long periods. Yet in this maze, if economic growth is to proceed steadily, there is need for a steady growth of building and for a steady rise in productive capacity, in some fields much more than in others. It is a major part of the planners' job to ensure that sufficient supply of non-inflationary financing is at hand to permit this steady growth, and that the over-all demand is such as will absorb the funds made available.

In a socialist State, this is presumably an obvious and not too difficult a task, as savings are obligatory and come out of the sales prices of goods. In a mixed economy, the need is not so obvious, and the means to assure the "proper" aggregate amount and the "right" allocation for high, sustained and non-inflationary growth, other than the forces of the market place and an inherited institutional framework, are not so easily available and usable.

In retrospect of the very recent past, it now appears obvious that a lag in interest payments behind prices means that savers are not only getting no return on their savings, but end a period with less capital than when they started saving. If this is not sufficient to lower the incentive to save, it certainly lowers the ability. On the other hand, rising prices increase the demand for loans at a negative rate of interest. Hence, with inflation, interest rates must rise. Instead of permitting rates to adjust to this rate, however, we permitted them to adjust in some markets but not in others, creating many distortions in the allocation of funds. Interest rates on mortgages were sticky and hence interest rates that thrift institutions could pay savers were also sticky. But other rates on obligations offering reasonable liquidity were permitted to rise. Hence, there was a massive flow of diminished real savings from the institutions financing building to those financing instalment debt and other short obligations offered by commercial banks and the government.

Funds literally become unavailable for mortgage financing and housing starts declined from an annual rate of 2.4 million to 1.1 million in a little over a year. While holding the line on mortgage and savings rates considerably below a positive rate, the United States Government competed for savings in the open market to secure the funds being withdrawn from thrift institutions to reloan these funds in the purchase of mortgages from the thrift organizations. The process was no secret. It was frequently commented on, as was the consequent bankruptcies of real estate organizations, contractors and developers. However, so enamoured were many economists of macro models that they did not weigh the dynamics of this process but assumed that the decline in building could safely be ignored by the reported enormous backlog of orders for industrial expansion and a continued rise in inventories. What was not appreciated was that one of the props for industrial expansion was building, and especially house building. Cutting this in half was bound to affect employment, the demand for materials and supplies and so forth. When, in the latter part of 1974, this was beginning to be felt, the backlog of orders for industrial expansion suddenly shrank. Orders were cancelled. Efforts were made to work off inventories. An outstanding consumer debt of $180,000 million inhibited further living beyond one's means.

There appears, unfortunately, to be no easy solution at hand. There are those who would accept the consequences of rigidities, resort to restrictive aggregate monetary and fiscal measures and maintain stable prices by forcing down the aggregate demand for goods. But with strong and weak groups in the community and the fierce resistance to lowered wage rates on the part of organized labour, the consequence of such a policy can be very grave. To wait until interest rates are forced down by lowered demand to a point where it is again profitable to build and funds are available, may be a long and painful wait. If, during this wait, real incomes are lowered by widespread unemployment, the ability to save and the demand for housing may likewise fall.

Monetary correction

Another type of solution would be to insulate the saving/mortgage market from the effect of inflation, make savings in thrift organizations exceptionally attractive (that is, give preference to such savings) and stimulate demand for building by providing low real rates of interest that will remain low regardless of what happens to prices. This could be done by monetary correction, i.e. indexing applied to this field. Here, again, such institutional change is easier to adopt in a developing country than in a developed country, where such enormous growth has already occurred. However, institutions are man-made and should serve the needs of man. When they cease to do so, they should surely be subject to change. The resistance to the application of monetary correction is an understandable resistance to far-reaching institutional change and, as always, weighty reasons can be adduced for not singling out an important sector of the economy for privileged treatment.

Opposed to these arguments, however, is the overriding importance of the building sector as one in which high and sustained growth rates can be secured independently of the over-all growth rates, where the capital requirements are potentially tremendous to build cities in developing countries or rebuild them in developed ones, and a field that can be utilized in developing countries to promote mobility, provide urban employment and lessen dualism. What is at stake in developing countries is nothing less than development itself, which requires a period of high and sustained growth to bring about the necessary structural transformation of the society and create an environment which offers an incentive for smaller families.

Monetary correction applied to the building/mortgage field is mentioned as one way of mobilizing the requisite large and growing volume of financial resources to carry through an urban building or rebuilding plan that would avoid the evils or drawbacks of urbanization that have been stressed in the literature. However, Singapore achieved the same effect by requiring obligatory worker-employer contributions to a provident fund which served for retirement and disability purposes and meanwhile, from the proceeds, to finance a very large building programme, possibly, in relative terms, the largest in the world. The important thing is not so much the means as the achievement by some means of the objective of increasing personal savings and channelling them through to the building sector. Industry should be encouraged to do its own saving through undistributed profits and depreciation reserves and not compete for personal savings which, for most countries and for many years, are badly needed to carry through the urban programme (and incidentally to provide funds indirectly to industry).

The funds made available in Singapore permitted building to reach 14 percent of GNP, which was itself growing at unprecedented rates of 10 to 14 percent. For a number of years the rate of increase in growth in building was sustained at from 30 to 40 percent per annum. This was both a cause and effect of the high over-all growth rates. A planned building programme required enormous savings and provided the outlet for the investment of the savings; together with manufactured exports it made possible the high rates of growth in income and consequently in savings. It permitted, in an astonishingly short period, the achievement of a very high (for developing countries) worker/participation ratio to the whole population and a dramatic fall in the birth-rate.

Something similar occurred in Colombia in 1973 and the first half of 1974 with the institution of a new system of savings/mortgage institutions based on monetary correction or indexing. Colombia had been a country of relatively low personal savings and building, despite a very rapid urban growth. Inflation had been chronic but became more acute in 1972-1973, so that interest rates on savings had been negative for some time, that is, did not compensate for the fall in purchasing power of the savings.

The national plan of development, adopted in December 1971, provided that special measures be taken to stimulate growth in two sectors — exports and building — as a means of stimulating growth in the whole economy and especially industry; that efforts be made to stimulate agricultural productivity to provide more food and raw material for cities and to export, and to release workers; and that differences in levels or styles of living be lessened; in short, a four-point programme.

The institutional change noted above was to provide the special stimulus for building. It was based on four basic assumptions: (1) that voluntary savings could be greatly increased by the institution of a positive rate of interest, or the protection of the principal of savings from monetary erosion; (2) that the bulk of these increased savings could be channelled to finance building; (3) that a very large latent demand for building existed that could be exploited, and (4) that, despite a rate of growth of over 6 percent achieved with the help of a rapid growth in exports, sufficient slack existed in the economy to permit the attainment of still higher rates of growth. All these assumptions proved valid. From the beginning of 1973 to March 1974, a volume of saving in the new system had been accumulated equal to that which had been accumulated in the previous 40 years by the Government Mortgage Bank. This saving was to a small extent at the expense of saving in obligations of the Mortgage Bank, but not of savings in commercial banks. What is equally significant is that the demand for mortgages outran the supply of savings by a ratio of 2 to 1. Building permits in terms of square metres, which had shown little growth from 1967 to 1971, increased by 30 percent in 1973 over 1972; in terms of estimated expenditures they rose by an estimated 20 percent in 1973 over 1972 and a further 20 percent or more in the first half of 1974, over the first half of 1973. The over-all rate of growth in the GNP rose 7 1/2 percent (nearly 8 percent if allowance is made for a decline in the production of petroleum). The over-all growth of employment in the four years 1969-1973 was a million new jobs, mostly urban, at an increasing rate in excess of the growth in the labour force. As unemployment declined, the participation rate rose.

Whether special measures have the effect of providing a stimulus to increased voluntary saving, as, for a time, in Israel and more recently in Colombia, or obligatory saving, as in Singapore and Brazil, is not as important as that there should be a stimulus. A rate of growth in personal saving of 6 percent of the disposable income (4.2 percent of the GNP) as in the United States in 1973, with increased competition for this reduced rate among various fields, leaves too little for building to play the role it is capable of playing. The lessons of the consequences of the lessening of personal saving and their diversion from the field of building finance, so dramatically brought out in 1973-1974 in the United States and the United Kingdom, must not be lost.

B. Capturing the Rise in Land Values

The rise in land values (and, to a small extent, building) that results from the growth in numbers and income of a community is a reflection of pure scarcity. It arises from the community and should belong to the community. It does not in any way arise from the work or saving of an individual owner and does not provide any incentive to work or save, since the supply of land is fixed. The rise in value in itself performs an economic function in assuring (more or less, and with exceptions and qualifications) — that the activities or people who can pay the most get the use of the land. In short, it is part of the economic land use allocation mechanism. But the economic use can be distinguished from the role played by the rise in land values in distribution. In other words, land can rise in value whether its owner is public or private. The capture of this value, after it has occurred, in no way affects the economic use to which the land is put. Indeed, as has also been stressed, reliance exclusively on the pricing mechanism for the allocation of land produces a planless and unlivable city. Consequently, even the resource allocation function of urban land must be subordinated to an over-all pattern of land use.

Not only should the allocative and property distributive functions be sharply distinguished, but in the latter, a distinction should be drawn between the part of the rise that merely reflects a fall in the value of money in general, and that part that reflects the growing scarcity of a resource fixed in supply. It is with the latter that this section is concerned. Even if the price level were absolutely stable, the concentration of people with rising incomes in a metropolitan centre of relatively small and fixed size would obviously give rise to an enormous increase in land values accruing to a relatively few owners of land in particularly favoured positions. Where there are no natural barriers, this rise in general is restrained by the outward extension of the urbanized area, which operates to transfer the cost of the land to the cost of transport, measurable and indirect. Where there are natural barriers, as in Manhattan Island, the rise can assume fantastic proportions. Even where there are no natural barriers and transport facilities are provided, the economic external advantages of proximity for certain activities and the social "advantage" of snobbishness for certain suburbs may result in very high rises.

It is a striking example of our economic illiteracy, or widespread inability to understand the functioning of the mixed economy under which so many people live, that we have more or less quietly acquiesced in the private appropriation of socially created gains, letting fortunate owners and their heirs levy tribute or claim a share of the national income to which they have contributed nothing. Where efforts have been made to capture this "betterment" (the British term, which is not very appropriate) the public interest has usually lost out to the private. The most successful instances to the contrary have been where public authorities have adopted the traditional private device of acquiring ownership and hence have availed themselves of all the protection and privileges accorded private property. Stockholm is often cited as a leading example, where public ownership of land in the suburbs was started many years ago (and is still being practised as the city grows). Orville Grimes of the World Bank has made a comprehensive compilation and discussion of the attempts made by various countries to capture "betterments."[2] There has been some measure of success, but generally the history is not too encouraging.

Generally, the case for capture of all or a large portion of the pure monopoly gain of rising urban land has been impaired by failure to distinguish between land and capital in general, between land and building, and between the rise reflecting inflation and that traceable to pure scarcity. In the first case the rise in land values has been subject to the capital gains tax which, since it applies to all properties, is naturally fixed at a relatively low rate. In the second case, buildings are not a fixed amount and their supply can be increased or be subject to deterioration. There would seem to be little object in attempting to capture the rise in their value, which generally is really the rise in the value of the site or reflects general inflation. In the third case, the implicit assumption of price stability in a world of chronic inflation leads to all sorts of distortions and inequities. If we are assuming stability, we should in logic separate the source of rises in land values. A good case on grounds of equity can be ruined by extending it to cases where the property owner can rightly claim that inequality arises from the application of a tax.

In addition to the lack of success in the capture of the "social increment," there is the universal practice of applying the tax or levy only at the time of realization or when the property in question is sold or passes

[2] Grimes, Orville F., Jr., "Urban Land and Public Policy: Social Appropriation of Betterment" (IBRD Working Paper No. 179, Washington, D.C., 1974).

as an inheritance. The levy can simply be evaded by refraining from sale, waiting for the law to be modified. Meanwhile the property can be leased. In some cases permission is given to write off a portion of the property yearly so that in a few years the amount subject to taxation is small. Again the tax can be evaded by waiting.

Assuredly, an important factor in the perpetuation of this glaring source of growing inequality of wealth and income has been the failure to exempt from liability small owner-occupied homes (land and houses) so that the owners of rapidly appreciating and very valuable lots of land could enlist the support of thousands (or millions) or small owner-occupied homes. Little damage would be done either to the principle or the yield by exemption of such homes. The main objective could be served by limiting the liability to the rise in the future to large and/or valuable lots. Moreover, this would enormously lighten the administrative load, which is a particularly important consideration in developing countries.

Another factor in the opposition is doubtless the fact that while urban land in general may be expected to rise more than the general rise in prices, specific areas may deteriorate. This factor can in part be offset by allowing larger owners of different properties to offset losses against gains. (Small owners would presumably not be subject to the recapture clause.)

It is generally considered that a tax or levy should have general application. But exceptions to this principle are constantly made. The proper application of the principle would be equal treatment to a group of persons who shared common taxable characteristics. Thus, for example, the recapture levy might apply to all land in certain cities having a population over a certain figure and whose owners have more than a certain area with a certain value. The canon of equal treatment of equal cases would be observed, but the acceptability of the levy would be enormously heightened and its administration improved without a sacrifice of the real benefits or the correction of the major abuses.

It is suggested, therefore, especially but not exclusively, that consideration be given to the capture of the social or unearned increment in urban land values along the following lines:

(1) The levy could be called a recapture (i.e. by the community that created the rise) and not a tax, which term should be better restricted to application to current income;

(2) Liability could be initially restricted to the largest cities or urban areas which are rising in value most rapidly;

(3) Within such areas, liability could be restricted to only land, and to "family" holdings above a certain size and value (this could exempt the great bulk of owner-occupied homes and avoid fragmentation of lots among a family);

(4) The recapture provision could apply only to rises in the future and not be retroactive;

(5) That part of the rise in value equal to the general rise in prices (as measured by the cost of living index) could be deducted from the rise in general, or the rise attributable to improvements (roads, for example) for which the owner has been assessed;

(6) The "true" rise (after deduction of items in (5)) could be assessed and payable every two years, whether or not the property has been transferred, or upon the date of transfer if within the two-year period;

(7) Land in the specified urban areas should be made exempt from the application of any general capital gains tax;

(8) Land owned by public urban corporations should not be liable to tax;

(9) The recapture could be as high as is feasible, considering the imperfections of assessment of commercial value, say 75 percent;

(10) Provision could be made for the extension of the recapture levy to other areas, suburban and urban, as experience is gained and large rises occur.

It has been objected that assessment every two years may result in forced sales of lands. This assumes, however, either that the land is yielding no revenue, that is, is vacant, or that the rise is very large and the owner has no other source of income. Owners can protect themselves by inserting escalator clauses in their leases to tenants, or providing for shorter-term leases. In general the rise in "true" value may be expected to be around 2 to 4 percent per annum and the payment of this should not occasion grave difficulty. In cases of manifest hardship, the liability might be funded as an indexed debt on which 8 percent need be paid.

The recapture provision would supplement the direct capture of the very high rise in land values that may be anticipated in the cities-within-cities, since it would apply to the more dramatic rises in land values in the privately owned sectors of the city, probably mostly in the traditional centre and in fashionable residential areas. A successful implementation of the proposal would remove one of the main sources of growing inequality in wealth and income and would provide a source of funds for investment in the purchase of land for new cities and in the provision of community facilities. It should probably not be used as revenue for current services, as payments for large accretions represent forced saving which would be dissaved in financing current expenditures. A developing country needs a large relative amount of saving to promote growth.

SOME CRUCIAL ISSUES IN PLANNING A NEW CITY-WITHIN-A-CITY

A. Adapting Plans to Sites

This may seem obvious and yet a great deal of time can be lost in discussing cash flows, the merits of high- and low-rise buildings, varying land uses and densities, and the range of factors and weights to be accorded them to determine location, and so forth, without reference to any specific site, unless, of course, one goes far out into farm land and plans a satellite community, which becomes in effect a separate new city, like most of the American Planned Communities and the British New Towns. In the end, in Colombia, the happy accident of being able to acquire large blocks of unbuilt-on land in otherwise suitable locations determined the choice of the first locations. Once the choice was made, the shape of the area, the nature of the surrounding area, the existing network of water mains and sewers, the nature and concentration of jobs, the variable bearing capacity of the soil, the nearness and size of playing fields, the main road network, all played a role in the choice of physical design, density, location of main shopping areas, the composition and character of apartments, and the height of buildings. It was very much borne in mind that in the case of a city-within-a-city, the adjoining area of influence will include all land use within 1 1/2 to 2 kilometres of the main shopping and office centre.

In short, planning an "ideal city" divorced from a specific site is of doubtful usefulness. In some cases the site may be adjoining a working class dormitory suburb. The problem then is to exercise one's ingenuity in bringing employment, a shopping centre (and centres), community facilities and playfields within walking distance or short internal busing distances of the existing suburb. For social reasons, every effort must be made to attract higher-income families, to reduce commuting, to attract offices and to add to the valorization potential, particularly of the commercial centre.

In another case the problem may be to create a residential and commerical area to balance an adjoining existing industrial zone. Pollution may have to be cleaned up, factories landscaped where possible, unsightly dumps bulldozed and planted and new industry required to be more economical in its use of space.

Finally, there may exist either a large vacant area or an area that can be remodelled in the midst of a rather dense mixture of workshops, commercial establishments and homes. A community centre with a better shopping area and high-rise apartments and community facilities may serve to pull the whole area together into a more compact and self-sustained community. Fitting pieces together and adding the missing elements is a challenging job which may yield high dividends with reduced expenditures.

None of these cases are as satisfying to a designer as a "green fields" site. They would constitute, however, an improvement in the existing state of affairs, would tend to create a community where one does not now exist. The difficulty with the green fields site is that it is likely to be too far out to form part of the metropolitan area and the task of attracting employment, offices and a modern shopping centre is almost as formidable as it would be in creating an entirely new satellite city. Rapid growth in employment must remain the indispensable characteristic to differentiate our design from a conventional dormitory suburb. Unless there is some assurance that primary employment can be attracted to a site, preference must be granted to other sites where there is such assurance. From this point of view alone, the remodelling of the actual centre itself deserves high priority and unplanned growth in the suburbs can thereby be restrained while the efficiency of the centre is enhanced.

B. Speed in Construction

The full benefits of a planned city are obtainable only when it nears completion. A commercial centre with a wide variety of shops, offices, professions and specialized occupations and skills suitable for a city of 400,000 can only be supported when the city actually has 400,000 people. The American Planned Communities and British New Towns were geared to slow growth, extending over 10 to 20 years, which meant that for a time they were rather ragged and unfinished-looking, the economies of scale were lacking and the rise in land values was slow. One of the few advantages in being a developing country is that the over-all rate of urban growth is very fast and hence the growth of a new city can be very rapid. If inducements are at hand to channel a portion of the growth into a new city, we can think in terms of 3 or 4 years of construction instead of 15, with all the economies that this implies.

The armory of instruments to be available for use in adopting a planned design for a city should ideally include the possession of land by a "land bank" or central agency to permit a choice of sites in the future, the ability to channel mortgage funds into a particular site at a time and make it unavailable to build in areas that do not fit into the over-all pattern and to back this up with building licensing powers. When there is widespread poverty this latter may prove to be far from effective, as much building may occur without licensing. The best remedy, apart from enforcement of the law, is full employment and a rapid addition to the total stock of housing so that, through the process of escalation or upgrading, there is assurance that there are always at least some houses or rooms available for the poorest groups. In addition, of course, there are possibilities of providing subsidies for existing housing as well as in the new cities.

The importance of speed in construction is one of the lessons to be learned from the French experience, which is very close, as a design, to what is here being suggested. No less than five large cities around Paris, as well as in six other metropolitan centres, were started at the same time. Growth in any one is naturally slow, especially as the growth in the over-all urban population of France itself is not very rapid. Hence it will be many years before the full benefits of all or any of the new cities can be obtained.

C. Controlling Density

The dream of a "house of one's own," or a house standing in its own grounds and surrounded by lawns and gardens, as an ideal for all, cannot be reconciled with the arithmetic of the problem, especially in developing countries. Where space is limited and we are dealing with numbers of 5 to 10 millions in a metropolitan area, the choice must be made between either rather high density in walkable cities, or an endless extension of single-family homes, with all the direct and indirect expense this occasions. Once the line is crossed to low-rise apartment houses, we may as well go the whole way to a compact, planned city. It makes little sense to erect apartments in the suburbs, as is now being done in Bogota, for example. On the other hand, the space requirements of a city of 10 million for single-family homes would quickly absorb all the arable lands near the larger cities of Colombia.

The relation of density to land area requirements is strikingly brought out by the following calculations. If, by 1985, the population of the larger cities of Latin America reaches 131 million, the land requirements would vary from 13,149,200 hectares (or 131,492 km^2) if the land density should be 10 per hectare (slightly higher than the present figure for the metropolitan area of Buenos Aires) to 292,204 hectare (or 2,922 km^2) for a density of 450 inhabitants per hectare, which is a density often recommended for efficient, low-cost public services and for an acceptable standard of urban environment.[3]

One troublesome problem of a planned city is the growth in families. A city composed of a number of apartments of varying sizes and prices will become too small if the families keep growing. The only answer would seem to be to stabilize employment in each city and provide inducements for new families to move to the new cities offering new employment.

---

[3] Jorge E. Hardoy, *Urban Land Policies and Land Use Control Measures*, vol. IV, Latin America, 1973 (United Nations document ST/ECA/167/Add.3), p. 11.

D. Renting Instead of Selling

Planned communities have been greatly influenced by the United States and British examples. In the former, single-family homes predominated and the private developers were anxious to sell lots as rapidly as possible in order to purchase more land to sell. The profit lay in the turnover. Similarly, the British public authorities adopted the practice of selling housing units. In the evolution of thinking about urban growth in Colombia, it was gradually appreciated that there were very weighty arguments for retaining public ownership and renting as much as possible.

In the first place, the basic interest or motivation of urban corporations and a ministry of urban affairs is very different from that of private developers. The concern is to capture the rise in land values in perpetuity, to provide a steadily rising quality of services, to ensure that people will live and work in the same community, and finally to provide common services such as maintenance to avoid deterioration and premature obsolescence.

For all these reasons, it appears preferable to retain ownership. Once an apartment is sold, it becomes very difficult to ensure that a person living in it but wishing to work in another part of the city can be discouraged from doing so. It is proposed, for example, that occupants in the new city of Pontoise in Paris will pay 22 percent lower rent than if they work elsewhere. This may at first seem rather drastic, but it is only through ownership that one can vary rents to poorer groups and for people depending on where they work. In Columbia, Maryland, generally considered to be the most successful planned community in the United States, the early sale of lots has led to more commuting than normally occurs in a community. People drive to Columbia every day from Baltimore to work in the General Electric plant and elsewhere; at the same time residents of Columbia drive to Washington to work in government and other offices. Hence one of the basic objectives is lost, even though considerable care was exercised to balance employment with residence. There is now no way by which lower rents or other inducements can be offered to lower-income groups to permit them to live in the city.

Another powerful reason for renting instead of selling is that a well situated and built community may hope to experience a rise in the rents above the cost of living index, especially in the commercial areas. This can be captured by the urban corporation and used to provide lower rents to low-income people or, what is perhaps preferable, better schools, health and play facilities.

If the urban corporation finances its construction with constant value 15-to-20-year mortages, the nominal debt service will rise as inflation proceeds. It will probably prove easier to raise rents accordingly to service the debt than it would be to adjust the principal monthly of mortages on properties of poorer individuals.

The corporation, as owner, would be in a better position to provide services of all kinds for the whole community than would the families of each apartment building. A case in point would be elevator servicing. The housing estates in Singapore provide maintenance and emergency services around the clock for the whole estate.

In short, there is a real danger that with sales of apartments, the city may soon lose its compact aspect of being a more or less self-contained community with its own peculiar image. The urban corporation, as owner, would be the jealous guardian in perpetuity of this image and identity.

Those who have a nostalgic feeling about ownership may be reminded that we are here discussing an apartment in a building anywhere from 5 to 20 stories high. Not too much pride of ownership can accompany the occupancy of such an apartment, and the headaches of condominium ("propiedad horizontal" in some Latin American countries) ownership are well known. It would seem easier to leave the management of the building and grounds in the hands of a professional corporation. After the first two or three years, occupants could elect one or more members of the Board, or elect representatives who would present the interests of the residents to the governing board of the corporation.

E. Mixing Income Groups

Although the first impulse is perhaps to concentrate resources on housing the low-income groups, the weightier arguments seem to be in favour of trying to obtain a good social mix, so that all the higher-income groups employed in the new city will be persuaded to live there and patronize the local shops and services and utilize the services of local professional people. For this reason also, in starting a new city, it would seem the counsel of wisdom, if not of popular impulse, to start with the higher-income apartments and stores and, with the resulting rise in land values and rents, to build and provide lower rents for the lower-income people working in the city. Otherwise, it will be difficult to provide the lower rents at first and even more difficult to attract the higher-income groups who will find employment in the city (and create it).

The investigations of Oscar Newman suggest that there is likely to be more crime and vandalism in a completely low-income development than in one in which income classes are mixed.[4]

F. Public Education

It was earlier suggested that the device of the urban corporation offers the possibility of a transition stage from wholly private education, especially in secondary schools, to wholly public by giving an opportunity for the corporation to build and run some schools in conformity with required standards but with somewhat better facilities and higher paid teachers than characterize wholly public schools in many developing countries.

G. Adjacent Areas and Suburbs

Within the designated perimeter of the new city will probably be many existing privately-owned homes, work shops and commercial establishments. The harmonization of this zone, which may use the shopping district of the newly built area, requires the closest kind of co-operation between the corporation and the neighbouring political unit, perhaps even the intervention of the ministry to ensure the proper degree of collaboration. A particularly delicate field will be that of licensing new buildings or alterations. In all such cases it would be very desirable for the corporation to have a voice in working out an agreement with the municipal authorities on a master plan for the zone and the adjacent region.

One of the principal reasons for the extension of the political boundaries of a single large city is to exert some control over the spread of the suburbs. We have proposed elsewhere that this be the special responsibility of a regional corporation surrounding a metropolitan area, whose main task will be non-development, that is, the preservation of land for agricultural and recreational purposes, under the watchful eye of a national ministry. Otherwise the flight to the suburbs and the use of the private car can defeat the city-within-a-city design and in time force, by numbers, other types of costly "solutions" to the transit and energy problems. It is proposed that regional corporations be joint building-licensing authorities in the political entities surrounding designated metropolitan areas. Their hand could be strengthened by greater restraints on the flow of mortgage money and in the provision of water, light, telephone, roads etc. From time to time, it may be necessary to select an area outside the main city as the site of a new member of the cluster or group of cities, and this must be done in collaboration with the regional authority.

H. Transport

In the first new city designed in Colombia (that of Salitre in Bogota), only 8 percent of the area was devoted to roads and parking areas, an exceptionally low percentage. The city was deliberately designed in the preliminary work to be both self-contained and walkable, having all the attributes of a complete city (with a zone of influence) of 500,000 — playfields, industries, a university — all within a little over a mile from the main commercial centre. The continuous one-way bus line was designed to provide local, internal transit to all residents, passing within 200 metres of all apartments.

Admittedly, this is a radical plan and will require considerable determination and persistence if it is to be adhered to. There will undoubtedly be much pressure to relax the enforcement or prohibition of sales and to permit garages in the basements of apartment buildings. From there it is an easy step to parking in congested streets and the "need" for costly provision of space for the private automobiles. It cannot be too strongly urged,

[4] Oscar Newman, *op. cit.*

therefore, that the rule that private cars must be kept in a guarded and enclosed parking space a short walk from a group of apartments, and the common servicing of that group, must be maintained at all hazards. The private car must become something for vacations and occasional trips but not for daily commuting. Otherwise many of the benefits claimed for the new design will be lost. The internal bus route should be linked with other routes leading directly to the traditional centre and to the airport.

CONCLUSIONS

A. The Problem

The problem is that of accepting the necessity and desirability of increasing urbanization, especially in developing countries, and of creating an urban design or form that permits and favours a greater concentration on activities that enhance life and more fully satisfies social needs. It must be a design that preserves the economies of scale and those externalities that are both economically and socially beneficial. Preferably, it should be a design that dispenses with the necessity of devoting so large a proportion of resources to movement and that will preserve for agricultural and recreational use lands near great concentrations of people. It should be a type of urbanization that decreases rather than increases inequality, especially in styles of living. Scarcity values arising from the growth of the community should accrue to that community rather than to individuals.

The focus was obviously on the urban problem in non-socialist economies where much more reliance is placed on the price mechanism in allocating resources and hence more attention in planning must be placed on providing incentives and disincentives within the framework of mixed economies.

B. The Solution

The solution proposed is variously known as cities-within-cities (or immediately adjoining cities) or the city cluster principle of metropolitan urban design.

It seeks to reconcile the social advantages of smaller community living with the economies of large concentrations of people. It is believed that if the design suggested is properly implemented, conglomerations of 10 to 20 millions can be made livable, which will hardly be true if we continue to treat them merely as indefinite enlargements of single villages or small towns.

It seeks to make the attainment of a livable urban design at the same time a motor of growth for the transformation of dualistic economies into more developed countries, with a change in the environment which will provide motivations to have smaller families, and avoid the reproach that we are only substituting urban for rural poverty and underemployment. For most countries, therefore, it rejects the basic assumptions on which the site and services and self-help solution is based, which are that resources are not only inadequate to do more, but also that they are fixed or limited.

One problem to which insufficient attention was devoted — the rising cost of fuel and energy in general — is one of the major problems confronting the suburban, low-density design of urban growth; and the solution of a cluster of compact walkable cities is in large part designed to reduce the impact of future higher costs of movement.

The provision of public services for ever-growing numbers was dealt with only to the extent that it was suggested that a change in urban design would permit a different allocation of resources in providing these services.

The cluster principle is applicable to larger cities in socialist countries but the discussion of legal and administrative problems of property and of the capture of the social increment is irrelevant.

4
Land and Human Settlements

H. Darin-Drabkin, Israel

The development of human settlements and the quality of life within them are dependent on many factors. One of the most important is the pattern of land use. The interdependence of different land uses which all use the same space makes the proper allocation of land particularly important. There exists an interdependence of different land uses similar to the close inter-relationships between different parts of a system, whereby the growth of any one part depends on the growth or non-growth of others. Hence, the undesirable growth of any one part threatens not only that part but others as well.

This can be applied to the development of the city, the city region, and rural areas (for both agricultural and recreational use), where there is competition between different uses, and where today the patterns of allocation are determined by the market mechanism on the basis of the most profitable current uses and the ability to pay, without considering the effects of one decision on land use on other uses and without viewing land as a limited resource. The recent development trends in the last 20 years, especially the high rate of technological progress, have increased general wealth and allowed a high rate of population growth, thus creating an increased demand for land for all types of uses, including urban, recreational and agricultural.

Intensive growth of population and rapid urbanization have posed the problem of the availability of land to meet the requirements for various uses in the future. The future supply of land is one aspect of the general problem of the availability of natural resources to satisfy demands that are increasing as a result of technological progress and economic growth.

The rapid rate of urbanization and the difficult living conditions that have been created in the large metropolitan areas lead to the question of whether the quality of life in the future is not threatened if urban growth continues according to the recently developed patterns.

The relationship between resources and needs is not only based on quantities of resources and the size of needs. The socio-economic system for utilizing the resources and for distributing them according to needs also influences this relationship. As the resources are changing with technological progress, so are needs changing, not only as the result of technological progress, but also as a result of the socio-economic structure. A socio-economic system based on planned action to satisfy the needs of the society may influence the limiting of some needs and the encouragement of others. Such a system may enable the fixing of a scale of priorities in allocating land for different uses.

Land, as one of the natural resources of the nation and limited in quantity, serves as a basis to satisfy different needs; the invested human labour creates the conditions which allow land to satisfy these needs. The invested human labour increases the capacity of land to satisfy needs — in agriculture by increasing the productivity through the use of better techniques, in recreation by constructing roads to open new areas for this purpose, and in housing through new means of construction which allow more people to live in a limited space.

There exists a close inter-relationship between different land uses, based on the limited land space and the impact of a particular land use on the availability of land for other essential uses. The difficulties in land use planning result from the contradiction between the rapid technological changes which influence urban growth and the slow process of planning which allocates land use. Land is the basis for structures which, once erected, have a long life, and fix the reality of urban life for a very long time.

There are different levels of conflicts in land-use planning:

1. The short-term needs of the population for housing, and the long-run consequences (due to the permanence of erected structures);
2. Different needs and socio-economic functions struggling over the same land space;
3. Individual, private needs versus collective land use needs and the conflict between local, regional and national interests over the use of land.

The use of land is influenced by the interplay of many factors, constantly changing their relationship to one another.

Land use forms the basis of city structure, and urban land is a reflection of a city's social structure. On the one hand, continual socio-economic changes influence the land use patterns of a city; on the other hand land use, by determining the location of various city functions, influences the future development of urban society.

The conflicts and common interests of different social strata are expressed in the city as a focus of human contacts. These internal contradictions and common interests influence the use of urban space. Each social group tries to influence the use of urban land to further its economic interests and improve its way of living. The most desirable space is utilized by the most powerful social groups. In this way changes in social relations affect the use of urban space.

One of the essential features of the modern economy is the big difference between the income of agriculture workers and those in industry and services. Another factor which influences the pattern of human settlements is the concentration of economic activity in the major metropolitan areas, because of the complementary effects of the concentration of industry, services, and qualified manpower in a large city region on the basis of the economics of scale. There is an inter-relationship between the concentration of economic activity and the concentration of population, whereby better employment prospects attract migration, while the larger market and manpower resources (even beyond economic needs) attract industry. Unbalanced development has become a common feature of all countries, with cultural and economic activity concentrated in some restricted areas, while the large rural areas not only lose population but become increasingly less desirable (in terms of employment and level of services) relative to the big city.

The extraordinary rate of population growth in urban areas in recent decades has emphasized the urgency of the problem of how to best use urban space and ensure a balanced national development. Rapid urbanization generates a demand for more new urban land; however it is the proper planning of all land use which is crucial in ensuring the quality of urban life.

The dominant role of agriculture in the developing countries in the past, and their rapidly increasing rate of urbanization at present, poses the question of whether these countries must follow the path of the industrialized countries, given our present knowledge of the likely consequences in the future. The need to use land in a rational way and the understanding of its nature as a limited resource may lead to the preventing, or at least the limiting of such development.

This is a particularly urgent problem, keeping in mind not only the growing needs for urban land but also the importance of the human factor in agricultural production; both land and skilled manpower are needed for efficient agriculture. The full utilization of land as a resource is therefore closely connected with the balanced development of rural settlements, which alone can attract the necessary human resources in order to properly develop agriculture to its highest possible level. Must the development of rural areas continue as it has been in the past on the basis of dispersed houses or would a more collective pattern of settlement be more successful in preventing the exodus from these areas? Is it possible to strengthen the rural areas through the spreading out of industrial processes, and cultural and educational services over a large region on the basis of planned development?

Such balanced development patterns are obviously desirable, but are they possible, keeping in mind the restricted resources of society?

The possibilities are determined in part by the allocation of natural and other resources in a society. This allocation is a function of the scale of priorities prevailing in such societies and the socio-economic system which affects the preservation or destruction of such resources.

Before discussing the utilization of land resources and manpower resources in order to secure a balanced development of human settlements, we should discuss the existing world potential of land resources and its present utilization for human settlements and agriculture, in order to demonstrate the importances of the problem. The next part will discuss the present pattern of land allocation on the basis of the free market mechanism, and some results of such dependence. Finally some brief evaluation of different policy measures and their effects will be made taking into account their social and cultural as well as economic effects.

Present and Future Land Utilization

The total land surface of the earth is estimated at about 134 million sq. km., which is today occupied by 4 billion people. But a high proportion of this land area cannot be used to fulfill any human needs, due to climatic or topographic conditions of inaccessibility (the Arctic regions, high mountains). It is estimated that 60 percent of the earth's surface is usable.

Agricultural Land Use

There are different estimates of the potential land space available for agricultural production. The FAO estimate is 32 million sq. km. Presently some 14.0 million sq. km. are in agricultural use in the world (therefore leaving a margin of "cultivatable land" of 18.5 million sq. km.). But there are wide variations in the degree of utilization of land in different regions, partly relating to the density of population in these regions (see Table 3). The most urgent problem is in Asia, where 83 percent of all potentially cultivatable land is already in use. Asia has the lowest per person allocation of agricultural land as well (0.7 acre per person, or 2800 m^2/person on average). Europe also had a low amount of agricultural land per person (0.9 acre/person or 3600 m^2/person) but it has a much higher agricultural productivity. Calculated in terms of the net agricultural production per male labourer employed, with France = 100, the following ratios have been estimated: USA 330; Latin America 9.8; Asia 4.8 (China 6.0, India 3.0); all developing countries 5.5 (see Table 2). These figures show that one US farmer is sixty times as productive as an average Asian peasant.

Obviously these figures demonstrate that the amount of agricultural production is not only a result of the space available, but is dependent on the human factor of the methods of use of land as a resource. The level of productivity is correlated with the use of modern agro-techniques, and therefore with the level of industrialization and education of the population. An additional factor which leads to higher productivity is the national infrastructure (especially transportation) which allows a close and beneficial relationship between the urban and rural areas, allowing the use of the most modern techniques everywhere. The fact that agricultural productivity in Western countries at the beginning of the industrial revolution was not too dissimilar to that in the developing countries today should give some basis for optimism for the future possibility of agricultural development in those currently less developed countries, based on the inter-dependence of agriculture and industrial development.

The enormous differences in productivity and the potential for future increases in some areas have led some experts to suggest that it would be possible to double present agricultural production (through irrigation and fertilizer) without increasing land space. These estimates point to the importance of irrigation and water supply in realising the potentially available land. It is the availability of water which puts the real limits on the amount of the earth's surface which could be cultivated. Here again the importance of the human factor (social organisation) is shown; for it must be pointed out that while the investment in irrigation needed is a large one relative to the current resources of a particular country or region, its long-term use means that its actual cost over generations is minimal. This is especially relevant to the developing countries. For example, in Africa it has been estimated that if the water resources of the Niger River, currently unused, were diverted northwards as a source of irrigation, a vast area of 10 million hectares could become fertile. By our estimates this means that (with productive methods of farming) a population of perhaps 50 million could be supported in a region where today millions are starving. This is not just theoretical; China is an example of a country which formerly had regular famines, but has become self-sufficient in food production through increased investment in irrigation since 1949.

The limit to this process will ultimately be set by the total water resources available. It has been estimated that technological improvements in desalination of sea water will soon make it economically viable to use this technique for providing water for irrigation.

Obviously the problem is one of costs and the more intensive use of a limited resource, balancing energy, mineral exploitation, water resources, and climate in order to preserve the balance of nature. The industrialized countries have demonstrated that more intensive land use is possible, leading to higher productivity; but the forecasted population growth, especially in Asia, means that it is important for the developing countries to manage their land resources carefully. Also needed is international cooperation in order to provide the needed industrial and energy resources to enable the utilization of the world's remaining agricultural land reserves (which are mainly in Africa and Latin America).

The estimates of most observers are that such measures would allow the earth to support a population of 10 billion. For a larger population, an enormous additional investment would be required, taking a part of the industrialized countries' GNP and redistributing it to other areas. The maximum exploitation of all possible cultivatable land may allow enough production to support 20 billion people if land used for human settlement purposes is carefully planned not to interfere with agricultural uses.

Human Settlement Land Use

The estimation of the land used for human settlements is based on varying definitions of "urban" in different countries. Some gross estimates are that 1 percent of total land surface in Japan, and the US is devoted to urban uses; 7 percent in the UK and 10 percent in the Netherlands and Germany. This leads to estimates of 400-600 m^2/person for urban land use in these countries. Obviously the land use for settlement purposes in rural areas (where agricultural and non-agricultural uses are intermixed) may be estimated as higher than in urban settlement (as it is more dispersed, although less allocation of land for nonhousing needs is made). We will use the figure of 500 m^2/person, or 2000 person/sq.km., as an average for all settlements, keeping in mind that some part of land so classified is actually in agricultural use.

The population of 4 billion thus occupies about 2 million sq.km. for settlement needs. This is in comparison with 14 million sq.km. in agricultural use in the world today. Thus, already human settlements occupy one-seventh of the space of agricultural land.

But these average figures only show the global patterns of land use. This does not pinpoint the land problem as it exists in particular urban areas. Some figures from particular cities show the problem is concentrated in the inadequate amount of land available per person in some larger cities, particularly (but not exclusively) in the less developed countries (see Table I). As indicated, land per person varies from 850 m^2/person in some American cities to 27 m^2/person in Calcutta. But even the figures for average urban land allocation do not show the real problem of land allocation for different purposes and for different population strata. A comparison between Stockholm and Calcutta may illustrate the point. In Stockholm the planned target (for the year 2000) is two rooms per person; while in Calcutta the target figure is two persons per room.

In the future, one can make estimates of land needs based on the adequate satisfaction of needs for all citizens in human settlements. A UN study by the author of land requirements for the various urban functions indicates that approximately 285 m^2/person will be sufficient for satisfying living conditions in urban regions (an average density of 35 persons per hectare). This figure is based on the following estimated land requirements for different urban land uses:

	m^2/person	Average m^2/person
Residential	67-144	125
Roads	30- 50	40
Green space	40- 56	48
Public services	20- 40	30
Industry	18- 44	30
Commercial services	10- 23	12

Future national recreational and transportation land needs can be estimated as equivalent to the total space needed for urban settlements. It should be noted that we have made a far more generous estimate of recreational space needs, both locally and nationally, than is currently the case. But we believe that as long as urban growth continues these needs are likely to become increasingly important for the majority of the population.

If we take as our estimate 250 m^2/person rather than 285 m^2/person for land allocation in new planned human settlements, then a doubling of the world population (by 4 billion) would require an additional 1 million km.^{2} of land (in addition to the 2 million km.^{2} already in use). But by also including adequate recreational and transport network space, the total non-agricultural land needs for an additional 4 billion population may be some 2 million km.^{2}, 6 billion would require about 3 million km.^{2}. If we look at a possible future population of 20 billion (which may be a maximum feasible on the basis of present methods of agricultural production), we see that the land space needed for such a population (10 million km.^{2} is equal to one third of the total estimated *potential* agricultural land in the world. If world urban development occurs on the California model of 1000 m^2/person, then a population of 10 billion would need 70 percent of all land in agricultural use today; 20 billion people would consume two thirds of all potential cultivated land.

This demonstrates the close inter-relationship between the allocation of land for human settlements and the allocation of land for agricultural production to supply growing population in the future. The planned use of land in human settlements is important not only for creating the appropriate quality of life within urban settlements, but also as the increasingly important basis of ensuring the future of humanity. Exaggerated land use patterns in urban settlements threaten the very possibility that mankind will be able to cope with the problems of feeding the exploding population.

The Land Market and Its Effects

The significant feature of land allocation today is that decisions about uses in most human settlements in market economy countries are based on the criteria of the landowners rather than those of the community. The deciding factor in land use decisions by landowners is the maximization of profit from the development of the site. The need of the community is for land use according to economic, social, cultural criteria, ensuring a good overall environmental balance between recreation space, housing, public services, and economic activity. Obviously the community's actual development programmes are influenced by the financial constraints of the local community and the nation.

The present land use patterns in human settlements are established on the basis of the mutual inter-dependence, and at the same time the conflict, between the interests of the individual, land owner, the neighbourhood, the city, the city region, and the rural areas and between the different uses of land for commercial services, industry, public institutions, residences, agriculture, recreation, and transport.

In the planned economies these conflicts are expressed in the discussions within the various local and national planning authorities over the criteria for fixing the allocation of land for different purposes, keeping in mind the costs of urban development and the need to strengthen the rural areas. One of the difficulties in such planning discussions is the permanent conflict between the present urgent needs and the long term requirements for land, as well as the financial limits, within the total local and national budget, to the funds that can be devoted to land acquisition and development. As the needs of human settlements are expressed in both public and private consumption expenditures, as well as investments in physical and social infrastructure which lay the basis for future growth, the general distribution of GNP between consumption, saving, and investment is a significant factor in such discussions.

In market economies the market mechanism is allocating land for different purposes. At the same time the community needs are partially achieved through the actions of the public authorities, who use various land policy measures to achieve their obejctives. Thus the present pattern of land use in human settlements is a result of two factors (the market and public allocation). We will discuss each of these separately, first considering the urban land market and its effects.

The urban land market is influenced by the peculiar character of urban land. That is, the general law of supply and demand does not influence the urban land market in the same way as it does other commodities. The demand for and the supply of land is always related to the characteristics of specific locations. Location affects land values in accordance with the use to which the land is put, and, as a general statement, it exerts a greater influence upon commercial land use than upon residential land use.

Land is physically undepreciable and is not influenced by time, while the quality of virtually all other commodities depreciates with time. Land is not transportable. Even if the use of land can be changed, the land itself is stationary. Land is limited in quantity, especially in areas of urban concentration. The high demand for land in these areas cannot be satisfied by the existence of vacant lands in other regions of the country. In such a way, urban land, especially in metropolitan areas, has a monopolistic feature because it cannot be substituted by supply in other areas.

The scarcity and the physically undepreciable character of land make it profitable to hold large reserves without using them as a basis for production. In contrast, investors in depreciable physical commodities will be forced to sell after some time, since their value diminishes with the physical depreciation of the goods. Obviously, money invested in land has its maintenance costs such as interest charges and taxes, but such costs are often minimal in comparison with the expected capital gains of sale. Such uses restrict the supply of land which might otherwise be used for building purposes.

These unique characteristics of urban land — the fact that the amount of land in the desired place is inherently limited, and the fact that land can be *not* used for production purposes with relatively little penalty — may lead to a permanent disequilibrium in the land demand.

This is demonstrated by the high percentage of vacant land in the metropolitan area despite the high demand. Some examples will show that this phenomenon plays a major role in the high rate of land price increases.

In Buenos Aires, according to a 1971 UN report, 70 percent of land was vacant in the metropolitan area. In Teheran in 1958, there was 12,760 ha. of urbanized land, 6,637 ha. of mixed built and vacant land, and 19,687 ha. of vacant land planned for building. In Tokyo, where there is not enough land on the market, there are some 270,000 hectares within a radius of 50 km. with a potential for building. In Tel Aviv (where housing extends over a 30 km. area) 30 percent of the land is vacant within the municipal borders. In the metropolitan area the percentage of vacant land is as high as 40 to 50 percent.

The existence of large vacant areas in a city region and a very high land price increase in such an urban area may be seen as two inter-related phenomena. The expected profit from future land use changes restricts the supply of land to the market. A taxation system which does not impose a high tax on the vacant land provided for future urban development makes the capital costs of maintaining vacant land low. Otherwise the economic decision will be based on the expected profit and the prevailing interest rate. Generally, in countries with restricted investment possibilities and a high rate of urbanization and of land price increase, the holding of vacant land is one of the most profitable economic enterprises. This is especially the case in countries with permanent inflation.

It is also important to understand that there is a "chain effect" by which high land prices affect the lower priced land throughout the city. The ability of a small segment to pay high prices for particularly desirable locations (either centrally located or suburban) pushes up prices in those areas. But the higher prices in certain areas influence land prices in adjoining areas as owners expect a change to a higher-price use. But the majority of the population has limited payment possibilities for housing (as it is already a rather large part of total individual's expenditure). Therefore they are forced to move to less desirable (usually distant) locations or to accept a worse standard of housing where they are (e.g. through overcrowding). This relentless search for cheaper land for housing, in turn, affects prices throughout the city region (where it is expected more land will be turned to urban use); while land will still be less valuable than closer urban land, it will be much more valuable in any urban than in non-urban use.

Thus in the urban land market, with its limited supply possibilities, a small segment of the market can have a large effect. Those countries which attempt to regulate land prices in only one sector of the land market (e.g. for social housing) do not understand the effect that prospective higher income uses of land have on *all* land prices. The high rate of land price increase in almost all cities in the world today demonstrates this point. There also exists a trend of land price increase as a side effect of planning decisions. The establishment of a commercial centre or construction of a new road will affect land price increases in a large radius from the area of increased value as a result of public authority decisions.

Some examples of land price increases from different industrialized countries may illustrate the effect of the market mechanism in areas where land is in short supply (i.e. the city and city region):

Land Price Increases
(Yearly Rate of Increase)

	Within the city	Urban expansion areas
Denmark (Copenhagen)	11.4	26-33%
France (Paris)	21	45
Italy (Milan)	15	25-34
Switzerland (Geneva)	8-24	34
USA (Columbus, Ohio)	6	25-30

As a result of such a high rate of increase, the role of land in housing costs has increased dramatically. Today land is 50-70 percent of total housing costs for residential housing within the big cities of Italy, France and Spain; the percentage reaches 80 percent for commercial development. Even for social housing erected far from the city frontier land is some 25-30 percent of total costs.

With such high rates of land price increase in the industrialized countries the developing countries show an even worse situation.

The following table illustrates the high rate of land price increase in some of the developing countries.

Comparison of Land Prices Increase of Selected Developing Countries

City	Period	Location	% Increase per annum Land prices (current prices)
Teheran	1940-60	Average of 18 districts	23
Tel Aviv	1951-71	Average of 4 districts	28
Seoul	1953-66	Average of land in city	41
Jamaica	1965-71	Average of whole land	22
Mexico	1939-58	Average of 2 districts	23

All of the capital gains which result from changes in land use are only made possible by the decisions of public authorities to allow development. It is the investment in infrastructure which creates the aggregate increase in value of land in newly developed areas but it is the planning decisions which determine the distribution of those windfall gains to particular individuals if it is rezoned for commercial use. One piece of land will increase in value a hundred times, while an adjacent piece (on which development was not permitted) will be little more valuable. Therefore there is great pressure for landowners to try to influence planning decisions, sometimes through illegal means.

Thus, planning decisions about the urbanization of large areas around the city are the result not only of the increasing needs for land for urban growth, but such needs within the context of the market economy. The power of the private landowners to decide not to use land influences planning decisions leading to enlarging the city. The interesting feature of the market mechanism is that the land values in newly urbanized areas are not based on their economic costs (which is the cost of the raw agricultural land plus the cost of infrastructure works) but on the level of land prices prevailing in the adjoining city. Therefore the highest *rate* of land price increase can be observed in these new urban areas, where the rate of increase often is measured in hundreds of percentage points. Such land price increases result from planning decisions to change land use from agricultural to urban; therefore the owners of agricultural land have strong reasons to be concerned with their influence on the planning authorities. The most active capital investment based on the expected future land use change is in the large metropolitan areas. There the rate of land price increase is the highest. Some representative examples from different developing countries may show the extraordinarily high increase in land prices resulting from a change in land use from agricultural to urban:

- Manila – Land in the metropolitan area between 1940 and 1969 showed an increase of 2,000 times or 30 percent yearly in one area (the Escolta), while only 100 times (12%) in the central area;

- Teheran – The new Mehrabad area has shown a price increase of 262 percent annually from 1952 to 1957;

- Tel Aviv — In towns 30 km from Tel Aviv price increases of 50 to 80 time in 14 years were shown.

There is only limited data on the role of land in housing costs in the developing countries but it is believed that the following examples are typical:

- Seoul — In 1957 the proportion of land costs in total housing expenditure was less than 20 percent in the peripheral suburban area; in 1967 land constituted 50 percent of the cost of low income housing, and 70-80 percent of housing costs in better locations;

- Lagos — In the metropolitan area land costs are 3-4 times higher than construction costs, making the former 75-80 percent of the total housing costs;

- Philippines — In the town of Legaspi the costs of erecting a small house from bamboo is only $100, but the 40m² of land for such a house costs $3,000.

- Tel Aviv — The price of land increased during one year (1973) by 25-50 percent (100% in newly urbanized areas). The proportion of land in housing costs reached 60 percent in the city center.

The increased land prices makes the housing problem for the low income strata in the developing countries extremely critical. According to the World Bank Report, 35-68 percent of the urban population in these countries cannot afford even the cheapest housing. A comparison of per capita income with housing costs will illustrate the severity of the problem. In the U.K. the average cost of a public housing unit is $20,000 and the per capita GNP $2,680, i.e. eight years of per capita GNP for a dwelling space of some 80 m². In Bombay, where the per capita GNP is $100, a dwelling of 17.3 m² cost $1,300, i.e. 13 years of GNP per capita for a space 4-5 times smaller.

The effect of high land prices as shown by the World Bank figures that raw land is 45 percent of the cost of single family low-income housing in Mexico City, and 30 percent of the cost of multi-family dwellings located on the periphery in Hong Kong. Obviously land is only one of the factors in housing costs, but of essential importance for those with low income.

The socio-cultural effects of the current patterns of land allocation have been deleterious. There has been an inadequate provision of public resources, such as parks, playgrounds, and an adequate transportation system ensuring accessibility for all to all city functions, while at the same time an overdevelopment of private luxury consumption. The demonstration effect of the consumer society creates unfulfilled expectations for more goods on the basis of unlimited competition, rather than the cooperative development of human potentialities through increased socio-cultural development. The permanent tension in the over-crowded city and neglected suburban areas and public housing developments without adequate services or facilities leads to many social problems.

In general the current pattern of urban development shows a neglect of the human factor. The concentration of development in order to meet certain economic goals of efficiency makes the human being a mere factor in economic growth, artifically developing services, consumption goods, etc., at the expense of a socially just allocation of resources. Urban growth based on the profitability to individuals does not ensure an adequate and full social and cultural life for all.

Evaluation of Urban Land Policies

Various policy measures have been used in different countries in order to ensure the supply of land for the urban growth requirements and to restrain excessive land price increases. The policy measures are based mainly on legal measures, including taxation and land use regulations, but sometimes include measures of direct intervention by the public authority in the land market.

Taxation

The general aim of taxation is to increase the income of the public authorities. The increasing needs of urban growth require increased expenditure, much of which must be publicly financed. Real estate and land taxes have traditionally been one of the sources of such finance. The extraordinary increase in land prices due to rapid urban growth has made the taxation of land profits another feasible source of revenue. At the same time the taxation system is often seen as a way of restraining speculation in land, thus increasing the supply of land and slowing the rate of land price increase. The taxation of vacant land in urban areas, and a high rate of taxation on land whose use is changed through public decisions (e.g. from agricultural to urban or to higher density urban uses) are means to such an end.

Property Tax

A property tax on land as well as on buildings has a mostly fiscal aim: to provide the financial means for municipal and central government authorities to cover permanently growing urbanization costs. At the same time the taxation of land property and real estate generally also has social and planning aspects. The method and rate of property taxation may serve in the redistribution of wealth, and may achieve some planning purposes if the tax is differentiated according to different land uses in urban areas.

Various forms of differential assessment may be increasingly important in property tax. Site value taxation, separate from buildings, will benefit owners of dwellings or firms located at the periphery of the city while imposing a higher part of taxation on commercial sites in the city centre.

A question is whether the rate of property tax should be equal for built sites and vacant land. There is also a question of whether a progressive tax on vacant land according to the value and size of a site should be introduced — this would be in order not to impose a high rate of taxation on land belonging to the low or middle income socio-economic groups who are trying to ensure land to improve housing conditions for themselves or their children. A differential rate of taxation on vacant land may allow a high rate of tax on land for speculative purposes, and low rate for prospective homeowners. It may be suggested that a differentiated rate of tax on improved sites could also be introduced distinguishing between commercial and residential buildings.

There exists also the problem of the taxation of land in an agricultural use within areas classified as urban. Should such land be taxed at agricultural or urban value? Are the public authorities interested in encouraging use of such land for agricultural purposes (as a result of low taxation)? This problem has recently been discussed in Denmark, Israel, in some states of the U.S.A., and in some other countries.

Land Profit Tax

Taxes on land profits include taxation of the additional value created through "normal" urban growth and general price increases as well as the profits resulting from specific public authority development works and planning decisions.

It might sometimes be difficult to separate the additional land value resulting from public authorities' investment and planning decisions, and that increase caused by the general price increase, inflation and urban growth process.

But there are some public authority decisions whose effect on land price increases might be measured easily. The planning decision to change land use from agricultural to urban, or from residential to commercial, or to increase building densities, leads to such a high rate of price increase that it is comparable to creating a new land value.

It might appear astonishing that in some countries with a high level of land prices the taxation on land profits is lower than on other kinds of capital gains. This may be explained by the fact that land profit taxation stems from a time period when urban land prices did not increase to such a high level as in the last twenty years.

Sweden and South Korea are examples of efficient land profit taxation. In Sweden the legislation of 1968 stipulated that profit from any transaction of land was to be taxed at normal income tax rates irrespective of the length of time that the land has been held in ownership by the vendor. Land profits from less than 2 years of ownership is 100 percent taxable while property sold after two years of ownership is taxable on 70 percent of the profit. The profit made is calculated as the difference between gross income and the purchase price (on the part of the vendor), bearing in mind the continuously declining purchasing value of money. The calculated amount of profit is therefore adjusted according to the increase shown by the Consumer Price Index during the period from the year of purchase to the year of sale. Additionally, the amount spent on improvements to the property during the period of ownership is deducted from the calculated gross income.

Land profits in South Korea are collected on the basis of the Real Property Speculation Check Tax which was introduced in 1967. The aim of this tax was to restrain land speculation by collecting the profits from land transfer. The rate of tax is 50 percent from "net assessible marginal profit." The profit is calculated as the difference between the selling price and the acquisition costs. The purchasing price is adjusted by the wholesale commodity index. Also, the cost of capital improvements and land maintenance and the expenses in connection with the land transaction are included.

Taxes on Vacant Land

For urban development purposes, special importance should be attributed to the taxation of vacant land in urbanized areas. For example, some countries have introduced a higher rate of taxation on vacant land than on improved land. The purpose is to make the maintenance costs of vacant land more expensive, in order to influence landowners to use the site for building purposes. Such taxation on unbuilt property in urbanized areas has already been introduced in some countries. Spain introduced a special tax on vacant land in areas declared as urbanized. After declaration as an urbanized area, the rate is 0.5 percent of the market value, or of the expected value after development. After provision of infrastructure, landowners must then pay a rate equal to 2 percent of market value, and after five years, if landowners keep the site unused for construction purposes, they must pay a rate of 5 percent of the market value.

Syria introduced a differential rate of property tax on vacant land according to the value of the site. The intent of the regulation is to keep the tax low on small low-valued sites which, e.g., owners are holding for housing construction for themselves or their family. The rate increases with increases in site value so that owners keeping land vacant in urbanized areas for speculative purposes will pay more. A regulation in 1966 introduced the following rates according to the site value:

less than $12,050 — 1%
$12,051 — $24,100 — 2%
$24,101 — $73,100 — 3%
$73,101 — $124,500 — 4%
$124,501 — up — 5%

Also, according to this regulation the municipality is entitled to put a site up for public auction if the landowner does not pay taxes for a three-year period. Of course, such a regulation is designed to influence the landowners to use the land themselves or sell to someone else who will use it for construction.

There is also a municipal tax on vacant sites in urban areas in Chile. The tax takes effect five years after a detailed planning scheme has been approved, and is levied at an increasing rate each year (starting at 1 percent of the assessed value and rising by 1 percent each year to 6 percent) until the land is used for construction purposes.

Taxes on Changes in Land Use

Some countries have introduced a system of payment of land price increases not at the time of purchase, but either periodically or when a land use change occurs as a result of public authority decisions.

Denmark recently introduced a land value tax when land is transferred from agricultural to urban use. The tax rate is 40 percent for the first 20,000 kr. ($50,000) of land profit and 60 percent for any higher amount. The tax is collected after a public authority decision to change land use. The municipal council is obliged to buy the land if the owner is not interested in keeping the land (since he has to pay the tax). The owner may obtain a delay of up to 4 years in paying the tax. He may also get a mortgage to pay the tax over 12 years. The estimation of the taxable additional value increase is based on the published evaluation of all land properties in Denmark carried out by the public authorities every 4 years.

Valuation Methods

The effectiveness of land taxation is in a large measure dependent on the evaluation system. The rate of tax on profits may be very high, but if the evaluation system does not function appropriately the actual tax rate (based on the difference between the original purchase price and the selling price) may be far lower.

An ineffective evaluation system is also likely to be an unfair one. Where there is no system which limits the freedom of an evaluator to rate property as he sees fit, while allowing public comparison of the evaluations of different properties, there is no guarantee that every citizen will be paying the tax equally. This problem of equity in turn creates resistance to payment.

In order for tax methods to be efficient, a periodically published evaluation carried out by the same system for the whole country would be appropriate. This would ensure that there was a check on the decisions of individual evaluators (who in the current system are under great pressure to change their evaluations in order that owners should avoid high taxes), and would also show all citizens that they had the same rights and the same obligations. It would also be extremely useful for determining compensation in the case of public appropriation procedures.

The most efficient evaluation system is in Denmark, which first introduced a periodic, variable evaluation system in 1922. A general evaluation of all properties takes place every four years, though a special evaluation takes place when a property has been transferred to urban use during the four-year period. Land value is assessed separately from the improvements on the land. It is important to note that the Danish evaluation system is based on the use of the same evaluative criteria for the whole country. Assessors are elected by the municipality and their work is supervised by appointed officials of the Ministry of Finance. It is the task of the ministry to prepare the needed material for formulating the criteria used by the assessors to evaluate property. The transactions which take place during the four-year period together with other factors associated with planning decisions and development works carried out during the period constitute one criterion for evaluation. The results of the tax evaluation are published as maps and made available to every citizen in Denmark. The evaluation serves as the basis for the property tax, for compensation in case of expropriation, and as a basis for collecting the benefit tax of land transactions.

Conclusions

There are no differences of expert opinion as to the view that a high rate of land taxation may provide the necessary means to cover growing urbanization costs. Analyzing the different methods of taxation, taxes may variously affect the land market, reducing or encouraging speculation.

Increased urbanization costs and increasing needs for municipal services are incongruous with the low rate of land taxation. Although the hopes that increased taxation rates may play a deciding factor in land supply to the market may be exaggerated, when combined with other measures of land policies, increased taxation rates may have a favourable influence in carrying out efficient urban land policy.

Planning Policies

The introduction of a planning system is a means to ensure the proper use of land by legal regulations. But in accordance with the planning regulations, while they can prevent some types of undesirable development, are unable by themselves to force the landowner to use his land according to plan. As a result, there are vacant and unused areas within the urbanized area, and new planning schemes must be introduced utilizing areas far from the city frontier for new urban development.

Examples of efficient use of planning regulations combined with other measures are furnished by Denmark and the Netherlands. In Denmark, through a planning implementation system, no agricultural land is released for urban development until all the land previously planned for urban extension is utilized. Plans are reviewed every 4 years, and a high rate of tax on vacant land planned for urban use (and on land price increase resulting from planning decisions) encourages compliance with planning schemes and influences the use of land for development purposes. In the Netherlands as well, the planning authorities will not release agricultural land for urban use unless it is part of the urban extension plan, based on public land acquisition by the municipality. In both of these countries such planning is based on the preparation of both macro and micro planning schemes, the first fixing the general land use categories for the entire country (i.e. agricultural, recreational, urban, future urban etc.), and the second being a detailed scheme for land use within the urban areas. The authorities therefore must make long-range plans for the location of future urban development.

Within urban areas, useful devices for efficiently implementing development programmes have been re-adjustment schemes. These require the rearrangement of the pattern of land tenures, in particular areas in order to release some land for public purposes. Such compulsory land pooling has been successfully used in Japan, India and South Korea for many years. The object has been to provide a specified area with adequate infrastructure (roads, parks, sewerage, etc.), to rearrange the land uses and to relocate housing sites on the basis of a new layout. Though the reconstituted plots must obviously be somewhat smaller in the new layout (with its additional public facilities) it has generally been found that the reduced plots are more valuable than the original plots as a result of improved facilities. In Japan such schemes are carried out either by various public bodies or by associations of the landowners themselves.

Another very important legal policy instrument of land use control is the designation of special areas where particularly stringent controls of both development and prices are to apply. France has perhaps the most advanced such system with the declaration of "Zones of Deferred Development" (ZAD). These are areas designated by the public authorities where it is intended that future development of some kind will occur. Land development is frozen in the ZAD for 16 years, the public authorities have priority rights of first purchase of any land offered for sale in the zone, and, if expropriation is necessary, it is payable on the basis of land prices one year before the ZAD area was declared. By this measure the French authorities have been able to purchase land needed for development (both of new towns, tourist centres, and commercial developments) without extensive investment of public money. Japan has also such a system, whereby prefectural governors can designate "control areas" where it is feared that speculative land transactions will result in a sharp rise in prices; all land transactions in such areas require the permission of the governor. If permission for sale and building has been given, and the land is still unused after three years, the governor endeavours to make the owner use his land.

The imposition of such positive land use control measures, forcing owners to use land rather than just prohibiting undesirable development, is a significant innovation in the planning system, and of great significance for the future. In Spain the right to build is considered not only a right, but a duty. If planning permission has been given for new urbanization work, the landowner must undertake construction within two or three years; if he does not, he is liable to expropriation. (Spain also has a high rate of tax on such vacant land.)

The procedures for the acquisition of public land have a major effect on the implementation of planning schemes, as it is very common to encounter long delays due to legal proceedings over expropriation and compensation. Therefore the introduction of pre-emption rights, which gives the public authorities the right to purchase any land which comes on the market before any other buyer, allows the bypassing of legal delays and, coupled with other measures, may ensure the provision of needed land (and also provides a way of monitoring land prices, as all transactions must be reported). As used in France, pre-emption rights are mainly envoked in the previously mentioned zones of deferred development. When a landowner declares his willingness to sell, the public authority must declare whether it is interested in the land. If not, the owner is free to sell privately. Even if the public authority is interested in buying, there is no obligation on either side to accept the price offered or asked. But the public authority may begin expropriation proceedings if no agreement on price is reached.

Expropriation

Expropriation and compensation procedures themselves could be considerably simplified and speeded up in order to improve implementation of public developments. Expropriation rights exist in all countries, allowing the public authorities to acquire land for public purposes with the payment of just compensation. The differences between countries stem from different definitions of public purpose, ranging from the restricted (essential infrastructure works only) to the more general (any land needed for urban development). The laborious procedures of expropriation, and the establishing of just compensation, have been the main reasons for the slowness of expropriation. Thus the Swedish procedures recently adopted are of some interest.

Here the public authorities may take possession of land and make use of it before legal title has been established, by means of a court order of "simple prior occupancy" if it can be established that this is a matter of extreme urgency. Sweden has also introduced a system of compensation whereby the prices 10 years previous to the date of expropriation will serve as the basis of compensation. Singapore has also set a period of seven years before expropriation as the basis of payment.

The experience of planning measures shows that it is the interaction of measures that is most effective. Macro and micro zoning may prevent undesirable development along with measures that force the use of land. The declaration of special areas and the efficient use of expropriation, compensation, and pre-emption procedures may also assist in the carrying out of urban development in designated areas of new developments. Expropriation is also a necessary part of any legal measures which attempt to impose development according to plan.

Evaluation of Planning and Taxation Measures

The experience of almost all countries shows that the use of different legal and taxation measures is able in some condition to achieve some restricted aims. But the essential goal of land policy — to supply all the land needed for development in the right location at the right time and appropriate price — has not been achieved. Land use policy measures in different countries have been able to preserve some areas from undesirable development and influence the proper type of construction on urban land through building regulations. But in the countries with market economies the use of land for different needs has depended on the calculations of private landowners of their prospective profits; thus the development of land has not necessarily been according to a planning scheme but depended on when and where land was made available for construction purposes by a developer or private landowner.

The taxation system might be helpful in making it unprofitable to keep land off the market through a high rate of tax on land for which planning permission has been given but not used. But the impact of taxation on the maintenance costs of land depends on the rate of tax in comparison with the rate of increase of land prices. The effectiveness of taxation is also limited by the methods of evaluating land values and by the efficiency of the collection system. Therefore the establishment of an efficient approach to the permanent evaluation of land and the collection of taxes is a precondition for efficient taxation methods.

In reality, different reports from the developing countries show that there is a gap between the high rate of land profit tax and the actual amount of collected revenue. One of the methods introduced to overcome such problems is the basing of evaluation for both expropriation and taxation on the declaration of the landowner. Such a system has been introduced in Mexico and other countries, and has been proposed for France, as well as the basis of an urbanization tax. Such a method, which is always used in connection with normal evaluation procedures, is an effective procedure for expropriation, as experience has shown that self-assessed values for tax purposes are generally lower than private market prices.

The analysis of land use and taxation legislation shows that in order to be efficient they should be connected with an efficient land acquisition and supply policy by the public authorities. Such a policy needs as a condition of success appropriate legislation for expropriation and compensation. The ability to expropriate at current use value in areas of future urban development (where land values will increase greatly with the carrying out of infrastructure works) — may allow the public authorities to acquire land without the price being influenced by the expectation of a future change in use. At the same time, such a policy may restrain the demand for land for speculative reasons. The legislation of Sweden and Singapore which set the payment of compensation on the basis of prices prevailing some years before may thus allow the acquisition of land by public authorities without exaggerated capital expenditure. The use of the self-declaration as a method of evaluation may serve as a substitute basis for land value estimation until an efficient evaluation system is created. At the same time, the introduction of special planned areas where pre-emption rights apply (as in France and Japan) may allow the control of land prices over a wide area while actually acquiring only a small amount of land. This has been the case in the French ZAD, where less than 1 percent of the land in these areas was actually purchased by the public authorities, yet land prices (as measured by prices offered for public purchase) decreased over time.

Land Acquisition Policies

Direct intervention by the public authorities in supplying the needed land for the development of human settlements exists in some measure in all countries. But the extent of intervention depends on the socio-economic structure of the country. Some countries use public land acquisition for all land needed for human settlements in urban and rural environments, while some only acquire land for restricted purposes or in some restricted areas.

In socialist countries it is the role of the local authorities to supply all needed land for development. But there are differences even within these countries according to varying concepts of land ownership rights and varying degrees of public and private ownership of land. In the USSR all land is nationalized and belongs in principle to the state: citizens have only land use rights which may be abolished if the land is needed for different public purposes. In other countries only land above a certain size was nationalized, while small plots remained in private ownership. This has meant that most urban and suburban land remained private. Acquisition of land for the development of human settlements is based on procedures of expropriation and compensation which vary among different socialist countries.

One of the problems of the countries with planned economies is the criteria of allocation of land for different purposes. The relevant public institutions often state that they require more land than that allowed by the planning scheme. Another problem is the evaluation of the costs of land, taking into account the importance of location as well as size in determining the value of land. These evaluation and allocation problems exist in all countries with systems of advance land acquisition as well.

The socialist countries are succeeding in supplying the land needed for human settlements in the framework of a general development scheme. The infrastructure works necessary to prepare land are carried out as part of general public investment on the basis of the planned allocation of resources between consumption, saving, and investment.

In the market economy countries there are major differences in land acquisition policy according to the role of the state in providing essential services. There is also a distinction between those countries in which the free market mechanism based on private initiative is considered central in the provision of almost all services, and those countries with a mixed economy where the State has an important role in economic and social development.

A large number of the developing countries are using policies similar to the mixed economy countries but adapted to their own particular historical and cultural traditions. The former traditional-communal patterns of land ownership influence land acquisition policy in these countries.

Most of the countries with a mixed economy are using an advance land acquisition policy for restricted purposes or in restricted areas only. The most comprehensive policies, with a long tradition behind them, have been in Sweden and the Netherlands. In these countries all land needed for urban development is acquired by the municipalities with the financial assistance of the central government. Such a policy has been able to ensure the continuous, planned development of Stockholm and Amsterdam while at the same time reducing the rate of land price increase there.

In the U.K., France, Israel and Spain some more restricted policies of acquiring land for new towns, housing projects and industrial development have been applied. The New Towns Development Corporations in the U.K. and the Paris Regional Land Acquisition Agency in France have proved efficient instruments for the acquisition of land for public purposes on the basis of public corporations granted legal powers of expropriation and borrowing. Spain has succeeded in creating "polygones," areas of new industrial and housing development near large cities, by means of a national land agency.

In the developing countries most examples of public land acquisition relate to programmes in limited areas or for certain purposes only. The most successful policy instruments have been created in Singapore, Chile, Israel, India (Bombay and Delhi), and Venezuela. In all these countries the creation of public corporations, with legal powers but not part of local government, has proved the most effective method of public land acquisition.

In Israel all public land was recently amalagamated in a national land agency, which allowed the comprehensive planning of regional and urban development. Some other examples:

- India — The most interesting experiment in land acquisition policy in India has been the experience of New Delhi. In 1959 the Delhi Development Authority was created with the task of the large-scale acquisition, development and disposal of land in Delhi in accordance with the new Master Plan. The Delhi Development Authority developed and sold a large number of plots through public auction at high rates and allotted a number of plots at low rates to low and medium-income groups on a lottery basis (subsidizing these by the sale of the high priced plots). All plots were sold on a leasehold basis. In 1969 a massive programme of house construction for low income groups was launched, both through direct construction by the D.D.A., financed through the newly created Federal Government Housing and Urban Development Corporation, and by means of loans for middle class housing from the Life Insurance Corporation of India. Recently a Regional Planning Agency (CIDCO) has been established to develop New Towns in the Bombay region. This body has the power to acquire land, execute development projects, raise finance and levy taxes. Other new towns have also been developed in India.

- Singapore — In order to effectively implement the housing programme of the Singapore Housing and Development Board, a Land Acquisition Act was passed in 1966 which gave the government wide powers to acquire private land on a compulsory basis. The Board is responsible for the land acquisition, development or redevelopment, planning, and construction of public housing. The Board acquires land through use of the compulsory powers mentioned and through reclamation of coastal waters. Resettlement of squatter settlements and the housing of the lower-income groups were its primary aims, though it has been intended that the development of industry and services should go hand-in-hand with the development of new public housing estates. The Singapore housing programme has had one of the highest rates of housing construction in the world, with more than 54,000 units constructed between 1960 and 1965, and 65,000 more until 1970. The third Five-Year Building Programme calls for the construction of 125,000 units (increasing the yearly rate of construction from 15,000 to 25,000). The Housing and Development Board has acquired some 2900 acres of land between 1968 and 1972 to accomplish this task, paying approximately US$18 million in compensation. In addition, over 1200 acres were acquired through reclamation. Densities of the new housing projects have been high, averaging some 650 persons per acre.

- Chile — According to a UN report, the Chilean Urban Development Corporation (CORMU) represents the most important of public land acquisition agencies that has been created in Latin America. CORMU was set up in 1964 as part of the newly created Ministry of Housing and Urbanism, along with the National Planning Office and the Housing Corporation (CORVI). It has its own funds and is autonomous in character, with a governing board appointed directly by the president and funds allocated to it from general revenues (as well as money derived from its own resources through the sale or lease of land, the issuance of loans, or received from general housing funds). The main function of CORMU was acquisition and development of urban land in conjunction with local authorities and CORVI projects for the development of social housing and infrastructure work. It was also in charge of all zoning and proposed changes in land use. Part of the land acquired was to be used as a land reserve for future urban development. In order to acquire land, CORMU was given wider powers of condemnation than previously existed — expropriation could be undertaken on all property considered necessary for the implementation of urban development schemes. Compensation could be in the form of land already owned by CORMU, securities, or other assets. From 1964 to 1967 CORMU succeeded in acquiring approximately 1,500 hectares per year, about half by direct purchase and half by expropriation. About half the land acquired was a land reserve for future urban development.

Site-Servicing

Also of great importance for land policy in the developing countries is site servicing and self-help housing. This concept is that the public authorities will provide only the land needed for housing and infrastructure works, while the housing will be constructed by those to whom the land has been given. The plan is to give the poor the right to a space for housing even where the public authorities do not have the resources to construct public housing for them. Land is leveled, roads, sewerage, electricity, etc., are provided, and schools, health clinics and some city services are provided. The World Bank has funded site servicing projects in 10 countries. India has independently initiated such an approach. The Cuban system is based on the organization of groups of future housing residents mainly working in industrial enterprises. Approximately one quarter of the group is released from the factory and undertakes construction of their housing, with building materials, land and technical assistance supplied by the government. The remainder of the cooperative housing group makes up for the loss of manpower in the factory by increased working and voluntary overtime. Such a system is based on the Urban Land Reform Law which transferred ownership of unused land in urban areas to the public authorities, thus enabling them to supply land for urban growth needs. In Spain self-help housing construction is organized to take place on Sundays and holidays, with the government giving loans in the form of tools and building materials.

The evaluation of land acquisition policies is difficult because of the comparatively restricted experience of application of such a policy. However, it is the view of many experts from different countries that the growing needs for land in urban areas can be more efficiently met through such policies of public land acquisition than through the traditional taxation and land use control measures. The lower rate of land price increase in those countries, such as Sweden and the Netherlands, which have such a policy is an indication of the truth of this assertion.

On the other hand, the experience of Israel, France, U.K., India and other countries has shown that a policy of public land acquisition or landownership by itself does not necessarily affect the urban land market, and may not even supply enough land for the growing areas of urban concentration. (See Table 5). It may be suggested that the effectiveness of a land acquisition policy mostly depends on the extent of land acquisition in comparison with the size of the needs. The most important part of a public land acquisition policy is that it allows the public authorities to fix the timing of land use development precisely, and thus they are able to effectively implement a long term development scheme.

The policy of public land acquisition is expected to lead to the municipality playing the dominant role in the execution of the development scheme, by acquiring land on a large-enough scale to serve as the basis for supplying the needs for the entire future expansion of the urban population.

In cases where public land acquisition is restricted to some purposes and some locations only, it has no effect on the land market and urban growth patterns. There is a danger that the public authorities (including the planning authority) may use their powers to adapt the planning scheme not to the needs of the growing urban community, but to the needs of public vested interests (i.e. in order to promote specific schemes by functional authorities).

Land Policy for Balanced Development

One policy objective, in order to prevent the exaggerated growth of large metropolitan areas, should be the strengthening of rural areas and the encouragement of the development of human settlements in the less populous regions of a country. It is suggested that the pressure on land resources in the large cities may be reduced by developing centres of economic and cultural activity in many regions of the country, combining industrial growth with agricultural development through agro-industrial human settlement units which are also the centres of cultural activity for large rural areas. Such a balanced development of human settlements should be seen as one of the most efficient means of economizing the land resource. The growing needs for food by the permanently increasing population can best be achieved by more intensive use of existing agricultural land rather than the mere extension of land area. But one of the preconditions for such an increase in agricultural productivity is the attraction of qualified manpower who will use modern techniques in the rural areas, which in turn depends on creating an adequate socio-cultural level in the human settlements in such areas. The development of industry and high level services in rural areas therefore will lead to more efficient use of agricultural land. At the same time, the development of regional-rural industry based on the processing of agricultural goods and the supplying of the means of agricultural production may economize transport costs that now involve wasteful frequent journies to the big cities. This is especially important for countries with a low GNP and poor national infrastructure.

A policy of balanced development is generally the aim of most countries as it is seen as the most desirable way to improve the quality of life in the metropolitan areas and achieve a more balanced use of land there as reduced growth can lead to more land devoted to recreation needs and other public purposes. But the effective implementation of such a policy objective depends on the use of various policy measures and particularly on the overall pattern of the allocation of a country's resources.

For a long time it was believed by decision makers that the high land prices in the metropolitan areas would in themselves lead to a lessening of the rate of growth there. Experience has shown that the exaggerated growth of a few centres cannot be prevented through the negative incentives of high land prices and deteriorating environmental conditions in these centres. This is similar to the limited effect that negative planning control measures have on urban development. The most successful results have been shown by those countries which have used more active measures to encourage the development of the rural areas. Such a policy is based on the assumption that the creation of job opportunities and the provision of an appropriate level of services is one of the preconditions to the development of many growth centres in rural areas. Another policy measure is the creation of agro-industrial units in order to secure integrated rural development. Obviously such a policy involves a major commitment as well as the re-education of a generation conditioned to orient themselves to big city life.

The combined use of economic and educational measures, in the framework of a scale of values which emphasizes economic development adapted to human needs, may be helpful in implementing such a policy. One may calculate the desirability of such a policy on a cost-benefit basis, looking at the return to capital investment. Such calculations are normally the basis of national economic policy. But there are different methods of calculating returns: looking only in the short term or also taking into account the long term effect; looking only at economic benefits or encompassing the whole range of socio-cultural effects. The investment in infrastructure for socio-economic development should be seen as a very long term investment with a return measured not only in monetary units but in terms of the improvement in the lives of people and the increased ability of people to use the benefits of economic growth.

Countries of different socio-economic structure have used such policies, and even achieved some important results over a period of one generation. The erection of new towns in less developed areas of a country is one way to ensure balanced development. The results achieved by the Soviet Union in erecting 800 new towns (mostly in rural areas or near natural resources) and by India, Israel, the U.K., and Brazil, are some examples of policies which have encouraged industrial development in less developed and less populated regions. The French and Italian examples show ways of strengthening existing cities and medium size and small towns in less developed regions.

Of particular importance are the measures that have been taken by the less developed countries with a predominantly agricultural economy. Tanzania, Sri Lanka, and Madagascar as well as India have attempted to encourage the cooperative organization of rural settlements as a way of achieving a higher socio-cultural level and improving agricultural productivity. Some countries have tried to encourage the resettlement of people from poor agricultural areas into more prosperous rural areas by erecting new settlements there — Egypt, Ghana and Mali have made major investments in implementing such a scheme. Interesting examples of a policy of creating strong mixed agro-industrial rural settlements are to be found on both sides of Asia — in China and Israel. The popularly-run communes in China, rural human settlements organized in a regional socio-economic framework, are based on the development of the land resource for both industrial production and more intensive agricultural cultivation. An additional element is the mobilization of all available manpower made more useful by the provision of increased education and training. The urban-rural cooperation by which the skills of urban intellectuals and the manpower of the rural areas are utilized together in the communes to carry out development is another important reason for their success. In Israel, the collective, rural settlements (kibbutz) succeeded in combining agro-industrial development with the development of cultural and educational services on the basis of regional cooperation with other agricultural cooperatives (moshav), sometimes reaching a higher level of productivity and educational achievement than in the urban areas.

Recently there has been increased regional cooperation between agricultural cooperatives and State farms in the Soviet Union, through the creation of regional agricultural-based industry and socio-cultural institutions. An interesting attempt to develop new patterns on the basis of traditional-communal land ownership has been the encouragement of Fokondo villages in Tanzania. Also, in some rural areas in Japan, collective farms and communes have been established in order to create a higher level of rural human settlements.

Financing and Mobilization of Human Resources

Financial difficulties are often seen as the main obstacle to the implementation of a public advance land acquisition policy. Those countries with a long experience of public land acquisition have financed their programmes through normal municipal budget sources, with the assistance of long and medium term loans from the central government. Other countries have financed land acquisition directly from national government revenues allocated to the national land acquisition agencies, with additional funds from private financial groups interested in participating jointly in development schemes. It is sometimes the case that private builders will transfer land to the public development agencies in order to participate in development schemes.

The experience of the Netherlands and Sweden shows that an advance land acquisition policy economizes public money by supplying land for building when needed on the basis of prices paid many years earlier. The rate of price increase of land in urban regions in nearly all countries is considerably higher than the capital costs of loans to finance advance land acquisition. Experience has shown that given the high rate of land price increase in new urban areas the costs of acquiring a land reserve for ten years future development, if done 10-15 years in advance, may be approximately the same as the cost of acquiring land for one year's present construction needs. Such a cost-benefit calculation has been made for some countries.

The understanding of the importance of the role of advance land acquisition in assuring more desirable urban growth patterns may lead to the mobilization of greater financial resources to carry out such a policy, not only from general revenue but also by collecting a proportion of the increase in land prices throughout the city as a result of the development of new areas. In addition, it might be possible to institute a greater degree of partnership between landowners and the development agency, whereby land owners put their land at the disposal of the public development agency, and in return get either shares in the public agency or construction rights on a piece of land equivalent to what they previously held (with some addition for the increase in value due to development).

There exists another method of alternative financing of the acquisition and development of land, especially appropriate to countries with a low level of economic development and a high percentage of underutilized manpower. By giving each family the right to a certain plot of land, on the condition that they carry out development works themselves (with the assistance of the public authorities supplying tools and organization), large manpower resources may be mobilized and a large number of minimally developed sites may be created. It is probably more important to ensure every person land for housing in the future on the basis of planned development than it is to carry out complete development which, given the limited financial resources of the authorities, will not supply enough housing for everyone. Many examples of such site preparation by less advanced methods in some of the developing countries show that such a policy may ensure a basis for future housing schemes and the development of new human settlements on a planned basis. The examples of the self-help housing schemes based on a cooperative organization of labour in Cuba and Spain, where the public authorities supply building materials and tools, show that such schemes are possible given more than one political orientation.

The mobilization of resources for financing development works is especially significant for developing countries who generally have a great problem of underemployment of labour in urban areas. An analysis of the composition of the costs of infrastructure, and even of housing projects and building materials, will show that human labour is the essential element in the overall costs. The organization of underutilized manpower, with the assistance of qualified personnel, may provide important means of financing infrastructure works as a basis for the development of human settlements.

Obviously the financing of land development (including land acquisition) is connected with the general evaluation of capital investment and return. Infrastructure works for human settlements and for agriculture give a return for many generations; some works constructed in ancient times (e.g. for irrigation) are still in use today. Therefore the present methods of financing should be based on the calculation of such a long-term return. Such an approach is connected with the general problem of the allocation of resources between the needs of present and future generations, as well as with the relationship between countries at different levels of economic development. The understanding of the nature of land as a natural resource, the danger of continuing the unplanned use of this resource, and the need to carefully plan land reserves for future urban development keeping in mind the growing needs for agricultural production — an appreciation of all these points may help to change the approach to land allocation and development, basing it more on the satisfaction of collective needs and less on private profit motivation.

Towards Urban Land Reform

The meaning of collective rights to use land space has been changing with technical progress and rapid urbanization. A human settlement is a framework of space used collectively by the people living in it. The individual's living conditions must insure his essential needs not only for a roof over his head, but also by providing the services vital to everyday life. All these are based on using land for collective needs. The close interrelationship between different land uses may allow one to define a town as a space which provides a framework for people to live together and share that space.

The literal concept of universal application of individual rights in the sphere of land should result, due to the interrelatedness of different land uses, in the transfer of ownership rights to the community in order to ensure for everyone individual land use rights. Such a transfer of rights has many legal, economic, social and physical aspects. It should be realized that the result of such a process, based on the integral rights of the community (preventing undesirable development and planning the use of land according to the long term needs of society), would be the transfer of ownership rights of all land needed for future development to the community, with land use rights given to individuals but ultimate ownership reserved for the use of future generations. Obviously such a transfer should be done simultaneously with the creation of institutional means for allocating land use rights for the whole population, based on establishing criteria of the value of space in relation to its location.

The public ownership of land needed for future urban development will ensure the proper planning of the city region as a whole. Enough land can be allocated for the recreational needs of the region's population and for new planned communities. That would not just mean housing but would include adequate employment opportunities and services. The ultimate aim would be the creation of a poly-city region, instead of the present pattern of one large town with many satellites.

An active role by the public authorities will not automatically solve all problems of future urban development. But it can create a framework of an urban land policy appropriate to the needs of society and more efficient than present methods. There will still be conflicts between local, regional and national interests. Public agencies with different functions may have their own vested interests even though private interests in land have been eliminated. The solution of such problems can only lie in the future; it can only be suggested today that they must be formulated in such a way as to take into account the interrelationships between the individual, the community, and the institutional structure.

There are few examples of such deep contradictions between the development of productive forces of the society and the ownership relations as in urban growth and urban land. The future of human settlements depends on the solution to this contradiction. Urban land should be seen as water, a scarce natural resource to be controlled and husbanded by the public authorities.

In previous centuries there has been a long struggle for *agricultural* land reform. It may be hoped that the urgent land needs for survival may allow this generation to carry out the necessary urban land reform in a shorter time period. It took 100 years to add one million people to the human population some centuries ago; today it only takes one week. This fast rate of growth is such that the time it takes to realize land reform should be adapted to the rate of population and urban growth.

BIBLIOGRAPHY

Marjura Acosta and Jorge Hardoy, Reforma Urbana en Cuba Revolucionaria, Caracas, 1971

Paul Bairoch, The Economic Development of the Third World since 1900, London, 1975

Colin Clark, Population Growth and Land Use, London, 1968

H. Darin-Drabkin, Land Policy and Urban Growth (forthcoming, Pergamon Press, London)

J. Gilli, Redefinir le Droit de Propriete, Paris, 1975

J. Klatzman, Nourir Dix Milliards d'hommes, Paris, 1975

Mesarovic, Milhajo and Eduard Pastel, Mankind at the Turning Point, London, 1975

A.R. Prest, Public Finance in Developing Countries, London, 1975

U.N., Urban Land Policies and Land Use Control Measures, 7 volumes, New York, 1973

The Use of Land, A Citizen's Policy Guide, A Report of the Rockefeller Brothers Task Force, New York, 1968

Woodruff, A.M., and J.R. Brown: editors, Land for the Cities of Asia, Hartford, Conn. 1971

World Bank, Urbanization, Sector Working Paper, June 1972

World Bank, Housing, Sector Policy Paper, 1975

International Bank for Reconstruction and Development 'Urban Land and Public Policy, Social Appropriation for Betterment,' May 1974

Table I Comparison of Actual Urban Land Requirements (sq. metre/person)

U.S.A.

	Central Cities	100,000-250,000	321.2
		250,000 and up	201.6
	Satellite Cities	10,000-25,000	529.6
		5,000-10,000	851.2
English Cities		Major Industrial	205.6
		Smaller Towns	318.0
European Cities		Zurich	68.0
		Zurich Region	120-150
		London	99.2
		Rome	74.6
		Paris	34.7
		Barcelona	58.9
		Madrid	27.5
		Moscow	55.3
		Stockholm	220.0
		Helsinki	320.0
		Copenhagen	110.0
Developing Countries		Calcutta	27.2
		Bombay	58.1
		Cairo	58.9
		Sao Paulo	428.1
		Porto Alegno	569.0

Table 2 Agricultural Productivity: Comparison of Developing Countries Today with Developed Countries Today and at the Beginning of Industrialization

France	1968-72	100	(index on the basis of man hours per unit production)
U.S.A.	1968-72	330	
France	1810	7	
U.S.A.	1840	21.5	
Belgium	1840	7.5	
Spain	1840	11	
Africa	1960/64-1968/72	4.7	
Latin America	1960/64-1968/72	9.8	
Asia	1960/64-1968/72	4.8	
Middle East	1960/64-1968/72	8.6	
Average Less Developed Countries		5.5	

Source: Bairoch p. 40.

Table 3   Present Population and Cultivated Land on Each Continent Compared with Potentially Arable Land

Continent	Pop. in 1965 (Millions of Persons) (1)	Areas in Billions of Acres			Acres of Cultivated Land per Person (5)	Ratio of Cultivated to potential Arable Land (Percent) (6)
		Total (2)	Poten- tially Arable (3)	Culti- vated (4)		
Africa	310	7.46	1.81	0.39	1.3	22
Asia	1,855	6.76	1.55	1.28	..7	83
Australia & New Zealand	14	2.03	.38	.04	2.9	2
Europe	445	1.18	.43	.38	.9	88
North America	255	5.21	1.15	.59	2.3	51
South America	197	4.33	1.68	.19	1.0	11
U.S.S.R.	234	5.52	.88	.56	2.4	64
Total	3,310	32.49	7.88	3.43	1.0	44

Table 4   Rates of Increase of Land Prices, Consumer Prices, and National Income Per Capita for Selected Countries   (Yearly Percentage)

	Period	Land Price Increase (current prices)	Consumer Price Increase 1948-67	National Income per capita 1948-67
Denmark (Copenhagen)	1956-69	11.4	4.2	6.5
France (Paris)	1950-66	21.0	4.3	5.5
Italy (Milan)	1950-62	12.0-19.0	3.0	5.6
Japan	1955-69	19.9	0.8	.8.2
Netherlands	1945-63	2.6-10.5	3.4	3.8
Spain (Madrid)	1950-69	20.5-27.5	5.3	7.5
Sweden (Stockholm)	1957-63	6.6	3.5	4.2
Switzerland (Zurich)	1950-68	13.0	1.9	3.0
United Kingdom (London)	1960-69	12.0	3.7	1.7
U.S.A.	1956-66	6.0	1.5	6.0
Iran (Teheran)	1940-60	23	12	6.2
Israel (Tel Aviv)	1951-71	28	6	5.9
Korea (Seoul)	1953-66	41	19.2	4.6
Japan	1955-71	21	10.9	8.2
Jamaica	1965-71	22	4	3.8
Mexico	1939-58	23	7	3.7

5
Supply and Pricing of Public Utilities

John D. Herbert, U.S.A.

The supply and pricing of utilities are potentially important instruments for guiding human settlement and affecting the quality of both urban and rural life in the developing areas. They are vastly underutilized as positive instruments at present. Indeed, they often are used presently in ways that increase, rather than decrease, inequities and environmental degradation.

The purpose of the present note is to initiate a discussion of the issues associated with utility supply and pricing and highlight their potential as development instruments. It does not attempt to present exhaustive analyses or proposals. If it results in constructive debate and the further development of ideas in preparation for the HABITAT Conference it will have served its purpose.

Only the major utilities are discussed — water supply, sewerage, drainage, refuse collection and disposal, power and communications. The geographic focus is urban, rather than rural, but many of the points made are believed to be just as relevant for rural areas as they are for urban areas.

No attempt is made to deal elaborately with each utility individually; however, where a particular utility has special characteristics that are relevant to a point being made, this generally will be noted.

Conditions in individual countries are not reviewed specifically since the purpose of the note is to identify shared problems and opportunities. Moreover, it is intended to be constructive rather than critical. The few data that are used are, however, data for specific cases during the period 1972-1975.

Issues

Survival

The most urgent issue associated with current deficiencies in utilities is the issue of survival. Within the last ten years several major metropolises have been on the brink of disaster because of water shortages. The next two years will see other cities, including at least one that already has a population of over 4 million, in a similar state. There are likely to be deaths from dehydration and many deaths from diseases contracted from the polluted ponds and streams that will be the only water sources available. There may be additional deaths from the consequent riots and disturbances that are almost inevitable.

The availability of sufficient water is only one of the factors threatening immediate survival. Polluted drinking water and inadequate or non-existent sewerage and drainage threaten the health and lives of hundreds of thousands of the desperately poor that constitute a majority of the urban population of the developing world. Cholera, malaria, typhoid and paratyphoid are among the major and obvious killers. More subtle are such things as the permanent brain damage resulting from water- and waste-borne diseases contracted in early childhood (damage that is permanent only in the sense that it precedes early death). The sewage treatment equipment of one major Asian city is capable of dealing with only 8 percent of the biological waste load generated daily; at present it is operating at half capacity and therefore dealing with only 4 percent of that load. Inadequate drainage results not only in disease but also, in many cases, in disability and death as a result of the floods to which the low-lying and densely populated parts of many developing-area cities are prone.

230

Gross Inequities

Those who suffer most severely from deficits in public utilities are generally the lowest income households who are least well equipped to seek alternatives in the private marketplace. The relatively well-off minority, often as little as 20 percent of an urban population or less, is served adequately, sometimes sumptuously, through public systems, while the vast majority must struggle to survive with minimal public services and courageous ingenuity.

The problem of inequity has at least two important aspects — the physical availability of services and their cost.

Conditions in a major Asian metropolis that is not atypical serve to illustrate the problem of physical availability. Only 30 percent of all households have piped water connections. Only 20 percent have sewer connections. Approximately 25 percent of the urban population lives at very high densities (400-1,000 persons per acre in one- to four-storey structures) in areas without proper drainage. Only about 50 percent of all households have electrical connections in their homes (but many of these have only one or two light connections, nothing more.) Only 6 percent of all households have individual gas connections, even though gas would be cheaper than other types of fuel (firewood, charcoal, kerosene or electricity) for cooking. Only households with monthly incomes of $100 or more (about 6 percent of all households) can afford a telephone.

In that city, and many others, current policies are systematically biased in favor of the affluent minority and a very small middle class — together constituting somewhere between 10 and 20 percent of the urban population. Public utility systems are extended, expensively, to serve the rich living at very low densities, or even to serve land they have purchased speculatively but do not occupy. The poor are left with minimal services or none, in terrible squalor, exposed to all of the diseases and physical danger associated with polluted water, the absence of sewerage, improper drainage and flood protection, only enough electricity to light dimly one room of the shacks in which they are forced to live. The 80 percent majority that are dependent on community taps, pit latrines and the like are not only vastly worse off in the levels of service available but they also pay much higher unit prices for the pitifully poor services they do receive. The inequity of the poor paying more seems sadly universal. A wealthy family in the midst of poverty may use 120-150 gallons of water per person per day, including water for liberal gardening, a swimming pool, car washing and the other necessities of affluence, yet it may pay only $0.15 to $0.20 per thousand gallons for that water. A desperately poor family that has to pay to have a water carrier bring water in, or pay a bribe for access to a communal tap, may pay as much as $2.00 per thousand gallons. (Poor households in a similar situation in a Caribbean city pay as much as $20.00 per thousand gallons!) The poor family, as a consequence, may be forced to consume as little as two gallons per person per day.

Absence of a Sound Foundation for Development

Beyond the obvious and urgent improvements in utilities needed for survival are the massive utility upgrading and expansion needed to provide a sound physical foundation for economic and social progress.

Fundamental to increasing the productivity and well-being of a nation's people is the achievement of at least minimal levels of health. It is impossible to do eight hours of productive work a day on a handful of rice, crippled with dysentery. It can be argued that the opportunity costs of the millions of man-days consumed by disease and disability each year in the developing areas is zero. Such a view may be academically correct in relation to existing capital investment and management capacity but it is far too static a view to be useful as a guide for policy. In the developing areas, a major part of the problem is not just allocating existing resources more efficiently but also increasing productive resources, including productive human resources. The achievement of at least minimal levels of health, for which adequate water supply and sanitation are essential, is likely to be a key part of any strategy for such resource augmentation.

At least minimal adequate utility systems — water supply, sewerage, refuse disposal, drainage, flood protection and power, are essential also to achieve viability in the manufacturing, trade, service, construction, transportation and other sectors whose growth is necessary to spearhead urban economic development. Although small establishments in the traditional sectors are able to persevere without adequate utilities, at least a rudimentary level of service is essential for establishments in the modern sectors. In most cases, quite modest improvements in utility systems could increase productivity in the traditional sectors substantially also.

Improvements in communications, as a part of the development of utility systems, are essential to economic modernization. The losses in managerial productivity that occur because telephone systems are defective or non-existent are themselves enormous and have repercussions which result in linked productivity losses throughout the sectors those managers are responsible for. The absence of a dependable telephone system, together with uncertainties about obtaining power, water, sewerage and drainage, is a major factor inducing the high-density clustering of economic activities in urban areas. Businessmen, in particular, must have face-to-face communication with one another if they cannot obtain satisfactory remote services of the kind that are taken for granted in North America and Europe. The productivity of even short-run improvements in communications in the developing areas is suggested by the figure of 50 percent as an achievable economic rate of return on investment.[1]

Deficits in utilities undoubtedly restrict greatly the density and locational options available for all types of activity. One has only to observe the way in which households and enterprises cling to the meager water, sewerage and power lines that are available in cities in most of the developing world to realize the extent to which these utility lines are, together with transport routes, literally "lifelines," and to appreciate the extent to which they influence private-sector locational decisions. Many alternatives for the geographic distribution of population and economic activity — including alternatives which would be economically, socially and even politically more desirable than present patterns of settlement — are simply denied to the developing world because it has not yet been possible to establish the basic utility networks needed to support them.

Economic Losses

The economic losses attributable to deficiencies in utilities are unmeasured, for the most part, but enormous. They occur every year through direct damage to equipment, structures and land and through production foregone as a result of interruptions in supply or flood damage, burst pipes and electrical fires; through production foregone as a result of health-related losses in labor productivity; and through loss of life. Taking a figure for value added per worker of $400 per year and assuming, very conservatively, that the capacity of a typical worker at this level is reduced 20 percent by debilitating disease, then the loss in value added per year for every thousand workers is $80,000; in a city of 2 million, with a labor force of 660,000-1,000,000, the annual loss in value added is of the order of $53 million — $80 million (assuming, of course, that there is an effective demand for the lost output). If water and sanitation could be improved to a level at which workers were able to operate at 95 percent capacity, instead of 80 percent capacity, then per-worker output could be increased 15 percent by this means alone — a dramatic improvement in situations in which gradual technological and other changes may be increasing average per-worker output by as little as one percent or two percent per year at present.

For such a city of 2 million, with a gross metropolitan product of $500,000,000 annually, if one adds a 5 percent loss due to interruptions in water and power supply and a loss of another million dollars annually for flood damage, the utility-related damage and the total losses that are utility-related are of the order of $79 million - $106 million — or approximately $40-$50 per capita. To these losses should be added part of the unnecessary capital and operating costs resulting from: 1) the inefficiency of utility systems and 2) the transport costs associated with the extravagant land use patterns found in middle- and upper-income areas in cities in most parts of the developing world.

Approximately $8,500,000 is a very crude estimate of the annual savings in operating costs that could be achieved in a city of just over 4 million population if total vehicle miles for automobiles, taxis, motorcycles, motor-rickshaws and buses could be reduced by only 15 percent through more efficient land use patterns.

Energy Waste

Substantial energy waste is associated with deficits in utility systems. The forms in which that waste occurs include, but are by no means limited to, the following (the figures shown are indicative, based on actual cases): avoidable use of electricity in water pumping (perhaps 15 percent of total pumping); losses in human energy as a result of seriously deficient communications systems (unmeasured but also probably very high); avoidable energy consumption in the construction and operation of the excessive utility systems and the

---

[1] World Bank. *Telecommunications: Sector Working Papers.* Washington, D.C.: World Bank, 1971. Page 6.

transportation associated with inefficient land use patterns (unmeasured but undoubtedly very high also).

Avoidable losses in electricity distribution systems have not been mentioned because they often are relatively small.

If the term "avoidable losses" is extended to include losses that could be eliminated if, instead of borrowing essentially "Western" technologies for water supply, sewerage, refuse disposal and power generation, the developing nations could create technologies tailored specifically to their own needs, reflecting their serious energy and resource constraints, then avoidable losses become many times greater than those indicated above.

Resource Conservation

The resource wastage that is attributable to utility systems includes at least the following: unnecessary depletion of coal, oil and natural gas for electricity generation; unnecessary use of oil for petroleum for the avoidable transportation that results from extravagant land use patterns permitted by the installation of utilities in inefficient networks; water wastage attributable to avoidable losses (of the order of 24 million gallons per day in a city of 4 million population, for example); wastage of materials (as well as electrical energy) for private ground reservoirs, pumps and roof tanks made necessary by inadequate public water supply systems; loss of the nutrient content of human and animal wastes because of inadequate sewerage systems; wastage of recyclable solid refuse as a result of the inadequacy of refuse collection and disposal services; wastage of the building materials and labor required for repairs to avoidable damage by flood, water system failure and electrical failures; and the wastage of human resources, referred to already, as a result of avoidable deaths and lowered productivity.

Environmental Degradation

The most obvious forms of environmental degradation associated with utility systems are: 1) the massive and terrible land pollution that results from totally inadequate sewerage, refuse and drainage systems; and 2) the air pollution associated with the production of electricity and the burning of refuse. A large city with a population of several million may have several thousand acres of its densely built-up land inundated almost continually with stagnant water and sewage.

A more subtle but pernicious form of degradation occurs through the waste and erosion associated with the extension of roads and settlements into vast tracts of medium and low-density development in extravagant land use patterns that permitted, or even encouraged, through policies which provide utilities to middle- and upper-income groups.

Globally, there probably are hundred of thousands of acres of urban land made unfit for human use by deficiencies in utility systems. The older central areas of some major cities in the developing world run a real risk of being literally inundated in their own sewage.

This brief review of the issues associated with the supply and pricing of utilities points up the varied and substantial impacts of utility systems (and deficiencies in those systems). Utilities must be of crucial concern in any development effort, not only because adequate levels of water supply, sewerage, drainage, refuse disposal, power and communications are themselves essential to decent human settlement, but also because deficiencies in these services undermine the very foundations of social and economic advancement. The supply and pricing of utilities can be used as instruments for increasing the level and improving the distribution of income through the generation of employment in the construction and operation of utility systems. They can be used to increase productivity and incomes selectively through their impact on health, production technologies and communication. They can be used to increase the output of essential goods and services, including food, clothing, shelter, health services and education. They can be used to reduce the prices of essential goods and services by increasing the efficiency of their production. They can be used to influence the level and distribution of capital accumulation (and, thereby, future income) through increasing selectively the productivity and value of existing land and other capital assets. They can be used to influence the value and distribution of the ownership of land and other new capital assets by making it possible to increase the supply of usable land and the production of capital assets. They can be used to influence the value of land and other capital assets also by influencing the spatial pattern of land use — thereby affecting the capital and operating costs of all land-using activities. They can be used to reduce energy and natural resource consumption through the introduction of more efficient utility technologies and by supporting more efficient production technologies for other goods and services. They can be used to reduce environmental degradation and enhance environmental quality by improving drainage and increasing erosion control, by the proper processing of pollutant wastes and by the use of low-grade water for landscaping and other environmental improvements. Communication systems, specifically, can be used to increase flows of information and, possibly, preferences for and the consumption of essential goods and services.

Objectives

In view of the concerns that appear to underly most national, regional and local policies in the developing areas and the potential impact of the supply and pricing of utilities, the following are suggested as objectives for utility programs:

1. The achivement of higher levels of essential consumption (including, of course, the consumption of water, power and other utilities themselves but including also the consumption of other essential goods and services such as food, clothing, shelter, health and education) — through a) improvements in the supply and pricing of utilities; b) consequent increases in the productivity of land, capital equipment, labor and management; and c) increases in employment and income associated with the development and operation of utilities.
2. The achievement of greater equity in the distribution of essential consumption, with high priority given to improvements in consumption for low-income households — through: a) direct improvements in the provision and pricing of utilities; b) improvements in income levels and income distribution associated with increases in employment and productivity resulting from the development and operation of utilities.

In choosing these two objectives as fundamental ones the term "consumption" is used purposely in a broad sense to encompass all of the types of essential "service" which normally are thought of as contributing to desirable living conditions — including, for example, food, water, sanitation, clothing, shelter, health services, educational services, opportunities for stimulating and satisfying social interaction, and the services that can be enjoyed through a stimulating physical environment. Improvement in other types of consumption, as well as the consumption of utility services, is included as an objective because improvements in utility systems are likely to be instrumental in achieving improvements in all types of consumption.

Because both of the objectives identified are to be pursued on a sustained basis, their achievement requires that appropriate trade-offs be made continually between increases in current consumption and the accumulation of physical and human capital necessary for increases in future consumption. There must therefore be a concern with the level of capital accumulation and the distribution of capital — including liquid savings, physical equipment, housing and other structures, land and human capital.

Also implicit in pursuing both objectives over a sustained period is the achievement of acceptably low levels of risk. Utility programs with very high benefits, if they succeed, but little chance of success, may be much less desirable than programs that are more modest but more sure. The concern with risk will have a major bearing on the types of program chosen. For example, it may be important to avoid water and power systems that would have a high risk of depleting water and fossil fuel resources; it may be important to avoid utility networks that are highly vulnerable to physical breakdown; and it may be important to avoid systems which, if they break down, will impact most adversely the disadvantaged households and enterprises that are least able to survive such impacts. (Utility systems in many of the developing areas at present are very risk-prone in all three of these respects.)

Even when the broad range of types of consumption and capital accumulation represented by the two objectives proposed is recognized, the concern with only two might be thought to be unduly restrictive. What about increased employment opportunities for the poor and increases in household income? What about a more equitable tax structure? What about greater efficiency in the production of essential goods and services? Things such as these are purposely not treated as objectives because they are merely instruments for achieving the two objectives that have been identified. To mix instruments and objectives is to risk confusion between what *must* be pursued (the objectives) and what *may* be used (assuming a variety of alternatives) as instruments for their achievement.

Opportunities for Action

If the two objectives suggested on the preceding page are accepted as a basis for utility programs there are two underlying factors which may be impacted to pursue those objectives:

1. The supply of utility services.
2. The effective demand for utilities.

It may be useful to differentiate current supply, future supply, current demand and future demand — even though the distinction between actions taken to affect "current" supply and demand and actions taken to affect "future" supply and demand is not always a sharp and unambiguous one. Such a distinction helps to indicate the variety of ways in which utility systems may be used as instruments of development and it helps to differentiate short-term and long-term action.

Specific ways in which utility programs may be used to impact the level and distribution of supply and demand are identified below. The suggestions made are a combination of types of action that have been tested to varying degrees and found effective and types of action which, although untested, appear promising.

Action to Impact Current Supply

Optimization of Existing Systems

In almost all cases there are large avoidable losses and wastage in existing utility systems. One of the most obvious (but not most observed) actions to be taken to augment current supplies at relatively low capital cost is therefore the achievement of the fullest possible equitable use of existing facilities.

In water supply, for example, avoidable losses from leakage and wastage (excluding evaporation losses from large surface reservoirs) may amount to as much as 40 percent of bulk supply. This should be reducible to something of the order of 25 percent through reductions in leakage, the introduction of balancing reservoirs (to maintain system pressures and reduce the need to leave intermittently-served faucets open), and through a more complete and systematic metering of users. (The introduction of metering where it has not existed before may not be a short-term measure because it may call for substantial meter maintenance and other actions.) Unnecessary system expenditures in water distribution often occur because the irregularity of supply results in very expensive private installation of ground reservoirs, pumps and roof tanks (by households who are fortunate enough to be able to afford this). The same total supply levels often could be achieved at lower cost if pressures and flows in the present system were dependable.

In sewerage, similarly, existing facilities often are operating well below capacity because of faulty maintenance and management. Pumps may be installed but not operating, grit screens may be inoperative, or heating and aerating equipment may be out of order — to name just a few of the more common problems.

In drainage systems it is not uncommon to find manhole covers missing, allowing street refuse and other solids to be dumped into channels which quickly clog as a result. Where sewerage and drainage are combined, this aggravates the problem of maintaining sewage treatment equipment.

In refuse systems, at least three types of problems are commonplace: underdeveloped collection and disposal systems; compressor trucks and other equipment inoperative because of improper maintenance; and complete loss of the soil-conditioning and fertilizer potential of refuse because of primitve disposal methods such as open dumping, burning, mechanical incineration or sanitary landfill.

Losses and wastage in power systems generally are much lower than in water supply, sewerage, drainage and refuse — in some cases because the former are operated privately on a commercial basis, whereas the latter are public and regarded as "free."

Although telephone and other modern communications cannot be considered vital for ordinary household activity, they are vital for business and their impact on productivity has been commented on already. Very often, existing deficiencies result partly from imbalances in system development — with instruments available (even manufactured locally in parts of Asia, for example) but with exchanges overloaded or with shortages of cable for connections and shortages of junction cable pairs or trunk pairs between exchanges. Overall system service levels could be increased quickly and relatively simply if these missing "links" could be installed.

In most utility systems there are extreme inequities in addition to avoidable losses — inequities that result from political favoritism for middle- and upper-income households in the supply of public services (water supply, sewerage, drainage and refuse) and from the inability of the poor to pay relatively high initial installation costs for privately-provided power. These inequities in physical supply typically result in middle- and upper-income households paying very low unit rates, while the poor pay extremely high rates for private supplements to the public supply. Very often, if the entire system were installed and operated efficiently, the poor majority could receive much better levels of service (perhaps five times present per capita supplies) and pay far less per unit (perhaps one-sixth of what they pay now). (These illustrative figures are for water supply and sanitation.)

Upgrading of Quality

In the case of water, in particular, more systematic testing, more regular treatment and the elimination or reduction of infiltration can be used to change the nature of the service and, in effect, increase supply. Even if a household receiving as little as four gallons per person per day of polluted water through a public distribution system were to receive the same amount of safe potable water the supply of services to that household would, in effect, be increased dramatically. In cases in which network layouts permit, the upgrading could be done selectively to improve the quality of supply to low-income households and thus reduce the gross inequities that are commonplace.

Pricing or Physical Rationing to Reduce Peak Loads

Where pricing or rationing can be introduced to reduce peaking of demand, current supply can be augmented in at least two ways: 1) by making it possible to extend services to a larger number of consumers with existing production and processing installations; 2) by reducing susceptibility to overloads and break-downs, thus achieving greater continuity in supply.

This measure is applicable in water supply, power and communications and could be used to achieve greater equity as well as increases in supply.

Physical Rationing to Reduce Inequities and Wastage

Physical rationing may be used to reduce extravagant uses by some consumers and ensure at least minimal adequate supplies for presently deficit groups — provided that appropriate controls can be introduced to avoid illicit redistribution or voluntary resale that would defeat the purpose of such a measure.

Rationing may be feasible, at least as a short-term measure for water supply, sewerage, refuse collection, power and communications.

Differentiation of Qualities of Service for Different Uses

Not all users require the same quality of service. If processing and distribution can be controlled to deliver lower qualities or levels of service to some users, reserving highest quality services for essential uses, then it may be possible to serve substantially larger groups of consumers at little or no extra cost. In water supply, for example, many industrial users can tolerate low-grade supplies.

In sewerage, there may be opportunities to provide lower levels of service (with latrines, cesspits with tanker pickup, etc.) for households at moderate densities — reserving piped systems and treatment for major institutional, industrial and high-density residential users whose wastes are serious environmental hazards if they are not dealt with adequately. It may be possible to differentiate refuse services similarly.

In power and communications there tend to be market and political rationing systems which differentiate levels of service already; there are, however, opportunities to modify existing rationing of these kinds to reduce inequities — by lowering service levels for non-essential high-income uses and increasing them for lower-income users within present total supply levels, adjusting prices to maintain commercial viability.

Emergency Modification of Distribution Networks

The great inequities that exist in the availability of utility services could be remedied partly and quickly be extending existing networks into low-income areas and other areas where there are major deficits, combined with the regulation of flows (physically, or by pricing) in well-served areas in order to stay within the limits of presently available supplies. Opportunities for this exist in water supply, power and communications.

Public Pricing to Achieve More Equitable Consumption

Even without changes in existing networks it is possible, in some cases, to introduce differential pricing to reduce high levels of consumption and to favor small, low-income consumers while preserving (sometimes achieving for the first time!) economic viability. This is possible with water supply and sanitation in many urban areas. It may be possible also with power.

Although price increases focused on selected consumer groups are likely to be difficult to implement politically, hard decisions simply must be made in a number of major cities because the choice now is between change and disaster.

The impact of such action is likely to fall on both supply (augmenting availability for previously deficit areas) and demand, with the impact depending on price elasticities.

Regulation of Private Pricing

If current private prices (including illicit surcharges on public systems) are exorbitant, as they often are, public price controls can have the effect of increasing the supply available at specific price levels and decreasing current inequities. Such controls might be introduced selectively to favor disadvantaged groups. As in the case of public pricing, such changes are likely to impact both supply and demand.

Opportunities for this type of action clearly are available in water supply in many localities, provided that prices are not reduced to such low levels that investment and activity in water supply are discouraged.

Emergency Support for the Production of Services

Where short-run supply bottlenecks are a result of shortages of capital, limited management capability or high production costs it may be possible to increase total supply with reduced prices to the consumer by means such as direct subsidies to producers, emergency credit programs, reductions in import duties on essential system components, emergency technical assistance to producers, or informational programs to alert potential producers to the opportunities available in both formal and informal utility services.

Such measures may be appropriate for all utilities and may be applied generally, to augment total supply, or selectively to support producers who tend to serve target consumer groups such as the poor.

Removal of Institutional Barriers

Formal institutional bottlenecks in supply may be reduced by means such as simplifying procedures for obtaining permits for utility connections and by improving utility management. Informal institutional bottlenecks such as corruption, which result in discriminatory pricing and/or generally exorbitant charges, may be reduced also where there is a political will to do so. Institutional barriers are commonplace in all utilities. Their removal or reduction can have a substantial impact on inequities as well as total supply.

Action to Impact Future Supply

To impact future supply, several of the measures identified for impacting current supply may be implemented on a permanent basis — for example, pricing to reduce peak demand, differentiation of service quality for different uses, public pricing to achieve more equitable consumption and the regulation of private pricing. There are several additional measures that are likely to be of special importance in impacting future supply.

Selective System Expansion with Present Technologies

The most obvious, but not necessarily the most effective, method of expanding total supply and reducing inequities in supply is simply the expansion of existing utility systems, using present technologies. If this is done selectively, with priority given to the most disadvantaged groups (the converse of what often happens today) existing inequities in supply can be reduced. If inequities in property ownership are reduced by other measures, the provision of utilities to presently disadvantaged groups can further reduce inequities in the distribution of capital assets, since it is likely to increase property values. Such action is likely to assist in decreasing income inequities also because of its long-term impact on health and productivity.

Selective System Expansion with Changes in Technology

If changes in technology are made at the same time as systems are expanded it is likely that additional advantages can be achieved. If the "existing" technologies are "developed-world" technologies, they are likely to be capital-intensive, high cost and very wasteful of basic resources. Since other alternatives exist, the possibility of making major changes in technology should be considered carefully.

In water supply, for example, there are opportunities to differentiate water quality for different uses, as noted earlier. In water supply, sewerage and refuse jointly there are major opportunities for the reuse of waste products that could reduce total requirements and resource waste dramatically. At present, most waste water is simply discharged into rivers or into the sea and lost. As much as 70 percent may possibly be reused for industrial, agricultural or even household purposes. One current proposal for an Asian metropolis suggests multi-stage regeneration of waste water for all three types of use, taking advantage of existing subsoils for large scale natural filtration, with the early stages of reuse in industry and agriculture and subsequent reuse, for household purposes, after further natural purification. That scheme, if it proves to be as feasible as preliminary studies suggest, would mean that the urban population, now just over 4 million, could at least triple without excessive demands on present bulk sources; large acreages of good soils (over 70,000 acres) could be brought into production; and the massive ground pollution that now results from inadequate sewerage would be eliminated. To achieve this would require the simultaneous development of an adequate sewerage system and substantial pumping capacity, but preliminary analysis suggests that it is economically feasible.

In power, some of the possibilities for technological change, such as the use of nuclear energy, are already apparent. The technical and economic feasibility of other changes that are very exciting remains still unclear. Solar energy seems likely to become feasible, at least for small-scale household applications. The possibility of modern wind-powered systems for small-scale uses is being explored actively.

In communications, modernization is already well under way in most of the developing areas. Increasing utilization of radio, telephone and television for domestic, commercial and mass-educational purposes is already expanding the supply of information enormously.

The combined impact of current and foreseeable changes in utility technology on the supply of utility services could be very substantial. So could their impact on productivity, on economies in energy and resource use and on the preservation and enhancement of environmental quality. One estimate suggests that, for water use alone, technological change could reduce urban requirements, per capita, to 1/20th of present U.S.A. levels.[2]

To the extent that changes in technology are associated with changes in incomes, prices and/or consumer preferences, they may impact the demand for utilities as well as their supply. Major opportunities to impact demand will be the subject of the next two sections.

Action to Impact Current Demand

Increased Efficiency to Reduce Prices to the Consumer

Several of the measures suggested for increasing current supply are important also as potential means of reducing production costs and delivery prices — the optimization of existing systems to reduce physical losses and wastage; the addition of missing system components to use presently idle capacity more fully; facilitation of imports for essential system maintenance; differentiation of service quality for different uses; reduction of

---

[2] Meier, Richard L. *Resource Conserving Urbanism: Progress and Potentials.* Berkeley, California: Institute of Urban and Regional Development. Reprint No. 70. Page 389.

peak loadings; basic improvements in management; and the reduction of corruption, which both increases costs to the consumer and biases distribution in favor of those who can pay.

Opportunities for increases in efficiency and reductions in price exist particularly in water supply, sewerage, drainage and refuse disposal. Similar opportunities exist, though generally to a lesser extent, in power and communications.

Selective Emergency Changes in Public and/or Private Pricing

The measures possible here include subsidies (possibly in the form of rebates), price controls and discriminatory pricing. Opportunities of this kind exist for all utilities, though subsidies and price controls generally can be only short-term measures.

Emergency Job Creation Through the Construction and Operation of Utility Systems

In some cases utility installations are overstaffed. However, there are many opportunities to use labor-intensive technologies for the optimization, upgrading or extension of existing systems — with the double benefit of achieving urgently needed improvements in service and job creation to utilize underproductive labor more fully, thereby improving both the level and distribution of incomes. In some situations it may be possible to use the contributed labor of households and enterprises to help to pay for installation costs that low income groups could not otherwise afford. With imaginative management, such an approach might be tried with private, as well as public, utilities.

Informational Programs

In some cases (especially with recent immigrants and the "disengaged" poor) low levels of demand result from lack of knowledge of what is available and/or lack of appreciation of the benefits of utilizing higher levels of services, as well as limitations in ability to pay for services. Informational programs focused on groups lacking such knowledge could increase the total number of demanders and shift the preferences of existing consumers to increase total demand and improve the distribution of demand.

Action to Impact Future Demand

Sustained application of some of the measures suggested for impacting current demand can be utilized to impact future demand also — increases in the efficiency of utility systems, job creation through the construction and operation of utilities, discriminatory pricing and informational programs designed to increase total markets and/or shift preferences. The following additional measures are potentially important also.

The Use of Utility Services to Increase Labor Productivity and Incomes

By focusing improvements in water supply, sanitation, power and mass communications on households in which health problems and illiteracy or lack of information are important causes of low productivity, both the level and distribution of incomes can be improved in the long run to increase demands for all types of essential consumption, including the consumption of utility services — with changes in demand for individual services depending, among other things, upon income elasticities of demand for individual services.

The Use of Utilities to Increase Entrepreneurial Activity and Productivity

As in the case of households, water supply, sanitation, power and communication services can be focused on existing and potential entrepreneurial groups to increase the total level of entrepreneurial activity and the distribution of productivity among entrepreneurs. In addition to increasing entrepreneurial incomes, this may trigger off a chain reaction in which additional employment is generated — thus increasing demands for utilities from both enterprises and households. Through a selective focusing of improvements both the distribution and level of demand can be affected.

The Use of Improvements in Utilities to Affect the Distribution of Productive Capital Assets

Selective improvements in utilities can be used to increase the total supply of usable land and increase the value of real property — thus impacting future demand as a result of changes in the value and distribution of capital assets. Here, as in other areas, present improvements in utilities may have a feedback effect which increases future demand for utility services themselves as well as the demand for other goods and services.

The Use of Improvements in Utilities to Decrease Capital and Operating Costs for the Production and Distribution of Other Goods and Services

As suggested earlier, improvements in utilities can be used selectively to increase productivity and to structure land use efficiently, thus reducing the capital and operating costs of a wide variety of commodities. Such cost reductions, if they are carried over into reductions in prices to the consumer may affect the level and distribution of demand for a wide variety of goods and services, including future demand for utilities.

Information Needed Urgently to Improve Utility Programs

Many of the actions that have been suggested can be taken immediately and some of them are being implemented, to varying degrees, in a number of developing areas presently. The relatively modest physical and financial resources required for implementing most of the measures suggested as means of impacting current supply and demand exist already in many countries. Moreover, the problems involved are understood well enough to make it possible to act now, without elaborate additional research or analysis. What is needed to take advantage of immediate opportunities is the political will and a highly-focused mobilization of management skills that are, in most cases, very scarce.

The resource requirements for some of the measures suggested for impacting future supply and demand are, however, much more substantial. Additional information is needed before major irreversible investment decisions can be made with reasonable confidence about their results. Perhaps part of the information required can be assembled prior to the HABITAT Conference in 1976 so that the Conference itself can result in at least initial guidelines for long-range utility strategies that are likely to be fruitful, as well as additional guidelines for urgently needed short-run action.

With this in mind, the following types of information are suggested as targets for Conference preparation. Since long-range research is not feasible for the Conference, emphasis is placed on types of quantitative data and informed judgement which are likely to be more or less readily available. Much of the information that will be most useful must come from the developing areas themselves, for it is their technicians, administrators and politicians who are grappling with the realities of the utility crisis. The types of information that appear to be among the most important are identified below. The preparation of a specific program for assembling such information might be a function of the pre-Conference meetings that are to be held later this year. The list makes no attempt to be exhaustive, but may at least serve to initiate productive pre-Conference activity.

1. Comparative data on existing levels of service for each utility in "major" urban areas, "intermediate" and "small" urban centers and rural areas — together with data on per capita development and non-development expenditures on utilities in these areas. These data should be related to specific household income levels, if possible.
2. Information on opportunities for optimizing the use of existing systems.
   a) Data on present levels of losses and wastage.
   b) Descriptions and evaluations of attempts that have been made, or are being made, to optimize existing systems — with comparisons of the relative effectiveness of the measures suggested in the present note and/or other measures that have been tried.
3. Information on experience with measures designed to reduce peak loadings.
4. Information on experience in the use of physical rationing as a device to reduce inequities and wastage.
5. Information on experience with the differentiation of service quality for different uses.
6. Information on experience with discriminatory pricing to achieve more equitable consumption.
7. Information on experience in the regulation of private utility pricing and its effectiveness as a device for increasing total supply and modifying the distribution of supply.

8. Information on the levels and types of employment that have been generated with different utility technologies.

9. Identification of the types of new technology for each utility that appear to be particularly well-adapted to the developing areas — comparing these with "Western" technologies in terms of their capital and operating costs, the service levels achievable and the population groups most likely to be impacted.

10. Information on experience with informational programs designed to expand consumer markets for utilities and/or shift consumer preferences.

11. Information on the types of economic activity, including activities in the "traditional" sectors, that are most likely to be responsive to improvements in utilities — with data on types and levels of response, relative to investment in utilities, where such data are available.

12. Judgements on the relative importance of utility systems as instruments for guiding land use — recognizing the importance of other instruments, such as transportation networks, and recognizing the fact that dense settlement often occurs even without utilities if employment opportunities and other factors are operative.

13. Data on the impact of improvements in utilities on land values.

14. Data relating health conditions to utility levels in individual parts of urban areas — recognizing other factors that may be operative also.

15. Judgements on specific "scenarios" that are likely to be effective in implementing the short-range and long-range actions that have been suggested in the present note, and/or alternative types of action.

The importance of obtaining better information for utility policies and programs should not be under-estimated, for the impact of utility systems extends far beyond the mere provision of improved water, sanitation, power and communications. Decisions made about the supply and pricing of utilities are decisions that will affect income levels and income distribution, the levels and distribution of capital accumulation, including land ownership, the output and prices of essential goods and services, energy requirements, natural resource requirements, land use patterns and environmental quality. Such decisions should reflect these impacts. They should be much more than the simple "engineering" decisions that they often have been in the past.

6
Improved Local Administration

Dilys M. Hill, United Kingdom

The future planning and management of human settlements depends on improved local administration. This includes reforms of the government structures; strengthening the executive function to carry out plans effectively; training more personnel in a broad spectrum of both administrative and modern management skills; and then using professional and expert staff in ways which will make maximum effective use of them.

Reform of Government Structures

The problems of structural reform are evident in all countries but tend to affect developing and more developed societies in rather different ways. In industrial societies there are representative institutions at central and local levels and a constitutional division of powers between different kinds of authorities. In addition to these legal structures there are long traditions of political and social action which make change difficult. Although units of local administration may no longer correspond to actual communities in terms of economic activity or of people's work, family and leisure activities, local authorities are reluctant to give up any of their powers to other bodies through amalgamation or radical reorganization of the local government structure. In some countries these traditions are reinforced by legal and philosophical defences of local autonomy and "home rule," which make reform difficult. In addition, political parties and social groups may defend the *status quo* because they fear that they would lose electoral power, or social and economic influence, if local jurisdictions were enlarged and local communities lost functions over their own property assessments, tax rates and services. The ease of inter-municipal cooperation, and of central government grants and loans to localities, have reinforced the ability of the unreformed structures to remain unchanged, often for long periods. Local authorities cooperate to provide services and, although this may remove control and direct participation from the hands of local citizens and give power to appointed boards, it superficially retains "local autonomy." Central finance similarly eases the pressure to reform, since service standards are maintained, and disparities between areas and classes of local authorities reduced, by specific and equalization grants and by help with capital funding.

The inadequacies of the unreformed system only becomes obvious slowly, as the small communities fail to provide services which need wider areas and larger resources to be viable, as boundaries become completely artificial in large urban areas, and as central governments take over certain services in order to rationalize them. A major force in the demand for the inadequacies to be faced is that of planning. If people are to be provided with adequate jobs, houses, schools and other facilities, then planning will have to become a larger and larger part of central, regional and local administration. Human settlements have to be planned; the defects of past development have to be eradicated, housing standards improved, facilities phased with each other, and surrounding areas considered an interrelated whole.

But the need to plan, both over wider areas and more comprehensively, has implications for government administration. This arises in two ways. If local units are to be persuaded to take part in large scale socio-economic and physical planning then either they must do so collaboratively in informal area-wide bodies, or governments must make institutional changes. The alternative is for central governments to take on the planning function itself, either by evaluating local plans at the centre or by using regional levels of their field administration to perform the scrutinizing and integrating function. In practical terms the impact of planning, short of total reorganization, drives authorities to cooperate to meet the need for increased scale of operation. At the same time, unreformed local governments face demands for greater equalization of tax burdens, for greater recognition of the special needs of the underprivileged, and for greater citizen participation in local public policy making. In one sense, this third demand is easier to meet than the other two. The neighbourhood movement, whether through informal groups or elected councils, are relatively easy to establish. But it is far harder to redistribute resources, or to improve the conditions of the under-privileged and encourage their greater involvement, without institutional changes. Developing countries face different problems of restructuring their local government and administrative framework. One of the main differences is that there may be no tradition of local autonomy, "home rule" or elected local government. Instead, traditional rural and community life are based on mutual and familial obligations rather than on administrative institutions. Developing societies normally have a strong centralized tradition of government. Greater decentralization can, however, enable more service planning and provision to be carried out at regional and local levels and greater and more reliable information and opinion to be fed back to the centre. This move, however, has to meet the equally strong need for effective plans and efficient services. Central governments are impatient with weak and possibly over-factionalized local units when economic and social development must be given a prime place in the nation's priorities. The central government sees the need for socio-economic development as paramount and may then make local councils adjuncts to development agencies at the regional or district level. Committees of local leaders may be nominated or elected to advise the development agency, or local councils may include members from the field administrations of various government ministries, or leading party members. This can be, nevertheless, a way of promoting the strength and development of more representative local government but the temptation is that governments are reluctant to hand over more functions to elected councils rather than to development agencies.

Developing countries share with advanced societies, however, both the dangers of overcentralization (though for different historical reasons) and the need for some form of popular participation in public policy-making. For a variety of reasons, however, where central governments in developing societies do wish to decentralize and to encourage local participation this is a smoother process. Localism and parochialism are obstacles but administrative change is normally easier to introduce *per se* because the system is not so financially and technically complex and so firmly entrenched as to present the daunting prospect faced by developed societies when they try to reform local government. A more powerful resistance to reform comes from field administration, since reforms would alter the authority of field officers as well as their particular functions. The success of reforms will then depend on the party and social structure of the country concerned and the role of the chief executive or ruling group in facilitating the decision to make changes without a long or complex consultative procedure. This does not mean that changes are automatically successful. Where schemes are introduced too quickly with too little explanation, or where the reforms do not fit well into the political and social climate of the country, then they will not be successful. This is as true of modern management and administrative techniques and structures as of governments.

The general consensus on reform is that the decentralization of functions to elected bodies should proceed gradually as the localities develop capacities to undertake them. This has two further elements. If decentralization and the promotion of representative local government is to succeed through gradualism then this argues against rigid uniformity. It also calls for new and additional functions to be allocated by ministerial orders and regulations, so that local authorities could be dealt with flexibly and quickly, rather than waiting for major legislative changes of basic statutes. The system of local government may then lack uniformity, as authorities have additional powers given to them according to their capacities, but this is not such a drawback as administrative rigidity.

Reform of administrative structures in both developing and developed countries should include an area-wide level. The main point is that the move by some countries to make the regional level the field units of central government is unfortunate from the view-point of democratic local government since general policy decisions about the whole area are taken at this level. It is essential, therefore, to create representative institutions at the area-wide level since this is where, increasingly, decisions will be taken and therefore where effective power lies. To achieve this, reorganization must be initiated by the central government. This may be difficult. Amalgamation and cooperation are then used to achieve the benefits of administrative reform without the upheaval of completely recasting the system.

Central government must take the initiative but is often reluctant to do so because of strong political and local opposition. In order to overcome this, the central government should provide financial inducements and a recast tax structure which will help to spread the burdens of the different authorities more equitably. It also helps if the local units in the combined scheme do not lose their identity completely but form the second-tier authorities in a new two-tiered system.

Cooperation will remain a major force in administrative reforms because of the difficulties of reorganization and forced amalgamation. Local authorities cooperate in many ways for different purposes, through joint boards or other machinery as well as through more informal methods. Central governments use this cooperation to encourage greater area-wide planning. Federal grants to local authorities in metropolitan areas in the United States for example, are given on the basis that individual project applications will be considered by the metropolitan Council of Governments (a voluntary confederal body of local authorities acting as equals) for their conformity to regional plans. Cooperation has disadvantages, however, for the future planning and management of human settlements. Cooperation is normally for a single, or a restricted range, of functions and this fragments both authority and participation. It becomes more difficult to relate services to each other. Responsible government becomes fragmented among different public bodies and responsible citizen participation is divided and its energies dissipated. To be successful, cooperation needs to be given an institutional structure and this in turn needs to be given real decision-making powers of its own as opposed to merely consultative powers under the veto of member local units.

Strengthening the Executive Capacity of Local Administration

While it is possible to allocate powers and responsibilities among different levels of government by law this will not eliminate the inevitable interplay of political factors. Equally, at the local level, the relationship between council and executive must be worked out in terms of a political and personal *modus vivandi* as well as constitutional rules. Effective administration rests on an effective relationship between representative councils and local executives whether appointed or elected. The tasks of planning and implementation depend on the machinery of administration used by the council, the relation of the council to its executive or board, and the use of committees and the question of who sits on them. The local authority may implement its plans through a single or a plural executive (board). The single executive may be elected from among members of the council, elected by the electors at large (as is the case in the position of the Mayor in American cities), or appointed by the central government or by the state or provincial government in federal systems. The single executive form has several advantages. The person concerned is a visible focus for responsible government to the electorate and this stimulates the citizen's involvement. The single executive, whether elected or appointed, is also the focus of accountable management in implementing the council's policies. He may also be, to a varying degree in different countries, the responsible agent of central government for the due performance of certain functions, particularly in relation to the council's budget, capital expenditure, and major planning decisions. The plural executive or board may similarly be either directly elected by the people at large or selected from or elected by the council. Inevitably, the plural executive is not such a publicly visible focus of accountable government as the single executive and may not arouse as much popular electoral interest.

The executive, whether appointed or elected, single or plural in form, is responsible to the whole council for the preparation of plans and the implementation of decisions. In this, the manner of election and the nature of the executive are important. The single executive may be appointed by the central government, and have a dual responsibility to the local council and to the central government. His post may be protected by special legislation which specifies his duties, the terms of his appointment and dismissal, and his relations to the council and to the staff.

The chief executive may be appointed by the central government and may be a member of the central government's Civil Service. Or the men appointed as chief executives of local authorities may be members of a special elite corps of the central civil service as with the French *corps préfetoral*. Chief executives appointed in this way are useful channels between localities and central government. Not all appointed executives are civil servants: some men may be appointed by the central government because of their political experience (either at central or local level) or because they are representatives of particular political parties or the ruling party. Ideally, however, the chief executive should be locally, not centrally, appointed and selected. One of the strong themes of this section is that for local government to play a major part in human settlements local people must be actively involved. But the council, in its turn, must make this participation a positive element of its work. It must, therefore, be able to take decisions and make real choices. To do this, it must have the major say in selecting, appointing, and dismissing (for due cause) its own personnel, including its chief executive. Clearly, however, there are still countries where, because of long tradition or because the centre is anxious to promote rapid development, the national government continues to insist on a centrally appointed executive.

The executive is responsible to the whole council and the relations between them will depend on a variety of factors. Among these are party politics; the personality of the chief executive and his powers including the preparation of the budget, the annual estimates and the council's capital programme; and the length of the term of office of the executive (whether this is a single appointed executive, with no set term of office or a plural executive which must be re-elected at specified intervals). With regard to the plural executive, relations with the council will depend on the duties of the board as a collective body and the duties which may be given to individual members of the board to carry out certain executive tasks. Such individual members of the executive board may or may not be executive heads of functional departments of the local authority, but they will in any case work closely with departmental heads. The powers of the plural executive lay down their duties for supervising the overall implementation of the council's decisions, and the preparation and control of the budget. It may also include responsibility for the hiring and firing of council staff and general personnel management, though this will be the responsibility normally of an appointed chief administrative head of the council's civil service.

One of the features of modern planning and implementation is the complexity of the chief executive's role, both in making policy and in explaining and promoting it among his colleagues and to the members of the elected council. In this the chief executive must be more than the person responsible for carrying out the decisions of the local authority. He must give leadership, both to the council's permanent staff and to the elected councillors. He must be able to develop new techniques of management and planning, show the relevance of these to the local authority's work, and use them in ways that help councillors to take a meaningful part in policy. This is crucial because, whether the executive is of the plural or single type, the basic question is the extent to which real alternatives are put to the elected council and whether they understand the complexities of the problems which they face. This places a great responsibility on the chief executive, who must be able to communicate ideas, explain them, and take councillors along with him. The chief executive's leadership role is also increasingly important *vis à vis* the community as a whole. In the industrialised countries, for example, local authorities face an educated and articulate electorate which is learning how to express its needs and which expects the local council to explain its policies and take the public into its deliberations. And in all countries, cities are facing a more heterogeneous population: different groups with different, and often conflicting, interests. These divisions may be based on many factors — age, class or ethnic groups, business and trade union interests, the rich suburbs and the slums — and their needs must all be taken into account. The council, and its chief executive, must go out and meet these citizens; council deliberations and policy-making can no longer be a remote, internal process. The chief executive's part in this can help to make participation by all groups a positive contribution to the wellbeing of the community and can help to prevent confrontation between the council and the public.

The way in which the council controls its budget, raises revenue, and controls and supervises its executive in making plans and carrying out services also depends on the way in which the council implements its policies through committees or by other means. Britain, and some Anglo-Saxon countries with similar administrative patterns, are virtually unique in combining deliberative and executive functions in the council's committees. In Britain, the council appoints committees for certain functions or services. These committees are made up of council members, normally reflecting the strength of the political parties on the council where the council is run on party lines. In addition, the majority party has normally exercised an overall policy-making role through an informal party group acting like an unofficial cabinet. In recent years, and particularly following the reorganization of local government in 1974, committee structures have been streamlined, with a strong emphasis on central policy mechanisms within the local authority and on the policy process, and new management techniques have been introduced. In most countries committees are used in a variety of ways but they do not normally act as both policy-making and implementing committees in the

British manner. Committees may have legislative, deliberative and advisory, initiative and policy-making, or ratifying and approving functions. Committees to administer or execute a service are, as we have seen, confined largely to the Anglo-Saxon experience.

Legislative committees. The local authority sets up one or more committees to enact by-laws or regulation of nuisances and so on. This work must normally be done within the framework of national legislation, that is, the local regulations must not clash with national laws. The central government regulates this law-making function and the responsible ministry may provide "model by-laws" which local authorities then use for their own particular circumstances. Legislative committees may also lay down regulations for the conduct and conditions of service of the officials and staff who work for the local authority but again the central government will normally lay down regulations and set guidelines.

Deliberative and advisory committees. Local authorities use committees to deliberate on the present and future policies of the local authority and its work and to advise on the implementation of these plans. Such committees may work closely with the chief executive; they may be set up to consider particular problems or special issues; they may be responsible for advising on the work of a particular department (though not supervising its day to day work); finally, advisory committees may be given a brief to enquire in future needs, either in one problem area or with regard to the development of the community as a whole. The success of this kind of committee depends on: the kind of responsibility which the council gives it, and the staff to help in their deliberations; their relation with the chief executive and with leading members of the staff and the council and consequently on the committee's own feelings of effectiveness and frustration; the personalities, including party members, of the committee; and, most of all, on whether the council and executive take their work seriously or whether the committees are merely debating chambers.

The Budgetary or Finance Committee is a special case of the deliberative or advisory committee. In countries where the local authority has a strong, centrally-appointed chief executive, and with administrative tutelage by higher authorities, then the Budgetary committee's advisory role is in practice rather circumscribed. But, whatever the extent of the Budgetary committee's freedom to control all aspects of local finance, it will be concerned with relating resources to needs, assessing the annual estimates, ordering priorities, and ensuring that the money is spent on items according to the budget's directives. In addition, a Finance committee will be responsible for the authority's overall financial policy and commitments, the raising of loans, credits and central government grants for capital projects, raising revenue and, in some cases, having responsibility for property valuation for tax purposes. The Finance committee may have overall responsibility for the annual budget, or this may be the responsibility of a separate committee. The Finance committee will also be responsible for seeing that correct auditing of the authority's expenditures has been carried out. In this field, there is a move from purely financial auditing to more sophisticated techniques of management accounting and performance budgeting, to show the various outputs of the council's programmes more effectively and how they relate to the progress of different policies.

Initiative and policy-making organs. The future development of settlements depends on the improved use of modern management and above all on a policy-making process which encourages the planned comprehensive approach. Informal mechanisms based on party or other private and *ad hoc* groups, are giving way to a more formal system in which there is a policy-making committee or a 'cabinet' at the top of the administrative structure. These policy-making bodies have a dual function: to initiate the search for ideas, and to bring programmes together in a coherent policy which charts priorities, shows the planned relation between resources and programmes, and demonstrates how the policy may be implemented over a period of time. The policy-making committee is a crucial element of council's work and this is reflected in its composition, which normally consists of the leading members of the council. The committee or board will also have a close relationship with the Finance committee and with the chief executive and these three bodies may form an 'inner council' — the really powerful core — of the local council.

Ratifying or approving committees. Ratifying and approving functions are normally carried out by the full council itself. But certain committees may be given special powers to approve particular acts of the council: passing the budget, for example, or approving the council's by-laws. There is always the danger in local government, however, that chief executives may use committees solely for this ratifying and approving function: the committees merely accede to the decisions which have been taken by the chief executive and play little effective part in the policy-making process.

Linking committees. In developing countries, these may form a bridge between local authorities with certain tasks and the development work of field agencies. Members of these committees may be drawn from the District Council, District Heads of Departments and from ruling political parties. In this way a meeting ground is provided for elected representatives of the people and the government's field agency personnel.

The use of committees in local government is often commended because it can be a way of drawing local people directly into the work of the council. In this way experts, interested laymen, and special groups and interests, can participate in making decisions that will affect them and the whole community. But it can also have disadvantages in that decisions are not implemented swiftly, factional divisions or even corruption weakens administration, or committees are merely mouthpieces for other interests whether of the executive, the party or the individual member. In many countries, for these reasons, committees are used to deliberate and advise but the execution of plans is carried out through a strong executive and his staff.

Training

One of the suggestions for strengthening local administration is to introduce an integrated personnel system to build up the local government service on the principle of a merit-based career structure. In developing countries only central government will have the facilities to do this by promoting or providing directly the essential training programmes.

The public personnel systems of different countries fall into three broad types. First, there is the localized type where individual local authorities have the power to select and appoint their own staff (although in some countries, their pay and conditions are governed by national agreements and negotiations). Second, there is the unified local government system. Under this system either all local government personnel, or certain categories of them, form a single career structure but this is separate from the national civil service. Finally, there is the integrated system under which central and local officials form a single personnel service and there is interchangeability between all parts of the system. In developing countries, the integrated system may not only help the best use of resources but also guard against possible nepotism and corruption of a service entirely controlled by individual local authorities.

But all systems of personnel management should ensure that the salaries and conditions of service in local government are comparable to those of the public service as a whole. Staff should have reasonable security of tenure, a system of merit promotions and a proper career structure. In-service training programmes for local government officers should be established. The universities, institutes of public administration, and the technical and professional schools should be the main source of this training, but if this is not possible then central governments will have to provide local government training establishments. Where a unified local government service is established, this usually involves the setting up of a local government service commission. But this should at most only have limited responsibility in the coordination of training while the main responsibility should remain with the ministry of local government.

Local government training falls into five broad categories: pre-entry preparation; orientation of new personnel and induction training; in-service training; on-the-job experience and post-experience courses. In addition there is the need to ensure that public servants are sympathetic to the aims of local government. There is the practice in some countries of assigning central or provincial government personnel to serve more or less permanently in local administration. These officers may become head of the administration in the local government areas concerned. It is vitally important, therefore, that they should be trained in the purposes and spirit of local administration. Although central government may have to assume leadership in training it should bring local authorities into direct participation in training activities as soon as possible by giving them opportunities to join in formulating policies and strategies of training. Central governments should also get local authorities to contribute to the costs of training, and persuade them to release their personnel for training and assist them in this by providing additional personnel on a rotation basis. Local authority Associations also help with training programmes. They, and the professional staff associations, have an important part to play in the maintenance of professional standards, providing technical and post-experience courses and refresher programmes.

In some countries there is a no centralized, overall direction of training. This is consistent with traditional doctrines of local self-government, and with recruitment by local authorities of their own staff (though there may be national standards of salaries and negotiating machinery).

In many couutries, National Associations of local authorities help their members with training and wide range of other kinds of help with problems. They offer advisory services on technical matters, and may also advise on salary and wage problems and negotiations. Practical cooperative services, such as centralized purchasing of commonly used items, municipal insurance, publications, salary and wage negotiations are also important. Training also forms a major part of their work, either through schools or correspondence courses, etc., or their own courses, or in collaboration with universities and other bodies. The associations have also been instrumental in disseminating information on new techniques of management and administration, including problem and system analysis, management services, personnel organization, and electronic data processing.

Management training is needed for technical officers and departmental heads as well as for the local authority's chief executive and his deputies. Management training can be divided into two main areas. One is the training of officers who are going to take up posts as general administrators and who need an extensive grounding in management, particularly in the new systems and policy-process approaches. The other is to add significant elements of management training to the professional and technical education of other officers. The nature of administrative problems has changed with the increased scale of organization and with the new methods of acquiring, storing and processing data, and the new techniques of planning and allocating resources. There is also a better understanding of the interdependence of administration and policy-making. There is also a new emphasis on the need for economic and social planning to be integrated with systems and ecological planning. But for many countries the search for ways of strengthening the administrative system begins with the efforts to improve data and its collection. Reliable statistics are essential and they must be capable of rapid and effective analysis. The computer aids this work and is frequently the beginning of a "management revolution."

Computers play an important part in planning and administration. But they also have the additional effect of tending to increase the size of operation (whether informal or formal) since only the largest authorities can afford to use them and because computers need a large 'population' of data to be economical. Initially, local authorities tend to use computers for processing certain routine operations such as pay-rolls and taxes rather than for developing better information systems. The next stage is to use them for traditional record-keeping and filing systems. This alters the traditional bureaucratic organization by reducing the numbers of clerks used, and changing the emphasis of clerical jobs from routine to more technical, and more highly-paid, operations. The centralizing influence of the computer within the political system (the concentration of data banks, for example at national and regional levels) is paralleled by similar centralizing trends within local administration itself. The power and expertise of top management is reinforced *vis-à-vis* lower management. Unless positive steps are taken to remedy this by the use of training and retraining schemes, management courses, secondment to other authorities and public bodies and so on, then the development of future top management will be seriously weakened.

Similar to the problem of computer data centralization, both within the political structure and within the administration of one authority, there is the problem of the integration of data. That is, data may be collected in such a way that it becomes harder, not easier, to integrate one set of statistics with another. This problem can operate both for statistics of the same authority (horizontal integration of data from different services) or between different authorities. But where these difficulties can be overcome then integrated data collection can offer better information at reduced cost and with fewer duplications. In developing countries there is a need for central units at national level with the capacity to guide computer policy and development.

A management revolution is occurring in many countries. The emphasis is on policy as a multi-faceted plan-making and plan-implementation process. Policy planning and corporate management seek the more efficient use of resources and manpower. At the same time these improved methods of decision-making must allow councillors to make real choices between alternatives which officers must present to them in intelligent and intelligible ways. The overall aim of policy planning is to set objectives and analyse alternatives. The focus on management must also be seen in the political context of local government and the principle of democratic control. There is a lively debate on the elected representatives' response to the new and complex management methods and techniques. Councillors' managerial role is part of their political, including party political, roles and of their values, perceptions, and relations with their constituents.

Planning, Programming, Budgeting Systems (PPBS) is essentially a means of allocating scarce resources in terms of a defined programme over a period of time and evaluating its progress at certain points or stages. PPBS shows the effects of alternative plans and the choices which are available. Outputs are measured in units of performance in real terms (numbers of teachers trained, etc.). Instead of annual expenditure budgeting the aim is to try to establish two, three and five year plans on the basis of programmes and their outputs. In this way the budget is changed from a short-term list of expenditure items to medium-term programmes of action. But to use this approach in developing countries calls for special versions which fit the circumstances of the countries concerned. In developing countries the introduction of PPBS and other techniques should build on rather than eliminate expenditure budgeting, and it should be introduced in stages. This also calls for the training of systems engineers, operations research experts, statisticians, and cost and management accountants. The feasibility of using the system depends both on the collection of more and better information on demographic and other data and on local leadership and the quality of administration. Performance budgeting has limitations, however, apart from the need for trained experts and relatively sophisticated data. The difficulty is that while it has proved useful where quality and quantity of outputs can be measured, such as the miles of road constructed or houses built, it is less successful in linking outputs with recourse inputs in the more personal services such as health, welfare and education.

In some countries the application of modern management techniques may be hindered by parochialism and sectionalism which claims that, for example, only the educationalist can speak about education administration or that only local people know the real problems of their area. On the other side, the management innovators may insist that the new techniques are applicable everywhere. This may not have regard to particular needs and conditions. But administrative capability is a major factor in economic and social development. Inadequate administrative capacity is the greatest bottleneck in the way of successful implementation of social and economic development programmes. The problems of using modern techniques must, however, be clearly recognised. First, it is difficult for administrators to keep themselves abreast of the new techniques. And secondly, it is difficult to identify the programmes which are suitable for the application of management techniques, and there is the added problem that mistakes are wasteful and disruptive. The central government, the local authority associations or other bodies and staff associations, all need to systematically assemble information on new techniques and processes. The United Nations has set up a number of workshops to evaluate new budget techniques and has made considerable efforts to introduce some form of programme budgeting. But the results so far have been limited and it is suggested that regionalization of the budget may be a more feasible goal together with review by higher authorities, and control of credit facilities by national municipal development banks and other means. We recognise that there is the danger that this can lead to greater centralization and bureaucratization. But it can also stimulate local authorities to action.

The wide variety of techniques — including PPBS, operational research, systems analysis, cost-benefit analysis, automatic data-processing and management information systems — all have a basic quantitative approach and a number of common features, particularly their stress on comprehensive and interdisciplinary approach. But they must be recognized as means to an end, useful only in the context of purposeful application. At the same time it should not be automatically thought they are not applicable in developing countries; they too need effective problem-solving techniques. It is true that in the 1960s many developing countries had only incidental experience of management and some had become disillusioned when their experience of the new methods did not live up to their expectations. The situation in the 1970s is different. The challenge is multi-deminsional: from the management of change, from information collection and dissemination, from new communication facilities, and from the tension arising from social change. The challenge to policy-makers and senior administrators is to manage an accelerated process of change in their public administrative systems away from the traditional trial and error and towards the effective use of modern management techniques and approaches.

In order to achieve this, there must be organizations or institutions to foster and evaluate the techniques and to stimulate a climate for their favourable reception. They also need to undertake research into the necessary modifications of the available technology, since the existing techniques were evolved in different circumstances. The main aim is to make more informed and rational choices, related more effectively to their environments. To do this, administrators must be able to see the consequence of the management innovations on the wider system as well as on the internal organization of regional and local authorities. Flexibility and open response are vital. But it is very difficult to move from the conventional bureaucracy to more adaptive systems. Human values must be changed also.

The Effective Use of Trained Staff

The value of the new management approach depends ultimately on the quality of the staff and, equally importantly, on the informed judgements of those who employ and use them, and of the elected representatives who must judge the application and relevance of the methods and techniques. Management technology has to compete for scarce resources along with other services. It also influences the social and political structure. In developing countries, for example, it can create new elites and positive efforts must be made to explain the new approach and the reasons for using it so that the public is not alienated from the influential management elite. The application of modern management techniques holds great promise for better services, but it may also result in a style of administration more orientated to efficiency than to service or to participation by ordinary people. This must be guarded against. The success of human settlements depends on strengthening the administrative framework at central and local levels. In many countries, this is severely limited by the availability and quality of administrative and technical personnel. There is also the problem of corruption and the dispute about the role of politics and political parties in the administration of programmes. But everyone acknowledges the need for trained staff, for better administration, and for impartiality and fairness. At the same time, the successful use of staff will depend on their sensitivity to the values and aspirations of local people and their willingness and ability to work with and for elected representatives. Trained staff must recognise the demand for participation and understand how this can aid, rather than frustrate, their own technical and administrative work.

The strengthening of the administrative framework reaffirms the belief in the need for powerful and responsible elected local authorities as part of the national and local policy for human settlements. The officials who help to prepare policy and implement plans must also be accountable. This is best achieved by their accountability to the local elected representatives and their responsibility to their professional colleagues through their training and their adherence to professional standards and normal. These aims depend on more than new techniques. They depend on organization, technical and personnel skills of a high order. The danger to be avoided is that, while central government becomes increasingly sophisticated and future-orientated, local authorities are left with the task of implementing plans to which they have not fully contributed. But there are also advantages to improved methods. Local authorities, especially the larger ones and the metropolitan bodies, can use the new management techniques to integrate social and economic planning with physical planning to achieve the truly comprehensive approach to human settlements which this paper has stressed.

But the progress which is being made in this field must be seen in perspective. New techniques and the management revolution must not be allowed to produce a gap between the administrators and those they serve. There is a real problem of accountability. Councillors must also be able to judge the work which the administrators do and how to make real — and not just token — choices. Administrators must be prepared, therefore, to take the elected representatives along with them in their work. They must also be able to explain to the citizens what they are trying to do and show the relevance of new and costly techniques in the search for a better life for ordinary people. Improved local administration must also be seen in the context of particular countries. All societies are using new techniques and are anxious to use the best modern methods of planning and of evaluating their plans. But these techniques must not be imposed from outside; they must be developed to meet the needs, ideologies and values of a country and its people. Here, in addition, the role of international cooperation is recognised and should be developed further.

7
Absorption of Newcomers in the Cities of Developing Countries

Otto H. Koenigsberger, United Kingdom

Up to the end of the 19th century most of the LDCs showed slow population growth. High birth rates compensated for high infant mortality and for losses from epidemics, feuds and wars. In the present century, improved public health services and medical care have reduced infant mortality and increased life expectation, thereby disturbing the precarious and unhappy balance of previous generations.

The reduction of death rates in the LDCs was not accompanied by corresponding reductions of birth rates. Measures that prevent disease and death are welcome. Changes in living habits and behaviour patterns that promise safety from disease are likely to overcome the resistance to innovation that is inherent in traditional as much as in Western societies.

Measures that prevent birth are not as obviously attractive, except to a small urbanised minority. For the vast majority, the odds are overwhelmingly in favour of large families. Agriculture based societies consider children above the age of five as a valuable auxiliary work force. Extended families need children to fulfil their social welfare functions, particularly the care of old or sick members. Tribal societies and local rulers derive their power from superiority of numbers. The combined interests of these institutions have — over the millenia — established traditions and customs that tie the status of women to the production of children. Religions have in many instances reinforced attitudes and traditions that had their origins in the economic needs and social structures of agricultural and pastoral societies. As a result, birth rates have remained constant or changed little while death rates have declined. The labile balance of past centuries has given way to a wave of population increase in third world countries, ranging from 1.8 percent per annum in Afghanistan to 3.8 percent in Mexico.

This rapid growth of Third World population has been called the "Demographic Revolution."[1] The name is apt because of the revolutionary changes in the lives of the countries involved. These changes have begun to make themselves felt only in the past thirty or forty years. There are still many among public administrators, planners and politicians who have not appreciated the inevitability and irreversibility of these changes and are hankering after a return to the "good old days" of zero population growth.

Others have reacted more positively and, under the leadership of U.N. sponsored or supported organisations, have campaigned for the reduction of birth rates through family planning. In 1974, nineteen percent of the countries of Africa, fifty percent of those of Asia and Oceania and fifty-six percent of the Latin American countries had official family planning programmes.[2] Results in urbanised communities are promising, progress in predominantly rural areas is slow. For most of the less developed countries the end of the demographic revolution is not yet in sight. Its consequences must be accepted and plans and policies formulated accordingly.

---

[1] The term was coined by C.D. Harris in *Urbanisation and Population Growth in the Soviet Union, 1959-1970*, Geogr. Review, Jan. 1971 pp. 102-124.

[2] I.B.R.D., *Population Policies and Economic Development*, Baltimore and London 1974, Table 25, p. 75.

Rural – Urban Migration

The most important consequence of rapid population growth is rural under-employment. Job opportunities in agriculture do not grow *pari passu* with the increase in population. Attempts to increase food production through improved farming methods and to extend arable land through irrigation and land reclamation are slow to produce results. Even when they eventually succeed in boosting production — as in the case of the green revolution and many irrigation projects — the growth in employment opportunities remains far below what is needed for the growing populations.

The same holds good for land reform. The cutting up of large estates into peasant holdings, desirable as it may be for other reasons, has rarely satisfied the accumulated demand for new viable holdings for the millions of young men and women who have reached working age and find themselves surplus to the manpower needs of the existing farming community.

Not all LDCs are short of land. A few have reserves of potentially cultivable land, most of it either semi-arid savannah or tropical rain-forest on lateritic soils. Neither is suited for food crops without major investment in public works, including irrigation, power supply, fertilizer production and above all marketing roads. Practically all LDCs have recognised the need for long term investment in rural development of this kind, and several have invested much of their limited resources and whatever capital they could obtain from international agencies and bilateral help into bold and imaginative multi-purpose projects. The Damodar Valley, the Bakra-Nangal and the Tunga-Badra projects in India, the Suqqur and Thal Valley projects in Pakistan, the Gal-Oya project in Sri Lanka, the Gezira project in the Sudan, the Assuan High Dam in Egypt and the Volta, Kainji and Kossou Dams in West Africa — to name only a few — are examples of far sighted investments by governments of basically poor countries that had the courage to forgo short term advantages for long term gains. Projects of this type benefit our children and grandchildren, but do little to increase job opportunities in our lifetime.

The only regions where employment has increased visibly and rapidly are the concentrations of industries and trade in and around big cities. The increase of output through the division of labour and specialization that is characteristic of urban economies throughout the world has shown itself capable of increasing job opportunities faster than long range projects of rural development. It has therefore exercised a much stronger influence on the young men and women entering the labour market.

Here lies the largest migratory movement in human history, the movement of people from rural areas to city regions that dominates the social scene of all LDCs without exception. The young people who find themselves redundant to the economy of their homesteads and villages have only two alternatives:

- they can either stay where they are, subsist when crops are good or perish with their friends and kinsmen when rains fail or floods or pests destroy the crops;
- or they can move to the city, either temporarily to earn a bride price or support their starving village or, more often, permanently to start a new life and career in what they see as the "brave new world" of urban opportunities.

Rural-urban migration is a phenomenon of our time that has been much studied and described. In the context of a "Conference on Human Settlements" it is essential that its nature be clearly understood. Emotionally coloured terminology can do a great deal of harm. What we are witnessing is neither a "drift" nor a "flood". The migrants are not "drifting aimlessly towards the attraction of the city lights," nor are they "refugees from a sudden disaster who flood into the unfortunate city." They are a self-selected group of men and women at the peak of their working power who have taken a deliberate decision about their own future. Contrary to common belief, the flow of information from city to village is considerable. Most migrants know from visits of friends or relations what to expect. They have kinsmen or people from the same village or town on whose help they can count and they often have a fair idea of prospects of employment in industry, petty trade or casual labour. In short, the rural urban migration is, with rare exceptions, a planned move of a group that represents one of the most valuable human resources on an otherwise poor country.

If an emotion charged term was needed to describe the city-bound migrants, I would suggest "*urban pioneers.*" Like the pioneers who developed the American West, they have broken with a past that holds no hope. Like the 19th century pioneers, they are moving to seek a better future — if not for themselves then for their children and grandchildren. They do not expect an early success and an easy life. On the contrary, they are prepared "to rough it," to work hard for low wages and to save patiently for a better future.

The U.N. Conference at Vancouver is to deal with human settlements, both urban and rural. The migrants — the urban pioneers — whom we have discussed are the urban settlers. The planning of their settlement, their reception in the city, their success or failure and their contribution to the building of the new nations of the Third World must be a major concern of the Conference.

The Response to Metropolitan Growth

it has taken a long time for the leaders of opinion in developed and developing countries to accept the inevitability of the demographic revolution and its results. There are many, even to-day, who do not see that rapid urban population growth has not created poverty. It has merely made poverty visible. The shock of coming face to face with large scale deprivation accounts for the frequency of negative responses to the growth of urban settlements.

There are the numerous voices who advocate investment in rural development and rural industrialization in order "to stop migration at the source;"

- there is the demand for new towns and even new metropolitan concentrations "to divert the stream of migration to alternative targets;"
- there is the fashionable call for decentralization of government departments, manufacturing industires and white collar employment in order "to create a better balance between regions;"
- there is even a faction that wishes to declare a particular metropolis a "closed city" and thus "put a stop to further population growth by force of law;"
- yet largest of all is the group that advises to do nothing at all, because "doing anything for the migrants would only induce more of them to come."

Investment in rural development is bound to play an essential part in the long term planning of any LDC. It requires carefully worked out development strategies at national and regional levels. Yet it must not be expected to have immediate effects on rural-urban migration. The increase in food production and the improvement of food distribution and storage are sufficient justification for allocating a high priority to agricultural projects, but such projects must not be expected to have short term effects on population movements.

Similarly, the building of new urban centres (ranging from new market towns to new mammoth cities) may form an important part of a country's development strategy, but it cannot be expected to make a noticeable impact on the growth rate of existing cities. Brasilia, the most famous and one of the largest new town ventures of our times, has done a lot to stimulate development in a hitherto under-populated and under-developed region, but its effects on the population growth in the metropolitan regions of Sao Paulo and Rio de Janeiro appear to have been negligible.

Decentralization of manufacture, trade and service industries (including the public sector which in LDCs is usually the largest service industry employer) has many advantages, most of them political and social. Its economic advantages are, to say the least, open to debate. During a demographic revolution, the rapid creation of new jobs for a rapidly growing population is a paramount need. Few LDCs have succeeded in meeting this need. From the evidence available so far, highly concentrated settlements such as Singapore or Hong Kong have done better in synchronising population growth and job creation than others with more decentralised settlement patterns.

Attempts to make it illegal for migrants to settle in capital cities are as old as cities themselves. To name only a few examples:

- The Egyptian Pharao Ech-N-Aton decided in 1385 B.C. that his capital city Thebes should be stopped from further growth by royal decree and replaced by a new "garden city in the desert." A few years later, his successor Tut-Ankh-Amun gave up the attempt and restored the court to Thebes.
- In 1600 A.D., Queen Elizabeth 1st of England decided that London with about 100,000 inhabitants was becoming too large and arranged for Parliament to pass legislation forbidding further settlement in the city.
- During the first Five-Year Plan, the Government of the U.S.S.R. legislated against further population growth in Moscow, but did not succeed any better than its predecessors. These attempts have failed —

and so have many others in more recent history, because their authors did not recognize the roots of urban population growth in demographic revolutions and failed to understand the essential role of large cities as motors of development and change.

The hypothesis that doing nothing for would-be urban settlers would discourage them from coming and thus retard migration is the only one that has been tested again and again over the last thirty years in cities of every size all over the developing world. It seems impossible to find a single case where it has shown itself to be true. Being ignored, being told not to expect help or housing on arrival and being denied access to services freely available to the older inhabitants has obviously failed to discourage migrants from making their way to the cities of the developing world in ever increasing numbers.

Moreover, the advocates of doing nothing have not only failed to prove their case, they have done harm to their countries and cities. As explained in the preceding chapter, the generation that decides to seek a new life and career in the city represents an important human resource which a poor country can ill afford to waste. By ignoring the pioneering spirit of the migrants, many countries have missed the opportunity of utilising their working power in the most productive way, their spirit of enterprise, their inventiveness and their readiness to endure temporary hardships. They have converted a potential asset of their cities into a long term liability.

There is no lack of apologists for those who put their heads into the sand and hope that urban migration and big cities "will go away" if they take no notice of them. An intellectual anti-big city movement is well established in the highly urbanised countries of Europe and North America. Many a learned paper has been written to prove that very large cities are uneconomical and a drain on a country's resources. It has been claimed that there are optimum sizes for cities and that urban problems become progressively more difficult to solve the more a city exceeds this theoretical optimum. Bombay, Lagos, Djakarta, Manila and Calcutta are commonly quoted in support of this view.

No doubt, the problems of health, housing, transport, utilities etc. of these cities are daunting, to say nothing of the difficulty of managing the affairs of a low per capita income community of such magnitude. Yet the fact that our past attempts have been less than successful is no proof that the problems of these cities are unsolvable. All it proves is that we were wrong in trying to leave the development of large urban concentrations to the forces of a free market, that it was a mistake to replicate in the large cities of Asia or Africa methods of city government and urban management that had evolved in Europe a hundred years earlier and that systems of urban planning are not transferrable to countries with different political, social economic histories and aspirations.

At the Receiving End of Migration

The scene at the point of arrival, if viewed dispassionately, is far from presenting a picture of unmitigated misery. It looks different from the different points of view of the groups that are affected by it.

There are, for instance, the established citizens, who include not only those born in the city, but also those first generation urbanites who have managed to establish themselves economically and are accepted socially. They react in the way established communities have reacted against newcomers since time immemorial: they resent them and, at the same time, exploit them. Xenophobia is one of the oldest features of human (and animal) societies, and it is not surprising that it has influenced local reactions towards in-migrants and indirectly also national and international attitudes and policies.

Resentment and dislike of newcomers has never prevented older inhabitants from taking advantage of the opportunities presented by the influx of large numbers of cheap and willing workers. The newcomers are not only a valuable pool of unskilled — yet imminently trainable labour, they also form a steadily growing market for consumer goods and services. At the same time, their arrival increases the pressure on the available accommodation. Prices for building land, houses and apartments rocket upwards and provide the owner of even the most modest piece of urban real estate with a vastly increased capital asset.

This conjuncture of an ample supply of labour with an expanding market and a windfall of capital produces local economic boom conditions in the formal as well as the informal sectors of the city. Examples abound, but are rarely publicised and even less often researched. Those who profit prefer to stay in the background. Their vociferous complaints of overcrowding, the spreading of slums, the deterioration of standards of public health, housing, urban services and amenities — all quite justified from the points of view of old inhabitants, visiting journalists and tourists — tend to divert attention from profits to problems.

The situation presents an entirely different picture to the newcomers themselves. The urban amenities, standards and services that, to the old inhabitants, seem so badly deteriorated appear still attractive and desirable by comparison with those of most villages. Moreover, questions of amenities and services are not foremost in the minds of migrants. Their main concern is employment. In the beginning, relations and friends from the home district or village provide contacts and guidance in the struggle for an urban job. Often they also help with food and shelter. Yet the economic life of the city where space is at a premium and food has to be paid for by hard earned cash limits hospitality and aid to kinsmen and friends. The newcomer soon realises that he must fend for himself.

He knows he has no access to official welfare services, labour exchanges and vocational training facilities are not for him. Authorities and established communities ignore him or treat him with hardly disguised hostility. He knows also that all he has to offer are his natural wit, a body that is used to physical labour and his willingness to do any work that might secure him a foothold in the urban economy or at least ensure survival for a few hours, days or weeks. It does not take him long to learn that his best chances of making a living are in areas of concentrated activity, such as central business districts, markets, bus and railroad stations, ports, fairgrounds and, above all, building sites. It is here where the action is and where a pair of willing hands is most likely to be needed, especially in moments of crisis and before and after official working hours.

Unfortunately for the newcomer, the places where he is most likely to find work are those where he is most unlikely to find accommodation. In central localities, he is in competition for space with the most powerful business interests in the city. Being pennyless, he is bound to lose out. However modest his space requirements are, he cannot afford to pay for them in the vicinity of likely work places. Yet, he cannot afford either to become a commuter. In the competition for casual work, his strength lies in his availability at all hours, particularly during the non-working hours of regular employees. Suburban housing and long journeys to work are unthinkable conditions for him. He has to snatch a few hours of sleep on pavements or benches in public parks or huddle up in a doorway, under a road bridge or in a public waiting room where he can shelter from rain and hope to escape the attention of the agents of law and order.

"Sleeping rough" is the first breach of the conventional code of behaviour or existing laws of the host city to which a newcomer is driven in his struggle for survival and for a foothold in the urban economy. The second is squatting. Squatting is the illegal occupation of land or buildings. In the United Nations report on Housing in Pakistan (1957/58), Charles Abrams described it aptly as a "trespass of desperation." It starts usually after a natural or man-made disaster when public opinion is on the side of the victims and ready to condone breaches of otherwise sacrosanct laws of property. Others quickly see their opportunity, and what started as an exception soon becomes common practice. Not all huts and shanties are built by the newcomers themselves. Many are put up by an earlier generation of squatters who have become "squatter landlords" and often do by letting rooms or bed spaces to later arrivals. Social surveys of squatter colonies have in some instances disclosed complex systems of letting and subletting of space in illegally occupied plots and buildings.

The location of squatter colonies follows the line of least resistance. Small groups occupy wide pavements, shopping arcades, unguarded public open spaces, parks and playgrounds, marginal land reserves along railway lines, banks of canals and temporarily unused plots of absentee landlords. Larger groups are driven to settle on stretches of land that suffer from defects which prevent their normal use, such as sites that are subject to flooding, steep hill sides, the neighbourhoods of refuse tips or sewage works. If such sites are near centres of intense urban activity, they usually harbour a majority of recent arrivals or "footholders". If they are on the outskirts, their occupants are likely to have reached the second stage of urban settlement. They have more regular employment and are therefore less dependent on proximity to their work places.

John Turner who has contributed a great deal to our understanding of the urban settlement process calls these suburban squatters "consolidators." In contrast to "footholders" for whom land ownership and housing are items of low priority, consolidators are prepared to make considerable sacrifices for the secure tenure of a piece of land and are ready and willing to invest in shelter for themselves and their families.

This striving for "a place to call their own" makes consolidators vulnerable to exploitation — not so much by squatter landlords as by equally illegitimate subdividers and land speculators. Almost all the fast growing cities around the Mediterranean and in Latin and Central America and many in Asia and Africa are surrounded by large tracts of formerly agricultural land that has been cut up into housing plots and sold to gullible newcomers with a promise of roads, services and public transport. The seller disappears with his gain, the buyer camps on a piece of land that is unconnected to the physical and social infrastructure network of the city. He starts building in the mistaken belief that by paying for his land he has acquired a right to the services and facilities enjoyed by the rest of the city population.

The third party involved in the reception of migrants from rural areas is the city government. The administrative and fiscal systems of most of the cities of the developing world date from the days of slow population growth. Many are replicas of pre- or post-demographic revolution models. Some are controlled by democratically elected councils, others by centralised administrations or political party machines. All are designed for a limited number of managerial functions which do not include planning for rapid population growth nor leadership in physical development.

The newcomers who try to settle in and around the city are almost without exception poor people. They make demands on the city's meagre financial and administrative resources, but make no contribution to the city's income. Neither housing nor infrastructure installations can be extended to keep pace with ever increasing numbers. The results are growing shortages of houses, schools, health centres and shopping facilities, inadequate road and public transport networks, water supply, drainage, waste and refuse collection systems, lack of administration and professional staff and — most important — shortages of funds to meet recurring costs and investment needs. The care and maintenance of a city at the receiving end of migration has become a nightmare job.

Local Authority Reactions

The obvious first reaction to increasing population pressure is public housing — preferably subsidised to benefit low income earners. Many countries and cities of the developing world have tried this remedy, only to find out soon that their resources were insufficient to make an impact. Lack of funds made it necessary to restrict public low income housing to city and state employees and a few demonstration or pilot projects for industrial labour. There are few growing cities where public sector built or aided houses represent more than 15 percent of the total stock. Exceptions are Singapore and Hong Kong. Both are city states that can devote much greater portions of the state's resources to public housing than other less highly urbanised states.

Local authorities have for many years operated in a climate of political and professional opinion which looked upon urban population growth as a disease and thought of newcomers as parasites. No wonder, they tend to alternate between policies of "laissez faire" and spells of radical surgery in the form of slum clearance — sometimes also euphemistically called "urban renewal." Squatters are evicted and their huts cleared by bulldozers. These operations solve nothing. The victims are forced to find shelter in other parts of the city where they form the nucleus of new slums. Scarce resources are spent on demolishing huts, instead of being used to create new accommodation. The result is the worsening of the overall housing shortage.

When slum clearance and urban renewal had failed to bring solutions, long suffering city administrators were told that the answer was resettlement. New houses had to be built *before* squatters could be moved. Land for large housing colonies was available only outside the city and cheap land only far outside. Resettlement meant therefore separation from the centres of urban activity where most of the newcomers have found a precarious living. For the "footholders," the recent or first-stage newcomers, compulsory resettlement is a severe blow. They cannot afford commuting, and the resettlement colonies themselves are ghettoes of uniformly poor families that offer few opportunities for local trade or service employment. Those who are still at the "footholder" stage drift back to the city centre. Their places in the resettlement colonies are taken by "consolidators" who are ready for suburban housing and commuting.

In contrast to the established urban communities that received very little attention from researchers, squatters have had abundant publicity and a great deal of attention from social scientists and students of urban affairs. A good deal has been published about their plight, their "un-aided selfhelp" and about the view from the barrias favellas, bidonvilles, bustees, shanty towns and gejecondas. This is one of the instances when research and publicity begin to have an effect on official policies. The world is becoming more tolerant of informal solutions. The legalisation and upgrading of squatter settlements is beginning to be preferred to eviction, demolition and forced resettlement.

Unfortunately, legalisation and upgrading often benefit also some of those who do not merit public sympathy. The term "squatter" applies not only to the pennyless newcomer who commits "a trespass of desperation"[3] by erecting his emergency shelter on land he does not own, but also the squatter landlord and

---

[3] Charles Abrams, 1957.

speculator/subdivider who exploits him. Upgrading projects help the exploiter as much as the exploited.

There is, however, a more fundamental objection to upgrading a policy: it is limited to correcting or mitigating the results of past mistakes and omissions. If cities had faced the fact of continuing population growth and planned for it, they would not find themselves compelled to spend the best part of their resources on the upgrading of unplanned settlements. Upgrading may be desirable or necessary, but it is no solution for the settlement problems of the present and the future.

Site and service schemes can be regarded as essential positive counterparts to upgrading projects. They represent two important steps forward in the thinking of city governments:

- on the one hand, they are a welcome attempt to wrestle the initiative from squatters and subdividers. It is the city that determines the location and pace of urban expansion by preparing housing plots for settlers and not waiting for them to help themselves and subsequently legalising their action;
- on the other hand, site and service schemes are an admission that the city cannot do the job alone. They are a welcome attempt at solving urban settlement problems through a sensible division of labour between public and private sector.

The formula is simple: the local authority devotes its limited resources to those parts of the job which the individual settler cannot do for himself, e.g. land and infrastructure. The newcomer is left free to do what he can do best and likes best to do: to construct a house in instalments according to the pace at which he can accumulate savings.

The fact that the practical results of the first generation of site and service projects are disappointing must not prevent us from acknowledging that they represent an impressive advance in official thinking. Many of the earlier schemes have achieved little more than the replacement of the private subdivider by an official agency. That alone is no mean feat, because it solves the age old problem of giving the city its due share of socially created land values.

Questions of project numbers and sizes are all important, if site and service schemes are to make an impact on the supply and demand situation. A one-off project of forming 15,000 housing plots over two years appears impressive, until one realizes that it is intended for a city region that grows at a rate of over 10,000 families per year. The need is not only for projects of appropriate magnitude, but also for programmes that extend over many years to meet the foreseeable demand from urban settlers.

Experience of recent years shows that plots end up in the wrong hands if site and service schemes are too small. Although plots are allotted to newcomers and other low income applicants at cost or even at subsidised rates, all manner of black market deals tend to occur and speculative deals are difficult to prevent in situations of extreme shortage. This tendency for serviced plots to end up in the hands of comparatively wealthy buyers is reinforced by rules and regulations regarding the quality and appearance of buildings. Insistence on high standards makes the buildings and thereby the plots too expensive for the groups for whom they were intended and defeats the purpose of a site and service project.

The fact that site and service schemes have been sponsored and supported by international agencies, particularly the I.B.R.D., permits feed back from one generation of projects to the other. Project evaluation surveys are due for publication. Three general rules can be distilled from the public learning process of the past years:

- Isolated (one-off) projects have little effect. Series of site and service projects are needed. They must be timed to keep pace with urban population growth.
- It is not enough to plan the production of service plots; the distribution of the plots to those for whom they are intended must form part of the project.
- Urban settlement means more than housing. Site and service schemes must form part of comprehensive plans and programmes for urban growth that encompass *all* aspects of urban life.

Towards a New Approach

The prevailing view of the economics of fast-growing cities defines the productive capacity of an urban system on the basis of formal — i.e. statistically-recorded — public and private sector production, income, consumption and investment and the volume of public revenues and expenditure which can be financed from these. Provision for fast-growing and poor populations over and above this system is considered as "welfare support" and therefore as a matter for subventions from the national exchequer. This view severely limits the field of action of local authorities.

The foregoing was intended to demonstrate:

a)   that there is more to a growing city than the conventional view takes into account, and

b)   that city and national governments have made valiant efforts to cope with their problems within the limiting framework of this conception. They may also serve to explain the feelings of despair that prevail among urban administrators when they view the widening gap between continuously-growing needs and the city's or government's capacity to satisfy them.

Substantial sums have been invested in slum clearance, urban renewal, resettlement, squatter colony upgrading and site and service schemes — to say nothing of investments in public housing, water supply and sewage schemes, traffic improvement, refuse collection and other infrastructure projects. Yet the gulf between public sector provisions and urban welfare needs is widening in all fields of municipal life and endeavour. Shortages continue and backlogs of unsatisfied demands are building up. Municipal revenues stagnate or grow at a much lower rate than expenditure. National governments become more and more reluctant to finance capital works and grant loans that are increasingly difficult to service.

Yet, life in the city goes on. Some sections clearly prosper (in conventional terms), others are busy building up a new style of life which appears as remote from that of the established citizenry as the life of the pioneers "out West" must have appeared to the brave citzens of Boston in the early nineteenth century. This is a new situation. There is clearly a case for a new approach.

According to the conventional wisdom of the "welfare approach" that has dominated urban policies for the past quarter century, newcomers are liabilities. Workers, manufacturers, traders and particularly tax or rate payers are assets. In several growing cities, the liabilities, i.e. the newcomers are more than half of the population. It is clear that charity alone — whether in the form of national or international subventions — is not enough to convert newcomers from liabilities into assets. It is equally clear that this conversion is vital for the future of the growing cities of the third world. The faster it can be achieved, the better for the economy of the cities concerned. The new approach must therefore begin with the quest for policies, plans and programmes that accelerate the process of urban settlement rather than oppose it, that assist the absorption of newcomers in the urban economy and society, that utilise the city building process itself for the creation of the jobs needed to absorb the newcomers, that produce cities that are economically viable and do not make continuous demands on natural resources. If such policies can be found, and if they are successful, they will foster the growth of cities that can support rural development not only as markets and service centres, but also through the productive absorption of a working force that is surplus to the rural economy.

The ingredients of the much needed new urban approach are best stated in the form of a brief:

There is an urgent need for policies, plans and programmes that

a)   concentrate on the potentials rather than on the problems of urban population growth,

b)   look upon migrants as a valuable national resource that needs developing,

c)   utilise the increase of job opportunities and productive capacity in the informal and formal sectors that result from concentration of populations in urban areas,

d)   assist and accelerate the absorption of newcomers in the urban community and economy,

e)   stimulate self-help and minimise the suffering inevitably associated with change and migration, and

f)   reduce the national investment needed to get the urban development process under way.

This brief covers plans and programmes for economic, physical, administrative and social development. A bundle of interlinked policies can succeed where separate efforts in one or two fields have remained ineffective. The total effort is likely to prove more powerful than the sum of its parts.

A great deal of work remains to be done before this general brief can be translated into programmes of action for particular cities. Our knowledge of the process of urban settlement needs deepening and the results of recent policies and programmes in fast growing cities need recording and evaluating in the light of the new approach.

8
Transportation and Human Settlements

Wilfred Owen, U.S.A.

Human settlements are affected in fundamental ways by three universal functions of the transportation system. First it is transportation that makes it possible for a community to exist and to survive, for it supplies the population with food and other necessities of life, it moves needed materials to factory, farm and workshop, and it delivers the products of the community to buyers elsewhere in the country and abroad. This is the role played mainly by long-distance railways, intercity highways, ships and port facilities, and more recently by national and international airlines. The human settlements of the world are in varying degrees the points of interchange along the global network of communications — road, rail, water and air. These arteries of commerce and travel differ widely among nations and regions in their ability to overcome distance and time, and to maintain the viability of the human settlements they serve.

A second and more visible function that transportation systems supply for human settlements falls in the category of local circulation of freight and passengers. Most of this occurs on community streets and highways, which accommodate the movement of pedestrians, motor vehicles, bicycles and animal-drawn vehicles. It is this internal circulation system that must be relied upon for the start and finish of every intercity freight movement or passenger trip. It is also the means of sustaining the constant flow of people, goods and ideas that is essential to the conduct of community affairs.

Thirdly, transportation is responsible, as much as any other single factor, for the quality of the environment. This is so not only because of its negative contributions to the noise, pollution and hazards of community life but because of the extent to which it is a user of land. The streets and other transportation rights of way of a community and the terminals and related concentration of transport space may absorb a fourth or more of all the space available, and these facilities therefore dominate human settlements and often determine their visual character and physical quality. More than that, these non-moving elements of the transportation system are the very framework of the community's development.

If one were to state in an abbreviated way how these three transportation functions are affecting the world's human settlements today, it would be correct to say that the transportation lifelines that feed and supply human settlements often function quite well — that modern carriers have done an especially remarkable job of making large cities accessible to their region and to the world. The major task still to be accomplished is to bring into the transportation network those smaller and intermediate-sized settlements that are still without good all-weather transport and that are poorly served by organized carriers.

With respect to internal transport systems, the opposite would generally be true. It is the larger human settlements that suffer from unsatisfactory services and the smaller communities that are often better able to handle local traffic. It is the growing capability of intercity transportation that has supported ever-larger metropolitan areas, but in the process traffic converging in the constricted space of high-density urban communities has resulted in heavy congestion. In recent years millions of automobiles have joined truck and bus traffic on the over-burdened streets of the world's great cities, multiplying the chaos of rush-hour traffic and creating enormous pressure for high-cost elevated expressways, rapid transit subways and other expensive infrastructure.

Concerning the non-transportation elements of the transportation networks located within human settlements, the impacts on the environment have been experienced by both large communities and small. Very often these impacts have been detrimental to the quality of life, largely because little thought has been given to the possibilities of locating, designing and using the streets as a means of enhancing the community. The spacious boulevards and quiet residential streets of many great cities are in sharp contrast to heavily travelled commercial arteries where uncontrolled development encroaches on the travelled way and adds to the undesirable condition of adjacent neighbourhoods. Most human settlements of any size have failed to recognize the important role of the streets in the daily life of the people and in the efficient operations of the community.

These positive and negative aspects of transportation in relation to human settlements demand much more consideration as we approach the time, late in the twentieth century, when this planet will be more urban than rural. The task ahead is first to supply the national and regional networks of transportation that will support a physical pattern of human settlement locations considered in the public interest. Second, a task of rapidly increasing complexity is to arrive at internal transportation system solutions that overcome the congestion and high social costs of urban concentrations. Third is the need everywhere to view transportation, location, and design decisions as integral parts of a strategy to improve the quality of life for human beings.

Transportation for Rural Settlement

Many millions of people engaged primarily in agriculture are living in human settlements that are almost completely isolated. At a time of growing concern over world food supplies, the ability of these settlements to be connected with the rest of the market economy is a universal concern. The importance of transportation is strikingly clear in the contrast between a village that has ready access to markets and one that is without an all-weather road connexion or perhaps any road whatever. In the latter case there is little knowledge of the outside world, no scientific methods of agriculture, no cash coming into the village, no health services, veterinary services or adequate means of education. Crops are disposed of for whatever they will bring locally. But the village with a good road and some degree of dependable bus and truck service presents a very different picture. Seed, fertilizer and other inputs to intensive agriculture find their way into this settlement, cash crops are marketed regularly, and consumer goods can be purchased at the market place. Children travel to neighbouring schools, the agricultural extension worker and the veterinarian reach this settlement, and transportation cost by truck falls sharply below what was incurred to move goods by human and animal power.

The relations between immobility and poverty and between mobility and affluence have been well documented. The question is what to do. Already many countries are allocating 20 to 30 percent of total public investment to transportation. Still there are countless miles of local rural roads to be built, and many major intercity routes need to be modernized at high cost. It is impossible to supply all human settlements with instant accessibility. The task is to supplement national economic planning with physical and spatial planning to assure that resources available for transportation are invested in the specific network of human settlements best able to carry out goals in other sectors. A rural road programme might focus on those human settlements selected to serve as market centres and potentially able to participate in intensive cultivation efforts. Or transport programmes might be determined by development plans for minerals, forestry or fisheries. Transportation priorities need to be derived from priorities in other sectors.

A strategy for transportation and national patterns of human settlement begins with the concept of resource conservation: how much transportation will be required to produce a given value of national product. In developed countries a given percentage increase in national product will generally involve a comparable percentage increase in the volume of freight. In earlier stages of development, freight burdens increase more rapidly than output. That is, where national product is increasing at the rate of 3 to 5 percent a year, it is likely that freight traffic by road and rail will be up 6 to 10 percent or more per year. A strategy for transportation should aim at avoiding unnecessary transportation in the creation of wealth, involving such factors as the choice of transport technology, stage construction methods, the location of human settlements to be included in the network, the extent to which processing and storage can reduce unnecessary movement, and in general the efficiency of transport operations. In these and other ways the nation, in earning a livelihood, will produce the greatest net increase in value of product for a given outlay in public infrastructure.

But the isolation of rural settlements is also a matter of what services are available in the area, rather than what means of transport are available to move people to where the desired services are situated. Thus a strategy for achieving a wider distribution of human settlements involves a concentration not only of transport resources but of schools, hospitals, telephone and other communications, job creation, and the introduction of opportunities and amenities comparable to those that are presumed to be available in the larger cities.

It is not intended in this brief report to do more than allude to the problems of intercity and rural transport. What is especially important to the subject of human settlements, however, is that with limited transport resources it is not possible to supply all-weather connexions to whatever planless pattern of community locations emerges. The need is to weigh the transportation and other infrastructure costs of alternative patterns of settlements that might be encouraged and to avoid those that so dissipate the nation's resources that even the need for equity among regions is not sufficient to defend them. In a word, wise transportation policy has to be based on a deliberate effort to introduce national land-use planning into national economic and social planning. Without the spatial context, transportation efforts become diffused and human settlements will not be well served.

Internal Transport for Large Urban Concentrations

In many parts of the world cities already overcrowded and suffering critical transportation problems will double their population by the end of this decade and triple their ownership of automobiles. Traffic congestion has reached staggering proportions, public transit is grossly inadequate, and pressures are mounting for costly engineering solutions. Countries in all stages of growth confront the problem of how the automobile is to be accommodated, what measures might be taken to make public transit work, and what urban growth policies and community designs might be adopted to reduce the causes of congestion that disrupt the free flow of people and freight.

The importance of a combined strategy for transportation and urban development stems not only from the critical problems of the moment but from population projections that assume nearly a thousand million more people in the cities of developing countries between now and the year 2000.[1] This massive increase in urban population will be accompanied by a continuing expansion of car ownership and use. In the face of these trends, the question is whether innovations in public policy can alleviate overcrowding, disorder, and pollution, all of which threaten developing countries in particular.

Motorization, urbanization and affluence go together, and the world is becoming more urban, its big cities more affluent, and its people more intent on driving. The 1970 world passenger car total was nearly double the 1960 figure, and car ownership is expected to double again by 1985. By the end of the century the world may have over 500 million cars in operation.[2] Developing countries accounted for fewer than 17 million cars in 1970, but they could own over 100 million by the year 2000. The uncertainty of petroleum supplies and prices remains, but the possibilities of more energy-efficient vehicles and of alternative methods of propulsion are also unknown. It is not yet clear if or when man will alter his age-old preference for private transport.

The impact of these growth trends is most threatening to the major cities. If the trends continue, Caracas is expected to double its population and triple the number of its automobiles in less than 20 years. In Lima the number of cars will quadruple between 1970 and 1985, and there will also be 2 million more people. Istanbul will have six times as many cars in 1990 as in 1970. Buenos Aires is expected to have 4 million more people by 2000, and 1.5 million more cars, while Sao Paulo will have 13 million more people and 2 million more automobiles. If these projections turn out to be right, today's traffic conditions are only a foretaste of the chaos to come.

Despite these nightmare statistics most people in big cities are too poor to own a car, and the majority will continue to be carless. As a general observation, therefore, it can be said that the automobile will play a limited role in most urban settlements of Asia, Africa and Latin America, and that most people will depend on walking, cycling, and public transport. In cities such as Seoul, Bombay, Calcutta, Lima, Bogotá, and

---

[1] See International Bank for Reconstruction and Development, *Urban Sector Paper*, 1972, p. 12.
[2] Projections to 1985 are based on OECD data. Figures to the year 2000 have been provided by Gerald Leach, "The motor car and natural resources," Working Paper No. 4, OECD, Paris, 1972.

Mexico City, four out of five trips today are by public transit, mostly bus.

The bicycle and more recently the motor cycle and motor scooter are also playing a significant role. In a selected group of 22 countries in the developing world there were 40 million motorized two-wheelers on the registration lists in 1970, and generally two to four times as many non-motorized two-wheelers. There was also substantial dependence on walking as a solution to the transportation problems of the centre city. Over half of all trips are made on foot in Dar es Salaam, and about one out of four in Seoul. The poor either operate outside the transport system or do not travel at all.

The motorist, the pedestrian and the bus rider represent the new classes of the modern world, and the major conflict of interest is between the car owners and the carless. In the United States and in developing countries, and to a lesser degree in Europe, the population of human settlements is becoming divided between the mobile and the immobile. Public transit is almost everywhere inadequate, from the overcrowded New York subway to the overloaded buses of Bangkok and the packed trains of Bombay. Public transportation is uncomfortable, unreliable and excessively slow, and the major transportation challenge is what can be done to improve it.

The question, once raised on the grounds of congestion and later of equity, has gained new importance from the standpoint of energy-efficiency. Current patterns of city travel create a highly unfavourable energy-output result. Most cars, with two people riding, get about the same number of passenger miles to a gallon of fuel as a Boeing 747. A city bus provides about three times as much transportation for a given amount of fuel as an ordinary car, and a city metro in rush hours will probably be four to eight times more energy-efficient than most automobiles.

The energy-efficiency of different methods of transportation varies not only with the technology, however, but with the number of passengers actually being transported, so that a group-riding taxi with four passengers is more energy-efficient than a bus with rush-hour load. Conversely, a subway that is little used in off-peak hours may be highly inefficient in terms of passenger miles generated per unit of energy. What is needed, therefore, is a system of transportation that incorporates vehicles that are energy-efficient for the purposes they are designed to serve, and which are then used in ways that take advantage of their inherent efficiencies. It is some such desirable combination of transportation methods that is needed to supply the levels of mobility required in urban areas.

Whether or not new rail rapid-transit systems offer solutions commensurate with the costs is a question still unresolved. On the positive side the speed, comfort and safety of new subway facilities are impressive, and they permit greater efficiency of movement for considerable numbers of people under high density conditions. Rapid transit saves space and supplies a fixed framework for the development of the urban area. When a rapid transit facility is constructed, a great many other structures follow, and the city becomes much more compact, with high-density development centring around the subway stations. This may be desirable or undesirable, depending on how these developments take place and how well they are planned, but the potentials are impressive.

The reasons given for doubts about rapid transit include its initial cost, its often unnecessarily high capacity, the inflexible nature of its fixed location, the fear of early obsolescence, the relatively limited percentage of total urban trips accommodated, and the fact that low-income families are generally unable to afford rapid transit.

An obvious drawback is that rapid transit cost trends have been steadily upward, and an extensive network capable of serving a large metropolitan area involves high total outlays. In the United States it can generally be expected that initial rapid transit investment will be about $1,000 per person living in the area served. Financial data indicate that no part of capital costs for rapid transit can be paid out of fare revenues, and large subsidies are required for operations as well. Rapid transit thus competes with other urgent needs such as housing, health and education, and low-income residents appear to benefit least. Fares on rapid transit systems are likely to be higher than bus fares, and for short trips typical of travel needs in the inner city the bus is likely to provide a better service. As Mexico and Tokyo attest, the subway may intensify congestion by promoting higher densities and greater concentration of people and economic activity in the central city, and by forcing residential neighbourhoods to move farther out.

The cost of rapid transit, however, may not be so high when viewed in relation to the cost of operating the whole urban system. Total urban costs may be less with rapid transit than without, and the benefits of concentration made possible by a subway may be greater. The latter depends on whether land use plans are carried out to assure locations and arrangements of economic activity that are consistent with the transportation made available, so that transportation supply and demand are kept in reasonable balance and over-crowding is avoided. Measures will need to be taken to control individual location decisions made in response to the additional transport capacity. Otherwise downtown will be converted to high-rise office buildings, residets will be pushed farther out from the centre by rising rents, and the added transport capacity will be filled by the new crop of commuters.

In assessing the desirability of rapid transit, therefore, it is necessary to extend the analysis beyond transportation to the urban system as a whole. If rapid transit makes possible large cost reductions through high-density land uses, as well as substantial benefits in the organization of economic activity, then the system may be warranted. It may not be the high cost of rail transportation relative to other transportation solutions that is critical, but rather the comparative total costs and benefits of alternative urban settlements supportable by selected transportation solutions.

The new San Francisco subway, moving at speeds up to 80 miles per hour, cannot fail to arouse considerable enthusiasm on the part of the rider, and it is understandable that Teheran, Manila, Bombay and other cities should consider the possibility of similar high standards of performance. The quality of the ride is not in question, however, but rather the cost, who pays the cost, and who benefits. Only 3 percent of Bay Area trip takers will be using the rapid transit system, each ride will cost the general taxpayer at least a dollar above what is collected in fares, and high-speed transit that requires long distances between stops to permit the train to accelerate and decelerate does not supply the easily accessible, cheap, short-haul travel that most people want.

Money spent for buses goes much farther. This is because the roadways for buses are mostly in place, and all the transit money goes for equipment. A further advantage of the bus is its shorter life — probably 10 years rather than the 40 to 50 years typical of rail rolling stock. The bus therefore involves less initial investment and takes less time and ingenuity to be brought into service. It can also provide low cost, frequent, short-haul travel over a very extensive geographic area. But the economic advantage of sharing the streets with other traffic is often a major physical drawback to good service, and successful bus operations may depend on setting aside city-wide networks of streets for the exclusive use of buses during peak hours. A combination of new buses, bus roadways, traffic control, and traffic regulation that excludes automobiles from specific routes or downtown areas could achieve effective results at reasonable economic cost, but not always at acceptable political cost.

If an effort to improve bus transport were undertaken for the larger cities of the developing world, the cost of the programme would be well within practical limits. Under existing practice, cities are operating about 500 buses per million urban residents. The gross overcrowding that is now customary and the lack of adequate geographic coverage suggest that double this number of buses might be required at the outset to furnish acceptable standards, assuming service improvement at the same time through traffic engineering.

It is estimated that developing countries in 1970 had about 270 million people in cities of over 500,000 population.[3] The size of their bus fleets is estimated at 135,000 units. Doubling this fleet to 270,000 units at a cost of $30,000 per bus would require an outlay of $4 billion. This is about equal to the investment required for eight subway systems comparable to the Mexico City Metro. The additional buses (assuming 1,000 passengers per bus per day) could carry 135 million passengers per day compared to a combined total capacity of 10 million passengers for the eight subway systems.

The bus alone, however, is unlikely to meet all transportation requirements, and it may be desirable to supplement this form of public transit by organizing the taxi as a more integral part of the system. Urban traffic patterns show that the popularity of the group-riding taxi, or public automobile, is rapidly expanding in such cities as Seoul, Teheran, Singapore, Caracas, Bogota and in many cases the bus has already lost considerable ground to the more convenient jitney taxi. If extensive and better organized public automobile fleets were used as a supplement to the bus, or as a substitute, they could supply service comparable to that of the automobile, eliminate parking problems, and reduce the social gap that separates car owners from the carless by providing all urban residents with physically comparable equipment. Sixteen thousand taxis could perform the work of 100,000 automobiles. But some means of separating automobile from other traffic and of reducing the use of private cars is essential.

---

[3] Based on UN population estimates contained in "Urbanization: Development Policies and Planning," *International Social Development Review*, No. 1, 1968, p. 19.

Methods of limiting traffic include three types: restraints, such as higher fees for urban street use or higher charges for parking; restrictions, such as the designation of vehicle-free zones; and avoidance, such as designing urban activity systems that reduce the need for vehicle movement.[4]

Pricing urban road services, banning street parking, and reflecting social costs in the fees paid by motorists could help reduce congestion quickly, with relatively minor investments in buses or other public transport. Pricing policy could act as a rationing device that would reduce the peaks and shift travel from private cars to public vehicles. One approach would be to use the proceeds of what the motorist pays to subsidize transit and reflect its social benefits. By keeping transit fares low, it might be possible to minimize the total transportation bill.

At the present time automobiles are generally able to park on the streets without charge. They are not paying the social costs of air pollution, accidents, and environmental destruction. In addition, automobile user charges are uniform regardless of where and when the travel is performed, so that peak-hour commuters are being subsidized by off-peak drivers. The simplest remedy appears to be the banning of free parking, which is a burden on the city, and introduction of parking charges for off-street facilities that reflect both the cost of parking and the costs incurred for peak-hour driving[5]

Other low-cost remedies for traffic congestion include the banning of automobile traffic in limited areas of the city and the dedication of the streets to pedestrians and transit vehicles. About 100 vehicle-free zones and pedestrian shopping streets have been created in European cities with moderate financial commitment and physical change, often by simply paving over streets and installing lights and landscaping. Other means of regulating vehicle use have been introduced in Goteberg, Sweden, where the division of the city into separate sectors and the prohibition of direct movement of cars from one sector to another has had favourable effects on traffic flow and on the environment.

A recent survey of opinion in Sweden, the most highly motorized country in Europe, shows that vehicle-free zones are gaining acceptance among car owners. A surprising 77 percent of all persons interviewed expressed the view that cars are unnecessary in central city areas. High value is placed on the automobile by farmers and residents of smaller cities and towns, but in the big city there is an "outspokenly negative attitude towards the automobile".[6]

What these data mean is that all big cities could solve their traffic congestion problems at relatively low cost if it were politically possible to restrict the use of private cars in certain areas or on specified major streets, and to cater instead to public transit vehicles, freight movement, and the needs of pedestrians and bicyclists. The result would be to save billions of dollars that would otherwise be spent for increasing transport capacity without providing the mobility and equity called for, and without ever coming to grips with the underlying causes of congestion.[7]

Transportation and the Total Environment

Human settlements are suffering from traffic congestion regardless of the prevailing transport technology. This reflects a global weakness of public policy, namely the tendency to focus exclusively on supplying transportation capacity and to neglect the factors creating the demand for transportation. Without measures designed to influence demand, efforts to assure an adequate supply of transportation often turn out to be futile. For example, central cities that ignore the need for shelter and concentrate on office buildings soon find that residents are forced by rising property values to live at increasing distances from the centre, resulting

---

[4] J. Michael Thomson, "Methods of traffic limitation in urban areas," Working Paper No. 3, OECD, Paris, 1972.

[5] For a fuller discussion of automobile and transit subsidies and user charges, see Wilfred Owen, *The Metropolitan Transportation Problem* (Brookings, 1966), pp. 142-164, and *The Accessible City* (Brookings, 1972), pp. 46-48.

[6] "The automobile in Swedish society," a social research project for the Swedish Road Federation, Stockholm, 1971.

[7] Singapore is making a full-scale demonstration of rush-hour automobile restraints through road pricing, parking fees, and the expansion of bus transport.

in expanded demand for commuter services. The resulting transportation problem is basically a problem in the organization of living and working space.

If the transportation problems of the cities are to be satisfactorily resolved, the locations, densities and patterns of urban activity cannot be ignored as elements in the picture. These elements are overlooked because existing transportation institutions require that transportation problems be resolved by transportation solutions. But efforts to ameliorate transportation problems cannot be divorced from the relentless addition to these problems created by urban growth. Transportation remedies do not lie exclusively in more buses, subways and highways but must also be found in locating job opportunities adjacent to housing developments, in efforts to clean up the environment to permit more close-in living, and in the design of structures for multiple uses, including housing, shops, offices, and recreation. Urban growth needs to be guided in ways that promote transport-saving communities.

The world must build urban settlements for a thousand million new residents by the end of this century, while rebuilding obsolete facilities for as many as a thousand million more. The massive urban development programmes that will have to be carried out one way or another offer great opportunities for resolving transportation problems while creating a better planned environment.

The planned cities of the world, granted their short-comings, have introduced new concepts of urban design that help us visualize how existing cities might be redesigned and further urban growth guided to create more satisfactory living environments that are also transportation efficient. The lessons are provided by the successes and failures of British New Towns, of Singapore, Brasilia, Chandigarh, Tema in Ghana and many others. If some of the best features of these planned communities were combined, urban development in the future would result in a rearrangement of housing and services, with neighbourhoods free from the intrusions of traffic, and housing accessible to jobs, shops, services and recreation. Mobility is one way of making things accessible, but accessibility can also be achieved by the way things are located and arranged. A series of clustered activities that provide easy access by local transport or pedestrian pathways to neighbourhood shopping centres, and that are provided with nearby employment opportunities and recreation, seem preferable to a planless urbanization that uses transportation to compensate for disorder.

The plan of Jarvafaltet in Sweden is an example. Instead of the usual town centre and clustered neighbourhoods, this largest Swedish new town is being laid out with a single linear employment and service area seven kilometres long and one kilometre wide. Two strips of housing are being built parallel to this employment strip, each about one kilometre wide. It is recognized that housing and work places need to be close together, but that it is undesirable to have large industrial plants intruding into housing areas. Housing is therefore insulated from the factory strip, but is made readily accessible to it by a short trip to the linear work area, at which point a shuttle service will provide longitudinal travel. Jarvafaltet is also being designed with all-bus streets, reserved bus lanes on expressways, and drive-through underground utility tunnels.[8]

This design is carried out in Mexico's new city of Cuautitlan Izcalli, now under construction 25 miles from Mexico City to accommodate 1.6 million people by 1980. The city is being built in parallel strips of housing, commercial establishments, and industrial development, using the main limited access highway as the major structural component of the linear community. The attraction of such a design from the standpoint of transportation is that expansion can take place by extending the development and housing strips, thus avoiding long commuter trips through built-up areas from distant suburbs to a city centre.

An important urban rehabilitation and growth plan in process today is that of Bogotá, Colombia, where the United Nations has been helping to finance a new pattern of development that will, it is hoped, reduce unnecessary transportation and help create better systems of public transportation. Every year 300,000 people are being added to the population of Bogotá, creating heavy congestion and severely taxing the available supply of transport services. The 1973 population of 3 million is expected to reach a total of 8 or 9 million by 1990. This growth and a moderate expansion in car ownership are expected to paralyse the central city as commuting from the high-income northside to the constricted centre continues to itensify street congestion. The choices offered by existing trends are either to allow the centre to deteriorate for lack of access or to build costly expressways and rapid transit. These would transform the centre into a daytime commercial area where residential uses of land would be replaced by offices and other commercial developments able to afford the rents that rising land values would impose. In the process an unplanned outward push of the population would absorb much of the vacant land now surrounding the city, which is an important source of food, and

[8] Igor Dergalin, "Planning of Jarvafaltet," Interregional Seminar on New Towns, London, 4-19 June 1973.

would extend commuting distances. The result would be a disorderly dispersal, a worsening environment, destruction of much of the city's natural beauty, and the elimination of needed recreation.

The United Nations-World Bank study of Bogotá has resulted in a recommendation to build three new satellite communities on the periphery to accommodate growth and to provide a mix of housing and jobs outside the congested area. The downtown area would be redeveloped to assure a mix of apartments and office building. Approximately 100,000 jobs that do not need to be downtown would be syphoned off into the new satellites. Extensive pedestrian walkways and good bus service on exclusive rights of way will be built into the satellites.

Unlike many other cities, Bogota has not included a subway in its plans, but has opted for surface rail lines from the city centre to the satellites, plus a reationalization of the bus system. Part of the plan is to reroute buses passing through the centre but having destinations elsewhere, which may eliminate 30 to 40 percent of the bus traffic now congesting the centre. Measures recommended to control the automobile include the creation of auto-free zones in the city's historic centre, restrictions on downtown parking, designation of exclusive bus lanes and bus streets, and higher taxes on peak hour use of private cars.

Karachi, Pakistan, indicates on a smaller scale how planned community growth can serve to minimize local transportation problems. There, a growth plan financed through the United Nations Development Programme has recommended the creation of a series of "metrovilles" or compact communities of 40,000 to 50,000 people, focusing on self-help housing and on public programmes of integrated water, sewer and street systems as well as close-by schools, clinics, markets and bus depot, and light industry capable of employing large volumes of local labour.[9] Four metrovilles are scheduled for the first year of the programme. The growth strategy, recognizing the inevitability of Karachi's expanding population, creates an orderly growth process designed to conserve resources, avoid unnecessary transportation, and reduce the distances between homes and work places.

These and other cities — Singapore and its satellites, Shah Alam in Malaysia and many others — are building a significant new partnership between transportation and urban development that promises to make the transport system a major contribution to the design of better human settlements, while the resulting designs help to reduce the causes of congestion and the intensity of transport problems. It is a partnership that may be one of the most hopeful signs that the growth of urban populations can contribute to economic and social advance rather than to congestion and confusion. A rapidly urbanizing world has begun to recognize that it is suffering from a conflict between the basic nature of communities and the changing nature of their communications. The community has traditionally provided communications by locating activities close together. The automobile, however, has provided a new means of communications which overcomes distance but in the process pre-empts a large percentage of available space and encourages dispersal at low densities. This has made it increasingly difficult to supply public transit, which requires higher densities to remain viable, and it has created major disadvantages for the carless, who must operate in an environment that presupposes the availability of a car. As a result, all three methods of communications are proving to be unsatisfactory: the city, the automobile and transit. The problem facing human settlements is how to come to grips with all three systems of communications in a way that will provide accessibility, enhance the environment, conserve resources and assure equity.

An Overview

The transportation problems relating to human settlements derive in part from over-all growth — the fact that more people, more food, more energy and more materials of all kinds will have to be moved from where they are to where their destinations lie. And since mankind is increasingly coming to concentrate in communities, large and small, the origins and destinations of movement are increasingly dependent on the location and size of these settlements. As many of these settlements grow to mammoth dimensions, internal transportation problems assume a higher priority while national and regional transportation problems tend to be neglected.

If trends in much of the world continue along existing lines, the transportation problem of human

[9]PADCO, Karachi Master Plan Project, 1974.

settlements will become acute for two reasons. One is that urbanized areas such as Cairo, Karachi, Calcutta, Sao Paulo, Caracas, Bangkok and Bogotá, ever-expanding in size and complexity, will demand very large increases in transport investments, both absolute and in relation to what is available to build the critical connexions that must be maintained with outside sources of supply. In other words, increasing efforts will be necessary just to combat congestion, and correspondingly less may be allocated to the larger network. The vital links between domestic food supplies and big cities may be threatened, and between major ports and rural hinterlands which may depend on global sources of food and fertilizer.

If we look ahead to the probable results of these trends, two types of problem come to mind. First, it is clear that the automobile and the big city are incompatible systems. The two together breed congestion, necessitate high-cost remedies, and defy ultimate solution because growth and response to growth never come into balance. The subway solution makes possible temporary relief of the situation existing at the time the decision is made to build. But the feedback effects (more growth and density, more job concentration and more automobile traffic) will make decongestion short-lived. Rapid transit solutions will not supply an answer without one or both of two other decisions: to limit the use of automobiles or to limit and restructure the growth of large human settlements.

To illustrate, a city that elects to build a rapid transit system (together with the necessary bus feeder lines and surface buses on non-rapid transit routes) might ban cars from congested areas in rush hours through appropriate regulations or pricing policies. It might also, as in the case of Bogotá, attempt to rearrange and limit the growth of the central city and to guide further expansion into satellite communities. The latter action would be designed to delineate efficient public transit corridors and to reduce traffic among different geographic areas of the city by making the various parts of the metropolis (especially the satellites) partially self-contained.

But a fundamental question is raised by this strategy. If effective operation of rapid transit and expressways is dependent on reducing automobile use and restructuring the metropolis, it should be possible to overcome congestion by taking these two courses of action first, to see whether the costly investments in high-capacity transportation are actually necessary. If good transportation is possible without them, then resources can be released for strengthening rural and intercity transportation linkages between the metropolis and the entire national network of human settlements. If this reallocation of transportation resources is accompanied by a reallocation of public funds to support community facilities and services in selected human settlements away from the primate city, then it may be possible to achieve another result. Instead of encouraging growth where the concentration of population is already burdensome, public investments can be made to encourage a greater dispersal of human settlements. This could lead to the creation of an integrated multicentred, regional economy capable of absorbing the growth potentials of human settlements without the devastating effects that now result from permitting a single city to grow to unmanageable proportions.

It is not suggested that there is an optimum size for cities, since we know that different people, technology and resources favor widely different living conditions. Rather, it is contended that cities of whatever size need to be brought into internal balance or consistency, and that in achieving such balance there is probably an optimal size for any given city, and something approaching an optimal network of human settlements for any given region or national economy.

9
Popular Participation in Housing

John F.C. Turner, United Kingdom

This section is intended as a contribution to the clarification of the issues of citizen and community participation in housing and local development, and to the proper statement of the operational problems that commonly arise. The most searching lights can be thrown on these problems by participants and by the administrators of programmes and institutions in which residents of local communities participate. This paper by an observer not currently either administering or participating in local development, is therefore written to clear the arena for debate between actors with present responsibilities, and so to help them to distinguish between issues of general concern and their own local problems in which the broad issues are manifest. This section is therefore addressed first to practitioners and others who are directly concerned with housing and local development problems that could be more effectively dealt with through citizen participation.

The problems which programmes for popular participation commonly set out to solve are presented here as the inevitable consequences of inappropriate uses of the same or similar organisations that often sponsor public participation. Even if central agencies funding programmes of popular participation do not themselves employ large-scale industrial and managerial organisations for planning, building and maintaining housing and dwelling environments, it is generally taken for granted that these represent the "efficient and modern way" and that local building must be converted "into a large-scale, efficient industry."[1] This latter assumption is challenged on its own material grounds of productivity and, therefore, the commonly asserted "problem" of popular participation is seen as a mis-statement in most instances. If large-scale industry is inefficient and even counter-productive when applied to the development of dwelling environments, as this paper suggests, then the problem of participation has more to do with participation of central authority in local affairs than the other way around. In Marshall McLuhan's terms, it is the penumbra which the vehicles for popular participation bring in their train that constitutes the problem.

The vital question for all concerned with participation wherever they are is: *Whose participation in whose decisions?* There are two possible answers to this question in most particular cases in all contexts: local participation in centrally administered programmes or central authorities' participation in locally controlled activities. Unless this issue is raised and appropriate positions are taken on particular cases or typical situations, the practical problems of participation will be misstated. As Georges Bernanos observed, there is no greater error than an improperly stated problem. As soon as the basic issue of who decides what for whom has been raised, it is clear that very different problems are seen to arise according to the position taken. The problem of integrating local participants into central decision making structures is an entirely different problem from that of the participation of central authority in local affairs. The common confusion of these essentially different problems, and the consequently inappropriate policies so often attempted is the greatest single reason for the common failures of programmes based on citizen and community participation.

This section concludes that both forms of participation are vital because they are complementary. The paradigms and their analysis show that *while local control over necessarily diverse personal and local goods and services – such as housing – is essential, local control depends on personal and local access to resources which only central authority can guarantee.* Evidence from all contexts shows that while the proper and full *use of the* most plentiful resources available for housing (and any other locally specific personal service) depends on local control, equal *access* to those resources, or the freedom to use them for those willing and able to do so in socially constructive ways, depends on central legislation and, of course, its administration. It follows that there are three principal problems: first, the intervention of central authority in local affairs in order to ensure that equal access to resources and, of course, the compatibility of complementary or adjacent forms of development; second, the participation of citizens and their local organisations and institutions in the formulation and administration of that legislation; and third, the drawing of boundaries between local control and central planning.

Two composite cases are used to illustrate the issues and problems, and to show the kind of evidence that supports the proposition. Although based on facts, the histories described are hypothetical, although the coincidences with some well-known cases are neither accidental nor unintended.

The first, an "uncontrolled urban settlement"[2] provides a paradigm used to illustrate the issues and problems of popular participation. It is based on a form of settlement best known through Latin American examples but, in its many variations, is very widely distributed both geographically and historically.[3] It is contrasted with the second, the centrally administered sites and services project, that also has historical precedents and is currently being employed by many governments of low-income countries, often with the persuasive support of international development agencies.[4] The critical difference between "self-governing" and the "centrally administered" forms of settlement is clear if King Edward II of England's terminology for Medieval "town plantation" are used: to devise, order and array. "The devising would select and procure the site; the ordering would organise the recruitment of townsmen and furnish them with privileges and legal security; the arraying would give the new town the physical accoutrements appropriate for its role." (The last sentence in this quotation is also significant but not immediately relevant to the present point: "The final purpose as expressed in the same writ, was the greatest profit for Ourselves and merchants.")[5] The squatters do their own devising, order their own recruitments and array their own settlements. Conventional housing projects are first "devised" by a government agency, then they are "arrayed" and only after that are they organised socially and institutionally. The more recent sites and services programmes, on the other hand, depart less from Edward II's eminently practical procedure. The central authority "arrays" some of the "accoutrements" in anticipation of recruitment and leaves the rest to the settlers. All the King's planners did was to draw the boundaries for the legally secured plots.

The Self-Governing Settlement[6]

The settlement is on the edge of a large and rapidly growing capital city in Latin America. The settlement has a present population of about 5,000 and is itself rapidly increasing but more in population than in area. The present gross density is about 75 persons to the hectare but this could double if current trends continue for another decade. It was established 10 years ago and the great majority of dwellings, mostly on plots between 140 m² and 160 m² in regularly laid out, conventional blocks, are built, or being built of brick and concrete. About one fifth of the plots are either underoccupied or underdeveloped and about one fifth are fully developed with structures of two stories or more, of relatively high construction standards but often of deficient design. (The most common defect are interior rooms with grossly inadequate daylighting and ventilation — a very serious matter in a society with high incidences of tuberculosis).[7] The remaining three fifths of the dwellings (and other community, commercial and small industrial premises) are at intermediate stages of construction but all have at least the rooms fronting on the street completed. (There are no set-backs — all private property is used up to the boundaries and these are generally defined by masonry walls where there is little or no permanent building within.) The only social characteristics that distinguished the locality from any other lower and moderate-income neighbourhood in the city is that the great majority of adults were born in the provinces — most, however, migrated long before they moved to their present homes. There are only a few households with members of professional and managerial status, nor are there very many of the lowest-income category; the great majority have incomes not far from the median for the city as a whole. The settlement has been recently made into a municipality with a mayor appointed by the metropolitan government, itself an appointed body. (Central government is elected, however.)

As mentioned above, the self-governing settlement started by "ordering" itself. A small group of inner-city renters threatened with eradication in a street-widening scheme got together to discuss their common problem.

Most of the neighbours were either unable or unwilling to accept the offer of a new rent-purchase unit in a planned public housing project. The unwillingness of some was due to suspicions that it would never be built or, if so, that it would be allocated to others as the result of some other crisis or political pressures that would overshadow their own. As demolition had already started at the other end of the street, it seemed highly unlikely that the new accommodation would be ready in time, assurances to the contrary notwithstanding. So, when the word was passed round that an association was to be formed that would seek alternative solutions its membership rapidly increased to about 300 families — rather more than the total number to be removed.

The initially self-appointed leadership, whose position was confirmed by formal nomination and a unanimous show of hands in the first general meeting, continued to meet with great frequency taking care that no outsiders had access to their deliberations. They met mainly to devise ways and means of getting land. The leadership made a largely symbolic application to the government for land on which to build their own homes, knowing that this was against government policy and that there were no precedents for such a seemingly obvious and simple response to popular demand (especially as the government owned huge tracts of commercially valueless and marginal desert land). While going through these legally and politically significant motions, the association committee got down to the serious business of finding a suitable site for a planned invasion. Eventually, one was found that had been improperly acquired by a landowner known to be unpopular with the government. An appropriate date was fixed, the eve of the national celebration of independence, and an appropriate name was chosen, that of the President's popular wife, and the invasion was successfully carried out with only nominal opposition from the authorities.

Immediately after the invasion, the site was surveyed, and a plan for its subdivision was drawn up by some members who worked as assistant surveyors helped by a group of students from the nearby university. Meanwhile, the 300-odd families who joined in the initial invasion, and about 200 latecomers subsequently admitted (for a somewhat larger fee) camped in a provisional settlement to one side of the site. As soon as the plans were completed and traced out on the ground, plots were distributed through a somewhat confusing mixture of chance by lottery, personal choice, bribery and subsequent exchanges. This resulted, in general, in those with the highest incomes possessing the sites with the highest potential values, and the poorest being relegated to the margins. Protests about these inequities were rare, however, as there is an obvious collective advantage in maximising the incentives to invest by those that have the most capital and in minimising the disincentives that follow from stagnation through a lack of investment.

Once the site was occupied and all or almost all plots allocated, and once *de facto* possession was evident from the inaction of the authorities, support for the organising committee fell off sharply. Rival groups appeared, interested in capitalising on discontented groups who had been poorly represented by the association leadership (especially the latecomers, who soon outnumbered the original membership). Until other problems began to be felt acutely, such as the lack of a running water supply and the high cost of water bought from privately owned tankers, and the lack of electricity, there were no general motives for collective action and neighbourhood politics. After a few years, these demands grew sufficiently to regenerate the association which, under a new leadership, began to agitate for recognition by central government and for the provision of basic utilities and other services which the community had failed to provide for itself. It was by no means ineffective, however, having succeeded in establishing bus routes, a flourishing retail trade and market, and elementary schools (subsequently incorporated into the state education system). But the association had failed in its attempts to install an electricity supply, in spite of a very substantial investment. It was beyond the association's capacity to install piped water supply, as the sources were beyond the area it controlled, and the owner of the intervening land (who claimed the site) impeded even subsequent government efforts to provide a service.

The third state of development started with central government intervention through which the settlers' top priority — security of tenure — was obtained with the official "recognition" of the *de facto* settlement. The ex-squatters were glad to pay a moderate land tax which confirmed their possession. This official 're-ordering' process was followed with the municipalisation of the settlement and the appointment of a mayor. As this was not an election, no chance was given to the community's own association of consolidating its institutional status — instead, it was destroyed. With the exception of converting some caretakers, secondary squatters and tenants into owners, the institutionalisation of the settlement did not affect the composition of the population, and the change was generally welcomed.

The complement of the government's popular settlement legalisation programme was an improvement programme in which utilities and other essential services that such communities were unable to provide for themselves are installed by government agencies. Although far from perfectly planned and administered — and though initially failing to take advantage of the major contributions the community was able and willing to make, both in skills and labour time, and in cash, this was also a popular and generally successful programme. Much progress has been made since toward the policy goal of providing government services in response to local community demands — and by right rather than its depending on short-term programmes subject to political whims and momentary changes. This necessarily central intervention in the "arrayment" of self-governing settlements demonstrates, or at least strongly suggests, a highly appropriate mode of settlement development — not at all unlike King Edward II of England's generally successful and highly economic "town plantation" strategy.

The vast scale of unauthorised, uncontrolled, and even outright squatter settlement emphasises the relative insignificance of sponsored low-income housing in most rapidly urbanising countries. During the past few decades many governments with low per capita budgets have attempted to substitute modern standard dwellings for the great mass of housing that reflects either their inhabitants' income levels, or distortions introduced by counter-productive legislation (such as high minimum standards and rent controls). Confronted by the relative successes of self-governing settlers and encouraged by international agencies, many governments are changing their policies now that many professionals and officials realise the absurdity of the "bottomless pit" definition of housing problems. (The recently published World Bank sector policy paper on housing reports that an average 70 percent of the populations of representative samples of six Third World cities cannot afford the cheapest complete housing units at a 15 percent rate on a 25 year mortgage.)[4c]

Two alternative approaches are currently debated. Both agree that "The problem . . . is not really one of inadequate physical resources but rather the absence of an institutional framework and public policy that can mobilise such resources as are in fact available." One approach is expressed by the author of the above quotation which continues with . . ."(mobilisation of resources) in an efficient and modern way (in order to) convert building into a large-scale, efficient industry." In the other view, adopted and developed in this section, large-scale building is a most inefficient way of mobilising most resources, whether financial and material or human. By doing so much with so little, the masses of low-income self-governing settlers show where the major resources lie and who has access to them. And by doing so little with so much the conventional modern housing programmes demonstrate their innefficiency. If, as their protagonists claim, the principal objective of centrally administered mass housing is to generate employment, then they must show how a few far more capital and managerially intensively large-scale "modern" industrial firms can do this more effectively, and smoothly, than large numbers of small-scale labour intensive enterprises using far less mechanical equipment and employing far fewer highly paid technicians and managers.

The types of projects described below reflect a partial understanding of the lessons that the mass of successfully urbanising people teach. When the two models are compared this crucial issue of alternative technologies and managerial organisations is clarified and the problems of popular participation can be properly stated.

A Centrally Administered Participatory Programme

If the government at the same time of the street-widening and consequent squatter settlement described above had had sites-and-services programmes it would have been a different story. Households threatened with removal would have been offered building plots with perhaps varying levels of servicing within a range of prices and repayment conditions the great majority could afford. There is therefore no need for intending participants in such programmes to organise themselves unless applications are received only from self-organised groups, or if groups get significantly greater benefits. Where the initiative lies between the sponsoring agency and the individual participant, community organisations will arise only after the community itself has been "ordered," or selected by the sponsor.

In most cases, applicants for participation in such programmes must file individually and follow standard procedures that typically include gathering documentary proofs of birth and citizenship, marriage, sobriety, and economic solvency — and of economic need. When strictly applied, qualifications such as these commonly exclude substantial proportions of any existing community and create new and highly stratified ones. The poorest cannot afford the lowest-priced alternatives, or they are disqualified because they cannot prove their economic capacity for making the minimum required investment (and the common solution of generating the capital through renting is usually explicitly forbidden, despite the fact that this is one of the most common ways in which lowest-income people house themselves and make a living at the same time). The better off, on the other hand, are frequently excluded because they cannot demonstrate a need for the subsidy represented. So, unless there are procedures by which the better-off may pay the full cost, many local community leaders and actual or potential entrepreneurs and specialists — professionals or para-professionals — will also be lost to the new community. Either because such procedures break up extended families and established local communities, or just because they take so long and cost the applicants so much, many qualified potential participants may be lost, it may be easier and cheaper, and even socially advantageous, to move to an unauthorised settlement of the kind described above.

The economies of self-governing settlements can be far greater for low-income households than those of centrally administered programmes, even where the latter are in the form of sites and services projects. Even if the initial charges are the same for both, so that they are at least initially comparable, it is usual that project participants are required to take out a mortgage loan in order to buy or improve their property. Not only do the interest charges greatly increase the net price paid, but the payments impose an inflexible overhead and represent a constant threat for those with low or insecure incomes. If Charles Abrams' observation that investment is proportionate to security of tenure — which all observations and analyses known to the writer confirm[8] — then the imposition of mortgage will deter many. The majority of those who make substantial investments in self-governing settlements over time do so in order to consolidate their security — the imposition of a mortgage, even if it provided a completed dwelling in one rather than ten years, would undermine the primary reason for investment. In fact, the demand for long-term financing by low-income households is very low indeed if recent studies and observations in South and Central America, and in North and Central Africa are indicative.[9] Unless the commonly preferred methods of financing (from savings and income, and from renting space or rooms) are allowed, along with the often necessarily lengthy periods of incremental construction, programmes will be limited to narrow ranges of families of upper-lower and lower-middle incomes, or the sponsors will have great difficulties in collecting payments.

Further disincentives are frequently created by the forms and requirements of credit provided, whether obligatory or optional. Participants may be required to join a self-help construction group in order to obtain credit, if credit is required, and credit may only be available in the form of building materials. If a participant must join an organised self-help construction team, the household must provide its share of labour at mutually agreed times — if it provides more it gets little or no direct benefit, and if it provides less, it may be fined or even lose the value of contributions already made. If the demands of jobs and child-minding conflict with those of the project, the household has to employ a substitute. Whether working as a group member or individually, if credit is supplied in the form of materials, the self-builders are dependent on the procurement and distribution system set up and administered by the agency. Where all credit is in the form of goods and services supplied by the sponsor, participants have no opportunities to use special personal or local advantages they may have, such as opportunities to get better or cheaper materials or skilled labour. Where participation takes the form of labour in an "aided and mutual self-help" project, standard designs will be required. These are also frequently required even where each participant household is responsible for its own dwelling. Where credit is provided, or building controls are administered with or without credit, participants must generally follow procedures for inspection and certified approvals.

Subsequent controls on uses of privately owned land and buildings in such projects, and on alterations or additions to existing structures, vary widely. The more closely controls resemble the modern urban-industrial models, the fewer the opportunities for commercial and industrial activities, as well as for renting. In practise, however, these controls tend to be weak and, to the extent that the location and physical design of the development and its social composition allow, locally typical neighbourhoods will develop in time.

These self-help and sites and services programmes are based on the assumption that the material and economic reason for popular participation in housing is the employment of their own labour and the consequent reduction of construction costs, and that these cost reductions and other social benefits outweigh the case for an employment generation and income redistribution strategy based on conventional mass-housing programmes (referred to above). The corollary of this assumption, of course, is that technical and administrative resources for appropriate forms of development are concentrated in the hands of the professions and public institutions that are free to serve commercially unprofitable demands. The urban-industrial models for zoned residential development have rarely been questioned, anyway until very recently.

With these assumptions, it is hard to criticise the valiant efforts currently being made by a growing number of national governments, many of which are being supported by international agencies. Given the social and institutional as well as the economic and technical constraints in contexts such as that described above, the further problems confronting the approved participant seem unavoidable. If the acquisition of a minimum standard dwelling unit depends on the future owner-occupier's labour, or "sweat equity" as it is called in North America, then the most reasonable way of mobilising this resource is to organise groups of mutual self-help builders and provide them with a technical assistance they are presumed to need, along with the necessary tools and materials — which they are also presumed to be incapable or very much less capable of obtaining for themselves at fair prices.[10]

The logistic and administrative problems in carrying out programmes of this kind are considerable, both for the sponsoring and executive agencies and for the participants themselves. The formation of compatible groups of self-helpers — commonly varying between one and three dozen — together with the scheduling of their spare-time and week-end labour, and the distribution and the individualised accounting for equipment and materials as well as their time, is obviously a heavy and extremely exacting task. (I report from experience, having introduced the method myself into a Latin American country.)[11] The not infrequent delays in the purchase, distribution, or final accounting for the 50-odd items required for even relatively simple construction jobs can cost the participants as well as the administration dearly. The total number of man and woman hours are at least double those demanded by conventional methods (Latin American women, by the way, are very active participants in both the manual and managerial operations of self-help building). It is not surprising when self-help housing programme participants pay substitutes to take their places — so that they are no longer participants at all, in the sense presumed for programmes of this kind. If acquiescence is the only way of getting a house, and especially if the market value of the property is high in proportion to the price the eventual owner must pay, then the intended participants are likely to put up with what seem to them to be capriciously eccentric views of what ordinary people are capable of doing for themselves and of what professionals and government officers are capable of doing better.

The abundant evidence contradicting the assumptions on which conventional self-help housing programmes are based suggest that this form of participation is mistaken. The unaided, and generally individual owner or squatter, in building that generated the official idea of programmes based on popular participation in the first place, is a very different procedure. The typical unauthorised builder, in a self-generating and more or less self-governing settlement, uses far more resources than the labour of the household. In many contexts, this is one of the less important contributions made from a wide range of resources. A list of over 30 resources commonly used by self-builders in metropolitan Mexico[12] includes the following: loans from employers, competitive buying of small lots of materials and the frequent use of used or remade components, the use of small or irregular sites, cooperation with friends or neighbours for specific operations, such as levelling a street, and perhaps most importantly of all, contracting locally available skilled and semi-skilled labour, closely supervised and often aided by resident members of the family whose house they are building.

The detailed evidence available from the highly industrialised North American context[13] as well as typical Latin American[3,6] and African contexts,[9] suggests that average self-help labour contributions in owner-built housing vary between 25 percent and 50 percent. The same scattered but detailed studies suggest that average cost reductions for owner-built housing vary between very similar limits (although the real differences with equivalent housing built in publicly sponsored programmes may well be considerably higher due to the usually very large differentials between private commercial and public housing construction). If the average of these averages is assumed, in order to be conservative, the general value of "sweat equity" is only a little more than one tenth (one third of one third). The two to four remaining tenths are generally due to "enterprise equity," that is to the often imaginative use of many different resources. But the infinitely variable use of many and highly variable local resources is inhibited or even totally frustrated by the well-meaning but misguided attempt to institutionalise self-help labour.

Whether the current programmes of sites and services will be more successful than the earlier vogue for aided self-help programmes remains to be seen. If the observations and deductions offered in this paper are correct the successes of sites-and-services projects will be inversely proportional to the specificity of participant selection and improvement works and procedures — the less "ordering" and pre-conceived "arrayment" attempted by the sponsors, the more investment and social development is likely to take place. Conversely, the more controls imposed by the sponsors, the more convincing will the arguments of the rival "direct construction" strategists become — and the whole cycle will start over once again.

Responsibility and Resourcefulness

While the spontaneous or autonomous local action succeeded by discovering and using its own resources, the sponsored programme failed to make use of the resources which the intending participants so evidently possess. In the view presented in this paper, this is not an insignificant coincidence, as those with different assumptions may suppose, but the usual and perhaps inevitable result of a misstated problem, itself a consequence of an unrecognised issue in which the wrong position has unconsciously been taken.

If the issue raised by the difference between local participation in government programmes and government participation in local action is recognised, then there are two alternative and quite different interpretations of the problem of realising the local and community action potential. If it is assumed that the mobilisation of personal and local community resources depends on local participation in government programmes — that local communities and their enterprises and institutions are less capable of organising themselves and managing their own affairs than centralised organisations and professionalised institutions — then the problem is clear: to find the most appropriate forms and procedures for programmed mobilisation of perceived popular resources and the mass replication of reordered and authorised versions of "spontaneous" popular settlements. On the other hand, if it is assumed that the mobilisation of personal and local community resources depends on local autonomy and on participation of government in locally controlled activities, then the problem is quite different: it is the identification of the underlying principles that generate local action, and the identification of the constraints so that these can be removed by changes of government policy — especially by the removal of counter-productive legislation and procedure.

This section presents the latter view, from which it is clear that the design and replication of standard models for centrally administered programmes is both uneconomic and socially undesirable. The categorisation of the demand (or intended beneficiaries) and its matching with the predesigned sets of goods and services (even when they are as basic as those provided in the most elementary sites and services schemes) impose constraints that inhibit a major part of the personal and local resources available for investment in housing and local amenities. Materially and socially economic and practical solutions are seen to depend on the *access* which households and local groups and enterprises have to the essential resources — as distinct from specific channels and forms. Evidence from all contexts and all world regions shows that effective local action and the full use of personal and local resources depend on local and personal freedom to organise, plan, build and manage in ways appropriate to the particular situation. Every situation of particular people in a place and time is unique and far too complex and variable to categorise and fit into standardised programmes. If personal and local resources are to be effectively used — or to be prevented from turning into destructive forces — then the dominant question is how can government participate in local decisions in ways that ensure the freedom to build.

Resourcefulness and genuine economy in housing is a function of local and personal responsibility for three simple reasons: because the greater part of the resources needed for housing are in the hands of local people; because people's efforts depend on their expected satisfactions, and because personal and local housing demands are infinitely variable.

Contrary to the implied and often explicit assumption of government housing agencies, most resources for housing are those possessed and controlled by households. Even where most dwellings do not have to be amortised by their users, their management and maintenance, and consequent durability and costs-in-use, depend on the user's behaviour. In addition to personal savings capacity and the margins of income households are able and willing to spend on their housing, there are entrepreneurial and managerial resources demonstrated by cases of the kind illustrated by the first of the two illustrations above. These are especially important in view of the fact that housing built or improved with these resources is generally cheaper and often better built in the first place, and naturally better kept and usually longer lived.

Of course, people can be and often are obliged to pay more for their housing than they wish, by sellers' markets, by law, or by considerations of social status and conformity. In the reverse order, these incentives weaken as incomes decline and are therefore exceptionally weak in most cities of the modern world in which the great majority are poor or very poor indeed by modern urban-industrial standards. Even in the wealthiest countries, however, dissatisfactions with housing, or with its usefulness and value for the price paid, lead to substantial decreases in the level of financial investment and personal care. Dramatic examples are becoming commonplace, even or especially in the wealthiest countries. Pruitt-Igoe in the United States is already notorious[14]; books have also been written on prematurely deteriorated housing estates in England,[15] and much local publicity has recently been given to the huge Nonoalco Tlatelolco housing scheme in Mexico City[16] – and similar examples can be cited from many other countries.[17]

Although far more empirical evidence must be gathered from in-depth case studies, those already carried out support the simplest common-sense interpretation of those failures as direct consequences of mismatches between the rigid standardised supply of centrally administered building and management organisations and effective demands. It is usual to find gross diseconomies, dislocations, insecurities of tenure, and even extreme physical discomfort suffered by the tenants of housing that is prematurely deteriorating. If prices are excessive in relation to the value of the services obtained, if sources of income, of commercial and community facilities, or relatives and friends and peer groups are inaccessible, if tenants have no security of tenure, if well-being is endangered by social violence or structural defects, then it is hardly surprising that households pay and do as little as they can for their housing. Recovery rates on "low-cost," low-income projects in rapidly urbanising countries are frequently one third of the (subsidised) dues.

Mismatches such as these are inevitable when housing is supplied by large organisations. The variety of personal and local demand is in direct conflict with the demands of large production and service organisations that must standardise their products and procedures in order to operate at all. To justify standardisation and mass production of housing on the pretext of economies of scale and productivity is illogical as centrally administered housing systems are intrinsically uneconomic and counterproductive (for the simple reason that they are incapable of responding to the variety of local and personal demands inhibiting plentiful and cheap resources and therefore depending on scarce and expensive resources).[18] In order to operate competitively – which must not be confused with economy or efficiency – centralised and large scale systems for housing must monopolise the market, whether this is "free" or "planned" or "mixed." (And, of course, the same is generally true of any personally and locally sensitive set of goods, services and procedures.) As observed above, citizens of highly institutionalised societies are relatively susceptible to social and institutional pressures to conform to standardised patterns of consumption and behaviour. This does not alter the fact that if a system is starved of personal and local resources, it is proportionately more dependent on the resources it does have access to and, as these are largely heavy and high energy technologies and large and highly paid managements, centrally administered systems are bound to be inflationary.

Local Control and Central Guarantees

While centralised administration and categorical programmes are incompatible with personal and local demands and are therefore starved of the relatively plentiful, renewable and cheap resources that people in their local communities possess, personal and local access to their own resources is directly or indirectly dependent on powers exercised by central authority. People cannot buy land, even if suitable sites exist, if the prices are too high in proportion to their financial resources, or even if they represent excessive proportions of building costs; people cannot organise their own building if management is monopolised by large organisations or institutions; and would-be builders or buyers who need access to credit cannot usually get it unless mortgage banks are backed by government guarantees.

This local dependence on central authority for access to even locally possessed resources extends to individual members of minorities in two common ways: in addition to personal as well as collective dependence on external powers, they can be excluded from local markets by local economic or social discrimination – the worst and most inescapable form of oppression. Individuals and small groups, as well as local communities must have guaranteed access to the resources they need in order to do what they are able to do. But if the actions taken with those resources are to benefit or, at least, if they are not to conflict with their neighbours' well-being, then those guarantees must be accompanied by limits to their use (where they are not provided in the form of limits).

Central legislation and, where necessary, resource planning, is the corollary of personal and local control over the use of resources. This crucial distinction reveals the complementarity of the two types of participation identified in the introduction: the rules setting the limits to personal and local use of resources, ideally restricted to the administration of those limiting rules, is necessary for the maintenance of local freedom – in the present case, to build, use and maintain dwelling environments that stimulate personal and social well-being.

Many of the recommendations made in recent official and unofficial analyses and reports on citizen participation are relevant to the legislative processes as distinct from the administration of acategorical programmes. This distinction is blurred however, by the increasingly *pre*scriptive nature of legislation — laws and regulations that lay down lines of action, rather than limits to action, and which therefore take on characteristics of categorical programmes. As already stated, legislation that complements and enables local action to take place must be predominantly *pro*scriptive — wherever possible, it must guarantee access to resources by setting *limits* to what local persons, enterprises or institutions *may* do, instead of laying down *lines* of action that *must* be followed. The centralised distribution of material resources by government is as likely to create rigidities and injustices as the inadequately controlled commercial market systems it replaces — and is equally or even more likely to inhibit the use of personal and local resources. This raises another (but subsequent) set of issues which exceed the present terms of reference. Before these highly critical issues of basic resources of technologies, land and finance — can be properly raised and clearly discussed, the primary issues of decision-making structures and their impacts on those resources must be clarified.

Actors and Their Roles[19]

The principal actors, or decision makers, in settlement and housing development are the households, the public authorities, and third parties contracted by or working in voluntary association with one or the other. The most critical questions in any enterprise or supply system for goods and services, are: Who decides what shall be supplied to whom and how? And who provides the goods and services? In these simplified terms, there are four primary alternative situations:

WHO PROVIDES?

		Government	People
WHO DECIDES?	Government	1. Government decides & government provides.	2. Government decides & the people provide.
	People	4. Government provides & the people decide.	3. The people decide & the people provide.

In the first situation there is no place at all for households and their local groups who are in the position of passive recipients or *consumers*. Third parties can only act as voluntary or involuntary assistants or spokesmen for the authority.

The second situation, in which government invites local residents to participate by adding their own resources to government sponsored programmes is much the most common form of popular participation. Experience from all parts of the world suggests that this is a rather unstable and generally unproductive relationship when applied to housing. Whether programmes attempt to organise voluntary labour directly, as in the case of aided and mutual self-help projects, increased administrative costs tend to outweigh the value of the sometimes reluctant labour provided by the intended beneficiaries. These overheads are generally disguised or hidden in the overall expenditures of the public administration or, as in the USA, by the intervention of non-government organisations (NGOs) as contracted administrators of government sponsored programmes. In this latter situation, the NGO or professional acts as the central agency's *surrogate* and the participants are *collaborators* in the programmes that they set up and administer. Where programmes are designed and controlled by NGOs with skilled and dedicated staff, as in the case of Self Help Enterprises of California,[20] overheads can be kept relatively low and real savings are made. Similarly, the private and self-financing Wadsworth Group in England also enable their self-help participants to achieve major savings while paying the full costs of the administration as well as the land and construction.[21] These and other similar cases suggest that these inevitably complex and locally specific aided and mutual self-help housing projects are best carried out by independent bodies with full control over the ways in which their programmes are administered.

More commonly, however, sponsored programmes for popular participation are also administered by central agencies. They are often staffed by young professionals committed to improving the lot of the poor and relatively powerless and often find themselves siding with the people they work with and for, even acquiring and articulating more radical views than those they brought to the job in the first place. The potential conflicts in the inherent contradiction of being paid by a central authority to work for local people conscious of the injustices maintained by the political system often break out and confrontations occur. Even where these are deliberate policy, as in the early days of the United States Office of Economic Opportunity, the wrath of local authorities may create political embarrassments. The suspension of the OEO VISTA programme in the United States, originally launched as a "domestic Peace Corps," and the very recent withdrawal of funds from the British Community Development Programme, are symptomatic and can be paralleled by many similar policy changes in the usually more tightly controlled and much less radical programmes of self-help and community development in countries with much larger proportions of low and very low income people. The continuing successes of private self-help organisers emphasize the conclusion.

Self-appointed advocates who find themselves out of a job having been accused of biting the hand that fed them, are naturally attracted to the rather rare third situations in which people are both deciding and providing for themselves as more or less autonomous *producers*. (Situations where this may occur are briefly described in the following paragraph.) Where professional advice is needed and sought, this is undoubtedly the most satisfactory and stable situation for the committed individual professional or NGO. This is the ideal position of the *associate* serving the local community. In any complex society no local group can be fully autonomous, of course. Any housing action group, anyway, must have access to resources that must be bought or transferred from others: land and building sites, in the first place, together with materials and tools, skills not possessed by the participants themselves, and, very often, financial credit with which to buy them. If — but only if — a local action group has already got all the resources it needs, or the credit with which to get them, can it be said to be fully autonomous, providing as well as deciding everything for itself.

Low-income groups, or individual households, very often have *de facto* powers to obtain resources they cannot afford to buy — especially land which is often the only essential resource that is legally inaccessible to urbanising, low-income populations. *De facto* autonomy, therefore, is quite common in rapidly urbanising countries with low per capita budgets and weak police powers. Where, as in Lima and most of the major cities of Peru for example, there has been an ample supply of land for squatting of no commercial value, relatively orderly autonomous settlement has taken place on a very large scale. Before an "informal" speculative land market in squatter plots develops, and while custom is reinforced by the rules of the residents' associations, these "progressive developments" are models for appropriate urban housing policy. As the case of Dar es Salaam also shows, as a result of the maintenance of customary land-use controls during the colonial period, a set of rules that minimise land speculation and maximise incentives to invest in improvements, leads to a relatively full use of available human and material resources and the economic development of socially supportive dwelling environments. These continue to improve as long as the control system, whether formal or informal, continues to ensure equal access to the essential resources as well as personal and local freedom to use them in socially compatible ways. In other words, the precedents where planning and development controls have taken the form of effective limits to what investors may do, which also guarantee access of all potential investors to the essential resources they need, full and productive use has been made of available resources. Where controls have taken the form of pre-planned or programmed designs and procedures, on the other hand, the greater part of personal and local initiative and resources have been inhibited and the centrally administered developments built are very costly and generally socially divisive and personally unsatisfactory. Government, therefore, has a critical role to play as the *legislator* of the enabling limits, guaranteeing access to the resources which local households, their associations, and the enterprises that serve them can use more effectively than any other sector.

In the more common instances where local community groups do not have the resources of those in the above-mentioned cases, the household or group is a *client*, often requiring the services of an *advocate* in order to obtain the additional resources required by soliciting central government agencies. Intending professional associates of local groups often find themselves working as advocates as the lack of resources, or of access to resources, becomes apparent and government, therefore, is called upon as a *supplier* of those goods or services which the local groups cannot obtain themselves. As the position of advocate is often unpaid, sometimes because the clients see themselves paying for what is theirs by right, it is an inherently unstable position, in a similar but opposite way in which the surrogate's position often becomes untenable: instead of being pushed into working directly with and for local groups by resentful employers, the advocate is often tempted to accept the invitation of those same public employers to rejoin them (as it were), especially when the erstwhile associates can no longer afford to pay fees.[22] In this way the circle is completed with the co-option of the initially troublesome radical who becomes a *subordinate* of the sponsor, perhaps recreating the situation described in the second case.

These definitions are suggested as a framework for the further consideration of alternative roles and relationships between principal actors where popular participation is at issue:

WHO PROVIDES?

	Government	People

WHO DECIDES?

Government

1.
Where government decides and provides it is the *executive*; professionals may act as *subordinates* and the people are the *consumers* of the goods and services provided.

2.
Where government decides and the people provide, government is the *sponsor* and supervisor; professionals may act as contractors or *surrogates*, and the people are *collaborators* in the actions decided by the authorities.

People

4.
Where the people decide and government provides, the latter is the *supplier* of resources the people cannot obtain; professionals may act as their *advocates* and the people are *clients*.

3.
Where the people decide and the people provide for themselves, government is the *legislator*; professionals may act as *associates* and the people themselves are the *producers*.

The ideal combination is clearly the third, in which the people both decide and provide for themselves, enabled by legislation that guarantees access to the necessary resources to all who are capable of using them in materially and socially constructive ways, aided, where necessary, by associated specialists. This ideal only applies to actions that can be taken locally, of course, and that are more economic if carried out locally rather than supplied by supra-local agencies and authorities. If the examples presented in this paper are representative, this model clearly applies to the design, construction, and management of housing or, in the broader view, to the assembly of the components of local dwelling environments. Many components, however, are dependent on subordinate parts of supra-local systems — such as a piped water supply, or a telephone system. The latter, of course, would be extremely inefficient if it were composed of an aggregate of autonomous local exchanges. Water, on the other hand, may or may not be best provided locally, depending on the sources. At a somewhat larger scale, similarly variable factors apply to the generation of electirc power — which many hold would be best provided by a multiplicity of small plants rather than a few very large ones.

When discussing the above, or any other forms and strategies for popular participation in personally and locally specific activities, it is most important to distinguish between these different "levels of action." Three have been identified above: 1) the *resources* without which no actions can take place and access to which must therefore be arranged (building land, finance, and technology in the case of housing); 2) the components of *infrastructure* which cannot be provided locally from the resources available (usually roads and transport, water, drainage, and electricity in the case of urban neighbourhoods); and 3) the assemblies of all components into specific *dwelling environments*. It is also necessary to recognise the different levels of authority that have been identified: a) **central government** that has the necessary powers for the formulation and administration of legislation controlling the accessibility of resources; b) **regional** or **city government** that generally has the necessary powers to formulate regulations controlling infrastructure and development, and to install and administer them where necessary; and c) **local institutions, groups,** and **persons** who must have sufficient freedom of local and personal action if local and personal resources are to be fully and properly used. A further useful frame of reference is provided by the basic combinations of these levels of action and authority:[23]

LEVELS OF AUTHORITY

LEVELS OF ACTION	Central Government	Municipal Government	Local Institutions, Enterprises and Persons
the assembly of *dwelling environments*	NO	?	YES
the provision of *infrastructure* components	?	YES	?
the maintenance of access to *resources*	YES	?	NO
(i.e. the elements without which no component or assembly can be made.)			

While it is possible for central government to provide dwelling environments, and for local groups to take the law into their own hands in order to provide themselves with otherwise inaccessible resources (such as land), both mismatches of action and authority are clearly undesirable and tend to be counter-productive. On the other hand, there is rarely any question of the competence of central authority to formulate law, of municipal authority to install infrastructure and administer related utilities and services, nor should there be — in the light of all the evidence — any question about the competence of local institutions, enterprises, cooperative groups and even individual households to build and manage local dwelling environments. Questions do remain, however, in the other areas: local inhabitants are often in better positions to install certain components of infrastructure than the municipal authorities when, for example, it is more economic to tap a local source of water than pipe it from a relatively distant source. Similarly, municipal governments are sometimes in better positions to maintain access to resources than central government, even when this is through the legislation of limits (the administration of government legislation naturally being carried out through subsidiary levels of government). Very often, municipal or intermediate levels of government are bound to provide dwelling environments where certain sectors of the population are unserved, or where particular areas cannot be developed by other and more local developers — and where the more appropriate alternatives of adjusting legislation or administration in order to remove the constraints creating these gaps cannot be made in time. Finally, there are many occasions in which central government is called on to provide infrastructure, especially in contexts where municipal resources are extremely limited.

The scope and meaning of popular participation is clearly different in all these seven viable alternatives. This paper, however, has focussed on participation at the local level of the dwelling environment — on assemblies from supra-local components of infrastructure and with resources subject to national law. Although it has been observed that most resources are local and personal, and can only be effectively used by people and their local institutions and enterprises, it is clear that the existence of those resources does not mean that they are *accessible*. Access, even to one's own capacity to work, depends on powers exercised by supra-local authority either directly, by permitting or prohibiting self-help construction, for example, or indirectly by ensuring adequate wages and full employment and, therefore, ensuring that would-be self-helpers have the time and energy to exercise their demands. The most important single resource, land, is especially subject to national law and policy. More can be done by increasing local and personal access to appropriate building sites — or to existing properties needing rebuilding or rehabilitation — than any other actions or, even, by all others together. In many contexts, the restructuring of land law, and the consequent prices and distribution of land, is a prerequisite as any other significant changes will simply exacerbate the inflation of land values and increase its inaccessibility for those who can make best use of it.[24] Sometimes all this means is confirmation of the tenure of its present occupiers.

Conclusion: Who Should Do What for Whom?

The opinion offered in this paper is based on the assumption that by seeking standard forms and procedures that can be turned into sponsored, categorical programmes, central authorities overlook the issue raised and are therefore vainly attempting to solve a misstated problem. The common denominators of successful community action do not lie in the particular ways and means employed but, rather, in the freedom of those concerned to find their own ways of using the means that they have access to, in order to match their own unique priorities and effective demands. Any potential local action group or enterprise is far more likely to be inhibited than stimulated by programmed sets of standard procedures and specifications. People need access to tools so that they can use their own resources in their own ways.

NOTES

1   CURRIE, Laughlin (A/CONF.70/RPC/BP/1)

2   TURNER, John F.C.: *Uncontrolled Urban Settlements: Problems and Policies*, Working Paper No. 11, United Nations Interregional Seminar on Development Policies and Planning in Relation to Urbanisation, University of Pittsburgh. October-November 1966. Reprinted (abridged) in BREESE, Gerald (Editor), *The City in Newly Developing Countries*, Prentice Hall, 1969.

3   Sources for case studies of urban settlement in rapidly urbanising countries include the following:

   3a   DWYER, D.J.: *People and Housing in Third World Cities*, Longman, 1975.

   3b   MANGIN, William P. *Peasants in Cities*, Houghton Mifflin, Boston, 1970.

   3c   OLIVER, Paul: *Shelter and Society* Barrie & Rockliffe, London, 1969.

   3d   PEATTIE, Lisa Redfield: *The View from the Barrio*, University of Michigan Press, Ann Arbor, 1970.

4   The most recent publications by international agencies with special reference to sites and services and self-help housing methods are:

   4a   UNITED NATIONS

   4b   VAN HUYCK, Alfred: *Planning Sites & Services Programmes*, USAID Ideas and Methods Exchange Bulletin No. 68, Washington, D.C.

   4c   WORLD BANK: *Housing Sector Policy Paper*, Washington, D.C., 1975.

5   BERESFORD, Maurice: *New Towns of the Middle Ages*. Lutterworth London, 1967.

6   This composite case history is drawn mainly from cases previously reported in:

   6a   MANGIN, William P.: "*Urbanisation Case History in Peru*," in (Turner, John F.C. Editor) *Architectural Design*, Vol. XXXIII August 1963. London, Reprinted in 3b. Op. Cit.

   6b   TURNER, John F.C.: "*Barriers and Channels for Housing Development in Modernising Countries*," in the *Journal of the American Institute of Planners*, Vol. XXXIII, May 1967. Reprinted in 3b. Op. Cit.

   6c   MANGIN, William P., and TURNER, John F.C.: "The Barriada Movement," in *Progressive Architecture*, New York, May 1968. Reprinted in 3c. Op. Cit.

   6d   KOTH, Marcia de Paredes: unpublished dissertation for Ph.D., Department of Urban Studies and Planning, M.I.T., Cambridge, Massachusetts.

   6e   UNITED NATIONS TV SERVICE (Film) *A Roof of My Own*, 1964.

7   A note by Margaret Grenfell in TURNER, John F.C.: "Barriada Integration and Development: A government programme in San Martin, Lima," in *Architectural Design*, Vol. XXXIII, August, 1973.

8   ABRAMS, Charles: *Man's Struggle for Shelter in an Urbanizing World*, M.I.T. Press, 1964 (published by Faber, London in 1966 as *Housing in the Modern World*.).

9. The author has carried out studies including observations on ratios between incomes, rents, construction costs and values in Peru (with Marcia Koth de Paredes (see 6d above), in Mexico with Tomasz Sudra (currently completing a doctoral dissertation for the Department of Urban Studies and Planning at M.I.T.), in Tanzania (for the World Bank) and in Egypt (for Messers Clifford Culpin and Partners, London).

10 TURNER, John F.C., "The Reeducation of a Professional," in *Freedom to Build* (Editors Turner, John F.C., and Fichter, Robert), Macmillan, New York, 1972.

11 Op. Cit. supra.

12 TURNER, John F.C.: "Housing Economy – Centralised Productivity or Localised Resourcefulness?" in *Architectural Design*, January, 1976 (fifth in a series of seven articles to be published as *Housing By People*, in the May, 1976), Marion Boyars, 18 Brewer Street, London W.1, in May 1976). This essay is largely based on information obtained in Mexico by Tomasz Sudra.

13 GRINDLEY, William C.: "Owner-Builders: Survivors with a Future," in Turner, John F.C. and Fichter, Robert, Editors, *Freedom to Build*, Macmillan, New York, 1972.

14 RIESMAN, David

15 RAVETZ, Alison. *Model Estate.*

16 Nonoalco Tlatelolco is a huge publicly sponsored and administered housing project near the central area of Mexico City, with 11,000 units. Extracts from newspaper reports published in 1975 indicate its history: "This gigantic time bomb" ... "7,000 people who live illegally in the servants' quarters" ... "Facades of inflammable fibreglass panels (that have had to be replaced at great cost)" ... "the index of criminality is perhaps the greatest in the city" ... "the 285 lifts that are mortal traps" ... "hundreds of structural faults which result in major cracks with minor earth tremors and intensified mini-gales created by bad orientation. . . ."

17 For example, the *Superbloques* of Caracas, built in the late 1940s and early 1950 by the Perez Jimenez administration during the oil boom of that time. This was reported in a study directed by Eric Carlson for the Banco Obrero, published by the Banco Obrero in Caracas, circa 1956. Publicity was given to the collapse of a block of flats built in an urban renewal (slum clearance) programme in Seoul, South Korea, in 1970.

18 This argument is set out in the forthcoming book *Housing by People* cited in note 12 above, and is contained in the first two essays of the series already published by *Architectural Design* in the issues for September and October, 1975.

19 This discussion is derived, in part, from a contribution by Ian Donald TERNER to "Increasing Housing Autonomy" in *Freedom to Build* (cited above).

20 An evaluation of the Self-Help Enterprises programme was made by the Organization for Social and Technical Innovation as part of a major study of Self-Help Housing in the USA. The study was directed by John F.C. Turner under the supervision of Donald A. Schon (President of OSTI) for the U.S. Department of Housing and Urban Development, 1969-70.

21 Colin Wadsworth & Co. Southern House, Hallfield Rd., Bradford, England.

22 See note 9 above.

23 See chapter of *Freedom to Build* cited in note 19 above.

24 A conclusion from a report to AURIS, Toluca, Mexico by John F.C. Turner, Robert Ledogar and Tomasz Sudra, 1971. (To be published in Spanish.)

Index